Communications in Computer and Information Science 872

Commenced Publication in 2007
Founding and Former Series Editors:
Phoebe Chen, Alfredo Cuzzocrea, Xiaoyong Du, Orhun Kara, Ting Liu, Dominik Ślęzak, and Xiaokang Yang

More information about this series at http://www.springer.com/series/7899

Youness Tabii · Mohamed Lazaar
Mohammed Al Achhab · Nourddine Enneya (Eds.)

Big Data, Cloud and Applications

Third International Conference, BDCA 2018
Kenitra, Morocco, April 4–5, 2018
Revised Selected Papers

Springer

Editors
Youness Tabii
Abdelmalek Essaâdi University
Tétouan
Morocco

Mohammed Al Achhab
Abdelmalek Essaâdi University
Tétouan
Morocco

Mohamed Lazaar
Abdelmalek Essaâdi University
Tétouan
Morocco

Nourddine Enneya
Université Ibn-Tofail
Tétouan
Morocco

ISSN 1865-0929 ISSN 1865-0937 (electronic)
Communications in Computer and Information Science
ISBN 978-3-319-96291-7 ISBN 978-3-319-96292-4 (eBook)
https://doi.org/10.1007/978-3-319-96292-4

Library of Congress Control Number: 2018948223

This Springer imprint is published by the registered company Springer Nature Switzerland AG
The registered company address is: Gewerbestrasse 11, 6330 Cham, Switzerland

Preface

We are happy to present you this book, Big Data, Cloud and Applications, which is a collection of papers that were presented at the 3rd International Conference on Big Data Cloud and Applications, BDCA 2018. The conference took place on April 04–05, 2018, in Kenitra, Morocco.

The book consisted of nine chapters, which correspond to the four major areas that are covered during the conference, namely, Big Data, Cloud Computing, Maching Learning, Deep Learning, Data Analysis, Neural Networks, Information System and Social Media, Natural Language Processing, Image Processing and Applications.

Every year BDCA attracted researchers from all over the world, and this year was not an exception – we received 99 submissions from 12 countries. More importantly, there were participants from many countries, which indicates that the conference is truly gaining more and more international recognition as it brought together a vast number of specialists who represented the aforementioned fields and share information about their newest projects. Since we strived to make the conference presentations and proceedings of the highest quality possible, we only accepted papers that presented the results of various investigations directed to the discovery of new scientific knowledge in the area of Big Data, Cloud Computing and their applications. Hence, only 45 papers were accepted for publishing (i.e., 45% acceptance rate). All the papers were reviewed and selected by the Program Committee, which comprised 96 reviewers from over 58 academic institutions. As usual, each submission was reviewed following a double process by at least two reviewers. When necessary, some of the papers were reviewed by three or four reviewers. Our deepest thanks and appreciation go to all the reviewers for devoting their precious time to produce truly through reviews and feedback to the authors.

July 2018

Youness Tabii
Mohamed Lazaar
Mohammed Al Achhab
Nourddine Enneya

Organization

The 3rd International Conference on Big Data, Cloud and Applications (BDCA 2018) was organized by Abdelmalek Essaadi University and IbnTofail University and was in Kenitra, Morocco (April 04–05, 2018).

General Chairs

Youness Tabii	National School of Applied Sciences (ENSA), Tetouan, Morocco
Nourddine Enneya	Faculty of Sciences, Kenitra, Morocco

Local Organizing Committee

Nourddine Enneya	FS, Ibn Tofail University, Kenitra, Morocco
Jihane Alami Chentoufi	FS, Ibn Tofail University, Kenitra, Morocco
Jalal Laassiri	FS, Ibn Tofail University, Kenitra, Morocco
Abdelalim Sadiq	FS, Ibn Tofail University, Kenitra, Morocco
Youness Tabii	ENSA, Abdelmalek Essaadi University, Tetouan, Morocco
Mohamed Lazaar	ENSA, Abdelmalek Essaadi University, Tetouan, Morocco
Mohamed Al Achhab	ENSA, Abdelmalek Essaadi University, Tetouan, Morocco
Mohamed Chrayah	ENSA, Abdelmalek Essaadi University, Tetouan, Morocco
Btissam Dkhissi	ENSA, Abdelmalek Essaadi University, Tetouan, Morocco

Program Committee

Hamid R. Arabnia	University of Georgia, USA
Abdelkaher Ait Abdelouahad	Ibn Zohr University, Morocco
Noura Aknin	FS, Abdelmalek Essaadi University, Morocco
Adel Alimi	REGIM, Sfax University, Tunisia
Mohammed Al Achhab	ENSA, Abdelmalek Essaadi University, Morocco
Naoual Attaoui	FS, Abdelmalek Essaadi University, Morocco
Abderrahim Azouani	Mohammed 1st University, Morocco
Jenny Benois-Pineau	Bordeaux University, France
Abdellah Abouabdellah	ENSA, Ibn Tofail University, Morocco
Amel Benazza	Supcom Carthage University, Tunisia

Kamal Baraka	Cadi Ayyad University, Morocco
Mohamed Batouche	Constantine University 2, Algeria
Lamia Benameur	FS, Abdelmalek Essaadi University, Morocco
Hamid Bennis	EST, Moulay Ismail University, Morocco
Mohamed Ben Halima	REGIM, Sfax University, Tunisia
Fadila Bentayeb	Lyon 2 University, France
Samir Bennani	EMI, Mohammed V University, Morocco
Thierry Berger	Limoges University, France
Kamel Besbes	FSM, University of Monastir, Tunisia
Mustapha Boushaba	Montréal University, Canada
Aoued Boukelif	University of Sidi-Bel-Abbès, Algeria
Abdelhak Boulaalam	FP, Sidi Mohamed Ben Abdellah University, Morocco
Abdelhani Boukrouche	Guelma University, Algeria
Jaouad Boukachour	ISEL le Havre, France
Omar Boussaid	Lyon 2 University, France
Anne Canteaut	Inria-Rocquencourt, France
Claude Carlet	Paris 8 University, France
Mohamed Chrayah	ENSA, Abdelmalek Essaadi University, Morocco
Habiba Chaoui	ENSA, Ibn Tofail University, Morocco
Btissam Dkhissi	ENSA, Abdelmalek Essaadi University, Morocco
Abdellatif El Afia	ENSIAS, Mohammed V University, Morocco
Nabil El Akkad	ENSA, Hassan 1st University, Morocco
Youssouf El Allioui	Hassan 1st University, Morocco
Younès El Bouzekri El Idrissi	ENSA, Ibn Tofail University, Morocco
Abdelaziz El Hibaoui	FS, Abdelmalek Essaadi University, Morocco
Mohammed Elghzaoui	FP, University Mohammed 1st, Morocco
Kamal Eddine El Kadiri	ENSA, University of Abdelmalek Essaadi, Morocco
Said El Kafhali	Hassan 1st University, Morocco
Yasser Elmadani Elalami	Sidi Mohamed Ben Abdellah University, Morocco
Abderrahim El Mhouti	FST, Mohammed 1st University, Morocco
Mourad El Yadari	FP, Moulay Ismail University, Morocco
El Mokhtar En-Naimi	FST, Abdelmalek Essaadi University, Morocco
Noureddine Ennahnahi	Sidi Mohamed Ben Abdellah University, Morocco
Karim El Moutaouakil	ENSA, Mohammed 1st University, Morocco
Nourddine Enneya	Faculty of Sciences, Kenitra, Morocco
Abdelkarim Erradi	Qatar University, Doha, Qatar
Mohamed Ettaouil	FST, Sidi Mohamed Ben Abdellah University, Morocco
Siti Zaiton Mohd Hashim	University Teknologi, Malaysia
Adel Hafiane	INSA Centre Val de Loire, France
Abdelhakim Hafid	Montréal University, Canada
Abderrahmane Habbal	Inria Sophia Antipolis, France
Faïez Gargouri	University of Sfax, Tunisia
Youssef Ghanou	EST, Moula Ismail University, Morocco
Khalid Haddouch	ENSA, Mohammed 1st University, Morocco

Contents

Image Processing and Applications

Natural Language Processing

Big Data

Informal Learning in Twitter: Architecture of Data Analysis Workflow and Extraction of Top Group of Connected Hashtags

Abdelmajid Chaffai(✉), Larbi Hassouni, and Houda Anoun

RITM LAB, CED Engineering Sciences, ENSEM, Hassan II University Casablanca, Casablanca, Morocco
majedchaffai@gmail.com

Abstract. The Advance of web-based technologies have brought radical changes to web site design and web service usage, primarily in terms of interactive contents and user engagement in collaboration and information sharing. In nutshell the web has been transformed from static media to the preferred communication media where the user is a key player in the creation of his experiences. The increase in the popularity of social networks on the Web has shaken up traditional models in different areas, including learning. Many individuals have resorted to social networking to educate themselves. Such learning is close to natural learning, the learner is autonomous to draw the pathway which best suits his individual needs in order to upgrade his skills. Several training organizations use the Twitter platform to announce the training they provide. We conduct an experiment on twitters data which are related to the training themes in Big Data and Data Science, we perform an exploratory analysis and extract the top group of connected hashtags using the Graph X library provided by the Spark framework. Data that come from the Twitter platform is produced at high speed and in a complex structure. This leads us to use a distributed infrastructure based on two efficient frameworks Apache Hadoop and Spark. Data ingestion layer is built by combining two frameworks Apache Flume and Kafka.

Keywords: Informal learning · Social network data · Distributed environment Apache spark · Graph · Connected components

1 Introduction

The learning is a long life process which takes place everywhere; it is divided in two categories [1] formal and non-formal or informal. Formal learning is often validated by official certifications; education occurs in structured environments such as schools and universities and is supervised by teachers. Knowledge and skills acquired outside the formal setting enable an informal learning. In today's world, communication between people occurs often through the use of social media platforms, wikis, micro-blogs which become the main channels for conveying and sharing information in a quickly manner. Communities and groups have been built around common points of interest. With advances in Web2 technologies, the user of social network platforms once authenticated,

Y. Tabii et al. (Eds.): BDCA 2018, CCIS 872, pp. 3–15, 2018.
https://doi.org/10.1007/978-3-319-96292-4_1

he can freely have several roles, read other people's posts, write messages, insert media and documents, search people and trend topics. Although social networks are considered as entertainment spaces, several universities are attracted by the insertion of informal learning via social networks like Twitter in their academic development [2]. In fact, in this new age of data and computing, many individuals, students in higher education or professionals have resorted to informal means to educate themselves and upgrade their skills for example in cutting edge of tools in information technologies by working on-line short courses and workshops. Informal learning through social media leads to empowerment and self-efficacy while saving time and money in the learning process and increase visibility in society.

Social network Analytics [3] is a set of methods and technologies that allow collecting a large datasets from social network platforms sources, transform them in a way that they become available and ready to be consumed by analysts. Text mining, Natural language processing, classification and clustering algorithms are used to extract the hidden insights in order to improve the best knowing of the user's experiences. New open source technologies like Apache Hadoop [4] and Spark [5] allow building infrastructures which aimed to manage massive datasets by distributing storage and computing across clusters of low cost machines, they handle and combine both structured and unstructured data that come from internal and external data sources. Depending on data production, data processing tasks is divided into two groups:

- Batch Processing: data are collected in big batches over period of time, it is stored in distributed file system, then processing and analysis jobs are applied at once, and batch results are generated.
- Streaming Processing: data come in continuous way; processing and analysis jobs are applied in near real time or in small time. In this work we use Apache Spark as data processing engine, it is a distributed framework developed in Scala programming language and works as a Java Virtual Machine, Spark is designed for fast scalable in-memory computing and relies on Hadoop to run in cluster mode and use HDFS [6] storage, it comes with a high level programming model that hides the partitioning of dataset in memory of cluster, using a novel data structure called Resilient Distributed Dataset RDD [7] which is an immutable distributed collection of objects partitioned across different nodes of the cluster. RDD data-sharing abstraction allows to use wide range of APIs provided by Spark: Spark SQL, Spark Streaming, MLlib (Machine Learning library), and GraphX (graph processing). Apache spark is suited to perform analytics that need iterative operations. It allows to process data directly, comparing to Map Reduce [8] programs which need several access to disk to retrieve intermediate result. Since twitter data are generated at high speed and in a complex structure, we implement a hybrid architecture which provides a faster ETL based on data pipeline that ensures the data collection and processing in a unified and distributed environment. We have conducted an experiment on twitters data filtered by keywords associated with 6 topics of big data technologies and data science which are of hot interests to developer and industrial communities.

In this paper we describe the necessary steps to carry out an exploratory analysis and the extraction of the top group of connected hashtags.

The rest of the paper is structured as follows. Section 2 discusses related work. Section 3 describes the Architecture of Data analysis workflow, Sect. 4 discusses the experiment and finally, Sect. 5 concludes the paper.

2 Related Work

Social network analysis is an emerging research field which aims to better understand how people seek and share information in social network platforms. Bonchi et al. in [9] provided an overview of what we consider to be key problems and techniques in social network analysis from a business applications perspective. The authors described each area of research in the context of a specific business processes classification framework (The APQC process classification framework), and then focused on several areas, giving an overview of the main problems and describing state-of-the-art approaches.

The explosion of the use of micro blogs by students offers opportunities to exploit this new communication channel in process-oriented learning. In paper [10], the authors proposed a platform which uses Twitter news in Education known as NIE in order to provide the latest news classified on various topics then enable discussion and debate groups. They implemented a prototype system which uses Twitter as source to the hot news and trends. For classification topics, each news tweet is cleaned and mapped into its words. The Naïve Bayes classifier is used to achieve the classification based on predefined number of keywords which correspond to the selected topics. The platform offers to learners a News Visualizer using treemap to facilitate the learner's query which is based on period, keywords, and desired topic. Cosine similarity method, Based on user document similarity and hierarchical agglomerative clustering is used to study the learners' preferences.

Aramo-Immonen et al. [11] employ Twitter data to study interactions between members of community of managers attending a conference. Data are retrieved two weeks before the conference. The process of data-driven visual network analytics and the Ostinato [12] process model are provided to extract insights into the informal learning of community managers. Quantitative and qualitative analyses of Twitter data are produced like analysis of the top hash tags over time before the conference and the network of hash tag co-occurrences.

In paper [13], the authors developed a workflow that consists to integrate both qualitative analysis and large-scale data mining techniques. They focused on engineering students' Twitter posts to understand issues and problems in their educational experiences. The authors conducted a qualitative analysis on samples taken from about 25,000 tweets related to engineering students' college life. They found engineering students encounter problems such as heavy study load, lack of social engagement, and sleep deprivation. A multi-label classification algorithm is implemented to classify tweets reflecting students' problems.

The majority of tweets do not contain the geographical location through exact GPS coordinates (latitude and longitude). The authors attempt in [14] to identify a location of the tweets. They employ twitter data to fit a Naive bayes model in order to classify a tweets based on features as users' timezone, the user's language, and the parsed users' location. The classifier with an accuracy of 82% was achieved and performs well on active Twitter countries such as the Netherlands and United Kingdom.

An analysis of errors made by the classifier shows that mistakes were made due to limited information and shared properties between countries such as shared timezone. A feature analysis was performed in order to see the effect of different features. The features timezone and parsed user location were the most informative features.

3 Twitter Data Characteristics and Architecture of Data Analysis Workflow

Twitter has become a largest social space in the world where 330 million monthly active users, discuss several topics and publish 500 million tweets per day. This data source offers tremendous opportunities to analyze social trends for multiple purposes. Twitter offers two types of APIs, Rest API and streaming APIs (for developers in real time) that allow different clients applications written in different languages [15] to consume the tweets. For example, in case of Java and Scala, Twitter4J is an open source Java library used for interfacing with Twitter's Application Programming Interfaces (APIs). Tweets data come in non-structured nature, they are encoded using Java Script Object Notation (JSON) based on key-value pairs. Each tweet has an author (user), a message, a unique ID, a timestamp of when it was created, and geo metadata often turned off by users. Each User has a Twitter name, an ID, a number of followers. Tweet contains 'entity' objects, which are arrays of contents such as hashtags, mentions, media, and links.

A typical SNA workflow consists of several interacting phases which are:

- Data collection
- Data preparation
- Data analysis
- Insights.

The different topics discussed in the context of informal learning and social learning in twitter are very varied, in this paper we propose a flexible data system (see Fig. 1) capable to receive data from different topics through multiple agents, each agent intercepts the stream data in real time based on keywords related to a given topic, Apache Flume [16] is used in the data collection layer. We are faced with a case where there will be several flume-agents, so we need a strategy to categorize the message, for this we use Apache Kafka [17] as an efficient publish-subscribe messaging system to separate the incoming data in topics and keep them in scalable and fault-tolerant way. In the rest of data pipeline, we use Spark streaming to consume, parse the incoming data in real time and store them in HDFS storage. Analysis tasks to extract insights can be performed by using Spark SQL and Spark ML.

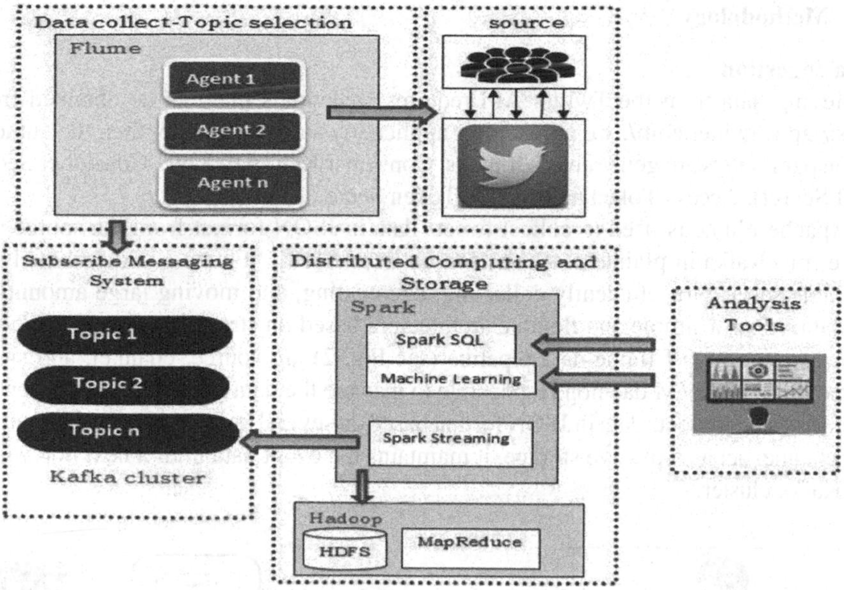

Fig. 1. Overall architecture of the proposed SNA workflow.

4 Experiment

4.1 General Description

Due to strong competition between organizations for integrating data into decision making, hiring opportunities for data specialists and data infrastructure specialists are much greater than those of other profiles. We will study this trend in the twitter social network as a case study, to try to extract useful information about users who are interested in acquiring new knowledge or who share their experiences in the field of big data. We employ data from twitter that is filtered based on the following keywords: “bigdata”, “datascience”, “machineLearning”, “hadoop”, “spark”, “analytics”.

4.2 Environment Experiment

We deployed a small local cluster for Hadoop and Spark on 11 nodes running Ubuntu 16.04 LTS and interconnected via one switch of 1 Gb/s. The Hadoop cluster is built using Hadoop version 2.7.3. The Spark cluster is built using Spark version 2.0.0. One machine is designed as Master for both Spark and Hadoop, the others nodes are both the Hadoop slaves and Spark workers. The following configuration is the same for all nodes: Intel(R) Core(TM) i5-3470 CPU 3.20 GHz(4CPUs), 1 Gb/s network connection, 300 GB hard disk, 8 GB Memory.

4.3 Methodology

Data Ingestion

Retrieving data from the Twitter API requires credentials that can be obtained from https://apps.twitter.com/, we register our application as a twitter app, then the authorization parameters are generated as follows: Consumer Key (API Key), Consumer Secret (API Secret), Access Token and Access Token Secret.

Apache Flume is used to collect tweets data in JSON format from the source and move it to Kafka in plaintext. As defined on its site [18], "Flume is a distributed and available service for efficiently collecting, aggregating, and moving large amounts of log data. It has a simple and flexible architecture based on streaming data flows." The main components of flume data pipeline (see Fig. 2) are source, channel, and sinks. Flume agent is a JVM daemon responsible to manage the data flow. The source continuously retrieves tweets data in JSON format based on several keywords from the Twitter. The channel act as a passive storage, it maintains the event data until a next hop which is a Kafka cluster.

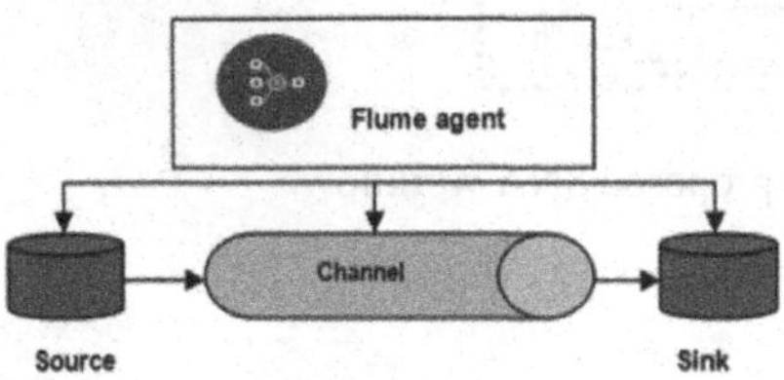

Fig. 2. Flume architecture.

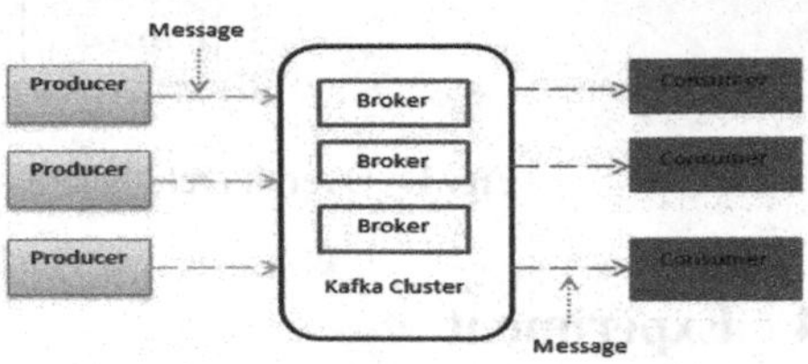

Fig. 3. Kafka concept.

The main components of Kafka-based architecture are shown in Fig. 3:

- Broker: Kafka is a cluster of nodes, each a node is a broker.
- Topic: is a category of related messages.
- Producer: each application that produces and sends the messages to Kafka topic for example our flume-agent.
- Consumer: each application that subscribes to kafka topic and consumes the messages.

Kafka relies on Zookeeper to manage his components and for monitoring the status of operations that occur on the cluster.

We create one topic with 3 replicated partitions as shown in the following statement: ***kafka-topics.sh –create –zookeeper localhost:2181 –replication-factor 3 –partitions 3 –topic bigdata_tweets***.

Bigdata_tweets represents the flume sink, it consumes the event data and remove it from the channel and act as storage for these messages that transit. Taking into account the proprieties of different components cited above we deploy the flume agent using a customized flume-agent configuration (see Fig. 4). The required jar files corresponding to the source and sink are added to the library folder of flume in order to interact with them.

```
#Flume Instance -Twitter_Flume_kafka_Agent
agent.channels = ch1
agent.sources = Twitter
agent.sinks = kafkaSink
agent.channels.ch1.type = memory
agent.channels.ch1.capacity = 1000000
agent.channels.ch1.transactionCapacity = 1000
# Twitter source and connection properties
agent.sources.Twitter.type = com.cloudera.flume.source.TwitterSource
agent.sources.Twitter.consumerKey = 2NHIZ8YCyy9upgE1Kq0IUwxjd
agent.sources.Twitter.consumerSecret =
QAf067Mu10RmrLzBLtU4ozFoltN1UcH5W8CDUK22PSpfmCtSpB
agent.sources.Twitter.accessToken = 90690287-
Adh9N226eLbt9fypeI6XWCSjMk8gag8DzsOSNHrJR
agent.sources.Twitter.accessTokenSecret =
uxWslwGjcKFF17cvJAoV4KmiaRu3Z55JGUrk2gT14aUx0
agent.sources.Twitter.keywords = bigdata, datascience, machinelearning,
hadoop, spark, analytics
agent.sources.Twitter.channels = ch1
#kafka sink proprieties
agent.sinks.kafkaSink.type=org.apache.flume.sink.kafka.KafkaSink
agent.sinks.kafkaSink.serializer.class
=org.apache.flume.sink.kafka.serializer.DefaultEncoder
agent.sinks.kafkaSink.brokerList=localhost:9092
agent.sinks.kafkaSink.topic=bigdata_tweets|
```

Fig. 4. Sample of Flume agent configuration

Data Processing

This phase consists to ingest data from Kafka topic for live processing in Apache Spark. Since Spark is a batch processing, we use Spark streaming to retrieve continuously the messages accumulated in Kafka topic. Spark streaming receives the input stream and divides it in a series of mini batches corresponding to input periods equal to batch interval, it creates a DStream (see Fig. 5) which is as a sequence of RDDs that can be processed in Spark core as a static data.

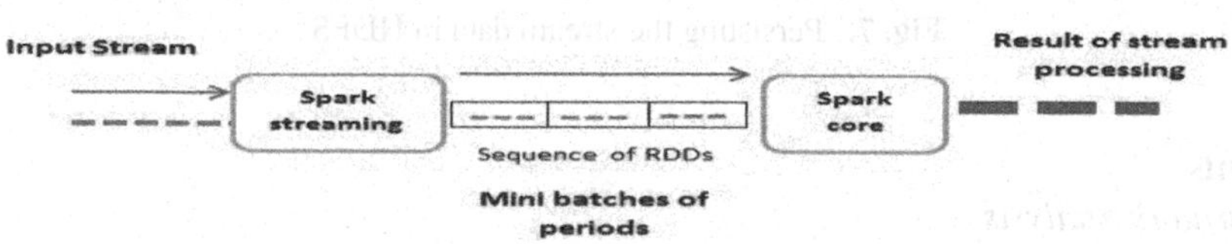

Fig. 5. Discretized data stream

Any streaming application needs a streaming context which is an entry point to the Spark cluster resources.

We create our application in Scala that involves the following steps:

(1) To interact with kafka cluster, we connect spark streaming adopting the direct approach using the DirectStream method in order to deploy a customized receiver (see Fig. 6) which requires the subscription to bigdata_tweets topic created above.

```
val kafkaParams = Map[String, Object](
"key.deserializer" ->classOf[StringDeserializer],
"value.deserializer" ->classOf[StringDeserializer],
"group.id" -> "mj-group",
"auto.offset.reset" -> "earliest",
"enable.auto.commit"-> "true",
"auto.commit.interval.ms"-> "1000",
"session.timeout.ms"-> "30000"
)
val kafkaTopics = " bigdata_tweets "
val topicsSet = kafkaTopics.split(",").toSet
//receive events from a Topic in plain text format
Val kafkaDstream =
KafkaUtils.createDirectStream[String,String](ssc,PreferConsistent,
Subscribe[String,String](topicsSet, kafkaParams)).map(_.2)
```

Fig. 6. Spark streaming receiver

(2) Once the stream is created we convert it to JSON format (see Fig. 7), in order to extract and process the interested fields in future analysis tasks. We store the stream data in HDFS in JSON Format.

```
val messages = kafkaDstream.map(gson.toJson(_))
messages.foreachRDD((rdd, time) => {
val count = rdd.count()
if (count > 0) {
val outputRDD = rdd.repartition(1)
outputRDD.saveAsTextFile("recherche/tweets_" + time.milliseconds.toString)
numTweetsCollected += count
if (numTweetsCollected> 20000) {
System.exit(0)
```

Fig. 7. Persisting the stream data in HDFS

Insights

Exploratory Analysis

We collected 20058 tweets, that we stored in HDFS in JSON format, then we converted them to DataFrame in a structured format appropriate to be queried. We create a table by selecting the entities and fields in interest like text, hash tags, urls, place, user.lang in order to extract insights using Spark SQL. Thus, we deduced that the tweets contain several links to a diversified resources for informal learning which can adapt to all styles of learning in the form of links to external pages, free tutorial and courses (see Table 1). We have noticed the presence of several companies specialized in the eLearning industry which publish their offers and course promotions to attract users interested in big data technologies and data science.

We found 9214 distinct users, although geo-location is disabled in the majority of tweets [14], but we can extract their origin from the time zone, and native languages, we found that 80% of users are Americans.

4264 distinct hashtags found in tweets data, we extract the top 10 most popular hashtags (see Fig. 8) with respectively the number of occurrences in all tweets.

Table 1. Summary of links to external resources

Topics	Total links to learning resources
Big data	157
Data science	84
Machine learning	408
Hadoop	70
Spark	390
Analytics	235

```
(#IoT,4272)
(#AI,3472)
(#BigData,3228)
(#MachineLearning,2566)
(#IIoT,2419)
(#DataScience,1974)
(#ML,1869)
(#DeepLearning,1618)
(#ArtificialIntelligence,1411)
(#DL,1221)
```

Fig. 8. Top 10 most popular hashtags.

Graph Data Structure and Finding Top Group of Connected Hashtags
Generally the raw data transformed for analysis tasks (see Fig. 9) are a set of records stored in a table or a DataFrame, they are structured and divided in two dimensions which are column and row.

```
+-----------------+-----------------+----------------------------------------------------------------------------------------------+
|id               |user             |hashtags                                                                                      |
+-----------------+-----------------+----------------------------------------------------------------------------------------------+
|951054872245428225|Jobs In BigData  |[BigData, DataScience, Database, BigData, jobs, Hiring, Careers, Horsham, UK]                |
|951073654032433152|Jason Schenker   |[BigData, tech, futureofwork, workforce, AI, IoT, data, technology, disruption, JobsForRobots]|
|951073655718662144|Infogix          |[BigData, insurers, datalakes, analytics]                                                     |
|951073658038050816|Tech Jobs        |[Developer, BigData, DataScience, Database, solr, jobs, Hiring, Careers, London, SE17]        |
|951073667609432069|UBDC             |[smartcities, futurecities, bigdata]                                                          |
```

Fig. 9. Sample of DataFrame created from raw data containing tweet identifier, user and hashtags.

In graph theory [19], graph is a data structure, conceptually described by a pair ***(S, A)*** where ***S*** is a finite set of nodes called vertices or vertex and ***A*** is a finite multi-set of ordered pairs of vertices called edges, an edge connects two vertices in a graph.

In real life applications, everything is interconnected, Graphs are mostly used to represent the networks and model the relations between nodes, like routers, airports, paths in cities, users in social networks.

A graph can be:

- Directed: the edges have a direction from the vertex source to the vertex destination
- Undirected: the edges have no direction.
- Directed multigraph: a pair of vertices is linked by one two or more edges, it describes a multiple relationships. The edges share the same source and destination.
- Property Graphs: is a directed multigraph where vertex and edges have proprieties.

A tweet can contain 0 to multiple hashtags, each hashtag represents a topic of discussion, the presence of multiple hashtags increase the engagement of the users and the value of the publication. Using Scala, we implement a graph analytics pipeline with Spark Graph X in order to convert the DataFrame (as shown in Fig. 9) to a graph and find the top connected hashtags.

Building a graph with Graph X requires two arguments: RDD of Vertices and RDD of edges, which can be instantiated based on two specialized RDD implementations:

- The VertexRDD[VD] is a parameterized class, it's defined as RDD[(VertexId, VD)], VertexId is a vertex identifier, it is an instance of Long, VD is the vertex attribute or property it can be a user type defined or other type of data information that are related to vertex.
- The EdgeRDD[ED] is a parameterized class which is an implementation of RDD[Edge[ED]], an instance of Edge represents VertexId source, VertexId destination, and the attribute of the property of the edge.

We build the structure of vertices from the hashtag name, for each hashtag we create a unique identifier (VertexId) in 64 bit by using the MurmurHash3 library [20], the vertex propriety takes the string value of the hashtag name.

For the edge which is the link between two nodes, a pair of hashtags is generated by using the combinations function, since we have no information about the relationship between hashtags except their presence in the same tweet we opt to use the Twitter username as propriety of the edge. A triplet represents an edge with two connected vertices. We employed data with the hashtags entities having a size greater or equal to 2 to avoid the appearance of isolated nodes in our graph. We present as follow (see Fig. 10) the steps to generate the structures of vertices and edges:

```
// vertices
val vertices:RDD[(Long,String)] = htagsDf.rdd.flatMap { row =>
val hashtagw = row.getAs[Seq[String]]("hashtags")
hashtagw.map(tw =>
val lowerTw = tw.toLowerCase()
val twHashCode=  MurmurHash3.stringHash(lowerTw).toLong

        (twHashCode, lowerTw)
}
}
//edges
val edges:RDD[Edge[String]] = htagsDf.rdd.flatMap { row =>
val hashtagw = row.getAs[Seq[String]]("hashtags")
val name = row.get(1).toString
val propriete= name
val combinations= hashtagw.combinations(2)
combinations.map( combs=>
val combHash_1= MurmurHash3.stringHash(combs(0).toLowerCase()).toLong
val combHash_2= MurmurHash3.stringHash(combs(1).toLowerCase()).toLong
Edge(combHash_1, combHash_2, propriete)
    })
```

Fig. 10. Steps to generate the vertices and edges.

From a pair of RDD vertices and edges, we create an instance of Graph class to generate a graph data structure as follows: ***val graph = Graph(vertices, edges)*** (Fig. 11).

```
Vertices:
(1493225160,robots)
(1036629328,fintech)
(-1672873777,logistics)
(-1688278873,carbon3d)
(-84935145,grctuesdays)
(-1744201873,dataanalytics)
```

```
Edges:
Edge(-2140377696,-1864478021,Nicolas Pinto)
Edge(-2140377696,-1461490338,Nicolas Pinto)
Edge(-2140377696,-1064716166,Nicolas Pinto)
Edge(-2140377696,617838906,Nicolas Pinto)
Edge(-2140377696,1848604945,Nicolas Pinto)
Edge(-2135946292,-86107614,R.lalhminglianaC)
Edge(-2135946292,572257391,R.lalhminglianaC)
Edge(-2132848384,-1717602248,Boston Technology)
```

```
Triplets
((-2140377696,mobileapp),(-1864478021,ai),Nicolas Pinto)
((-2140377696,mobileapp),(-1461490338,bots),Nicolas Pinto)
((-2140377696,mobileapp),(-1064716166,chatbots),Nicolas Pinto)
((-2140377696,mobileapp),(617838906,roboadvisors),Nicolas Pinto)
((-2140377696,mobileapp),(1848604945,machinelearning),Nicolas Pinto
((-2135946292,computing),(-86107614,artificialintelligence),R.lalhm
((-2135946292,computing),(572257391,medicine),R.lalhminglianaC)
```

Fig. 11. Sample of graph vertices, graph edges and graph triplets.

Total of vertices = 3329, Total of edges = 208973, Total of triplets = 208973

Connected component is a subgraph whose vertices is a subset of the set of vertices of the original graph and whose edges is a subset of the set of the original graph. In nutshell connected component is a subgraph whose vertices are interconnected by a set of edges, if a vertex A is not linked directlty or indirecty to vertex B via another vertex C, then A and B aren't in the same connected component (Fig. 12).

```
(-2141701353,3078)  <--------- Component number 1
(-2140883310,17)
(-2076771034,8)
(-2135941161,7)
(-749294443,7)
(-2062995470,6)
```

Fig. 12. Sample of total vertices per component.

Connected components are generated by using the connectedComponents method as follows: ***val connectedComponentsGraph = graph.connectedComponents***

We extract the total of vertices and respectively the components to which they belong as follows: ***connectedComponentsGraph.vertices.map(_._2).countByValue.toSeq.sortBy(_._2). reverse.take(10)foreach(println)***

A top group of connected component is performed using an InnerJoin method in order to join vertices of the original graph and the vertices of the connected Components based on VertexId, then we can filter the hashtags that belong to the component number 1, the result can be stored as a text file (see Fig. 13). The top group of connected component contains 3078 hashtags, which represents 92.40% of all the original graph verticcs, they are strong interrelated to our six topics: big data, data science, machine learning, hadoop, spark and analytics.

robots	iot	dataanalysis	knowledgeengineering	autonomous	creepy
fintech	datalakes	industrialiot	networkscience	cosmosdb	diagnostics
logistics	java	remarketing	dataanalytcs	greentech	crm
analyticsplatform	informatics	datastrategy	clustering	zendesk	cdo
datamining	sparkr	automated	cassandra	codingflux_	iomt
grctuesdays	informatics	apachekafka	digitalliteracy	dataanalytcs	serverless
dataanalytics	digitization	intelligenthealthcare			

Fig. 13. Sample of hashtags that belong to the top group of connected component

5 Conclusion

In this paper we propose a social network analysis system designed around a Twitter API source. This system is in the form of a real time data pipeline capable to capture events which are the tweets related to informal learning and categorize them in topics in order to extract valuable information. We combine Apache Flume and Kafka to build the data ingestion layer which is responsible to retrieve live data. Apache Kafka cluster is used for categorizing the data that transit. To process data in real time we use Spark Streaming library. HDFS is used as a persistence layer.

This work is based on a real experience where we have collected a dataset of 20058 tweets, then we accomplished some steps to achieve the data pipeline analysis, and finally we extracted the top group of connected hashtags using Spark Graph X API.

During this work we have identified new directions concerning the eLearning. The first is to study the use of social network platforms by Moroccan students for informal learning purposes, and the second is to study how to integrate social networks channels in formal learning settings like eLearning platforms.

References

1. Cameron, R., Harrison, J.L.: The interrelatedness of formal, non-formal and informal learning: evidence from labour market program participants. Aust. J. Adult Learn. **52**(2), 277–309 (2012)
2. McPherson, M., Budge, K., Lemon, N.: New practices in doing academic development: Twitter as an informal learning space. Int. J. Acad. Dev. **20**(2), 126–136 (2015)
3. Wadhwa, P., Bhatia, M.P.S.: Social networks analysis: trends, techniques and future prospects. In: Fourth International Conference on Advances in Recent Technologies in Communication and Computing (ARTCom 2012), Bangalore, India, pp. 1–6 (2012)
4. White, T.: Hadoop: The Definitive Guide. O'Reilly Media, Inc., Newton (2012)
5. Zaharia, M., Chowdhury, M., Franklin, M.J., Shenker, S., Stoica, I.: Spark: cluster computing with working sets. In: Proceedings of the 2nd USENIX Conference on Hot Topics in Cloud Computing (2010)
6. Ghemawat, S., et al.: The Google File System. ACM SIGOPS Operating Systems Review (2013)
7. Zaharia, M., et al.: Resilient distributed datasets: a fault-tolerant abstraction for in-memory cluster computing. In: Proceedings of 9th USENIX Conference on Networked Systems Design and Implementation, p. 2 (2012)
8. Dean, J., Ghemawat, S.: MapReduce: simplified data processing on large clusters. Commun. ACM **51**(1), 107–113 (2008)
9. Bonchi, F., Castillo, C., Gionis, A., Jaimes, A.: Social network analysis and mining for business applications. ACM Trans. Intell. Syst. Technol. (TIST) Arch. **2**(3), 37 (2011). Article 22
10. Kim, Y., Hwang, E., Rho, S.: Twitter news-in-education platform for social collaborative and flipped learning. J. Supercomput. Springer, 1–19 (2016). https://doi.org/10.1007/s11227-016-1776-x
11. Aramo-Immonen, H., Kärkkäinen, H., Jussila, J.J., Joel-Edgar, S., Huhtamäki, J.: Visualizing informal learning behavior from conference participants' Twitter data with the Ostinato model. J. Comput. Hum. Behav. Arch. **55**(PA), 584–595 (2016)

12. Huhtamäki, J., Russell, M.G., Rubens, N., Still, K.: Ostinato: the exploration-automation cycle of user-centric, process-automated data-driven visual network analytics. In: Matei, S., Russell, M., Bertino, E. (eds.) Transparency in Social Media, pp. 197–222. Cham, Computational Social Sciences, Springer (2015). https://doi.org/10.1007/978-3-319-18552-1_11
13. Chen, X., Vorvoreanu, M., Madhavan, K.: Mining social media data for understanding students' learning experiences. IEEE Trans. Learn. Technol. **7**(3), 246–259 (2014)
14. Chandra, S., Khan, L., Muhaya, F.B.: Estimating Twitter user location using social interactions–a content based approach. In: IEEE Third International Conference on Privacy, Security, Risk and Trust and 2011 IEEE Third International Conference on Social Computing, Boston, MA, pp. 838–843 (2011)
15. Twitter libraries homepage. https://developer.twitter.com/en/docs/developer-utilities/twitter-libraries. Accessed 24 Feb 2018
16. Shreedharan, H.: Using Flume. O'Reilly Media, Inc., Sebastopol (2014)
17. Vohra, D.: Apache kafka. In: Practical Hadoop Ecosystem. Apress, Berkeley, CA Apache (2016)
18. Apache Flume homepage. https://flume.apache.org/. Accessed 24 Feb 2018
19. Bondy, J.A., Murty, U.S.R.: Graph Theory with Applications. American Elsevier Publishing Company, New York (1976)
20. MurmurHash3 documentation. https://www.scala-lang.org/files/archive/api/2.11.0-M4/index.html#scala.util.hashing.MurmurHash3$. Accessed 24 Feb 2018

A MapReduce-Based Adjoint Method to Predict the Levenson Self Report Psychopathy Scale Value

Manal Zettam(✉), Jalal Laassiri, and Nourdddine Enneya

Informatics, Systems and Optimization Laboratory, Department of Computer Science, Faculty of Science, Ibn Tofail University, Kenitra, Morocco
{manal.zettam,laassiri,enneya}@uit.ac.ma

Abstract. The Levenson Self Report Psychopathy serves as a measure to spot persons with psychopathic disorders able to commit crime or offend others. Indeed, predicting the Levenson Self Report Psychopathy factors would help investigator and even psychologist to spot offenders. In this paper, a statistical model is performed with the aim of predicting the Levenson Self Report Psychopathy scale value. For this purpose, the multiple regression statistical method is used. In addition, a parallelized algebraic adjoint method is performed to solve the least square problem. The MapReduce framework is used for this purpose. The Apache implementation of Mapreduce developed in Java untilled Hadoop 2.6.0 is deployed to tackle experiments.

Keywords: Levenson Self Report Psychopathy scale · MapReduce HDFS · Multiple regression analysis · Prediction

1 Introduction

Psychopathy refers to a disorder characterized by antisocial behaviors and exploitative interpersonal relationships [1,19]. According to [2], psychopathic traits involve manipulative and callous use of others, shallow and short-lived affect, irresponsible and impulsive behavior, egocentricy and pathological lying. Nonetheless, psychopaths lack of basic prosocial personality traits such as empathy, guilt, and perspective-taking [3–6]. Psychopaths generally exhibit glibness, superficial charm, grandiosity and deception [4,19].

In literature several measures have been developed to assess psychopathic personality traits [1]. The Hare psychopathic Checklist-Revised (PCL-R) and The Levenson Self Report Psychopathy (LSRP) are the most widely used measures to assess psychopathic personality traits. The PCL-R measure was developed on a criminal population and showed a strong reliance on corroborating file data thereby PCL-R measure is not appropriate for use in non-incarcerated samples. In contrast with PCL-R, the LSRP measure was developed on a collegial population it is appropriate for use in non-incarcerated samples.

Y. Tabii et al. (Eds.): BDCA 2018, CCIS 872, pp. 16–28, 2018.
https://doi.org/10.1007/978-3-319-96292-4_2

The LSRP measure was validated using a two factor model in which the first factor is related to affective/interpersonal deficits, and the second factor is related to an antisocial, impulsive lifestyle [4]. A numerous studies in literature on psychopathic disorders dig on the relationship binding the first and the second factors with different behaviors such as [7].

Ian Mitchell from Birmingham University provides datasets of Sexual offenders available at http://reshare.ukdataservice.ac.uk/852521/. The datasets were extracted and collected by means of emotional facial expression recognition procedures in conjunction with eye tracking and use of personality inventories. Ian Mitchell also provides the LSRP factors in his datasets.

In literature and during the last decades, numerous studies contributed to the criminal investigations such as [8,9]. Providing clear and accurate descriptions of each mental disorder is the main purpose of the Diagnostic and Statistical Manual of Mental Disorders DSM IV [8]. Thus, physicians and investigators could diagnose and treat patient on the basis of DSM IV. The reference [10], in addition to introduction of clinical prediction models, highlights the necessary steps to develop an accurate pediction model via regression analysis. Those steps are as follows:

- Expliciting the prediction problem by defining predictors and data,
- Defining the advantage and disadvantage of stepwise selection methods,
- Estimating model parameters,
- Determining the quality of the estimated model,
- Considering the validity of the new model,
- Considering the presentation of a prediction model.

Besides the multiple regression method explained above other predictive statistical methods are used in the literature. Indeed statistical models for prediction can be discerned in three main classes: regression, classification, and neural networks [11].

The multiple regression have been parallelized using the MapReduce Framework. Indeed, several works in literature such as [12,13] present parallelized versions of multiple regression. To the best of our knowledge, the parallelized algebraic adjoint method has been presented briefly for the first time by our previous work in [14]. Thus, the main contribution of the current work is to detail the parallelized algebraic adjoint method. Furthermore, the analysis tools available for multiple regression limit the number of predictors. Thus, presenting a solution capable of tackling a limitless number of predictors would allow the consideration of a great number of predictors thereby producing more accurate models.

In this paper, the prediction model of LSPR is constructed via regression method. The rest of this paper is organized as follows. The second section briefly introduces the MapReduce framework as well as the multiple linear regression. The third section of this paper, introduces the MapReduce-based adjoint method. Then the fourth section, contains the computational results as well as accuracy tests to verify the robustness of the statistical model.

2 Background

2.1 MapReduce and HDFS Technologies

MapReduce is considered both as a programming model for expressing distributed computations and an execution framework for large-scale data processing on clusters of commodity servers [15]. MapReduce was developed by Google and built on well-known parallel and distributed processing principles [16]. Hadoop is an open-source implementation of MapReduce.

2.2 Linear Regression Analysis

Multiple linear regression analysis aims to establish a relationship between a given dependent variable (the LSPR value) and two or more independent variables [17], also called the predictors, in the following form:

$$Y_i = \beta_0 + \beta_1 X_{i1} + \beta_2 X_{i2} + \cdots + \beta_p X_{ip} + \varepsilon_i \qquad (1)$$

In this equation $\beta_{i\in[0,p]}$ are the regression coefficients to be estimated based on a record of observations. The regression coefficients are estimated by means of resolving the least square problem. The adjoint method is one of methods resolving the least square problem.

2.3 Heap's Algorithm

Heap's algorithm, first proposed by [20], generates all possible permutations of n objects. Indeed, it generates a new permutation on the basis of previous one. The new permutation is obtained by interchanging a single pair of elements of the previous permutation. The authors of [21] describe Heap's algorithm as the most effective algorithm for generating permutations.

Let us consider the case of permutation containing n different elements. Heap found a systematic method for choosing at each step a pair of elements to switch, in order to produce every possible permutation of these elements exactly once.

For this purpose, initialize a counter by 0. Then, perform the following steps repeatedly until is equal to:

- Generate permutations of the first elements.
- Adjoining the last element to each of the generated permutation,
- Then if is odd, switch the first element and the last one,
- While if is even we can switch the element and the last one (there is no difference between even and odd in the first iteration).
- We add one to the counter and repeat.

The Heap's algorithm produces an exhaustif set of permutations ending with the element moved to the last position. The Heap's algorithm code in java programming language is detailed thereafter.

Heap's algorithm code in java programming language

```
int sum = 0;
public static int permute(String[ ] ourArray,
String[ ] ourArray1, int currentPosition,
int[ ][ ] M) {

int a = 0;
int sign = 0;
if (currentPosition == 1) {
   for (int j = 0; j < ourArray.length; j++) {
        a = a + M[j][Integer.parseInt(ourArray[j]) - 1];
        if (Integer.parseInt(ourArray[j]) != Integer.parseInt(ourArray1[j]))
sig = sig + 1;
   }
   if (sign % 2 == 0) {
        sum = sum + a;
        sign = 0;
        a = 0;
   }
   else if (sign % 2 == 1) {
        sum = sum - a;
        sign = 0;
        a = 0;
   }

} else {
   for (int i = 0; i < currentPosition; i++) {
        permute(ourArray, ourArray1,currentPosition - 1, M);
        if (currentPosition % 2 == 1) {
           swap(ourArray, 0, currentPosition - 1);
        } else {
           swap(ourArray, i, currentPosition - 1);
        }
        }
}
return sum;
    }
```

2.4 The Adjoint Method

The adjoint of the matrix A denoted $adj(A)$ or A^{+} is the transpose of the matrix obtained from A by replacing each element a_{ij} by its cofactorA_{ij}. A numerical example to explain step by step the calculation of the adjoint matrix is given below. Let consider the following A matrix:

$$A = \begin{pmatrix} 1\,2\,3 \\ 0\,5\,2 \\ 1\,0\,4 \end{pmatrix}$$

The matrix of cofactors is given by:

$$\begin{pmatrix} A_{11} & A_{12} & A_{13} \\ A_{21} & A_{22} & A_{23} \\ A_{31} & A_{32} & A_{33} \end{pmatrix} = \begin{pmatrix} 20 & 2 & -5 \\ -8 & 1 & 2 \\ -11 & -2 & 5 \end{pmatrix}$$

Since the adjoint matrix is the transpose of the matrix of cofactor, the adjoint is calculated as follows:

$$A^{+} = \begin{pmatrix} 20 & -8 & -11 \\ 2 & 1 & -2 \\ -5 & 2 & 5 \end{pmatrix}$$

As well known the adjoint method is defined as the steps undertaken to find the inverse of a matrix with the aim of solving the least square problem. The pseudo-code of the adjoint method is given thereafter.

Algorithm 1. The adjoint method pseudo-code

Data: A sample of patients
Result: the inverse of the A matrix
Construct the A matrix from the patient sample;
Initialize a $p \times p$ matrix denoted A' ;
foreach $a_{ij} \in A$ **do**
    Define $(p-1) \times (p-1)$ matrix denoted B ;
    Calculate $Det(B)$;
    $a'_{ij} = (-1)^{(i+j)} Det(B)$;
end
foreach $a'_{ij} \in A'$ **do**
    $temp = a'_{ij}$;
    $a'_{ij} = a'_{ji}$;
    $a'_{ji} = temp$;
end

---

3 Mapreduce-Based Adjoint Method

A MapReduce-based adjoint method (MR-AM) is proposed by this paper to make conventional adjoint method work effectively in distributed environment. Our method has two steps. The following part describes in detail the two steps of our method.

MapReduce breaks the processing into two phases: The map phase and the reduce phase. Each phase has (key, value) pairs as input and output.

In the current study, a text input format represents each line in the dataset as a text value. The key is the first number departed by a plus sign from the reminder of the line. Let consider the following sample lines of input data:

$$
\begin{array}{c}
0 + 067 - 011 - 95 \ldots \\
0 + 143 - 101 - 22 \ldots \\
\vdots \ddots \ddots \vdots \\
\vdots \ddots \ddots \vdots \\
1 + 243 - 011 - 22 \ldots \\
1 + 340 - 310 - 12 \ldots \\
\vdots \ddots \ddots \vdots \\
\vdots \ddots \ddots \vdots \\
4 + 44 - 301 - 265 \ldots
\end{array}
$$

The keys is the line numbers of the matrix. The map function calculates the determinant for B matrix. The output of the Map function is as follows:

$$
\begin{array}{c}
(0, 0) \\
(0, 22) \\
\vdots \\
\vdots \\
(1, -11) \\
(1, 111) \\
\vdots \\
\vdots \\
(4, 78)
\end{array}
$$

The pseudo code of Map Function is as follows:

Algorithm 2. The Map function pseudo-code

Data: LongWritable *Key*, Text *value*, Context *con*
Result: a set of (*outputkey*, *outputvalue*)
foreach $v \in$ *value* **do**
  Define the *outputkey* based on v;
  Pass the *outputkey* to the *con* parameter;
  Construct a Matrix denoted B from v;
  Calculate the determinant of B ;
  Define the *outputvalue* as $Det(B)$;
end

The output from the map function is processed by the MapReduce framework before being sent to the reduce function. This processing sorts and groups the key-value pairs by key. So, continuing the example, our reduce function sees the following input:

$$(0, [0, 22, \ldots])$$
$$(1, [-11, 111, \ldots])$$
$$\vdots$$
$$(4, [78, \ldots])$$

The reduce function returns (i, β_j) as output. The output of the reduce function is as follows:

$$(0, 20)$$
$$(1, 13)$$
$$\vdots$$
$$(4, 0.5)$$

The pseudo code of Reduce Function is as follows:

Algorithm 3. The reduce function pseudo-code

Data: Text word, Iterable <IntWritable> values, Context con
Result: a set of (i, β_j)
foreach $v \in value$ **do**
  $sum = sum + \frac{1}{Det(XX')}(vYX[i])$;
  $i++$;
end
Define the *outputKey* as the *word* variable;
Define the *outputvalue* as the *sum* variable;

The above steps are described in Fig. 1.

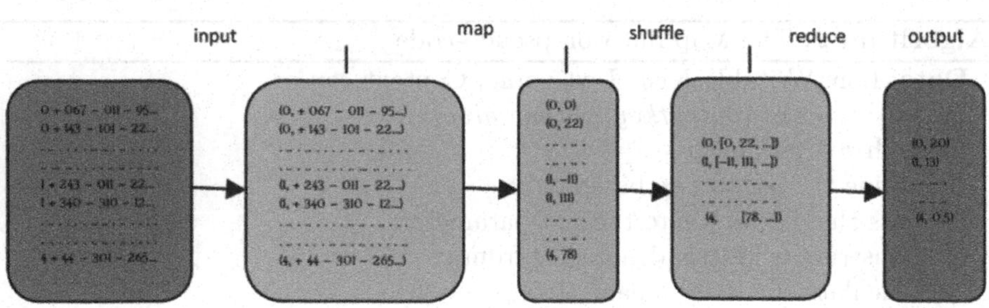

Fig. 1. MapReduce logical data flow.

4 Model Evaluation and Computational Results

4.1 Dataset Description

In this paper, a case study is presented on predicting the Levenson Self Report Psychopathy scale for a person on the basis of several factors. The data used to construct the prediction model is similar to the one used to spot sexual offenders available at http://reshare.ukdataservice.ac.uk/852521/. Based on the factors provided in the studies of Ian Mitchell we aim to predict the value of the first and the second factors of LSRP measure. The following variable codes are relevant to aaFHNeyesAccuracyData, aaFHNeyesDwellTime and aaFHNeyesFixCount datasets:

- Participant = Identification number assigned to participant
- Eye tracker = Method of eye tracking (1 = head mounted; 2 = tower)
- Primary = Primary subscale of the Levenson Self Report Psychopathy Scale
- Secondary = Secondary subscale of the Levenson Self Report Psychopathy Scale

Variable names for each trial type are coded as follows [Emotion]_[Intensity]_[Sex]_[Region] using the following values:

- Emotion: ANG = Angry expression, DIS = Disgust expression, FEAR = Fear expression, HAP = Happy expression, SAD = Sad expression, SUR = Surprise expression
- Intensity: 5 = 55, 9 = 90
- Sex: F = Female, M = male
- Region: Eyes = Eyes, Mouth = Mouth

Thus, ANG_ 5_ F refers to an angry expression at 55% intensity, expressed by a female face and ANG_ 5_ F_ Eyes refers to the eye region of the same face. The Fig. 2 illustrates the variation of primary and seconde subscale of LSRP.

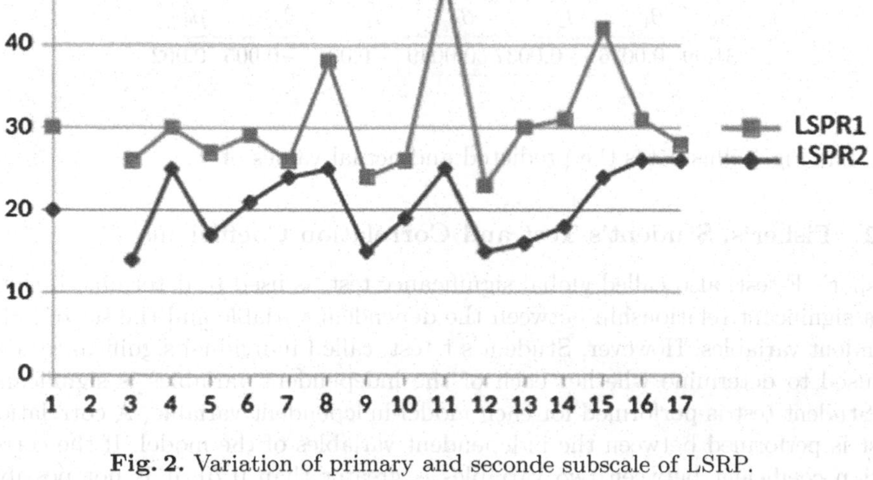

Fig. 2. Variation of primary and seconde subscale of LSRP.

In our case we consider an illustrative example where we consider that only six variables are responsible for the variation of the primary LSRP subscale.

For the first example the first predictor X_1 denotes an angry expression at 55% intensity, expressed by a female face in eye region (ANG_ 5_ F_ eyes). The second variable X_2 denotes an angry expression at 55% intensity, expressed by a female face in mouth region (ANG_ 5_ F_ mouth). The third variable X_3 denotes a surprise expression at 10% intensity, expressed by a female face in mouth region (SUR_ 1_ M_ mouth). The fourth variable X_4 denotes a surprise expression at 55% intensity, expressed by a female face in eye region (SUR_ 5_ F_ eyes). The fifth variable X_5 denotes a surprise expression at 90% intensity, expressed by a female face in eye region (SUR_ 9_ F_ eyes). The sixth variable X_6 denotes a surprise expression at 90 % intensity, expressed by a female face in mouth region (SUR_ 9_ F_ mouth).

Let assume that X_{i1} is the random variable associating an angry expression at 55% intensity, expressed by a female face in eye region to an individual. X_{i2} is the random variable associating an angry expression at 55% intensity, expressed by a female face in mouth region to an individual. X_{i3} is the random variable associating a surprise expression at 10% intensity, expressed by a female face in mouth region to an individual. X_{i4} is the random variable associating a surprise expression at 55% intensity, expressed by a female face in eye region to an individual. X_{i5} is the random variable associating a surprise expression at 90% intensity, expressed by a female face in eye region to an individual. X_{i6} is the random variable associating a surprise expression at 90% intensity, expressed by a female face in mouth region to an individual. The obtained regression model is as follows (Table 1):

$$Y_i = \beta_0 + \beta_1 X_{i1} + \beta_2 X_{i2} + \beta_3 X_{i3} + \beta_4 X_{i4} + +\beta_5 X_{i5} + \beta_6 X_{i6} + \varepsilon_i \qquad (2)$$

Table 1. Parameters' values of Eq. 2

β_0	β_1	β_2	β_3	β_4	β_5	β_6
31.09	0.0036	−0.0037	0.0049	−0.001	−0.005	0.002

The Fig. 3 illustrates the predicted and actual values of Y.

4.2 Fisher's, Student's Test and Correlation Coefficient

Fisher's F-test, also called global significance test; is used to determine if there is a significant relationship between the dependent variable and the set of independent variables. However, Student's t test, called individual significance test, is used to determine whether each of the independent variables is significant. A Student test is performed for each model-independent variable. A correlation test is performed between the independent variables of the model. If the correlation coefficient between two variables is greater than 0.70, it is not possible

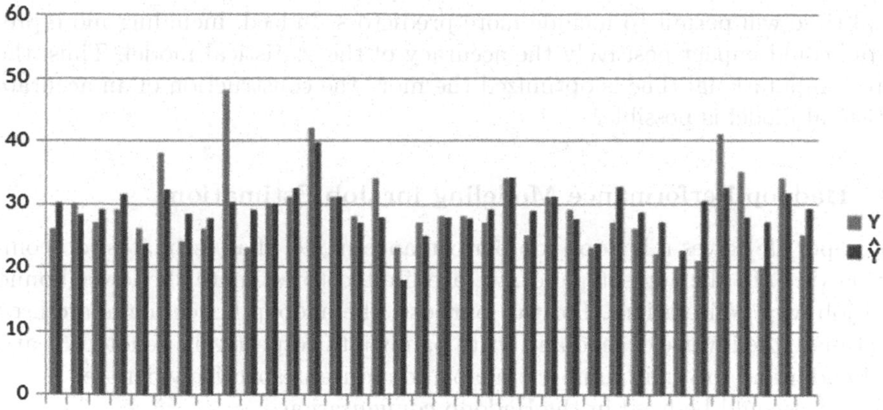

Fig. 3. Predicted and actual values of Y.

to determine the effect of a particular independent variable on the dependent variable.

A Fisher test, based on Fisher's distribution, can be used to test whether a relationship is meaningful. With a single independent variable, the Ficher's test leads to the same conclusion as the Student test. On the other hand, with more than one independent variable, only the F test can be used to test the overall meaning of a relationship.

The logic underlying the use of the Ficher's test to determine whether the relationship is statistically significant or not, is based on the construction of two independent estimates of σ^2. A table similar to the ANOVA table summarizes Fisher's significance test.

Table 2. Fisher's significance test.

Source	DF	SS	MS	F	P
Factor	6	475,67	79,28	2,56	0,04
Error	29	898,63	30,99		
Total	35	1374,31			

Table 2 represents the Fisher's significance test where DF denotes the degrees of freedom in the source. SS denotes the sum of squares due to the source. MS denotes the mean sum of squares due to the source. F denotes the F-statistic. P denotes the P-value. In java a framework called `edu.northwestern.utils.math.statistics.FishersExacttest` is available for performing the Fisher's test.

The numbers contained in Table 2 proof that the use of six variables is not enough to predict accurately the LSRP value therefore reducing the computational time will permit to include more predictors. Indeed, including more predictors could impact positively the accuracy of the statistical model. Thus, the more computational time is optimized the more the construction of an accurate statistical model is possible.

4.3 Hadoop Performance Modeling for Job Estimation

The paper [18] gives a hadoop job performance model that estimates job completion time. In the current paper, we are limited to estimate the lower bound for a job with N iterations. For this purpose, the hadoop benchmarks are used to estimate the inverse of read and write bandwidth respectively denoted β_r and β_w. In addition, the limit number of map and reduce, respectively denoted m_{max} and r_{max}, should be fixed in the Hadoop configuration.

The Lower bound for a job with N iterations, denoted T_{lb}, is estimated on the basis of the following formula:

$$T_{lb} = \sum_{j=1}^{N} \frac{R_j^m \beta_r + W_j^m \beta_w}{p_j^m} + \frac{R_j^r \beta_r + W_j^r \beta_w}{p_j^r} \tag{3}$$

subject to

$$p_j^m = min(m_{max}, m_j) \tag{4}$$

$$p_j^r = min(r_{max}, r_j, k_j) \tag{5}$$

$$R_j^m = number\ of\ data\ read\ in\ the\ j^{th}\ map \tag{6}$$

$$W_j^m = number\ of\ data\ write\ in\ the\ j^{th}\ map \tag{7}$$

$$R_j^r = number\ of\ data\ read\ in\ the\ j^{th}\ reduce \tag{8}$$

$$W_j^r = number\ of\ data\ write\ in\ the\ j^{th}\ reduce \tag{9}$$

where k_j is the number of distinct input keys passed to the reduce tasks for step j and where m_j and r_j are respectively the number of map and reduce tasks for step j.

We conduct several groups of experiments on a local machine equipped with only 2 cores. To estimate β_r and β_w, we used Hadoop benchmarks. The computed lower bounds are illustrated in Table 3.

Table 3. Computed lower bounds

HDFS size (GB)	T_{lb} (secs.)
1	23
16	115
32	102

5 Conclusions

In this paper, a parallelized algebraic adjoint method based on MapReduce is presented. This solution aims to efficiently predict the Levenson Self Report Psychopathy scale value based on a colossal number of factors. For the sake of clarity and simplicity, throughout the current paper example with small number of factors is presented. The parallelized algebraic adjoint method proofs its efficiency by reducing the calculation time. Thus the consideration of colossal number of predictors become possible and predicted model become more accurate.

References

1. Brinkley, C., Schmitt, W., Smith, S., Newman, J.: Construct validation of a self-report psychopathy scale: does Levenson's selfreport psychopathy scale measure the same constructs as Hare's psychopathy checklist-revised? Pers. Individ. Differ. **31**(7), 1021–1038 (2001)
2. Cleckley, H.: The mask of sanity; an attempt to reinterpret the so-called psychopathic personality. Oxford, England (1941)
3. Gummelt, H., Anestis, J., Carbonell, J.: Examining the Levenson self report psychopathy scale using a graded response model. Pers. Individ. Differ. **53**(8), 1002–1006 (2012)
4. Hare, R.D.: The psychopathy checklist-Revised (2003)
5. Lykken, D.T.: The Antisocial Personalities. Lawrence Erlbaum Associates, Mahwah (1995)
6. Marcus, D.K., John, S.L., Edens, J.F.: A taxometric analysis of psychopathic personality. J. Abnorm. Psychol. **113**(4), 626 (2004)
7. Dotterer, H.L., Waller, R., Neumann, C.S., Shaw, D.S., Forbes, E.E., Hariri, A.R., Hyde, L.W.: Examining the factor structure of the self-report of psychopathy short-form across four young adult samples. Assessment **24**(8), 1062–1079 (2017)
8. Bell, C.: Dsm-iv: diagnostic and statistical manual of mental disorders. JAMA **272**(10), 828–829 (1994)
9. Pramanik, M.I., Lau, R.Y.K., Yue, W.T., Ye, Y., Li, C.: Big data analytics for security and criminal investigations. Wiley Interdiscip. Rev.: Data Min. Knowl. Discov. **7**(4) (2017)
10. Steyerberg, E.W.: Clinical Prediction Models: A Practical Approach to Development, Validation, and Updating. Springer, Heidelberg (2008). https://doi.org/10.1007/978-0-387-77244-8
11. Hastie, T., Tibshirani, R., Friedman, J.H.: The Elements of Statistical Learning: Data Mining, Inference, and Prediction. Springer, Heidelberg (2001). https://doi.org/10.1007/978-0-387-84858-7
12. Adjout, M.R., Boufares, F.: A massively parallel processing for the multiple linear regression. In: Tenth International Conference on SignalImage Technology and Internet-Based Systems, pp. 666–671 (2014)
13. Padua, D. (ed.): Encyclopedia of Parallel Computing. Springer, Heidelberg (2011). https://doi.org/10.1007/978-0-387-09766-4
14. Zettam, M., Laassiri, J., Enneya, N.: A software solution for preventing Alzheimer's disease based on MapReduce framework. In: 2017 IEEE International Conference on Information Reuse and Integration (IRI), pp. 192–197 (2017)

15. Lin, J., Dyer, C.: Data-intensive text processing with MapReduce. Synth. Lect. Hum. Lang. Technol. **3**(1), 1–177 (2010)
16. Ghemawat, S., Gobioff, H., Leung, S.: The Google file system. In: ACM SIGOPS Operating Systems Review, vol. 37, pp. 29–43. ACM (2003)
17. Sen, A., Srivastava, M.: Multiple regression. In: Regression Analysis. Springer Texts in Statistics. Springer, New York (1990)
18. Khan, M., Jin, Y., Li, M., Xiang, Y., Jiang, C.: Hadoop performance modeling for job estimation and resource provisioning. IEEE Trans. Parallel Distrib. Syst. **27**(2), 441–454 (2016)
19. Gummelt, H.D., Anestis, J.C., Carbonell, J.L.: Examining the Levenson self report psychopathy scale using a graded response model. Personal. Individ. Differ. **53**(8), 1002–1006 (2012)
20. Heap, B.R.: Permutations by interchanges. Comput. J. **6**(3), 293–298 (1963)
21. Sedgewick, R.: Permutation generation methods. ACM Comput. Surv. **9**(2), 137–164 (1977)

Big Data Optimisation Among RDDs Persistence in Apache Spark

Khadija Aziz(✉), Dounia Zaidouni, and Mostafa Bellafkih

Networks, Informatics and Mathematics department,
National Institute of Posts and Telecommunications, Rabat, Morocco
{k.aziz,zaidouni,bellafkih}@inpt.ac.ma

Abstract. Nowadays, several actors of digital technologies produce an infinite number of data coming from several sources such as: social networks, connected objects, e-commerce, and radars. Several technologies are implemented to generate all this data which is incremented quickly. In order to exploit this data efficiently and durably, it is important to respect the dynamics of their chronological evolution. For fast and reliable processing, powerful technologies are designed to analyze large data. Apache Spark is designed to make fast and sophisticated processing, but when it comes to process a huge amount of data, Spark becomes slower until it doesn't enough memory to process the data and it has to pay for more memory consumption. In this paper, we highlight the implementation of the framework Apache Spark. Thereafter, we conduct experimental simulations to show the weakness of Apache Spark. Finally, to further enforce our contribution, we propose to persist RDDs (Resilient Distributed Dataset) in order to improve performances for computing data.

Keywords: Big Data · Apache Spark · Processing · Computing Performances · Persistence · RDDs · Memory · Velocity

1 Introduction

Big Data is a set of techniques and architectures that allows to analyze and process a large amount of varied data. According to Gartner [1], Big Data is a concept that brings together a set of tools that address the three issues: volume: a considerable amount of data to process, variety: varied data from several sources, and speed: the frequency of creation, collection, and processing of these data.

Data volume mainly refers to all types of the data which is generated from different sources and continuously expands over time. In today's generation, the storing and processing includes exabytes (10^{18} bytes) or even zettabytes (10^{21} bytes) whereas almost 10 years ago, only (10^6 bytes) were stored on floppy disks.

Two technologies have facilitated the exponential growth of data: first, the Cloud Computing which allows to offer a set of service for the management and the storage of data. Second, data processing technologies such as Hadoop [2] and

Y. Tabii et al. (Eds.): BDCA 2018, CCIS 872, pp. 29–40, 2018.
https://doi.org/10.1007/978-3-319-96292-4_3

Spark [3], and the integration of MapReduce [4] which allows a high performance parallel computing.

In this study, we use Apache Spark to study the velocity of data processing. We chose Apache Spark because it is very fast for processing Big Data, and it is very powerful for distributed data processing. Developed by AMPLab of UC Berkeley University in 2009 [5], Apache Spark is built to perform Big Data analysis and it is designed primarily for speed and ease of use. Moreover, we present Resilient Distributed Datasets (RDDs), it lets process data across the cluster in memory and persist intermediate results in memory, also if data in memory is lost, it can be recreated.

The rest of paper is structured as follows: Sect. 2 provides Spark overview and describes functioning mechanisms of RDDs for processing data. While Sect. 3 details our implementation and experimental settings. The experimental evaluation of data analysis with Spark using persistence RDDs the drawbacks of using Spark in case of using a large amount of data and how Spark pays for more memory consumption are discussed in Sect. 4. Finally, Sect. 5 entails the concluding remarks and future work.

2 Literature Review

2.1 Apache Spark

Apache Spark is an open source Big Data processing framework built to perform analysis and designed for speed and ease of use. Spark offers a framework to meet the needs of Big Data processing for different types of data from different sources. This system provides APIs (Application Programming Interface) in different programming languages such as Scala, Java and Python. Apache Spark supports in-memory computing across DAG (Directed Acyclic Graph) that allows it to do a fast processing [19]. Apache Spark has an advanced DAG execution engine, Spark can be faster up to 10x than MapReduce for batches processing on disk, and up to 100x faster data analysis in memory [3].

The functions of the Spark engine are very advanced and different than other technologies. This engine is developed for processing in-memory and on disk [6], this internal processing capacity makes it faster compared to traditional data processing engines.

2.2 RDD (Resilient Distributed Datasets)

The RDD [7] is the basic component of Apache Spark. The most instructions for processing data in Spark consist of performing operations on RDDs. RDD (Resilient Distributed Dataset) refers:

- **Resilient**: If data in memory is lost, it can be recreated.
- **Distributed**: Data is processed across the cluster.
- **Dataset**: Initial data can come from a source such as a file, or it can be created programmatically.

The RDD is immutable [8], Data in an RDD is never changed and transform in sequence to modify the data as needed. Each data or dataset in RDD is divided into partitions, and this partitions are computed among different nodes of the cluster.

The RDDs are a read-only [8], it is a set of partitioned collection. There are three ways to create an RDD: From a file or set of files, from data in memory, and from another RDD.

2.3 RDD and Fault-Tolerance

Fault-tolerance is one of important features in Apache Spark [9], it refers the capacity to recover loss data after a failure occurs. Generally, data is partitioned across worker nodes. Partitioning is done automatically three times by Spark as shown in Fig. 1, thus we can control how many partitions can be created.

By default, Spark partitions file-based RDDs by block [10]. Each block loads into a single partition. If a partition in memory becomes unavailable in any node, the driver starts a new task to recompute the partition on a different node, then Lineage is preserved, data is never lost.

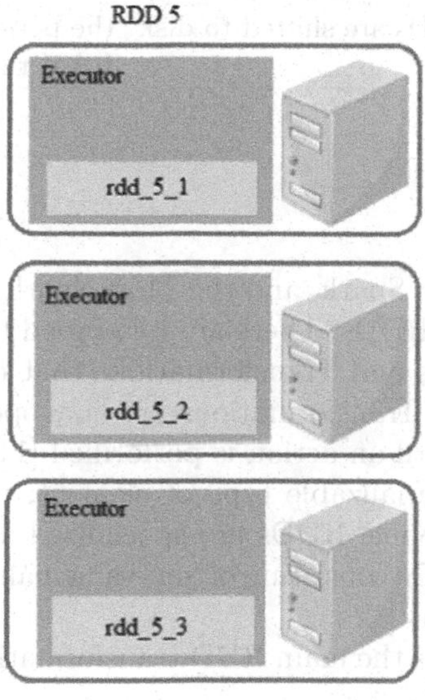

Fig. 1. RDDs on th cluster.

2.4 The Benefits of RDDs

The main idea behind RDD is to hold and optimize iterative and interactive algorithms. The RDD is immutable, Data in an RDD transforms in sequence to modify as needed. Data in RDD is divided into partitions and this partitions are computed through several nodes. To understand the benefits of RDD.

We compare the RDD (resilient distributed dataset) with DSM (Distributed Shared Memory) in Table 1, this comparison will show the main differences that make RDD the basic component in Apache Spark.

Table 1. RDD vs DSM.

	RDD	DSM
Read	The read operation is coarse grained or fine grained	The read operation is fine-grained
Write	The write operation is coarse grained	The Write operation is fine grained
Consistency	The consistency of RDD is trivial at means the RDD is immutable in nature. The level of consistency is high	The system lets the memory being consistent and the results of memory will be predictable
Fault-recovery	Each lost data is recovered using lineage	lost data is recovered by a checkpointing technique
Straggler mitigation	Possible to mitigate stragglers using backup task	Very difficult to use straggler mitigation
Case of not enough memory	The RDDs are shifted to disk	the performance decreases if the RAM runs out of storage

2.5 RDD Operations

RDDs are a key concept in Spark, and the Most Spark programming consists of performing operations on RDDs. There are two broad types of RDD operations: Actions that return values and Transformations that define a new RDD based on the current RDD. The Transformations are lazy operations because Data in RDDs is not processed until an action is performed [11].

RDDs can hold any serializable type of element: primitive types, sequence types, and mixed typed. Some RDDs are specialized and have additional functionality: Pair RDDs (RDDs consisting of key-value pairs), Double RDDs (RDDs consisting of numeric data) [12].

The following table lists the main RDD transformations and actions available in Spark.

2.6 Spark Architecture and Processing Data

Apache Spark runs applications independently through its architecture [13]. Figure 1 represents Apache Spark architecture.

- Spark runs the applications independently in the cluster, these applications are combined by SparkContext Driver program.

Table 2. RDDs transformations and actions available in Spark.

Actions	count(): it returns the number of elements
	take(n): it returns an array of the first n elements
	collect(): it returns an array of all elements
	saveAsTextFile(dir): it saves to text file(s)
Transformations	map(function): it creates a new RDD by performing a function on each record in the base RDD
	filter(function): it creates a new RDD by including or excluding each record in the base RDD according to a Boolean function
	flatMap: it maps one element in the base RDD to multiple elements
	distinct: it filters out duplicates
	sortBy: it uses the provided function to sort
	intersection: it creates a new RDD with all elements in both original RDDs
	union: it adds all elements of two RDDs into a single new RDD
	zip: it pairs each element of the first RDD with the corresponding element of the second
	subtract: it removes the elements in the second RDD from the first RDD

- Spark connects to several types of Cluster Managers (such as YARN, Mesos) to allocate resources between applications to run on a Cluster.
- Once connected, Spark acquires executors on the cluster nodes, which are processes that perform calculations and store data for the application.
- Spark sends the application code passed to SparkContext to the executors.
- SparkContext sends tasks to executors to execute.

Figure 2 shows how data is processed in Spark. Spark process data through different stages:

- A RDD is created by parallelizing a dataset in the driver program or by loading the data from the external storage system as HBase.
- Results of RDDs are recorded to apply to the data.
- Each time a new action is called, the entire RDD must be recalculated. Intermediate results are stored in memory.
- The output is returned to the driver.

Spark copies the data into RAM (processing in-memory). This type of processing reduces the time needed to interact with physical servers and this makes Spark faster. For data recovery in case of a failure, Spark uses RRDs (Fig. 3).

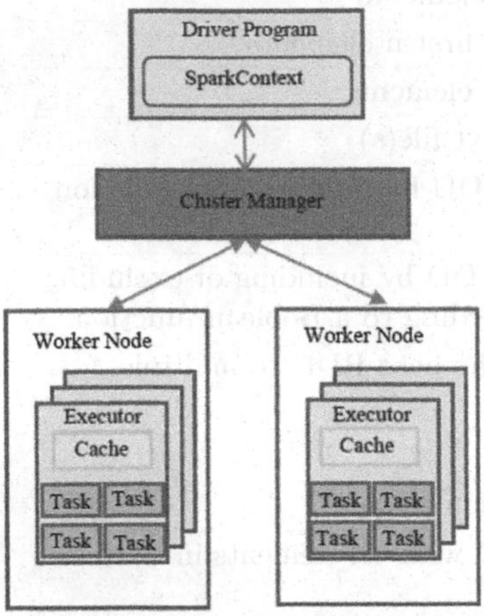

Fig. 2. Spark architecture.

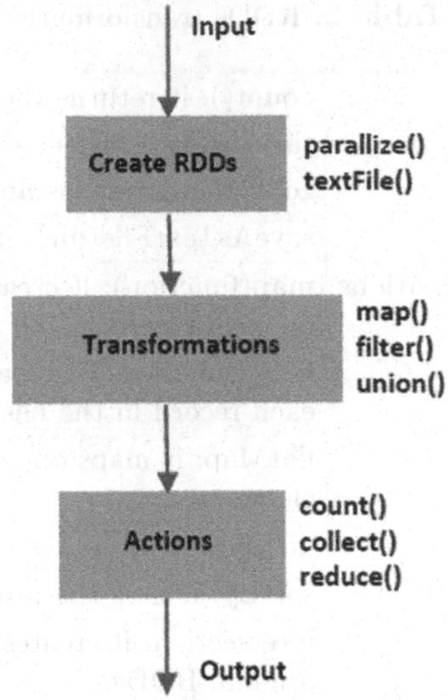

Fig. 3. Data flow in Spark.

3 Implementation

3.1 Cluster Architecture and Environment

The cluster of this implementation is composed of three machines, one of them is master and the other two machines are designed as workers. Figure 4 shows the architecture of this implementation.

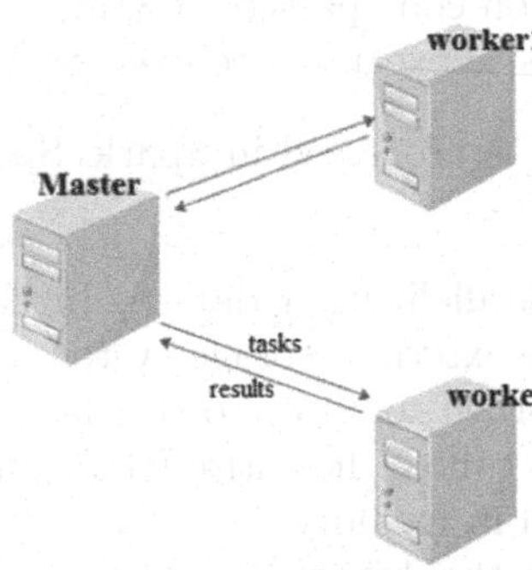

Fig. 4. Cluster architecture.

Table 2 shows information about the cluster deployed in our study: Hostname, IP address, Memory, OS, processors and hard disk. Table 3 shows information about software configuration.

We have implemented Spark 2.0.1 and then we have stored data in HDFS, because spark can read from any Hadoop input such as HBase and HDFS. In this study we choose different data size (up to 10 GB) to analyze and test the capacity of Spark. After each processing experimental, spark saves results in HDFS (Table 4).

Table 3. Informations of Spark cluster.

Hostname	Master	Worker1	Worker2
IP address	192.168.1.1/24	192.168.1.2/24	192.168.1.3/24
Memory	3 GB	1 GB	1 GB
OS	Linux (Ubuntu)	Linux (Ubuntu)	Linux (Ubuntu)
Processors	1	1	1
Hard disk	40 GB	40 GB	40 GB

Table 4. Software configuration.

Software name	Version
OS	Ubuntu 14.04/64 bit
Spark	2.0.1
JRE	Java(TM) SE Runtime Environment (build 1.8.0_131-b11)
Virtualization platform	VMware Workstation Pro 12

3.2 WordCount Overview

Word Count lets to find the frequency of words in a file or a set of files, and it is classic example of big data analysis. We care about word count because it rates the ranking of online content like blogs, articles or any digital content, and it optimizes content length from search engine to audience actions (For example in search engine Google).

3.3 WordCount on Spark

Algorithm 1 is the Word Count program implemented in Spark. First, we load data from HDFS using the function textFile(). Next, the functions flatMap(), map(), and reduceByKey(), are invoked to record the metadata of how to process the actual data. And then, all of transformations are called to compute data. Finally the result is saved in HDFS using function saveAsText().

To optimize processing data we use RDD persistence that saves the result of RDD evaluation. We use different storage levels according to our need to improve performance. This experimental step will be discussed in further detail in next section.

Algorithm 1. Word Count

```
val wc = sc.textFile(input).
  flatMap(line ⇒ line.split(’’)).
  map(word ⇒ (word,1)).
  reduceByKey((v1,v2) ⇒ v1+v2)
  wc.saveAsTextFile(output)
```

4 Evaluation

We evaluated Spark through several experiments by increasing data up to 10 GB to visualize how Spark behaves according to the data size, moreover we optimized data by persisting RDDs. Overall, our experimental studies shows the following results:

- Spark becomes slower by increasing data, especially when it comes to process a huge amount of data.
- Increasing memory driver to 4G improves the velocity of processing up to 8.33%.
- RDDs persistence improves performances and it decreases the execution time.
- Storage levels of persisted RDDs have different execution times.
- MEMORY_ONLY level has less execution time compared to other levels.

4.1 Running Times on Spark

We conduct several experiments by increasing data to evaluate running time of Spark according to data size. When data is small, Spark makes very fast processing. We increase the data size, Spark becomes slower, as shown in Fig. 4. When data is extremely large, the memory is not enough to store newly intermediates results, moreover, Spark crashes (Figs. 5 and 6).

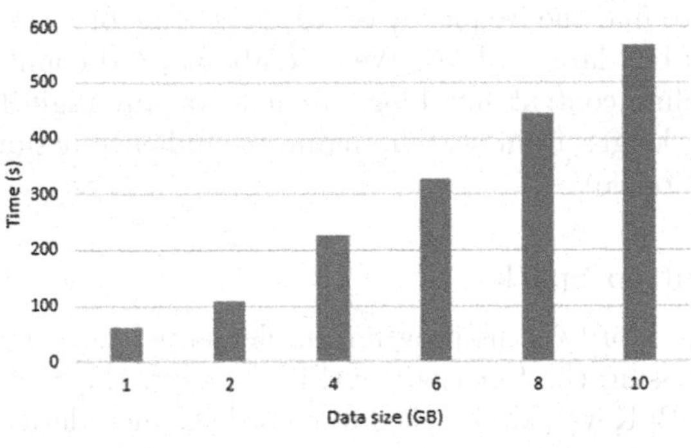

Fig. 5. Running times for Word Count on Spark, processing increasingly larger input datasets.

To improve the processing time, we proposed increasing memory driver to 4G, and this approach improves the capacity of processing up to 8.33%.

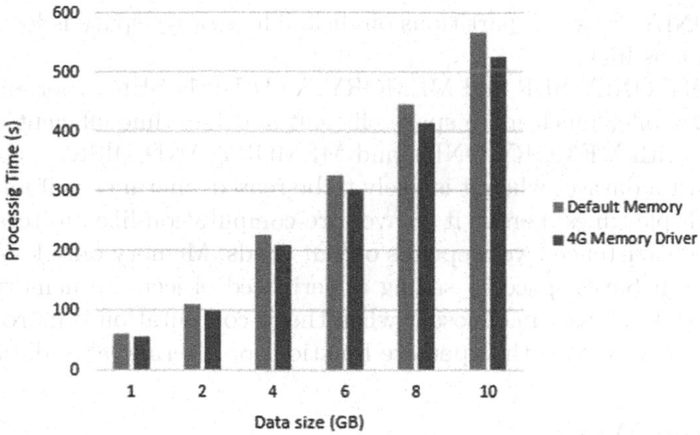

Fig. 6. Running times for Word Count on Spark, using default memory and 4G in memory diver.

4.2 RDD Persistence

In this step, we use an optimization method, it is called RDD persistence, and this lets the storage of intermediates results of RDD. By persisting RDD, we can use saved intermediates results later if it is requisite.

We conduct experimental simulations to evaluate RDD persistence using different storage levels. In this case we use 1 GB of data (Fig. 7).

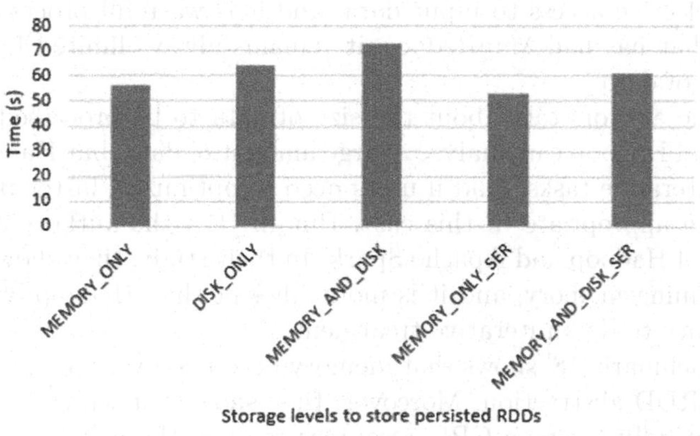

Fig. 7. Running times according to storage levels to store persisted RDDs.

MEMORY_ONLY: Store data in memory if it fits. In this level the storage space is very high and the computation time is low.

MEMORY_AND_DISK: Store partitions on disk if they do not fit in memory. In this level the storage space is high, the computation time is high.

DISK_ONLY: Store all partitions on disk. The storage space is low, the computation time is high.

MEMORY_ONLY_SER and MEMORY_AND_DISK_SER to serialize data in memory, they offer much more space efficient and less time efficient, compared successively with MEMORY_ONLY and MEMORY_AND_DISK.

We persist a dataset when it is likely to be reused, that means if an RDD will be used multiple times, persist it to avoid re-computation like an iterative algorithms. The persistence level depends on our needs. Memory only level has best performance, it Saves space by saving as serialized objects in memory if necessary. For Disk level, we can choose it when the re-computation is more expensive than disk read such as with expensive functions or filtering large datasets.

5 Related Work

Several architectures and technologies have been implemented to realize an optimal treatment on big data. In addition, several studies focused on technologies that perform treatments in an effective way in meeting the needs of data scientists. In this section, some points need to be discussed.

In [14], the authors say that Hadoop is designed to analyze and process a large amount of data, and MapReduce is a programming paradigm that allows parallel processing on a large data set. So both of them are used to analyze an enormous amount of data. But In [15], the authors describe the weaknesses of MapReduce witch are related to its performance limits and the originally of this paradigm. The authors identified a list of problems related to the processing of Big Data with MapReduce, for example: MapReduce consume very high communication, it makes a selective access to input data, and it is wasteful processing Despite the success that has had MapReduce, it remains always limited for analysis a huge amount of data.

In [16], the authors talk about the size of data to be processed. They said that Spark and Hadoop can analyze a large amount of data, but Hadoop remains too slow for iterative tasks. And if users need to optimize Cluster performance, Spark is more appropriate in this case. But In [17], the authors evaluate the performance of Hadoop and Apache Spark. In their study, they show that Spark is very consuming memory, and it is more efficient than Hadoop when there is enough memory to do an iterative treatment.

Spark Benchmark [18] shows that memory becomes a very high resource even if the use of RDD abstraction. Moreover, they show that while increasing task parallelism to fully leverage CPU resources reduces the execution time, overcommitting CPU resources lead to CPU contention and adversely impact the execution time.

6 Conclusion and Future Work

In this article, we have shown how Spark performance did decrease when using a huge large of data. Moreover, we have proposed to increase memory driver, as obtained in our experimental setup, this technique have helped to improve the velocity of processing. Therefore we have used resilient distributed datasets (RDDs) in order to optimize processing time and storage space according to our needs, this method did improve performance and did decrease the execution time.

As part of our future work, we will study a very important direction that consists of adjusting the various configuration parameters to improve the processing speed and the storage space of Spark. We will also evaluate Spark through a series of experiments for example Amazon EC2. In fact, we are currently working on a model that finds the equivalence between processing time and memory usage for optimal processing.

References

1. Beyer, M.: Gartner Says Solving 'Big Data' Challenge Involves More Than Just Managing Volumes of Data. Gartner. Archived from the original on 10 (2011)
2. Hadoop. http://hadoop.apache.org/
3. Spark. https://spark.apache.org/
4. Dean, J., Ghemawat, S.: MapReduce: a flexible data processing tool. Commun. ACM **53**(1), 72–77 (2010)
5. https://spark.apache.org/research.html
6. Shi, J., Qiu, Y., Minhas, U.F., Jiao, L., Wang, C., Reinwald, B., Özcan, F.: Clash of the titans: MapReduce vs. Spark for large scale data analytics. Proc. VLDB Endow. **8**(13), 2110–2121 (2015)
7. Zaharia, M., Chowdhury, M., Das, T., Dave, A., Ma, J., McCauley, M., Franklin, M.J., Shenker, S., Stoica, I.: Resilient distributed datasets: a fault-tolerant abstraction for in-memory cluster computing. In: Proceedings of the 9th USENIX Conference on Networked Systems Design and Implementation, p. 2. USENIX Association, April 2012
8. Xin, R.S., Gonzalez, J.E., Franklin, M.J., Stoica, I.: Graphx: a resilient distributed graph system on spark. In: First International Workshop on Graph Data Management Experiences and Systems, p. 2. ACM, June 2013
9. Zaharia, M., Xin, R.S., Wendell, P., Das, T., Armbrust, M., Dave, A., Meng, X., Rosen, J., Venkataraman, S., Franklin, M.J., Ghodsi, A.: Apache spark: a unified engine for big data processing. Commun. ACM **59**(11), 56–65 (2016)
10. Xu, L., Li, M., Zhang, L., Butt, A.R., Wang, Y., Hu, Z.Z.: MEMTUNE: dynamic memory management for in-memory data analytic platforms. In: 2016 IEEE International Parallel and Distributed Processing Symposium, pp. 383–392. IEEE, May 2016
11. Sehrish, S., Kowalkowski, J., Paterno, M.: Exploring the performance of spark for a scientific use case. In: 2016 IEEE International Parallel and Distributed Processing Symposium Workshops, pp. 1653–1659. IEEE, May 2016
12. Karau, H., Konwinski, A., Wendell, P., Zaharia, M.: Learning Spark: Lightning-Fast Big Data Analysis. O'Reilly Media, Inc., Sebastopol (2015)
13. Spark architecture. https://spark.apache.org/docs/latest/cluster-overview.html
14. Landset, S., Khoshgoftaar, T.M., Richter, A.N., Hasanin, T.: A survey of open source tools for machine learning with big data in the Hadoop ecosystem. J. Big Data **2**(1), 24 (2015)

15. Doulkeridis, C., Nørvåg, K.: A survey of large-scale analytical query processing in MapReduce. VLDB J. **23**(3), 355–380 (2014)
16. Singh, D., Reddy, C.K.: A survey on platforms for big data analytics. J. Big Data **2**(1), 8 (2015)
17. Gu, L., Li, H.: Memory or time: performance evaluation for iterative operation on hadoop and spark. In: 2013 IEEE 10th International Conference on High Performance Computing and Communications and 2013 IEEE International Conference on Embedded and Ubiquitous Computing (HPCC_EUC), pp. 721–727. IEEE, November 2013
18. Li, M., Tan, J., Wang, Y., Zhang, L., Salapura, V.: Sparkbench: a comprehensive benchmarking suite for in memory data analytic platform spark. In: Proceedings of the 12th ACM International Conference on Computing Frontiers, p. 53. ACM, May 2015
19. Gibilisco, G.P., Li, M., Zhang, L., Ardagna, D.: Stage aware performance modeling of DAG based in memory analytic platforms. In: 2016 IEEE 9th International Conference on Cloud Computing (CLOUD), pp. 188–195. IEEE, June 2016

Cloud Computing

QoS in the Cloud Computing: A Load Balancing Approach Using Simulated Annealing Algorithm

Mohamed Hanine(✉) and El Habib Benlahmar

Faculty of Sciences Ben'Msiq, Hassan II University, Casablanca, Morocco
Mohamedhanine24@gmail.com

Abstract. Recently, Cloud computing has known a fast growth in term of applications and the end users. In addition to the growth and evolution of the Cloud environment, many challenges that impact the performances of the Cloud applications emerged. One of these challenges is the Load Balancing between the virtual machines of a Datacenter, which is needed to balance the workload of each virtual machine while hoping to get a better Quality of services (QoS). Many approaches were proposed in hope of offering a good QoS. But due to the fact that the Cloud environment is exponentially evolving, these approaches became outdated. In this axis of research, we are proposing a new approach based on the Simulated Annealing and different parameters that affect the distribution of the tasks between the virtual machines. A simulation is also done to compare our approach with other existing algorithms using Cloudsim.

Keywords: Cloud computing · Load balancing · Quality of service
Workload · Simulated annealing · Virtual machine

1 Introduction

Cloud Computing is a new technology that is constantly evolving and growing fast. Many services are being provided by the Cloud's operators such as Infrastructure as a Service (IaaS), Platform as a Service (PaaS), Software as a Service (SaaS) solutions [1], Data Integrity as a Service (DIaaS) [2], Database as a Service [3], Logging as a Service [4], Provenance as a Service [5], Security as a Service [6], Big Data as a Service [7] and Storage as a Service [8]. Nowadays, more users are using some of the Cloud's services, which is an indicator at the evolution and exponential growth of the Cloud environment. It is also an indicator of the emergence of different issues that affect the Cloud's performances in term of Quality of Services (QoS) such as: the complexity of the Cloud's infrastructure, and the weakness of the Load Balancing algorithms at providing a better task distribution between the VMs. While aiming at solving this issue, we will expose our approach on balancing the workload of each virtual machine by using the Simulated Annealing algorithm, to ensure that all the virtual machines will work at their optimal capacities while offering better task distribution.

Y. Tabii et al. (Eds.): BDCA 2018, CCIS 872, pp. 43–54, 2018.
https://doi.org/10.1007/978-3-319-96292-4_4

The article will be structured as follow: in part two, we will present a state of art on the recent technics used for load balancing. In part three, we will detail our approach. In section four, we will implement our approach on CloudSim simulator, then we will discuss the results. And finally, in section five, we will conclude.

2 State of the Art

Different researches were made on existent Load Balancing approaches [9, 10]. Knowing that the load balancers are constantly increasing, we will try to summarize them in the next part, while trying to expose their inability to balance the Load of the Virtual machines. In our Stat of the Art, some load balancing algorithms will be presented. Then we will present some meta-heuristics algorithms while trying to explain why the meta-heuristic algorithm that we chose is more appropriate.

2.1 Load Balancing Algorithms

We will present briefly in this part, some load balancing algorithms that were presented in previous studies [10].

General Algorithm-Based Category. This category includes Load balancing algorithms that don't take into consideration the Cloud's architecture. In other words, this category contains all the classical algorithms. Some of these algorithms are: Round Robin [11], Weighted Round Robin [12], Least Connection [13] and weighted Least Connection [14].

We will now explain briefly the algorithms stated above:

Round Robin. Based of FCFS [15], Round Robin is a simple algorithm for dispatching workload between VMs in turns using a Server controller. Overall, it is a good algorithm but it does not have a control over the workload distribution.

Weighted Round Robin. Similar to Round Robin, Weighted Round Robin gives to VMs with higher specs, more tasks.

Least-Connection. This algorithm is based on the connection between each server. The server with less connection will be given new workload.

Weighted Least-Connection. Similar to Least Connection algorithm in calculating the connection of each server. Weighted Least-Connection attributes new workloads to servers based on a value given by multiplying the server's weight by its connections.

Architectural Based Category. This category contains load balancing approaches that are represented through architecture components like: Cloud Partition Load Balancing [16], VM-based Two-Dimensional Load Management [17], DAIRS [18] and THOPSIS Method [19].

The algorithms stated above can be explained as follow:

Cloud Partition Load Balancing. This algorithm improves the efficiency in the public Cloud's environment. It uses non-complex algorithms for underloaded situations in partitions. This algorithm is not yet implemented.

VM-based Two-Dimensional Load Management. This algorithm aims at reducing system overhead by reducing migration. But, it is only considering applications with seasonal attribute change.

DAIRS. This approach balances the workload in data centers by taking into consideration the CPU, memory, network bandwidth and four queues (waiting queue, requesting queue, optimizing queue and deleting queue).

THOPSIS. This approach selects which VM that should migrate and the Server that should receive it.

Artificial Intelligence Based Category. All load balancers based on an Artificial Intelligence concept join this category. They can also be considered a part of the Architecture category. Some of these Algorithms are: Bee-MMT [20] and Ant Colony Optimization [21].

Bee-MMT. This approach is based on the artificial bee colony with the feature of minimal migration time.

Ant Colony Optimization. This algorithm is based on the behavior of ants. It will, at first, detect the location of under-loaded or over-loaded nodes. Then it will update the resources utilization table.

2.2 Meta-Heuristics Algorithms

Unlike all the optimization algorithms, Meta-heuristic algorithms are known for their robustness and their ability to solve complex problems, including the load balancing which is highlighted in this contribution. Many studies opted for the usage of Meta-heuristic algorithms to solve the Scheduling problems [22]. We will proceed by explaining some of these Meta-Heuristics:

Tabu Search. Tabu search is a metaheuristic method based on the local search methods used for mathematical optimization. Initially, it has a random solution of the problem, then it starts comparing it with neighbor's solutions to find an improved solution [23, 24].

Genetic Algorithm. Genetic algorithms are an optimization technic used to solve non-linear optimizations problems. They are based on the evolutionary biology to look for a global minimum for an optimization problem. Initially, the algorithm generates some initial solutions that are tested against the objective function. Then these solutions evaluate which help the convergence to the global minima [25].

Bat Algorithm. Based on the bats' echolocations, Bat algorithm is a meta heuristic algorithm that is utilizing a balanced combination of the advantages of existing successful algorithms. The main purpose of the Bat algorithm is to identify the shortest iteration to the solution [26].

Before explaining our contribution, we will discuss about the Simulated Annealing in the following subpart in hope to explain why we based our approach on it.

2.3 Simulated Annealing

The simulated annealing technique (SA) was initially proposed to solve the hard-combinatorial optimization problems by trying random variations of the current solution. The main feature is that a worse variation may be accepted as a new solution with a probability, which results in the SA's major advantage over other searching methods, that is, the ability to avoid becoming trapped at local minima. Theoretically SA is able to find the global optimal solution with probability equal to 1 [27]. This advantage can be illustrated by the acceptance probability P which allows SA to accept worst scenarios as solutions. The acceptance probability is as follow:

$$P = e^{-E_i - E_{i+1}/T} \tag{1}$$

Where T is the temperature (initially T has a high value and has to slowly decrease between each iteration). $E_i - E_{i+1}$ is the energy variation of the material at different time lapses. SA improves the research of the global solution by taking risks and accepting worse solutions [28]. The Pseudo-code of SA [29] can be found below:

```
PSEUDO-CODE of the Simulated Annealing

Initialize the system configuration;
Initialize s as the initial state;
Initialize T with a large value;
Set temperature change counter t = 0;
  Repeat
  Set repetition counter n = 0→N;
  Repeat:
    Generate a neighbor state of s: s' = s + Δs.
    Evaluate ΔE = E (s) - E (s'):
    if ΔE(s) < 0
      keep s as the actual state;
    else if random (0,1)> e^(-ΔE/T)
      s' is the new state;
    n=n+1;
    until n=N;
  t=t+1 ;
  until t=T
until stopping criterion true.
```

We chose to use the Simulated Annealing to develop out algorithm due to the fact that it has a great fault tolerance which will lead it to the best solution easily compared to the other Meta-Heuristics. There is also the fact that it can work with any complicated problem.

3 Our Approach

After the study of the different Load Balancing algorithms, we noticed that even if they provide some QoS, there is still an issue regarding the task distribution between the VMs [30].

Each VM has a value of million instruction it can process per second (MIPS) [31], which is directly related to the number of core a VM has. The tasks also have a length (TL) which is the million instructions that have to be treated in order to execute the task [31]. From [31]'s study, we know that the MIPS of a VM and the length of a task are related.

We can also determine the maximum number of tasks a VM can process by calculating the Strip Length (2):

$$S = MIPS_i / \sum_i MIPS * (\text{length of the tasks' list}) \tag{2}$$

Now that we have the maximum number of tasks a VM can process at a given time. The task distribution can be improved to prevent the overload or the underload of a VM.

The approach that we are proposing is illustrated by the flowchart (Fig. 1), and the algorithm below.

Initially, the length of the task j will be compared to the MIPS of the VMi

$$C_{i,j} = MIPS_i - TL_j \tag{3}$$

If Ci, j > 0, then the task j will be added to the workload of the VMi in the next iteration, then the length of the next task j + 1 is compared with the MIPS of VMi. This process will continue until Ci, j < 0.

If Ci, j < 0, the next steps will be taking into consideration the acceptance probability P of the VMi that is defined as follow:

$$P = e[-(MIPSi - MIPSi + 1)/Ts] \tag{4}$$

Where MIPSi + 1 is the MIPS of the VM i + 1, MIPSi is the MIPS of VMi.

Then a random value R will be generated and will illustrate the acceptance probability of the VMi + 1

If P > R, then VMi←Taskj.
If P < R, then VMi + 1←Taskj.

This process will continue until all the tasks are allocated.

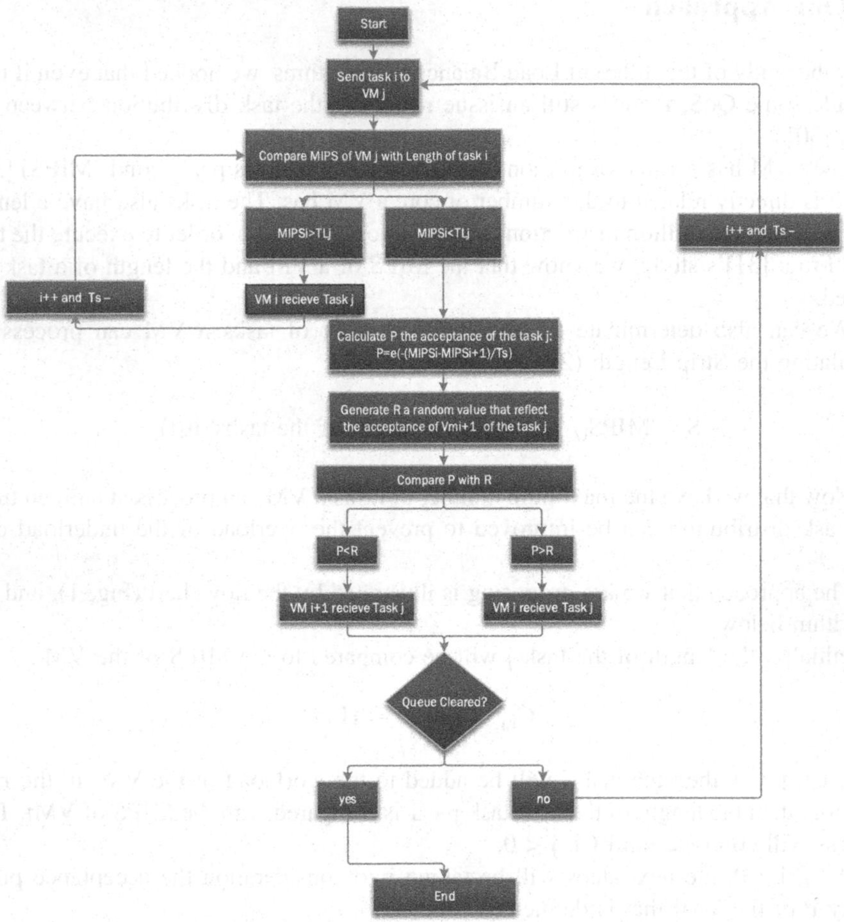

Fig. 1. Tasks distribution using the simulated annealing algorithm

```
Length based Simulated Annealing

Initialize the system configuration;
Initialize the initial state of the VMs;
Initialize Ts the number of tasks in the queue;
Initialize CH a Boolean list of the same size as Ts
with false values;
For (v:0→the list of the VMs)
{
Get the MIPS of VM(v);
Calculate S(v)= MIPS(v)*T/∑v MIPS;
Set I=0;
For (c:0→the list of the Tasks)
{
  Get the length of the Task(c);
  While (Ts !=0 && CH != true && I !=S(v))
  {
    If (MIPS(v)>=TL(c))
    {
      VM(v)←Task(c);
      Ts--;
      I++;
      CH(c)=true;
    }
    Else
    {
      For (b: v+1→the list of the VMs)
        {
          Calculate S(b)= MIPS(b)*T/∑b MIPS;
          Set U=0;
          While (U !=S(b))
          {
            Calculate P= exp(-(MIPS(c)-MIPS(b))/T);
            Generate R= random (0,1);
            If (P>R)
            {
              VM(v)←Task(c);
              Ts--;
              I++;
              CH(c)=true;
            }
            Else
            {
              VM(b)←Task (c);
              Ts--;
              U++;
              CH(c)=true;
            }
          }
        }
      }
    }
  }
}
```

4 Experiments and Results

4.1 Experiments

In order to test our proposed algorithm, we implemented it on the CloudSim simulator which main purpose is to simulate a cloud-based environment and present the different stages of our proposed solution.

We used the scenario of having only one physical machine. Initially. The configuration details are given in Table 1.

Table 1. Cloud setup configuration details.

Entity	Number
Data center	1
Number of HOSTS in DC	1
Number of CORES of the CPU	10
The Core's processing capacity	10 MIPS
HOST RAM capacity	2048 MB
Number of VM	2
Number of cores attributed to a VM	6-3
VMS' processing capacity	6-3 MIPS
VM RAM	512 MB
VM Manager	Xen

The user has initially sent 10 tasks with different lengths that are between 1 and 9 (just for an easier demonstration) as follow:

Table 2. Tasks' length

Task	Length
Task 0	5
Task 1	7
Task 2	4
Task 3	6
Task 4	2
Task 5	3
Task 6	1
Task 7	7
Task 8	2
Task 9	2

The virtual machines MIPS is also chosen randomly between a value between 1 to 9. Here in this example, the first VM has 6 MIPS, and the second VM has 3 MIPS.

We will now proceed by explaining the results.

4.2 Results

We compared the overall process time of all task between our approach and some classical Algorithm. All the Algorithms were given the exact same conditions: 10 tasks of the same length (Table 2), and two virtual machines with 6 and 3 MIPS respectively.

The first thing that was noticed is the tasks' allocation between the VMs. VM0 got 7 tasks while VM1 got only three tasks (Fig. 2). This distribution of the tasks means that the VMs are balanced. It can be demonstrated by calculating the Strip length of each VM as follow:

- VM 0:
  $S(VM0) = 6 * 10/9 \approx 7$
- VM 1:
  $S(VM1) = 3 * 10/9 \approx 3.$

This can explain why VM0 took 7 tasks while VM1 took 3 tasks.

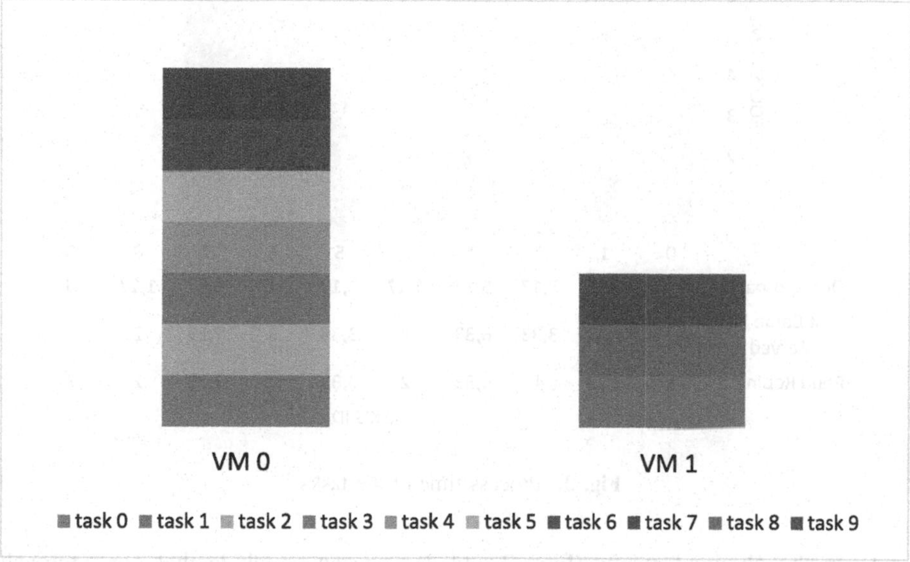

Fig. 2. Tasks allocation

The second result obtained (Fig. 3) shows a comparison of the execution time of each task for different Algorithms. As we can see in Fig. 3, our approach processed all the tasks at 6.17 s while it took 7.33 s for both FCFS and Round Robin algorithms. This show that our approach outperforms greatly Round Robin and FCFS Algorithms in term of process speed while providing a better task distribution to the VMs (Fig. 2). From Table 2, we noticed that Task 1 has a length that is greater than the MIPS value that VM 1 has and task 7 had a length greater than the MIPS of VM0. But because we are using the Acceptance Probability P, and by comparing it with R we can explain why the task was given to the VMs:

- Task 1

  $P = \exp[-(6-3)/9] = 0.72$

  $R = 0.895$

  $P < R \rightarrow$ VM1 will take Task 1.

  The same thing is noticed for Task 7 and VM 0:

- Task 7

  $P = \exp[-(6-3)/3] = 0.37$

  $R = 0.318$

  $P > R \rightarrow$ VM0 will take Task 7.

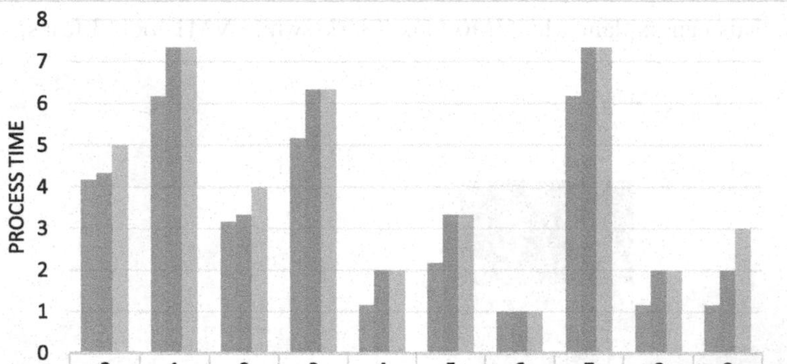

	0	1	2	3	4	5	6	7	8	9
Our Approach	4,17	6,17	3,17	5,17	1,17	2,17	1	6,17	1,17	1,17
First Come First Served	4,33	7,33	3,33	6,33	2	3,33	1	7,33	2	2
Roud Robin	5	7,33	4	6,33	2	3,33	1	7,33	2	3

TASK'S ID

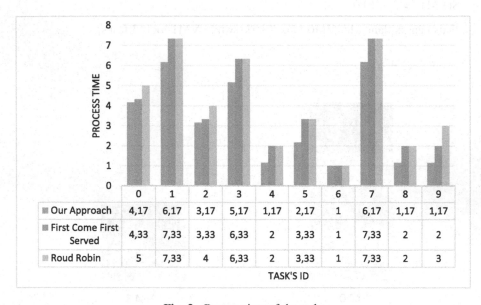

Fig. 3. Process time of the tasks

From the obtained results (Figs. 2 and 3), we can conclude that our approach provides a better tasks' distribution. In other words, The VMs are more balanced, and it can reflect on the process time of each task being shorter and faster than the process time given from the other Load Balancers.

5 Conclusions

Nowadays Cloud users are exponentially growing. This fast growth leads to many QoS issues regarding the Load Balancing. In an attempt to find a solution which allows a better Load Balancing, we propose a load balancing approach based on the Simulated Annealing. Our approach will: send a task to it adequate VM so that we may process more tasks at a given time T without risking a VM being overloaded Our approach's main feature is the fact that it has a high fault tolerance, which allows a better task allocation than normal.

References

1. Gaspard, G., Jachniewicz, R., Lacava, J., Meslard, V.: Equilibrage de Charge et ASRALL, 22 April 2009
2. Nepal, S., et al.: DIaaS: data integrity as a service in the cloud. In: 2011 IEEE International Conference on Cloud Computing (CLOUD). IEEE (2011)
3. Curino, C., et al.: Relational cloud: a database-as-a-service for the cloud. In: 5th Biennial Conference on Innovative Data Systems Research, CIDR 2011, Asilomar, California, 9–12 January 2011
4. Frenot, S., Ponge, J.: LogOS: an automatic logging framework for service-oriented architectures. In: 2012 38th EUROMICRO Conference on Software Engineering and Advanced Applications (SEAA), pp. 224–227 (2012)
5. Hammad, R., Wu, C.-S.: Provenance as a service: a data-centric approach for real-time monitoring. In: 2014 IEEE International Congress on Big Data (BigData Congress), pp. 258–265 (2014)
6. Al-Aqrabi, H., Liu, L., Xu, J., Hill, R., Antonopoulos, N., Zhan, Y.: Investigation of IT security and compliance challenges in security-as-a-service for cloud computing. In: 2012 15th IEEE International Symposium on Object/Component/Service-Oriented Real-Time Distributed Computing Workshops (ISORCW), pp. 124–129 (2012)
7. Zheng, Z., Zhu, J., Lyu, M.: Service-generated big data and big data-as-a-service: an overview. In: 2013 IEEE International Congress on Big Data (BigData Congress), pp. 403–410 (2013)
8. Calder, B., Wang, J., Ogus, A., Nilakantan, N., Skjolsvold, A., McKelvie, S., Xu, Y., Srivastav, S., Wu, J., Simitci, H., Haridas, J., Uddaraju, C., Khatri, H., Edwards, A., Bedekar, V., Mainali, S., Abbasi, R., Agarwal, A., Haq, M.F.U., Haq, M.I.U., Bhardwaj, D., Dayanand, S., Adusumilli, A., McNett, M., Sankaran, S., Manivannan, K., Rigas, L.: Windows Azure storage: a highly available cloud storage service with strong consistency. In: Proceedings of the Twenty-Third ACM Symposium on Operating Systems Principles, pp. 143–157. ACM, New York (2011)
9. Sharma, S., Singh, S., Sharma, M.: Performance analysis of load balancing algorithms. World Acad. Sci. Eng. Technol. **38**, 269–272 (2008)
10. Mohammadreza, M., et al.: Load balancing in cloud computing: a state of the art survey. Mod. Educ. Comput. Sci. PRESS **8**(3), 64–78 (2013)
11. Aditya, A., Chatterjee, U., Gupta, S.: A comparative study of different static and dynamic load-balancing algorithm in cloud computing with special emphasis on time factor. Int. J. Curr. Eng. Technol. **3**(5) (2015)
12. Mesbahi, M., Rahmani, A.M.: Load balancing in cloud computing: a state of the art survey. Int. J. Mod. Educ. Comput. Sci. **3**, 64–78 (2016)
13. Vashistha, J., Jayswal, A.K.: Comparative study of load balancing algorithms. IOSR J. Eng. (IOSRJEN) **3**(3), 45–50 (2013). e-ISSN 2250-3021, p-ISSN 2278-8719
14. Lee, R., Jeng, B.: Load-balancing tactics in cloud. In: International Conference on Cyber-Enabled Distributed Computing and Knowledge Discovery, pp. 447–454, October 2011

15. Stattelmann, S., Martin, F.: On the use of context information for precise measurement-based execution time estimation. In: 10th International Workshop on Worst-Case Execution Time Analysis, December 2010. ISBN 978-3-939897-21-7
16. Xu, G., Pang, J., Fu, X.: A load balancing model based on cloud partitioning for the public cloud. Tsinghua Sci. Technol. **18**(1), 34–39 (2013)
17. Wang, R., Le, W., Zhang, X.: Design and implementation of an efficient load-balancing method for virtual machine cluster based on cloud service. In: 4th IET International Conference on Wireless, Mobile and Multimedia Networks (ICWMMN 2011), pp. 321–324 (2011)
18. Tian, W., et al.: A dynamic and integrated load-balancing scheduling algorithm for Cloud datacenters. In: 2011 IEEE International Conference on Cloud Computing and Intelligence Systems (CCIS). IEEE (2011)
19. Ma, F., Liu, F., Liu, Z.: Distributed load balancing allocation of virtual machine in cloud data center. In: 2012 IEEE 3rd International Conference on Software Engineering and Service Science (ICSESS). IEEE (2012)
20. Ghafari, S.M., et al.: Bee-MMT: a load balancing method for power consumption management in cloud computing. In: 2013 Sixth International Conference on Contemporary Computing (IC3). IEEE (2013)
21. Teoh, C.K., Wibowo, A., Ngadiman, M.S.: Artif. Intell. Rev. **44**, 1 (2015). https://doi.org/10.1007/s10462-013-9399-6
22. Nishant, K., et al.: Load balancing of nodes in cloud using ant colony optimization. In: 2012 UKSim 14th International Conference on Computer Modelling and Simulation (UKSim). IEEE (2012)
23. Ikonomovska, E., Chorbev, I., Gjorgjevik, D., Mihajlov, D.: The adaptive tabu search and its application to the quadratic assignment problem. In: Proceedings of 9th International Multi conference - Information Society 2006, Ljubljana, Slovenia, pp. 26–29 (2006)
24. Said, G.A.E.N.A., Mahmoud, A.M., El-Horbaty, E.S.M.: A comparative study of meta-heuristic algorithms for solving quadratic assignment problem. Int. J. Adv. Comput. Sci. Appl. **5**(1), 1–6 (2014)
25. Neumann, F., Witt, C.: Bio Inspired Computation in Combinatorial Optimization. Springer, Heidelberg (2010). https://doi.org/10.1007/978-3-642-16544-3
26. Yang, X.S.: A new metaheuristic bat-inspired algorithm. In: González, J.R., Pelta, D.A., Cruz, C., Terrazas, G., Krasnogor, N. (eds.) Nature inspired cooperative strategies for optimization (NICSO 2010). SCI, vol. 284, pp. 65–74. Springer, Heidelberg (2010). https://doi.org/10.1007/978-3-642-12538-6_6
27. Van Laarhoven, P.J.M., Aarts, E.H.L.: Simulated annealing. In: van Laarhoven, P.J.M., Aarts, E.H.L. (eds.) Simulated Annealing: Theory and Applications. MAIA, vol. 37, pp. 7–15. Springer, Dordrecht (1987). https://doi.org/10.1007/978-94-015-7744-1_2
28. Kirkpatrick, S., Gelatt Jr., C.D., Vecchi, M.P.: Optimization by simulated annealing. Science **220**(4598), 671–680 (1983)
29. Du, K.-L., Swamy, M.N.S.: Simulated Annealing. In: Du, K.-L., Swamy, M.N.S. (eds.) Search and Optimization by Metaheuristics. Techniques and Algorithms Inspired by Nature, pp. 29–36. Springer, Switzerland (2016). https://doi.org/10.1007/978-3-319-41192-7_2
30. Fahim, Y., Ben Lahmar, E., Labriji, E.H., Eddaoui, A., Elouahabi, S.: The load balancing improvement of a data center by a hybrid algorithm in cloud computing. In: Third International Conference on Colloquium in Information Science and Technology (CIST). IEEE (2014)
31. Sudip, R., Sourav, B., Chowdhury, K.R., Utpal, B.: Development and analysis of a three-phase cloudlet allocation algorithm. J. King Saud Univ. – Comput. Inf. Sci. **29**, 473–483 (2016)

A Proposed Approach to Reduce the Vulnerability in a Cloud System

Chaimae Saadi(✉) and Habiba Chaoui

Systems Engineering Laboratory, Data Analysis and Security Team,
National School of Applied Sciences, Campus Universitaire, B.P 241,
14000 Kénitra, Morocco
chaimaesaadi900@gmail.com

Abstract. Today, cloud computing is becoming more and more popular as a Pay-as-You-Go model for providing on-demand services over the Internet. In this paper, we will propose new detection and prevention mechanisms for cloud systems to protect against different types of attacks and vulnerabilities by improving a new architecture that provides a security mechanism including a virtual firewall and IDS/IPS (Intrusion Detection and Prevention System) which aims to secure the virtual environment.

Keywords: Correlation · Cloud computing · Virtualization · Security issues Vulnerability · Security as a service · Cloud firewall · HIDS · Hypervisor OSSEC

1 Introduction

Virtual security is a new type of cloud services. Thus, many security vendors exploit systematically cloud computing models to offer security solutions (online antivirus, virtual firewalls, etc.) [1]. Therefore, this technology remains a major problem to solve and a big challenge for researchers.

Indeed, the data is following through different places in the cloud, which means that providers have more places to protect their system from several threats. In this context, it is very important to search for these threats and learn how to deal with them, This allows us to provide the level of trust and security needed for information flows in the cloud environment.

The outline of this paper is as follows: In Sect. 2, we focus on the current state of security solutions. In Sect. 3 we describe our contribution to secure the cloud infrastructure. Experimental setup and results are discussed in Sect. 4. Finally, Sect. 5 concludes the paper, and presents our future work.

2 Related Work of Security Solutions in Cloud Computing

Cloud computing does indeed increases the efficiency and scalability of enterprises, but, it poses new challenges for security levels. Indeed, the basic solutions for security in the cloud for companies are outdated as the majority of virtual network traffic leaves

Y. Tabii et al. (Eds.): BDCA 2018, CCIS 872, pp. 55–66, 2018.
https://doi.org/10.1007/978-3-319-96292-4_5

the physical server and therefore does not allow a sustainable control [2]. A new cloud computing services appeared called Security as a service in order to face these limitations [3]. Thus, new mechanisms have been proposed to prevent and protect the companies' business against different types of attacks inside the Cloud [4].

Authors in [5] proposed security services that a Cloud provider could offer to its clients to deal with Rootkit attacks, insider attacks and malware injection, their threat model includes the administrator of the cloud system that manage tenant user who utilize the applications offered by the provider and the tenant virtual machines. This architecture is based on the IaaS platform owing to the fact that attacks generated in SaaS or PaaS are limited to the platforms or the application software which they may have access.

In [6] authors spelled IAMaaS framework Identity and Access Management as a Service. It consists in managing the access to resources by firstly verifying the identity of an entity then the access is being granted at the appropriate level based on policies of the protected resource. Thus, an architecture system has been proposed called POC (Proof-of-Concept).

Authors in [7] proposed a solution completely based on the Cloud. It gives a cloud provider the possibility to offer a Firewalling services to its clients in order to increase the capacity of analysis by distributing traffic across multiple virtual firewalls. A secure authentication architecture and effective identity management solution for firewall service has been deployed to insure a high level of security in order to prevent attacks such as Man in the Middle and session hijacking using the EAP-TLS technology-based smart cards. The proposed architecture for authentication is based on smart card technology, precisely smart cards supporting the EAP-TLS. Obviously, the smart card is a device that includes a CPU, Ram and ROM. Thus, it includes a certificate and RSA algorithm. This architecture is based on processing and filtering packets in destination to a data center's clients in order to prevent and protect them from internal and external attacks. Accordingly, this solution does not provide security to the data hosted by the cloud provider. Moreover, authors in [7] affirm that one of the major challenges of the deployment of firewalls is relative to the dynamic resources allocation.

Authors in [8] affirm and assume that traditional firewall mechanism for dealing with network's packets is not suitable for a cloud computing environment due to sophisticated attacks that target the cloud system. Besides, traditional firewalls cannot handle the diversity of the traffic that transits the network. Hence the idea of proposing a new architecture for the cloud based on firewalls, it's a mechanism of detection events designed for the cloud with a dynamic allocation of resources. The firewall will take place between the cloud platform and Internet so that all incoming traffic will be filtered and examined by sensors until the detector indicates a correspondence. Thus the request will be blocked or rejected.

Distributed environment such as Cloud computing for organizations is the most targetable place to launch cyber-attacks. To protect public or a private Clouds, an IDS which supports scalable and virtual environment is required. Authors in [9] from the University of Morocco have proposed a Framework, which can detect intrusion as a service that monitors Cloud networks in order to detect any malicious activity, called

CBIDS (Cloud-based Intrusion Detection Service). The boundary of this Framework is that if the proxy server which is responsible for collecting information from each VM's user, has been identified by the attacker, it can steal sensitive information or attacks the entire server.

In the same context, to detect malicious traffic, [10] has shown that the power of cloud computing can be employed to perform DDoS (Distributed Denial of Service) attacks by using the main benefit of cloud. Cloud services are provided as "pay-per-use". Accordingly, the attackers try to exhaust available resources of legitimate users. From there, the 3 authors showed different deployment models IDS in the cloud infrastructure, nonetheless there is only a single management unit called IDS Management System which is responsible for gathering and preprocessing alerts from all sensors. Thus, we will have a single point of failure on the system.

The most important thing over the internet is the security of information because it is the key to success. By the Internet traffic growth, the malicious traffic growth too, hence the need of prevention and detection against malicious web users.

Therefore, [11] proposed a scalable Honeynet into the cloud computing system. It is not the only way to secure a cloud infrastructure but it is a network that takes place behind a firewall where all the traffic is being captured and analyzed. It requires a high performance for hardware and the processing. In addition to this, if the true identity of a Honey net has been discovered to hackers, its efficiency reduces and attackers can bypass the honey net or implant into it false data. Thus the data analysis would be useless or misleading. Moreover, another limit is that major power of processing dedicated to the Honey net remains unused [11].

The One Time Password (OTP) or the password for single use [12] is a valid password used for one session or transaction. The use of multi-factor authentication with OTP reduces risks associated with the connection to the system from a non-secure workstation. OTP is like a validation system that provides an additional layer of security to data and sensitive information by wondering a password that is only valid for a single connection, which will eliminate some deficiencies associated to static passwords, such as simplicity of a password or the brute force attack. To secure the system, the generated OTP must be difficult to estimate, find or draw by hackers [12].

In order to enhance security in the cloud computing, we describe the proposed approach based on cloud firewall in the next section.

3 Proposed Work

Cloud computing becomes the most important target for several attacks in the whole world, which is the real reason behind the fact that the data security that resides beyond the company's infrastructure is the only obstacle for companies to outsource their data, in the case of sensitive data the concern is very high. Firewalls come in the first line when defending against malicious traffic, but as we have clarified before, traditional packet level firewall mechanism is not suitable for cloud computing environment and only little work have been done on cloud firewall. One of the solutions they have proposed is a centralized cloud firewall. However, the resource limitations of physical security devices such as firewalls and Intrusion detection System without Prevention mechanism had not decreased the seriousness of the threats. In addition to this, traditional Detection System does not perform a better understanding of alerts, to ensure a high level of security and to prevent internal as well as external attacks, we have deployed a secure architecture, strong and efficient as shown in Fig. 1. It includes a decentralized cloud-firewall for protecting user tenant and applications that are hosted in cloud infrastructure, a Host-based Intrusion Detection and Prevention System (IDS/IPS) to oversee all traffic destined to each host in order to detect any malicious traffic, and we use a correlation strategy so that to make it possible to have a better understanding of alerts.

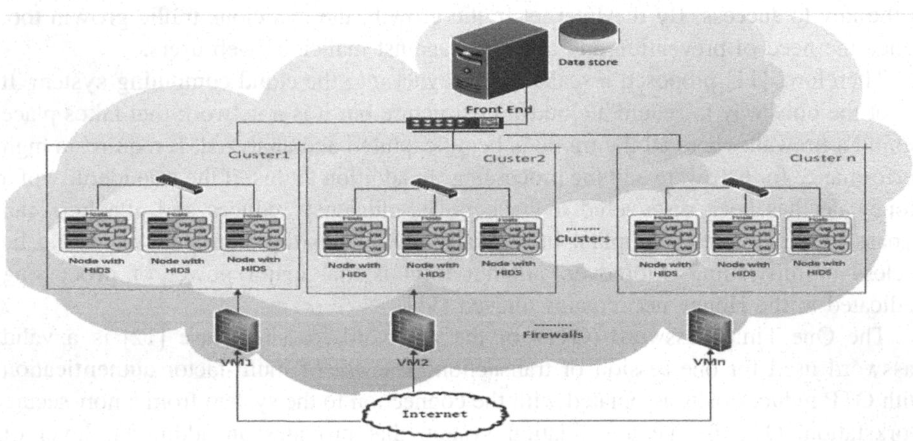

Fig. 1. Proposed architecture

- **Cloud Firewall**

Certainly the Firewall is the first line in the security policy against malicious traffic, but the change of environment brings additional challenges that a traditional firewall may not be able to handle.

As a result, the diversity of services, complex attacks, and high packet arrival rate make traditional firewalls not suitable for Cloud environment. However it is difficult to guarantee a quality of service (QoS) to customers. Thus, we propose a cloud firewall framework for individual cloud cluster as shown in Fig. 2.

The cloud firewall is offered by the cloud service provider and placed between Internet and the cloud data center, cloud customer rents the firewall for protecting his tenant and applications which are hosted in the cluster, the Firewall resources are dynamically allocated to set up an individual firewall for each cluster. All these parallel firewalls will work together to monitor incoming packets.

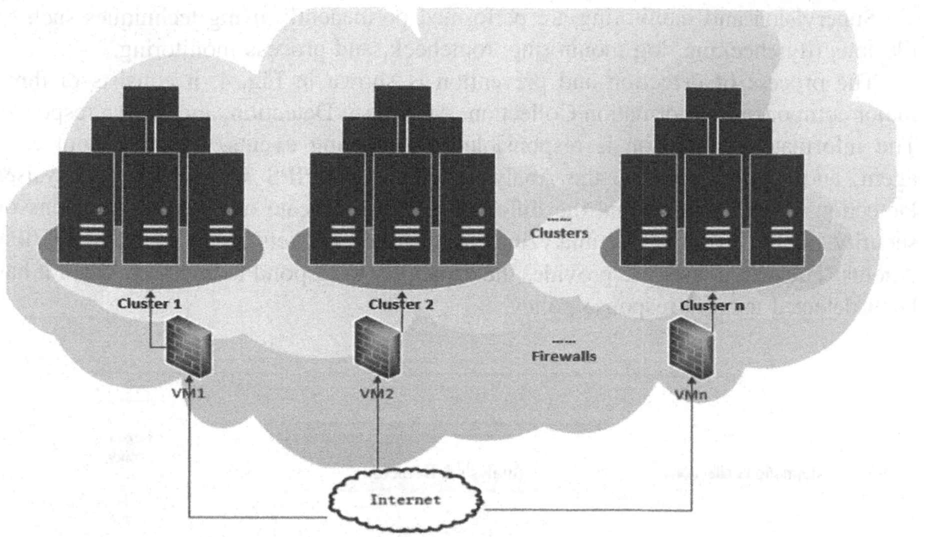

Fig. 2. Decentralized cloud firewall

- **Host Based Intrusion Detection System (HIDS)**

To protect all virtual machines against various attacks, an intrusion detection and prevention system (IDS/IPS) is required, it has the ability to detect known attacks as well as unknown attacks, so the main goal of this system is to identify and remove any type of intrusion in real time. Therefore To resist attack attempts, an intelligent intrusion detection system is proposed in Fig. 3. The IDSs are controlled by the cloud provider, and we consider that this approach is conducted on signature based way.

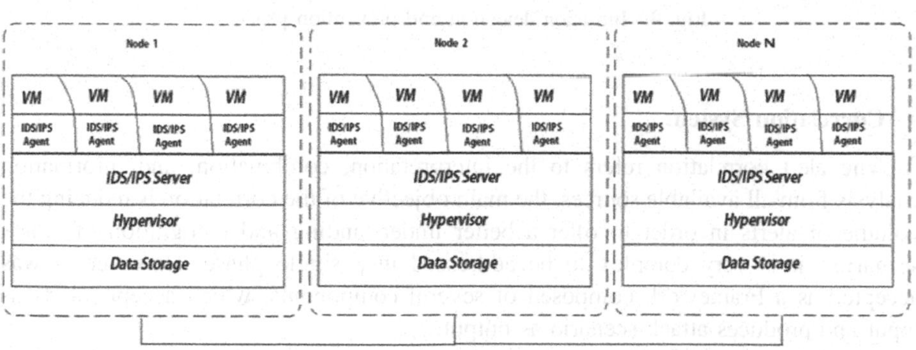

Fig. 3. IDS/IPS architecture

The management system is called IDS/IPS server, it runs on each node as a virtual machine, and IDS/IPS agent is needed on each VM, the agent scans the entire machine to check if the VM is not infected, then sends events to the server using the key shared between them.

Supervision and monitoring are performed permanently using techniques such as file integrity checking, log monitoring, rootcheck, and process monitoring.

The process of detection and prevention is shown in Fig. 4, it consists of three major components: Information Collection, Analysis& Detection, and Active response. The information collection is responsible for gathering events, log files from each agent, and sending them to the Analysis System (IDS/IPS server). The Analysis& Detection system implements the different rules to indicate and detect intrusions or security policy breaches, by analyzing the different packets received from IDS/IPS Agents. The active response provides the capability to respond to an attack when it has been detected using a response policy.

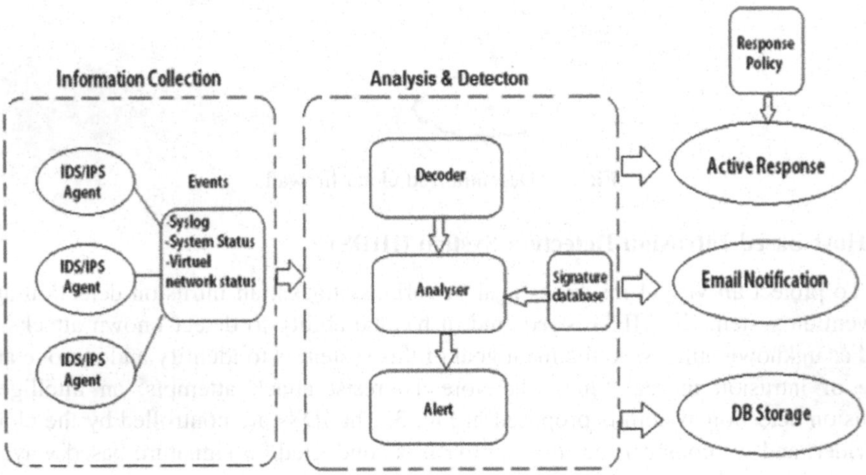

Fig. 4. Intrusion detection and prevention process

- **Correlation System**

The alert correlation refers to the interpretation, combination, and information analysis from all available sources, the main objective of the correlation is reducing the volume of alerts in order to offer a better understanding and recognition of attack scenarios, it is very complex to be addressed in a single phase. However, it was accepted as a Framework composed of several components, which accepts alerts as input and produces attack scenario as output.

The following block diagram shows the architecture of alert correlation, it will be achieved by gathering the various alerts generated by the detection system to facilitate the alert's management by the analyst, this module Fig. 5 performs five main functions.

The basis of alerts management, collects events generated by different IDS sensors, and records them in a database to analyze them by other functions. All the alert files are formatted, in order to normalize these events into a standardized format (e.g. Intrusion Detection Message Exchange format – IDMEF). After that, the Redundancy elimination function removes events that are generated following the observation of a single event, thus reduces the alerts number to be processed. The aggregation function takes as input the alerts triggered by different sensors and generates packets (cluster) alerts as output. In fact a packet is a set of events corresponding to the same attack instance. Afterwards each packet is sent to fusion function which is used to create a new alert, called a global alert, this alert combine symptoms based on the 'similarity' among events attributes.

Finally, events are analyzed by the "correlation" function using one of several techniques. The goal of this function is to identify and recognize the plan that the attacker is trying to achieve. In this approach an attack scenario is modeled by pre-condition and post-condition attacks. A pre-condition is a logical condition that specifies the requirements to be satisfied to achieve the attack. Apost-condition is logical condition that specifies the impact of the attack when it is achieved.

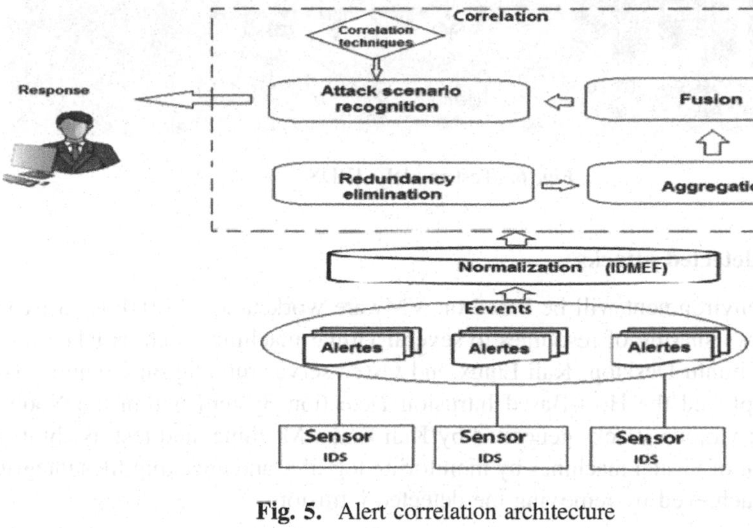

Fig. 5. Alert correlation architecture

4 Test and Result

To ensure the normal state of every virtual machine deployed in the node, we will be working on a host-based intrusion detection and prevention system called OSSEC to test the Intrusion Detection and Prevention IDS/IPS performance to protect the virtualized environment in the infrastructure cloud.

The following figure shows the model on which we tested our HIDS detection system. Indeed, all the machines are interconnected by a virtual network, using the technology of virtualization (Fig. 6).

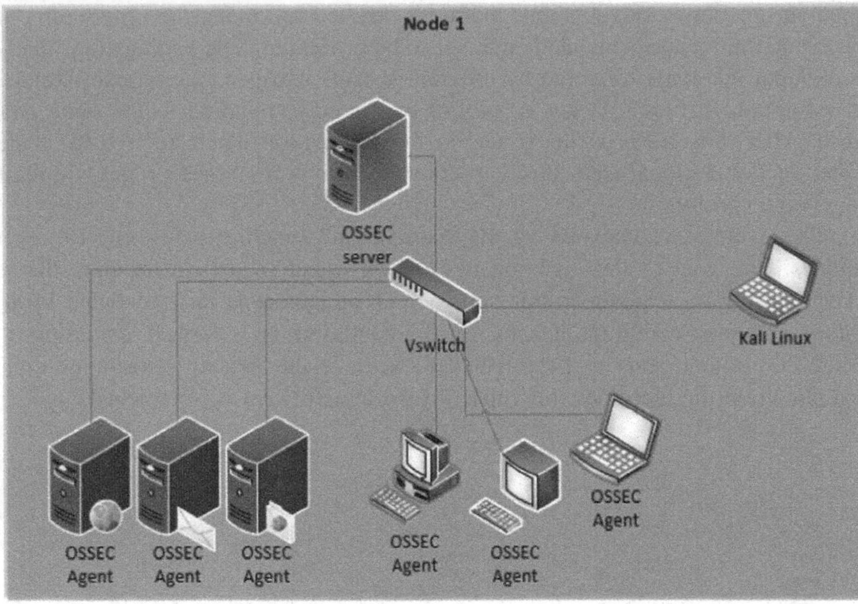

Fig. 6. Test model - HIDS

- **Types of detected attacks**

First test environment will be based on VMware workstation 11.0.0 as an hypervisor that allows sharing of resources to several virtual machines such as FTP server, Web server, Ubuntu Desktop, Kali Linux and Ossec-server running on Ubuntu server 14.04. We deployed the Host-Based Intrusion Detection System within the Node in order to detect various attacks generated by Kali Linux Machine, and test its ability to oversee the stat of virtual machines by monitoring log files and checking files integrity. Prevention is achieved by removing the detected intrusions.

Types of attacks	Figures
File integrity checking: Syscheck is the internal processor of OSSEC. Attackers still leave traces of system change. OSSEC is looking to make changes to the MD5/SHA1 checksums. Figure 7. Illustrates the triggered message alerts	**Level:** 7 - Integrity checksum changed again (2nd time). **Rule Id:** 551 **Location:** (desktop_agent) 192.168.10.13->syscheck Integrity checksum changed for: '/var/ossec/etc/ossec.conf' Size changed from '3031' to '3029' Old md5sum was: 'd01024ae1ca49cd13082bef7fab5ae0f' New md5sum is : 'cb1ea13a853dcb739fc1e167abd294ba' Old sha1sum was: '811ea6b594dce55a403c98721680821e8ef1a557' New sha1sum is : '8cf531a4d1d6816f631efc04e3809e0b8ea4cfd2' **Fig. 7.** OSSEC alert message for integrity checksum

Website attack:
the web application attacks are harmful in our case we have deployed a web software named WordPress to create a website, a brute force attack of the Kali Linux machine to access a site, it tries usernames and passwords using a word list, until it comes into play. it is successfully initiated by the wpscan command from Kali OS as the sending host to the Ubuntu server 12.04 target virtual machine. Figure 8 illustrates driving and performance degradation and making system availability

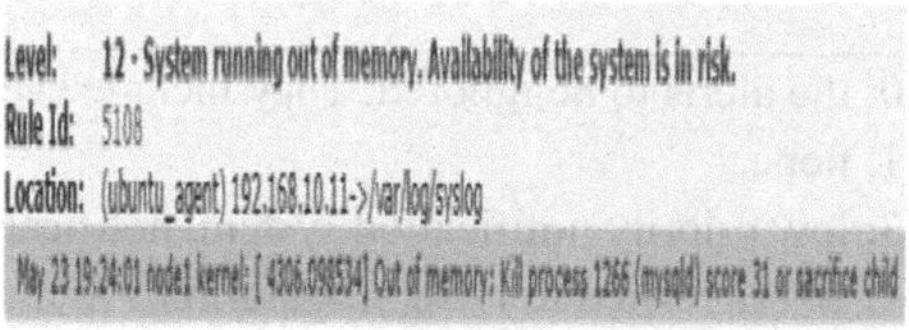

Level: 12 - System running out of memory. Availability of the system is in risk.
Rule Id: 5108

May 23 19:24:01 node1 kernel: [4306.098534] Out of memory: Kill process 1266 (mysqld) score 31 or sacrifice child

Fig. 8. OSSEC Alert message for web site brute force

FTP and SSH Brute Force:
We used the brute force attack to obtain the user's credentials, such as username and password. a remote machine using SSH. Figure 9 shows an alert message generated by OSSEC after the detection of brute force.

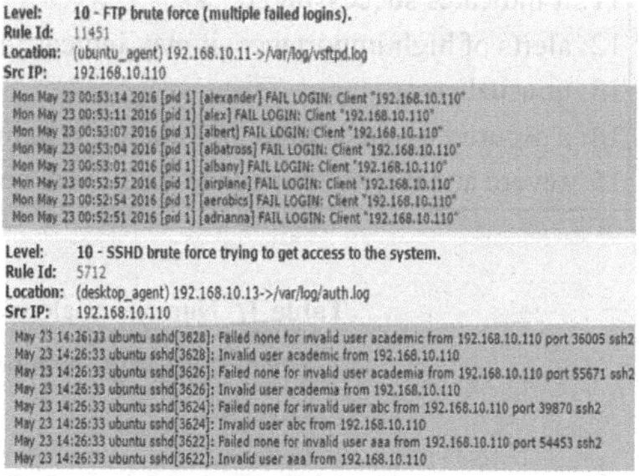

Level: 10 - FTP brute force (multiple failed logins).
Rule Id: 11451
Location: (ubuntu_agent) 192.168.10.11->/var/log/vsftpd.log
Src IP: 192.168.10.110
Mon May 23 00:53:14 2016 [pid 1] [alexander] FAIL LOGIN: Client "192.168.10.110"
Mon May 23 00:53:11 2016 [pid 1] [alex] FAIL LOGIN: Client "192.168.10.110"
Mon May 23 00:53:07 2016 [pid 1] [albert] FAIL LOGIN: Client "192.168.10.110"
Mon May 23 00:53:04 2016 [pid 1] [albatross] FAIL LOGIN: Client "192.168.10.110"
Mon May 23 00:53:01 2016 [pid 1] [albany] FAIL LOGIN: Client "192.168.10.110"
Mon May 23 00:52:57 2016 [pid 1] [airplane] FAIL LOGIN: Client "192.168.10.110"
Mon May 23 00:52:54 2016 [pid 1] [aerobics] FAIL LOGIN: Client "192.168.10.110"
Mon May 23 00:52:51 2016 [pid 1] [adrianna] FAIL LOGIN: Client "192.168.10.110"
Level: 10 - SSHD brute force trying to get access to the system.
Rule Id: 5712
Location: (desktop_agent) 192.168.10.13->/var/log/auth.log
Src IP: 192.168.10.110
May 23 14:26:33 ubuntu sshd[3628]: Failed none for invalid user academic from 192.168.10.110 port 36005 ssh2
May 23 14:26:33 ubuntu sshd[3628]: Invalid user academic from 192.168.10.110
May 23 14:26:33 ubuntu sshd[3626]: Failed none for invalid user academia from 192.168.10.110 port 55671 ssh2
May 23 14:26:33 ubuntu sshd[3626]: Invalid user academia from 192.168.10.110
May 23 14:26:33 ubuntu sshd[3624]: Failed none for invalid user abc from 192.168.10.110 port 39870 ssh2
May 23 14:26:33 ubuntu sshd[3624]: Invalid user abc from 192.168.10.110
May 23 14:26:33 ubuntu sshd[3622]: Failed none for invalid user aaa from 192.168.10.110 port 54453 ssh2
May 23 14:26:33 ubuntu sshd[3622]: Invalid user aaa from 192.168.10.110

Fig. 9. OSSE alert message for brute force attack

- **Numbers of detected alerts**

The OSSEC web interface is a better solution for diagnosis. It allowed us to have a global view of the different agents of our node, the last modified files, to perform alerts searches from a specific date or to have statistics that can be used to make decisions about the security strategy.

Our test was done for 48 h whose purpose is to monitor traffic flowing through the node, in order to detect suspicious packets. Each VM has a OSSEC agent, which is responsible for transmitting the information to the server, it analyzes all received data from its agents by using a shared key and if there is a match with the signature database, an alert is generated.

The alert numbers displayed during the two days (Table 1) 1224 alerts grouped by severity of each alert, going from 0 to 15. The alert level 0 are numerous (912 notifications), followed by user error alerts (level 5: attack for access to Wordpress website administrator account) with 101 alerts. However, the alert that has great importance is that of denial of service with a single alert (level 12).

0: the alerts to be ignored. They include events with no security risk.
1: none.
3: low priority notification system, notification or system status message.
4: errors related to misconfiguration.
5: user error, lack of password.
6: weak attack, a worm or virus that have no effect on the system.
7: the correspondence of the "Bad word" includes "error" "Bad".
8: first seen event, first login of a user.
9: error: invalid source, includes login attempts as an unknown user or an invalid source.
10: generation of errors by multiple users, example of dictionary attack.
11: it indicates successful attacks.
12: alerts of high importance, it may indicate an attack against a specific application.
13: unusual error.
14: a security event of high importance, it indicates an attack.
15: severe attacks, an immediate reaction is necessary.

Table 1. Number of alerts according to severity

Level of severity	Number of alerts	%
Level 4	1	0.1%
Level 12	1	0.1%
Level 9	2	0.2%
Level 8	3	0.2%
Level 7	13	1.1%
Level 10	16	1.3%
Level 2	43	3.5%
Level 1	55	4.5%
Level 3	77	6.3%
Level 5	101	8.3%
Level 0	912	74.5%
Total alerts	1224	100%

The signature database of OSSEC is composed of a set of XML files, each file represents an attack signature, and each signature (rule) has its own ID. Indeed, the rule ID represents the type of detected attack. Table 2 shows the number of alerts generated by OSSEC grouped by the number of signatures (rules) and the percentage of each rule in relation to total alerts.

Table 2. Number of alerts according to the rule ID

Rule ID	Number of alerts	%
11310	12	1.0%
5521	17	1.4%
5522	17	1.4%
12100	23	1.9%
2900	24	2.0%
532	26	2.1%
1002	43	3.5%
11403	45	3.7%
5523	50	4.1%
11401	51	4.2%
5503	51	4.2%
535	55	4.5%
509	143	11.7%
530	598	48.9%

- **Prevention mechanism**

The OSSEC solution not just as a HIDS, but also as a HIPS that can take steps to reduce the impact of an attack and prevent the incident to spread in the host. This feature provides the ability to block communications by disabling ports or network interfaces for example. The prevention feature can be configured to launch rules, block source addresses, or disable interfaces for a period determined by the administrator. In our test, OSSEC has terminated any suspicious communication by blocking the source address as shown in the following figure (Fig. 10):

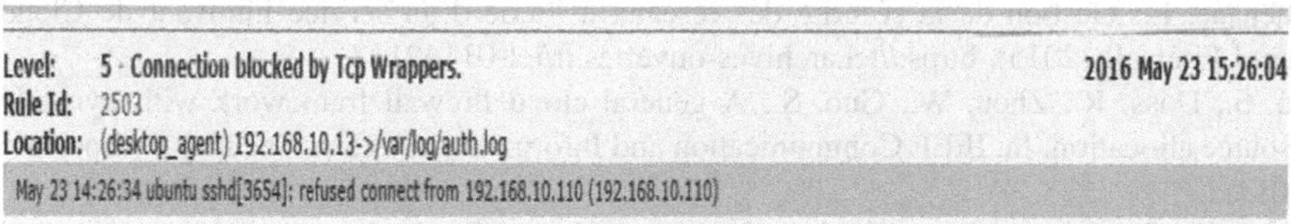
Level: 5 - Connection blocked by Tcp Wrappers.
2016 May 23 15:26:04
Rule Id: 2503
Location: (desktop_agent) 192.168.10.13->/var/log/auth.log
May 23 14:26:34 ubuntu sshd[3654]: refused connect from 192.168.10.110 (192.168.10.110)

Fig. 10. Prevention mechanism

We simulate different types of attacks in our cloud environment, using VMware workstation as a hypervisor, our intrusion detection and prevention system may be appropriate to detect these intrusions and remove malicious packets using the active response feature. Since virtualization is a fundamental part of cloud computing, we believe that the proposed solution can be exploited in a real-world cloud environment to reduce security threats in such a system.

5 Conclusion and Perspectives

The cloud is designed to meet the needs of customers using the minimum of resources. All we need is a browser and an internet connection. As a result, the ongoing threat and attacks are facing this evolving technology, they remain challenges in terms of management tools, control and security.

In this paper, we focused on cloud computing security issues, identified various threats related to such an environment, and then proposed a decentralized cloud-firewall to monitor incoming packets and a prevention and detection system. intrusion. new threat as well as to attack and improve our security system.

In the future, we will deploy event correlation for HIDS components and implement all the proposed architecture within a cloud infrastructure to validate it. The test results will be given in the extended version of this document.

References

1. Cloud Security Alliance: Cloud Computing Top Threats in 2013, February 2013, unpublished
2. Mazhar, A., Khan, U., Vasilakos, V.: Security in cloud computing: Opportunities and challenges. Inf. Sci. **305**, 357–383 (2015)
3. Memari, N.: Scalable Honeynet based on artificial intelligence utilizing cloud computing. Int. J. Res. Comput. Sci. **4**, 27–34 (2014)
4. Raghavendra, S., Lakshmi, S., Venkateswarlu, S.: Security issues and trends in cloud computing. Int. J. Comput. Sci. Inf. Technol. **6**(2), 1156–1159 (2015)
5. Varadharajan, V.: Security as a service model for cloud environment. IEEE Trans. Netw. Serv. Manag. **11**(1), 60–75 (2014)
6. Sharma, D., Dhote, C., Potey, M.: Identity and access management as security-as-a-service from clouds. In: Proceedings of International Conference on Communication, Computing and Virtualization (2016)
7. Guenane, F.: Gestion de la sécurité des réseaux à l'aide d'un service innovant de Cloud Based Firewall (2015). https://tel.archives-ouvertes.fr/tel-01149112
8. Yu, S., Doss, R., Zhou, W., Guo, S.: A general cloud firewall framework with dynamic resource allocation. In: IEEE Communication and Information Systems Security Symposium (2013)
9. Saadi, C., Chaoui, H.: Intrusion detection system based interaction on mobile agents and clust-density algorithm "IDS-AM-Clust". In: Information Science and Technology (CiSt IEEE) (2016)
10. Saadi, C., Chaoui, H.: Cloud computing security using IDS-AM-Clust, Honeyd, Honeywall and Honeycomb. Procedia Comput. Sci. CMS **85**, 2016 (2016)
11. Saadi, C., Chaoui, H.: Make the intrusion detection system by IDS-AM-Clust, Honeyd, Honeycomb and Honeynet. Advances in Computer Science, pp. 177–188. Wseas Press, November 2015. ISBN 978-1-61804-344-3
12. Zayed, A., Mostafa, H., Mamouni, A.: Cloud computing et sécurité: approches et solutions. Int. J. Res. Comput. Sci. **30**(1), 11–14 (2015)

A Multi-factor Authentication Scheme to Strength Data-Storage Access

Soufiane Sail(✉) and Halima Bouden

Laboratory Modélisation et théorie de l'information, University AbdelMalek Essaadi, Tétouan, Morocco
Soufiane.sail@gmail.com, bouden.halima@gmail.com

Abstract. Nowadays Cloud Computing is one of the most useful IT technology in the world, many companies and individuals, adopt this technology due to its benefits, such as high performance infrastructure, scalability, cost efficiency etc.

However Security remains one of the biggest problems that make this technology less trustful. With the big success of the Cloud, many Hackers started focusing on it, and many attacks that use to be exclusively targeting the web, are now used against Cloud system especially the SaaS.

That's why authentication to the SaaS and data storage systems is now a serious issue, in order to protect our system and client information. This paper describes a scheme that strength the authentication system of data storage, using multi-factor authentication such as OTP, smart card and try to bring an alternative system that manage authentication Error issues.

Keywords: Security · Cloud computing · Software as a service · OTP · Smart card Captcha · Data storage

1 Introduction

Clouds computing nowadays represent one of the most and fastest growing technologies in IT industry, offering several services such as SaaS, PaaS and IaaS.

This technology brings many advantages to their client, since that a client will pay for what he use, which means saving money by using some excellent infrastructure (servers, data center, computer…), also the user will no longer worry about IT problems, since that all is managed by the owner, who offer a service available 24/24.

On the other hand, this technology has several fails, especially when it comes to security issues, hackers are more and more interested in Cloud, and attacks are increasingly aggressive, SaaS remain one of the biggest targets, that's why Cloud Service Providers are invited to improve their security strategies in order to protect their systems by working on many aspects such as authentication… etc.

Y. Tabii et al. (Eds.): BDCA 2018, CCIS 872, pp. 67–77, 2018.
https://doi.org/10.1007/978-3-319-96292-4_6

2 Cloud Computing and Security Issues

Cloud had made many tasks easier for enterprises especially SME, who benefits from high quality infrastructure without the need of investing a huge amount of money. But this technology still under critics, principally for its security problems, such as Data loss, Data branches, accounts hijacking [1, 2] Third party trust etc. (Fig. 1).

Fig. 1. Security issues in the cloud environment.

- Data Breaches: happen when we have two or more virtual machines of different customers in same server, Side Chanel Attacks is a threat where an attacker could attempt to compromise the cloud by placing a malicious virtual machine in the immediate vicinity of a target cloud server and then launching a lateral channel attack [3].
- Data Loss: there are many ways that can cause data loss, such as physical problems of the infrastructure, fail in cryptography and key management, malicious injection, absence of backup etc. [1].
- Insider attacks: These attacks are orchestrated or executed by people that are trusted with varying levels of access to a company's systems and facilities, and who have intimate knowledge of the company's infrastructure which an external attacker would take a significant period of time to develop [4]. Such attacks are extremely dangerous, and they are hard to detect.
- Account Hijacking: Generally attacks based on using login information of a person, gained by the attackers with some tools or methods such as phishing, exploitation of software vulnerabilities etc. [1, 2].
- Third Party Trust: Such issues are generally related, to the relation between the client the cloud provider and a third party, it can be dangerous, since that the third party can have access to the client information which is a violation of our client privacy.

- Malicious Injection: Attacks that aims to inject malicious service implementation or virtual machine into the cloud service [5]. Once this malicious is in the system, it is executed as part of the system and can damage the system easily.
- Denial of service: In cloud computing, hacker attack on the server by sending thousands of requests to the server. That server is unable to respond to the regular clients in this way server will not work properly [6].
- Insecure APIs: APIs are used by cloud service providers and software developers to allow customers to interact, manage, and extract information from cloud services [7]. An unsecure API can be very dangerous, especially if the API use an unsecure channel for transporting information, containing fails at the authentication and authorization level, or event allowing some scripting attacks such as Sql Injection and XSS [8, 9].

3 Related Work

One of proposed solution to authenticate was proposed by Banyal [10], a Multi-factor authentication for different level of data. This work had classified data, based on their importance (low, medium, high) and in order to access to each level there are some different challenge's, and we should past by the start, which means that for having access to medium information, the client must first access to the low level then the medium one, with no direct access.

Classification of data might be used to find the encryption solution for each one, for example data with high sensibility we can encrypt them with a very complex cryptography, and less for medium and low sensible information to save cost, and not to exhaust our server. But using classification in order to find the right authentication solution can be harmful, because if a hacker will have access to the first level he will be able to lunch attacks such as side channel attacks which it might allow him to access to other levels and maybe attacks other users.

Also this scheme had proposed a solution at the high level, the system ask the user to enter his EMEI code, and this is not secure at all, since that the EMEI is not a real secret code, simply we can get this code event if we don't have the mobile, for example Google do memories anything of its client event somewhat might appears as useless information, EMEI are one of those information that Google keep in their client database, so if someone get access to the Google+ client space, he can easily find this code in the dashboard. Finally EMEI are not static to each mobile there are tools which allow the modification of this code.

Other works proposed some solution such as the facial recognition [11] which was add recently to Appel IPhone to authenticate, problem that this system contain a big fail, recently a group of researchers did broke the Appel phone authentication using the 3D printing of the client face [12].

4 Proposed Solution

Scheme that we are proposing is a multi-Factor authentication, based on the use of a double OTP (one time password) and smart card.

This system combine the use of a smart card and a mobile phone, by sending two OTPs, generated differently to limit risks in case one of the tools will be hacked, which is probable, also the system will prevent attacks if the mobile or smart card will be lost. The scheme also provides a Captcha to limit DoS attacks.

4.1 Key Entities

We consider that the communication between the client and server is protected by SSL-128 or SSL-256 for maximal protection, in order to prevent some network attacks such as Man in The Middle.

Also the smart card is well configured, and we considered that the client is trusted also.

Authentication is based on a multi-factor; in order to authenticate a user must have his mobile phone and a secure smart card (Table 1).

Table 1. Key entities.

Notation	Example
Us	Username
Pwd	Password
UPo	User mobile phone
MP	Private email
OTP1	One time password sent to the smart card
OTP2	One time password sent to the mobile phone

Phase 1 - Registration

Each member must do a registration, and bring some important and required information's for authentication, such as phone number and private email, and maybe a second phone line in case the second will be lost.

Phase 2 - Authentication

Step1- the user enter his username and password, and then he past the Captcha test in order to prevent BoT attacks.

Step2- the server will check the authentication of information sent, if information are correct past to step3 if not the system will send a message and/or an email to the user, to report him that someone had tried to connect to the system, the user must confirm if his is the responsible of what happened or not, if he did a recovery system will be launched in order to help him remembering his password or having a new one… if the user confirm that he has nothing to do with what happened the system will consider it as an attack, and he will memories the ip from where the request came, put it in a blacklist and blocked (Fig. 2).

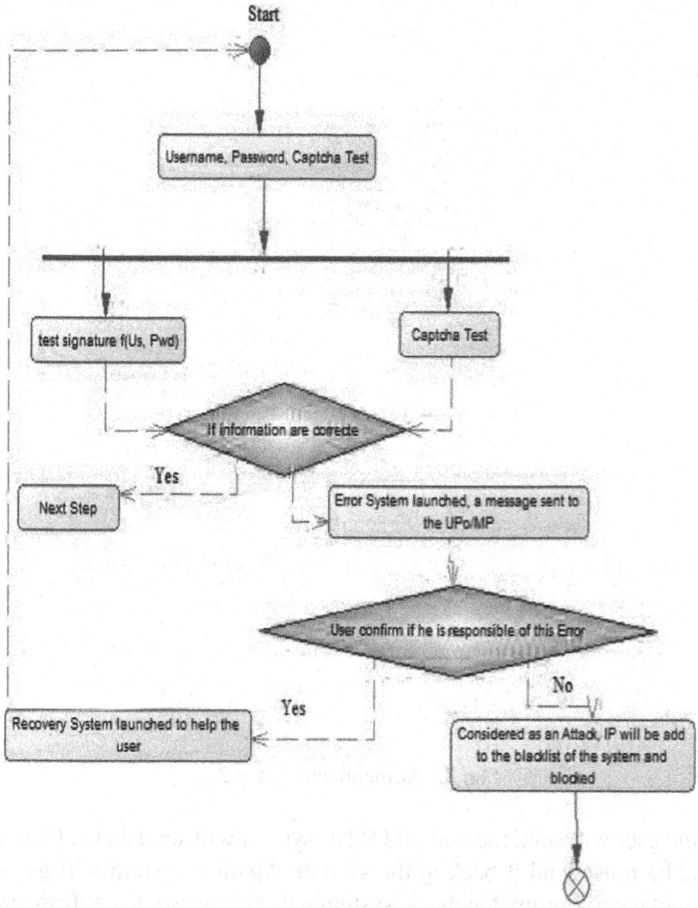

Fig. 2. Authentication step1.

Step3- if information are correct the system will send an OTP1 (one time password) to the user smart card.

Step4- The user must enter the OTP1 sent by the system in order to past to the next level. In case the system will generate many OTPs without receiving any answer, a message will be sent to the user. If the user will confirm that he did lose his smart card, the system will automatically block it, and will ask him to use a new one (Fig. 3).

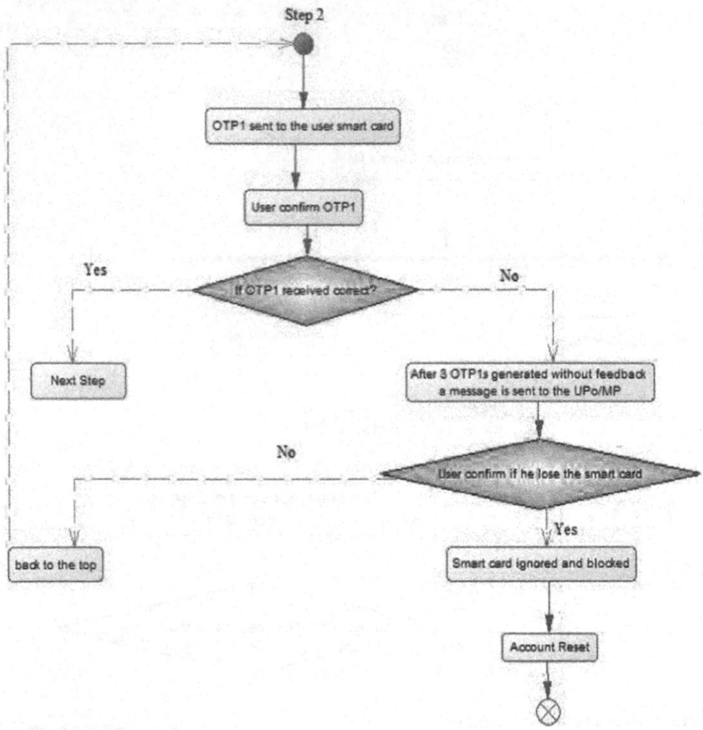

Fig. 3. Authentication step 2.

Step5- If the user will send the correct OTP1, system will send an OTP2 to his mobile phone, and he must send it back to the system. Again if system will generate many OTPs without receiving any feedback, system will ask the user to confirm that he didn't lose his phone. If he did system will no longer generate OTPs to that mobile phone and he will ask the user to bring a new one or skip to the second phone line.

Step6- If the user will bring the correct OTP2 the system will send him the permission to access the Cloud (Fig. 4).

Phase 3 - Reset

Case 1 Smart card:

In case the Smart Card will be lost, we ask the user to move to the agency or a trusted third part who will manage the deliverance of configured smart card for our client.

Case 2 user Phone:

In this case, if the user had a second line we will keep contact through it, if not we will ask him by his personal email to bring us a new phone number and configure the phone in order to be able to receive messages of OTPs.

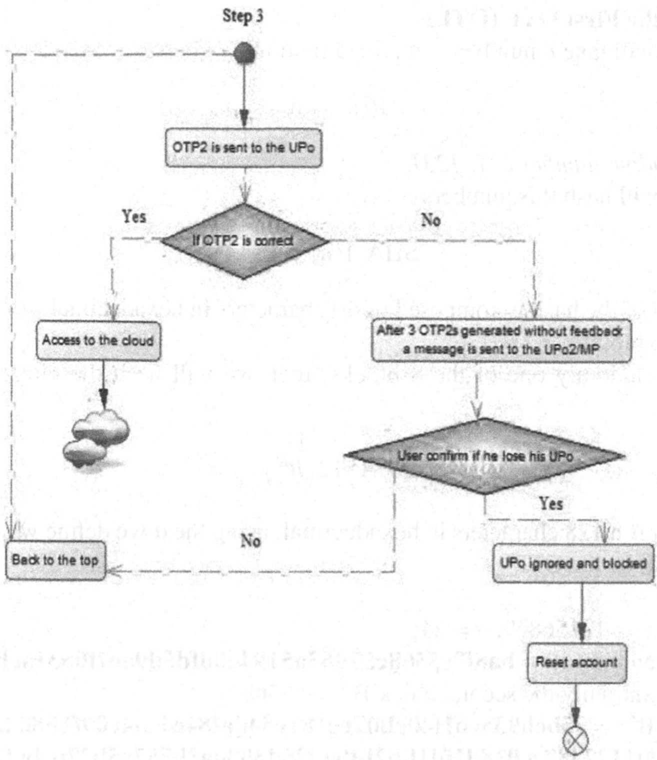

Fig. 4. Authentication step 3.

4.2 Captcha

Captcha which means (Completely Automated Public Turing Test to Tell Computers and Humans Apart) is a security mechanism that is used to distinguish human users from malicious computer programs trying to gain illegitimate access to resources [13].

Many type of Captcha exist, linguistic Captcha, text-based Captcha, image Captcha, audio Captcha and also video Captcha. Many solution can be used, some works focused on video Captcha such as kurt [14] who proposed a video Captcha based on tags, so that the user can watch the video and select what he did saw on the video. Rao [15] has proposed Captcha based on commercial video, where the user must select what type of commercial product it concern.

4.3 One Time Password

One time password is a code generated for each session. In our scheme we need two OTPs generated differently (two functions of OTP's generation) which will limit damage in case one of those functions will be hacked.

Generating the First OTP (OTP1)

First step we will take 8 numbers generated randomly where:

$$R(x) = n$$

And a random number α[1, 123];

Then we will hash this numbers

$$SHA\text{-}1(n) = k;$$

The result of the hash is composed of 40 characters in hexadecimal format; we split the result to 8 blocks.

We take randomly one of the 8 blocks, then we will hash the block again with SHA512,

$$SHA512\left(B^K\right)$$

The result is a 128 characters in hexadecimal, using the α we define wish block of 6 characters will be the OTP.

Example:

Random(x) = 12156849, α = 24;

SHA-1(Random(x)) = **ba8f9c5568c57965a519460dfd5d9ae7f0531aeb**

We take randomly the second block B^K = **c5568**

SHA512(B^K) = **35bcb935cb1f40cb07ec181c54daf84e4cd4c09f1b8022632d50f527c8be0e3ebd01122482ec018d1fd1bb2f4ba225d3030a5b757e5b276ebaf2df06e4dc8b84**

α = 24;

$$OTP1 = \mathbf{c54daf}$$

Generating the Second OTP (OTP2)

First step we randomly take:

$$\gamma[1, 35], \beta[1, 123] \text{ and } 8 \text{ numbers } R(x) = 8n.$$

Then we hash the number token randomly

$$SHA\text{-}1(R(x)) = m;$$

We replace m by OTP1 at position γ

$$Replace(m, OTP1)_\gamma = K;$$

And we hash the result K with SHA512.

$$SHA512(K)$$

And through the value of β we take the block B_β of 6 characters which will be the OTP2.

Example:

R(x) = 25986539, $\gamma = 5$, $\beta = 42$.

We hash the R(x) ⇔ SHA-1(R(x))

SHA-1(R(x)) = **d5f1b12050787e0ebfa31ea4704c02df4fbcd313.**

Then we replace the block at the position $\gamma = 5$ by the OTP1.

Replace (**d5f1b12050787e0ebfa31ea4704 c02df4fbcd313,** *c54daf*)5 = **d5f1c54daf787e0e bfa31ea4704 c02df4fbcd313.**

Finally we hash the result using SHA512.

SHA512(d5f1c54daf787e0ebfa31ea4704c02df4fbcd313) = cdd7809b65fd110fe64420ab7b60de57ccf6d78090c76c8fa811758248101f971e9f88ae 80c3ecd0636b795dc115e6137a2358d6a51ec9ad9912d69e7697a29b.

Using the value $\beta = 42$ we find the position of the block.

OTP2 = **0c76c8.**

5 Data Storage

Once the user authenticate, he will be able to choice the way his data will be stored based on their importance. If the user has very important information he can encrypt them using a very complicated algorithm, and less complicated encryption for less important information, in order to save time in accessing information and to prevent exhausting our servers (Fig. 5).

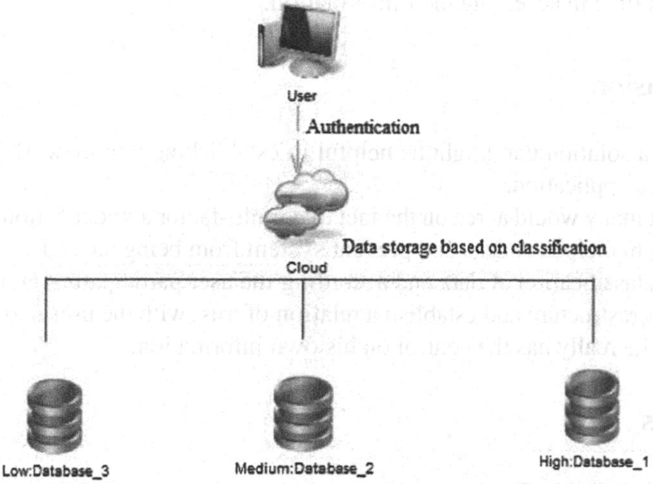

Fig. 5. Overview of data storage system.

6 Results and Discussion

The use of a double OTP, generated differently and sent to different device will limit the probability of being hacked event if one of those devices will be lost, or one of those OTP's generator will be discovered, they will be useless since that we have two completely different OTPs.

Also the use of a captcha, will limit BoT attacks, which will prevent our system from being exhausted by receiving useless request.

SSL will secure the transit of our information in a secure way, also will help to authenticate users while they send their login and password, and also when they make registration and reset their accounts.

The main idea of using a multi-factor authentication in data storage and the classification of data in storage will maximize the security of our system, and minimize directly threatens, and will prevent servers and computers from being exhausted, and will allow to client to participate in the way of storing there information, and adept for very complicated algorithm for their top secrets data etc.

This solution is in favor of Cloud computing providers since using such scheme will unifying the access for information and will protect all information in same way, and prevent from many threatens such as Side channel attacks, man in the middle, DoS attacks etc. Also classification using complicated encryption for just some data will not be a problem for servers and machines.

Also this scheme is in favor of Client too, since they participate in the way of their information will be stored which will establish a relation of trust Client/Provider; they will also gain time in accessing their information.

7 Conclusion

This work is a solution that might be helpful in establishing a framework of accessing to data storage application.

Since that many would agree on the fact that multi-factor authentication is a solution to prevent all malicious attacks and prevent system from being hacked.

Also the classification of data and according the user participating in it will help to protect our infrastructure and establish a relation of trust with the user in order to make him feel that he really has the control on his own information.

References

1. Pandey, S., Farik, M.: Cloud computing security: latest issues & countermeasures. Int. J. Sci. Technol. Res. **4**(11), 2–30 (2015)
2. Ma, J.: 14 December 2015 https://www.incapsula.com/blog/top-10-cloud-security-concerns.html. Accessed 9 Sept 2017
3. Luo, Q., Fei, Y.: Algorithmic collision analysis for evaluating cryptographic system and side-channel attacks. In: International Symposium on H/w – Oriented Security and Trust (2011)

4. Duncan, A., Creese, S., Goldsmith, M.: Insider attacks in cloud computing. In: 2012 IEEE 11th International Conference on Trust, Security and Privacy in Computing and Communication, pp. 857–862 (2012)
5. Jensen, M., Schwenk, J., Gruschka, N., Iacono, L.L.: On technical security issues in cloud computing. In: 2009 IEEE International Conference on Cloud Computing (2009)
6. Vani Mounika, S., Preetiparwekar: Survey on cloud data storage security techniques. In: National Conference on Advanced Functional Materials and Computer Applications in Materials Technology (CAMCAT-2014), pp. 95–98 (2014)
7. Simon Leech 2016: Cloud Security Threats - Insecure APIs. https://community.hpe.com/t5/Grounded-in-the-Cloud/Cloud-Security-Threats-Insecure-APIs/ba-p/6871684#.Wbw0b_PyjIV. Accessed 9 Sept 2017
8. Shackleford, D.: Cloud API security risks: how to assess cloud service provider APIs. http://searchcloudsecurity.techtarget.com/tip/Cloud-API-security-risks-How-to-assess-cloud-service-provider-APIs. Accessed 9 Sept 2017
9. Rodero-Merino, L., et al.: Building safe PasS clouds: a survey on security in the multitenant software platforms. Comput. Secur. **31**(1), 96–108 (2012)
10. Banyal, R.K., Jain, P., Jain, V.K.: Multi-factor authentication framework for cloud computing. In: 2013 Fifth International Conference on Computational Intelligence, Modelling and Simulation (2013)
11. Chakraborty, S., Singh, S.K., Chakraborty, P.: Local quadruple pattern: a novel descriptor for facial image recognition and retrieval Comput. Electr. Eng. **62**, 1–13 (2017)
12. Saunders, S.: Cyber Security Firm Uses a 3D Printed Mask to Fool iPhone X's Facial Recognition Software, 13 November 2017. https://3dprint.com/194079/3d-printed-mask-iphone-x-face-id/
13. Roshabin, N., Miller, J.: ADAMAS: interweaving unicode and color to enhance CAPTCHA security. Future Gener. Comput. Syst. **55**, 289–310 (2014)
14. Kluever, K.A.: Evaluating the usability and security of a video CAPTCHA. Master's thesis, Rochester Institute of Technology, Rochester, New York, August 2008
15. Rao, K., Sri, K., Sai, G.: A novel video CAPTCHA technique to prevent BOT attacks. In: International Conference on Computational Modeling and Security (2016)

A Novel Text Encryption Algorithm Based on the Two-Square Cipher and Caesar Cipher

Mohammed Es-Sabry[1(✉)], Nabil El Akkad[1,2], Mostafa Merras[1], Abderrahim Saaidi[1,3(✉)], and Khalid Satori[1(✉)]

[1] LIIAN, Department of Mathematics and Computer Science, Faculty of Sciences, Dhar-Mahraz, Sidi Mohamed Ben Abdellah University, B.P. 1796, Atlas, Fez, Morocco
{mohammed.es.sabry, abderrahim.saaidi}@usmba.ac.ma, khalidsatori@gmail.com

[2] Department of Mathematics and Computer Science, National School of Applied Sciences (ENSA) of Al-Hoceima, University of Mohamed First, B.P. 03, Ajdir, Oujda, Morocco

[3] LSI, Department of Mathematics, Physics and Informatics, Polydisciplinary Faculty of Taza, Sidi Mohamed Ben Abdellah University, Taza, Morocco

Abstract. Security of information has become a popular subject during the last decades, it is the balanced protection of the Confidentiality, Integrity and Availability of data, also known as the CIA Triad. In this work, we introduce a new hybrid system based on two different encryption techniques: two square cipher and Caesar cipher with multiples keys. This homogeneity between the two systems allows us to provide the good properties of the two square cipher method and the simplicity of the Caesar cipher method. The security analysis shows that the system is secure enough to resist brute-force attack, and statistical attack. Therefore, this robustness is proven and justified.

Keywords: Text encryption · Two square cipher · Caesar cipher
Brute-force attack · Statistical attack

1 Introduction

In parallel with the rapid development of multimedia and network technologies, digital information has been applied to many fields in real world applications. However, as people transmit and obtain information more easily, the problem of information security has become crucial during the communication process. Cryptography [1–13] is one of the basic methodologies for information security by coding messages to make them unreadable.

So encryption is the process of encoding a message or information (Fig. 1) in such a way that only authorized parties can access it and those who are not authorized cannot. Encryption does not itself prevent interference, but denies the intelligible

Y. Tabii et al. (Eds.): BDCA 2018, CCIS 872, pp. 78–88, 2018.
https://doi.org/10.1007/978-3-319-96292-4_7

content to a would-be interceptor. In an encryption scheme, the intended information or message, referred to as plaintext, is encrypted using an encryption algorithm – a cipher – generating cipher text that can be read only if decrypted. For technical reasons, an encryption scheme [16–33] usually uses a pseudo-random encryption key generated by an algorithm. It is in principle possible to decrypt the message without possessing the key, but, for a well-designed encryption scheme, considerable computational resources and skills are required. An authorized recipient can easily decrypt the message with the key provided by the originator to recipients but not to unauthorized users.

The rest of this work is organized as follows: the second part presents the proposed method. Experimentation is covered in the third part. A conclusion of this work is presented in the fourth part.

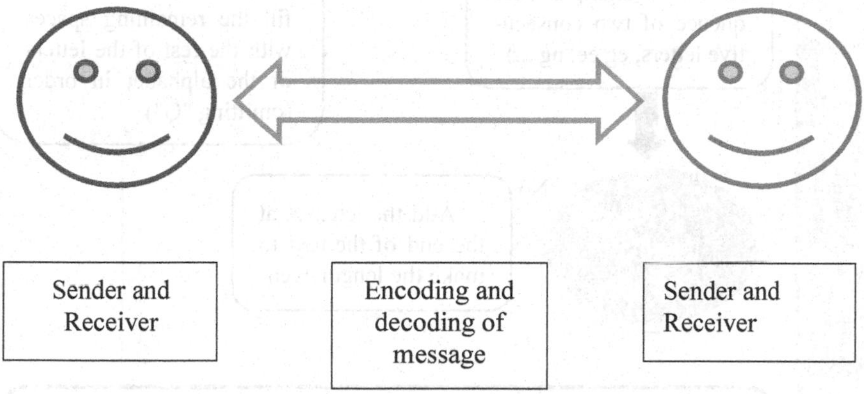

Fig. 1. Operation of encryption and decryption

2 Proposed Method

The proposed method takes advantage from the good properties of the two square cipher method and the simplicity of the Caesar cipher [14, 15] method.

Our system is initialized by a text document that we will encrypt, first we use the method of two square cipher to encrypt the text with two different keys, and each key is used to build a square. These squares represent 5 * 5 matrices are used to encrypt the text for each digraphs (Sequence of two consecutive letters, e.g. ee, th, ng…).

Then we take the result and we also crypt it using the method of Caesar cipher with multiples keys for each letter, the keys chosen are the indices of the letters.

2.1 Text Encryption

2.1.1 Flowchart of the Encryption Phase for Proposed Method

The flowchart below (Fig. 2) illustrate the various steps used to encrypt the original text.

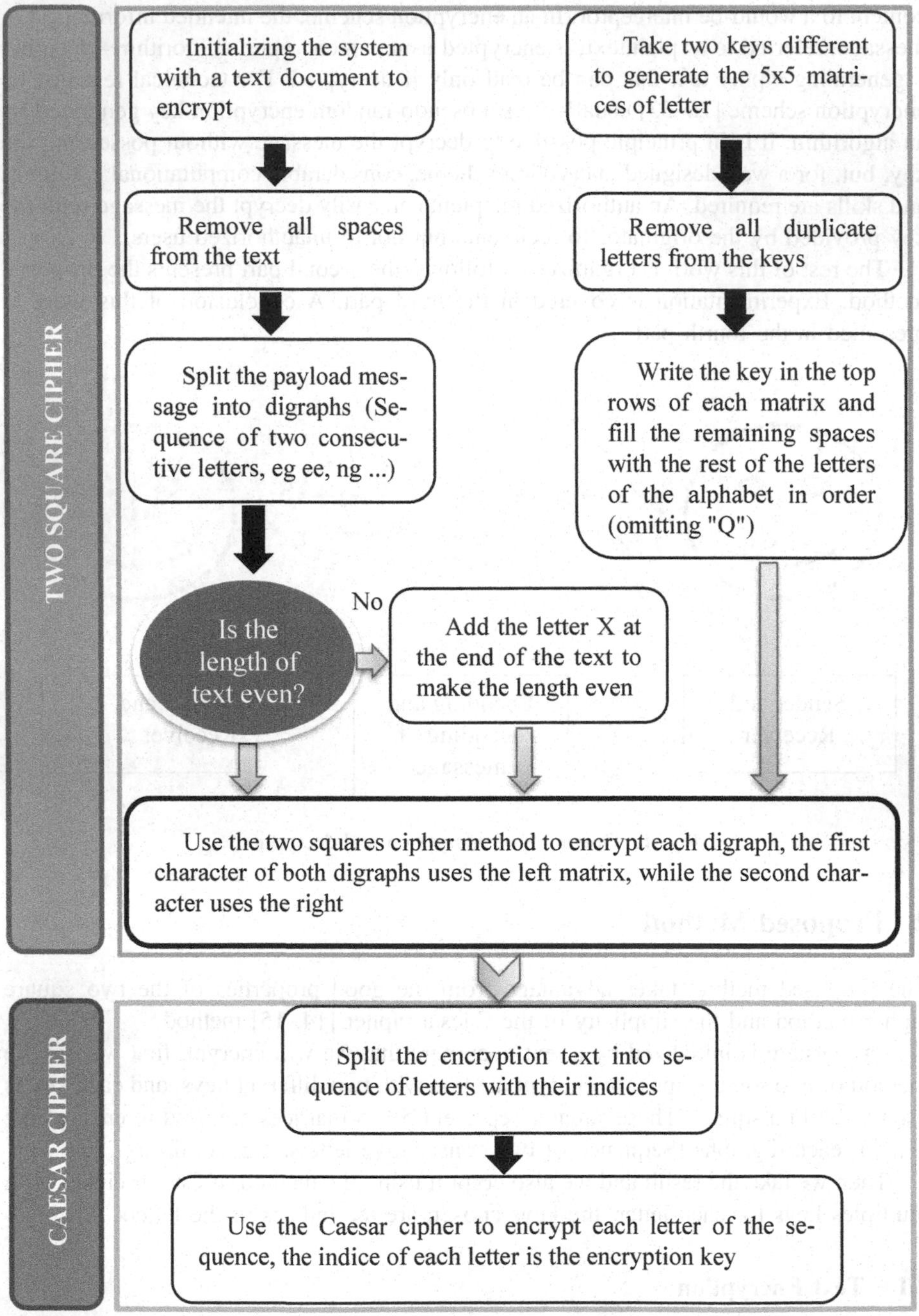
TWO SQUARE CIPHER
Initializing the system with a text document to encrypt
Take two keys different to generate the 5x5 matrices of letter
Remove all spaces from the text
Remove all duplicate letters from the keys
Split the payload message into digraphs (Sequence of two consecutive letters, eg ee, ng ...)
Write the key in the top rows of each matrix and fill the remaining spaces with the rest of the letters of the alphabet in order (omitting "Q")
Is the length of text even?
No
Add the letter X at the end of the text to make the length even
Use the two squares cipher method to encrypt each digraph, the first character of both digraphs uses the left matrix, while the second character uses the right
CAESAR CIPHER
Split the encryption text into sequence of letters with their indices
Use the Caesar cipher to encrypt each letter of the sequence, the indice of each letter is the encryption key

Fig. 2. Flowchart of the steps used to encrypt the original text

2.1.2 Explanation of the Algorithm

The two-square cipher comes in two varieties: horizontal and vertical. The vertical two-square uses two 5 × 5 matrices, one above the other. The horizontal two-square has the two 5 × 5 matrices side by side. Each of the 5 × 5 matrices contains the letters of the alphabet (usually omitting "Q" or putting both "I" and "J" in the same location to reduce the alphabet to fit). The alphabets in both squares are generally mixed alphabets, each based on some keyword or phrase.

To generate the 5 × 5 matrices, one would first fill in the spaces in the matrix with the letters of a keyword or phrase (dropping any duplicate letters), then fill the remaining spaces with the rest of the letters of the alphabet.

In order (again omitting "Q" to reduce the alphabet to fit). The key can be written in the top rows of the table, from left to right, or in some other pattern, such as a spiral beginning in the upper-left-hand corner and ending in the center. The keyword together with the conventions for filling in the 5 × 5 table constitute the cipher key. The two-square algorithm allows for two separate keys, one for each matrix (Fig. 3).

E	L	A	K	D
B	C	F	G	H
I	J	M	N	O
P	R	S	T	U
V	W	X	Y	Z

E	S	A	B	R
Y	C	D	F	G
H	I	J	K	L
M	N	O	P	T
U	V	W	X	Z

Fig. 3. Example of horizontal two-square matrices for the keywords "essabry" and "elakkad"

The letters of the clear message are encrypted by digraph. For example, let us encrypt the digraph **CM**. We find the **C** in the left square, thc **M** in the right square, then we search in these squares the letters that complete the rectangle: in our example, the **I** in the left square and the **F** in the right square. **CM** is encrypted **FI**, because by convention the first of the two encrypted letters is on the same line as the first clear letter (Fig. 4).

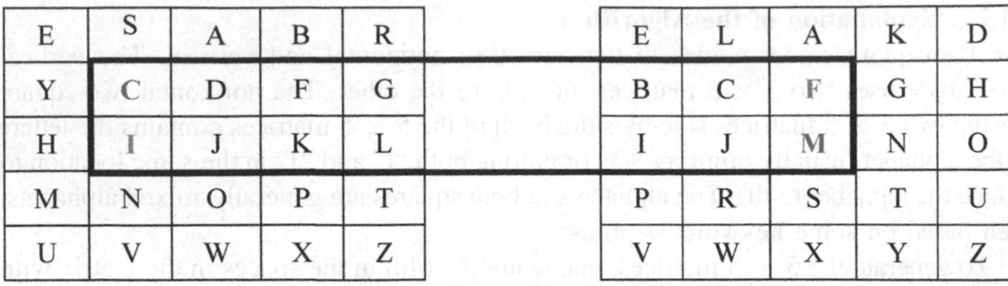

Fig. 4. Example of encrypting the digraph CM

If the two clear letters are in the same line, their inversion forms the encrypted digraph. For example, **CH** becomes **HC** (Fig. 5).

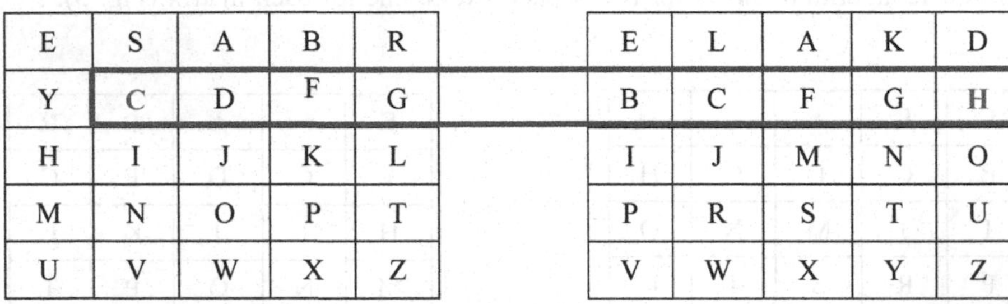

Fig. 5. Example of the two clear letters are in the same line

Like most pre-modern era ciphers, the two-square cipher can be easily cracked if there is enough text. Obtaining the key is relatively straightforward if both plaintext and cipher text are known. When only the cipher text is known, brute force cryptanalysis of the cipher involves searching through the key space for matches between the frequency of occurrence of digraphs (pairs of letters) and the known frequency of occurrence of digraphs in the assumed language of the original message.

To work around this problem, we used the method of Caesar cipher with multiple keys for each letter encrypted by the two squares cipher.

Caesar cipher [17, 18] is one of the simplest and most widely known encryption techniques. It is a type of substitution cipher in which each letter in the plaintext is replaced by a letter some fixed number of positions down the alphabet.

The encryption can be represented using modular arithmetic by first transforming the letters into numbers, according to the scheme, A → 0, B → 1, …, Z → 25. Encryption of a letter X by a shift N can be described mathematically as,

$$E_N(X) = (X + N)\ mod\ 26 \tag{1}$$

Decryption is performed similarly,

$$D_N(X) = (X - N)\ mod\ 26 \tag{2}$$

For example (Fig. 6), with a left shift of 3, A would replace D, E would become B, and so on. The method is named after Julius Caesar, who used it in his private correspondence.

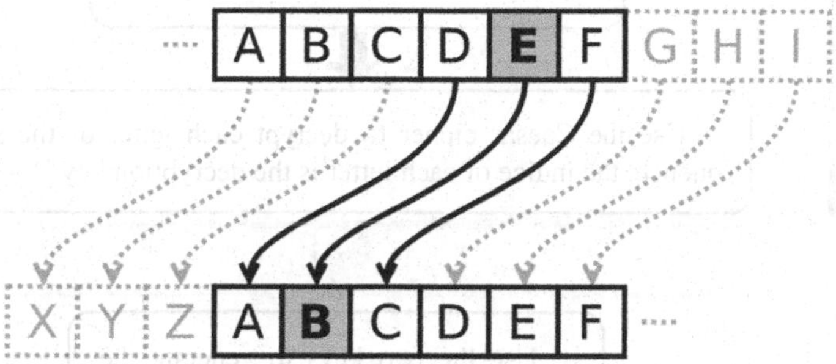

Fig. 6. Caesar cipher encryption

The difference between the classic method of Caesar cipher and the method we will use is that instead of using the same key for all the text, we will use a key for each letter, this key is defined by the formula

$$K(X) = ind(X)\ mod\ 26 \tag{3}$$

With:
X: Letter to encrypt
$ind(X)$: Indcx of the letter X
$K(X)$: The corresponding key to the letter

2.2 Text Decryption

2.2.1 Flowchart of the Decryption Phase for Proposed Method

The flowchart below (Fig. 7) illustrate the various steps used to decrypt the encrypted text.

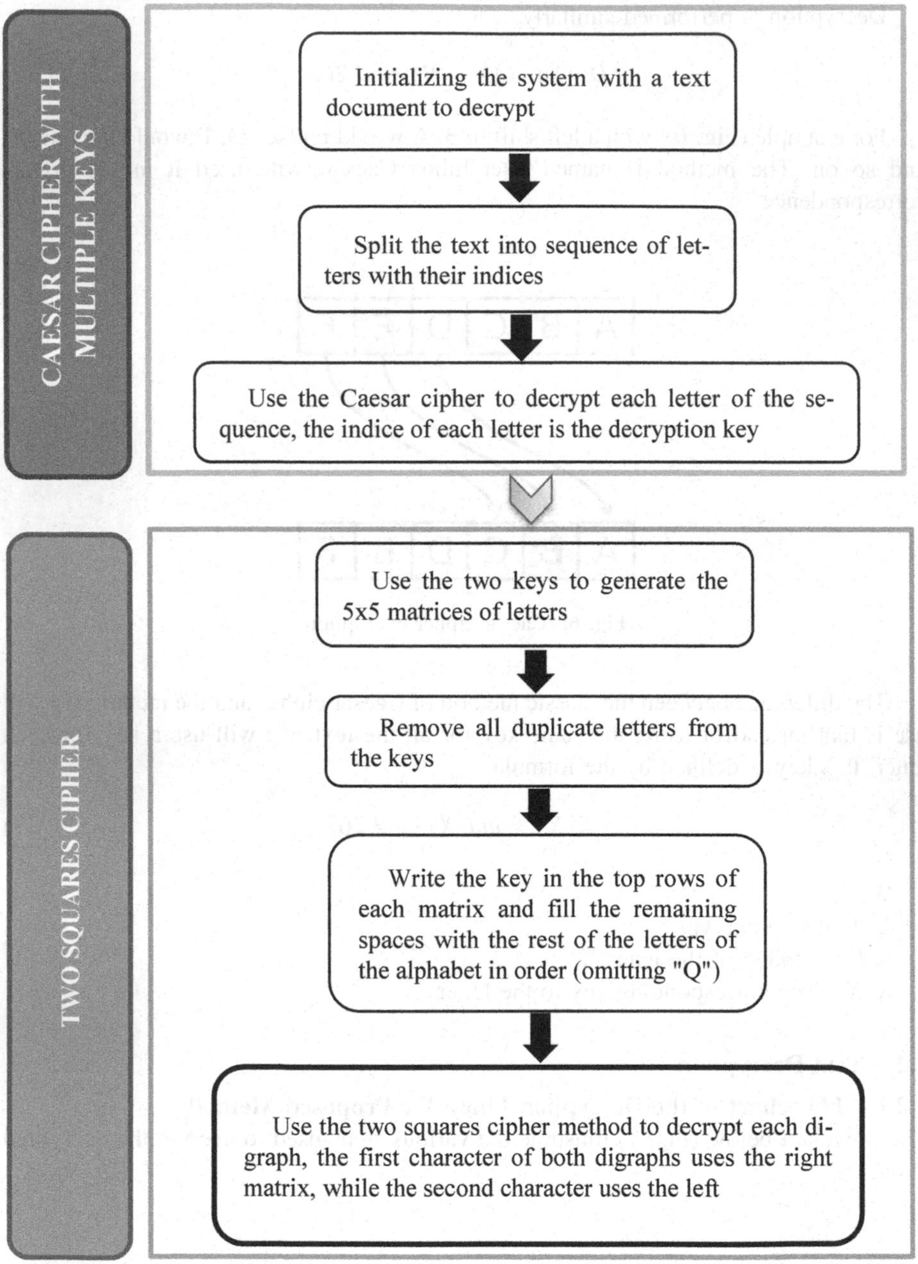
CAESAR CIPHER WITH MULTIPLE KEYS
Initializing the system with a text document to decrypt
Split the text into sequence of letters with their indices
Use the Caesar cipher to decrypt each letter of the sequence, the indice of each letter is the decryption key
TWO SQUARES CIPHER
Use the two keys to generate the 5x5 matrices of letters
Remove all duplicate letters from the keys
Write the key in the top rows of each matrix and fill the remaining spaces with the rest of the letters of the alphabet in order (omitting "Q")
Use the two squares cipher method to decrypt each digraph, the first character of both digraphs uses the right matrix, while the second character uses the left

Fig. 7. Flowchart of the steps used to decrypt the encrypted text

3 Experimentation

In this phase, we took different paragraph with multiple length of text without punctuation. The first paragraph is composed of 131 letters; the 2 keywords used for the two square method are "nabil" and "mohammed".

The second paragraph is composed of 130 letters; the 2 keywords used for the two square method are "elakkad" and "essabry" (Table 1).

The same keywords are used to decrypt the text with changing the order of squares, square 1 becomes square 2 and square 2 becomes square 1 (Table 2).

Table 1. Encryption of the original text

Text Encryption			
Text	**Key-words**	**2 Squares**	**Encrypted text**
Cryptography prior to the modern age was effectively synonymous with encryption the conversion of information from a readable state to apparent nonsense	"nabil" and "mohammed"	Square 1 | Square 2 N A B I L | M O H A E C D E F G | D B C F G H J K M O | I J K L N P R S T U | P R S T U V W X Y Z | V W X Y Z	CRYXWOICVB WHEDDYKJEOI JGGFAVLHHGD OZOORUSDBO WCQNUIKMUI OWUBFZUVQM EIGDDYRHGH WJJTASQMQSQ MLUKSAMNFD YRUKUGERYL DPFHPYYHZOC WXCDDHXCNG IKRZGPDZ
The detailed operation of a cipher is controlled both by the algorithm and in each instance by a key The key is a secret ideally known only to the communicants	"elakkad" and "essabry"	Square 1 | Square 2 E L A K D | E S A B R B C F G H | Y C D F G I J M N O | H I J K L P R S T U | M N O P T V W X Y Z | U V W X Z	TKGIKYTRNV MMHBIQGEGIG CEBLTOPSNXK UWADWARZQT CMCWTPKLZJC NSNXOSQVMP YSPRDVEMMZ FDLZXILIBXOJ SOHSFUFRULSI GBWXHZZOM MDTTHPHDWG ABQDZANICBB HRT

Table 2. Decryption of the encrypted text

Text Encryption			
Text	**Key-words**	**2 Squares**	**Encrypted text**
CRYXWOICV BWHEDDYKJ EOIJGGFAVL HHGDOZOOR USDBOWCQN UIKMUIOWUB FZUVQMEIGD DYRHGHWJJ TASQMQSQM LUKSAMNFD YRUKUGERY LDPFHPYYHZ OCWXCDDHX CNGIKRZGPD Z	"nabil" and "mohammed"	Square 1 | Square 2 M O H A E | N A B I L D B C F G | C D E F G I J K L N | H J K M O P R S T U | P R S T U V W X Y Z | V W X Y Z	CRYPTOGRAPHYP RIORTOTHEMODE RNAGEWASEFFEC TIVELYSYNONYM OUSWITHENCRYPT IONTHECONVERSI ONOFINFORMATIO NFROMAREADABL ESTATETOAPPARE NTNONSENSEX
TKGIKYTRNV MMHBIQGEGI GCEBLTOPSN XKUWADWAR ZQTCMCWTP KLZJCNSNXO SQVMPYSPRD VEMMZFDLZ XILIBXOJSOH SFUFRULSIGB WXHZZOMM DTTHPHDWG ABQDZANICB BHRT	"elakkad" and "essabry"	Square 1 | Square 2 E S A B R | E L A K D Y C D F G | B C F G H H I J K L | I J M N O M N O P T | P R S T U U V W X Z | V W X Y Z	THEDETAILEDOPE RATIONOFACIPHE RISCONTROLLEDB OTHBYTHEALGORI THMANDINEACHIN STANCEBYAKEYT HEKEYISASECRETI DEALLYKNOWNO NLYTOTHECOMMU NICANTS

According to the results shown in the Tables 1 and 2, we can conclude that our approach gives good results; the encrypted text is very different from the original text. We note that for the deciphering of the first paragraph, we got one more letter; it is the letter X, because the length of the original text is odd, this letter does not interfere with the overall meaning of the text.

The weakness of the original method is seen at the level of the repeated digraphs of the original text, and as a result, the number of iterations for a brute-force attack will greatly diminish. That is why we have added another simple method based on the indices of each letter so that each digraphs of the original text will not be encrypted with the same letters.

4 Conclusion

In this work, we have treated an approach to encrypt text using the strength of the two squares cipher and the simplicity of Caesar cipher with multiple keys. This new hybrid system allowed us to work around the problem of the brute force cryptanalysis of the two squares cipher (searching through the key space for matches between the frequency of occurrence of digraphs and the known frequency of occurrence of digraphs in the assumed language of the original message). Therefore, our approach is strong enough to resist any cryptanalysis attack.

References

1. Bellare, M., Boldyreva, A., Micali, S.: Public-key encryption in a multi-user setting: security proofs and improvements. In: Preneel, B. (ed.) EUROCRYPT 2000. LNCS, vol. 1807, pp. 259–274. Springer, Heidelberg (2000). https://doi.org/10.1007/3-540-45539-6_18
2. Bellare, M., Desai, A., Jokipii, E., Rogaway, P.: A concrete security treatment of symmetric encryption: analysis of the DES modes of operation. In: Proceedings of the 38th Symposium on Foundations of Computer Science. IEEE (1997)
3. Bellare, M., Rogaway, P.: Optimal asymmetric encryption. In: De Santis, A. (ed.) EUROCRYPT 1994. LNCS, vol. 950, pp. 92–111. Springer, Heidelberg (1995). https://doi.org/10.1007/BFb0053428
4. Bellare, M., Sahai, A.: Non-malleable encryption: equivalence between two notions, and an indistinguishability-based characterization. In: Wiener, M. (ed.) CRYPTO 1999. LNCS, vol. 1666, pp. 519–536. Springer, Heidelberg (1999). https://doi.org/10.1007/3-540-48405-1_33
5. Cramer, R., Shoup, V.: A practical public key cryptosystem provably secure against adaptive chosen ciphertext attack. In: Krawczyk, H. (ed.) CRYPTO 1998. LNCS, vol. 1462, pp. 13–25. Springer, Heidelberg (1998). https://doi.org/10.1007/BFb0055717
6. ElGamal, T.: A public key cryptosystem and signature scheme based on discrete logarithms. IEEE Trans. Inf. Theory **31**, 469–472 (1985)
7. Dolev, D., Dwork, C., Naor, M.: Non-malleable cryptography. In: Proceedings of the 23rd Annual Symposium on Theory of Computing. ACM (1991)
8. Håstad, J.: Solving simultaneous modular equations of low degree. SIAM J. Comput. **17**(2), 336–341 (1988)
9. Goldwasser, S., Micali, S.: Probabilistic encryption. J. Comput. Syst. Sci. **28**, 270–299 (1984)
10. Naor, M., Reingold, O.: Number-theoretic constructions of efficient pseudorandom functions. In: Proceedings of the 38th Symposium on Foundations of Computer Science. IEEE (1997)
11. Rackoff, C., Simon, D.R.: Non-interactive zero-knowledge proof of knowledge and chosen ciphertext attack. In: Feigenbaum, J. (ed.) CRYPTO 1991. LNCS, vol. 576, pp. 433–444. Springer, Heidelberg (1992). https://doi.org/10.1007/3-540-46766-1_35
12. Stadler, M.: Publicly verifiable secret sharing. In: Maurer, U. (ed.) EUROCRYPT 1996. LNCS, vol. 1070, pp. 190–199. Springer, Heidelberg (1996). https://doi.org/10.1007/3-540-68339-9_17
13. Tsiounis, Y., Yung, M.: On the security of ElGamal based encryption. In: Imai, H., Zheng, Y. (eds.) PKC 1998. LNCS, vol. 1431, pp. 117–134. Springer, Heidelberg (1998). https://doi.org/10.1007/BFb0054019

14. Luciano, D., Prichett, G.: Cryptology: from caesar ciphers to public-key cryptosystems. Coll. Math. J. **18**(1), 2–17 (1987)
15. Savarese, C., Hart, B.: The Caesar Cipher, 15 July 2002
16. Buchmann, J., Ding, J. (eds.): PQCrypto 2008. LNCS, vol. 5299. Springer, Heidelberg (2008). https://doi.org/10.1007/978-3-540-88403-3
17. Barkan, E., Biham, E., Keller, N.: Instant ciphertext-only cryptanalysis of GSM encrypted communication. J. Cryptol. **21**(3), 392–429 (2008)
18. Bogdanov, A., et al.: PRESENT: an ultra-lightweight block cipher. In: Paillier, P., Verbauwhede, I. (eds.) CHES 2007. LNCS, vol. 4727, pp. 450–466. Springer, Heidelberg (2007). https://doi.org/10.1007/978-3-540-74735-2_31
19. Byod, C.A., Mathuria, A.: Protocols for Authentication and Key Establishment. Springer, Heidelberg (2003). https://doi.org/10.1007/978-3-662-09527-0
20. Eisenbarth, T., Kumar, S., Paar, C., Poschmann, A., Uhsadel, L.: A survey of lightweight cryptography implementations. IEEE Des. Test Comput. **24**(6), 522–533 (2007). Special Issue on Secure ICs for Secure Embedded Computing
21. Guneysu, T., Kasper, T., Novotny, M., Paar, C., Rupp, A.: Cryptanalysis with COPACOBANA. IEEE Trans. Comput. **57**(11), 1498–1513 (2008)
22. Kaps, J.-P., Gaubatz, G., Sunar, B.: Cryptography on a speck of dust. Computer **40**(2), 38–44 (2007)
23. Kumar, S., Paar, C., Pelzl, J., Pfeiffer, G., Schimmler, M.: Breaking ciphers with COPACOBANA – a cost-optimized parallel code breaker. In: Goubin, L., Matsui, M. (eds.) CHES 2006. LNCS, vol. 4249, pp. 101–118. Springer, Heidelberg (2006). https://doi.org/10.1007/11894063_9
24. Lim, C.H., Korkishko, T.: mCrypton – a lightweight block cipher for security of low-cost RFID tags and sensors. In: Song, J.-S., Kwon, T., Yung, M. (eds.) WISA 2005. LNCS, vol. 3786, pp. 243–258. Springer, Heidelberg (2006). https://doi.org/10.1007/11604938_19
25. Preneel, B.: MDC-2 and MDC-4. In: van Tilborg, H.C.A. (ed.) Encyclopedia of Cryptography and Security. Springer, Boston (2005). https://doi.org/10.1007/0-387-23483-7
26. Robshaw, M., Billet, O. (eds.): New Stream Cipher Designs. LNCS, vol. 4986. Springer, Heidelberg (2008). https://doi.org/10.1007/978-3-540-68351-3
27. Rolfes, C., Poschmann, A., Leander, G., Paar, C.: Ultra-lightweight implementations for smart devices – security for 1000 gate equivalents. In: Grimaud, G., Standaert, F.-X. (eds.) CARDIS 2008. LNCS, vol. 5189, pp. 89–103. Springer, Heidelberg (2008). https://doi.org/10.1007/978-3-540-85893-5_7
28. Trimberger, S., Pang, R., Singh, A.: A 12 Gbps DES encryptor/decryptor core in an FPGA. In: Koç, Ç.K., Paar, C. (eds.) CHES 2000. LNCS, vol. 1965, pp. 156–163. Springer, Heidelberg (2000). https://doi.org/10.1007/3-540-44499-8_11
29. Whiting, D., Housley, R., Ferguson, N.: RFC 3610: counter with CBC-MAC (CCM). Technical report, Corporation for National Research Initiatives, Internet Engineering Task Force, Network Working Group, September 2003
30. Wiener, M.J.: Efficient DES key search: an update. CRYPTOBYTES **3**(2), 6–8 (1997)
31. Wollinger, T., Pelzl, J., Paar, C.: Cantor versus Harley: Optimization and analysis of explicit formulae for hyperelliptic curve cryptosystems. IEEE Trans. Comput. **54**(7), 861–872 (2005)
32. Schnorr, C.-P.: Efficient signature generation by smartcards. J. Cryptol. **4**, 161–174 (1991)
33. Shamir, A.: Factoring Large Numbers with the TWINKLE Device. In: Koç, Ç.K., Paar, C. (eds.) CHES 1999. LNCS, vol. 1717, pp. 2–12. Springer, Heidelberg (1999). https://doi.org/10.1007/3-540-48059-5_2

Machine Learning

Improving Sentiment Analysis of Moroccan Tweets Using Ensemble Learning

Ahmed Oussous[1], Ayoub Ait Lahcen[1,2(✉)], and Samir Belfkih[1]

[1] LGS, National School of Applied Sciences (ENSA),
Ibn Tofail University, Kenitra, Morocco
ahmed.oussous@uit.ac.ma, {ayoub.aitlahcen,
samir.belfkih}@univ-ibntofail.ac.ma
[2] LRIT, Unité associée au CNRST URAC 29,
Mohammed V University in Rabat, Rabat, Morocco

Abstract. With the proliferation of the internet and the social media, increasing huge contents are generated each day across the world. Such huge data mines attract the attention of many entities. Indeed, by analyzing sentiments expressed in such content, government, businesses and particulars can extract valuable knowledge in order to enhance their strategies. Many approaches have been proposed to classify the posted content. Most of them are based on a single classifier. However, it has been proved that combining multiple classifiers and ensemble learning may give better performance. It is noticed from the literature, that sentiment classification in Arabic language based on the ensemble learning has not been well explored. Therefore, we aim through this study to improve the Arabic sentiment classification by combining different classification algorithms. So, we investigated the benefit of multiple classifier systems on Moroccan sentiment classification. First, three classification algorithms, called Naive Bayes, Maximum Entropy and support vector machines, are adopted as base-classifiers. Second, stacking generalization is introduced based on those algorithms with different settings and compared with the majority voting. The experimental results show that combining classifiers can effectively improve the accuracy of Moroccan datasets sentiment classification. Results show that this combination based on the majority voting is consistently effective, works better and needs less time to build the model than any other combination approach.

Keywords: Sentiment analysis · Ensemble learning · Machine learning
Arabic

1 Introduction

Since the emergence of Web 2.0 concept and social networking sites, the Internet has become the most sophisticated way to communicate. So, users express themselves through social networks, blogs and forums. The size of the generated information is tremendously expanding. Such information constitutes a mine of various opinions and comments on different issues in different fields. Therefore, those data mines have become the subject of several research areas and mainly "Sentiments Analysis" or "Opinion Mining".

Y. Tabii et al. (Eds.): BDCA 2018, CCIS 872, pp. 91–104, 2018.
https://doi.org/10.1007/978-3-319-96292-4_8

Since many years, opinion mining has attracted the attention of many researchers to extract valuable knowledge from such huge data mines. Indeed, opinion mining called sentiment classification enables to classify the expressed online opinions. It determines the semantic orientation of a text as either positive, negative or neutral. Such sentiment analysis can be carried at many granularity levels: expression or phrase level, sentence level, and document level [1]. Choosing the level of granularity depends on the objectives of applications. In this work, we decided to tackle sentiment classification at the sentence level.

There are various techniques of sentiment analysis. They can be categorized into: corpus-based machine learning, lexicon-based and hybrid approaches [2].

The corpus-based approach classifies text according to the sentiment orientation. First, it uses a large dataset of manually annotated examples to train the classifier. Then, it uses cross validation to evaluate the performance of the classifier. However, the lexicon-based approach works differently. It uses a lexicon composed of terms along with their sentiment values. More precisely, this approach searches through the lexicon for the sentiment values of the terms composing the text and combines them. The hybrid approach (called the weakly-supervised approach [3]) is a combination of the two precedent approaches. According to literature, the machine learning approaches are more suitable for the case of twitter than the lexical-based approach [2, 4, 5]. However, their performance depends on the features extracted for the language and domain of application.

In the last years, many works tackled ensemble learning in order to fuse the advantages of classification techniques for more performance and accurate results.

However, additional work is still needed for sentiment classification especially for morphologically complex languages. Limited studies are done on sentiment analysis for the Arabic language.

Thus, in our study, we investigate sentiment analysis for the Arabic language with a focus on reviews written in Moroccan. We choose the Arabic language for several reasons: on one hand, the Arabic language is well spread among various countries and used by millions of people across the world [6]. It is an important language for its historical, cultural and social aspects. Furthermore, Arabic raises important issues and challenges due to its complex structure and morphology [7]. On the other hand, we notice in the literature that currently limited Arabic resources are offered for sentiment and opinion analysis (Only a few freely available Arabic corpora). Research for building Arabic corpora is limited when compared with the English language. Arabic resources become scarcer when we consider the sentiment classification of Arabic dialects text such as that found in social media.

It is worth mentioning that there are other challenges facing the analysis of Moroccan tweets. This is because users tend to use multiple languages and dialects in Twitter or Facebook. So, a sentence in a Moroccan tweets may contain words from Standard Arabic, Moroccan Arabic "Darija", Moroccan Amazigh dialect "Tamazight", French, Spanish, and English. This is because Moroccans like to mix words from multiple languages in their casual communications. Therefore, analyzing Moroccan tweets is so complex.

In addition to the specificity of Moroccan tweets, there are other classical challenges faced in any sentiment analysis. Indeed, the majority of the text produced by the social websites is considered to have an unstructured or noisy nature. This is due to the lack of standardization, spelling mistakes, missing punctuation, nonstandard words, repetitions and more. So the text preprocessing is important.

To fill this research gap, we propose an ensemble of machine learning framework to handle the Arabic sentiment classification. Thus, Base classifier, voting, and stacking methods were investigated in this study. The novelty of this work is the integration of three classifiers and the comparative assessment of all models for Moroccan sentiment classification. The main contribution is threefold:

- We build a new Arabic corpus for sentiment analysis that combine standard Arabic and Moroccan dialect;
- We develop a multiple classifier based model for Arabic sentiment classification based on three classifiers Naive Bayes, Support Vector Machines and Maximum Entropy;
- We compare two ensemble methods, namely the fixed combination and meta-classifier combination (Stacking);
- We proved that multiple classifier systems increase the performance of individual classifiers on Moroccan sentiment classification.

The remainder of this article is structured as follows: Sect. 2 discussed the related work. Section 3 explains the used methodology. Section 4 presents the experiment results and Sect. 5 presents the conclusion.

2 Related Works

We notice that the most of the researches achieved in the SA is related to English. Therefore, many high quality frameworks and tools are now available for English text. However, for other languages such as Arabic, the community still needs research efforts to propose additional complete tools.

There exist resources and SA systems for the Arabic language. However, the available Arabic datasets and lexicons for SA are still limited in size, availability and dialects coverage. For instance, the highest proportion of available resources and researches are devoted to MSA [8]. Regarding Arabic dialects, the Arabic dialects, the Middle Eastern and Egyptian dialects received a great attention of research effort and funding. Whereas, low amount of research tackles' dialects such as those of Arabian Peninsula, Arab Maghreb and the West Asian Arab countries [9]. This is in spite of the large coverage of the Arab Maghreb dialects and social media in such countries. So, additional work is required to fulfill the need for SA regarding those dialects.

Table 1 summarizes the freely available SA corpora for Arabic and dialects that we were able to find.

The machine learning methods have been evaluated or enhanced in many sentiment classification studies. But, most of the studies were carried out for a specific domain with narrow datasets. Therefore, it is hard to determine which classification model performs better than other for a sentiment classification task. Indeed, there is a lack of consensus regarding the methodology, algorithm and type of combination to adopt for

Table 1. Freely available Arabic SA corpora

Data set name	Size	Source	Language	Cite
OCA	500	Movie reviews	Dialectal	[10]
Twitter data set	2000	Twitter	MSA/Jordanian	[11]
ASTD	10000	Twitter	MSA/dialects	[12]
LABR	63000	www.goodreads.com	MSA/dialects	[13]
Sentiment analysis resources for Arabic language	33000	TripAdvisor.com elcinema.com souq.com, qaym.com	MSA/dialects	[14]
Syria tweets	2000	Twitter	Syrian	[15]
Multi-domain Arabic sentiment corpus	8861	Jeeran/qaym/ Twitter/Facebook	Dialects	[16]

a given sentiment classification case. As a result, many researchers construct multiple classifiers and then create an integrated classifier based on the overall performance.

Studies are still limited and more in-depth empirical comparative work is needed for sentiment classification based on ensemble methods. This section presents some of the interesting works.

Paper [17] compares the performance of three popular ensemble methods (Bagging, Boosting, and Random Subspace) based on five base learners (Naive Bayes, Maximum Entropy, Decision Tree, KNearest Neighbor, and Support Vector Machine) for sentiment classification. Random Subspace has the best results.

Paper [18] introduces an approach that automatically classifies the sentiment of tweets by using classifier ensembles and lexicons. Their experiments show that classifier ensembles formed by Multinomial Naive Bayes, SVM, Random Forest, and Logistic Regression can improve classification accuracy.

The study of [19] investigated multiple classifier systems concept on Turkish sentiment classification problem and proposes a novel classification technique. Vote algorithm has been used in conjunction with three classifiers, namely Naive Bayes, Support Vector Machine (SVM), and Bagging. Their experiments showed that multiple classifier systems increase the performance of individual classifiers on Turkish sentiment classification datasets and meta classifiers contribute to the power of these multiple classifier systems.

The paper [20] presents the ensemble learning framework, stacking generalization is introduced based on different algorithms with different settings, and compared with the majority voting. Results prove that stacking has been consistently effective over all domains, working better than majority voting.

The authors of paper [21] pursue the paradigm of ensemble learning to reduce the noise sensitivity related to language ambiguity and therefore to provide a more accurate prediction of polarity. The proposed ensemble method is based on Bayesian Model Averaging, where both uncertainty and reliability of each single model are considered. They addressed the classifier selection problem by proposing a greedy approach that evaluates the contribution of each model with respect to the ensemble. Experimental results on gold standard datasets show that their proposed approach outperforms both traditional classification and ensemble methods.

It is noticed from this reviewed literature that combining classifiers may improve the classification performancc. Unfortunately, they are few works on ensemble classifiers for Arabic sentiment analysis. The published article that we found is as follow:

The study [22] proposes an ensemble of machine learning classifiers framework for handling the problem of subjectivity and sentiment analysis for Arabic customer reviews. Three text classification algorithms, called Naive Bayes, Rocchio classifier and support vector machines, are adopted as base-classifiers. They made a comparative study of two kinds of ensemble methods, namely the fixed combination and meta-classifier combination. The results showed that the ensemble of the classifiers improves the classification effectiveness in terms of macro-F1 for both levels.

Paper [23] presents a combined approach that automatically extracts opinions from Arabic documents. They used a combined approach that consists of three methods. At the beginning, lexicon based method is used to classify as much documents as possible. The resultant classified documents used as training set for maximum entropy method which subsequently classifies some other documents. Finally, k-nearest method used the classified documents from lexicon based method and maximum entropy as training set and classifies the rest of the documents. their experiments showed that in average, the accuracy moved (almost) from 50% when using only lexicon based method to 60% when used lexicon based method and maximum entropy together, to 80% when using the three combined methods.

Paper [24] conducts a comparative study between some base classifiers and some ensemble-based classifier with different combination methods. The results showed that MaxEnt, SVM and ANN combined with majority voting rules have achieved the best results with a macro-averaged F1-mesaure of 85.06%.

Paper [25] compares the performance of different classifiers for polarity determination in highly imbalanced short text datasets using features learned by word embedding rather than hand-crafted features. Several base classifiers and ensembles have been investigated with and without SMOTE (Synthetic Minority Over-sampling Technique). Using a dataset of tweets in dialectical Arabic, obtained results showed that applying word embedding with ensemble and SMOTE can achieve more than 15% improvement on average in F 1 score over the baseline.

3 Methodology

In this section, we present our methodology used for the task of classifying the tweets orientations. It precise our text models, the used datasets and the applied classifiers. We detail also our pre-processing schemes and the normalization techniques used to deal with the informal Arabic language nature. At the end, we present the measurement techniques used to evaluate the performance of sentiment classification.

We can summarize our methodology as follows: First, generating different Arabic datasets that can be used to support supervised sentiment analysis systems in Arabic context. Second, applying different pre-processing stage (including tweets annotation, noise elimination, conversion of the emotion icons into text and more) to the generated datasets which in turn leads the polarity classification performance to increase. Third, classifying the Arabic text using three classifiers; SVM, NB, and ME. Finally ensemble's algorithms (voting and stacking) have been used as meta-classifier to combine the output of the three algorithms.

3.1 Data Collection and Preparation

To face the challenges related to the Moroccan dialect and Arabic, we decided to create a publicly available SA data set. This data set was prepared manually by collecting reviewers' opinions from many sources:

- Reviewers' opinions from Hespress website against various published articles
- A combination of reviews and comments from Facebook, Twitter, and YouTube.

The collected corpus, called MSAC (Moroccan Sentiment Analysis Corpus) [26] is a multi-domain corpus consisting of the text covering a maximum vocabulary from sport, social and politics domain.

We noticed that our collected Corpus (MSAC) for annotation suffer from several problems. In fact, they include a high number of duplicated tweets which may be the result of re-tweeting. In addition, some of the collected tweets are empty and contain only the sender's address. So, we removed such tweets from our dataset. We also removed all user-names (e.g. @username), hash tags (e.g. #topic), URLs (e.g. www.example.com), re-tweet sign (e.g. RT), punctuations and additional white spaces. In addition, we removed punctuation at the start and ending of the tweets and all non-Arabic word from the tweets. In this manner, the tweets can be easily manipulated and processed.

Our final corpus contains about 1,000 of positive tweets and 1,000 of negative ones.

To better evaluate our Framework, we use two different corpora, so the second dataset is generated by collecting tweets posts and comments from SemEval-2017 task 4 in many topics such as sports, technology and political. It is freely available for research purposes [27]. We have extracted 2000 reviews: 1000 positive reviews and 1000 negative reviews. All written in MSA and Arabic dialect by professional reviewers with high quality.

3.2 Tweets Pre-processing

The pre-processing techniques are an essential step in the SA for Arabic text. Especially the Arabic dialectal text because of its unstructured form. Indeed, the posts and texts generated by social media include informal writing, errors, the use of abbreviations, missing punctuation, no respect of grammatical rules. So, we need to process unstructured text that lack grammar standardization. We have also to eliminate spelling mistakes and noise. To minimize the effect of those issues we decided to pre-process Arabic posts before classification.

To enhance the results of SA for Arabic text, we created our own text preprocessing scheme to deal with the informal Arabic language nature. We describe below the different preprocessing tasks performed.

Tokenization and Normalization. Tokenization consists of splitting the text into words (tokens) separated by whitespaces or punctuation characters. The result of this operation is a set of words. Our framework offers various types of tokenization including NLTK library.

The normalizing process puts the Arabic text in a consistent form. It converts all the forms of a word into a common form. Our framework offers a normalizer that performs the tasks according to the following rules:

- Removing the "tatweel" character "_" (for example using tatweel the word "رحـــــيم" (mercy) may look like " رحيم"),
- Removing the Tashkeel (مُشْكِلة (problem) > مشكلة)
- Looking for two or more repetitions of character which expresses affirmation and accentuation and replace them with the character itself (جميييييل جداااا --> جميل جد)
- Replacing of final letter ي with ى,, ة with ه, and replacing آ ,إ, and أ with ا

Stop-Words Removal. Consists of eliminating words that frequently occurred in the documents and do not give any hint or value to the content of their documents such as articles, prepositions, conjunctions, and pronouns ("في" (in), "انت" (you), "من" (of) …). There is no standard stopwords list to use in a SA experiment for the Arabic language. That is why; in this research the list of stop words (called stoplist) is manually established.

Stemming. This technique standardizes words by reducing each word to stem, base or root form [28]. The application of the derivation makes it possible to reduce the corpus dataset size into a small dimensional space. Two types of stemming approaches can be cited: light stemming and root extraction [29]. The goal of light stemming is to extract the stem of the word by deleting the identified prefixes and suffixes. On the contrary, the goal of root extraction is to extract the word's root by removing all the types of the word's affixes (including infixes, prefixes and suffixes). Studies showed that light stemming outperforms aggressive stemming than other stemming approaches [33]. That is why we use light stemmer in this study.

3.3 Feature Extraction

After text pre-processing, the next step is Feature extraction/selection. This later is used to find the most relevant features for the classification task by removing irrelevant, redundant and noisy data [30]. It enables to reduce both the dimensionality of the feature space and the processing time.

Many text features are considered for SA [31] such as n-gram models and part-of-speech (POS). The later is used to find adjectives that contain opinion information. An n-gram is a contiguous sequence of n terms from a given sequence of text. An n-gram of size 1 is referred to as a unigram; an n-gram of size 2 is a bigram; an n-gram of size 3 is a trigram. N-grams of larger sizes are referred to by the value of n and keeping the words with the highest score according to a predefined threshold (predetermined measure of the importance of the word). We used unigrams (bag of words) during our experiments because it provided the best performance.

In the feature extraction step, the text is transformed to a vector representation. The weight of the word (feature) is calculated according to the document containing that word. There are several weighting schemes such as: Boolean weighting, Term Frequency (TF) weighting, Inverse Document Frequency (IDF) weighting, and Term Frequency Inverse Document Frequency (TFIDF).

In this research, binary weighting (presence) is applied to our datasets. The weight of every token or word is determined using the Binary Model where a token is given a weight equals to 1 if it is present in the tweet under consideration. Otherwise, the token is given a weight equals to 0 if the token is absent from the tweet.

3.4 The Classifiers Used

Our framework is based on three algorithms. The data was classified using three supervised machine learning algorithms: Naive Bayes classifier (NB), Support Vector Machine classifier (SVM), Maximum Entropy (ME) and the combinations of these classifiers, using majority vote rule and stacking as ensemble learning methods. The goal is to test if ensemble learning methods can improve Arabic sentiment classification by combining different classification algorithms. In the following, we explain those algorithms:

A Nave Bayes classifier [32] is a probabilistic classifier which is based on the probability models. The main assumption in this approach is the independency of the features. Nave Bayes is a popular technique for text classification used in various research studies such as [33–35]. This classifier can be applied in various fields such as personal email sorting, document categorization, language detection, sentiment detection as well as the detection of spams in emails. It can ensure good results.

The SVM [36] is a linear classification/regression algorithm. It identifies a best hyper-plane that separates two classes of data with the largest possible margin. Many studies confirmed that SVM ensures very good performance and high accuracy in the case of sentiment analysis. [37] proved that SVM ensured good results in the case of English language in comparison to other classifiers. In addition, [1] confirmed that SVM shows good results for reviews sentiment analysis that are written in Chinese. In our experience, we implemented Linear Support Vector Classification (LinearSVC). BernoulliNB and LogisticRegression can also be used instead of LinearSVC.

The Maximum Entropy classifier [38] is a probabilistic classifier which belongs to the class of exponential models. Unlike the Naive Bayes classifier, the Max Entropy does not assume that the independence of features. The ME is based on the Principle of Maximum Entropy and from all the models that fit our training data; it selects the one which has the largest entropy. The Max Entropy classifier consumes more time for training the model in comparison to Naive Bayes. However, The Max Entropy is useful for various text classification problems such as language detection and topic classification. We used Generalized Iterative Scaling (GIS) algorithm. The other available algorithms are Improved Iterative Scaling (IIS) and LM-BFGS.

Ensemble Learning Technique. It uses multiple learners. Unlike ordinary machine learning approaches that try to learn one hypothesis from the training data, ensemble methods construct a set of hypotheses and combine them. Experiments in other fields have shown that the combination of a set of models or classifiers may lead to more accurate and reliable results in comparison to a single classifier. [19, 39].

In this paper, we will use two models to combine classifiers in order to improve the classification of Arabic tweet: the majority voting and stacking.

Majority Voting. It combines predictions from various classifiers. Each classifier has a single vote. The collective prediction and the class label are determined using the majority vote rule. In order to verify the effectiveness of ensemble learning for Arabic sentiment analysis, we combined the three base learners SVM, NB and ME. The majority voting method is implemented with the three base learners.

Stacked Generalization. Or stacking [20], is a method for constructing classifier ensembles. A classifier ensemble, or committee, is a set of classifiers whose individual decisions are combined to classify new instances. Stacking combines multiple classifiers to induce a higher-level (meta-level) classifier with improved performance.

4 Results Discussion

We carried out two types of experiments. The first type evaluates a set of base learning algorithms. The second type compares a set of ensemble based classifiers. The objective is to find the combination configuration for the best and stable performance across different domains.

4.1 Base Classifiers Evaluation

In this part, we compare the performance of the ML classification methods (SVM, Naive Bayes, and Maximum Entropy) without using ensemble method. The objective is to determine the best accurate base algorithm in each dataset. The two data sets described in the first section were used.

Table 2 presents the results achieved from different classifiers in terms of precision, accuracy, recall, F-Measure and Time taken to build model. It reveals that SVM has better results than NB and ME classifiers in almost all the evaluation measures. It reached 82.5% of accuracy and 82.9% of precision on our dataset. It achieved also the best results on SemEval dataset with 82.91% of accuracy and 82.8% of precision.

Through the experiment, NB shows less performance than ME and SVM. In fact, in our dataset the best performance outputs achieved by NB are 70.1% as accuracy and 73.2% as precision. ME achieved 81.55% in term of accuracy and 81.6% in term of precision.

The same results are obtained with SemEval dataset; the results confirm that the performance of the NB algorithm on sentiment analysis is slightly less than what has been achieved by SVM and ME.

To summarize, the SVM's algorithm proved to be the best performing classifier over all datasets scoring a significant difference than the rest of the classifiers. In fact, SVM is used by many sentiment analysis studies for its various advantages. For instance, SVM can handle efficiently high dimensional spaces. SVM considers all features as relevant and they show robustness when dealing with sparse set of samples.

Table 2. Performance results of single classifiers

	Our dataset (MSAC)					SemEval dataset				
	Accuracy	Precision	Recall	F	Time (s)	Accuracy	Precision	Recall	F	Time (s)
SVM	82.5	82 .9	82.5	82.6	1.5	82.91	82.8	82.9	82.9	3.14
ME	81.55	81.6	81.6	81.5	26.59	82.86	82.9	82.9	82.9	35.66
NB	70.1	73.2	70.1	69.1	0.58	75.07	75.8	75.1	74.9	0.7

This behavior was observed in more than one study as usually SVM produces more accurate results than the NB. This is because NB is based on probabilities, thus it is more suitable for inputs with high dimensionality [13].

4.2 Results of Ensemble of Classification Algorithms

In addition to the evaluation of base classifiers, we conducted another set of experiments to evaluate ensemble classifiers with the same datasets and various evaluation metrics. The combination of the classifiers is performed according to the two methods: voting and stacking. SVM, ME and NB are used as base classifiers, in stacking method each of this base classifiers are used as meta classifier. The results achieved in each experiment are illustrated in Table 3.

Table 3. Performance results of ensemble classifiers

	Our dataset (MSAC)					SemEval dataset				
	Accuracy	Precision	Recall	F	Time (s)	Accuracy	Precision	Recall	F	Time (s)
Voting	83.45	83.9	83.5	83.4	31.78	83.91	83.9	83.9	83.9	36.76
(Staking, SVM)	81.7	81.8	81.7	81.7	344.52	83.36	83.4	83.4	83.4	429.3
(Stacking, ME)	83	83.1	83	83	523.92	84.07	84.1	84.1	84.1	427.73
(Stacking, NB)	83.15	83.2	83.2	83.1	379.43	84.17	84.2	84.2	84.2	433.28

Compared to Table 2, Table 3 indicates that most of the selected ensemble classifiers have exceeded the results yielded by base classifiers in terms of precision, accuracy, recall and F-measure. In particular, majority voting of ME, SVM and NB has achieved the best results in SemEval dataset with accuracy of (83.91%), recall of (83.9%), precision of (83.9%), and F-measure of (83.9%). The same results are obtained in our datasets (MSAC), the Table 3 shows that the majority voting rule achieved the highest accuracy (83.45%), recall (83.5%), precision (83.9%), and F-measure (83.4%). The time required to build the model is 36.76 s.

So, for both datasets, this ensemble classifier has performed better results than the best base classifiers.

Compared to the individual classifiers, our results show also that stacking these base classifiers gives high classification accuracy with the two used datasets. Stacking achieved a high classification accuracy, 83.15% in MSAC dataset and 84.17% in SemEval dataset using Naïve Bayes as meta classifiers. When using SVM as meta classifier, stacking model achieved a classification accuracy of 81.7% in MSAC dataset and 83.36% in SemEval dataset. It achieved also 83% in MSAC dataset and 84.07% in SemEval dataset when using ME as meta classifier.

Stacking needs a long time to build the models, which is 433.28 s using naïve Bayes, 429.3 s using SVM and 427.73 s using ME, since it consists of two stages of learning.

When considering the effectiveness of ensemble methods, we notice that ensemble of classification algorithms perform better than all the other individual classifiers. However, those methods require more time for processing than the individual classifiers. The time needed to build the models depends on both the number of classifiers used and the type of combination. Indeed, the more classifiers are used the more time is needed. The stacking method requires more time than the other tested approaches.

Whereas the fixed combination rules need less time to build the model than any other combination method. This is because the fixed approach simply calls a non-trainable combiner.

By considering those outputs, we can confirm that it is recommended to use a multiple classifier systems for sentiment classification. One advantage is to aggregate the results of all the selected models and thus reducing the probability of selecting by chance a wrong or unsuitable single classification model for a dataset.

But we may investigate why ensembles models are more effective. One of the possible explanations is the following. Each of the single models may perform well but it may overfit to a different part of data sets. So, individual models have different mistakes on different part of data. By combining such single models, the mistakes made by each model tend to be reduced by reducing the risk of over-fitting. Thus, the accuracy and precision may be improved without affecting the prediction performance of the model.

Our conclusion from this study regarding Arabic text confirms the conclusions obtained in other studies for English language, which confirm that ensemble methods improve the performance of individual base learners for sentiment classification [18, 19].

5 Conclusion

In this study, we compare the performance and the efficiency of two approaches for sentiment analysis. Indeed, the individual classifiers and the ensemble methods are investigated for the Arabic sentiment analysis specifically on the Moroccan reviews. We built a new Moroccan Arabic dataset which consists of 2000 tweets/comments, with a good balance between negative and positive sentiments. The data used include informal structures, non-standard dialects and many spelling errors. First, we used various techniques for the preprocessing of Arabic SA (stemming, normalization, tokenization, stop words, etc.). Then, the ensemble method was applied to sentiment classification for more accuracy by integrating three classification algorithms: NB, ME and SVM. Third, we made a comparative study of two types of ensemble methods, the voting and meta-classifier combinations. The experiments of individual classifiers on Arabic sentiment analysis showed that SVM performed better than other algorithms. The results showed that ensemble of classification algorithms performed better than all individual classifier. The only drawback is the increase of the computational time. For all the ensemble methods, a group of different learners must be trained as opposed to a single learner to make all classifications.

References

1. Medhat, W., Hassan, A., Korashy, H.: Sentiment analysis algorithms and applications: a survey. Ain Shams Eng. J. **5**(4), 1093–1113 (2014)
2. Boudad, N., Faizi, R., Thami, R.O.H., Chiheb, R.: Sentiment analysis in arabic: a review of the literature. Ain Shams Eng. J. (2017, in press). https://doi.org/10.1016/j.asej.2017.04.007
3. Al Shboul, B., Al-Ayyoub, M., Jararweh, Y.: Multi-way sentiment classification of arabic reviews. In: 6th International Conference on Information and Communication Systems (ICICS), pp. 206–211. IEEE (2015)
4. Godsay, M.: The process of sentiment analysis: a study. Int. J. Comput. Appl. **126**(7), 26–30 (2015)
5. Mostafa, A.M.: An evaluation of sentiment analysis and classification algorithms for Arabic textual data. Int. J. Comput. Appl. **158**(3) (2017)
6. Biltawi, M., Etaiwi, W., Tedmori, S., Hudaib, A., Awajan, A.: Sentiment classification techniques for Arabic language: a survey. In: 7th International Conference on Information and Communication Systems (ICICS), pp. 339–346. IEEE (2016)
7. Shaheen, M., Ezzeldin, A.M.: Arabic question answering: systems, resources, tools, and future trends. Arab. J. Sci. Eng. **39**, 4541 (2014). https://doi.org/10.1007/s13369-014-1062-2
8. Assiri, A., Emam, A., Aldossari, H.: Arabic sentiment analysis: a survey. Int. J. Adv. Comput. Sci. Appl. **6**(12), 75–85 (2015)
9. Medhaffar, S., Bougares, F., Esteve, Y., Hadrich-Belguith, L.: Sentiment analysis of Tunisian dialects: linguistic ressources and experiments. In: Proceedings of the Third Arabic Natural Language Processing Workshop, pp. 55–61 (2017)
10. Rushdi-Saleh, M., Martín-Valdivia, M.T., Ureña-López, L.A., Perea-Ortega, J.M.: OCA: opinion corpus for Arabic. J. Assoc. Inf. Sci. Technol. **62**(10), 2045–2054 (2011)
11. Abdulla, N.A., Ahmed, N.A., Shehab, M.A., Al-Ayyoub, M.: Arabic sentiment analysis: lexicon-based and corpus-based. In: IEEE Jordan Conference on Applied Electrical Engineering and Computing Technologies (AEECT), pp. 1–6 (2013)
12. Nabil, M., Aly, M.A., Atiya, A.F.: ASTD: Arabic sentiment tweets dataset. In: EMNLP, pp. 2515–2519 (2015)
13. Aly, M.A., Atiya, A.F.: LABR: a large scale Arabic book reviews dataset. In: ACL, vol. 2, pp. 494–498 (2013)
14. ElSahar, H., El-Beltagy, S.R.: Building large Arabic multi-domain resources for sentiment analysis. In: Gelbukh, A. (ed.) CICLing 2015. LNCS, vol. 9042, pp. 23–34. Springer, Cham (2015). https://doi.org/10.1007/978-3-319-18117-2_2

15. Salameh, M., Mohammad, S., Kiritchenko, S.: Sentiment after translation: a case-study on Arabic social media posts. In: HLT-NAACL, pp. 767–777 (2015)
16. Al-Moslmi, T., Albared, M., Al-Shabi, A., Omar, N., Abdullah, S.: Arabic senti-lexicon: constructing publicly available language resources for Arabic sentiment analysis. J. Inf. Sci. **44**(3), 345–362 (2017)
17. Wang, G., Sun, J., Ma, J., Xu, K., Gu, J.: Sentiment classification: the contribution of ensemble learning. Decis. Support Syst. **57**, 77–93 (2014)
18. Da Silva, N.F., Hruschka, E.R., Hruschka, E.R.: Tweet sentiment analysis with classifier ensembles. Decis. Support Syst. **66**, 170–179 (2014)
19. Catal, C., Nangir, M.: A sentiment classification model based on multiple classifiers. Appl. Soft Comput. **50**, 135–141 (2017)
20. Su, Y., Zhang, Y., Ji, D., Wang, Y., Wu, H.: Ensemble learning for sentiment classification. In: Ji, D., Xiao, G. (eds.) CLSW 2012. LNCS (LNAI), vol. 7717, pp. 84–93. Springer, Heidelberg (2013). https://doi.org/10.1007/978-3-642-36337-5_10
21. Fersini, E., Messina, E., Pozzi, F.A.: Sentiment analysis: Bayesian ensemble learning. Decis. Support Syst. **68**, 26–38 (2014)
22. Omar, N., Albared, M., Al-Shabi, A.Q., Al-Moslmi, T.: Ensemble of classification algorithms for subjectivity and sentiment analysis of Arabic customers' reviews. Int. J. Adv. Comput. Technol. **5**(14), 77 (2013)
23. El-Halees, A.: Arabic opinion mining using combined classification approach (2011)
24. Bayoudhi, A., Ghorbel, H., Belguith, L.H.: Sentiment classification of Arabic documents: experiments with multi-type features and ensemble algorithms. In: PACLIC (2015)
25. Al-Azani, S., El-Alfy, E.S.M.: Using word embedding and ensemble learning for highly imbalanced data sentiment analysis in short arabic text. Procedia Comput. Sci. **109**, 359–366 (2017)
26. https://github.com/ososs/Arabic-Sentiment-Analysis-corpus
27. Rosenthal, S., Farra, N., Nakov, P.: SemEval-2017 task 4: sentiment analysis in Twitter. In: Proceedings of the 11th International Workshop on Semantic Evaluation (2017)
28. Mustafa, M., Eldeen, A.S., Bani-Ahmad, S., Elfaki, A.O.: A comparative survey on Arabic stemming: approaches and challenges. Intell. Inf. Manag. **9**(02), 39 (2017)
29. Haraty, R.A., Khatib, S.A.: T-Stem-A superior stemmer and temporal extractor for Arabic texts. J. Digit. Inf. Manag. **3**(3), 173 (2005)
30. Liu, B., Zhang, L.: A survey of opinion mining and sentiment analysis. In: Aggarwal, C., Zhai, C. (eds.) Mining Text Data, pp. 415–463. Springer, Boston (2012). https://doi.org/10.1007/978-1-4614-3223-4_13
31. Pang, B., Lee, L., Vaithyanathan, S.: Thumbs up?: sentiment classification using machine learning techniques. In: Proceedings of the ACL-02 Conference on Empirical Methods in Natural Language Processing, vol. 10, pp. 79–86. Association for Computational Linguistics (2002)
32. Saloot, M.A., Idris, N., Mahmud, R., Ja'afar, S., Thorleuchter, D., Gani, A.: Hadith data mining and classification: a comparative analysis. Artif. Intell. Rev. **46**(1), 113–128 (2016)
33. Duwairi, R.M., Alfaqeh, M., Wardat, M., Alrabadi, A.: Sentiment analysis for Arabizi text. In: 7th International Conference Information and Communication Systems (ICICS), pp. 127–132. IEEE (2016)
34. Tripathy, A., Agrawal, A., Rath, S.K.: Classification of sentiment reviews using n-gram machine learning approach. Expert Syst. Appl. **57**, 117–126 (2016)
35. Abbas, M., Smaïli, K., Berkani, D.: Evaluation of topic identification methods on Arabic corpora. JDIM **9**(5), 185–192 (2011)
36. Ye, Q., Zhang, Z., Law, R.: Sentiment classification of online reviews to travel destinations by supervised machine learning approaches. Expert Syst. Appl. **36**(3), 6527–6535 (2009)

37. Wan, X.: Co-training for cross-lingual sentiment classification. In: Proceedings of the Joint Conference of the 47th Annual Meeting of the ACL and the 4th International Joint Conference on Natural Language Processing of the AFNLP, vol. 1, pp. 235–243. Association for Computational Linguistics (2009)
38. El-Halees, A.M.: Arabic text classification using maximum entropy. IUG J. Nat. Stud. **15**(1) (2015)
39. Oussous, A., Benjelloun, F.Z., Lahcen, A.A., Belfkih, S.: Big data technologies: a survey. J. King Saud Univ.-Comput. Inf. Sci. (2017, in press). https://doi.org/10.1016/j.jksuci.2017.06.001

Comparative Study of Feature Engineering Techniques for Disease Prediction

Khandaker Tasnim Huq(✉), Abdus Selim Mollah(✉), and Md. Shakhawat Hossain Sajal(✉)

Khulna University of Engineering and Technology (KUET), Khulna 9203, Bangladesh
swadtasnim@gmail.com, salim9326@cse.kuet.ac.bd, sajalhsn13@gmail.com

Abstract. Feature engineering is essential for desigining predictive models using online text. To fit appropriate machine learning models for text analysis, feature extraction and selection is need to be done rightfuly. This paper presents a comparative study of a number of feature extraction and feature selection techniques useful for text analysis and also presents a feature selection technique inspired from the existing methods. In particular the problem focused here is predicting diseases based on symptoms descriptions collected from online free text. A good number of well known machine learning models are also applied in various setup along with the feature engineering techniques to build predictive model for the disease prediction. The experiments show promising results.

Keywords: Feature engineering · Feature selection
Feaure extraction · Medical text classification · LDA · NMF

1 Introduction

Identifying diseases is the 1st step towards better medication. A person once identify right disease, can then choose right healthcare professionals for better medication. This task is particularly challenging because of various reasons such as collecting online data, Language processing, feature extraction and selection, and training machine learning models and evaluating the model using challenging testing data. Similar to spam filtering, sentiment analysis and language identification, disease prediction is an important text classification problem. Text classification is a classic machine learning problem that deals with the categorization of a set of documents using various classifier algorithms or models. This paper presents a collection of feature extraction, selection and machine learning techniques appropriate for text classification. A number of machine learning models like Naive Bayes, Decision Tree, Support Vector Machine with Kernel "RBF" (Radial Basis Function), Stochastic Gradient Descent, Nearest Centroid, K Nearest Neighbour, Multiple Layer Perceptron, Multinomial Logistic regression have

Y. Tabii et al. (Eds.): BDCA 2018, CCIS 872, pp. 105–117, 2018.
https://doi.org/10.1007/978-3-319-96292-4_9

been evaluated on textual health data collected from online. Feature extraction techniques such as Term Frequence-Inverse Document Frequency (TF-IDF), Latent Dirichlet Allocation (LDA), Non-Negative Matrix Factorization (NMF) etc. and Feature selection methods such as Chi-Square, ANOVA, Recursive Feature Elimination (REF) and Classwise Feature Elimination (CFE) etc. are added as pre-processing step that resulted in a promising outcome.

The paper is organized as follows: Sect. 2 describes some of the related works on the domain, Sect. 3 encompasses the methodological description of the methods and techniques considered for the experiment. In Sect. 4, experimental details are explained with the outcome of the experiment. Finally the conclusion is included in Sect. 5.

2 Related Works

Beckhardt et al. [1] created an interactive disease classification application based on symptoms collected from the websites like Mayo Clinic, Freebase as training dataset and text from Wikipedia and generated by a user as testing dataset. It gives the top five most likely diseases as outputs with their probabilities.

Subotin and Davis [2] also built an automated tagging system which takes clinician notes and predicts a standardized disease code. They collected training and testing dataset from Electronic Health Records (EHRs) and used regularized logistic regression model.

Quwaider and Alfaqeeh [3] used social networks benchmark dataset for classifying diseases of 3 classes using 3 machine learning classifier models.

Kononenko [4] described how machine learning eases intelligent medical data analysis in details as well as its historical overview and some trends which will be applied in future as a subfield of applied artificial intelligence.

McCowan et al. [5] investigated the classification of a patient's lung cancer stage based on analysis of their free-text medical reports using SVM.

Yao et al. [6] investigated features and machine learning classification algorithms for traditional Chinese medicine (TCM) clinical text classification. He used Clinical Records Classification, Features, Classification Algorithms, TCM domain knowledge.

Li et al. [39] also worked with TCM using cross-domain method focusing topic modeling with datasets from three different medical record books.

Parlak and Uysal [7] evaluated various feature selection techniques on medical text data from MEDLINE and OSHUMED datasets by combining the feature selection models in several ways using Bayesian Network classifier model.

In another research paper [8], they compared the performance of three classifier models: Bayesian network, C4.5 decision tree, and Random Forest trees with two different cases: with stemming and without stemming.

Zhu et al. [40] compared among various feature extraction techniques and classifier models on TCM.

Al-Mubaid and Shenify [38] proposed an improved bayesian method for disease document classification of two classes using medical dataset collected from MEDLINE and PUBMED.

3 Methodology

3.1 Feature Extraction

A handful of feature extraction techniques have been performed and evaluated in this experiment:

- Term-Frequency (TF):
  A very naive way of extracting feature is to compute the term frequency for each training documents. According to [26], the weight of a term that occurs in a document is simply proportional to the term frequency. It is estimated by the equation from [30]-

$$TF(t) = \frac{\text{number of times term t appears in a document}}{\text{total number of terms in a document}} \tag{1}$$

  CountVectorizer from [27] was used in experiment.

- Term-Frequency and Inverse Document Frequency (TF-IDF):
  Tf-idf is a weighting of the importance of a term to a document in a corpus [28]. Inverse Document Frequency is estimated by the equation from [30]:

$$IDF(t) = log_e(\frac{\text{Total number of documents}}{\text{Number of documents containg term t}}) \tag{2}$$

  Then tf-idf(t) = TF X IDF. In experiment, maximum DF value was kept in range from .3 to .75 using TFidfVectorizer from [27].
- Latent Dirichlet Allocation (LDA) with TF:
  According to the LDA model, each document consists of several topics and each term can be attributed to the document's topics [31]. Term-frequency matrix is fed to LDA model generating document-topic probability and topic-term probability and returns document-topic distribution. LatentDirichletAllocation from [27] was applied using 400–700 topics.
- Non Negative Matrix Factorization (NMF) with TF-IDF:
  NMF is used to factorize TF-IDF Document-term matrix 'X' into two matrices [32]. One is the feature matrix 'W' and other is the coefficient matrix 'H', where the elements are non negative. The column number of feature matrix was chosen in a way for which the $||X - WH||$ is minimized [33,34], using Frobenius norm [9].

3.2 Feature Selection

Feature Selection simplifies the model by reducing high dimensionality and it increases generalization to avoid overfitting. The following techniques were used to select features-

- Chi Square (chi2):
  It seeks the rank of independence between two events [35]. Which are the occurrence of a specific feature and the occurrence of a specific class. It is defined by:

$$X^2(D,t,c) = \sum\nolimits_{e_t \in \{0,1\}} \sum\nolimits_{e_c \in \{0,1\}} \frac{N_{e_t e_c} - E_{e_t e_c}}{E_{e_t e_c}} \tag{3}$$

  Here $e_t = 1$ if term t is in document D, otherwise 0. $e_c = 1$ if D is in class c, otherwise 0. N is the observane frequency and E is the expected frequency in D. If the rank of a feature is high in a class, it is selected. Otherwise, it is removed
- Analysis of variance (ANOVA):
  It computes F-value [15],

$$F = \frac{\text{variance between classes}}{\text{variance within classes}} \tag{4}$$

  By this manner, those feature set was kept for which F-value is high and rest of the features were reduced.
- Recursive Feature Elimination (RFE):
  RFE is basically a backward selection process [16]. A classifier or estimator estimates weights according to the coefficient attribute or the feature importances attribute and assigns to features to recursively select the subset of features which is a smaller set of main feature set. The least scored features are eliminated from the main set of features. Finally, the best combination of feature set is chosen. To select feature, Logistic Regression and SVC model were used. Logistic Regression performed better.
- Classwise Feature Elimination (CFE):
  This is the implemented technique which is inspired by Recursive Feature Elimination method. Instead of choosing recursively, the best features are chosen using two estimators. Multinomial naive bayes and LinearSVC have been used for estimating the importance of features. The steps of the Algorithm 1 were followed to obtain best features (Figs. 1 and 2).

Algorithm 1. Classwise Feature Elimination

1: Train/Fit a classifier model with a given training set.
2: Declare variables C for classes and F for storing features.
3: Calculate the importance score or coefficient of all the features.
4: **for** each class C_i, where i=1,2,3... number of classes, **do**
5: Sort the features in descending order according to the coefficient.
6: Choose first N number of features, where N is the desired number of feature to keep.
7: Store the chunk of chosen features in F_i, where i is the number of current class.
8: **end for**
9: [Optional] Follow the same steps within the loop for other classifier model, obtain F_i features and merge them with features obtained from previous classifier.
10: In training set, for each class C_i, where i=1,2,.... number of classes, search features that are not in F_i and reduce them from the class C_i and so on.
11: Use classifier models with newly created training set.

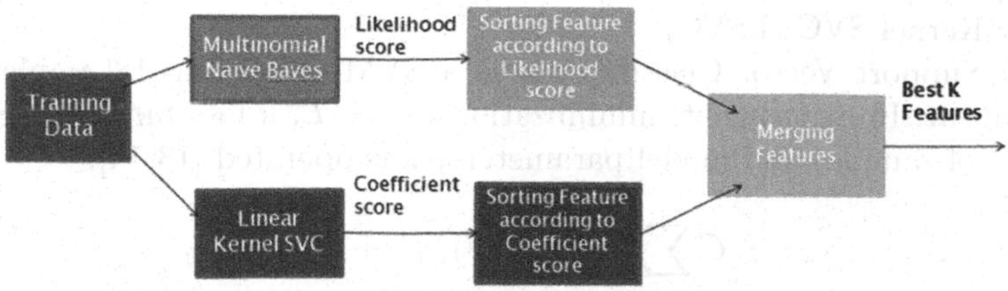

Fig. 1. Classwise feature elimination process (stage 1)

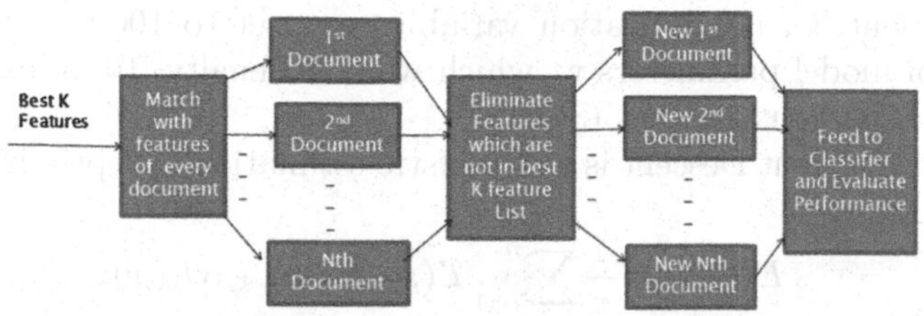

Fig. 2. Classwise feature elimination process (stage 2)

3.3 Classifier Models

The models used in experiment to classify symptoms are explained below:

- Naive Bayes:
  Given a class variable y and a dependent feature vector x_1 through x_n, Bayes theorem states the following relationship [27]:

$$P(y|x_1, x_2...x_n) = \frac{P(y)\prod_{i=1}^{n} P(x_i|y)}{P(x_1, x_2....x_n)} \tag{5}$$

  where P(a|b) is the probability of event a given event b. In Experiment two Naive bayes methods were used:

  - GaussianNB (GNB):
    The likelihood of the feature:

$$P(x_i|y) = \frac{1}{\sqrt{2\pi\sigma}} exp(-\frac{(x_i - \mu_y)^2}{2\sigma_y^2}) \tag{6}$$

    where, σ is the variance and μ is the mean of x vector.

  - MultinomialNB (MNB):
    The likelihood of the feature:

$$P(x_i|y) = \frac{N_y i + \alpha}{N_y + \alpha n} \tag{7}$$

    where, $N_y i$ is number of time x_i occures in class y and N_y is the total features in class y. In Experiment, $\alpha = .20$ is the smoothing prior.

- Linear Kernel SVC (LSVC):
  Linear Support Vector Classification is a SVM algorithm [18] implemented in liblinear. In experiment, minimization of the $\mathcal{L}$, a loss function "Squared Hinge" of samples and model parameters, was operated [13,14]:

$$C\sum_{i=1}^{n} \mathcal{L}_i(f(x_i), y_i) + \Omega(w) \tag{8}$$

  where, $f(x) = w^T x + b$ and $y \in \{1, -1\}^n$ and these are subject to- $y_i f(x_i) > 1 - \mathcal{L}_i$ for i = 1, 2,...n.
  In experiment, C, regularization variable, was set to 1000. Ω is a penalty function of model parameters w, which was L2 Penalty [10] in experiment.
- Stochastic Gradient Descent (SGD):
  Stochastic Gradient Descent is a stochastic estimation for optimizing a target function [11]:

$$E(w, b) = \frac{1}{n}\sum_{i=1}^{n} \mathcal{L}(y_i, f(x_i)) + \alpha R(w) \tag{9}$$

  where, $f(x) = w^T x + b$ is the target function. In experiment, Linear SVM and Logistic Regression were used as Loss function $\mathcal{L}$. R is the regularization term and α was $1e^{-8}$ iterating over 1000–3000 times.
- Decision Trees (DT):
  This method predicts target value by learning simple decision rules inferred from the data features. Let D is training data node and O = (j,t_d) to be splitted where j is the feature and t_d is threshold. Partitioning will be like- [37]

$$D_{left}(O) = (x, y)|x_j <= t_d, D_{right} = D \backslash D_{left}(O) \tag{10}$$

  If H() is the impurity function "Gini", then:

$$G(D, O) = \frac{n_{left}}{N_d} H(D_{left}) + \frac{n_{right}}{N_d} H(D_{right}) \tag{11}$$

  Here, $O = argmin_O G(D, O)$
- Nearest Centroid (NC):
  NC method was successfully used in [12] for protein mass spectrometry. It uses cluster mean or centroid to determine class of new testing data sample:

$$\mu_{C_l} = \frac{1}{|C_l|}\sum_{i=1}^{n} x_i \tag{12}$$

  where, C_l is the set of features of class l and $x_i \in C_l$. Then a class 'C' is assigned to a testing data set x, for which, $C(x) = argmin_{C_l} d(\mu_{C_l}, x)$. Here, d(a,b) is distance function which was set as "euclidean" in experiment.
- K Nearest Neighbours (KNN):
  Given N training vectors, K Nearest Neighbour algorithm identifies the K nearest neighbors of class 'C'. Weight function in KNeighborsClassifier [27] to predict class 'C' was set to "distance". So that the closer K number of neighbors of class 'C' will impose greater influence than distant neighbors.

- Multinomial Logistic Regression (LR):
  Logistic regression classifies observation by estimating the probability that an observation is in a particular category. It minimizes the following cost function from [36]:

$$C\sum_{i=1}^{n} log(-exp(y_i(x_i^T w + c)) + 1) + \Omega(w) \tag{13}$$

  where, $y \in \{1, -1\}^n$ and $\Omega(w)$ is the regularization function of model parameter w. In experiment, both L1 and L2 regularization [10] were used. C is the amount of regularization, which was set to 1000 in experiment.
- Multi-Layer Perceptron (MLP):
  Multi-layer Perceptron consist of one or more hidden layer and an output layer. The training of the network is done by the error back propagation algorithm [17]. In experiment, 300 hidden layers were used. As activation function, hyperbolic tan f(x) = tanh was used.

4 Experiment Setup and Result Analysis

See Fig. 3

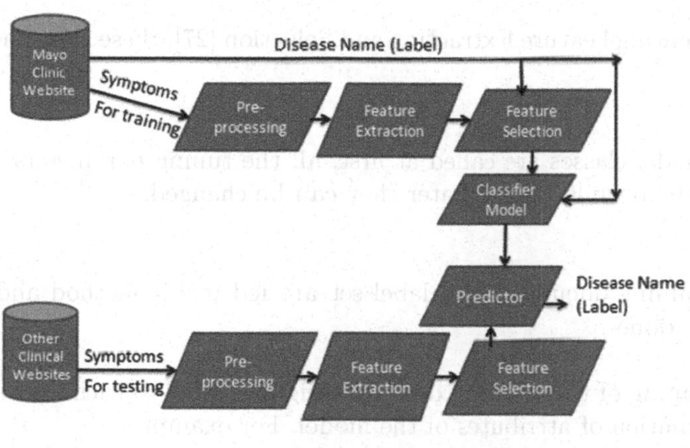

Fig. 3. Experiment setup

4.1 Data Collection

Data, the Symptoms, was collected as free text for training from Mayo Clinic website [19]. By HTML web scrapping process [20], both a list of symptoms and a description for each disease from the website were extracted. There are 200 different possible disease classes. Examples from several medical websites [21–23] were used as test dataset. In experiment, cross validation process was not used because each example set is consist of only one example of each disease for which it is not possible to split any of the data sets.

4.2 Data Pre-processing

Following steps, inspired from [24], were maintained for text preprocessing:

- Punctuation and White-space Removal:
  Regular expression rules were created to remove all the punctuations and white-spaces from text.
- Stemming (Lemmatization):
  This process converts words into a more basic form. For example, the words "fishing", "fished", "fisher", and "fishes" converts into "fish" after stemming. SnowballStemmer from [25] was used for stemming.
- Stopword removal:
  Stopwords are the words which do not carry information that can contribute to the statistical evaluation. Examples: Articles, prepositions, auxiliary verbs, pronouns etc.
- Case folding:
  Every character in corpus were turned into lower case so that there will be no difference between words start from upper case and lower case.

4.3 Implementation of Feature Extraction and Selection

For implementing Feature Extraction and Selection [27], these class and methods are called-

- Model:
  When model classes are called at first, all the tuning parameters are initialized by the default values. Later they can be changed.

- Fit:
  Only Training document and label set are fed to Fit method and following tasks are done-

  - Grouping of the training data by assigning label to each document.
  - Estimation of attributes of the model. For examples-
    (a) CountVectorizer, as bag of words, learns vocabulary.
    (b) Besides vocabulary, TfidfVectorizer learns IDF value.
    (c) LatentDirichletAllocation learns topic-feature matrix.
    (d) NMF learns Frobenius norm of the matrix difference between training data X and reconstructed matrix WH.
- Transform:
  Both Training and Testing data are assigned to the Transform method. then-

  - for CountVectorizer and TfidfVectorizer, returns Document-term matrix.
  - for LatentDirichletAllocation and NMF, returns document-topic matrix.

4.4 Applying Classifier Models

During implementing classifier models according to [27], these stages have been to go through-

- Model Declaration:
  Tuning Parameters are manipulated. e.g. For Nearest Centroid, parameters are metric, shrink-threshold.
- Fit:
  Features and label set are fed to Fit method and following tasks are done-
  - Grouping of the training data by assigning label to the feature set of each document.
  - Estimation and updating the attributes of the model (e.g. MultinomialNB learns log probability of classes and features etc.).
  - Assignment of weights or coefficient or importance score to each feature of the training set.
- Predict:
  Testing data or document is assigned to the Predict method. This method then-
  - operates the functions according to classifier model algorithms and obtains score.
  - obtains the index of class for which the score is suitable (e.g. for Nearest Centroid, find index for which pairwise distance is minimum) and returns the class label.

4.5 Experiment and Result

The results of 4 feature selection techniques using TF-IDF values are shown in Fig. 4. Here, chi2, ANOVA and RFE selected 1700–1800 features from around 2300 extracted features of 100 disease training set. In case of CFE, 40–60 terms were selected from each class where each class has 80–300 unique terms. For testing, symptoms of 30 disease classes were used here.

It is observed that all the techniques were very much competitive. Among them, CFE technique did best for most of the classifiers except MNB and SGD. Second best was ANOVA and lastly, chi2 and RFE did nearly similar performance.

Figure 5 shows the overall performance of feature extraction, selection and classifier models. For evaluation, there were two rounds, Round 1 for 100 diseases training dataset with 30 diseases testing dataset, and Round 2 for 200 training samples with 50 testing samples. Feature selection technique of round one was similar to the time of evaluation shown in Fig. 4.

In case of round two, overall 3000 features were selected from 3500 unique features counted from [29].

Here it is observable that, TF-IDF performed best among all the feature extraction techniques in both round. Best accuracy score was 80% from round

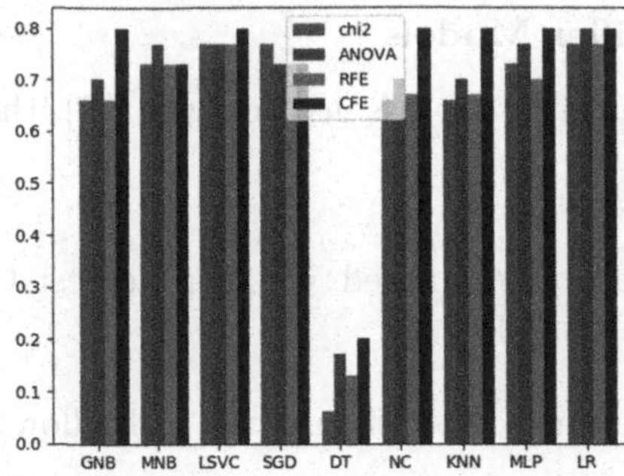

Fig. 4. Accuracy of Tf-idf with various feature selection methods

1 of TF-IDF without CFE using LR and with CFE using most classifiers except MNB and SGD.

In each feature extraction technique, round 1 gives better accuracy than round 2 depicting additional training dataset includes more noises than the small dataset.

In most cases, CFE improves accuracy which is most observable in both round of TF-IDF, round 1 of LDA, TF and round 2 of NMF.

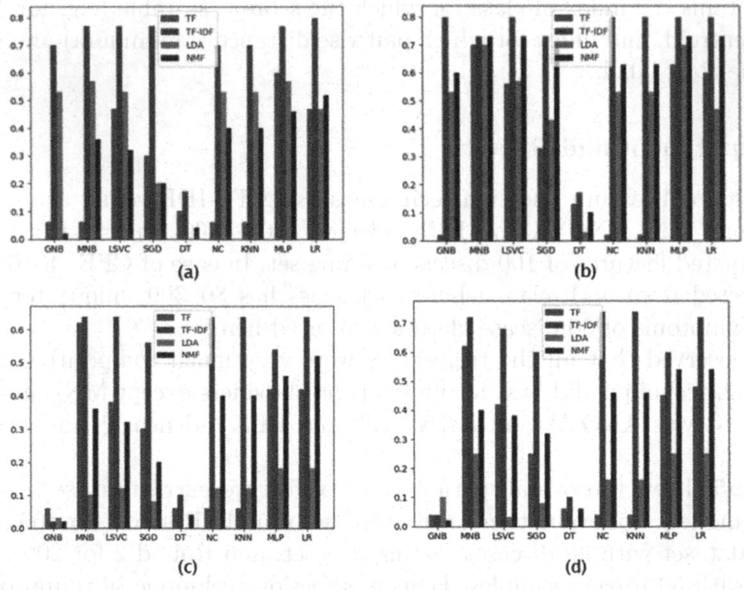

Fig. 5. Accuracy of Tf, Tf-Idf, LDA and NMF in Round-1: (a) without CFE, (b) with CFE and in Round-2: (c) without CFE, (d) with CFE

Among the topic extraction techniques, NMF did better than LDA in both round as it was much more accurate and even performed faster than LDA. Inspite of that, in round 1, LDA improves accuracy of TF features.

Among all classifier models, LR, MNB and MLP performed better. Most of the time MNB gave consistent results. It is also noticeable that GNB, NC and KNN performed pretty much similarly in a number of cases. The worst performance was from DT classifier.

5 Conclusion

This paper has presented the work on building a system that can determine disease from symptoms represented in text. The goal of this experiment was to determine best feature selection and extraction technique and classifier model. Also this experiment investigated an approach of feature selection. This approach can be improved further by making it more general to prevent the overfitting situation. Further investigation will also be imposed on improving the minimization of the noises of training data and improving the application of Topic Modeling efficiently.

Acknowledgment. Thanks to Bishnu Sarker (www.kuet.ac.bd/cse/bishnu/) for the guidelines.

References

1. Beckhardt, B., Keselman, L., Perez, A.: CS229 Project: Doctor Bayes (2015)
2. Subotin, M., Davis, A.R.: A system for predicting ICD-10-PCS codes from electronic health records. In: Proceedings of BioNLP, pp. 59–67, June 2014
3. Quwaider, M., Alfaqeeh, M.: Social networks benchmark dataset for diseases classification. In: IEEE International Conference on Future Internet of Things and Cloud Workshops (FiCloudW), pp. 234–239. IEEE, August 2016
4. Kononenko, I.: Machine learning for medical diagnosis: history, state of the art and perspective. Artif. Intell. Med. **23**(1), 89–109 (2001)
5. McCowan, I., Moore, D., Fry, M.J.: Classification of cancer stage from free-text histology reports. In: 28th Annual International Conference of the IEEE Engineering in Medicine and Biology Society 2006. EMBS 2006, pp. 5153–5156. IEEE, August 2006
6. Yao, L., Zhang, Y., Wei, B., Li, Z., Huang, X.: Traditional Chinese medicine clinical records classification using knowledge-powered document embedding. In: 2016 IEEE International Conference on Bioinformatics and Biomedicine (BIBM), pp. 1926–1928. IEEE, December 2016
7. Parlak, B., Uysal, A.K.: The impact of feature selection on medical document classification. In: 2016 11th Iberian Conference on Information Systems and Technologies (CISTI), pp. 1–5. IEEE, June 2016
8. Parlak, B., Uysal, A.K.: Classification of medical documents according to diseases. In: 2015 23th Signal Processing and Communications Applications Conference (SIU), pp. 1635–1638. IEEE, May 2015

9. Frobenius Norm (n.d.). http://mathworld.wolfram.com/FrobeniusNorm.html. Accessed 27 Aug 2017
10. Regularization: Simple Definition, L1 & L2 Penalties (n.d.). http://www.statisticshowto.com/regularization/. Accessed 27 Aug 2017
11. Stochastic Gradient Descent (n.d.). http://scikit-learn.org/stable/modules/sgd.html. Accessed 29 Aug 2017
12. Levner, I.: Feature selection and nearest centroid classification for protein mass spectrometry, 23 March 2005. https://bmcbioinformatics.biomedcentral.com/articles/10.1186/1471-2105-6-68. Accessed 29 Aug 2017
13. Support Vector Machines (n.d.). http://scikit-learn.org/stable/modules/svm.html#svm-mathematical-formulation. Accessed 29 Aug 2017
14. Scaling the regularization parameter for SVCs (n.d.). http://scikit-learn.org/stable/auto_examples/svm/plot_svm_scale_c.htm. Accessed 29 Aug 2017
15. Fisher, R.A.: On the probable error of a coefficient of correlation deduced from a small sample. Metron **1**, 3–32 (1921)
16. Kuhn, M.: The caret Package 23 July 2017. https://topepo.github.io/caret/recursive-feature-elimination.html. Accessed 27 Aug 2017
17. Buscema, M.: Back propagation neural networks. Subst. Use Misuse **33**(2), 233–270 (1998)
18. Rumpf, T., Mahlein, A.K., Steiner, U., Oerke, E.C., Dehne, H.W., Plumer, L.: Early detection and classification of plant diseases with support vector machines based on hyperspectral reflectance. Comput. Electron. Agric. **74**(1), 91–99 (2010)
19. Mayo Clinic: Symptoms (n.d). http://www.mayoclinic.org/symptoms
20. Reitz, K.: HTML Scraping (2016). http://python-guide-pt-br.readthedocs.io/en/latest/scenarios/scrape/
21. WebMd: Symptoms A-Z (n.d). http://symptomchecker.webmd.com/symptoms-a-z
22. NHS choices: Health A-Z Conditions and treatments (n.d). http://www.nhs.uk/Conditions/Pages/hub.aspx
23. Healthline: Health Topics (n.d). http://www.healthline.com/directory/topics
24. Zhu, X.: Basic Text Process (2010). http://pages.cs.wisc.edu/jerryzhu/cs769/text_preprocessing.pdf. Accessed 14 June 2017
25. NLTK Project: Source code for nltk.stem.snowball [Scholarly project]. In: NLTK 3.2.4 documentation, 21 May 2017. http://www.nltk.org/_modules/nltk/stem/snowball.html. Accessed 14 June 2017
26. Luhn, H.P.: A statistical approach to mechanized encoding and searching of literary information. IBM J. Res. Dev. **1**(4), 309–317 (1957)
27. Pedregosa, F., Varoquaux, G., Gramfort, A., Michel, V., Thirion, B., Grisel, O., Blondel, M., Prettenhofer, P., Weiss, R., Dubourg, V., Vanderplas, J., Passos, A., Cournapeau, D., Brucher, M., Perrot, M., Duchesnay, E.: Scikit-learn: machine learning in Python. J. Mach. Lear. Res. **12**, 2825–2830 (2011). http://scikit-learn.org/stable/about.html#citing-scikit-learn
28. Rajaraman, A., Ullman, J.D.: Data Mining. Mining of Massive Datasets (PDF), pp. 1–17 (2011). http://doi.org/10.1017/CBO9781139058452.002. ISBN 978-1-139-05845-2
29. AP: Unique words count (n.d.). https://planetcalc.com/3205/. Accessed 30 Aug 2017
30. Tf-idf: A Single-Page Tutorial - Information Retrieval and Text Mining (n.d.). http://www.tfidf.com/. Accessed 29 Aug 2017
31. Blei, D.M., Ng, A.Y., Jordan, M.I.: Latent dirichlet allocation. J. Mach. Lear. Res. **3**(Jan), 993–1022 (2003)

32. Dhillon, I.S., Sra, S.: Generalized Nonnegative Matrix Approximations with Bregman Divergences (2005). http://papers.nips.cc/book/advances-in-neural-information-processing-systems-18-2005. Accessed 12 July 2017
33. Lee, D.D., Seung, H.S.: Learning the parts of objects by non-negative matrix factorization. Nature **401**, 788–791 (1999). https://doi.org/10.1038/44565
34. Lin, C.J.: Projected gradient methods for nonnegative matrix factorization. Neural Comput. **19**(10), 2756–2779 (2007)
35. Chi2 Feature selection, 04 July 2009. https://nlp.stanford.edu/IR-book/html/htmledition/feature-selectionchi2-feature-selection-1.html. Accessed 29 Aug 2017
36. Generalized Linear Models (n.d.). http://scikit-learn.org/stable/modules/linear_model.html#linear-model. Accessed 29 Aug 2017
37. Decision Trees (n.d.). http://scikit-learn.org/stable/modules/tree.html. Accessed 30 Aug 2017
38. Al-Mubaid, H., Shenify, M.: Improved Bayesian based method for classifying disease documents. In: 2016 World Symposium on Computer Applications and Research (WSCAR), pp. 47–52. IEEE, March 2016
39. Li, Y., Wei, B., Chen, H., Jiang, L., Li, Z.: Cross-domain learning based traditional chinese medicine medical record classification. In: 2015 10th International Conference on Intelligent Systems and Knowledge Engineering (ISKE), pp. 335–340. IEEE, November 2015
40. Zhu, W., Zhang, W., Li, G.Z., He, C., Zhang, L.: A study of damp-heat syndrome classification using Word2vec and TF-IDF. In: 2016 IEEE International Conference on Bioinformatics and Biomedicine (BIBM), pp. 1415–1420. IEEE, December 2016

Business Process Instances Scheduling with Human Resources Based on Event Priority Determination

Abir Ismaili-Alaoui[1,2(✉)], Khalid Benali[2], Karim Baïna[1], and Jamal Baïna[3]

[1] Alqualsadi, Rabat IT Center, ENSIAS, Mohammed V University, Rabat, Morocco
karim.baina@um5.ac.ma

[2] Université de Lorraine, CNRS, Inria, LORIA, 54000 Nancy, France
{abir.ismaili-alaoui,khalid.benali}@loria.fr

[3] Angel Assistance, Nancy, France
jamal.baina@angel-assistance.fr

Abstract. Business Process Management (BPM) is concerned with continuously enhancing business processes. However, this cannot be achieved without an effective Resource allocation and a priority-based scheduling. These are important steps towards time, cost and performance optimization in business processes. Even though there are several approaches and algorithms for scheduling and resource allocation problems, they do not take into consideration information gathered from past process executions, given the stateless aspect of business processes. Extracting useful knowledge from this information can help achieving an effective instance scheduling decisions without compromising cost or quality of service. In this paper, we pave the way for a combination approach which is based on unsupervised machine learning algorithms for clustering and genetic algorithm (GA) to ensure the assignment of the most critical business process instance tasks, to the qualified human resource while respecting several constraints such as resource availability and reliability, and taking into consideration the priority of the events that launch the process instances. A case study is presented and the obtained results from our experimentations demonstrate the benefit of our approach and allowed us to confirm the efficiency of our assumptions.

Keywords: Business process · Instance scheduling
Priority determination · Genetic algorithm · Machine learning

1 Introduction

Business Process Management (BPM) is about "continuous improvement and optimizing process to ensure high performance by achieving agility and flexibility as a tool to gain competitive advantages" [1]. Most of the existing studies in BPM focused on maintaining and enhancing the process business logical correctness, or improving the process performance at both levels: build-time and run-time, by focusing on the optimization of process modeling issues at build-time

Y. Tabii et al. (Eds.): BDCA 2018, CCIS 872, pp. 118–130, 2018.
https://doi.org/10.1007/978-3-319-96292-4_10

and process scheduling issues at run-time. The process scheduling is considered as a crucial step in the journey of business process performance improvement, since there is an important relationship between the effective resource allocation and the business process improvement [2]. However, scheduling in general tends to become more complicated in near-real time systems. In general, business processes are different from scientific workflows as they may contain automatic tasks and non automatic tasks. Human resources are more difficult to manage as a human resource can execute other tasks that do not belong to the main process [3] or they may be available for only a specific time slots. Besides, several characteristics must be taken into consideration in order to choose the right human resource to execute a critical task (especially in critical sectors like health-care or banking), such as availability [3], competence [4], Seniority or reliability [5]. In this paper, we deal with a case of a process defined in an organization that can not control the arrival of tasks (online scheduling [3]), but at the same time it should maintain a balance between multiple constraints such as (priority, time, quality of service, lack of resources) to better manage resources and to minimize the overall execution time without compromising the quality of service. We only deal with human resources in this article. We address the challenges mentioned above with the following major contributions: (1) Business process instance priority determination based on the criticality of the events that launched these instances. In this step, we analyze the historical data from past business process execution using unsupervised machine learning algorithms for clustering to estimate the priority of incoming events and then the priority of the instances. (2) We propose a genetic algorithm to solve our optimization problem which aims to achieve an effective assignment of the most critical process instance (result of the first step) to the most available human resource, while respecting several constraints such as resource availability and reliability.

The remainder of the paper is organized as follows. In the next section, we present an overview of related work to the problem of scheduling and human resource allocation in business processes. In the third section we introduce the objective and our context of work. Section 4 outlines our approach and methodology. Section 5 is devoted to the presentation of our experimental results and discussions. We conclude the paper in Sect. 6 and we give an outlook on future work.

2 Related Work

This section will describe some of the related researches that have been done to solve the problem of scheduling and human resource allocation in business processes. Human Resource Allocation Problem (HRAP) is considered as a special case of assignment problem. S.Bouajaja et al. write a survey on human resource allocation problems [6], where they present the main approaches proposed in the literature to solve HRAP in different real life applications. Among these approaches, we find exact methods [7] or meta-heuristics [8]. But to deal with human resource allocation problem in the context of business processes and achieve an efficient resource allocation and scheduling in business processes, several approaches have been proposed in the literature. In [9] authors focus on the integration of the priority aspect for human resource allocation in business process based on preferences. This approach provides also a mechanism for ranking resources. Another approach for resource allocation in business processes has been proposed in [10], where the authors tackle the problem of resource scheduling for several number of process instances by proposing two approaches based on heuristic rules to achieve a rational scheduling at build time and to take into consideration different dependencies that may exist between instances at run time. To the best of our knowledge, only few of these works present an effective instances scheduling based on event priority determination in incident management business processes. However, they do not take into account the stateless aspect of these processes, as such a process does not distinguish between events and it treats each event independently and without taking into consideration information that can be gathered from the previous executions. In the next section, we present in details the main idea and the problematic of this paper.

3 Objective and Context of Work

Each company must submit its business processes to a continuous improvement mechanism respecting their life cycle. However, achieving a high level of enhancement cannot be done without integrating business process instances priority determination systematically with business processes improvement approaches. In fact, an optimized resource allocation based on instances priority ensures a positive impact on business processes performance, as it addresses time constraints and cost requirements without compromising the output quality. Some works on resource allocation focus more on changing and adapting the structures of the business process to better fit the resources available in the enterprise [2], others try to ensure an equitable sharing of resources between the different tasks or process instances [3]. Regardless of the adapted approach, managing efficiently resource allocation and time consumption could become a very important competitive advantage especially for organization where time and resources are crucial for their business improvement. Scheduling approaches in business process management take into consideration a lot of constraints related to instances of a business process, such as execution start time, finishing time and dependencies between tasks, in order to determine their priority. Despite this, instances of the same business process can still be executed in first in first out order, which hinder the efficiency of the service especially when one of these instances is launched by a critical event. Besides, this situation become more complicated when most of the tasks in this business process are executed by human resources.

3.1 Context of Work and Motivation Example

The case study of our research work belongs to silver economy domain which is a new industrial sector officially launched in 2013 in France [11], in order to create personalized services and new technologies that are expected to improve disability-free life expectancy or to help dependent elderly people and their caregivers on a day-to-day basis. The risk of falls increases with age. In fact, losing physical capacities due to age or some kind of accidents can lead to serious falls of elderly people and those falls can have adverse repercussions. Let us consider a video surveillance company that edits an automatic falls detection system for elderly people and offers a 24/7 automatic alert solution and a quick rescue without the intervention of the person in danger. The incident management process used in this case study is based on a real-time analysis of alerts received from 24/7 streaming cameras for detecting elderly people's falls. This process is compliant to ISO 9001 corrective/preventive actions process. Besides, the global business process of this case study is simple but it represents several hard functional constraints such as: Business scaling, real-time data analysis and the obligation to maintain limited resources for the viability of the business. When an old person falls, the camera automatically detects it, takes a picture of the scene, and then saves the scene image and information about the event in a table in a data base. Those events are classified and qualified by human agents into 4 categories: False alerts (level 0): Empty place. False alerts (level 1): Active person. Alerts with average level (level 2): Seated person. High level alerts (level 3): Person lying down. The agent determines whether an assistance action is necessary or not (see Fig. 1). That's why, each received alert (event) requires a quite vigilant treatment, in order to be sure of its category, because the margin of error in this type of system must be very small, as those falls, in case of a delayed intervention or an incorrect qualification, may have an adverse impact on the person concerned. The growing needs of these type of companies (24/7 Streaming HD camera, increasing number of clients, unpredictable elderly people's falls), increase also the need to have more dynamic, adaptable and proactive business processes that ensure an appropriate responding to emerging customer events while maintaining an effective management of resources and without compromising one business process value (time, cost, quality, efficiency, flexibility, etc.) over the other. It turns out that time and resources are the

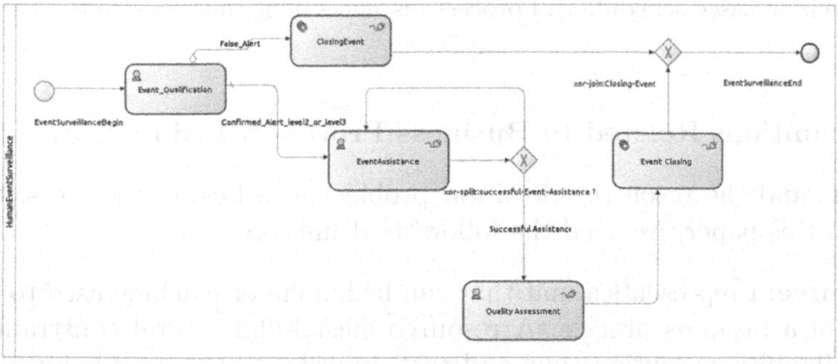

Fig. 1. Qualification and assessment of the risk level of alerts Process

most critical values in these cases, and a non efficient management of resources preclude the organization from achieving an effective scheduling, and this consequently hinder the continuous improvement of these business processes. In the next section we present our approach that is based on genetic algorithm and clustering algorithm.

4 Approach and Model

We propose in this paper an approach based on two main steps to achieve a dynamic and flexible scheduling: (1) Estimate the priority of several business process instances using an event priority determination approach: in this step we ensure a dynamic clustering for the events source using unsupervised learning algorithms. We attribute in fact the highest score to the cluster that contains the most critical cases. After that, each incoming event will be characterized by a score based on its cluster, so that the most critical event has the highest score. And then, the instance launched by the event that has the highest score has the highest level of priority. (2) Assign the most critical instance tasks to an available human resource: in this step, we use genetic algorithm to select the most suitable human resource and instance tasks matching, taking into consideration the availability and reliability of those human resources and the priority of each business process instance. In Fig. 2, we schematize the ent-to-end process to achieve a priority and reliability based resource allocation for our approach.

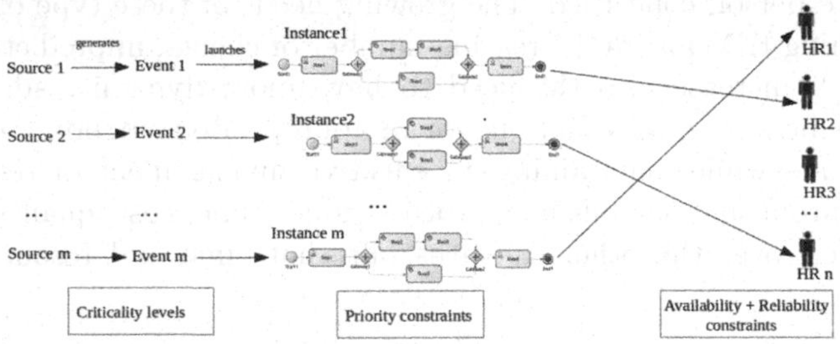

Fig. 2. Priority-based scheduling of process instances under human resource constraints

4.1 Definitions Releted to Business Process Scheduling Problem

To understand the resource allocation problem in a business process, that we discuss in this paper, we need the following definitions:

Resource: r represents a unit that can be human or machine used to execute tasks of a business process. A resource must fulfill several constraints such as availability, execution time and cost, in order to be suitable for a specific task. A is a set of agents (human resources), with n its cardinality.

Task: t is a logical unit of work in a business process that can be executed by a set of human or machine resources, depending on whether this task is automated or not. T is a set of tasks, with m its cardinality.
Business process: is a set of activities and tasks that exploit different resources to achieve one or more objectives.
Process instance: is a specific execution of a business process which is characterized by execution start time and execution finishing time for each task in this instance.
Resource allocation: is a matching between a task t of a process instance and an appropriate resource r.
Constraint: is a rule that control the execution tasks in a business process instance.
Priority: is a parameter used to choose between two or more tasks that need the same resource at the same time. The lowest priority task must wait for the resource occupied by the highest priority task.

4.2 Formulation of Priority-Based Business Process Scheduling Problem

The main objective of our approach is to ensure an effective and optimal human resource allocation and instances scheduling, while respecting the following constraints: (1) Priority of a process instance: the priority in our approach depends not only on the execution time interval, but also on the criticality of the event that triggers the instance. (2) Availability of human resources: in our approach we have two type of availability: The initial availability, which is related to SLA (Service-level agreement) between the hired human resource and the company. And the availability at time t, which is related to whether a human resource is assigned to execute a task or not. To determine the time that a human resource will spend to execute the allocated tasks in order to determine his availability, existing approaches proposed several methods to estimate the available time slot of each resource based on the time that a specific task require to be executed. However to gain more flexibility and to ensure a real time service we propose in our approach to manage the availability of each human resource using an online system that shows whether a specific human resource is available to receive a new task or he /she is not available (absent or allocated to an other task). (3) Reliability R_i of each human resources r_i: Since we are dealing with an incident management business processes, the error rate must be very small especially for the critical tasks. That's why, we include this metric which is calculated based on the number of errors that a specific human resource has made in a determined time interval.

$$Reliability = \frac{1}{\sum_{j=1}^{k} P_j N_j} \quad (1)$$

with P represents a weight which is proportional to the criticality level of the event. And N represents the total number of errors a human resource has committed while qualifying previous events, for each criticality level k.

The objective of our model is to minimize the total cost-reliability ratio for all available human resources. While respecting the constraints in order to ensure that a human resource can be assigned to one task at a time, but we must also respect the human resource initial capacity and also his/her availability in order to assign to them only tasks that occur in their availability time slot.

$$min \sum_{i=1}^{n} \sum_{j=1}^{m} \frac{C_{i,j}}{R_i} x_{i,j} \tag{2}$$

Subject to

$$\sum_{i=1}^{n} x_{i,j} = 1, j = 1, ..., m \tag{3}$$

$$\sum_{j=1}^{m} a_{i,j} x_{i,j} \leq Init\_Availability(r_i), i = 1, ..., n \tag{4}$$

The objective function represents the cost-reliability ratio, where c_{ij} represents the cost of the allocation of human resource r_i to task t_j, and R_i refers to the reliability of each human resources r_i (Eq. 1). x_{ij} in the first constraints, represented by Eq. (3), represents the decision variable ($x_{ij} = 1$ if human resource r_i is allocated to execute task t_j; 0 otherwise). This constraint means that each task is assigned to only one human resource. In Eq. (4) a_{ij} represents the total time used by the human resource r_i when assigned to execute a task t_j, and this equation means that the total time used by each human resource cannot exceed his/her initial availability.

4.3 Event Priority Determination Step

As mentioned previously, in order to schedule our business process instances according to their priority, we estimate this priority based on the criticality of the events that launch those instances. We proceed to a dynamic clustering in order to score and to estimate the priority of the incoming event based on the cluster of its source. We opted for clustering algorithms to discover groups in our dataset, we choose K-means clustering algorithms and we tested several criteria such as the frequency of falls or total number of falls, in order to have the most representative clustering for our data. We apply K-means algorithm on a set of events sources in order to classify those sources on different clusters using a score that we calculate for each event's source (a patient in our case) based on the frequency of previously generated events and their criticality value given previously by the agents (human resources) in the qualification step (see Fig. 1). This first step of our proposed method uses basic iterations of K-means algorithm. The event criticality is ranged from low level (0) to very serious (3), and there is a bijection between event criticality levels and instance priority. Two scenarios are encountered when applying this approach: (a) The sources of the incoming events belong to different clusters: in this case, the score of each cluster helps us to determine the criticality level of each event, which help us to estimate the priority level of the business process instance launched by this event. So, the instance launched by an event that was generated from a source that belongs to the critical cluster has a higher priority than the other instance. (b) Both sources, that generate the events, belong to the same cluster : in this case, the criticality level of each event is determined by the comparison of the score (used to cluster the sources) of each event source.

4.4 Instance Tasks and Resource Matching Step

Meta-heuristics present a potential solution for scheduling problems when exact methods are unable to find an optimal solution within a reasonable computational time [6]. Genetic algorithm is a meta-heuristic that has been proposed in 1975 by John Holland, it belongs to evolutionary algorithms group, and it aims to solve optimization problems by simulating the intelligence of natural selection and genetics [12] following specific steps as shown in this pseudo-code:

The use of a meta-heuristic in our approach is intuitive as we are facing an optimization problem, and meta-heuristics have proven their efficiency and their capability to obtain near-optimal results, through several works previously done by researchers. But we opted for genetic algorithm instead of other meta-heuristics such as Artificial Bee Colonies algorithm (ABC) or Ant Colony Optimization algorithm (ACO), as it was more adaptable to our case. Besides the phases of GA offer more flexibility in order to propose modified or adapted versions of the algorithm. Our optimization approach consists on of the following phases:

Algorithm 1. Genetic algorithm

Begin
1: Randomly generate an initial population of different individuals
2: Evaluate the fitness of each individual of the population
3: **repeat**
4: Select two parents from the population
5: Generate offspring by the selected parents
6: randomly Mutate the offspring
7: Evaluate the fitness of the offspring
8: Replace the less important individuals in the initial population by the best ones from the offspring
9: **until** convergence criterion is met // time limit or specific number of iteration

---

Input Parameters and Population Initialization. Like other population-based search and optimization algorithm, the initial phase of genetic algorithm starts by generating the initial population and set the initial parameters. A population in genetic algorithm (GA) represents all the possible solutions for the problem, and an adequate representation of a population of candidate solution increases the efficiency of GA results. For our approach, each individual from the initial population is encoded as vector where the first element of this vector represents the human resource index and the second one represents the task index. An individual in our case is represented as a possible one-to-one matching between a human resource and process instance tasks. So our population will have the following representation (see Fig. 3).

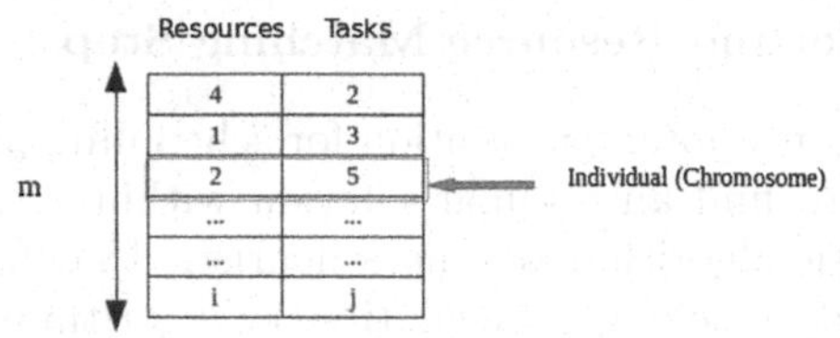

Fig. 3. Representation of population of candidate solutions

Population Fitness-Based Evaluation. As we mentioned before, our purpose is to ensure one-to-one matching between a human resource and process instance tasks. We evaluate the fitness value of each individual in the population. This fitness represents the total cost-reliability ratio of the available human resources that will be allocated to the current tasks (see Eq. 2).

Parent Selection and Population Reproduction. In this phase, the individuals of the initial population (parent) are sorted based on their fitness values. Among the different selection technics in literature (Tournament Selection, Roulette Wheel Selection, Rank Selection, ...), we apply rank selection. This technic consists on sorting the individuals by their fitness score and after that we randomly choose the parents from the individuals with higher ranks.

Crossover Phase. Is a step in genetic algorithm which consists on selecting two random individuals (chromosomes) and switch between their elements (genes) to generate a new population. In our approach, we can only use the one point crossover strategy to the individuals of our population given their representation (see Fig. 3).

Mutation Phase and New Generation. Represent an operation in genetic algorithm that consists on randomly modifying an individual. In our case, we opted for selecting the first element of the individual (chromosome) which represents the human resource index and modify it with an index of another available human resource. To obtain the future population we use the "Elitism" with a fitness based selection approach, which consists on keeping the fittest individuals of the current population, and those individuals replace the least fit offspring in the new generation.

Termination Condition. Time is a crucial factor in our case study, since we are dealing with critical events. So we use time as a limit condition.

5 Experimental Results and Discussions

In the following, we present a summary of the results obtained from our experiments, in order to demonstrate the effectiveness of the combination of the two proposed approaches. All our experiments were conducted on an Intel(R) Core(TM) i5-540 M 2.53 GHz. For the first step in our proposed approach, which aims to estimate the priority level of each business process instances based on the criticality level of each incoming events that launch these instances, we used K-means algorithm that we coded in R language. For this, we took a dataset of patients falls over the period from 01-02-2016 to 12-06-2017, this dataset is consisted of 238228 observations generated by 81 patients: 89312 alerts are of level 0 (low), 148466 of level 1(average), 275 of level 2 (serious) and 175 of level 3 (very serious). This dataset represents historical data gathered from our previous business process past instances (see Fig. 1). As shown in (Fig. 4), we obtain four clusters with the K-means algorithm based on the score of each patient calculated using the total number of his/her falls, taking into consideration level 2 and 3 only.

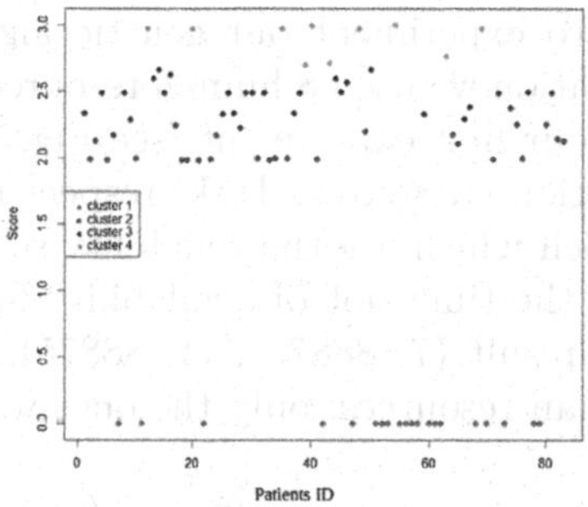

Fig. 4. Clustering of patients based on their score

Analyzing the historical data of each patient, helped us to cluster the patients into categories and find similarities between different patients. Each time a new event has been processed, the clustering is dynamically restarted in batch to ensure that the clusters are continuously updated and conclusive regarding the evolution of the patient's health level. In fact, this helps us to keep the score and the cluster of each patient updated in our database since we are using these two criteria to estimate the priority of the incoming events, in order to execute the instances linked to those events in priority order instead of first in first out order, as shown in the (Fig. 5). The first part of this figure represents the contents of the Json file that we send to our API (Application Programming Interface) in order to sort the incoming event by priority using the score and the cluster ID of each patient. The second part of this figure shows the received results. As we can see the score obtained for each event corresponds to the result of our clustering, and those events are sorted based on the score and the cluster ID of their sources.

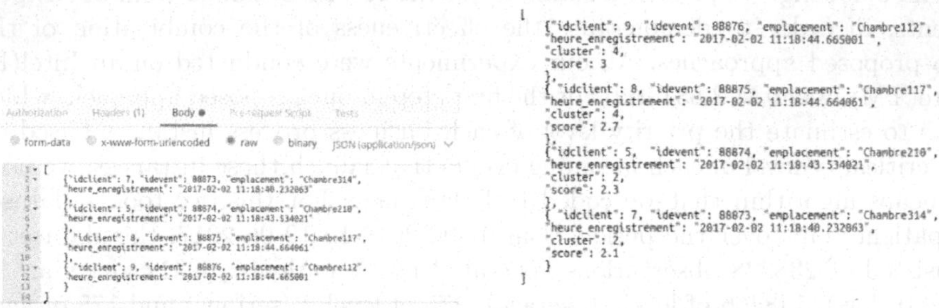

(a) Received events (b) Sorted events

Fig. 5. Event priority determination

In the second step, which represents the human resources allocation step in our approach, genetic algorithm and all other algorithms were coded in Java programming language. To experiment our genetic algorithm based approach for human resources allocation we used 8 human resources (see Table 1) with the same sorted events from our first experiment (see Fig. 5). The results obtained from this matching operation (Resource, Task) respect the two constraints that we propose in our approach which are the reliability score and the initial availability which is linked to the time slot of availability for each human resource. We obtain the following result (7, 88876), (1, 88875), (2, 88874), (5, 88873). Among the available human resources, only the ones with high reliability score were selected.

Table 1. List of human resources

Human resource ID	Reliability score	Initial availability	Time slot of availability
1	0.13	4 h	8AM–12 (Noon)
2	0.20	4 h	8AM–12 (Noon)
3	0.25	8 h	2PM–8PM
4	0.19	3 h	2PM–5PM
5	0.57	4 h	8AM–12 (Noon)
6	0.31	4 h	4AM–8AM
7	0.12	2 h	10AM–12 (Noon)
8	0.43	6 h	6PM–12 (Midnight)

In addition to the constraints related to human resources (availability and reliability) and to business process instances (priority), response time is also an important criterion that we should take into consideration in our approach since we are dealing with a critical tasks that should be allocated to human resources in near real-time. For this, we conduct another series of experiments in which we keep a fixed number of human resources, but we have modified alternately the number of tasks and the number of generation that we used within our genetic algorithm. The following figure (Fig. 6) represents the obtained results.

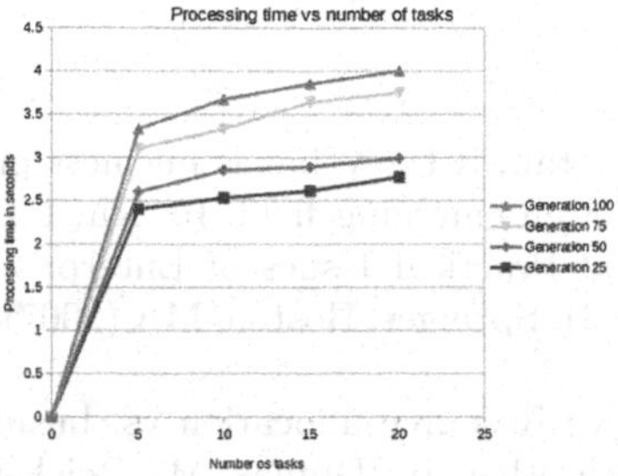

Fig. 6. Variability of the processing time according to number of tasks and number of generation

We observe that our priority based scheduling approach allows us to schedule up to 20 events in just a few seconds. Increasing generation number causes a slight increase in processing time, but the final result of resource allocation is the same. Thus we have limited the number of generations in our genetic algorithm to 50.

6 Conclusion and Future Work

In this paper, we introduced a two-phase approach to ensure an effective scheduling in the case of critical tasks that must be executed by human resources. The first phase represents a solution for event priority determination to ensure an effective instance scheduling in business process. This solution is based on the analysis of historical data from past business process execution using unsupervised machine learning algorithms for clustering, in order to manage the priority of several events that launch business process instances. The second phase is about resource allocation. In fact, the problem of scheduling in business processes, has several constraints at the same time such as resource availability and reliability, and time. As this problem is considered as an optimization problem, we propose a genetic algorithm to solve it in order to achieve an effective matching between the most critical process instance and the most available human resource. Our solution ensures that the events are processed according to their order of priority, by exploiting the result of our clustering step to estimate the criticality of the incoming events. In our future work, we project to improve our approach by introducing other technics to provide a real-time scheduling in business process management.

Acknowledgments. The authors would like to thank the French Embassy in Morocco for their financial support, Angel Assistance for providing us with the necessary data to accomplish our work, and a groupe of students from M2 MIAGE SID for their participation in implementing some parts of our experimentation platform.

For privacy management, all data has been anonymized.

References

1. Møller, C., Maack, C.J., Tan, R.D.: What is business process management: a two stage literature review of an emerging field. In: Xu, L.D., Tjoa, A.M., Chaudhry, S.S. (eds.) Research and Practical Issues of Enterprise Information Systems II. ITIFIP, vol. 254, pp. 19–31. Springer, Boston, MA (2007). https://doi.org/10.1007/978-0-387-75902-9_3
2. Xu, J., Liu, C., Zhao, X.: Resource allocation vs. business process improvement: how they impact on each other. In: Dumas, M., Reichert, M., Shan, M.-C. (eds.) BPM 2008. LNCS, vol. 5240, pp. 228–243. Springer, Heidelberg (2008). https://doi.org/10.1007/978-3-540-85758-7_18
3. Bessai, K.: Gestion optimale de l'allocation des ressources pour l'ex ecution des processus dans le cadre du Cloud. Ph.D. thesis, Université Paris1 Panthéon-Sorbonne (2014)
4. Hachicha, R.M., Dafaoui, E., EL Mhamedi, A.: Assignment problem under competences and preferences constraints: modelling and resolution. IFAC Proc. Vol. **45**(6), 1170–1176 (2012)
5. Volgenant, A.: A note on the assignment problem with seniority and job priority constraints. Eur. J. Oper. Res. **154**(1), 330–335 (2004)
6. Bouajaja, S., Dridi, N.: A survey on human resource allocation problem and its applications. Oper. Res. Int. J. **17**(2), 339–369 (2017)
7. Younas, I., Kamrani, F., Schulte, C., Ayani, R.: Optimization of task assignment to collaborating agents. In: 2011 IEEE Symposium on Computational Intelligence in Scheduling (SCIS), pp. 17–24. IEEE (2011)
8. Gutjahr, W.J., Rauner, M.S.: An aco algorithm for a dynamic regional nurse-scheduling problem in austria. Comput. Oper. Res. **34**(3), 642–666 (2007)
9. Cabanillas, C., et al.: Priority-based human resource allocation in business processes. In: Basu, S., Pautasso, C., Zhang, L., Fu, X. (eds.) ICSOC 2013. LNCS, vol. 8274, pp. 374–388. Springer, Heidelberg (2013). https://doi.org/10.1007/978-3-642-45005-1_26
10. Xu, J., Liu, C., Zhao, X.: Resource planning for massive number of process instances. In: Meersman, R., Dillon, T., Herrero, P. (eds.) OTM 2009. LNCS, vol. 5870, pp. 219–236. Springer, Heidelberg (2009). https://doi.org/10.1007/978-3-642-05148-7_16
11. Silvereco: Silver économie. http://www.silvereco.fr/
12. Holland, J.H.: Adaptation in Natural and Artificial Systems: An Introductory Analysis with Applications to Biology, Control, and Artificial Intelligence. MIT press, Cambridge (1992)

Hashtag Recommendation Using Word Sequences' Embeddings

Nada Ben-Lhachemi(✉) and El Habib Nfaoui(✉)

LIIAN Laboratory, Sidi Mohammed Ben Abdellah University, Fez, Morocco
nada.benlhachemi@usmba.ac.ma, elhabib.nfaoui@usmba.ac.be

Abstract. Nowadays, billions of people use social networks such as Twitter. Twitter users create and use hashtags in their tweets to classify them corresponding to topic or theme. Hashtags have been progressed into a multifaceted instrument to tag and track content, emphasise a standpoint or galvanise communal support across published posts on social networks. Although, by dint of the free hashtag creation strategy, users are having a broad toughness to choose suitable hashtags for their posts. In this paper, we introduce an approach for hashtag recommendation in Twitter based on tweets embeddings. We first make use of multiple techniques to calculate embeddings of the tweets in the corpus. Next, we use the k-means clustering algorithm in order to divide the heterogeneous tweets into clusters of similar tweets. Afterwards, we compute the similarity between the entered tweet embeddings and the centroids embeddings of each obtained cluster to recommend the most appropriate hashtags to the user. Through miscellaneous experiments, we introduce an itemized study on how the techniques used for tweet embeddings influence on the final set of the recommended hashtags.

Keywords: Word2vec · Word embeddings · Doc2vec · Twitter
Hashtag · K-Means

1 Introduction

Social media include a broad spectrum of websites such as social networking sites, microblogs, websites and blogs such as Twitter, that play a fundamental role in the creation and sharing of information, ideas and emotions within online social networks in teal time. Recently, social media have become gradually popular; Twitter as example; has more than 313 million active users and monthly 1 billion unique visits to sites with embedded tweets [1]. Tweets are restricted to only 140 characters, comprising text and special components such as media, hashtags, urls, emoticones, user_mentions, and media. A hashtag is a word or words sequence preceded by a hash sign (#), adopted on social networks, especially Twitter, to pick out blogs on a specific topic. Anyone sharing content on a relevant topic can use hashtag in its post. Other connected people in the same platform looking for that topic, can search for that hashtag to find other related

Y. Tabii et al. (Eds.): BDCA 2018, CCIS 872, pp. 131–143, 2018.
https://doi.org/10.1007/978-3-319-96292-4_11

posts. Twitter users make use of hashtags in their tweets in order to: (a) classify tweets in a manner that makes it straightforward for users to find and follow tweets about a precise topic or theme. (b) Track trending topics, and look for people with the same interests. Consequently, the task of recommending hashtag has been experienced to be relevant for natural language processing (NLP) applications.

Current research on methods for recommending hashtags has as objective to surmount the constraints of classical techniques based on the syntax and lexicon of tweets instead of their semantics. Hashtag recommendation is one of the primary challenges in analyzing data in microblogging platforms because of their special features: (a) the concision of tweets (140 characters in maximum), which makes it complicated to use formal language to express much information, and thus bloggers feel free to use aliases/morphs, uncanny language, high contextualization, and informal writing. (b) Traditional issues of text understanding; polysemy, synonymy and ambiguity, added to the frequent use of acronyms and abbreviations, caused by the restriction of the character number.

Not long ago, word embeddings became one of the most effective and victorious applications of unsupervised learning. Their primary advantage is that they don't demand costly annotation, however they can be extracted from huge unannotated data set that are willingly available. Current work aim to enhance the computation techniques of syntactic and semantic embeddings of sentences, paragraphs, micro-blogs, short and long documents, with straightforward methods such as a simple additional composition of the word vectors or more advanced methods such as recurrent neural networks (RNNs) and convolutional neural networks (CNNs). (e.g.: Le and Mikolov [20], Arora et al. [2], Iyyer et al. [3], Wieting et al. [4] and Wang et al. [5]). Here, in the current paper, we make use of two simple additional methods (Average of word2vec vectors and average of word2vec vectors with TF-IDF) to calculate tweet embeddings, and doc2vec model to learn tweet embeddings.

In this paper, we propose a method of hashtag recommendation that compute tweet embeddings using word2vec features (dimensionality = 300), use three different methods to compute embeddings of each given tweet, then combining these features with K-Means algorithm to select candidate hashtags in each cluster in order to recommend the top k suitable hashtags to the blogger.

The remainder of this paper is structured as follows. Section 2 presents related work. Section 3 discusses the details of the proposed system and the selected algorithms to automatically recommend the top k hashtags. In Sect. 4, we evaluate our system using a real Twitter dataset and we evaluate the three different approaches of calculating embeddings and their impact in the task of hashtag recommendations. Section 5 concludes this work and discusses future prospects.

2 Related Work

In this section, we discuss different methods published by researchers lately, addressing the task of hashtag recommendation in micro-blogging platforms, particularly Twitter.

Numerous published works are based on methods of topic distribution as Latent Dirichlet Allocation (LDA) [6]; She and Chen [7] introduced a supervised topic-model based on a modified solution from Twitter-LDA to recommend suitable hashtags in Twitter. Seeing that hashtags are labels, they identify the relationships between topics of tweets, hashtags, and the followers of users, to compute the probability that a given hashtag will be used in a tweet, and recommend the most probable hashtags. Ding et al. [8] adopt the LDA model with the topic-specific translation model to assess the topic specific word-alignment probabilities between a given tweet and existing hashtags, thereby extracting relevant hashtags. Chen and Kao [9] introduced a system of recommending hashtags founded on a semi supervised learning that use non-hashtags tweets (the tweets that do not hold hashtags) for training. These researchers rely on the hypothesis that a given hashtag can be the topic of tweet, appropriately; they use the labeled LDA which specify a one-to-one connection between real labels and the topics generated by the LDA. Then, they consider the non-hashtags tweets with self-labeling hashtags in the data set as auxiliary set and real-annotated set as training set. Thus, they adjust weights by applying a classifier based on Transfer AdaBoostTrAdaBoost to filter out the useless parts of non-hashtag tweets.

Several other works are based on the supposition that tweets that are similar are ordinarily tagged by the same hashtags. Sedhai and Sun [10] proposed a hashtag recommender system for hyperlinked tweets to pick candidate hashtags, they first considered similar tweets, similar documents, and named entities in a document and the link domain. Then they formulated the hashtag recommendation task as a learning-to-rank problem and used SVMRank to rank and suggest suitable hashtags. Zangerle et al. [11] compared four methods in which text similarity is adopted to suggest the top five hashtags to the user: cosine similarity on TF-IDF, cosine similarity on BM-25, Jaccard similarity and the Lavenshtein distance. These researchers also proposed three ranking methods: ScoreRank, RecCountRank and GlobalPopularityRank. Cosine similarity on TF-IDF with ScoreRank is examined the best methods for recommending the five most appropriate hashtags. Jeon et al. [12] proposed a system for recommending hashtags based on user interests, similar tweets and popularity of hashtags. They extracted keywords from collected tweets using TF-IDF and used Naïve Bayes to classify these keywords into pre-defined classes before ranking the candidate hashtags so as to recommend appropriate hashtags to the blogger. The main limitation of these techniques is that they use a large corpus of tweets; a tweet must be compared with all the others in the data set to extract similar tweets based essentially on the syntax and lexicon of words.

Other recent researches are based on the use of semantic knowdlege bases to recommend the top-k appropriate hashtags to the users. Ben-Lhachemi and Nfaoui [15] introduced a hashtag recommendation system, based on a extended version of the spreading activation technique using various semantic knowdlege bases (WordNet, DBpedia and Wikipedia), in order to compute a semantic similarity between an entered tweet and a set of recent existing hashtags to recommend the most k relevant hashtags to the blogger. Kalloubi et al. [16] propose a method for hashtag recommendation based on the use of semantic similarity; they adopt a tweet entity linking approach, to pick a set of DBpedia entities, afterwards they calculate semantic based similarity between entities within tweets, to collect a collection of nominee hashtags from similar tweets to recommend the top-k hashtags to the user.

Lately a lot of researchers are interested in embeddings adopted for learning vector representation of words and document using huge corpus. Gong and Zhang [13] use the convolutional neural networks (CNNs) to execute the hashtag recommendations task. They used attention mechanisms; (local attention channel to compute each word embeddings of a given post and a global channel to model the whole post), afterwards they use a convolutional layer with several features maps to combine the outputs of the local attention channel and the global channel, to compute hashtags scores, at last they use these scores to rank hashtags for a given post and suggesting relevant hashtags to the blogger. Weston et al. [14] introduced a system appointed by #TAGSPACE that learn to rank hashtags by analyzing short text blogs features and adopting hashtags as a supervised signal. They depict hashtags and each word of the entered text using d-dimensional embedding, afterwards they make use of a scoring function based on the document embeddings to rank suitable hashtags.

In accordance with Le and Mikolov [20]; word2vec is an effective technique for learning high-quality distributed vector representations that catch a huge number of accurate semantic and syntactic word intercourses. By opposite of LDA or TF-IDF, word2vec vectors consider various types of similarities between words (syntactic and semantic similarities), but it doesn't have a careful consideration on word co-occurrence patterns. In our application case, it is a relevant choice to compute continuous vector space representation of tweets. Yet, we evaluate three techniques for calculating tweets embeddings, the first and the second one make use of Google News pre-trained model [19] of word2vec to load word vectors, then they adopt a simple averaging value with and without TF-IDF, and the third one uses the doc2vec approach to learn tweets embeddings, afterward we use the K-Means clustering algorithm to gather similar tweets into clusters, in order to pick nominee hashtags from where we can suggest the top-k appropriate hashtags to the blogger.

3 Methodology

This section describes our proposed system designed to automatically recommend the top-k hashtags for an entered tweet. The computation of these recommendations is described in the following steps:

(a) Calculate tweets embeddings in the corpus according to the three methods presented in next subsections.
(b) Divide the heterogeneous tweets featuring at least one hashtag into clusters of similar tweets based on their embeddings.
(c) Calculate the cosine similarity between the entered tweet and each cluster centroid.

(d) Extract the hashtags contained in the tweets of the most similar clusters. These hashtags are the elements of the hashtag recommendation nominee set.
(e) Rank the candidate hashtags.
(f) Suggest the top-k relevant hashtags to the user.

The method of computing the embeddings of a short text; in our case the whole tweet embeddings is crucial for the further calculation of recommendation candidates. Hence, we evaluated the following word sequences methods:

(a) Average of word2vec vectors.
(b) Average of word2vec vectors with TF-IDF.
(c) Doc2vec.

3.1 Preprocessing

Every tweet is affected by the 140-character length restriction; because of this, users use often a lot of abbreviations, shortening words, symbols and emoticons, which make the content of tweets very noisy and unclear. Furthermore, tweets encompass other special fields such as urls, media, hashtags, retweets and user mentions. Preprocessing tweets is a basic first step to reduce the impact of their noise and perplexity. In our work, we use these preprocessing steps: (a) Hold only tweets that contain at least one hashtag, (b) Clean all urls, stop words, emoticons and symbols, (c) Perform stemming and lemmatization, (d) Keep just tweets that gather at least one valid english word.

3.2 Word2vec

The word2vec [18] (word to vector) is a two-layer neural network that is trained to rebuild linguistic contexts of words. Its input is a text corpus and its output is a collection of vectors, typically of several hundred dimensions (feature vectors for words in that corpus) such as there is a small distance between words that have similar context in space.

Word2vec was created by a Google team guided by Mikolov, theses researchers published it as open source tool for research intention [19]. Word2vec provides two architectures to produce a distributed representation of words [18]: The Continuous Bag-of-Words Model (CBOW) and The Continuous Skip-gram Model (CSG); The CBOW tends to predict the probability of a word given a window of surrounding context words. A context may be a single word or a set of words, the best performance was reaching by adopting the four words before and after the current word for predicting the current word. The CSG follows the same architecture of the CBOW. The aim of skip-gram is to predict the surrounding window of context words; it assigns hefty weights for words that have similar context to the current word.

Word vectors generated by the layer neural networks are powerful at predicting the nearby words in terms of semantics and syntactic senses: word vectors are very good at answering analogy questions of the type; x is y as z is to ?. For example, "man" is to "woman" as "uncle" is to ? (aunt) using a simple vector offset method based on cosine distance. In other hand, mainly in the semantic axis, embeddings of "Windows" and "Linux" are close since they have the same semantic context and in the syntactic sense, "oranges" minus "orange" is close to "apples" minus "apple".

In this paper, we use the Google News pre-trained model [19], to extract continuous vector space representation of words (words embeddings) of a given tweet. It contains word vectors for a vocabulary of 3 million words trained on around 100 billion words from the Google news dataset. Afterwards, we make use of three different methods to generate the whole tweet embeddings. Hence, in this paper we evaluated them as explained in the next subsections.

3.3 Tweet Embeddings

So as to calculate the tweet embeddings, we use three different methods to compute the whole tweet embeddings, Hence, in this paper we evaluate them.

Average of Word2vec Vectors. Calculate the average value of all the word embeddings of a given tweet computed using word2vec. This average vector will represent the embeddings of the whole tweet as follows:

$$V(t) = \frac{1}{N}\sum_{i=0}^{N} V(Wi) \tag{1}$$

Where N is the number of words composed the tweet t, and V(Wi) is the word Wi embeddings.

Average of Word2vec Vectors with TF-IDF: Averaging embeddings of all words in a text has proven to be a strong baseline or feature across a multitude of tasks [17], such as short text similarity tasks. An alternative would be to weight word vectors with their TF-IDF to reduce the impact of the most common words. Thus, we calculate a given tweet embeddings by the average value of word2vec embeddings of each word of this tweet with its TF-IDF as follows:

$$V(t) = \frac{1}{N}\sum_{i=0}^{N} V(Wi) * TF(Wi) * IDF(Wi) \tag{2}$$

Where N is the number of words composed the tweet t, and V(Wi) is the word Wi embeddings.

Notes and Comments. In this work, we make use of Google News corpus [19] which is a pre-trained model of Word2vec on a part of Google News dataset. It includes word vectors for a vocabulary of 3 million words and phrases that google researchers trained on approximately 100 billion words from a Google

News dataset. The vector length is 300 features. Here, we use it to extract the continuous vector space representation of words of a given tweet. Hence, we compute the embeddings of the whole given tweet as clarified in the previous and the current subsections.

Doc2vec: A prolongation of word2vec to construct embeddings from full documents (instead than the individual words) has been proposed. As word2vec calculates a feature vector for each word in a given corpus, doc2Vec calculate a feature vector for each document in a given corpus. Doc2vec is an unsupervised method to calculate embeddings for word sequences regardless of it's length (paragraphs,documents,sentences...) [20]. But contrary to words, word sequences do not come in logical structures such as words, that it is why Le and Mikolov [20] have added another feature vector, which is the document-unique parameter with the word2vec model. Hence, we use doc2vec to calculate a given tweet embeddings in the following manner: for training, a set of tweets is intended, a word embeddings is calculated for each word, and a tweet vector is generated for each tweet. Such as word2vec, the doc2vec model trains weights for a softmax hidden layer, All weights are fixed to compute the tweet embeddings while a new tweet may be presented in the inference stage.

3.4 K-Means

K-means [21] is a simple unsupervised learning algorithm for data clustering. The main idea is to classify the input data set through a certain number of clusters (k clusters). It is a way of partitioning a set of input data points into a certain number of clusters (k clusters) or sets of data points which are similar. The first step is to define randomly k centroids (The centroid is a representative point of each cluster) one for each cluster. The better choice to place these centroids is to place them as much as possible far away from each other. The next step is to take each point of a given data and associate it to the nearest centroid. When all points have been assigned, then recalculate the positions of the k centroids. Afterwards, a new binding should be done between the same data points and the new centroid. Thus, a new loop is generated which the k centroids change their location step by step until no more changes are done. In other words, this process continues until the centroids settle down and stop moving. Finally, this algorithm aims at minimizing an objective function, in this case a squared error function as follows:

$$F = \sum_{i-1}^{n} \sum_{j-1}^{m} \left\| x_j^i - m_i \right\|^2 \quad (3)$$

Where: n is the cardinal of data points, $\left\| x_j^i - m_i \right\|^2$ is the chosen distance measure between a data point x_j^i and the cluster centroid m_i.

For measuring the distance between cluster vectors, or between new data points and the randomly chosen centroid, there is various distance metrics, in our work, we use the most used one which is the Euclidian distance for k-means clustering it minimizes the mean distance between points and centroids. In order to validate the number of initial clusters, we use the elbow method. The aim of this method is to run the k-means algorithm on the corpus for a range of values of k (e.g. k = 10, 50, 100, 200, 500), and for each value of k compute the sum of squared errors SSE. The SSE is specified as the sum of the squared distance between each member of the cluster and its centroid. Basically k gets larger as the SSE decreases, since the number of clusters increases, this number should be smaller, so distortion is also smaller. The concept of the elbow method is to pick the k value at which the SSE decreases suddenly.

3.5 Hashtag Recommendation

In order to recommend the top-k appropriate hashtags to the user, we propose to process the entered tweet in the same way of the preprocessing done to tweets in the data set. We first process the entered tweet to extract valid english words, next we use Google News model pre-trained using word2vec [22] (dimensionality = 300) to extract word vectors, then we apply the three proposed methods to compute the embeddings of the whole entered tweet. Correspondingly, we compute the cosine similarity between the entered tweet embeddings and the kmeans-centroids embeddings, then, this process avoids comparing the entered tweet embeddings with all tweets in the dataset, which helps speeding up computation. If the entered tweet embeddings is near a given centroid, then this tweet share semantic and syntactic contexts with approximately the majority of the tweets in this cluster. As a result of this, we have a nominee set of hashtags, which are the hashtags adopted by tweets of the most similar clusters to the entered tweet. Then, we will depend on the occurrence score of each hashtag to rank them; if a candidate hashtag is used in more than one tweet, it will have the highest occurrence score.

4 Evaluation

4.1 Data Set Description

The approach proposed in this paper was evaluated using the UDI Twitter Crawl-Aug2012 dataset [23]. This dataset contains 147,909 files; each file containing up to 500 tweets published by a user. We established a preprocessing which we extracted 1.212.300 tweets that contain hashtags. Next, we did another preprocessing to hold just tweets that contain at least one valid english word, which we extracted 851.496 English-language tweets. Then, we splitted this data set into a dev set (75%) (which we optimized and trained our method) and a test set (25%) (which we tested our method).

4.2 Results and Discussions

The evaluation was performed by implementing a Python project and was based on the formerly reported data set. Various machine learning libraries were used.

Scikit-Learn [24] was adopted to implement the K-Means algorithm. Gensim [25] to load and use the Google News word2vec model, and to calculate the whole tweet embeddings using doc2vec model.

We use hashtags annotated in test set as the golden set. To assess the efficiency and suitability of the recommendations of hashtags provided by our system to the user, we use precision (P), recall (R), and F1-score (F1) metrics as shown in Table 1, with k = 1.

We contemplate recall@k as the most important quality metric for our approach, for the purpose that our method is aiming at recommending the blogger an optimal number of relevant hashtags, which usually may not be provided by the user in its entered tweet.

Table 1. Precision, Recall and F1-score of our method using three different methods to calculate the whole tweet embeddings

Method	Precision	Recall	F1-score
word2vec	0.426	0.392	0.408
word2vec with tf-idf	0.485	0.421	0.541
doc2vec	0.419	0.381	0.399

Figures 1, 2 and 3 show the recall@k, the precision@k and the F1-score@k respectively (k = 1, 2, 3, 4, 5) plot of the recall, precision and F1-score values of the three methods of calculating the whole tweet embeddings used by our system. In our evaluation, we consider that several tweets contain more than one hashtag, that is why we assess the top-k recommended hashtags by our system on the test data, with k ranging from 1 to 5 as shown in the three figures. In most set of circumstances, a range of 1–5 hashtag recommendations is most preferable by users to pick from.

As shown in Figs. 1, 2 and 3, our system achieves good results, especially when it uses the average value of word2vec vectors with TF-IDF, as embeddings of the whole tweets. The performance of our system using the average value of word2vec or doc2vec for computing the tweets embeddings is approximately equal when we applied it on our data set.

As shown in Figs. 2 and 3, the precision and the F1-score values decrease when the hashtag number increases, it may be for the reason that word embeddings do not consider ambiguity of words; a given word should be represented by multiple embeddings if it has more than one semantic meaning. Withal our system performs better when using as embeddings of tweets, the average value of word2vec with TF-IDF than the other evaluated methods and recommends appropriate hashtags to the blogger. Yet, we propose recommending only one or two hashtags for each tweet to have better performance for the three methods.

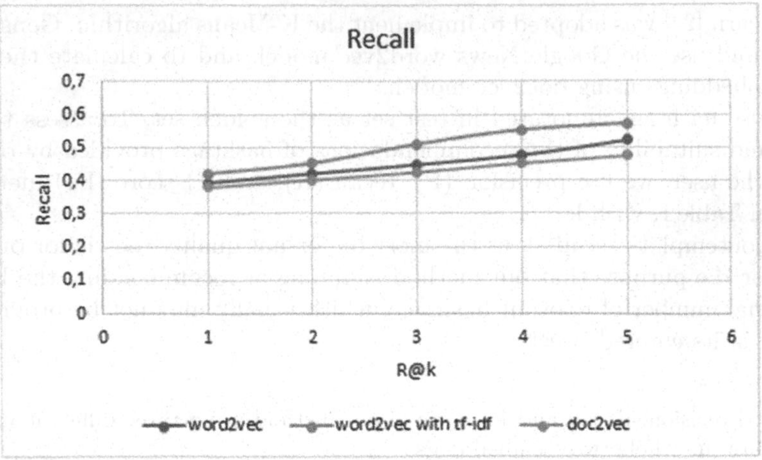

Fig. 1. Recall of our system using three different methods to compute the whole tweet embeddings with the top-k recommended hashtags with k ranging from 1 to 5

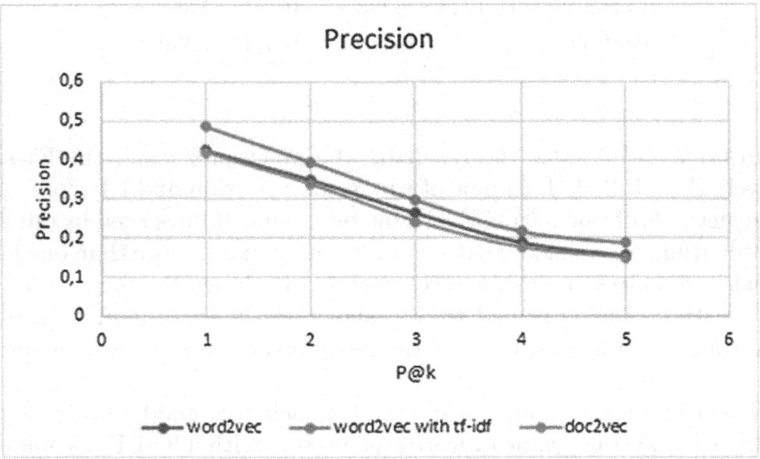

Fig. 2. Precision of our system using three different methods to compute the whole tweet embeddings with the top-k recommended hashtags with k ranging from 1 to 5

We call to mind that our proposed system needs mainly a suitable use of the preprocessing techniques. Thereby, it is based on the use of doc2vec to calculate embeddings of tweets, or the use of Google news pre-trained model of word2vec to extract word embeddings which can not work if there is no valid english words in tweets.

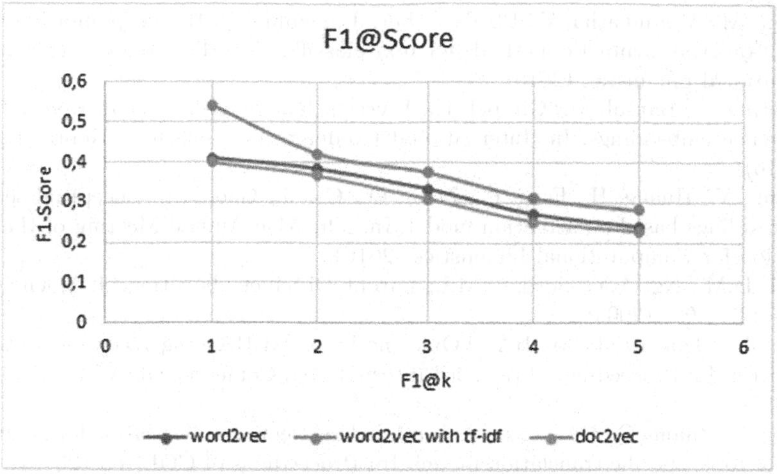

Fig. 3. F1-Score of our system using three different methods to compute the whole tweet embeddings with the top-k recommended hashtags with k ranging from 1 to 5

5 Conclusion and Future Work

In the current paper, we introduce an approach for recommending hashtags in Twitter that is based on the use of one of the most famous pre-trained models of word2vec (Google News model) to extract vector representations of words, several methods use these representations to calculate tweets embeddings. Our method is based on the use of K-Means algorithm to assemble similar tweets under one umbrella. Moreover, the nominee set of hashtags is picked corresponding to their co-occurence in the closest clusters to the entered tweet. The results show that the techniques used for calculating the whole tweet embeddings influence on the final set of the recommended hashtags.

The present paper regard only the textual part of tweets without considering their other fields (emoticones, urls, named entities ...) in the recommending hashtags task. Our next work will concentrate on using new components of tweets such as geographical and temporal information. Alternatively, we will focus to expand more complicated DL architectures and train them on various semantic knowledge bases such as Dbpedia or BabelNet to enhance the accuracy of results.

References

1. Twitter Company. https://about.twitter.com/fr/company.html. Accessed 29 Jan 2018
2. Arora, S., Liang, Y., Ma, T.: A simple but tough-to-beat baseline for sentence embeddings. In: The 5th International Conference on Learning Representations (2017)

3. Iyyer, M., Manjunatha, V., Boyd-Graber, J., Daume III, H.: Deep unordered composition rivals syntactic methods for text classification. The Association for Computational Linguistics (2015)
4. Wieting, J., Bansal, M., Gimpel, K., Livescu, K.: Towards universal paraphrastic sentence embeddings. In: International Conference on Learning Representations (2016)
5. Wang, Y., Huang, H., Feng, C., Zhou, Q., Gu, J., Gao, X.: Conceptual sentence embeddings based on attention model. In: The 54th Annual Meeting of the Association for Computational Linguistics (2016)
6. Blei, D.M., Ng, A.Y., Jordan, M.I.: Latent Dirichlet allocation. J. Mach. Learn. Res. 993–1022 (2003)
7. She, J., Chen, L.: TOMOHA: TOpic model-based HAshtag recommendation on Twitter. In: Proceedings of the 23rd International Conference on World Wide Web (2014)
8. Ding, Z., Zhang, Q., Huang, X.: Automatic hashtag recommendation for microblogs using topic-specific translation model. In: Proceedings of COLING (2012)
9. Chen, J.D., Kao, H.Y.: LDA based semi-supervised learning from streaming short text. In: 2015 IEEE International Conference on Data Science and Advanced Analytics (2015)
10. Sedhai, S., Sun, A.: Hashtag recommendation for hyperlinked tweets. In: SIGIR Proceedings of the 37th International ACM SIGIR Conference on Research and Development in Information Retrieval (2014)
11. Zangerle, E., Gassler, W., Specht, G.: On the impact of text similarity functions on hashtag recommendations in microblogging environments. Soc. Netw. Anal. Min. (2011). https://doi.org/10.1007/s13278-013-0108-x
12. Jeon, M., Jun, S., Hwang, E.: Hashtag recommendation based on user tweet and hashtag classification on Twitter. In: Chen, Y., et al. (eds.) WAIM 2014. LNCS, vol. 8597, pp. 325–336. Springer, Cham (2014). https://doi.org/10.1007/978-3-319-11538-2_30
13. Gong, Y., Zhang, Q.: Hashtag recommendation using attention-based convolutional neural network. In: Proceedings of the Twenty-Fifth International Joint Conference on Artificial Intelligence (IJCAI-16) (2016)
14. Weston, J., Chopra, S., Adams, K.: #TAGSPACE: semantic embeddings from hashtags. In: Proceedings of the 2014 Conference on Empirical Methods in Natural Language Processing (EMNLP), pp. 1822–1827 (2014)
15. Ben Lhachemi, N., Nfaoui, E.H.: An extended spreading activation technique for hashtag recommendation in microblogging platforms. In: The 7th International Conference on Web Intelligence, Mining and Semantics (2017)
16. Kalloubi, F., Nfaoui, E.H., El Beqqali, O.: Harnessing semantic features for large scale content based hashtag recommendations on microblogging platforms. Int. J. Semant. Web Inf. Syst. **13**(1), 6381 (2017)
17. Kenter, T., Borisov, A., de Rijke, M.: Siamese CBOW: optimizing word embeddings for sentence representations. In: Proceedings of the 54th Annual Meeting of the Association for Computational Linguistics (2016)
18. Mikolov, T., Sutskever, I., Chen, K., Corrado, G., Dean, J.: Efficient estimation of word representations in vector space. arXiv:1301.3781 (2013)
19. https://code.google.com/archive/p/word2vec/. Accessed 3 Dec 2017
20. Le, Q., Mikolov, T.: Distributed representations of sentences and documents. In: 2014 Proceedings of the 31st International Conference on Machine Learning, Beijing, China, vol. 32. JMLR: W&CP (2014)

21. MacQueen, J.B.: Some methods for classification and analysis of multivariate observations. In: Proceedings of 5-th Berkeley Symposium on Mathematical Statistics and Probability (1967)
22. https://code.google.com/archive/p/word2vec/. Accessed 16 Nov 2017
23. Illinois Wiki. https://wiki.cites.illinois.edu/wiki/display/forward/Dataset-UDITwitterCrawl-Aug2012. Accessed 21 Oct 2017
24. http://scikit-learn.org/stable/. Accessed 25 Nov 2017
25. https://radimrehurek.com/gensim/ Accessed 24 Nov 2017

Towards for Using Spectral Clustering in Graph Mining

Z. Ait El Mouden[1(✉)], R. Moulay Taj[2], A. Jakimi[1], and M. Hajar[2]

[1] Software Engineering & Information Systems Engineering Team, FSTE, UMI, Errachidia, Morocco
mouden.zakariyaa@outlook.com

[2] Operational Research & Computer Science Team, FSTE, UMI, Errachidia, Morocco

Abstract. This paper presents an approach of community detection from data modeled by graphs, using the Spectral Clustering (SC) algorithms, and based on a matrix representation of the graphs. We will focus on the use of Laplacian matrices afterwards. The spectral analysis of those matrices can give us interesting details about the processed graph. The input of the process is a set of data and the output will be a set of communities or clusters that regroup the input data, by starting with the graphical modeling of the data and going through the matrix representation of the similarity graph, then the spectral analysis of the Laplacian matrices, the process will finish with the results interpretation.

Keywords: Community detection · Spectral clustering · Laplacian matrices Similarity graphs

1 Introduction

Recently, with the Big Data revolution, many works are born to exploit the maximum of knowledge from data while respecting the cost and time factors.

Among those works we find the researches of L. Jourdan that deal with the knowledge extraction from massive data by introducing the methods of optimization and Dataminig such as the use of metaheuristics to optimize the association rules [1, 2], one of those applications use the genetic algorithms, and the result of those works is the algorithm MOCA-I as the first algorithm for the classification of heterogeneous and poorly distributed data using optimization methods, published in 2013 by J. Jaques under the supervision of L. Jourdan [3]. Other approaches use the multi-objective optimization [4]. On other side, we find the works that focus on the graphs, and the knowledge extraction from data modeled by graphs [5], those works are based in general on the frequent pattern search.

In this paper, we are going to present our approach to classify graph modeled data, starting with the citation of some related works in the next section. Section 3 will be the presentation of the approach that contains five main parts; each part will be details thereafter. We will close our paper in Sect. 4 with a conclusion and some perspectives for our future works.

Y. Tabii et al. (Eds.): BDCA 2018, CCIS 872, pp. 144–159, 2018.
https://doi.org/10.1007/978-3-319-96292-4_12

2 Related Works

The knowledge extraction from graphs are based on the frequent pattern search in the graph, this field has started with the attribute pattern search, then it have been upgraded to the sequential pattern, trees pattern and finally the graphs pattern mining.

A sequential pattern is a set of subsequences of attributes patterns separated in time where each subsequence contains the items that occurs in the same moment [6]. The first published algorithm of sequential patterns search was `GSP` [7] as an improvement of `Apriori` [8] by adding the sequential constraint. After `GSP` other algorithms were born by adding the sequential constraint to existing works, which was the case for `Sprade` [9] as an improvement of `Eclat` [10], `FreeSpan` [11] and `PrefixSpan` [12].

The same principle was applied for the trees patterns, which are the structure the most similar to graphs. Trees are useful for the case of information seeking and the representation of semi-structured data such as XML. The algorithms of frequent trees patterns search depend on the type of the tree (Fig. 1) and the type of the inclusion (sub-trees) (Fig. 2), the main algorithms are presented in the table below (Table 1).

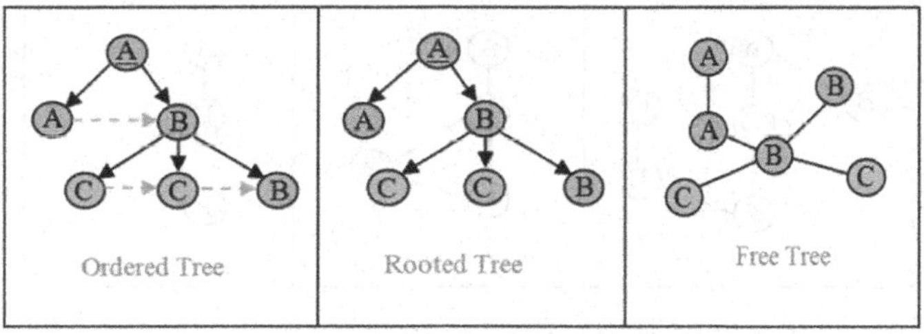

Fig. 1. Types of trees.

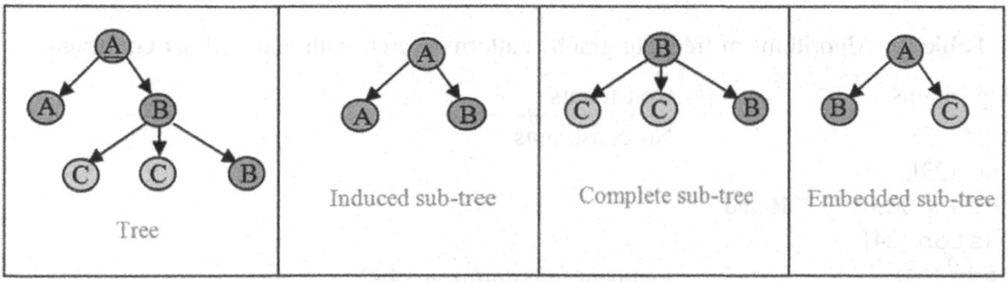

Fig. 2. Types of inclusions in trees (sub-trees).

Table 1. Algorithms of frequent trees patterns search.

Trees	Inclusions	Algorithms
Ordered	Induced	FREQT [13], DryadeParent [14]
	Embedded	TreeMiner [15], Dryade [16]
Rooted	Induced	HybridTreeMiner [17], CMTreeMiner [18]
	Embedded	SLEUTH [19]
Free	Induced	FreeTreeMiner [20], HybridTreeMiner [17], Gaston [21, 24]

After sequential patterns and trees patterns, the first algorithm for frequent graphs patterns search was AGM [22] as an evolution of Apriori by adding the case where the patterns are in the form of connected graphs, its frequency is defined as the number of induced sub-graphs (Fig. 3) that are isomorphic to the searched patterns.

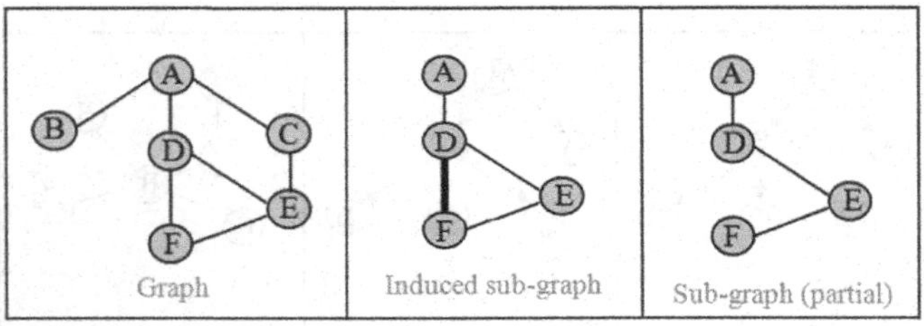

Fig. 3. Types of subgraphs

The next table (Table 2) summarizes the most used algorithms in frequent graphs patterns search sorted by constraints.

Table 2. Algorithms of frequent graphs patterns search with and without constraints.

Algorithms	Constraints
AGM FSG [23], Mofa, gSpan, FFSM and Gaston [24]	No constraints
SPIN [25]	Frequent maximum graphs
CloseGraph [26]	Frequent closed graphs
CloseCut and Splat [27]	Connectivity between nodes higher that a given threshold
gPrune [28]	Constraints on data depending or not depending of patterns
ORIGAMI [29] LEAP [30]	α-orthogonal graphs

A graph G is α-orthogonal if the similarity index between any pair of patterns of G is less than a given threshold $\alpha \in [0, 1]$. This constraint formalizes the redundancy between patterns; the patterns should not be similar as possible.

3 Proposed Approach

In this section we are going to present our approach to classify the graph modeled data using spectral clustering; this approach is composed of five major parts. In the first part we will start with the data definition which can be summed up by the collection of information relating to the treated individuals and the components of each individual. The second part is the graphical modeling of the defined data; in this part we will see the different similarity graphs that we can build from a set of data and the factors that influence the quality of the constructed graph. The third part we will define the various matrix representations of the similarity graph built in the previous section, we will focus on the normalized Laplacian matrices. The fourth part of the process is the heart of the matter; using the spectral analysis of the Laplacian matrices we will try to extract the main clusters from the input data defined in the first section of the process, through the spectral clustering algorithms. The fifth and the last part of the approach is the interpretation of the results provided by the process and the classification of the communities.

3.1 Data Definition

The data definition starts with the collection of the n (heterogeneous) individuals that makes up the treated problem: X_1, X_2, ..., X_n. The next step defines for each individual the set of its p components $X_i = (x_j)_{j \in [1,p]}$.

Let's consider the set of 3 heterogeneous actors in a faculty; the data definition can be summed up as a table (Table 3):

Table 3. Example of Data Definition

	X_1	X_2	X_3
Nom	Student_1	Professor_1	Technician_1
CNE	10-100010	Null	Null
Num	Null	202020	303030
Sector	Software Engineering	Null	Null
Department	Computer Science	Mathematics	Computer Science
Grade	Null	PA	Null

The definition of the components of an individual is to limit for each component the interval of its accepted values; for example, in the case of the component Grade, if the individual is a professor, there is three possible values (AP: Assistant Professor, HP: AP + Habilitation or FP: Full Professor), else it takes `Null` as value.

3.2 Graphical Modeling

The input of the graphical modeling process is the set of the n individuals $\{X_1, X_2, ..., X_n\}$ defined in the previous step, and using a formula to calculate similarities s_{ij} between any pair of data points x_i and x_j, we will connect the vertices v_i and v_j if their similarity value is positive of higher than a given threshold. The result of this step is a similarity graph defined as $G = (V, E)$ where V is the set of vertices and E the set of edges between the vertices of V. We distinguish between three types of similarity graphs; the fully connected graph, the ϵ-neighborhood graphs and the k-nearest neighbor graphs.

Fully Connected Graphs. In this type of graphs, we connect all the pairs of vertices v_i and v_j when $s_{ij} > 0$, the weight w of each existing edge $\{i, j\}$ is the similarity value $s_{ij}(w_{ij} = s_{ij})$. One of the used formulas (1) to calculate similarities is the Gaussian similarity where:

$$s_{ij} = exp\left(-\frac{\|x_i - x_j\|^2}{2\sigma^2}\right) \quad (1)$$

With $\|x_i - x_j\|$ the Euclidian distance between x_i and x_j, and $\sigma > 0$ a parameter to control the size of the neighborhood. In the case of $i = j$ the distance is supposed null. The output is a weighted and undirected graph (Fig. 4).

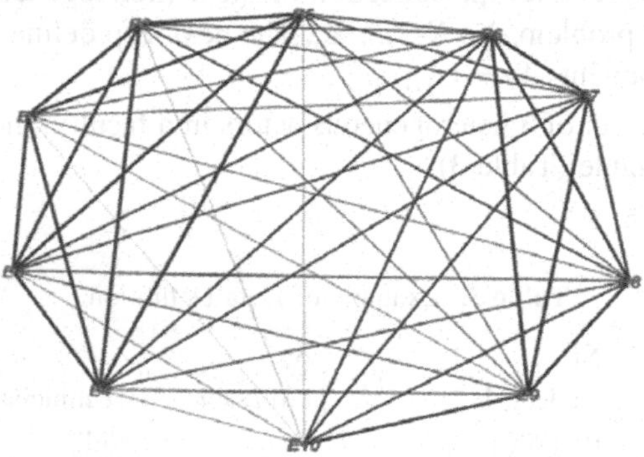

Fig. 4. Example of a fully connected graph with degree 10.

From a similarities table, we can build a fully connected graph, where all the vertices are connected. To visualize this graph we propose the use of an open source graph visualization and manipulation software named Gephi [31], this tool can read an input of similarity values as an Excel table. Gephi gives also the possibility to import and export graphs in GEXF files (Graph Exchange XML Format) (Fig. 5). It gives also the possibility to create and visualize 3D graphs.

```
<graph>
   ...
   <nodes>
      <node id="1" label="x1">
          <viz:size value="10.0"></viz:size>
          <viz:position x="-176.66779" y="233.71866"
                               z="0.0">
          </viz:position>
          <viz:color r="153" g="153" b="0"></viz:color>
      </node>
     ...
   </nodes>
   <edges>
      <edge source="1" target="2" weight="0.27">
      </edge>
        ...
     </edges>
</graph>
```

Fig. 5. GEXF schema example

As we can see, a whole graph can be presented as an XML format file, were we define each node by its properties id, label, position (we add the z coordinate for 3D graphs) and the size to express the importance of the node in the graph where the nodes has different weights. The same thing for the edges, we express each edge by the ids of its source and destination nodes and the weight. This GEXF format can give us the possibility to share and transfer graphs as XML files and apply the algorithms of binary search trees when needed.

One of the main limits of the fully connected graphs is the presence of all the vertices which is not an important information in the case where the weight of the vertex is almost null, on the contrary it increases the complexity of the graph and the time of its generation.

ϵ-Neighborhood Graphs. In this type of graphs, we fix a threshold $\epsilon > 0$ and we connect all the pair of vertices v_i and v_j where $s_{ij} \geq \epsilon$. The weight w_{ij} of a vertex $\{i, j\}$ is given by (2):

$$w_{ij} = \begin{cases} 1 & \text{if } s_{ij} \geq \epsilon \\ 0(i.e\{i,j\} \notin E) & \text{else} \end{cases} \tag{2}$$

The output is a binary and undirected graph.

The major challenge in building ϵ-neighborhood graphs is to choose the parameter ϵ (Fig. 6). An unsupervised choice of this parameter will can give better results than a static or a supervised choice.

The results shown in (Fig. 6) models the same set of individuals, with the same links between them, which are the same data visualized by the fully connected graph in (Fig. 4).

***k*-Nearest Neighbor Graphs.** We fix the parameter k, and we calculate the similarities s_{ij} between all pairs of data points x_i and x_j $(i \neq j)$ and we store the values in a list of similarities l_i associated to x_i. After filling the list, the values have to be sorted, and if s_{ij} is one of the k highest values of l_i, then we consider v_j as a k-nearest neighbors of v_i and we connect them with a directed edge from v_i to v_j weighted with the value of s_{ij}.

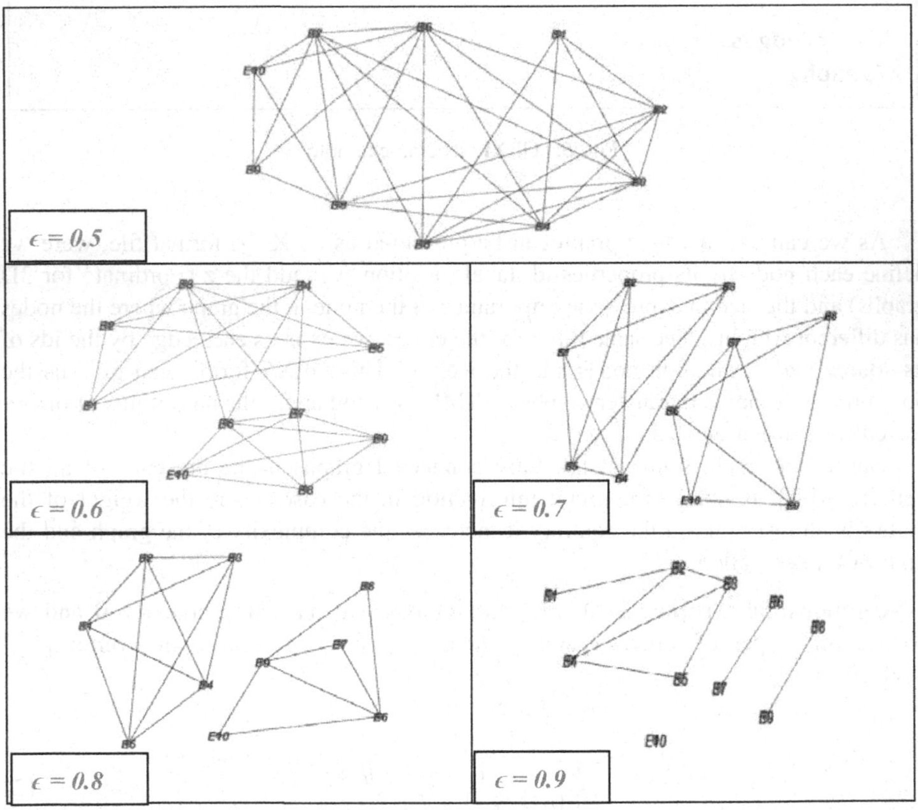

Fig. 6. The influence of the parameter ϵ on the generated ϵ-neighborhood graphs.

The output is a weighted and directed graph.

Note: The value of k is always strictly lower than the order n of the graph; we add the constraint on the parameter k: $k \leq n - 1$.

As the case of the ϵ-neighborhood graphs, the parameter k plays a critical role in the output results provided by the construction algorithm of k-nearest neighbor graphs (Fig. 7); A higher value of k generates a higher number of links between the nodes, when a lower value of k risks of disappearing edges that carries an information about the visualized data.

The minimal degree of a vertex in a k-nearest neighbor graph is k ($d_v \geq k$, $v \in V$); for each vertex v_i, the number of the edges having v_i as source is k, so initially the degree of v_i is equal to the parameter k, but in the other way v_i can be considered as a k-nearest neighbor of another vertex v_j which adds other edges having v_i as a destination vertex and increase its degree.

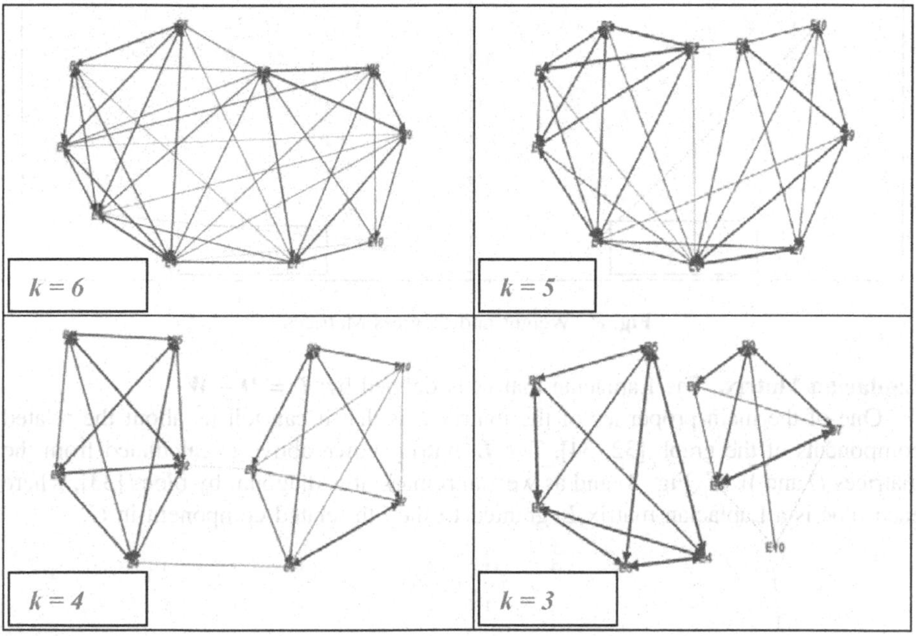

Fig. 7. The influence of the parameter k on the generated k-nearest neighbor graphs

3.3 Matrix Representation

We consider a Graph $G = (V, E)$. The weight matrix W is defined as follow (3):

$$W_{ij} = \begin{cases} w_{ij}, & if \{i,j\} \in E \\ 0, & else \end{cases} \quad (3)$$

Where w_{ij} is the weight of the vertex v_{ij}. And the Degrees matrix D (Fig. 8) is also a square matrix where the degrees are stored in the diagonal of the matrix: $d_i = \sum W_{ij}$, with $(i \neq j)$.

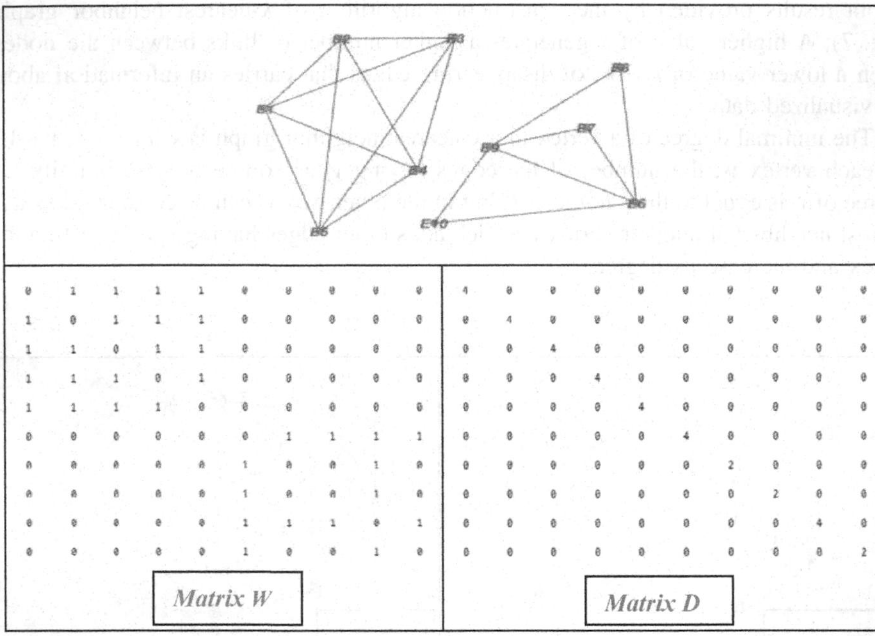

Fig. 8. Weight and Degrees Matrices.

Laplacian Matrix. The Laplacian matrix is defined by: $\boldsymbol{L} = \boldsymbol{D} - \boldsymbol{W}$

One of the main properties of the matrix L is that it can tell us about the related components of the graph [32, 34]. The $\boldsymbol{L}$ matrix shown above is calculated from the matrices D and W of (Fig. 8) and as we can remark, it is diagonal by blocs [33], where each bloc is a Laplacian matrix L_i granted to the i-th related component in G.

$$\begin{pmatrix} 4 & -1 & -1 & -1 & -1 & 0 & 0 & 0 & 0 & 0 \\ -1 & 4 & -1 & -1 & -1 & 0 & 0 & 0 & 0 & 0 \\ -1 & -1 & 4 & -1 & -1 & 0 & 0 & 0 & 0 & 0 \\ -1 & -1 & -1 & 4 & -1 & 0 & 0 & 0 & 0 & 0 \\ -1 & -1 & -1 & -1 & 4 & 0 & 0 & 0 & 0 & 0 \\ 0 & 0 & 0 & 0 & 0 & 4 & -1 & -1 & -1 & -1 \\ 0 & 0 & 0 & 0 & 0 & -1 & 2 & 0 & -1 & 0 \\ 0 & 0 & 0 & 0 & 0 & -1 & 0 & 2 & -1 & 0 \\ 0 & 0 & 0 & 0 & 0 & -1 & -1 & -1 & 4 & -1 \\ 0 & 0 & 0 & 0 & 0 & -1 & 0 & 0 & -1 & 2 \end{pmatrix}$$

L_1 (upper-left block), L_2 (lower-right block)

In this case L_1 is the Laplacian matrix associated to the first related component $Cc_1 = \{E_1, E_2, E_3, E_4, E_5\}$ and the same for L_2 and $Cc_2 = \{E_6, E_7, E_8, E_9, E_{10}\}$

Specter of *L* [32, 34]
Complete graphs: A complete graph K_n is a fully connected graph with n nodes where all the pair of vertices i and j are connected by a vertex $\{i, j\}$. The eigenvalues of the associated Laplacian matrix to K_n are 0 of multiplicity *1* and n of multiplicity $n-1$.
Stars: A star S_n is a graph of n nodes where all the nodes are connected to the central node (except the central node). The eigenvalues of the associated Laplacian matrix to S_n are 0 of multiplicity *1*, n of multiplicity *1* and 1 of multiplicity $n-2$.

Normalized Laplacian Matrix. The normalized Laplacian matrix is defined by:

$$L_N = I - D^{-1/2} W D^{-1/2}$$

L_N is a symmetric matrix since W is symmetric and D diagonal [32]. And I is the identity matrix with the same size of W and D. The matrix $D^{-1/2} W D^{-1/2}$ is a matrix *Temp* where each element is: $mp_{ij} = W_{ij} / \sqrt{d_i d_j}$, with d_i is the degree of the vertex v_i. So the matrix L_N can be defined otherwise:

$$L_{Nij} = \begin{cases} 1 & \text{if } i = j \text{ and } d_i \neq 0 \\ -W_{ij}/\sqrt{d_i d_j} & \text{if } i \neq j \text{ and } \{i,j\} \in E \\ 0 & \text{else} \end{cases} \tag{4}$$

Another normalized Laplacian matrix can be calculated from L_N, we can call it the Absolute Laplacian matrix, which is defined by:

$$L_{abs} = D^{-1/2} W D^{-1/2} = I - L_N$$

$$\begin{pmatrix} 0 & 0,25 & 0,25 & 0,25 & 0,25 & 0 & 0 & 0 & 0 & 0 \\ 0,25 & 0 & 0,25 & 0,25 & 0,25 & 0 & 0 & 0 & 0 & 0 \\ 0,25 & 0,25 & 0 & 0,25 & 0,25 & 0 & 0 & 0 & 0 & 0 \\ 0,25 & 0,25 & 0,25 & 0 & 0,25 & 0 & 0 & 0 & 0 & 0 \\ 0,25 & 0,25 & 0,25 & 0,25 & 0 & 0 & 0 & 0 & 0 & 0 \\ 0 & 0 & 0 & 0 & 0 & 0 & 0,35 & 0,35 & 0,25 & 0,35 \\ 0 & 0 & 0 & 0 & 0 & 0,35 & 0 & 0 & 0,35 & 0 \\ 0 & 0 & 0 & 0 & 0 & 0,35 & 0 & 0 & 0,35 & 0 \\ 0 & 0 & 0 & 0 & 0 & 0,25 & 0,35 & 0,35 & 0 & 0,35 \\ 0 & 0 & 0 & 0 & 0 & 0,35 & 0 & 0 & 0,35 & 0 \end{pmatrix}$$

There is a relation between the specters of L_{abs} and L_N; generally, if we note λ_1, λ_2,.., λ_n as the n eigenvalues associated to L_{abs} sorted in descending order ($\lambda_i \leq \lambda_{i+1}$, $1 \leq i \leq n-1$)

And Λ_1, Λ_2, ..., Λ_n as the n eigenvalues associated to L_N sorted in ascending order ($\Lambda_i \geq \Lambda_{i+1}$, $1 \leq i \leq n-1$)

We notice that $\Lambda_i = 1 - \lambda_i$ ($i \in [1, n]$), with always $\lambda_n \approx 1$ and $\Lambda_1 \approx 0$.

L_{abs}	L_N
-0.7414	0
-0.25	0.0086
-0.25	1
-0.25	1
-0.25	1.25
-0.25	1.25
0	1.25
0	1.25
0.9914	1.25
1	1.7414

Specter of L_{abs} [32]

Bipartite graphs: A bipartite graph $G = (V, E)$ is a graph where $V = V_1 \cup V_2$, with $V1 \cap V2 = \emptyset$, we can say a graph is bipartite if the specter of its associated L_{abs} is symmetric.

Complete graphs: The eigenvalues of a matrix L_{abs} associated to a complete graph K_n are 1 of multiplicity 1 and $\alpha = -1/(n-1)$ of multiplicity $n-1$. The Form L_{abs} associated to a complete graph is always as following.

$$\begin{bmatrix} 0 & \alpha & \alpha & \cdots & \alpha \\ \alpha & 0 & \alpha & \cdots & \vdots \\ \vdots & \vdots & 0 & \cdots & \vdots \\ \vdots & \cdots & \cdots & 0 & \alpha \\ \alpha & \cdots & \cdots & \cdots & 0 \end{bmatrix}$$

3.4 Spectral Clustering Algorithms

Spectral Clustering is an unsupervised classification based on the spectral analysis of the input; generally using the eigenvectors of a similarity matrix (Laplacian matrices in our case). Thereafter we are going to focus on the normalized Spectral Clustering which uses the normalized Laplacian matrices [33]. We distinguish between two types of normalized SC algorithms; the first uses the L_N matrix and the second uses the L_{abs} matrix.

Normalized Spectral Clustering [35] (2002)

//Input : The matrix W and the number of clusters k
//Output : Clusters C_1, …, C_k partitioning the vertices

1- Calculate the Normalized Laplacian matrix L_N
2- Calculate the k eigenvectors $u_1,\ldots,u_k$ associated to the k smallest eigenvalues of the matrix L_N
3- Build a matrix U *with the size* n x k where the columns are $u_1,\ldots,u_k$
4- Build the matrix T with the size n x k which normalizes the lines of U to an Euclidian norme i.e $t_{ij} = u_{ij} / \sqrt{\sum_k (u_{ik})^2}$
5- Create the clusters C_1, ..., C_k on the n lines of T using k-means

Absolute Spectral Clustering [36] (2011)

//Input : The matrix W and the number of clusters k
//Output : Clusters C_1, …, C_k partitioning the vertices $\{v_1, \ldots, v_n\}$

1- Calculate the Normalized Laplacian matrix L_{abs}
2- Calculate the k eigenvectors $u_1,\ldots,u_k$ associated to the k largest eigenvalues of the matrix L_N in absolute value.
3- Build a matrix U *with the size* n x k where the columns are $u_1,\ldots,u_k$
4- Create the clusters C_1, ..., C_k on the n lines of T using k-means

To see the behavior of the last Absolute Spectral Clustering algorithm, we consider the graph following, with $k = 2$. And we calculate the matrix L_{abs} and its eigenvalues and eigenvectors.

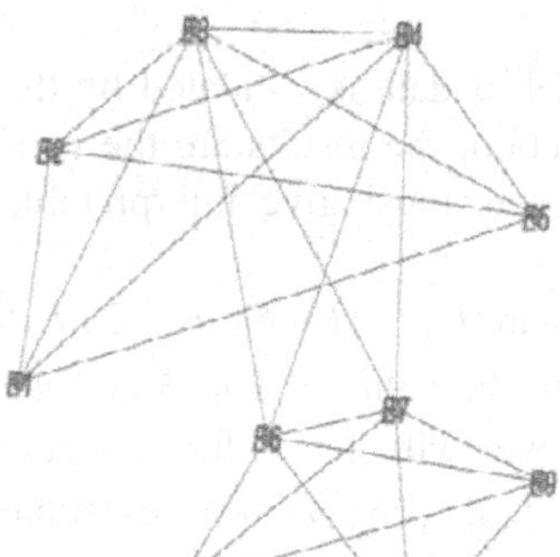

$$\begin{pmatrix}
0 & 0,25 & 0,2 & 0,2 & 0,25 & 0 & 0 & 0 & 0 & 0 \\
0,25 & 0 & 0,2 & 0,2 & 0,25 & 0 & 0 & 0 & 0 & 0 \\
0,2 & 0,2 & 0 & 0,17 & 0,2 & 0,17 & 0,17 & 0 & 0 & 0 \\
0,2 & 0,2 & 0,17 & 0 & 0,2 & 0,17 & 0,17 & 0 & 0 & 0 \\
0,25 & 0,25 & 0,2 & 0,2 & 0 & 0 & 0 & 0 & 0 & 0 \\
0 & 0 & 0,17 & 0,17 & 0 & 0 & 0,17 & 0,2 & 0,2 & 0,2 \\
0 & 0 & 0,17 & 0,17 & 0 & 0,17 & 0 & 0,2 & 0,2 & 0,2 \\
0 & 0 & 0 & 0 & 0 & 0,2 & 0,2 & 0 & 0,25 & 0,25 \\
0 & 0 & 0 & 0 & 0 & 0,2 & 0,2 & 0,25 & 0 & 0,25 \\
0 & 0 & 0 & 0 & 0 & 0,2 & 0,2 & 0,25 & 0,25 & 0
\end{pmatrix}$$

L_{abs}

The eigenvalues associated to L_{abs} in this example are:
$\lambda_1 = -0.4285$; $\lambda_2 = \lambda_3 = \lambda_4 = \lambda_5 = -0.25$; $\lambda_6 = \lambda_7 = -0.17$; $\lambda_8 = 0.0151$; $\lambda_9 = \mathbf{0.7585}$ and $\lambda_{10} = \mathbf{0.9949}$.

Table 4. The matrix U and the result clusters.

Matrix U		***k-means***
λ_9	λ_{10}	
u_1	u_2	***Cluster number ϵ [1,k=2]***
-0.3611	0.2872	2
-0.3611	0.2872	2
-0.2333	0.3554	2
-0.2333	0.3554	2
-0.3611	0.2872	2
0.2333	0.3554	1
0.2333	0.3554	1
0.3611	0.2872	1
0.3611	0.2872	1
0.3611	0.2872	1

For $k = 2$, the 2 largest eigenvalues are λ_9 and λ_{10}. So, we consider the eigenvectors associated to λ_9 and λ_{10}, noted respectively u_1 and u_2. Then the matrix U composed of u_1 and u_2 will have the form of a table (Table 4).

3.5 Results Interpretation

The process of the knowledge extraction from any model of data is validated by the results interpretation, in the case of the community detection; the results are the generated clusters in the output of the process; those clusters must give interpretable information about the processed data points.

In the case of the matrix U in (Table 4), the clusters are $\boldsymbol{C_1} = \{E_1, E_2, E_3, E_4, E_5\}$ and $\boldsymbol{C_2} = \{E_6, E_7, E_8, E_9, E_{10}\}$ (Fig. 9). And if we increase the value of k to 3 and we restart the Absolute Spectral Clustering Algorithm we will have the clusters $\boldsymbol{C_1} = \{E_3, E_4\}$, $\boldsymbol{C_2} = \{E_1, E_2, E_5\}$ and $\boldsymbol{C_3} = \{E_6, E_7, E_8, E_9, E_{10}\}$ (Fig. 9). For example in the case when we deal with a set of people in university, we will remark that in a first time the algorithms classify students in a cluster, professors in another one, and other individuals in the other clusters. But when we run the algorithm with higher number of clusters we'll see that even the student cluster will be divided into other clusters that group the students by their common components such as the students studying in the same class or the students having the diploma in the same year or with the convergent degrees.

Running the algorithm with variable thresholds can give us other information about the input data points, some information are even not expected or waited, and this is the advantage of the knowledge extraction process.

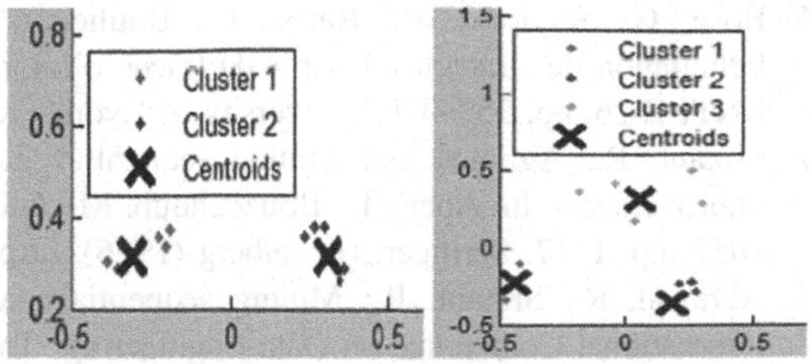

Fig. 9. *k*-means with $k = 2$ and $k = 3$.

The choice of the similarity graph and the selection of the variable parameters of the different phases of the process play an important role in the classification of the nodes of a graph; the parameter ϵ for the ϵ-neighborhood graphs, the parameter σ in the case of the use of a Gaussian similarity and the parameter k for the k-nearest neighbors graphs.

4 Conclusions

In this paper, we have presented our approach for the classification of modeled data by graphs, starting with matrix representation of the chosen similarity graph and the spectral analysis of the normalized and unnormalized Laplacian matrices. This approach can be adapted to several use cases where the set of data can be modeled by graphs using a similarity function. The limits of the spectral clustering are generally encountered in the unnormalized case, where the adding of a set of data points can change the partitioning indefinitely [37] and generate a meaningless clusters from the dataset. Therefore, the normalized version of spectral clustering algorithms proofs its strengths in both theoretical and practical cases. As perspectives, we have already started to adapt our approach to a use case and the result seems to be satisfying for a medium number of data points, waiting for a large dataset to see the performances of the process. In addition we are studying the possibility to link the first phase of the process which is the data definition to an object relational model; in this case the data will be extracted automatically from a database without defining each data point.

References

1. Jourdan, L.: Métaheuristiques pour l'extraction de connaissances: Application à la génomique. Thesis. University of Lile 1, France (2003)
2. Alaoui, A.: Application des techniques de métaheuristiques pour l'optimisation de la tache de la classification de la fouille de données. Thesis. Algeria (2012)
3. Jaques, J.: Classification sur données médicales à l'aide de méthodes d'optimisation et datamining, appliquée au pre-sceening dans les essais cliniques. Thesis. France (2013)
4. Jourdan, L.: Optimisation multiobjectif pour l'extraction de connaissances floue sur données massives et mal réparties. Thesis subject proposed by L. Jourdan. France (2017)
5. Pennerath, F.: Méthodes d'extraction de connaissances à partir de données modélisables par des graphes, application à des problèmes de synthèse organique. Thesis. Chapter 1 and 2. University of Nancy 1, France (2009)

6. Bosc, G., Kaytoue, M., Raïssi, C., Boulicaut, J.: Fouille de motifs séquentiels pour l'élicitation de stratégies à partir de traces d'interactions entre agents en compétition, vol. RNTI-E-26, pp. 359–370. University of Lyon, France (2014)
7. Srikant, R., Agrawal, R.: Mining sequential patterns: generalizations and performance improvements. In: Apers, P., Bouzeghoub, M., Gardarin, G. (eds.) EDBT 1996. LNCS, vol. 1057, pp. 1–17. Springer, Heidelberg (1996). https://doi.org/10.1007/BFb0014140
8. Agrawal, R., Srikant, R.: Mining sequential patterns. In: Proceedings of the Eleventh International Conference on Data Engineering, Taiwan (1995)
9. Zaki, M.: SPADE: an efficient algorithm for mining frequent sequences. Mach. Learn. **42**(1–2), 31–60 (2001)
10. Zaki, M.: New algorithms for fast discovery of association rules. In: Proceedings of the KDD 1997 (1997)
11. Han, J., et al.: FreeSpan: frequent pattern-projected sequential pattern mining. In: Proceedings of the sixth ACM SIGKDD International Conference on Knowledge Discovery and Data Mining, pp. 355–359 (2000)
12. Han, J., et al.: Prefixspan: mining sequential patterns efficiently by prefix-projected pattern growth. In: Proceedings of the 17th International Conference on Data Engineering, pp. 215–224 (2001)
13. Asai, T., et al.: Efficient substructure discovery from large semi-structured data. In: Proceedings of the 2nd Annual SIAM Symposium on Data Mining (2002)
14. Termier, A., et al.: DryadeParent, an efficient and robust closed attribute tree mining algorithm. In: IEEE Transactions on Knowledge and Data Engineering (2008)
15. Zaki, M.: Efficiently mining frequent trees in a forest. In: Proceedings of the SIGKDD'02 Conference, Edmonton, Alberta (2002)
16. Termier, A., et al.: Dryade: a new approach for discovering closed frequent trees in heterogeneous tree databases. In: 4th IEEE International Conference on Data Mining (2004)
17. Chi, Y., et al.: HybridTreeMiner: an efficient algorithm for mining frequent rooted trees and free trees using canonical forms. In: Proceedings of the 16th International Conference on Scientific and Statistical Database Management, 2004, Santorini Island (2004)
18. Chi, Y., et al.: CMTreeMiner: mining both closed and maximal frequent subtrees. In: Proceedings of the 8th Pacific-Asia Conference, PAKDD 2004, Sydney (2004)
19. Zaki, M.: Efficiently mining frequent embedded unordered trees. Fundamenta Informaticae **66**(1–2), 33–52 (2005)
20. Chi, Y., et al.: Indexing and mining free trees. In: IEEE International Conference on Data Mining ICDM 2003 Third, Melbourne (2003)
21. Nijssen, S., et al.: The gaston tool for frequent subgraph mining. Electron. Notes Theor. Comput. Sci. **127**(1), 77–87 (2005)
22. Inokushi, A., et al.: An apriori-based algorithm for mining frequent substructures from graph data. In: European Conference on Principles of Data Mining and Knowledge Discovery, pp. 13–23 (2002)
23. Kuramochi, M., et al.: Frequent subgraph discovery. In: Proceedings IEEE International Conference on Data Mining ICDM 2001, San Jose (2001)
24. Wörlein, M., et al.: A quantitative comparison of the subgraph miners MoFa, gSpan, FFSM, and Gaston. In: Proceedings of the 9th European Conference on Principles and Practice of Knowledge Discovery in Databases, Porto (2005)
25. Huan, J., et al.: SPIN: mining maximal frequent subgraphs from graph databases. In: Proceedings of the Tenth ACM SIGKDD International Conference on Knowledge Discovery And Data Mining, pp. 581–586, Seattle (2005)

26. Yan, X., Han, J.: CloseGraph: mining closed frequent graph patterns. In: Proceedings of the Ninth ACM SIGKDD International Conference on Knowledge Discovery and Data Mining, pp. 286–295 (2003)
27. Yan, X., et al.: Mining closed relational graphs with connectivity constraints. In: Proceedings of the Eleventh ACM SIGKDD International Conference on Knowledge Discovery in Data Mining, pp. 324–333 (2005)
28. Zhu, F., et al.: gPrune: a constraint pushing framework for graph pattern mining. In: Pacific-Asia Conference on Knowledge Discovery and Data Mining, pp. 388–400 (2007)
29. Al Hasan, M., et al.: ORIGAMI: mining representative orthogonal graph patterns. In: Seventh IEEE International Conference on Data Mining. IEEE (2007)
30. Yan, X., et al.: Mining significant graph patterns by leap search. In: Proceedings of the 2008 ACM SIGMOD International Conference on Management of Data, pp. 433–444 (2008)
31. Gephi, The Open Graph Viz Platform (open source). https://gephi.org/
32. Matias, C.: Analyse statistique des graphes (2015)
33. von Luxburg, U.: Technical Report No. TR-149: A tutorial on Spectral Clustering. Max Planck Institute for Biological Cybernetics (2007)
34. Chung, F.: Lectures on Spectral Graph Theory, Chapter 1. University of Pennsylvania, Philadelphia, Pennsylvania 19104 (1997)
35. Ng, A., Jordan, M., Weiss, Y.: On spectral clustering: analysis and an algorithm. Adv. Neural. Inf. Process. Syst. **14**, 849–856 (2002)
36. Rohe, K., et al.: Spectral clustering and the high-dimensional stochastic blockmodel. Ann. Stat. **39**(4), 1878–1915 (2011)
37. von Luxburg, U., et al.: Limits of spectral clustering. Advances in Neural Information Processing Systems (NIPS) 17, pp. 857–864. MIT Press, Cambridge (2005)

Automatic Classification of Air Pollution and Human Health

Rachida El Morabet[1(✉)], Abderrahmane Adoui El Ouadrhiri[2,3(✉)], Jaroslav Burian[2], Said Jai Andaloussi[3], Said El Mouak[1], and Abderrahim Sekkaki[3]

[1] Department of Geography, LADES, CERES, FLSH-M, Hassan II University of Casablanca, B.P. 546, Mohammedia, Morocco
rachidaelmorabet@yahoo.fr, mouaksaid@gmail.com

[2] Department of Geoinformatics, KGI, FS, Palacky University, 17. listopadu 50, 771 46 Olomouc, Czech Republic
jaroslav.burian@upol.cz

[3] Department of Mathematics and Computer Science, LR2I, FSAC, Hassan II University of Casablanca, B.P. 5366, Maarif, Casa, Morocco
{a.adouielouadrhiri-etu,said.jaiandaloussi, abderrahim.sekkaki}@etude.univcasa.ma

Abstract. We are entering an era of data, which are spatially and temporally referenced, this paper offers an opportunity to enhance geographic understanding, more especially in the term of air pollution and its relationship with human health, especially in the city of Mohammedia (Northern part of Morocco). Authors build a tool in the form of data mining scheme, to couple the data with machine learning, in order to automatically align the features of massive and complex data sets for human interaction in environmental social systems. New proposed approach is based on PCA (Principle Component Analysis) and K-SVM (Kernel Support Vector Machine). The system tests result is accomplished, an accuracy of 93% in testing data taken from daily values during 3 years.

Keywords: Air pollution · Weather conditions · Human health Machine learning · PCA and K-SVM

1 Introduction

Air pollution is a biological, chemical or physical alteration of the air in the atmosphere, affecting people of all ages through many countries and regions, especially among children [1]. It occurs when the components of harmful gases, dust, smoke accumulate and enter into the atmosphere in the air in high enough concentrations, so that, humans, animals, and plants have a difficulty to survive. It is often caused by human activities, like transportation, agriculture, mining, construction, industrial work, etc.

Y. Tabii et al. (Eds.): BDCA 2018, CCIS 872, pp. 160–170, 2018.
https://doi.org/10.1007/978-3-319-96292-4_13

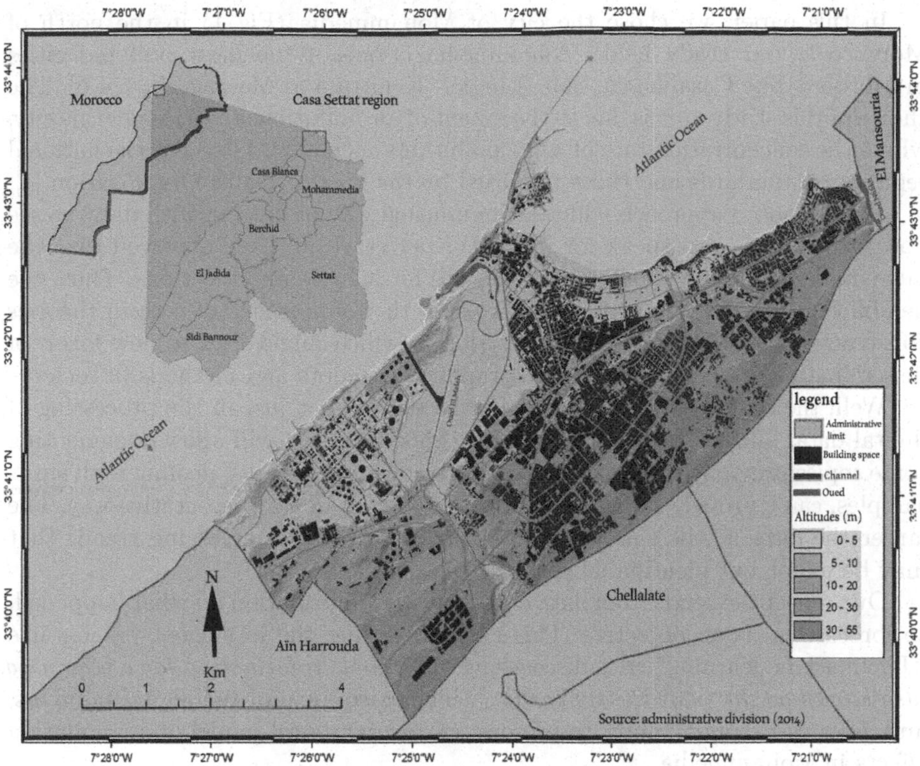

Fig. 1. Mohammedia

In addition, the proximity of industrial and urban areas has led to a situation of cohabitation of the population with air pollution. Therefore, the study will be focusing on the city of Mohammedia.

Well, even if the air pollution divides the city of Mohammedia into two regions, one is very polluted, the other has a lesser degree of pollution, so the population is not immune to its consequences due to its compulsory movements and also the atmospheric conditions (e.g. the wind's speed).

We find, on the other side, that the air quality is not localized and affected by several factors, such as the geographic and wind characteristics. Therefore, the study should not focus on one region only; for instance, EL ALIA and/or FDALAT; where the air quality monitoring stations are located.

Plus, as what has been indicated in [2], some air pollutants are able to displace far from the sources, even at regional scale, due to the long atmospheric lifetimes.

In general, Kampa and Castanas [3] and *(MassDEP)* indicated that a high number of people who were exposed to high levels of certain air pollutants suffer from diseases, ranging from simple symptoms like coughing and the irritation of the respiratory tract, to chronic, like lung and asthma, breathing difficulties, risks of heart attack *(MassDEP)* and cancer in long-term.

In this paper, we chose the city of Mohammedia (Fig. 1) in the north of Morocco as our study field. Mohammedia is one of the most polluted cities in Morocco, like Casablanca, Safi, Tangier, Kenitra and Marrakech [1,4,5]. The choice of this study area is due to the extent of air pollution standards in this city, where the concentration rate of some pollutants such as PM exceeds the national regulatory standards and those tolerated by the World Health Organization [4].

The proposed approach will take an unusual way of dealing with data, to see how far the data can speak for itself. Wiener et al. [6] have observed that the huge amount of data somehow compensate for it little imperfections. Thus, the flexibility of resolution would allow revising the foundations of certain theories constructed for other levels of observation in which might lead to new forms of dissemination of geographical, cartographical concepts and methods in society.

Well, the real evolution brought by the data is not just in the processing of digital data, but especially in the scale of this data that will allow documenting some topics previously out of reach. Since traditional surveys, dealing with small samples, can't provide sufficient data to treat them in a representative way. The larger the data is, the easiest it is or will be to identify emerging trends that may be minor but identifiable with the big data.

Our concept extends from data capture to get information on what happened, to forecasting as an objective. This challenge using the intelligent process like "The machine learning" tries discovering *any simple information for a beginning also known as the invisible dimension*, which exists behind the digital numbers, and gives us an opportunity to present a spatiotemporal model of air pollution effects in Mohammedia.

Therefore, the main idea is the ability to learn during a training phase and then generalize the knowledge acquired to predict new weather situations.

In air pollution, smog and soot are the most prevalent types. Thus, the change in the atmospheric composition is primarily due to the combustion of fossil fuels, used for the generation of energy and transportation [3]. Therefore, Air pollutants have the ability to transit short or long distances and impact on the human health. There are four categories of Air pollutants:

- Gaseous pollutants (e.g. SO_2, NO_2, CO, Ozone, Volatile Organic Compounds),
- Persistent organic pollutants (e.g. Dioxins),
- Heavy metals (e.g. Lead, Mercury),
- Particulate Matter.

Many works have been presented in this field, such as the work of Akbari et al. [7] who studied the elevated temperatures that increases cooling-energy use and accelerate the formation of urban smog, plus how to reduce energy use and improve air quality. Kampa and Castanas [3] presented a brief review of air pollutants on human health, supported by a number of epidemiological studies. Moreover, Ghorani-Azam et al. [8] added practical measures to reduce air pollution (Normalization) and indicated some long-term diseases complications and diseases.

On the other side, Wyborn and Evans [9] presented an environmental research interoperability platform that could help in High-Performance Computing Data. Wiener et al. [6] suggested "*A Conceptual Architectural Framework for Spatio-Temporal Analytics at Scale*".

While for human health, the study is focussing only on the aspect of health effects that related to air quality. According to this study relationship analysis between air quality and health effects will be carried out only on the outdoor air quality of Mohammedia.

Conferring to Ghorani-Azam et al. [8], "*In terms of health hazards, every unusual suspended material in the air, which causes difficulties in a normal function of the human organs, is defined as air toxicants*". The effects of air pollutants are ophthalmologic, cardiovascular, respiratory, ophthalmologic, neuropsychiatric, hematologic, dermatologic, immunologic, and reproductive systems diseases, and may also induce a variety of cancers in the long term [10,11].

On the other hand, even with the spread of few air toxicants, it is dangerous for vulnerable groups, children, and elderly people as well as patients suffering from respiratory and cardiovascular diseases.

This work is prepared on the basis of the information provided by:

- Weather data in Mohammedia 2014, 2015 and 2016. Directorate of National Meteorology, Morocco, (details in Proposed Approach Section),
- Report on the Assessment of Ambient Air Quality in Mohammedia 2014, 2015 and 2016. Directorate of National Meteorology, Morocco,
- Field investigations of 2015: the analysis of the diseases files related to air pollution of the Social Security System known as Caisse Nationale de Securite Sociale (CNSS) and the files of five health centers.

The remainder of the paper is organized as follows; the proposed approach is described in Sect. 2. The experimental results and discussions are reported in Sect. 3. Finally, the conclusion is given in Sect. 4.

2 Proposed Approach

Machine learning algorithms are automatic analytic models that are allowing a computer to work, evaluate decisions and predict future options. They can compare the data for each component with the history of variations. From this comparison, the algorithms can determine the best forecasting programs based on real-time information and historical data.

The interpretation of information in 2 to 3 dimensions is easier. Thus, the main idea is to transform the data from high-dimensional data to lower dimensional space while retaining as much of the information as possible. After that, the classification of information will take two classes by K-SVM. Finally, we calculate the accuracy level of forecasting and show its influence on human health.

2.1 PCA

The principal component analysis is an approach that is both geometric and statistical, its strategy is: First, to extract linear structure from high-dimensional data. Thus, it defines a linear relationship between the original variables of a dataset by finding new principal axes. Second, the Principal Component Analysis could be viewed as a linear mapping from a dataset to a lower dimensional set, when we want to compress a set of N variables, to n [12]. Therefore, the main axes of principal component analysis are a better choice, from the point of view of inertia or variance.

The basic equation of Principal component analysis is, in matrix notation, represented by

$$Y = W'X \tag{1}$$

$$y_{ij} = w_{1i}x_{1j} + w_{2i}x_{2j} + w_{3i}x_{3j} + w_{4i}x_{4j} + ... + w_{pi}x_{pj} \tag{2}$$

Where W is a matrix of coefficients that is determined by PCA [12]. The out factors of the original variables are formed by a set of p linear equations. And the matrix of weights, W, is calculated from the variance-covariance matrix, S.

$$s_{ij} = \frac{\sum_{k=1}^{n} (x_{ik} - \bar{x_i})(x_{jk} - \bar{x_j})}{n-1} \tag{3}$$

2.2 SVM and Kernel

Support vector machine is a set of techniques supervised learning to solve problems of discrimination and regression.

SVMs could be used to resolve discrimination problems, that is, define which class a sample belongs to, or regression, and predict the numerical value of a variable [13]. Solving these two problems involves building a function h in which an input vector x matches an exit y:

$$y = h(x) \tag{4}$$

In addition, SVMs could expeditiously perform a non-linear classification utilizing the kernel [14]:

$$k(\boldsymbol{x}_i, \boldsymbol{x}_j) \tag{5}$$

2.3 Proposed Method

The dataset on which we based on this work was defined as the reported data from 2014 to 2016 (3 years) by two stations of air quality measurement in Mohammedia, with daily frequency of Min/Max of Temperature, Pressure, Humidity, Air Quality Index, Nitrogen dioxide (NO_2), Ozone (O_3), Particulate Matter (PM_{10}), Sulfur Dioxide (SO_2), Wind speed and temperature, plus Rainfall with Heat index.

Our concept is to choose the relevant data of the elements indicated previously and presented by PCA, we focus on 2-dimensional principal axes, the axes

1 and 2 preserve more than 85% of relevant data after dimension reduction from the original (weather information and value of pollutant substances). Besides that, the objective of the adoption of kernel SVM was to classify our data into 2 parts, *Safe: 0* and *Dangerous: 1*.

The kernel adopted is Radial Basis Function (6), in which the non-linear distribution of data could be treated. The dataset is divided into 2 parts with random selection, Training and Testing sets, 80% and 20%, respectively. The forecasting of air pollution was based on the following binary classes defined for Mohammedia (Table 2):

- Class 0 - Good (Safe)
- Class 1 - Unhealthy (Dangerous)

$$k\left(\boldsymbol{x}_i, \boldsymbol{x}_j\right) = exp\left(-\frac{\left\|\boldsymbol{x}_i - \boldsymbol{x}_j\right\|^2}{2\sigma^2}\right) \tag{6}$$

$$P = \frac{TP}{TP+FP}$$

$$S = \frac{TP}{TP+FN} \tag{7}$$

$$A = \frac{TP+TN}{TP+FP+FN+TN}$$

Table 1. Confusion matrix for binary classification

		Classifier	
		Class 0	Class 1
Truth	Class 0	TN	FP
	Class 1	FN	TP

Moreover, to evaluate the performance of this approach, it was measured in terms of the positive predictive value *P*, sensitivity *S*, and accuracy *A* (Table 1, 7) to identify any abnormal values, and to show their influence on human health. This part briefly summarizes the main idea that is for harvesting the good content "feature selection" from the original data by PCA and examines its effectiveness by k-SVM that is an excellent classification of detection, regression, to detect the "safe" and "dangerous" situation of air under a non-linear distribution of data using a Python dictionary implementation.

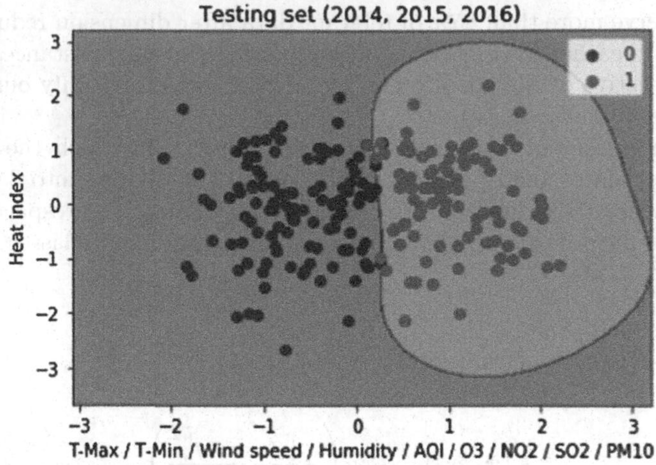

Fig. 2. Testing 20% (2014, 2015, 2016). (Color figure online)

3 Results and Discussion

According to the experiences based on our approach, we could display the classification of the air pollution by independent parameters (Temperature, SO_2, NO_2, etc) and the heat index, we were able to find the results listed in Figs. 2 and 3, and Tables 2 and 3.

Our approach presented a good report based on the training dataset of 2014, 2015 and 2016 taken from two stations in Mohammedia. Thus, in testing, we observed that the red and green segmentations, which present the Unhealthy and the Good (acceptable) zone, are well determined; we can also say that more than 90% of classification was correct. We notice that our algorithm was adaptable in the part of 2017 (Testing 2017), in which we took the data of random 20 days of the year 2017 (between January and June), and we found a good classification accuracy. We note also that the sensitivity was reaching 92% in testing data, the precision and the accuracy have 94% and 93% respectively.

Thus, we were able to forecast the situation of the air pollution rapidly. Moreover, we can now even mention an alarm signal in critical cases.

On the other side, once the substances SO_2, NO_2 etc. are released into the air, they are transported under the effect of winds, rain, temperature gradients in the atmosphere and according to heat index, they may undergo transformations by chemical reactions[1], and they are able to lead to bad influences on the human health.

In comparison with the work of Squalli Houssaini et al. [15] our work does not just focus on asthma among schoolchildren in Mohammedia, but we took in our investigation a great consideration of different ages and diseases related

[1] World Organization for the Protection of the Environment (OMPE: 2017) http://www.ompe.org/les-consequences-de-la-pollution-de-lair/.

Table 2. Confusion matrices for training, testing data (2014, 2015, 2016) and test 2017.

		Training (80%)		Testing (20%)		Test 20 days on 2017	
		Classifier		Classifier		Classifier	
		Class 0	Class 1	Class 0	Class 1	Class 0	Class 1
Truth	Class 0	396	31	098	006	014	001
	Class 1	19	431	009	107	000	005

Table 3. Performance evaluation [2014, 2015, 2016 and 2017].

		Training (80%)	Testing (20%)	Test 20 days on 2017
Performance	*S*	95%	92%	100%
	P	93%	94%	83%
	A	75%	93%	95%

Table 4. Distribution of diseases registered in (CNSS) in 2003 and 2015

The diseases	2003 [16]	2015
Respiratory diseases	237	1500
Gastrology	118	350
Diseases of the eye, nose, ear and throat	106	309
Neurosurgery	101	500
Skin diseases	92	250
Diabetes	58	150
Cardiovascular+ BLOOD DISEASES	102	900
Bones and joints	39	110
Mental and psychological	23	500
Urology	18	130
Others	13	165

Table 5. Respiratory diseases infections at children under 5 years (Health center)

Health center years	Target population	Pneumonia	Throat	Ear	Asthma	Tuberculosis
2000 [16]	17788	1285	635	817	49	288
2015	18700	1459	1712	944	350	362

to air pollution. Thus, we could present more details. By the way, if we take the CNSS results of 2003 [16] and 2015 (Field of investigation), we note that, in 2015, the diseases related to air pollution were *respiratory diseases, diseases of the eye, nose, ear, and throat, cardiovascular + blood diseases* outweigh all other diseases and a very large increase in diseases involving air pollution as mental and psychological diseases.

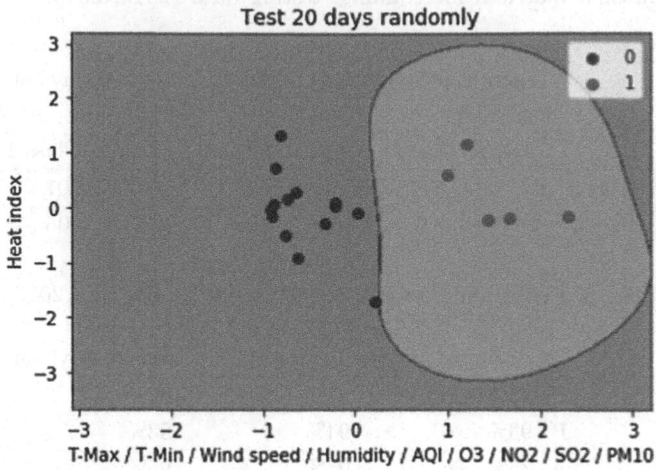

Fig. 3. Test 20 days randomly in 2017. (Color figure online)

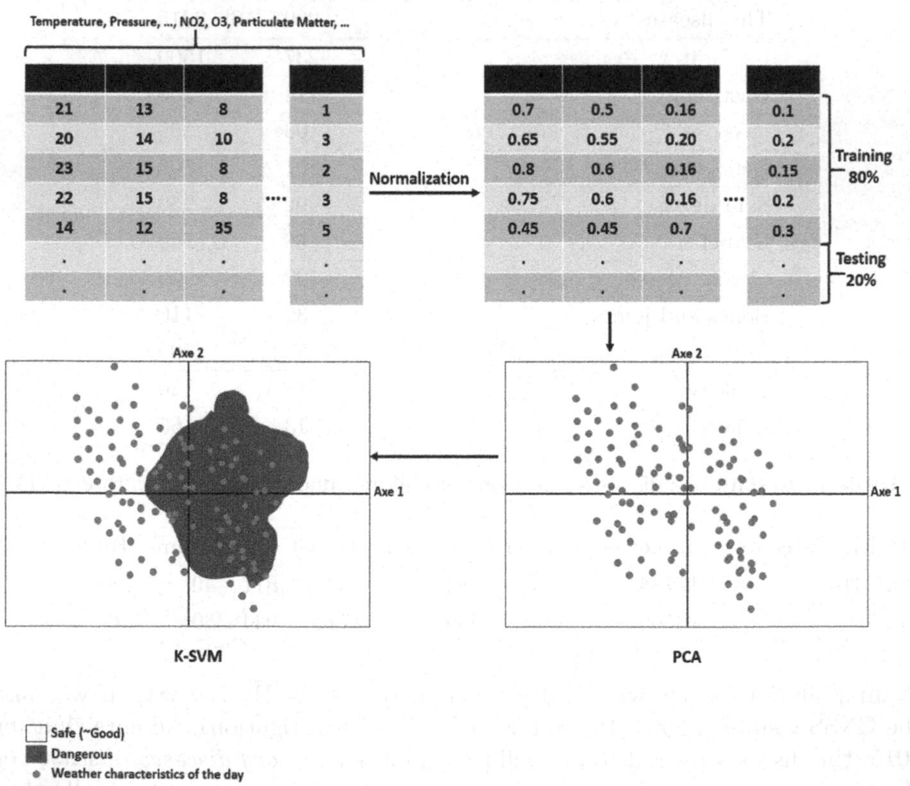

Fig. 4. The classification system of air pollution.

On the other side, the average population growth rate between 2004 and 2014 was 0.96% (188619 and 207670, respectively)[2]. According to Table 4, the result of the average disease growth rate is 16.24% for diseases caused by air pollution and 19.00% for neuronal and psychological diseases. The increase in the disease rate is higher than the population growth. Moreover, the augmentation of diseases related to air pollution of children aged less than 5 years increased from 20% in 2000 to 25.8% in 2015 (Table 5), and with other factors like smoking, genetic and infectious diseases, they will increase and present a high-risk threat. Thus, this result is significant and probably a red alert for new generations.

In general, this approach (Fig. 4) gives us an air quality forecast, adding the above results, we conclude that the chronic exposure to air pollution for the adult and children (future generation) leads to the most dangerous impacts on the health.

4 Conclusions

The collection and analysis of statistical data, in real time, can provide concrete support for decision-making, especially during disruptions, and more particularly on a very important subject such as human health and pollution. We mention that machine learning opens up another alternative to prediction. Thus, with 93% of accuracy in testing data, we could, in general, predict the air pollution situation, and its influence on human health in the city of Mohammedia. Our perspective is to study the city area by area and delve into the data with more precision in terms of air quality, heat and each type of disease.

References

1. El Morabet, R., Aneflouss, M., Mouak, S.: Air pollution effects on health in Kenitra. In: Kallel, A., Ksibi, M., Ben Dhia, H., Khélifi, N. (eds.) EMCEI 2017, pp. 1971–1973. Springer, Cham (2018). https://doi.org/10.1007/978-3-319-70548-4_570
2. Mabahwi, N.A., Leh, O.L.H., Omar, D.: Urban air quality and human health effects in Selangor, Malaysia. Procedia-Soc. Behav. Sci. **170**, 282–291 (2015)
3. Kampa, M., Castanas, E.: Human health effects of air pollution. Environ. Pollut. **151**(2), 362–367 (2008). Proceedings of the 4th International Workshop on Biomonitoring of Atmospheric Pollution (With Emphasis on Trace Elements)
4. The United Nations Economic Commission for Europe (ECE): Environmental performance review of Morocco. In: The Environmental Performance Review, A Powerful Tool for Achieving Sustainable Development (2014). e-ISBN 978-92-1-056517-2
5. Inchaouh, M., Tahiri, P.M.: Air pollution due to road transportation in Morocco: evolution and impacts. J. Multidiscip. Eng. Sci. Technol. (JMEST) **4**(6) (2017). ISSN: 2458–9403

[2] Report (Statistics) of High Commission for Planning (Morocco) 2014 https://www.hcp.ma.

6. Wiener, P., Simko, V., Nimis, J.: Taming the evolution of big data and its technologies in BigGIS - a conceptual architectural framework for spatio-temporal analytics at scale. In: Proceedings of the 3rd International Conference on Geographical Information Systems Theory, Applications and Management, GISTAM, vol. 1, pp. 90–101. INSTICC/SciTePress (2017)
7. Akbari, H., Pomerantz, M., Taha, H.: Cool surfaces and shade trees to reduce energy use and improve air quality in urban areas. Sol. Energy **70**(3), 295–310 (2001). Urban Environment
8. Ghorani-Azam, A., Riahi-Zanjani, B., Balali-Mood, M.: Effects of air pollution on human health and practical measures for prevention in Iran. J. Res. Med. Sci. **21**(1), 65 (2016)
9. Wyborn, L., Evans, B.J.K.: Integrating 'big' geoscience data into the petascale national environmental research interoperability platform (NERDIP): successes and unforeseen challenges. In: 2015 IEEE International Conference on Big Data (Big Data), pp. 2005–2009, October 2015
10. Nakano, T., Otsuki, T.: Environmental air pollutants and the risk of cancer. Gan to kagaku ryoho. Cancer Chemother. **40**(11), 1441–1445 (2013)
11. Mabahwi, N.A.B., Leh, O.L.H., Omar, D.: Human health and wellbeing: human health effect of air pollution. Procedia - Soc. Behav. Sci. **153**, 221–229 (2014). AMER International Conference on Quality of Life, AicQoL2014KotaKinabalu, The Pacific Sutera Hotel, Sutera Harbour, Kota Kinabalu, Sabah, Malaysia, 4–5 January 2014
12. Hintze, J.L.: Principal components analysis. In: NCSS Statistical Software, chap. 425, pp. 425.1–425.23. https://goo.gl/GHjKKJ
13. Scholkopf, B., Smola, A.J.: Learning with Kernels: Support Vector Machines, Regularization, Optimization, and Beyond. MIT Press, Cambridge (2001)
14. Chang, Y.-W., Hsieh, C.-J., Chang, K.-W., Ringgaard, M., Lin, C.-J.: Training and testing low-degree polynomial data mappings via linear SVM. J. Mach. Learn. Res. **11**, 1471–1490 (2010)
15. Squallio Houssaini, A.S., Messaouri, H., Nasri, I., Roth, M.P., Nejjari, C., Benchekroun, M.N.: Air pollution as a determinant of asthma among schoolchildren in Mohammedia. Morocco. Int. J. Environ. Health Res. **17**(4), 243–257 (2007)
16. Aneflouss, M.: Transformations of the Moroccan field and society: a study in the geography of health in the urban environment (thesis in Arabic). Thesis of the Doctor of State in Geography, Faculty of Arts and Humanities, Hassan II University, Mohammedia, Morocco (2007)

Deep Learning

Deep Semi-supervised Learning for Virtual Screening Based on Big Data Analytics

Meriem Bahi(✉) and Mohamed Batouche

Computer Science Department, Faculty of NTIC,
University Constantine 2 - Abdelhamid Mehri,
Biotechnology Research Center (CRBt) & CERIST,
Constantine, Algeria
{meriem.bahi,mohamed.batouche}@univ-constantine2.dz

Abstract. Nowadays, scientists and researchers, are facing the problem of massive data processing, which consumes relatively too much time and cost. That is why researchers have turned to Deep Learning (DL) techniques based on Big Data Analytics. On the other hand, the ever-increasing size of unlabelled data combined with the difficulty of obtaining class labels has made semi-supervised learning an interesting alternative of significant practical importance in modern data analysis. In the same context, drug discovery has reached a state and complexity that we can no longer avoid using Deep Semi-Supervised Learning and Big Data Processing Systems. Virtual Screening (VS) is a computationally intensive process which plays a major role in the early phase of drug discovery process. The VS has to be made as fast as possible to efficiently dock the ligands from huge databases to a selected protein receptor. For these reasons, we propose a deep semi-supervised learning-based algorithmic framework named DeepSSL-VS for pre-filtering the huge set of ligands to effectively do virtual screening for the breast cancer protein receptor. The latter combines stacked autoencoders and deep neural network and is implemented using the Spark-H2O platform. The proposed technique has been compared to twenty-four different machine learning algorithms applied all on the same reference datasets, and preliminary performance assessment results have shown that our approach outperforms these techniques with an overall accuracy performance more than 99%.

Keywords: Drug discovery · Virtual screening · Deep learning
Stacked autoencoders · Big Data · H2O · Spark

1 Introduction

The emergence of computer sciences in recent decades has forever changed the pursuit of explorations and scientific discoveries. With experience and theory,

Y. Tabii et al. (Eds.): BDCA 2018, CCIS 872, pp. 173–184, 2018.
https://doi.org/10.1007/978-3-319-96292-4_14

computer simulation is now a "third paradigm" confirmed for science [1]. Its value lies in exploring areas where solutions cannot be found analytically, and experiments are not feasible or take too much time, as in the formation of galaxies and bioinformatics applications.

We are living now in an age where older storage and processing technologies are not enough, computing technologies must scale to handle the huge volume of data. The main difficulty in managing these amounts of data is due to the speed with which they are about to increase, and it is much faster than the computer resources. The acquisition and processing of those big amounts of data make this paradigm more useful for researchers in various fields; it is now completely changing the way researchers work in almost all scientific fields.

One of these scientific fields is Drug search and discovery. It is the process which aims to find a molecule able to bind and activate or inhibit a molecular target. Discovering new treatments for human diseases is increasingly hard, costly and time-consuming. Thousands of molecules must be processed and selected, to reach a very limited number of candidates. The drug discovery process can take between 12−15 years and costs over one billion dollars with a risk of failure along the way.

Drug discovery uses many techniques including virtual screening [18]. This latter is a computational technique used to search libraries of small molecules (ligands) for the purpose to identify structures that most likely bind to a drug target. Indeed, a drug target is a protein receptor that is involved in a metabolic or signaling pathway through which one designates a specific disease condition or a pathology [11].

These libraries are developing rapidly at an exponential rate. The number of ligands which have to be tested has increased considerably. We are now talking about 10^{60} ligands and still counting [12], which makes traditional techniques for the virtual screening like docking-based techniques impractical. The docking process consumes a lot of time; many hours or even days are spent. To cope with this problem, a new era of techniques which are based on modern machine learning has emerged [15,23]. A small part of these ligands is used to train a binary classifier that can classify very large sets of ligands into two classes: dockable ligands and non-dockable ones. In other terms, machine learning is used to develop a kind of filter for classifying huge database of ligands given a protein target and a small database of ligands for training. Deep Learning belongs to modern machine learning and is garnering significant attention. It is a kind of ANN with many hidden layers and more sophisticated parameter training procedure. As the overall complexity of the virtual screening problem has limited the impact of machine learning in drug discovery, deep learning should be applied, to achieve greater predictive power and speed up the VS process. It provides a flexible paradigm for synthesizing large amounts of data into efficient predictive models. Therefore, the search space is considerably reduced, and the VS process becomes very fast.

On the other hand, the ever-increasing size of unlabeled data and the rarity of label information which is expensive and even impossible to obtain, have made difficulties to develop new computational methods for accelerating the virtual screening process and potentially increasing the prediction performance. A semi-supervised learning method is a significant practical way to address this problem by using labeled and unlabeled data. The semi-supervised learning or in the other terms the unsupervised pre-training is used to improve decision boundaries and to allow for classification that is more accurate than that based on classifiers constructed using the labeled data only.

To this end, we propose an effective computational technique based on deep semi-supervised learning termed as DeepSSL-VS, to accurately filter the huge databases of ligands by classifying small molecules as active or inactive relative to the breast cancer protein target. Firstly, we use the unsupervised stacked autoencoders both to convert high-dimensional features to low-dimensional representations and to initialize the weights of a supervised deep neural network model. Then we apply labeled data to build an efficient classification model based on deep neural network.

Consequently, the rest of the paper is organized as follows. In the next section, we present recent works related to machine and deep learning in drug discovery. In Sect. 3, we explain some concepts related to our work. Section 4 is dedicated to the description of the proposed approach for Virtual Screening based on stacked autoencoders and deep neural network. In Sect. 5, the experimental results accompanied by some comments are presented. Finally, conclusions and perspectives for future work are drawn.

2 Related Work

In this section, we start by explaining the motivation and the objective behind our work. Then, we try to compare and situate our work among the state of the art techniques for drug discovery.

As explained before, VS is the process that uses computer-based methods to discover new drugs on the bases of chemical structures. Virtual screening methods can be grouped into structure and ligand based approaches depending on the amount of structural and bioactivity available [15]. The structure-based methods or molecular docking simulate physical interactions between the compound and a protein target. The limitation of these methods is that they require the three-dimensional (3D) structure of a target which is a problem because not all proteins have their 3D structures available. In addition, The process of molecular docking takes about 5–6 h to treat only 400 ligands. By contrast, the ligand-based approach is based on the concept that similar ligands (or small molecules) tend to have similar biological properties [21]. One of these methods is Quantitative Structure-Activity Relationship (QSAR) that predict the bioactivity of a ligand on a specific target. Unfortunately, the problem with this category of methods is that many target proteins have little or no ligand information available.

Machine learning (ML) is another important resource that has been extensively used in drug development and discovery to overcome the drawbacks of previous methods [10]. It can be found mainly as a ligand-based virtual screening approach. The commonly used machine learning method is to build a binary classification model which is a kind of filter to classify ligands as active or inactive with regard to a specific protein target. These techniques require less computational resources and find more diverse hits than other earlier methods due to its generalization ability.

There are many studies in the literature that explored the performances of the machine learning methods for virtual screening. For example, Korkmaz et al. [13] used support vector machines (SVM) to filter the set of ligands while Garcia-Sosa et al. [9] applied a logistic regression on the same datasets. The density estimation was proposed in [17] for target prediction. Byvatov et al. [3] compared performances of SVM and neural networks (NN) on drug-like/nondrug-like classification problem and they concluded that SVM outperformed NN.

With the increasing of experimental data and increasing complexity of the machine learning algorithms that perform poorly, deep learning methods have been widely applied in many fields of bioinformatics, biology, and chemistry [19]. Deep learning has attracted much attention recently thanks to its relatively better performance and ability to learn multiple levels of representation and abstraction [16]. Therefore, Deep Learning has rapidly emerged in pharmaceutical industries as a viable alternative to aid in the discovery of new drugs.

Deep learning algorithms have been proved to be well suited for the classification task. Alexander Aliper et al. [2] demonstrated how deep neural networks (DNN) trained on large transcriptional response data sets, can classify various drugs into therapeutic categories solely based on their transcriptional profiles. Aries Fitriawan et al. [8] proposed a framework of ligand-based virtual screening using Deep Belief Networks.

In this paper, the objective is to optimize the time spent into the virtual screening operation when it comes to select dockable ligands in a very large set because increasing the number of ligands influences greatly the quality of the solution, and to deal with the problem of the imbalance data between labeled and unlabelled which degrades the prediction performance. For these reasons, we propose the use of the deep semi-supervised learning algorithm that is specialized in resolving problems with the huge amount of data. To our knowledge, this is the first time deep semi-supervised learning method for virtual screening is employed.

The proposed method comprises two steps. Firstly, we use the unsupervised stacked autoencoders both to convert high-dimensional features to low-dimensional representations and to initialize the weights of a supervised deep neural networks model. Then we apply labeled data to build an efficient classification model based on deep neural networks. Our approach can be used as a filter which precedes the virtual screening operation that selects the set of ligands which have the higher chance to bind to a target protein. This will considerably help researchers and biologists in their quest of new drugs by accelerating the drug discovery process.

3 Background

This section explains the main concepts underlying the proposed method.

3.1 Basic Autoencoder

An Autoencoder (AE) is considered as a one-hidden-layer neural network. Its objective is to reconstruct the input using its hidden activations so that the reconstruction error is as small as possible. The AE takes the input and puts it through an encoding function to a new representation (input encoding), and then it decodes the encodings through a decoding function to reconstruct the original input [24]. More formally, let $x \in R_d$ be the input,

$$h = f_e(x) = s_e(W_e x + b_e) \tag{1}$$

$$x_r = f_d(x) = s_d(W_d h + b_d) \tag{2}$$

where $\mathbf{f_e}$: $\mathbf{R_d} \mapsto \mathbf{R_h}$ and $\mathbf{f_d}$:$\mathbf{R_h} \mapsto \mathbf{R_d}$ are encoding and decoding functions respectively, $\mathbf{W_e}$ and $\mathbf{W_d}$ are the weights of the encoding and decoding layers, and $\mathbf{b_e}$ and $\mathbf{b_d}$ are the biases for the two layers. $\mathbf{s_e}$ and $\mathbf{s_d}$ are element wise non-linear functions in general, and common choices are sigmoidal functions like tanh or logistic.

3.2 Stacked Autoencoders

Stacked Autoencoders (SAE) is one of popular deep learning model, built with multiple layers of neural networks that tries to reconstruct its input [24]. In general, an N-layer deep autoencoder with parameters $\mathbf{P} = \{\mathbf{P^i} | \mathbf{i} \in \{\mathbf{1}, \mathbf{2}, ..., \mathbf{N}\}\}$ where $\mathbf{P^i} = \{\mathbf{W^i_e}, W^i_{\mathbf{d}}, \mathbf{b^i_e}, \mathbf{b^i_d}\}$ can be formulated as follows:

$$h^i = f^i_e(h^{i-1}) = s^i_e(W^i_e h^{i-1} + b^i_e) \tag{3}$$

$$h^i_r = f^i_d(h^{i+1}_r) = s^i_d(W^i_d h^{i+1}_r + b^i_d) \tag{4}$$

$$h^0 = x \tag{5}$$

The stacked autoencoders architecture contains multiple encoding and decoding stages made up of a sequence of encoding layers followed by a stack of decoding layers. SAE can automatically take advantage of large amounts of unlabeled data and can learn higher level features from raw data and increase the performance of features. It plays a fundamental role in semi-supervised learning which is based on a greedy layer-wise unsupervised [7].

4 Materials and Methods

In this section, we explain how we developed the proposed approach for virtual screening in drug discovery. First, we will describe the dataset and how we obtained it. And then, we will present the chosen algorithms and platforms and how we use them to accomplish our goal.

4.1 Data Preparation

The labeled dataset used in this study were collected from a recent publication of Korkmaz et al. [14]. They consist of 847 ligands (409 druglike and 438 non-druglike). The unlabeled data (one million of ligands) were got from the Chem-Bridge Library [6]. For this experiment, a therapeutic target has been identified which is the breast cancer protein. We have selected the receptor 4JLU which is a crystal structure of BRCA1.

4.2 Dataset Representation

The ligands used in this work are represented by sets of descriptors (i.e., feature vectors). The molecular descriptors of all ligands were calculated using the chem-informatics software Dragon 7. The features that have been used to represent ligands are descriptors related to constitutional, topological, geometrical descriptors and other molecular properties. They include logP, polar surface area (PSA), donor count (DC), aliphatic ring count (AlRC), aromatic ring count (ArRC) and Balaban index (BI). On the whole, there are 5270 molecular descriptors.

After collecting the molecular descriptors, each ligand is represented by a feature vector $[d_1, d_2, d_3, ..., d_{5270}]$. At the end, we refer to these ligands as instances and we assign a label (+1 or −1) for each labeled sample.

4.3 DeepSSL-VS: The Proposed Method for Virtual Screening

Given the ever-growing volumes of unlabeled data and the cost of labeling, it is hard to use only the small part of labeled data to represent the whole sample space and applicability of the model may bias [4]. In this case, it is imperative to develop an additional pre-training step in a supervised setting for exploiting a better the amounts of unlabeled data for drug discovery.

The unsupervised pre-training followed by supervised fine-tuning is a way of successfully applying the semi-supervised deep learning method. The first part of pre-training aims typically at building deep feature hierarchy, and is performed in an unsupervised mode. The latter stage is supervised fine-tuning of the deep neural network parameters. Pre-training is essentially obsolete, given the success of semi-supervised learning which accomplishes the same goals more elegantly by optimizing unsupervised and supervised objectives simultaneously [5].

The training procedure of our deep semi-supervised learning model DeepSSL-VS can be divided into two consecutive processes: the layer-wise unsupervised pre-training process using a stacked autoencoders [4,5], and the supervised fine-tuning process of deep neural network.

The supervised fine-tuning process is as follows:

1. After training the stacked autoencoders with the layer-wise unsupervised pre-training procedure, we use the weights of the stacked autoencoders to initialize the parameters of deep neural network model (DNN) in a region such that the near local optima overfit less the data.

2. Train the whole deep neural network as supervised learning which is performed as in a regular feed-forward network with back-propagation.
3. All parameters are tuned for the supervised task to get the classification model using labeled data.
4. The representation is adjusted to be more discriminative.

The pseudocode of our procedure is given below. For the sake of simplicity, we explain how unsupervised pre-training with supervised fine tuning is employed with only two-layered.

Pseudocode

In the following pseudocode, we will use the following notations. **L** is a number of hidden layers. **x** represents the input data. **h** is the hidden layer. **D** represents the domain of training. **T** is the number of hidden units in each layer. $\mathbf{b}^{(1)}$ is the bias vector for level **l**.

Phase of Pre-training:

- For l= 1 to L (L := 2) Build unsupervised training set (with $h^{(0)}(x) = x$) :

$$D = \{h^{(l-1)}(x^{(t)})\}_{t=1}^{T}$$

- Train greedy layer wise of stacked autoencoders on D.
- Use hidden layer weights and biases of greedy module to initialize the deep network parameters $W^{(l)}$, $b^{(l)}$ (see Fig. 1).

Phase of Fine-Tuning:

- Initialize randomly the output layer parameters $W^{(L+1)}$, $b^{(L+1)}$ of deep neural network.
- Train the whole neural network using supervised stochastic gradient descent with Backpropagation (as depicted in the Fig. 1).

4.4 The Benefit of Using Unsupervised Pre-training

Training deep neural networks can be difficult since there are many local optima in the search space and the complex models are prone to overfitting. Indeed, with random initialization, the gradient-based training process may lead to many different local minima leading to poor performance. That is why an additional mechanism to optimization with regularization is required [7].

Unsupervised pre-training initializes a discriminative neural net from one which was trained using an unsupervised criterion such as a deep belief network or a deep autoencoder. This unsupervised algorithm can help for both the optimization and the overfitting issues, and therefore it helps to obtain a better

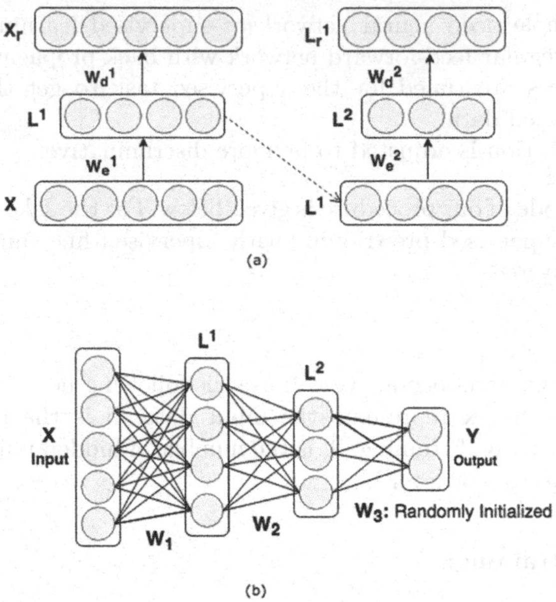

Fig. 1. Architecture of the proposed deep neural network: (a) Pre-training of SAE. (b) Training of supervised DNN using SAE weights for initialization.

generalization after the network is trained [22]. Moreover, unsupervised learning along with supervised learning is particularly beneficial to improve decision boundaries and to allow for classification that is more accurate than that based on classifiers constructed using the labeled data only.

Unsupervised pre-training is not only still relevant for tasks for which we have small labeled datasets and large unlabeled datasets, but it can also exhibit much better performance in data representation and classification [22]. It is often noticed that unsupervised pre-training helps in extracting important features from the data, as well as in setting initial conditions for the supervised algorithm in the region in the parameter space, where better local optimum may be found. Some hypothesis claims that the pre-training phase is a kind of very particular regularization, which is performed not by changing the optimized criterion or introducing new restriction for the parameters, but by creating a starting point for the optimization process. Regardless of the reason, unsupervised pre-training helps in creating efficient deep architectures. We can summarize the main advantages of the unsupervised pre-training process as follows:

– A better initialization of the weights in the deep neural network instead of randomly initialized weights which may lead to better convergence and better performing classifiers.
– It acts as some special kind of regularization process which yields a better generalization power.

4.5 Implementation: Spark-H2O Platform

The DeepSSL-VS algorithm was implemented in Sparkling Water (Spark + H2O) platform. This latter combines the fast, scalable deep learning algorithms of H2O with the capabilities of Spark. H2O is very suitable for fast scalable deep learning. It is an open source in-memory, parallel processing prediction engine for Big Data [5]. Spark-H2O can handle billions of data rows in-memory, even with a fairly small cluster.

5 Experimental Results

5.1 Measurement of Prediction Quality

To assess the performance of the proposed method based on deep semi-supervised learning for virtual screening in drug discovery, we used six measures namely the accuracy rate (AR), the sensitivity (SE), the specificity (SP), the positive predictive value (PPV), the F-Score (FS) and the Matthews correlation coefficient (MCC) with 10-fold cross-validation.

5.2 Cross-Validation Results

We compared our approach (DeepSSL-VS) with twenty-four machine learning methods reported in the literature [14,20] like ANN, SVM, Naïve Bayes, KNN, and MKL, applied all on the same reference datasets. The obtained results are summarized in Table 1 and show that the proposed method competes with and even outperforms other techniques. Ligands are classified into two classes: drug-like or nondrug-like.

As shown in Table 1, the results obtained by our method DeepSSL-VS with the Spark-H2O platform have more than 0.99 (99%) in almost measurements where the specificity, sensitivity, and Positive Predictive Value are equal to 100%. The obtained results are clearly better than the ones reported in [14,20]. The multiple kernel learning is the second best performing algorithm with accuracy more than 0.81 in almost all measurements. The least squares support vector machines with radial basis function kernel (LsSVMrbf), the flexible discriminant analysis (FDA) and the C5.0 were the third best-performing algorithms with accuracy close to 79%. Besides this, the specificity obtained by these methods is between 51% and 71%, which means that it fails to identify negative ligands (nondrug-like). The F-score results values are between 71%- 78%. The cross-validation between the results of the proposed approach and those of the twenty-four different machine learning algorithms applied all on the same datasets, clearly demonstrates that the DeepSSL-VS method gives the best compromise between the Accuracy rate (AR), the Specificity (SP), the Sensitivity (SE), Positive Predictive Value (PPV), the (MCC), and the F-score, while the other methods yield to heterogeneous results. These results indicated that the deep semi-supervised learning model surpassed the threshold to make virtual screening rapid and have the potential to become a standard tool in industrial drug design and discovery.

Table 1. Performance assessment of the proposed method

Classification model	AR (%)	SE (%)	SP (%)	PPV (%)	F score (%)	MCC (%)
Our proposed classifier (DeepSSL-VS)	99.34	100	100	100	99.40	99.07
Multiple kernel learning	81.35	81.92	80.82	80.17	80.81	80.23
Discriminant classifiers						
Linear discriminant analysis	72.69	89.80	58.47	64.23	74.89	49.89
Robust linear discriminant analysis	75.93	91.84	62.71	67.16	77.59	55.96
Quadratic discriminant analysis	69.91	87.76	55.08	61.87	72.57	44.53
Robust quadratic discriminant analysis	73.61	80.61	67.80	67.52	73.49	48.37
Mixture discriminant analysis	75.93	90.82	63.56	67.42	77.39	55.53
Flexible discriminant analysis	78.24	89.80	68.64	70.40	78.92	58.92
Nearest shrunken centroids	74.07	91.84	59.32	65.22	76.27	53.03
Decision tree classifiers						
Classification and regression trees	72.22	88.78	58.47	63.97	74.36	48.71
C5.0	78.24	89.80	68.64	70.40	78.92	58.92
J48	77.31	89.80	66.95	69.29	88.76	57.40
Conditional inference tree	73.61	86.73	62.71	65.89	74.89	50.19
Kernel-based classifiers						
Support vector machine with linear, kernel	76.39	87.76	66.95	68.80	77.13	55.16
SVM with radial basis function kernel	77.78	90.82	66.95	69.53	78.76	58.53
Partial least squares	74.07	91.84	59.32	65.22	76.27	53.03
Least squares SVM with linear kernel	73.15	90.82	58.47	64.49	75.42	51.09
Least squares support vector machine with radial basis function kernel	78.70	87.76	71.19	71.67	78.90	59.05
Ensemble classifiers						
Random forest	76.85	88.78	66.95	69.05	77.68	56.27
Bagged support vector machine	76.39	88.78	66.10	68.50	77.33	55.51
Bagged k-nearest neighbors	75.46	90.82	62.71	66.92	77.06	54.79
Other classifiers						
Naïve Bayes	68.06	88.78	50.85	60.00	71.60	41.99
Neural networks	77.31	86.73	69.49	70.25	77.63	56.39
K-Nearest neighbors	76.85	90.82	65.25	68.46	78.07	57.03
Learning vector quantization	74.07	87.76	62.71	66.15	75.44	51.33

6 Conclusion and Future Work

In this study, we proposed a deep semi-supervised learning method that can improve the virtual screening process in the drug discovery field. The proposed method deals with imbalanced data by using a small number of labeled data in conjunction with many unlabeled data. We concentrate our focus on the breast cancer which is a perilous disease that is taking every day more and more lives. Our approach uses a stacked autoencoders to effectively abstract raw input vectors and to initialize the weights of a deep neural network. To this end, we have used well known big data processing platforms such as Spark combined with the H2O platform. The obtained results have shown that our method (DeepSSL-VS) achieves a high prediction performance with 99% of precision.

As we believe that more data will improve the model we designed, we will run it on a bigger cluster of machines where we will be able to use a huge number of ligands in relatively better execution time. In addition, we expect to explore more big data algorithms for deep learning in the context of drug discovery and repositioning.

References

1. Agrawal, A., Choudhary, A.: Perspective: materials informatics and big data: realization of the "fourth paradigm" of science in materials science. Apl Mater. **4**(5), 053208 (2016)
2. Aliper, A., Plis, S., Artemov, A., Ulloa, A., Mamoshina, P., Zhavoronkov, A.: Deep learning applications for predicting pharmacological properties of drugs and drug repurposing using transcriptomic data. Mol. Pharm. **13**(7), 2524–2530 (2016)
3. Byvatov, E., Fechner, U., Sadowski, J., Schneider, G.: Comparison of support vector machine and artificial neural network systems for drug/nondrug classification. J. Chem. Inf. Comput. Sci. **43**(6), 1882–1889 (2003)
4. Candel, A., Parmar, V., LeDell, E., Arora, A.: Deep learning with H2O. H2O. ai Inc. (2016)
5. Cook, D.: Practical Machine Learning with H2O: Powerful Scalable Techniques for Deep Learning and AI. O'Reilly Media, Beijing (2016)
6. ZINC Database: Chembridge full library (2011). http://zinc.docking.org/
7. Erhan, D., Bengio, Y., Courville, A., Manzagol, P.A., Vincent, P., Bengio, S.: Why does unsupervised pre-training help deep learning? J. Mach. Learn. Res. **11**(Feb), 625–660 (2010)
8. Fitriawan, A., Wasito, I., Syafiandini, A.F., Azminah, A., Amien, M., Yanuar, A.: Deep belief networks for ligand-based virtual screening of drug design. In: Proceedings of 2016 6th International Workshop on Computer Science and Engineering (WCSE 2016) Tokyo, Japan, pp. 655–659 (2016)
9. García-Sosa, A.T., Oja, M., Hetényi, C., Maran, U.: Druglogit: logistic discrimination between drugs and nondrugs including disease-specificity by assigning probabilities based on molecular properties. J. Chem. Inf. Model. **52**(8), 2165–2180 (2012)
10. Gertrudes, J., Maltarollo, V., Silva, R., Oliveira, P., Honorio, K., Da Silva, A.: Machine learning techniques and drug design. Curr. Med. Chem. **19**(25), 4289–4297 (2012)

11. Howard, A.D., McAllister, G., Feighner, S.D., Liu, Q., Nargund, R.P., Van der Ploeg, L.H., Patchett, A.A.: Orphan G-protein-coupled receptors and natural ligand discovery. Trends Pharmacol. Sci. **22**(3), 132–140 (2001)
12. Irwin, J.J., Sterling, T., Mysinger, M.M., Bolstad, E.S., Coleman, R.G.: Zinc: a free tool to discover chemistry for biology. J. Chem. Inf. Model. **52**(7), 1757–1768 (2012)
13. Korkmaz, S., Zararsiz, G., Goksuluk, D.: Drug/nondrug classification using support vector machines with various feature selection strategies. Comput. Methods Programs Biomed. **117**(2), 51–60 (2014)
14. Korkmaz, S., Zararsiz, G., Goksuluk, D.: MLVis: a web tool for machine learning-based virtual screening in early-phase of drug discovery and development. PloS One **10**(4), e0124600 (2015)
15. Lavecchia, A.: Machine-learning approaches in drug discovery: methods and applications. Drug Discov. Today **20**(3), 318–331 (2015)
16. LeCun, Y., Bengio, Y., Hinton, G.: Deep learning. Nature **521**(7553), 436 (2015)
17. Lowe, R., Mussa, H.Y., Nigsch, F., Glen, R.C., Mitchell, J.B.: Predicting the mechanism of phospholipidosis. J. Cheminform. **4**(1), 2 (2012)
18. Mannhold, R., Kubinyi, H., Folkers, G.: Virtual Screening: Principles, Challenges, and Practical Guidelines, vol. 48. Wiley, Hoboken (2011)
19. Min, S., Lee, B., Yoon, S.: Deep learning in bioinformatics. Br. Bioinform. **18**(5), 851–869 (2017)
20. Mohamed, B., Kamel, Z., Meriem, B., Amira, K., Anouar, B.: An efficient compound classification technique based on multiple kernel learning for virtual screening. In: Proceedings of The Thirteenth International Conference on Computational Intelligence methods for Bioinformatics and Biostatistics (CIBB2016) Stirling, UK (2016)
21. Pérez-Sianes, J., Pérez-Sánchez, H., Díaz, F.: Virtual screening: a challenge for deep learning. In: Saberi Mohamad, M., Fdez-Riverola, F., Domínguez Mayo, F., De Paz, J. (eds.) 10th International Conference on Practical Applications of Computational Biology & Bioinformatics, pp. 13–22. Springer, Cham (2016). https://doi.org/10.1007/978-3-319-40126-3_2
22. Rusiecki, A., Kordos, M., et al.: Effectiveness of unsupervised training in deep learning neural networks. Schedae Inform. **24**(2015), 41–51 (2016)
23. Senanayake, U., Prabuddha, R., Ragel, R.: Machine learning based search space optimisation for drug discovery. In: 2013 IEEE Symposium on Computational Intelligence in Bioinformatics and Computational Biology (CIBCB), pp. 68–75. IEEE (2013)
24. Zhou, Y., Arpit, D., Nwogu, I., Govindaraju, V.: Is joint training better for deep auto-encoders? arXiv preprint arXiv:1405.1380 (2014)

Using Deep Learning Word Embeddings for Citations Similarity in Academic Papers

Oumaima Hourrane(✉), Sara Mifrah, El Habib Benlahmar, Nadia Bouhriz, and Mohamed Rachdi

Laboratory for Information Processing and Modeling, Faculty of Sciences Ben M'sik, Hassan II University of Casablanca, Cdt Driss El Harti, BP 7955 Sidi Othman, Casablanca, Morocco

oumaima.hourrane@gmail.com, mifrah.sara@gmail.com, h.benlahmar@gmail.com, bouhriz.nadia@gmail.com, rachdi.simo@gmail.com

Abstract. The citation similarity measurement task is defined as determining how similar the meanings of two citations are. This task play an significant role in Natural Language Processing applications, especially in academic plagiarism detection. Yet, computing citation similarity is not a trivial task, due to the incomplete and ambiguous information presented in academic papers, which makes necessity to leverage extra knowledge to understand it, as well as most similarity measures based on the syntactic features, and other based on the semantic part still has many drawbacks. In this paper, we propose a corpus-based approach using deep learning word embeddings to compute more effective citation similarity. Our study explores the previous works on text similarity, namely, string-based, knowledge-based and corpus-based. Then we define our new basis and experiment on a large dataset of scientific papers. The final results demonstrate that deep learning based approach can enhance the effectiveness of citation similarity.

Keywords: Word embedding · Deep learning · Text similarity

1 Introduction

Textual information is omnipresent. Processing semantic connections between textual information empowers to prescribe articles or items identified with given query, to take after patterns, to investigate a particular subject in more subtle elements, and so forth. Be that as it may, writings can be altogether different various: a Wikipedia article is long and elegantly composed, tweets are short and regularly not syntactically right.

Thus, determining the similarity between sentences is one of the critical undertakings in natural language processing. To appraise the exact score produced from syntactic similarity to semantic similarity. Processing text similarity

Y. Tabii et al. (Eds.): BDCA 2018, CCIS 872, pp. 185–196, 2018.
https://doi.org/10.1007/978-3-319-96292-4_15

isn't an inconsequential assignment, because of the changeability of natural language articulations. Estimating semantic similarity of sentences is firmly identified with semantic similarity between words. In data recovery, similarity measure is utilized to dole out a positioning score between an inquiry and text in a corpus. Recent utilizations of natural language processing present a requirement for a powerful strategy to process the similarity between short texts or sentences [1]. The work of text similarity can altogether streamline the specialist's information base by utilizing normal sentences instead of basic examples of sentences. In text mining, sentence similarity is utilized as a rule to find concealed information from literary databases [2]. Likewise, the joining of short-content closeness is gainful to applications, for example, Plagiarism detection [3], machine translation, text classification and text summarization. These model applications demonstrate that the registering of text similarity has turned into a non specific segment for the exploration group associated with content related information portrayal and revelation. Generally, methods for identifying similarity between long texts have fixated on dissecting shared words. Such techniques are normally successful when managing long texts on the grounds that comparative long text will as a rule contain a level of co-occurring words. Be that as it may, in short texts word co-occurrence might be uncommon or even invalid. This is chiefly because of the inborn adaptability of natural language, empowering individuals to express similar meanings utilizing very unique sentences as far as structure and word content.

In this proposed approach, we focused on computing the semantic similarity between citations in scientific papers. Citation embeddings will be found from word embeddings in which words are represented as word embedding vectors with respect to context they occurs. From that point, the similarity measure is finished by discovering relationship of the features in the citation embedding. Remaining paper insights about the related works done on text similarity in Sect. 2, point by point approach clarification is given in Sect. 3, including the data pre-processing, words vectors representation, citation embeddings and the similarity measurement we used in our approach and evaluation, then the experiment and observations are explained in Sect. 4.

2 Previous Works

In this section we discusses the existing works on text similarity that fall into two categories: String-based similarity and Semantic similarity.

String-based similarity is a metric that measures distance between two text strings for approximate comparison, this category requires a fulfilment of the triangle inequality. For example, the strings “Sam” and “Samuel” can be considered to be close [4] This kind of similarity does not require knowledge of the language and do not take into account structural changes. The upper hand of this can detect similarity between different types of text. Among the best known algorithms of this category, there is the Longest Common SubString lCS [5] which is an alternative approach to word-by-word comparison, This is a two-step method. The first step is to make an intersection of two texts, in order to obtain a table of the words present in both texts while maintaining the position they have in one of the two. While the second step is to build, from the table obtained in the previous step, the longest common sequences between two texts. The main weakness of the LCS length as a measure of string similarity is its insensitivity to context. Another approach to determine this kind of similarity is the N-grams [6, 7], N-gram similarity algorithms compare the n-grams from each character or word in two given sentences. Where we can compute the distance by dividing the number of similar n-grams by maximal number of n-grams. Though, there are some other metrics which can be used on strings matching, The most widely known is the Cosine similarity which measures the similarity between two vectors of an inner product space measures the cosine of the angle between them. Also, the Euclidean distance which takes the square root of the sum of squared differences between corresponding elements of two vectors, and finally the Jaccard similarity [8] that is measured as the number of shared words over the number of all unique words in both sentences.

As for the second category the Semantic similarity, where its main idea is based on the similarity of the words meaning or semantic content. This approach can be divided into two other sub-categories as well. Corpus-based and Knowledge-based similarities.

Knowledge-based approaches use information retrieved from semantic dictionaries, or other lexical resources. Those techniques use the connection between words to determine the relation between them. There is a well-know example of semantic dictionary WordNet [9] or Roget's [10], which categorize the English language words by their part of speech as well as into sets of synonyms. Otherwise, WordNet contains many linguistic relations, making it suitable for the detecting the semantic similarity. However, the major drawback of knowledge-based approaches is that focus on lexical information about individual words, and contain few information on the different word senses, as well as the limited natural language lexicon. On the other side, Corpus-based approaches like hyperspace analogue to language [11], Latent Semantic Analysis LSA [12], Explicit Semantic Analysis ESA [13], Salient Semantic Analysis SSA [14], Pointwise Mutual Information PMI [15], and PMI-IR [16]. Those methods utilize the contextual information to extract semantic information, and learn semantic relations from patterns of word co-occurrence in the corpus. According to this principle, For example, LSA examines the similarity between the contexts in which a word appears and creates a new vector space with fewer dimensions. LSA uses Singular Value Decomposition SVD to discover the most important relationships between terms in a document collection. Unlike knowledge-based methods, which suffer from limited coverage, corpus-based measures are able to induce the similarity between any two words, sentences or texts.

The words embeddings, like deep learning based architectures, are another type of approaches in this category. One of the popular works on this type of words representations is by Mikolov et al. [17], and Global Vector GloVe [18]. Where they used probabilistic feed forward neural network language model to estimate word representations in vector space. As such, for all these methods, the similarity between words can be computed in terms of cosine similarity between corresponding vectors. Our methodology in this paper is an extension work based on word2vec which can be discussed in the next section.

3 Our Approach

The citation similarity method we propose uses word2vec [17] model for word embedding. It consists of three steps: dataset preprocessing, the word embeddings, and citation embeddings where we take the output of the words embedding in a given citation and aggregate it into one vector.

3.1 Dataset Pre-processing

The goal of this step is to reduce inflectional forms of words to a common base form. At first, we extract all the metadata of the given papers, namely, the Id, Title, Authors, Year and the full text in each paper. Then we took the full text and thrown away all the unwanted parts, and then we segment the text into sentences and extract just the citation, namely, the sentences that contains some references. After that, we save the result in an CSV file, then we tokenize all citation by chopping them up into tokens and throwing away punctuation and other unwanted characters. Those tokens serve like and input for the next step word embeddings.

3.2 Word Embeddings

The word2vec tool that we used in our approach provides an efficient implementation of the continuous bag of words and skip-gram models for computing vector representations of words. Those are the two main learning algorithms for distributed representations of words whose aim is to minimize computational complexity.

- The Continuous Bag of Words CBOW, where the non-linear hidden layer is removed and the projection layer is shared for all words. This model predicts the current word based on the N words both before and after it. E.g. Given N = 2, the model is as the Fig. 1 showed.
  And by ignoring the order of words in the sequence, CBOW uses the average value of the word embedding of the context to predict the current word.
- The Skip-gram model, which is similar to CBOW, but instead of predicting the word from context, it tries to maximize the classification of a word based on another word in the same sentence. The Skip-gram architecture works a little less well on the syntax task than on the CBOW model, but much better on the semantic part of the test than all the other models.

In our approach, we considered the extended model that go beyond word level to achieve sentence-level representations [19] which called Doc2vec. This

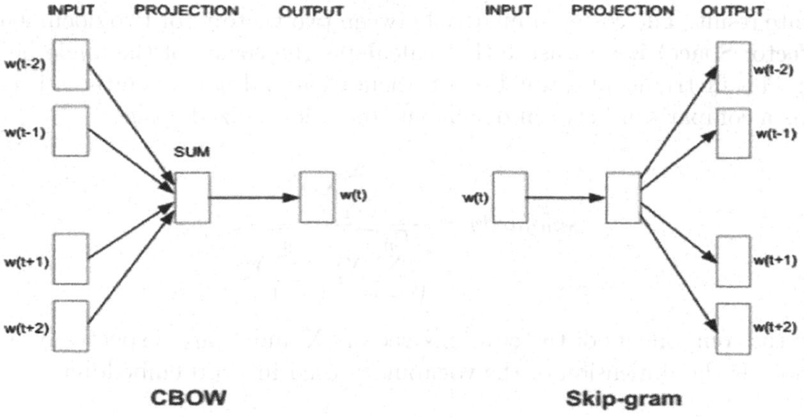

Fig. 1. The CBOW and Skip-gram architectures [17]

model represents one of the skip-gram techniques previously presented, in order to remove the limitations of the vector representations of the words, correspond to the composition of the meaning of each of its individual words. Thus, These representation takes our dataset as input and produces the word vectors as output. It first constructs a vocabulary from the training text data and then learns vector representation of words. The resulting vectors can be used as features in the next and final step for computing the similarity between the citations in our corpus.

3.3 Citation Embeddings

As we already mention that the word embeddings is very useful in many natural language processing tasks. For plagiarism in academic papers however, citation need to be compared. The simplest way to represent a sentence is to consider it as the sum of all words without regarding word orders. Yet, in our method we utilize Vector weighted average of words with their TF-IDF where each weight gives the importance of the word with respect to the corpus, and decrease the influence of the most common words.

$$\overline{x} = \sum_{i=1}^{n} \frac{1}{n} x_i \tag{1}$$

where the word vectors of each sentence represented by $[x_1, x_2, \ldots, x_n]$.

According to Kenter et al. [20], averaging word embeddings of all words in a text has proven to be a strong baseline or feature across a multitude of tasks", such as text similarity tasks.

3.4 Similarity Measurement

After the citation embeddings phase, we can then compute the similarity between the given citation vectors, simply by using cosine distance, and that can give an accurate result. The cosine similarity between two vectors (or two documents on the Vector Space) is a measure that calculates the cosine of the angle between them. This metric is an estimation of orientation and not magnitude, it can be seen as a comparison between documents on a normalized space.

$$similarity = \frac{\sum_{i=1}^{n} X_i Y_i}{\sqrt{\sum_{i=1}^{n} X_i^2} \sqrt{\sum_{i=1}^{n} Y_i^2}} \quad (2)$$

where the components of the citations vectors X and Y are respectively X_i and Y_i, and n is the dimension of the vocabulary used in word embeddings.

4 Experiments and Results

On part of the freely-available Google News word2vec model, we trained our word2vec models on NIPS papers corpus. This dataset includes the Id, Title, Authors, and extracted text for all NIPS papers to date ranging from the first 1987 conference to the current 2016 conference). The paper text has been extracted from the raw PDF files and are releasing in CSV files. The full text is then segmented and tokenized and cleaned as mentioned in our approach explanation, resulting in 30 Millions words. Then we trained a Skip-gram model on that dataset. The Table 1 below shows an example of the preprocessed dataset given two first papers and their three first citations.

After we have trained our skip-gram model, we projected 200 words of our vocabulary in a vector space model VSM which represent embed words in a continuous vector space where semantically similar words are mapped to nearby points. We have visualized the learned vectors by projecting them down into 2 dimensions by using the t-SNE dimensionality reduction technique [21]. When we inspect these visualizations it becomes apparent that the vectors capture some general, and in fact quite useful, semantic information about words and their relationships to one another. It was very interesting when we first discovered that certain directions in the induced vector space specialize towards some semantic relationships as the Fig. 2 shows below.

In order to evaluate our embeddings as shown in Table 2, one simple way is to directly use them to predict syntactic and semantic relationships. By examining the example above, we can first see that the word "Good" becomes increasingly related the resulted words, which makes sense.

As for citation embeddings phase, we aggregate the citation's word vectors as demonstrated in our methodology, and then we project first 50 vectors of citations as well in another vector space model using the same tool T-SNE, as Fig. 3 shows below.

Thus, to evaluate this task, we gave some example that compute the cosine similarity of different citations, as Table 3 shows below.

Table 1. NIPS dataset structure sample.

Id	Year	Title	Authors	Citation
2	1987	The Capacity of the Kanerva Associative Memory is Exponential	P.A. Chou	1. Towards the capacity of the Hopfield associative memory 2. This exponential growth in capacity for the Kanerva associative memory contrasts sharply with the sublinear growth in capacity for the Hopfield associative memory 3. Assuming the coordinates of the k-vector are drawn at random by independent flips of a fair coin
9	1987	Learning on a General Network	Atiya Amir F.	1. In our model y is governed by the following set of differential equations, proposed by Hopfield 2. Independently, other work appeared recently on training a feedback network 3. Neural network models having feedback connections, on the other hand, have also been devised for example the Hopfield network, and are shown to be quite successful in performing some computational tasks

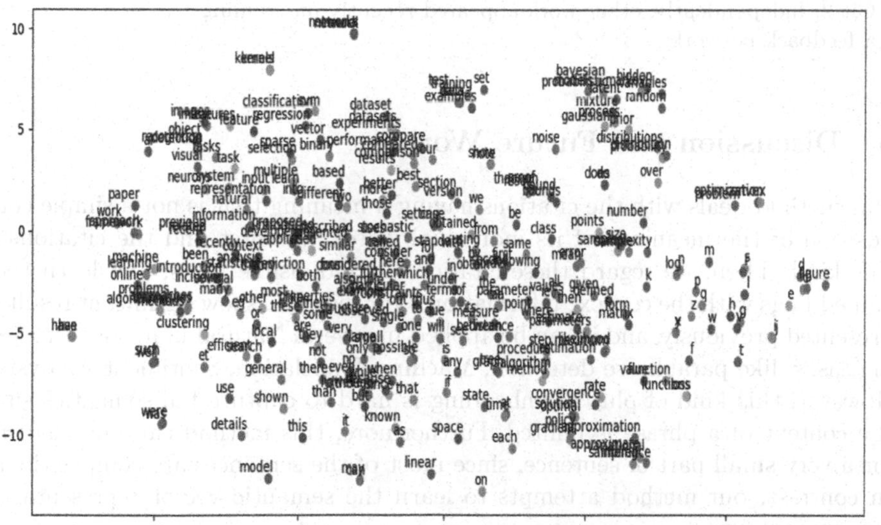

Fig. 2. NIPS Word2vec visualization with t-SNE

Table 2. The most similar words of "Good": an example.

Better	0.7271568179130554
Very	0.7213494777679443
Still	0.6984521150588989
Satisfactory	0.6695748567581177
Superior	0.6594116687774658
Simpler	0.6512424349784851
Practical	0.6487882137298584
Difficult	0.6476009488105774
Poor	0.6368283629417419
Slow	0.6296271085739136

Table 3. Example of the similarities between two citations using cosine similarity.

Citations	Cosine similarity
Cit. 1: Towards the capacity of the Hopfield associative memory Cit. 2: This exponential growth in capacity for the Kanerva associative memory contrasts sharply with the sub-linear growth in capacity for the Hopfield associative memory	0.810165
Cit. 1: Kanerva and Keeler have argued that the capacity at 8 = 0 is proportional to the number of memory locations Cit. 2: In our model y is governed by the following set of differential equations, proposed by Hopfield	0.463798
Cit. 1: In our model y is governed by the following set of differential equations, proposed by Hopfield Cit 2: Independently, other work appeared recently on training a feedback network	0.167626

5 Discussion and Future Work

Our method deals with the citations having a meaning that is not a simple composition of the meanings of its individual words. We first find the citations of this kind. Then, we regard these citations as indivisible units, and learn their embeddings with the context information. Our method, show significant result as presented previously, and it can be applied in several Natural Language Processing tasks, like paraphrase detection, Machine Translation, Sentiment Analysis... However, this kind of phrase embedding is hard to capture full semantics since the context of a phrase is limited. Furthermore, this method can only account for a very small part of sentence, since most of the sentences are compositional. In contrast, our method attempts to learn the semantic vector representation for any sentence.

To tackle this limit, we can get inspired in our future work on some other specific deep learning methods on sentence embedding, and advance the state of the

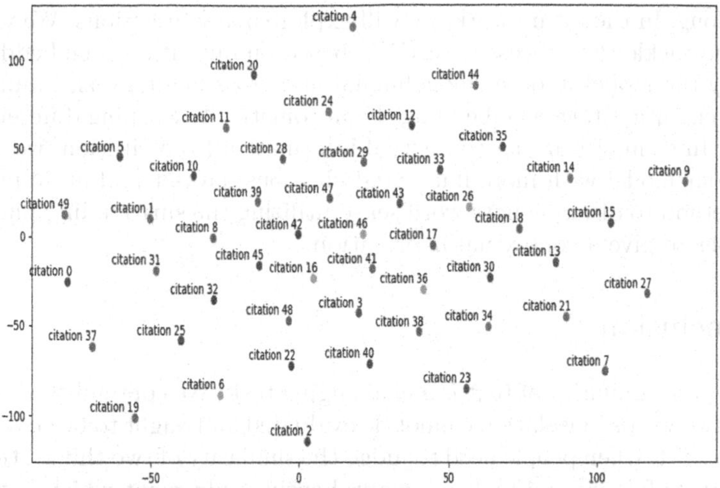

Fig. 3. Citation embeddings visualization with t-SNE.

art. For example using Long short-term memory and Recurrent Neural network as presented in [22], came to identify a dense and low dimensional semantic representation by sequentially and recurrently processing each word in a sentence and mapping them into a low dimensional vector. As for any RNN architecture, the global contextual features of the sentence will be presented in the semantic representation of the last word in the sentence, additionally, a word hashing layer is used to the model, which converts the high dimensional input into a relatively lower dimensional letter tri-gram representation. Another proposed model that represents effectively the hierarchical structure of sentences and the rich matching patterns at different levels, by using a deep Convolutional Neural Network [23]. It takes as input the embeddings of words, and then summarize the meaning of a sentence through layers of convolution and pooling. the convolution operates on sliding windows of words resulting some convolution units for a large feature map that model the rich structures in the composition of words, then max-pooling is applied in every two-unit window after each convolution this operation shrinks the size of the representation by half, thus quickly adsorbs the differences in length and it filters out undesirable composition of words. This models perform also significantly. However, however the models is less salient when the sentences have deep grammatical structures and the matching relies less on the local matching patterns. Additionally, a deep learning method [24] come to focus on learning phrase embeddings from the view of semantic meaning, by proposing a Bilingually-constrained recursive Auto-encoders. In this method the phrase embeddings pre-trained using an recursive auto-encoder in order to minimize the reconstruction error, then the Bilingually-constrained model learns to fine tune the phrase embeddings by minimizing the semantic distance between translation equivalents and maximizing the semantic distance between non-translation pairs. This model learns the semantic meaning for each phrase no matter whether it is short or long. In the future work, we will explore many directions. We will try to model and tackle the process with DNN based on our citation embeddings. We will apply the model in other monolingual and cross-lingual tasks, and we plan to learn semantic citation embeddings by automatically learning different weight matrices. In term of learning contextual information from citation, we are going to learn our model with more fluctuated citations dataset and an improvement to the method to disambiguate word sense utilizing the surrounding phrases and paragraphs to give a contextual information.

6 Conclusion

Surveying the similarity of text is a challenging task. We contend that similarity between two words in isolation cannot be evaluated and ought to be characterized in context. Yet, when people need to judge the similarity of two things, they think about various factors and make a comprehensive judgement which is the thing that the mix of various similarity techniques are presumably catching.

In this paper, We portrayed another set of results on citations vectors demonstrating they can viably be utilized for estimating semantic similarity between citations in academic papers. Firstly, semantic similarity is derived from a knowledge-base and a corpus-based approach. The lexical knowledge-base approach regular human knowledge about words in a natural language, this knowledge is generally steady over an extensive variety of natural language application. A corpus mirrors the genuine use of expressions and words. In this manner our semantic similarity not just catches basic human knowledge, yet it is likewise ready to adjust to an application utilizing a corpus particular to that application. Furthermore, the proposed technique considers the effect of word embeddings on sentence meaning. To assess our similarity calculation, we take a huge dataset of NIPS papers, which contains an a huge number of citations sets and an a large number of words from an variety of articles in Neural Network subject. An introductory experiment on this dataset shows that the proposed approach gives similarity that are genuinely consistent with human knowledge.

Our future work will incorporate the development of a more fluctuated citations dataset and an improvement to the method to disambiguate word sense utilizing the surrounding phrases and paragraphs to give a contextual information. And after that we ca apply this method in a particular applications, namely, sentiment analysis of citations, and plagiarism detection in academic papers. Presently, the comparison with some of the alternate approaches is extremely troublesome because of the absence of some other published results on citation similarities.

References

1. Michie, D.: Return of the imitation game. Electron. Trans. Artif. Intell. (2001)
2. Atkinson-Abutridy, J., Mellish, C., Aitken, S.: Combining information extraction with genetic algorithms for text mining. IEEE Intell. Syst. **19**(3), 22–30 (2004)

3. Hourrane, O., Benlahmar, E.H.: Survey of plagiarism detection approaches and big data techniques related to plagiarism candidate retrieval. In: Proceedings of the 2nd International Conference on Big Data, Cloud and Applications. ACM (2017)
4. Lu, J., et al.: String similarity measures and joins with synonyms. In: Proceedings of the 2013 ACM SIGMOD International Conference on Management of Data. ACM (2013)
5. Hirschberg, D.S.: Algorithms for the longest common subsequence problem. J. ACM (JACM) **24**(4), 664–675 (1977)
6. Barrón-Cedeno, A., et al.: Plagiarism detection across distant language pairs. In: Proceedings of the 23rd International Conference on Computational Linguistics. Association for Computational Linguistics (2010)
7. Buscaldi, D., et al.: LIPN-CORE: semantic text similarity using n-grams, WordNet, syntactic analysis, ESA and information retrieval based features. In: Second Joint Conference on Lexical and Computational Semantics (2013)
8. Niwattanakul, S., et al.: Using of Jaccard coefficient for keywords similarity. In: Proceedings of the International MultiConference of Engineers and Computer Scientists, vol. 1, no. 6 (2013)
9. Miller, G.A.: WordNet: a lexical database for English. Commun. ACM **38**(11), 39–41 (1995)
10. Roget's, I.I.: The new thesaurus (1995). http://www.thesaurus.com/. Accessed 18 Mar 2016
11. Azzopardi, L., Girolami, M., Crowe, M.: Probabilistic hyperspace analogue to language. In: Proceedings of the 28th Annual International ACM SIGIR Conference on Research and Development in Information Retrieval. ACM (2005)
12. Landauer, T.K., Dumais, S.T.: A solution to Plato's problem: the latent semantic analysis theory of acquisition, induction, and representation of knowledge. Psychol. Rev. **104**(2), 211 (1997)
13. Gabrilovich, E., Markovitch, S.: Computing semantic relatedness using Wikipedia-based explicit semantic analysis. In: IJCAI, vol. 7 (2007)
14. Hassan, S., Mihalcea. R.: Semantic relatedness using salient semantic analysis. In: AAAI (2011)
15. Church, K.W., Hanks, P.: Word association norms, mutual information, and lexicography. Comput. Linguist. **16**(1), 22–29 (1990)
16. Turney, P.D.: Mining the web for synonyms: PMI-IR versus LSA on TOEFL. In: De Raedt, L., Flach, P. (eds.) ECML 2001. LNCS (LNAI), vol. 2167, pp. 491–502. Springer, Heidelberg (2001). https://doi.org/10.1007/3-540-44795-4_42
17. Mikolov, T., et al.: Efficient estimation of word representations in vector space. arXiv preprint arXiv:1301.3781 (2013)
18. Pennington, J., Socher, R., Manning, C.: Glove: global vectors for word representation. In: Proceedings of the 2014 Conference on Empirical Methods in Natural Language Processing (EMNLP) (2014)
19. Mikolov, T., et al.: Distributed representations of words and phrases and their compositionality. In: Advances in Neural Information Processing Systems (2013)
20. Kenter, T., Borisov, A., de Rijke, M.: Siamese CBOW: optimizing word embeddings for sentence representations. arXiv preprint arXiv:1606.04640 (2016)
21. van der Maaten, L., Hinton, G.: Visualizing data using t-SNE. J. Mach. Learn. Res. **9**(Nov), 2579–2605 (2008)
22. Palangi, H., et al.: Deep sentence embedding using long short-term memory networks: analysis and application to information retrieval. IEEE/ACM Trans. Audio Speech Lang. Process. (TASLP) **24**(4), 694–707 (2016)

23. Hu, B., et al.: Convolutional neural network architectures for matching natural language sentences. In: Advances in Neural Information Processing Systems (2014)
24. Zhang, J., et al.: Bilingually-constrained phrase embeddings for machine translation. In: Proceedings of the 52nd Annual Meeting of the Association for Computational Linguistics, Long Papers, vol. 1 (2014)

Using Unsupervised Machine Learning for Data Quality. Application to Financial Governmental Data Integration

Hanae Necba[1(✉)], Maryem Rhanoui[1,2], and Bouchra El Asri[1]

[1] IMS Team, ADMIR Laboratory, Rabat IT Center, ENSIAS, Mohammed V University, Rabat, Morocco
hnecba@gmail.com, mrhanoui@gmail.com, b.elasri@um5s.net.ma
[2] Meridian Team, LYRICA Laboratory, School of Information Sciences, Rabat, Morocco

Abstract. Data quality, means, that data are correct, reliable, accurate and valid to be used and to serve its purpose in a given context. Data quality is crucial to make right decisions and reports in every organization. However, huge volume of data produced by organizations or redundant and heterogeneous data integration make manual methods of data quality control difficult, for that using intelligent technologies like Machine Learning is essential to ensure data quality across the organization. In this paper, we present an unsupervised learning approach that aims to match similar names and group them in same cluster to correct data therefore ensure data quality. Our approach is validated in the context of financial data quality of taxpayers using scikit learn the machine learning library for the Python programming language.

Keywords: Machine Learning · Data quality · Name matching
Affinity propagation · Levenshtein distance · Clustering · Unsupervised learning
Scikit learn · Data integration problems

1 Introduction

Each year, companies lose millions as a result of inaccurate and missing data in their operational databases [1]. Organizations create millions of critical and sensitive data, their bad management and bad quality could lead to catastrophic results. Because having data quality involved obtaining certain, reliable and correct results that we hope to get out of it. The challenge of analysts and scientists is to detect and correct errors to enhance data quality, therefore derive value from data and help managers to make relevant decisions from historical reliable data. This challenge has been amplified these last years by the increasing volume of processed data and Big Data analysis. Analyze big data, discover anomalies and determine if data is accurate, complete and correct with minimum effort and time, intelligent tools and automatic manners, let analysts obligatory get rid of traditional methods and adopt robust and advanced technologies in the top of them Machine Learning.

Y. Tabii et al. (Eds.): BDCA 2018, CCIS 872, pp. 197–209, 2018.
https://doi.org/10.1007/978-3-319-96292-4_16

One of the major causes that affect data quality is bad data integration by integrating redundant and erroneous or incorrect data either in terms of validity or in terms of typo mistakes or other unknown causes. Due to having huge integration data volume and different problems that cannot be listed and identified, get general or standard rules that could be applied to solve all problems is impossible. For that, it is essential to use more sophisticated and smart methods that can be flexible, adaptable and that put their own intelligent rules that can solve heterogeneous problems. Hence, the importance of using Machine Learning.

Through this paper, we propose a non-supervised name matching approach, to enhance and ensure data quality in a Machine Learning environment. The names will be weighted using Levenshtein Distance and then clustered with affinity propagation unsupervised learning algorithm. Our solution aim to validate and correct name of taxpayers to get unique identification of each one and merge their scattered data throughout database. This solution will improve data quality in the database using Machine Learning and help users to base their decisions and researches on reliable, correct and complete data.

This paper is organized as follow: the second section provides the general background of our work, the third one exposes some related works, the fourth one presents an overview of the proposed approach for our solution which is validated in the fifth and final section using financial organization's data case of study.

2 Background and Context

In this section, we will first present the relation between data integration and data quality. Then expose the problems caused by bad data integration. Finally define the name matching algorithms as the tool that help unsupervised machine learning algorithms to cluster data, therefore enhance data quality and remedy the problem of data integration.

2.1 Public Data Integration

The integration of erroneous and heterogeneous data in a database, negatively affects the quality of data in an organization in terms of:

- **Making decisions:** If data are correct, therefore reliable, its affect positively decisions by reducing the risk of having incorrect analysis and reports.
- **Efficiency/Gain time:** Having good data quality help employees to do their work efficiently with spending the minimum time, this could be released if only data are already valid, employees will focus on their work instead of spending time to validate and fix data errors.
- **Competitiveness:** Enterprises basing their decisions on invalid data and data with poor quality, will absolutely lose opportunities in terms of competitiveness compared to competitors that make the right decisions based on correct data.
- **Reputation:** Having unreliable, invalid and incorrect data therefore incorrect statistics, reports and decisions can lead to reputation damage especially if the enterprise have sensitive data.

Data integration problems and bad data quality, causes many problems.

2.2 Data Integration Problems

Bad data integration could lead to serious problems in an organization by having heterogeneous, incorrect and inaccurate data. One of the major result of data integration problems is name conflicts due to typos mistakes and bad data quality. Name conflicts means having same object with redundant names, spelling mistakes, incorrect information… etc.

In order to solve the data integration problems, an unsupervised Machine Learning is the appropriate solution, because we have heterogeneous problems that do not obey to a specific rule. To use an unsupervised Machine Learning algorithm to group together those having same characteristics, we must pass to it as an entry the proximity and similarity between data. For that, we will resort to the name matching algorithm.

2.3 Name Matching Algorithms

Name matching algorithm is used in unsupervised learning and consist on calculating similarity/distance between data, based on mathematic functions, which reflect and translate the approximation of data between them. Output similarity indices will be used as input for the unsupervised learning algorithm to cluster in the same class similar data. There are too many name matching algorithms, some of them are [2–5]:

- **Hamming distance:** calculate the number of different characters between two names having obligatory same length.
- **Jaccard distance** = number of common characters between two names/number of different characters between them.
- **Jaro distance:**

$$d_{jaro}(A, B) = \frac{1}{3}\left(\frac{m}{|A|} + \frac{m}{|B|} + \frac{m - t/2}{m}\right)$$

With:

- m: number of common characters between A and B.
- t: number of transpositions among the common characters between A and B.

In this paper, we use the levenshtein distance as it is the most name matching algorithm known for spellchecking. Moreover, is the most appropriate to compare names having unequal lengths, or names that can be inserted, deleted or replaced.

To enhance data quality and solve data integration problems, we will use an unsupervised Machine Learning based on name matching. The next section present relative works to data quality in different contexts.

3 Related Works

Data quality is an important step in every organization, in previous related works (Table 1) they are limited to explain the importance of data quality and how to ensure it – data quality management. Our proposed approach aim to enhance financial data quality in a Machine Learning environment. The added value of our approach is that we have applied data quality in an organizational context and in an unsupervised Machine Learning environment by using name matching as input.

Table 1. Summary of related works

Data quality	Organizational context	Name matching	Unsupervised Machine Learning	Summary
[6]	No	No	No	Authors review the methods of assessing data quality and identify causes of problematic survey questions
[7]	No	No	No	Data quality is one of the major concerns of using crowdsourcing websites such as Amazon Mechanical Turk (MTurk) to recruit participants for online behavioral studies
[8]	Yes	No	No	In this study, a research model is proposed to explain the acquisition intention of big data analytics mainly from the theoretical perspectives of data quality management and data usage experience
[9]	Yes	No	No	Poor data quality (DQ) can have substantial social and economic impacts. The purpose of this paper is to develop a framework that captures the aspects of data quality that are important to data consumers
[10]	Yes	No	No	This article, describe the subjective and objective assessments of data quality, and present three functional forms for developing objective data quality metrics
[11]	Yes	No	No	This paper, introduce the data quality problem in the context of supply chain management (SCM) and propose methods for monitoring and controlling data quality
[12]	No	No	No	Increasing demand for better quality data and more investment to strengthen civil registration and vital statistics (CRVS) systems will require increased emphasis on objective, comparable, cost-effective monitoring and assessment methods to measure progress

4 Proposed Approach: Unsupervised Clustering

Our approach (Fig. 1) aim to validate financial data using affinity propagation the unsupervised learning algorithm, to correct data, therefore ensure data quality.

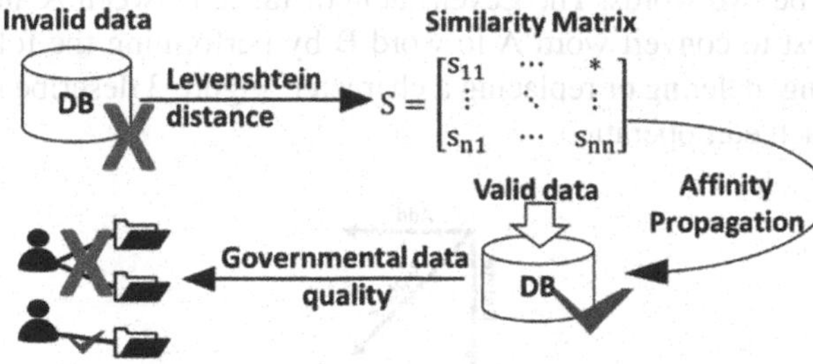

Fig. 1. Proposed approach to ensure data quality

4.1 Overview

To ensure data quality in an organization context, data must be correct and valid. We propose three major steps to process unsupervised Machine Learning:

- **Step1:** Calculate the similarity matrix using Levenshtein Distance. The smaller the distance, the greater the similarity.
- **Step2:** Clustering data using affinity propagation algorithm based on the previously calculated similarity matrix.
- **Step3:** Validate the performance of our clustering results with the ROC curve.

Figure 2, presents the technical environment used in our approach.

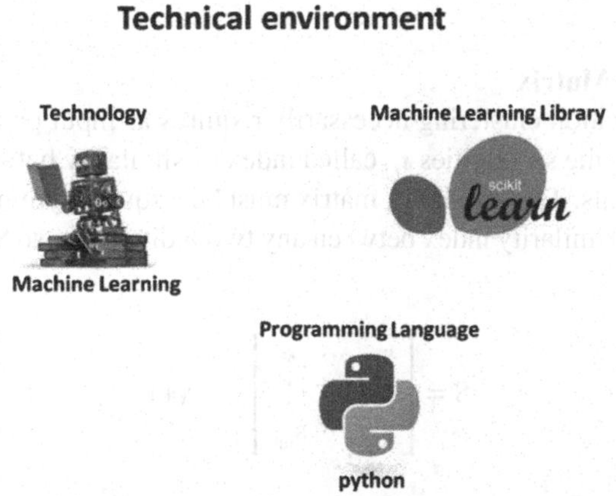

Fig. 2. Technical environment used in our proposed approach

4.2 Levenstein Distance

The Levenshtein distance (also called Edit-Distance), owes its name to the Soviet mathematician Vladimir Levenshtein who proposed it and defined it in 1965. This distance of Levenshtein is the most used to remedy the problems of misspelling (or of typos).

Let A and B be two words. The Levenshtein distance between A and B is equal to the minimum cost to convert word A to word B by performing the following editing operations: adding, deleting or replacing a character. Figure 3 describe the direction of movement for each edit operation.

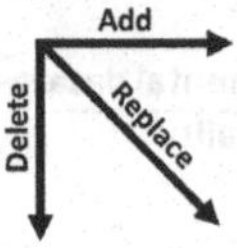

Fig. 3. Direction of movement of editing operations

Each operation carried out is worth 1 cost except in the case of a replacement of a character by another identical, we associate for this operation 0 cost.

4.3 Affinity Propagation Algorithm

The method of affinity propagation (AP) [13–16] is a method proposed by Frey and Dueck in 2007, based on graphs and the principle of message passing. AP consists on electing representatives, exemplars, around whom clusters are built. This algorithm takes as input parameter the similarity matrix S of size N * N with N the number of individuals to classify. Gradually, we will scan the fundamental concepts to understand the Affinity Propagation algorithm that automatically groups similar individuals that look like homogeneous clusters.

4.3.1 Similarity Matrix

The affinity propagation clustering necessarily requires as input parameter a similarity matrix S measuring the similarities $s_{i,j}$ called index of similarity between all the pairs (i, j) of the N individuals. This similarity matrix must be a square symmetric matrix ($*$) i.e. $s_{i,j} = s_{j,i}$ with s_* the similarity index between any two individuals, so S must have N rows and N columns.

$$S = \begin{bmatrix} s_{11} & \cdots & * \\ \vdots & \ddots & \vdots \\ s_{n1} & \cdots & s_{nn} \end{bmatrix} \quad (*)$$

Similarity matrix based on Levenshtein distance using Python
Entry: Let X be the N individuals to classify $X = \{I_1, I_2, I_3, \ldots, I_N\}$
Output: Similarity matrix of size N * N.
$s_{i,j} = -1 * \text{np.array}([[\text{distance.levenshtein}(i,j) \text{ for i in X}] \text{ for j in X}])$

After calculating the similarity matrix, the various similarity indices must be transformed into a graphical representation making possible to translate the similarity/dissimilarity relations between the individuals and facilitate message passing between data.

4.3.2 Message Passing

As already mentioned, the Affinity Propagation method is a method based on the message passing between the data, after having built a similarity matrix, which facilitate the exchange of messages between data in order to elect the exemplars and form all the clusters gathering the data having common characteristics.

Initially, all the data are considered as exemplars, which will themselves exchange two types of messages, responsibility and availability, to determine which are the best representatives around which the clusters will be formed.

In fact, the availabilities and responsibilities are calculated in an iterative way for each data towards others, in order to answer two important questions:

- What data would be the representative of all others to form a cluster?
- For each data, what is its good representative?

For each data i his representative k will be the one who will maximize the sum of availabilities and responsibilities (1):

$$\arg\max_{k} (A(i, K) + R(i, k)) \tag{1}$$

Below is an illustration of the exchange of the two types of messages "Responsibility R (i, k)" (Fig. 4) and "Availability A (i, k)" (Fig. 5) between the data k considered as exemplar and the data i:

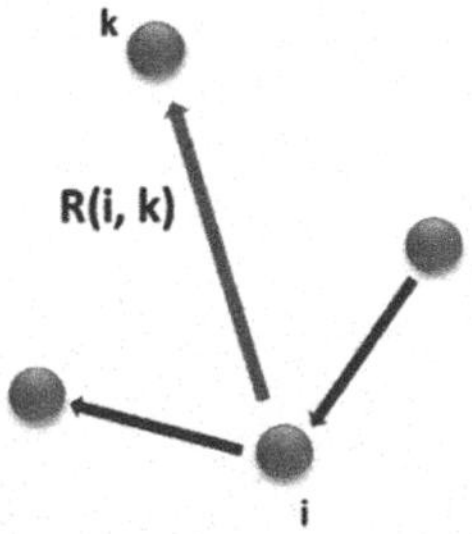

Fig. 4. Responsibility message R(i,k) from i to k

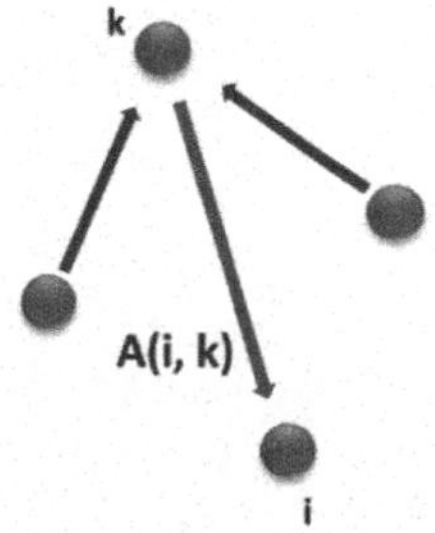

Fig. 5. Availability message A(i,k) from k to i

The responsibility R (i, k) exchanged between an exemplar candidate k and a data i, indicates how much k would be a good representative of i, i.e. the degree of responsibility of k on i compared to the other potential candidates available k′. R (i, k) is calculated as follows (2):

$$R(i,k) = s_{i,k} - \max_{k' \neq k}\{A(i,k') + s_{i,k'}\} \tag{2}$$

The availability A (i, k) exchanged between data i and an exemplar candidate k, indicates how appropriate would it be for i to choose k as its representative? In other words, after sending a responsibility message from i to k, k responds i with an availability message indicating whether it is still available to represent it or it has already been taken by another data i′ as its representative.

A (i, k) is calculated as follows (3):

$$A(i,k) = \min\left\{0, R(k,k) + \sum_{i' \notin \{i,k\}} \max\{0, R(i',k)\}\right\} \tag{3}$$

From (2) and (3) we can conclude that:

- The responsibility R (i, k) depends on the availability A (i, k) and vice versa.
- The responsibility R (i, k) depends on the computation of the similarity $s_{i,k}$ between the exemplar candidate k and the data i, as well as the similarity $s_{i,k'}$ between the data i and the other representatives k′ according to their availability A (i, k′).
- The availability A (i, k) depends on the responsibility of the representative k on himself or on his self-responsibility R (k, k), as well as the responsibility $R(i',k)$ of k on other data i′, with i′ ≠ i. The self-responsibility R (k, k) is high if k has no representatives.

"Affinity Propagation" algorithm [17]

Input: The similarity matrix S between the individuals to be classified.
Output: Clusters grouping individuals who are alike.

1.Construction of the graph from S.
2.Initialization of availabilities to 0: A (i, k) = 0
3.Update of availabilities and responsibilities as follows:

$$R(i,k) = s_{i,k} - \max_{k' \neq k}\{A(i,k') + s_{i,k'}\}$$

$$A(i,k) = \begin{cases} \min\left\{0, R(k,k) + \sum_{i' \notin \{i,k\}} \max\{0, R(i',k)\}\right\} & i \neq k \\ \sum_{i' \notin \{i,k\}} \max\{0, R(i',k)\} & i = k \end{cases}$$

4. For each iteration the availabilities and the responsibilities are updated until convergence according to a damping factor $\lambda \in [0,1]$ with 0.5 the default value of λ, and t the number of current iteration:

$$R^{(t+1)}(i,k) = (1-\lambda)\, R^{(t+1)}(i,k) + \lambda\, R^{(t)}(i,k)$$
$$A^{(t+1)}(i,k) = (1-\lambda)\, A^{(t+1)}(i,k) + \lambda\, A^{(t)}(i,k)$$

5. Determination of the representative k for each individual i:

$$\arg\max_{k}(A(i,k) + R(i,k))$$

5 Working Example

In order to validate our approach, we apply it to a real case of financial organization's data, but for confidential reasons we will anonymize the name of the organization, the system and taxpayers.

The treasury public organization has opted for a migration from its ancient system, which has been decentralized to a new centralized tax management system (TMS) regrouping data of taxpayers all over Morocco. After this migration, we find in the database of the system TMS lot of different taxpayers having same identification, CIN, number of the national ID card. The limitations of the TMS system have several negative impacts on the activity of the treasury, in terms of Efficiency and time like already explained in the section "2.1. Public Data Integration" and in terms of the most important and serious one which is money. The treasury loses in terms of money when it does not recover it debts, for example: If the taxpayer named "Necba Hanae" request for a tax clearance, the system reveals that the taxpayer is in a regular situation, whereas in fact he still has to pay taxes registered under the name of "Nesba Hanaa". However, taxpayers are exempt by law from paying taxes if they become prescribed.

Our objective aim to create a unique folder to each taxpayer by grouping together in the same cluster taxpayers having same ID, different names in terms of errors in spelling but represent same person. In other words, we must group and fusion the taxpayers that represent same person despite of having different spelling.

5.1 Data Integration Problems

The "CIN", is a unique identifier for every individual in the world regardless of its gender, its function, its origins… etc. Therefore, we cannot find two persons with same CIN, in other words:

- For the same CIN, we can only find one individual
- For the same individual, we can only find one CIN

Contrary in TMS system, we find for the same CIN several individuals or taxpayers, in the same CIN three categories of problem could be found:

- *Duplicate redundant taxpayers: Taxpayers having same name and are the same person, Ex:* Taxpayer 1 = "Necba Hanae" and Taxpayer 2 = "Necba Hanae".
- *Taxpayers having different name, incorrect spelling, but are the same person, Ex:* Taxpayer 1 = "Necba Hanae", Taxpayer 2 = "Nesba Hanaa", Taxpayer 3 = "Nesba-Hanae" and Taxpayer 4 = "Nesba Hanaa".
- *Taxpayers having different name and are actually two different people, Ex:* Taxpayer 1 = "Nesba-Hanae" and Taxpayer 2 = "Idrissi Mohamed".

5.2 DataSets

The database of the system TMS, include multiple tables with millions of data. In our case, we have worked with 25 million data. This huge mass of data is heterogeneous, therefore enumerate all existing errors in the database is impossible, thus we couldn't establish an exhaustive list of rules to correct name errors. For that, we have used Machine Learning technology instead of standard traditional programming.

5.3 Results and Evaluation

Results are as follow:

- Each similar taxpayers are clustered in a class.
- Similar taxpayers that represent the same person are clustered and merged under the correct name and CIN.

Since our solution is a clustering, that consists on grouping similar taxpayers in classes or clusters.

For this, we will use the ROC curve acronym of "Receiver Operating Characteristic", to evaluate performance and measure the validity of the results.

The "Affinity Propagation" algorithm we used for clustering, can be considered as a binary classifier since for the results obtained an individual is either classified in the correct class or not.

The ROC evaluation method is the representation of the FPR (False Positive Rate) according to the TPR (True Positive Rate).

To confirm the performance of the classifier, it is necessary to calculate the area under the curve of ROC or AUC. The closer the AUC gets to 1, the better the classifier and the predicted classes are accurate and 100% correct [18].

In order to calculate the TPR and FPR parameters of the ROC curve, it is necessary to go through the construction of confusion matrix Table 2 as shown below:

Table 2. Confusion matrix

		Prediction	
		Unclassified	Classified
Actual	Unclassified	TN	FP
	Classified	FN	TP

For our case:

- **True positives (TP):** Taxpayer classified in a class and in reality should be classified in this class.
- **True negatives (TN):** Taxpayer unclassified in a class and actually should not be classified.
- **False positive (FP):** Taxpayer classified in a class but in reality should not be classified at all.
- **False negatives (FN):** Unclassified taxpayer but in reality must be classified in a class.

TPR and FPR rates are:

- **True Positive Rate (TPR):** Among taxpayers who actually must be classified, how many times did the algorithm actually classified them?

  The following equation shows the method of calculating the TPR:

$$TPR = \frac{TP}{TP + FN}$$

- **False Positive Rate (FPR):** Among the taxpayers who actually must be unclassified, how many times did the algorithm classified them?

  The following equation shows the FPR calculation method:

$$FPR = \frac{FP}{FP + TN}$$

Graphically the performance of the Machine Learning algorithm “Propagation of affinity” in our case Fig. 6:

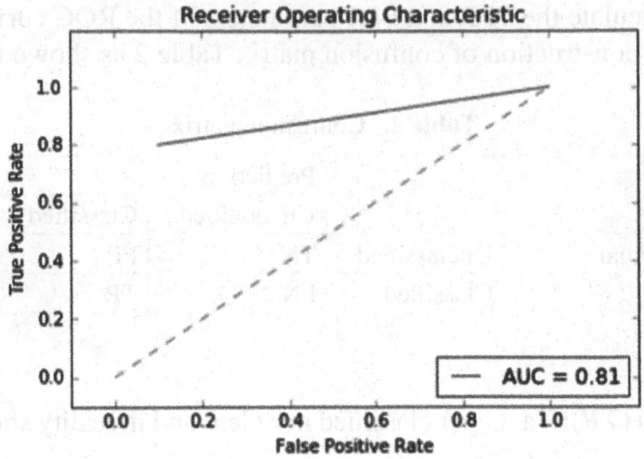

Fig. 6. ROC curve to evaluate the performance of the Machine Learning algorithm "Propagation of affinity" in our case

Figure 6 above shows that the "Affinity Propagation" algorithm is a good classifier since the AUC is 0.81 and therefore closer to 1, so the predicted classes of similar taxpayers to be merged are accurate and correct to 80%.

6 Conclusion

This paper presents a non-supervised Machine Learning approach that takes as input the matrix resulting from name matching algorithm, to solve data integration problems consequently ensure and enhance data quality. The proposed approach is applied to financial governmental data integration use case. From this paper, we aim to validate the contribution of new intelligent technologies such as Machine Learning to solve the most complex data integration problems, therefore enhance data quality of big data in an organizational context.

References

1. English, L.P.: Improving Data Warehouse and Business Information Quality: Methods for Reducing Costs and Increasing Profits. Wiley, New York (1999)
2. Recchia, G., Louwerse, M.M.: A Comparison of String Similarity Measures for Toponym Matching, pp. 54–61 (2013)
3. Christen, P.: A comparison of personal name matching: techniques and practical issues. In: IEEE, pp. 290–294 (2006)
4. Cohen, W.W., Ravikumar, P., Fienberg, S.E.: A comparison of string distance metrics for name-matching tasks. Paper Presented at the Proceedings of the 2003 International Conference on Information Integration on the Web, Acapulco, Mexico (2003)
5. Bilenko, M., Mooney, R., Cohen, W., Ravikumar, P., Fienberg, S.: Adaptive name matching in information integration. IEEE Intell. Syst. **18**(5), 16–23 (2003)
6. Pasick, R.J., Stewart, S.L., Bird, J.A., D'onofrio, C.N.: Quality of data in multiethnic health surveys. Public Health Rep. **116**, 223–243 (2016)

7. Peer, E., Vosgerau, J., Acquisti, A.: Reputation as a sufficient condition for data quality on Amazon Mechanical Turk. Behav. Res. Methods **46**(4), 1023–1031 (2014)
8. Kwon, O., Lee, N., Shin, B.: Data quality management, data usage experience and acquisition intention of big data analytics. Int. J. Inf. Manag. **34**(3), 387–394 (2014)
9. Cordier, T., Esling, P., Lejzerowicz, F., Visco, J., Ouadahi, A., Martins, C., Cedhagen, T., Pawlowski, J.: Predicting the ecological quality status of marine environments from eDNA metabarcoding data using supervised machine learning. Environ. Sci. Technol. **51**(16), 9118–9126 (2017)
10. Pipino, L.L., Lee, Y.W., Wang, R.Y.: Data quality assessment. Commun. ACM **45**(4), 211–218 (2002)
11. Hazen, B.T., Boone, C.A., Ezell, J.D., Jones-Farmer, L.A.: Data quality for data science, predictive analytics, and big data in supply chain management: an introduction to the problem and suggestions for research and applications. Int. J. Prod. Econ. **154**, 72–80 (2014)
12. Mikkelsen, L., Phillips, D.E., AbouZahr, C., Setel, P.W., De Savigny, D., Lozano, R., Lopez, A.D.: A global assessment of civil registration and vital statistics systems: monitoring data quality and progress. Lancet **386**(10001), 1395–1406 (2015)
13. Frey, B.J., Dueck, D.: Clustering by passing messages between data points. Science **315**(5814), 972–976 (2007)
14. Sharma, I., Motwani, M.: An efficient text clustering approach using biased affinity propagation. Int. J. Comput. Appl. **96** (1) (2014)
15. Hung, W.-C., Chu, C.-Y., Wu, Y.-L., Tang, C.-Y.: Map/reduce affinity propagation clustering algorithm. Int. J. Electron. Electr. Eng. **3**(4), 311–317 (2015)
16. Zhang, X., Furtlehner, C., Germain-Renaud, C., Sebag, M.: Data stream clustering with affinity propagation. IEEE Trans. Knowl. Data Eng. **26**(7), 1644–1656 (2014)
17. Limin, W., Li, Z., Xuming, H., Qiang, J., Guangyu, M., Ying, L.: An improved affinity propagation clustering algorithm based on entropy weight method and principal component analysis. Int. J. Database Theor. Appl. **9**(6), 227–238 (2016)
18. Hanley, J.A., McNeil, B.J.: The meaning and use of the area under a receiver operating characteristic (ROC) curve. Radiology **143**(1), 29–36 (1982)

Advanced Machine Learning Models for Large Scale Gene Expression Analysis in Cancer Classification: Deep Learning Versus Classical Models

Imene Zenbout(✉) and Souham Meshoul

Computer Science Department, Faculty of NTIC,
University Constantine 2 - Abdelhamid Mehri Biotechnology Research Center (CRBt) & CERIST, Constantine, Algeria
{imene.zenbout,souham.meshoul}@univ-constantine2.dz

Abstract. Analysis of large gene expression datasets for cancer classification is a crucial task in bioinformatics and a very challenging one as well. In this paper, we explore the potential of using advanced models in machine learning namely those based on deep learning to handle such task. For this purpose we propose a deep feed forward neural network architecture. In addition, we also investigate other classical yet very popular machine learning classifiers namely, support vector machine, naive bayes, k-nearest neighbours and shallow neural networks. The main objective is to appreciate the extent to which they are able to deal with the increasing size of these datasets. We conducted our experimental study using a high-performance computing platform with 32 compute nodes, each consisting of two Intel (R) Xeon (R) CPU E5-2650 2.00 GHz processors. Each processor is made up of 8 cores. Five data sets available at the omnibus library have been used to test the five models . Experimental results show the effectiveness of deep learning and its ability to deal with large scale data.

Keywords: Gene expression · Machine learning · Deep learning
Neural network · Classification · Cancer classification · Big data

1 Introduction

In the last decades, the remarkable advances in microarrays technology opened huge opportunities in genomic research and especially in cancer researches to move from clinical decisions and standard medicine toward personalized medicine. The analysis of gene expression level may reveal a lot of informations about the cancer type, its outcomes also allow the possibility to predict about the best therapy in order to improve the survival rate.

Gene expression microarrays is a new breakthrough technology developed in the late 1990s [1] that can measure the gene expression level of thousands

Y. Tabii et al. (Eds.): BDCA 2018, CCIS 872, pp. 210–221, 2018.
https://doi.org/10.1007/978-3-319-96292-4_17

of genes corresponding to different samples or experiments simultaneously [2]. Many solution schemes for cancer classification and therapy process on molecular and cellular levels may be concluded from the analysis and the comparison of the generated data through different experiments [3]. Microarrays technology has two variants in the market [3], (1) cDNA microarrays-*On Spotted array*- and (2) oligonucleotide microarrays-*On GeneChip*-. cDNA microarrays are cheaper and more flexible as custom-made arrays, it was developed at Stanford University. While oligonucleotide arrays (developed at Affymetrix) are more automated, stable, and easier to be compared through different experiments [3,4]. The data produced by microarrays technology represent the result of thousands of genes for few experiments where this matrix can be used to evaluate the variation of gene through samples or the interaction of genes in different samples.

Since DNA microarray technology allows to analyse the gene data quickly and at one time in order to get the expression pattern of a huge amount of genes simultaneously [5], gene expression data are unique in their nature due to three reasons: (1) their high dimensionality (more than thousands of genes), (2) the publicly available data are very small just hundred or fewer of samples, (3) a big partial of the genes are irrelevant in cancer classification and analysis, where the problem is to find the difference between cancerous gene expression tissues and non-cancerous tissues. For these reasons, and in order to handle those kind of data researchers proposed that feature selection and/or dimensionality reduction is a relevant process in order to take advantage of the data and to converge toward accurate classifiers. Several machine learning methods have been used in caner classification, yet recently deep learning start to be investigated as well in this process due to its ability to work on raw and high dimensional data.

The paper investigates the use of advanced machine learning to handle large scale gene expression data to enhance cancer classification. Also it explores the potential of deep learning based classifiers to manage such datasets. Hence, we propose a simple feed forward neural network and implement four yet powerful classical classifiers namely, support vector machine (SVM), k-nearest neighbours (KNN), bayes naive (BN) and shallow neural network (SNN). We tested the four classifiers along with the deep classifier on publicly available five cancer datasets in the omnibus library. the cancer types are: Leukemia cancer, inflammatory breast cancer, lung cancer, bladder cancer and thyroid cancer

The remainder of the paper is organized as the following: the first Sect. 2 highlights the used classification methods. Then Sect. 3 presents an overview on the recent works related to machine learning and deep learning for gene expression and cancer classification. In Sect. 4 we explained our proposed deep feed forward neural network for the discussed problem. Then the used datasets are described in Sect. 5. Section 6 deals with the experimental study and presents the obtained results and our discussion. Finally in Sect. 7 conclusions are drawn.

2 Classification Methods

Many classification methods have been introduced through time. In the following we present four main methods.

2.1 K-Nearest Neighbours

K-nearest neighbours (KNN) classifier is the simplest supervised classifier that attempts to find the class membership of an unknown instance in the testing dataset $\{X\}$ on the basis of the majority vote of the k-nearest neighbours [6]. KNN is a *lazy learning* or an instance based learning, where the function is approximated locally and all the computation is postponed until classification [5]. When classifying a sample x, the KNN classifier finds in the testing set $\{X\}$ the most similar k examples to x and then chooses the most appropriate label class among this examples, by calculating the similarities between the attributes of the object x and the k samples. The simplest or the most used way to calculate the similarity between x and y is the geometric distance [7].

2.2 Support Vector Machine

Support Vector Machine (SVM) is also a supervised machine learning tool, that was introduced and implemented in 1995 [8] for pattern recognition. SVM was widely used for both classification and regression tasks [9]. The concept of SVM is based on [8, 10–12]:

The $\{X\}$ instances of the training data set are plotted in some high-dimensional features space, where the task is to find the support vectors that maximise the margin (also the optimal hyperplane) not between the vector and the data but between the classes in the space (see Fig. 1).

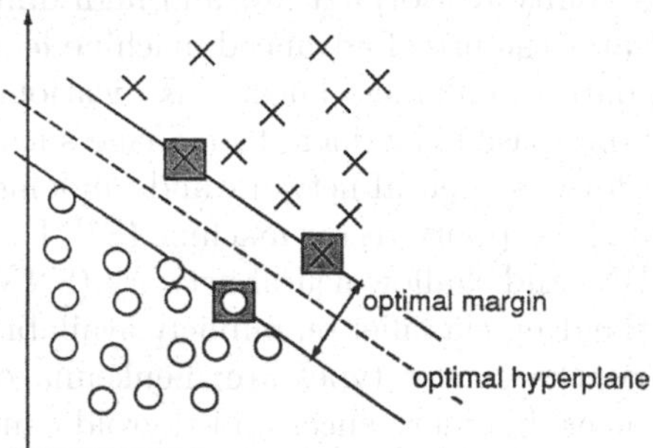

Fig. 1. An SVM example represents the maximum margin between classes in two dimensional space [8]

2.3 Naive Bayes Classifier

Naive Bayes classifier (NB) as well is one of the first simple supervised machine learning. It is a probabilistic model based on the Bayesian formula to calculate the probability of class A given the values B_i of all attributes for an instance to be classified [13]. NB classifiers follow the assumption that all attributes of a given example are independent of each other, which facilitates the learning phase because every parameter can be learned separately, especially in the scalable data [14]. Naive bayes classifier have been intensively used in different fields such as document classification [14], Medical application like EGG signal analysis [15], music emotion classification [13] based on lyrics (text) analysis, and for image classification [16] as well.

2.4 Deep Learning

Deep Learning (DL) is the new breakthrough in machine learning and Artificial intelligence. DL migrates with machine learning technique from hand-designed features toward data-driven features-learning, where deep learning can learn complex models through simple features learned from raw data [17].

Deep Neural Networks (DNN) were the best showcase of deep learning with the aspect of multilayer that offers the possibility to explore the hierarchical representation of data by increasing the level of abstraction [18]. This properties allowed DNN to demonstrate state-of-the-art performance in different domains [19–21].

In deep learning we can find: (1) deep neural networks (DNN), (2) convolution neural network (CNN) and (3) recurrent neural network (RNN). DNN is the simplest representation of multilayer neural network. It may be either a multilayer perceptron , auto encoders (AE), stacked auto encoders (SAE), deep belief networks (DBN) or boltzman machine. While (2), convolution neural networks are built upon three majors layers convolution layers, max-pooling layers and and non-linear layer. At each convolutional layer a group of local weighted sums called features are obtained. At each pooling layer, maximum or average sub sampling of non-overlapping regions in feature maps is performed which allows CNNs to identify more complex features [17,18]. RNNs, they are designed to use sequential information, and they have a basic structure with cyclic connection. Past information is implicitly stored in the hidden units called *state vectors* using an explicit memory *long short term memory*, and the current output is computed based on all the previous input through this state vector [17].

3 Machine Learning in Gene Expression Cancer Analysis Related Work

Both supervised and unsupervised methods have been used in gene expression data analysis. in 1998 a cluster analysis based on graphical visualisation method to reveal correlated patterns between genes were proposed in [22]. Supervised machine learning served microarrays data analysis intensively and effectively [5]. Neural network were proposed in [23] for Cancer classification and diagnostic prediction. Li et al. [24] proposed a genetic algorithm/k-nearest neighbours approach in order to select effective genes that can be highly discriminative in cancer sample classification, by splitting the set of genes into several subsets and then calculate the frequency of genes' membership to the subset. After a number of iterations the genes with high frequency are the most relevant to the classification. The latter was used recently in [25] in order to select the most discriminative genes to classify the TCGA data of 31 different cancer type. SVM also was used in the field [10], where in [26] a new SVM ensemble based on Adaboost (ADASVM) and consistency based feature selection (CBFS) was proposed for leukemia cancer classification, SVM was used to overcome the problems of regular ensemble methods based on decision trees and neural network. Where the authors cited in the former the issue of the tree size and overfitting problem in the latter. Another approach based on Battcharya distance was implemented in [27] for colon cancer and leukemia cancer. The features were selected based on their ranking score, where the genes with larger Battcharya distance are the most effective in classification. Then the subset with the lowest error classification rate is selected as the marker genes. In [28] a shallow neural network was proposed for colon cancer classification with a variation on parameter setting that uses the Monte-Carlo algorithm with SVM theory.

Recently researchers start to apply deep learning in the context [29]. Table 1 illustrates the top recent researches in the literature, where we compared the works based on the used features selection model, the classification model and its accuracy.

Table 1. Deep learning cancer classification recent research. **H/L** the highest and lowest accuracy score of the classifier depends on the dataset

Reference	Feature selection	Classification method	Accuracy	
[30]	PCA+ Sparse AE	Softmax classifier	L 35.0%	H 97.5%
	PCA+ Stacked AE		L 33.71%	H 95.15%
[31]	Adversarial net + CNN +RBM	Segmoid+CNN	—	
[32]	SDAE	SVM	98.04%	
		ANN	96.95%	
[33]	Desq	(KNN,SVM,DT,RF, GBDTs)+ANN	H 98.80%	L 98.41%

Fakoor et al. [30] present the use of deep learning for cancer classification through unsupervised features learning. The proposed approach is a two phases process. The feature learning phase, where Principal Component Analysis (PCA) was used for dimensionality reduction. Since PCA is a linear representation of data, some raw features were added to capture the non-linearity of the features. Then sparse auto encoders (Stacked auto encoders in the second test) were used for the unsupervised features selection. In the second phase, the set of learned features with some of the labelled data were passed to the classifier to learn the classifier, as well fine-tuning was used to tune the weights of the features and generalize the features set to adapt to different cancer types.

Bhat et al. [31] used adversarial model based on convolutional neural network and restricted boltzmann machine for gene selection and classification of Inflammatory Breast Cancer. The proposed generative adversarial network (GAN) is a combination of two network. The first network represent a generator that tries to mimic examples (wrong inputs) from the training data set and fed them among the real inputs to the second network. The latter works as a discriminator that tries to distinguish the true inputs from the false ones and classify the samples as accurately as possible. The process continues until the discriminator can no longer distinguish noise input from the real ones. The learnt features are passed to a sigmoid layer for supervised classification.

Danaee et al. [32] proposed stacked denoising auto encoders (SDAE) for breast cancer classification. The paper used SDAE to addresses the high dimensionality and noisy gene expression issues and to select the most discriminative genes in breast cancer classification. The selected genes have been evaluated by ANN and SVM.

In [33], a deep learning approach that combines five classical classification methods was proposed for the classification of lung cancer, stomach cancer and inflammatory breast cancer. The paper used DeSeq for features selection, then the selected features were passed through the five classifiers namely, KNN, SVM, Decision Trees (DTs), Random Forest(RF) and GBDTs in the first classification stage. The output of the first stage is used as the input for a five layer neural network to classify the samples.

4 Deep Forward Neural Network for Cancer Classification

The tackled cancer classification problem can be formulated as follows: Given a matrix $\{X\}$ of NxM dimension where N represent the number of samples and M is the number of genes, each $x_{i,j}$ represents the expression level of the gene j related to the sample i, and each sample X is associated to a class that can be either cancerous or not cancerous for binary classification. It can also refer to the the corresponding subtype of the cancer for multiclass classification. Then the problem can be binary classification or multiclass classification.

The architecture is a multilayer feed forward neural network organized as the following:

- The input layer receives the set of features that represent the gene expression values of each sample.
- Seven hidden layers have been used. Four are fully connected layers, and between the layers we added three dropout layers that applies a dropout penalty to avoid overfitting.
- An output layer with a softmax classifier is used to assign the set of received features from the Seventh hidden layer to their corresponding class.
- We applied a regularization *l2()* on the input data at the input layer level.
- For the activation of layers we used the non-linear *tanh* and *relu* functions.

Algorithm 1: Proposed architecture pseudo-code

```
Data: X,y
Apply one of [KPCA, FRE, UFS] for dimensionality reduction;
X_train, X_test <-Split(X);
y_train, y_test <-Split(y);
Build the Deep forward classifier;
Initialized the Deep forward classifier;
Define the number of epochs and the batch size;
while iteration less than or equal to the number of epochs do
    while batch_size less than or equal to the number of samples do
        X_batch, y_batch <- next_batch(X_train, y_train);
        Train model(X_batch, y_batch);
        Update batch_size;
    end
    Evaluate model(X_test, y_test);
    Reset batch_size;
end
```

The pseudo-code (Algorithm 1) outlines the different steps of our proposed classifier building. We used batch training to train the network with *adam*optimizer and a *categorical crossentropy* loss. Also, we applied *hold-out* cross validation (70% training data, 30% testing data) to asses the performance of the classifier. The used performance metrics are accuracy and the loss function where the objective is to maximize the accuracy and minimize the loss without dropping in overfitting and underfitting issues.

For dimensionality reduction we used three methods namely, Kernel Principal Component analysis (KPCA) for non-linear problems, Recursive Feature Elimination (RFE) and Univariate Feature Selection (UFS). In this way we can evaluate the performance of the proposed classifier on different reduced data space.

5 Datasets

The datasets (Table 2) are publicaly available in the GEO bank (https://www.ncbi.nlm.nih.gov/geo/query/acc.cgi). They represent the expression level of patient genes that define if the samples are cancerous or not cancerous, the type and the stage of the disease. We applied data preprocessing and imputation on some of the data sets in order to handle the missing values of some genes that appear in few samples.

- *Leukimea Cancer (DS1):* The data set is stored under the key *GSE15061* [34], it represents a case study of the transformation of leukemia cancer from AML to MDS stage. the samples are all bone marrow distributed as 164 MDS patients, 202 AML patients and 69 non leukemia. The total set is 870 samples with 54613 genes.

- *Inflamatory Breast Cancer (DS2):* Stored under the key *GSE45581* [35]. The samples are the expression of IBC tumor cells and non-IBC cells. The dataset is a total of 45 samples of Inflammatory Breast Cancer (IBC) and non-IBC with 40991 genes.
- *Lung Cancer (DS3):* The dataset is stored under the key *GSE2088* [36]. It represents a set of 48 samples of squamous cell carcinoma (SSC), 9 samples of adenocarcinoma and 30 normal lung cancer samples. The total set is 87 samples of 40368 genes.
- *Bladder Cancer (DS4):* The access key is *GSE31189* [37], it represents the gene expression of human urothelial cells, it contains 52 samples of urothelial bladder cancer patient and 40 non-cancer samples. The set is 92 samples represented through 54675 genes.
- *Thyroid Cancer (DS5): GSE82208* [38], this data set has been used to differentiate between malignant and benign follicular tumours. The set is a collection of 27 samples of follicular thyroid cancer (FTC) and 25 follicular thyroid adenomas (FTA) with the dimensionality of 54675.

Table 2. The data sets description (* preprocessed data set)

Data set	Genes	Samples	Classes
DS1	54613	870	MDS, AML, non-leukemia
DS2	40991	45	IBC, non-IBC, Normal
DS3(*)	40368	87	Normal, Squamous carcinoma=SSC, Adenocarcinoma
DS4	54671	92	Cancerous , Normal
DS5	54671	52	FTC, FTA

6 Results and Discussion

For the aforementioned classical machine learning models (SVM, BN, KNN) we used the scikit-learn python package models, for the shallow network and deep neural network architecture we used sequential model of keras package with tensorflow back-end.

The experimental results (Table 3) shows the variation of the classification accuracy rate, depending on the classifier and the dimensionality reduction method. The obtained results demonstrate the usefulness of supervised machine learning in tumour classification. Yet the results also prove that the deep classifier was able to achieve better performance and score a higher accuracy (up to 100% in different cases) than the classical models.

The proposed DNN model was able to achieve the highest possible accuracy between the classifiers in many situations for the five datasets. Citing the dataset DS4, with the new feature space obtained by univariate feature selection, deep learning overcomes the other classifiers. While in DS1, DS2 respectively DS3, the deep classifier achieved the highest accuracy score in both RFE and UFS. Whereas in DS5, for the three dimensionality reduction models deep learning was able to conquer the other classifiers.

Table 3. Comparative study results in terms of accuracy. Bold values represent the best obtained score.

Datasets	FS	SVM	KNN	BN	DNN	Shallow net
DS1	KPCA	0.44	0.**0.47**	0.40	0.45	0.44
	RFE	0.64	085	0.66	**0.90**	0.88
	UFS	0.63	0.79	0.57	**0.80**	0.79
DS2	KPCA	0.29	0.64	**0.86**	0.64	0.36
	RFE	0.28	0.42	0.64	**0.78**	0.71
	UFS	0.29	0.57	0.79	**0.85**	0.51
DS3	KPCA	0.59	**1.0**	**1.0**	0.81	0.70
	RFE	0.70	0.96	**1.0**	**1.0**	0.96
	UFS	**1.0**	**1.0**	0.96	**1.0**	0.96
DS4	KPCA	0.60	0.57	**0.82**	0.68	0.57
	RFE	0.57	0.60	**0.78**	0.64	0.60
	UFS	0.57	0.93	0.92	**0.96**	0.79
DS5	KPCA	0.38	0.56	0.81	**0.87**	0.81
	RFE	0.87	0.87	0.87	**1.0**	0.93
	UFS	0.81	**0.88**	0.81	**0.88**	0.87

Compared to SVM and shallow networks, BN and KNN performance was very promising as well. Both classifiers were able to achieve the highest score in three out of five datasets. The Bayes naive classifier performance was at its best with kernel principle components and recursive feature elimination in DS2, DS3, DS4. While KNN performed better with KPCA and UFS in DS1,DS3 and DS5. The overall performance of SVM and shallow network was good yet in the studied cases, it was not good enough compared to the deep classifier performance.

For the case where the proposed classifier was not able to achieve the best accuracy, we believe that an improved architecture (in its density, depth and parameters setting) and a better feature selection model would improve its performance. It is worth noting that the worst cases for the deep network (DS1,DS2,DS3, and DS4) was where we used KPCA as a dimensionality reduction method. This let us to make the assumption that the new feature space was not quite discriminative in order to train the deep classifier to perform accurately.

7 Conclusion

In the era of information and massive datasets, classification and machine learning have been intensively applied by computational, statistical and data analysis researchers to mine, organize, and categorize huge data sets in order to extract a valuable knowledge and acceptable patterns in a variety of field for decades.

Recently with the advances in biological data generation and the migration of biological and medical community toward personalized medicine and cancer advanced treatment systems, scientists start to apply classification and machine learning in order to classify and extract biomarker genes that may help in the therapy process. Through this paper we have seen that machine learning was widely used from the first and classical models to the new deep learning innovation. Therefore we think it may be a key for new achievements in medical informatics. Also the experimental results and the theoretical research mainly in cancer classification problem, have proved to us that every classification model have its strength and weakness and the variation between the performance of each classifier, mainly classical models, depends on the data and the experimental environment. Also we have seen that deep learning is very effective and powerful to handle biological large scale data sets, and was able to conquer other models in their discrimination and classification accuracy. In our future contributions we will try to use deep models for the selection and identification of relevant biomarkers for cancer diagnosis, therapy process.

Acknowledgement. We express our sincere gratitude to every one that help us to accomplish this work. This was granted access to the HPC ressources of UCI-UFMC '(Unité de Calcul Intensif)' of the University FRERES MENTOURI CONSTANTINE1. This work has been supported by the national research project CNEPRU under-grant N:B*07120140037.

References

1. Bumgarner, R.: Overview of DNA microarrays: types, applications, and their future. Curr. Protoc. Mol. Biol. 22.1.1–22.1.11 (2013)
2. Zhang, X., Zhou, X., Wang, X.: Basics for bioinformatics. In: Jiang, R., Zhang, X., Zhang, M.Q. (eds.) Basics of Bioinformatics, pp. 1–25. Springer, Heidelberg (2013). https://doi.org/10.1007/978-3-642-38951-1_1
3. Xu, Y., Cui, J., Puett, D.: Omic data, information derivable and computational needs. In: Xu, Y., Cui, J., Puett, D. (eds.) Cancer Bioinformatics, pp. 41–63. Springer, New York (2014). https://doi.org/10.1007/978-1-4939-1381-7_2
4. Harrington, C.A., Rosenow, C., Retief, J.: Monitoring gene expression using dna microarrays. Curr. Opin. Microbiol. **3**(3), 285–291 (2000)
5. Bhola, A., Tiwari, A.: Machine learning based approaches for cancer classification using gene expression data. Mach. Learn. Appl.: Int. J. **2**, 01–12 (2015)
6. Kriti, Virmani, J., Agarwal, R.: Evaluating the efficacy of gabor features in the discrimination of breast density patterns using various classifiers. In: Dey, N., Ashour, A., Borra, S. (eds.) Classification in BioApps, LNCVB, vol. 26, pp. 105–131. Springer, Cham (2018). https://doi.org/10.1007/978-3-319-65981-7_5
7. Kubat, M.: Similarities: nearest-neighbor classifiers. An Introduction to Machine Learning, pp. 43–64. Springer, Cham (2015). https://doi.org/10.1007/978-3-319-20010-1_3
8. Cortes, C., Vapnik, V.: Support-vector networks. Mach. Learn. **20**(3), 273–297 (1995)

9. Cleophas, T.J., Zwinderman, A.H.: Support vector machines. In: Cleophas, T.J., Zwinderman, A.H. (eds.) Machine Learning in Medicine, pp. 155–161. Springer, Dordrecht (2013). https://doi.org/10.1007/978-94-007-6886-4_15
10. Vanitha, C.D.A., Devaraj, D., Venkatesulu, M.: Gene expression data classification using support vector machine and mutual information-based gene selection. Procedia Comput. Sci. **47**(Supplement C), 13–21 (2015). Graph Algorithms, High Performance Implementations and Its Applications (ICGHIA 2014)
11. Kubat, M.: Inter-class boundaries: linear and polynomial classifiers. An Introduction to Machine Learning, pp. 65–90. Springer, Cham (2015). https://doi.org/10.1007/978-3-319-20010-1_4
12. Shalev-Shwartz, S., Ben-David, S.: Understanding Machine Learning: From Theory to Algorithms. Cambridge University Press, New York (2014)
13. An, Y., Sun, S., Wang, S.: Naive Bayes classifiers for music emotion classification based on lyrics. In: 2017 IEEE/ACIS 16th International Conference on Computer and Information Science (ICIS), pp. 635–638, May 2017
14. McCallum, A., Nigam, K., et al.: A comparison of event models for Naive Bayes text classification. In: AAAI-98 Workshop on Learning for Text Categorization, Madison, WI, vol. 752, pp. 41–48 (1998)
15. Sharmila, A., Geethanjali, P.: Dwt based detection of epileptic seizure from EEG signals using naive bayes and k-NN classifiers. IEEE Access **4**, 7716–7727 (2016)
16. Karthick, G., Harikumar, R.: Comparative performance analysis of Naive Bayes and SVM classifier for oral X-ray images. In: 2017 4th International Conference on Electronics and Communication Systems (ICECS), pp. 88–92, February 2017
17. Yann, L., Yoshua, B., Geoffrey, H.: Deep learning. Nature **521**, 436–444 (2015)
18. Min, S., Lee, B., Yoon, S.: Deep Learning in Bioinformatics. ArXiv e-prints, March 2016
19. Elleuch, M., Maalej, R., Kherallah, M.: A new design based-SVM of the CNN classifier architecture with dropout for offline arabic handwritten recognition. Procedia Comput. Sci. **80**(C), 1712–1723 (2016)
20. Wen, X., Fuhrman, S., Michaels, G.S., Carr, D.B., Smith, S., Barker, J.L., Somogyi, R.: Large-scale temporal gene expression mapping of central nervous system development. Proc. Natl. Acad. Sci. **95**(1), 334–339 (1998)
21. Alipanahi, B., Delong, A., Weirauch, M.T., Frey, B.J.: Predicting the sequence specificities of DNA-and RNA-binding proteins by deep learning. Nat. Biotechnol. **33**(8), 831–838 (2015)
22. Michaels, G.S., Carr, D.B., Askenazi, M., Fuhrman, S., Wen, X., Somogyi, R.: Cluster analysis and data visualization of large-scale gene expression data. Pac. Symp. Biocomput. **3**, 42–53 (1998)
23. Khan, J., Wei, J.S., Ringner, M., Saal, L.H., Ladanyi, M., Westermann, F., Berthold, F., Schwab, M., Antonescu, C.R., Peterson, C., et al.: Classification and diagnostic prediction of cancers using gene expression profiling and artificial neural networks. Nat. Med. **7**(6), 673–679 (2001)
24. Li, L., Darden, T.A., Weingberg, C., Levine, A., Pedersen, L.G.: Gene assessment and sample classification for gene expression data using a genetic algorithm/k-nearest neighbor method. Comb. Chem. High Throughput Screen. **4**(8), 727–739 (2001)
25. Li, Y., Kang, K., Krahn, J.M., Croutwater, N., Lee, K., Umbach, D.M., Li, L.: A comprehensive genomic pan-cancer classification using the cancer genome atlas gene expression data. BMC Genomics **18**(1), 508 (2017)

26. Begum, S., Chakraborty, D., Sarkar, R.: Cancer classification from gene expression based microarray data using SVM ensemble. In: 2015 International Conference on Condition Assessment Techniques in Electrical Systems (CATCON), pp. 13–16, December 2015
27. Ang, J.C., Haron, H., Hamed, H.N.A.: Semi-supervised SVM-based feature selection for cancer classification using microarray gene expression data. In: Ali, M., Kwon, Y.S., Lee, C.-H., Kim, J., Kim, Y. (eds.) IEA/AIE 2015. LNCS (LNAI), vol. 9101, pp. 468–477. Springer, Cham (2015). https://doi.org/10.1007/978-3-319-19066-2_45
28. Chen, H., Zhao, H., Shen, J., Zhou, R., Zhou, Q.: Supervised machine learning model for high dimensional gene data in colon cancer detection. In: 2015 IEEE International Congress on Big Data, pp. 134–141, June 2015
29. Urda, D., Montes-Torres, J., Moreno, F., Franco, L., Jerez, J.M.: Deep learning to analyze RNA-seq gene expression data. In: Rojas, I., Joya, G., Catala, A. (eds.) IWANN 2017. LNCS, vol. 10306, pp. 50–59. Springer, Cham (2017). https://doi.org/10.1007/978-3-319-59147-6_5
30. Fakoor, R., Ladhak, F., Nazi, A., Huber, M.: Using deep learning to enhance cancer diagnosis and classification. In: Proceedings of the International Conference on Machine Learning (2013)
31. Bhat, R.R., Viswanath, V., Li, X.: Deepcancer: detecting cancer through gene expressions via deep generative learning. CoRR abs/1612.03211 (2016)
32. Danaee, P., Ghaeini, R., Hendrix, D.A.: A deep learning approach for cancer detection and relevent gene identification, pp. 219–229. World Scientific (2016)
33. Xiao, Y., Wu, J., Lin, Z., Zhao, X.: A deep learning-based multi-model ensemble method for cancer prediction. Comput. Methods Programs Biomed. **153**, 1–9 (2018)
34. Mills, K.I., Kohlmann, A., Williams, P.M., Wieczorek, L., Liu, W.M., Li, R., Wei, W., Bowen, D.T., Loeffler, H., Hernandez, J.M., Hofmann, W.K., Haferlach, T.: Microarray-based classifiers and prognosis models identify subgroups with distinct clinical outcomes and high risk of AML transformation of myelodysplastic syndrome. Blood **114**(5), 1063–1072 (2009)
35. Woodward, W.A., Krishnamurthy, S., Yamauchi, H., El-Zein, R., Ogura, D., Kitadai, E., Niwa, S.I., Cristofanilli, M., Vermeulen, P., Dirix, L., Viens, P., van Laere, S., Bertucci, F., Reuben, J.M., Ueno, N.T.: Genomic and expression analysis of microdissected inflammatory breast cancer. Breast Cancer Res. Treat. **138**(3), 761–772 (2013)
36. Fujiwara, T., Hiramatsu, M., Isagawa, T., Ninomiya, H., Inamura, K., Ishikawa, S., Ushijima, M., Matsuura, M., Jones, M.H., Shimane, M., Nomura, H., Ishikawa, Y., Aburatani, H.: ASCL1-coexpression profiling but not single gene expression profiling defines lung adenocarcinomas of neuroendocrine nature with poor prognosis. Lung Cancer **75**(1), 119–125 (2012)
37. Urquidi, V., Goodison, S., Cai, Y., Sun, Y., Rosser, C.J.: A candidate molecular biomarker panel for the detection of bladder cancer. Cancer Epidemiol. Prev. Biomark. **21**(12), 2149–2158 (2012)
38. Wojtas, B., Pfeifer, A., Oczko-Wojciechowska, M., Krajewska, J., Czarniecka, A., Kukulska, A., Eszlinger, M., Musholt, T., Stokowy, T., Swierniak, M., Stobiecka, E., Chmielik, E., Rusinek, D., Tyszkiewicz, T., Halczok, M., Hauptmann, S., Lange, D., Jarzab, M., Paschke, R., Jarzab, B.: Gene expression (mRNA) markers for differentiating between malignant and benign follicular thyroid tumours. Int. J. Mol. Sci. **18**(6) (2017)

Stemming and Lemmatization for Information Retrieval Systems in Amazigh Language

Amri Samir(✉) and Zenkouar Lahbib

LEC Laboratory, EMI School, University Med V, Rabat, Morocco
amri.samir@gmail.com

Abstract. Stemming and lemmatization are two language modeling techniques used to improve the document retrieval precision performances. Stemming is a procedure to reduce all words with the same stem to a common form whereas lemmatization removes inflectional endings and returns the base form of a word.

The idea of this paper is to explain how a stemming or lemmatization in Amazigh language can improve the search outcomes by providing results that fit better with the query the user introduced.

In Document retrieval systems, lemmatization produced better precision compared to stemming. Overall the findings suggest that language modeling techniques improves document retrieval, with lemmatization technique producing the best result.

Keywords: Search engine · HMM · Lemmatization · Stemming
Machine learning

1 Introduction

The process of lemmatization and stemming is the same: given a set of affixes, for each word in a list, after check if the word ends with any of the affixes, and, if so, and apart from a few exceptions, remove the affix from the word. The challenge is that this process is sometimes not efficient to retrieve the base form of a word, in most cases; the stem is not the same as the lemma [2].

For the search query procedures, the traditional approach has been stemming but due to its limitations it seems necessary to look for another method, and there is where lemmatization shows up [3].

The goal of both stemming and lemmatization is the same: they reduce the inflectional forms and derivations from each word to a common root.

When we are running a search, we want to find as many results as possible, and that includes not only the exact word we typed on the search bar but also the ones that have the same root. For example, when we look for the word sewer, it will enrich our findings if we have results containing words like sew or sewerlike.

So, words appear in Amazigh language in many forms:

– Inflections: adding a suffix to a word, that doesn't change its grammatical category, such as (-iwn, -iwin) for plural in nouns (s). (afr → afriwn, wing → wings in English)

Y. Tabii et al. (Eds.): BDCA 2018, CCIS 872, pp. 222–233, 2018.
https://doi.org/10.1007/978-3-319-96292-4_18

- Derivations - adding a suffix to a word that changes its grammatical category, such as iffr (verb) => iffri (noun) (hide → cave in English).

Stemming and lemmatization are useful for many text-processing applications such as Information Retrieval Systems (IRS); they normalize words to their common base form [4].

- Lemmatization is the technique of converting the words of a sentence to its dictionary form. To have the proper lemma, it is necessary to check the morphological analysis of each word.
- Stemming is the method of converting the words of a text to its invariable portions. Different algorithms are used in the stemming, but the most common in English is Porter stemmer. The rules contained in this algorithm are divided in five different phases numbered from 1 to 5. The aim of these rules is to reduce the words to the base form.

The essential difference is that a lemma is the dictionary form of all its inflectional forms. However, the stem can be the same for the inflectional forms of different lemmas, providing then noise to our search results. Also, the same lemma can have forms with different stems.

The remainder of the paper is structured as follows: the related works are discussed in the following section. This is then followed by language background and the research design which focuses on the stemming and lemmatization techniques, experiment setup and the evaluation metrics used. The results and discussion follow next.

2 Related Work

Users create in a language model a query to describe the information that they need and the system will choose keywords from the query that are deemed to be relevant. These keywords will be matched against the documents in a collection. When similarities are found between the given query and a document in the collection, that document is retrieved and then matched against the rest of the retrieved documents for ranking purposes [1]. Stemming and lemmatization usually help to improve the language models by making faster the search process.

So, there are three classifications of stemming and lemmatization algorithms: truncating methods, statistical methods, and mixed methods. Each of these types has a typical manner of obtaining the stems or lemmas of the word variants. These categories and the algorithms are shown in the Fig. 1.

- **Truncating Methods**: these methods are related to removing the suffixes or prefixes of a word. In this method words shorter than n are kept as it is. The chances of over stemming increases when the word length is small.
- **Statistical Methods**: These are based on statistical analysis and techniques. Most of the methods remove the affixes but after implementing some statistical procedure.

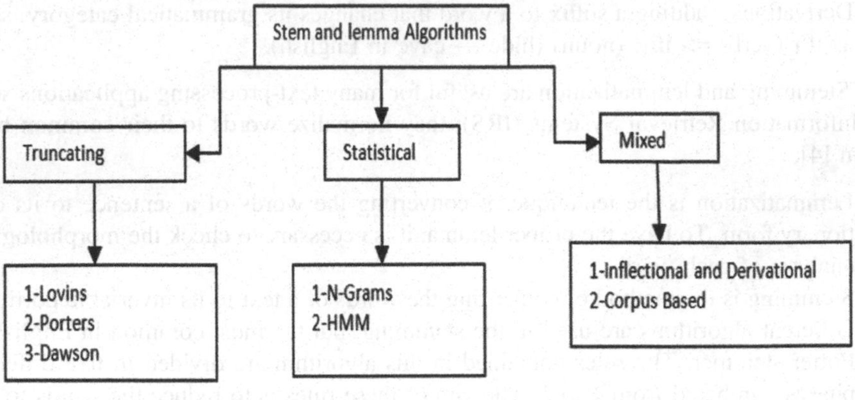

Fig. 1. Types of stemming and lemmatization algorithms

- **Inflectional and Derivational Methods**: This involves both the inflectional as well as the derivational morphology analysis. The corpus should be very large to develop these types of stemmers and hence they are part of corpus base stemmers too. In case of inflectional the word variants are related to the language specific syntactic variations like plural, gender, case, etc. whereas in derivational the word variants are related to the part-of-speech (POS) of a sentence where the word occurs.
- The stemming is used in IRS to make sure that variants of words are not obsolete when text is retrieved [5]. The process is used in removing derivational suffixes as well as inflections, so that word variants can be conflated into the same roots or stems. Stemming methods have been used in a lot of language research areas such as Arabic [6], cross-lingual retrieval [7] and multi-language manipulations [8].
- The lemmatization technique has been used in several languages for IRS. For instance, the authors of [11] compared three different lemmatizers to retrieve information on a Turkish collection. Their results showed that lemmatization indeed improves the retrieval performance utilizing only a minimum number of terms in the system. Moreover, they also found that the performance of information retrieval was better when the maximum length of lemmas is used. In 2012, the authors of [12] combined stemming and partial lemmatization and tested their model on the Hindi language. Their model yielded significant improvements compared to the traditional approaches.

Let's see an example in Amazigh to illustrate the differences of using stemming and lemmatization (Table 1).

Table 1. Examples in Amazigh using stemming and lemmatization

Input	Stem	Lemma
ddan verb: to go	Dda	Ddo
ddan noun: hide	Dda	Ddan
tazla noun: running	Tazl	Azla
tazla verb: run	Tazl	Azl

Stemming and lemmatization are very important when it comes to increase relevance and recall capabilities of IRS [9]. When these language model techniques are used, the number of indexes used is reduced because the system will be using one index to present a number of similar words which have the same root or stem [10].

3 Language Background

3.1 Amazigh Language

The Amazigh language is a branch of the Afro-Asiatic (Hamito-Semitic) [13, 14]. Since the ancient time, it has its own writing that has been undergoing many slight modifications.

Amazigh language became an official language in 2011. Many Imazighen also speak Arabic, and Tamazight is taught in schools. French is an important secondary language.

Tamazight-speaking inhabitants are divided into three ethnolinguistic groups: the Rif people of the Rif Mountains, the people of the Middle Atlas, and the people of the High Atlas and the Sous valley. While there are differences among these variants, they are mutually comprehensible.

In 2003, it has also been changed, adapted, and computerized by the Royal Institute of the Amazigh Culture (IRCAM), in order to provide the Amazigh language an adequate and usable standard writing system. This system is called Tifinaghe-IRCAM. This system has become the official graphic system for writing Amazigh in Morocco. It contains:

- 27 consonants including: the labials (ⴼ, ⴱ, ⵎ), dentals (ⵜ, ⴷ, ⵟ, ⴹ, ⵏ, ⵔ, ⵕ, ⵍ), the alveolars (ⵙ, ⵣ, ⵚ, ⵥ), the palatals (ⵛ, ⵊ), the velar (ⴽ, ⴳ), the labiovelars (ⴽⵯ, ⴳⵯ), the uvulars (ⵇ, ⵅ, ⵖ), the pharyngeals (ⵄ, ⵃ) and the laryngeal (ⵀ);
- 2 semi-consonants: ⵢ and ⵡ;
- 4 vowels: three full vowels ⴰ, ⵉ, ⵓ and neutral vowel (or schwa) ⴻ.

3.2 Amazigh Morphology

Amazigh morphology in contrast with English, is a highly inflected language. It has three main syntactic categories: noun, verb, and particle.

Noun

Nouns distinguish two genders, masculine and feminine; two numbers, singular and plural; and two cases, expressed in the nominal prefix. The feminine is used for female persons and animals as well as for small objects. The productive derivation masculine feminine is quite regular morphologically, using noun prefixes and suffixes.

- The plural has three forms: the external plural consisting in changing the initial vowel, and adding suffixes; the broken plural involving changes in the internal noun vowels; and the mixed plural that combines the rules of the two former plurals.

– The annexed (relative) case is used after most prepositions and after numerals, as well as when the lexical subject follows the verb; while, the free (absolute) case is used in all other contexts.

Verb

The verb has two forms: basic and derived forms.

– The basic form is composed of a root and a radical.
– The derived one is based on a basic form in addition to some prefix morphemes.

Whether basic or derived, the verb is conjugated in four aspects: aorist, imperfective, perfect, and negative perfect. Person, gender, and number of the subject are expressed by affixes to the verb. Depending on the mood, these affixes are classed into three sets: indicative, imperative, and participial.

In Amazigh, some simple verb forms obtain their intensive by just epenthesizing a prefinal vowel. Behaving this way, these verbs align with the derived forms that involve the causative morpheme.

Examples:
- skr skar 'to do'
- srm srum 'to whittle'
- sti staj 'to choose'
- zri zraj 'to pass'

Particles

Particles contain pronouns; conjunctions; prepositions; aspectual, orientation and negative particles; adverbs; and subordinates. Generally, particles are uninflected word. However in Amazigh language, some of these particles are flectional, such as the possessive and demonstrative pronouns [15, 16].

4 Algorithm and Preliminary Results

A user enters the search query via the interface. The query is then passed to the search engine which will in turn invoke the stemming and lemmatizing algorithm. The stemming algorithm is applied to the search query and the resulting stemmed text is returned to the search engine. The next step is for the search engine to pass the stemmed or lemmatized text to the database so that it can be matched against the documents that are available in the collection. The results in the selection of matching data or documents which will be passed to the search engine and displayed to the user for viewing, all these steps of algorithm are illustrated in the data flow diagram in Fig. 2.

The stemmer or lemmatizer is widely used in IRS [10]. When the stemming function of the system is called, it will search the keyword and follow a set of rules. Firstly it will remove all stop words.

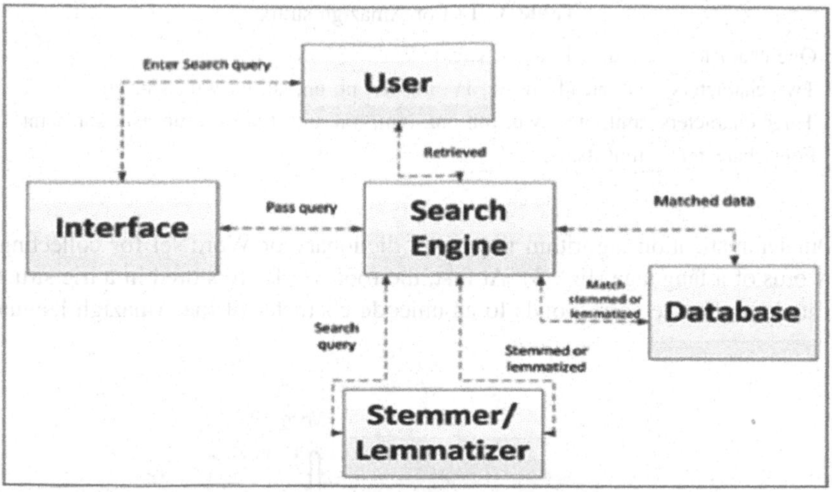

Fig. 2. Data flow diagram for stemming/lemmatizing

These are generally words that frequently occur in search queries, such as "d" (and), "s" (to) and "ta" (this), etc. The prototype designed in our study contains 230 of these words. The next step will be to remove endings that make the keyword plural (e.g. -iwn, -awn), past tense in plural (-t, -nt or -m). The stemmer then moves on to check and convert double suffixes to single suffix. Other suffixes are listed in Table 2, just to mention a few are removed as well. The latter is a very influential characteristic as the proposed search engine might have just one query word or a sentence structure.

The stemmer or lemmatizer is widely used in information retrieval [10]. When the stemming function of the system is called, it will check the keyword and follow a set of rules. Firstly it will remove all stop words (i.e. a list of words specified by the system to be ignored). These are generally words that frequently occur in search queries, such as "d" (and), "s" (to) and "ta" (this), etc.

The prototype designed in our study contains 230 of these words. The next step will be to remove endings that make the keyword plural (e.g. -iwn, -awn), past tense in plural (-t, -nt or -m).The stemmer then moves on to check and convert double suffixes to single suffix. Other suffixes and prefixes are listed in Tables 2 and 3, just to mention a few are removed as well. The latter is a very influential characteristic as the proposed search engine might have just one query word or a sentence structure.

Table 2. List of Amazigh prefix

One character	a, I, n, u, t
Two characters	na, ni, nu, ta, ti, tu, tt, wa, wu, ya, yi, yu
Three characters	itt, ntt, tta, tti
Four characters	itta, itti, ntta, ntti, tett
Five characters	tetta, tetti

Table 3. List of Amazigh suffix

One character	a, d, I, k, m, n, v, s, t
Two characters	an, at, id, im, in, IV, mt, nv, nt, un, sn, tn, wm, wn, yn
Three characters	amt, ant, awn, imt, int, iwn, nin, unt, tin, tnv, tun, tsn, snt, wmt
Four characters	tunt, tsnt

Our lemmatization algorithm requires a dictionary or WordNet for collecting the root words of a language (Fig. 3). At first, the root words are stored in a trie structure. Each node in the trie corresponds to an unicode character of the Amazigh language.

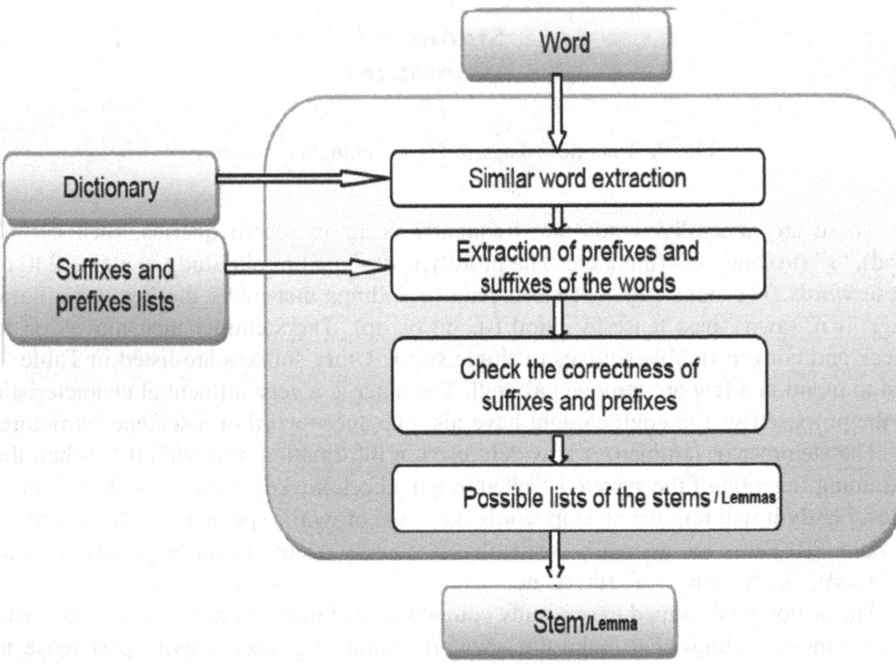

Fig. 3. Steps of stemming and lemmatization process

The nodes that end with the final character of a root word are marked as "final" nodes. To find the lemma of a surface word, the trie is navigated starting from the initial node. Navigation ends when either the word is completely found in the trie or after some portion of the word there is no path present in the trie to navigate. While navigating, some situations may occur, depending on which we are taking decision to determine the lemma. The examples (Fig. 4) show the implementation of our algorithm.

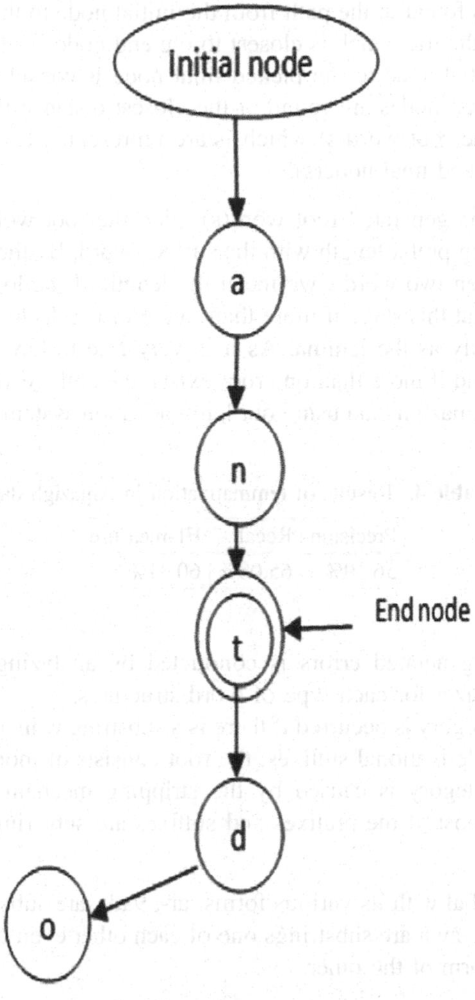

Fig. 4. An example with the word "antdo"

If the surface word is itself a root word, then we will reach to a final node. If the surface word is not a root word, then the trie is navigated up to that node where the surface word completely ends or there is no path to navigate. We call this node as the end node.

Now two different cases may occur here.

1. In the path from initial node to the end node, if one or more than one final nodes are found, then pick that final node which is closest to the end node. The word represented by the path from initial node to the picked final node is considered as the lemma.

2. If no root word is found in the path from the initial node to the end node, then find the final node in the trie which is closest to the end node. The word represented by the path from initial node to the picked final node is considered as the lemma. If more than one final nodes are found at the closest distance then pick all of them. Now, generate the root word(s) which is/are represented by the path from initial node to those picked final node(s).

Finally among the generated root word(s), pick the root word(s) which has/have maximum overlapping prefix length with the surface word. By the phrase "overlapping prefix length" between two words, we mean the length of the longest common prefix between them. Even at this stage if more than one root is selected, and then select any one of them arbitrarily as the lemma. As it is very rare to have more than one root words in this stage and if more than one root exists, then all are viable candidates. The results obtained on Amazigh data using our lemmatization system are given in Table 4.

Table 4. Results of lemmatization in Amazigh data

Precision	Recall	F1-measure
56.19%	65.08%	60.31%

The analysis of generated errors is conducted by analyzing the results of both stemmer and lemmatizer for each type of word structures.

The first error category is occurred if there is a substring w in a root, such that w is a part of prefixes and derivational suffixes, the root consists of more than two syllables. The second error category is caused by the stripping mechanism. This mechanism causes errors since most of the prefixes and suffixes are substrings of each other.

For example:

- The prefix preverbal with its various forms. ar-, 9ad-, are substrings of each others.
- Suffixes -iwn and -awn are substrings one of each other even though one of them is not the various form of the other.

The Amazigh stemmer and lemmatizer also suffer from the third kind of error, but it is because of its shortest possible match. This case happened especially with the infixes -an and -in. The last type of errors occurred because of the difficulty in the implementation of derivational rules for Amazigh language that contain ambiguities. Both stemmer and lemmatizer suffer from this kind of errors.

Furthermore, compound words and out-of-vocabulary words are not considered in our algorithm. Root words are taken from dictionary but if the coverage of the dictionary used is not good, then that will cause errors. However, as there is no such good language independent lemmatizer for Amazigh language.

The study is not without its limitations, with the main drawback being the test collection. During the evaluation, it was found that most of the queries were not suitable to be used for Amazigh language model as they do not contain items that require stemming or lemmatization. Future studies should look into using other test collections.

5 Conclusion and Perspectives

In this paper we demonstrate that creating a lemmatizer is more difficult than a stemmer for Amazigh language, lemmatizer requires more knowledge of linguistics to create the dictionaries that allow the algorithm to look for the base form of the words.

To create a lemmatizer still remains a lot to be done to improve recall as well as precision. There is a need for a method and a system for efficient stemming and lemmatization that reduces the heavy tradeoff between false positives and false negatives.

We still hope to improve the lemmatizer by addressing some minor but troublesome issues, such as integrating more morphological features. There are cases where elements of composed and hyphenated words, when put apart, belong to different categories.

Appendix

Tifinaghe Unicode		Transliteration		Chosen writing system
Code	Character	Latin	Arabic	
U+2D30	ⴰ	A	ا	A
U+2D31	ⴱ	B	ب	B
U+2D33	ⴳ	G	گ	G
U+2D33&U+2D6F	ⴳⵯ	Gw	گ	Gw
U+2D37	ⴷ	D	د	D
U+2D39	ⴹ	ḍ	ض	D
U+2D3B	ⴻ	E		E
U+2D3C	ⴼ	F	ف	F
U+2D3D	ⴽ	K	ک	K
U+2D3D&+2D6F	ⴽⵯ	Kw	گ+	Kw
U+2D40	ⵀ	H	ه	H
U+2D43	ⵃ	ḥ	ح	H
U+2D44	ⵄ	E	ع	E
U+2D44	ⵅ	X	خ	X

U+2D45	ⵇ	Q	ق	Q
U+2D47	ⵉ	I	ي	I
U+2D47	ⵊ	J	ج	J
U+2D47	ⵍ	L	ل	L
U+2D47	ⵎ	M	م	M
U+2D47	ⵏ	N	ن	N
U+2D47	ⵓ	U	و	U
U+2D47	ⵔ	R	ر	R
U+2D47	ⵕ	ṛ	ر	R
U+2D47	ⵖ	Y	غ	G
U+2D47	ⵙ	S	س	S
U+2D47	ⵚ	ṣ	ص	S
U+2D47	ⵛ	C	ش	C
U+2D47	ⵜ	T	ت	T
U+2D47	ⵟ	ṭ	ط	T
U+2D47	ⵡ	W	و	W
U+2D47	ⵢ	Y	ي	Y
U+2D47	ⵣ	Z	ز	Z

References

1. Chowdhury, G., Chowdhury, S.: Introduction to Digital Libraries. Facet Publishing, London (2002)
2. Belkin, N.J.: Anomalous states of knowledge as a basis for information retrieval. Can. J. Inf. Sci. **5**, 133–143 (1980)
3. Heaps, H.S.: Information Retrieval, Computational and Theoretical Aspects. Academic Press, Cambridge (1978)
4. Baeza-Yates, R., Ribeiro-Neto, B.: Modern Information Retrieval, vol. 463. ACM Press, New York (1999)
5. Lovins, J.B.: Development of a stemming algorithm. Mech. Trans. Comput. Linguist. **11**, 22–31 (1968)

6. Larkey, L.S., Ballesteros, L., Connell, M.E.: Improving stemming for Arabic information retrieval: light stemming and cooccurrence analysis. In: Proceedings of the 25th Annual International ACM SIGIR Conference on Research and Development in Information Retrieval, pp. 275–282. ACM (2002)
7. Xu, J., Fraser, A., Weischedel, R.: Empirical studies in strategies for Arabic retrieval. In: Proceedings of the 25th Annual International ACM SIGIR Conference on Research and Development in Information Retrieval, pp. 269–274. ACM (2002)
8. Wechsler, M., Sheridan, P., Schäuble, P.: Multi-language text indexing for internet retrieval. In: Proceedings of the 5th RIAO Conference, Computer-Assisted Information Searching on the Internet, vol. 5, pp. 217–232 (1997)
9. Hull, D.A.: Stemming algorithms: a case study for detailed evaluation. J. Am. Soc. Inf. Sci. **47**, 70–84 (1996)
10. Hooper, R., Paice, C.: The Lancaster stemming algorithm, December 2013. http://www.comp.lancs.ac.uk/computing/research/stemming/
11. Ozturkmenoglu, O., Alpkocak, A.: Comparison of different lemmatization approaches for information retrieval on Turkish text collection. In: Innovations in Intelligent Systems and Applications (INISTA) International Symposium, pp. 1–5 (2012)
12. Gupta, D., Kumar, R., Yadav, R., Sajan, N.: Improving unsupervised stemming by using partial lemmatization coupled with data-based heuristics for Hindi. Int. J. Comput. Appl. **38**, 1–8 (2012)
13. Greenberg, J.: The Languages of Africa. The Hague (1966)
14. Ouakrim, O.: Fonética y fonología del Bereber. Survey at the University of Autònoma de Barcelona (1995)
15. Ameur, M., Bouhjar, A., Boukhris, F., Boukous, A., Boumalk, A., Elmedlaoui, M., Iazzi, E. M., Souifi, H.: Initiation à la langue Amazigh. The Royal Institute of Amazigh Culture (2004)
16. Boukhris, F., Boumalk, A., El Moujahid, E.H., Souifi, H.: La nouvelle grammaire de l'Amazigh. The Royal Institute of Amazigh Culture (2008)

Data Analysis

Splitting Method for Decision Tree Based on Similarity with Mixed Fuzzy Categorical and Numeric Attributes

Houda Zaim[1(✉)], Mohammed Ramdani[1], and Adil Haddi[2]

[1] FSTM, Hassan II University of Casablanca, BP 146, 20650 Mohammedia, Morocco
houdazaime@gmail.com, ramdani@fstm.ac.ma
[2] EST, Hassan I University of Settat, 218, Berrechid, Morocco
adil.haddi@gmail.com

Abstract. Classification decision tree algorithm has an input training dataset which consists of a number of examples each having a number of attributes. The attributes are either categorical, when values are unordered or continuous, when the attribute values are ordered. No previous research has considered the induction of decision tree using a wide variety of datasets with different data characteristics. This work proposes a novel approach for learning decision tree classifier which can handle categorical, discrete, continuous and fuzzy attributes. The most critical issue in the learning process of decision trees is the splitting criteria. Our splitting approach is based on similarity formula as feature selection strategy by choosing the greatest similarity attribute as splitting node. An illustrative example is demonstrated in multiple test dataset to verify the validity of the proposed algorithm which is less affected by the type and the size of training dataset.

Keywords: Fuzzy membership degree · Class · Record · Decision node · Branch Root · Leaf · Splitting threshold · Splitting attribute

1 Introduction

Decision tree algorithm is to get classification rules based on instance learning where training samples are assumed to belong to a predefined class, as determined by one of the attributes, called the target attribute. Once derived, the classification model can be used to categorize the newly coming data. The widely used classification methods include Decision Tree, K-Nearest Neighbor, Neural Networks, Naive Bayesian Classifiers, etc. A well-accepted method of classification is the induction of decision trees. A decision tree is a classifier which consists of nodes and a root. Each internal node represents a decision, and each branch corresponds to a possible outcome of the test. Each leaf node represents a class. This paper focuses on the most critical point of decision tree induction algorithms: The choice of a splitting attribute in a considered node. There are many splitting methods for decision tree construction algorithms. In 1986, Quinlan invented ID3 decision tree algorithm that chose the largest information gain value as the splitting attribute, where the information gain of the attribute was calculated based on

Y. Tabii et al. (Eds.): BDCA 2018, CCIS 872, pp. 237–248, 2018.
https://doi.org/10.1007/978-3-319-96292-4_19

the entropy of data. Its successor, C4.5 algorithm, was later introduced in 1993 to add continuous attribute process. However, when it comes to numerical attributes, C4.5 is not very effective. Furthermore, Breiman et al. proposed classification and regression tree (CART) which used the Gini index as its attribute selector index. At first designed for non-numerical attributes, this algorithm was not a particularly good way to process continuous numerical attribute. Another option is to use Fayyad's method and extend it to Gini index, as for CHAID algorithm [1].

While the most commonly used splitting methods are based on information entropy, information gain, information gain ratio, distance measure, weight of evidence, etc. to manage the cases of categorical attributes and attributes with values in continuous intervals. There is no splitting method that will give the best performance for all type of datasets; discrete, continuous, categorical and also fuzzy attributes with less complexity. Our approach has the objective of proposing a new splitting method using a wide variety of datasets with different data characteristics by proposing a novel splitting criteria based on similarity function. The value of this function is calculated for all attributes and the attribute that provides the highest value of split measure is chosen as the splitting one. The training set contains categorical attributes, continuous attributes and membership degrees of fuzzy sets. The proposed algorithm divide data set into several subsets according to class value, if the similarity between each subset of data is highest, indicating that splitting effect is best. The average similarity is calculated of both the attribute that is selected for a given node of the decision tree and also the partitioning of the numeric values of the selected attribute to find the threshold split (Fig. 1).

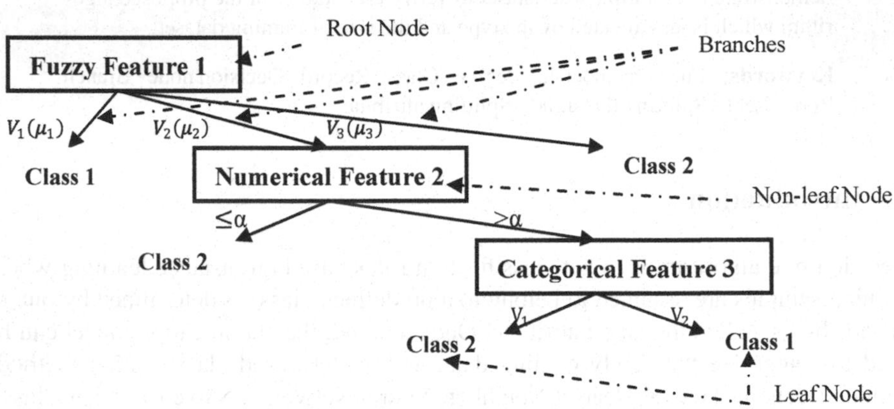

Fig. 1. Schematic of the decision tree

The literature review and problem statement are presented in Sect. 2. Section 3 discusses the method of similarity computation. An illustrative example is presented in Sect. 4 to show the applicability of the proposed splitting criteria procedure. In Sect. 5, we draw the conclusions and pointed out the work which needed to be solved in the future.

2 Review of Split Measure for Decision Tree Induction

2.1 Literature Review

A lot of heuristic algorithms have been proposed to construct near-optimal decision trees. Most algorithms require discrete valued target attributes, over-sensitivity to training sets, and issues (both at the level of learning and performance) related to standard univariate split criteria. Contributing to resolving the issue of computational complexity of learning in trees with multivariate splits is the main focus of [2] which used conventional gradient-based optimization techniques to derive univariate and multivariate optimal splitting criteria. Finding the best threshold value is an important issue. [1] Used the golden-section search (GSS) method to find the extremum of a strictly unimodal continuous function to search the best threshold for discrediting continuous attribute data. [3] Proposed Tsallis Entropy Information Metric (TEIM) algorithm with a new split criterion and a new construction method of decision trees which treats numeric, categorical and mixed datasets. Traditional decision tree induction models with continuous valued attributes only consider the frequencies of classes, which fail to differentiate the candidate cut point (CCPs) with the same or approximately equal splitting performance. In order to tackle this problem, the concept of segment is proposed in [4]. Theoretical analysis demonstrates that the expected number of segments has the common features of frequency based measures such as information entropy and Gini-index. The hybrid of frequency and segment is then used as a measure to split nodes. Constructing an optimal decision tree is to find a path which reduces the information entropy the quickest in essence. Therefore, [5] proposed a new method based on the shortest path planning which convert the categorical attributes set to a directed graph and use the common path planning method depth-first search and greedy algorithm to find an optimum solution, and finally get an ultimate decision tree. [6] Developed a family of new splitting criteria for classification in stationary data streams. The new criteria, derived using appropriate statistical tools, were based on the misclassification error and the Gini index impurity measures. For continuous valued (real and integer) attribute data, [7] proposed a new K-ary partition discretization method with no more than $K - 1$ cut points based on Gaussian membership functions and the expected class number. A new K-ary crisp decision tree induction is also proposed for continuous valued attributes with a Gini index, combining the proposed discretization method. A lot of heuristic algorithms have been proposed to construct near-optimal decision trees. Most of them, however, are greedy algorithms that have the drawback of obtaining only local optimums. Besides, conventional split criteria they used Shannon entropy, Gain Ratio and Gini index, cannot select informative attributes efficiently. To address the above issues, [8] proposed a novel Tsallis Entropy Information Metric (TEIM) algorithm with a new split criterion and a new construction method of decision trees. Existing binary decision tree models do not handle well the minority class over imbalanced data sets, to address this issue, a Cost-sensitive and Hybrid attribute measure Multi-Decision Tree (CHMDT) approach is presented by [9] for binary classification with imbalanced data sets to improve the classification performance of the minority class. While diversity has been argued to be the rationale for the success of an ensemble of classifiers, little has been said on how uniform use of the feature space influences classification error. The existence of the link between uniformity in the feature use frequency and classification error opens a new avenue for [10] to explore and exploit this relationship with the goal of creating more accurate ensemble classifiers. [11] Estimated the class prior in positive and unlabeled data through decision tree induction. A classifier may only have access to positive and unlabeled examples, where the unlabeled data consists of both positive and negative examples. [12] Designed a partially monotonic decision tree algorithm to extract decision rules for partially monotonic classification tasks. Authors proposed a rank-inconsistent rate that distinguishes attributes from criteria and represented the directions of the monotonic relationships between criteria and decisions.

Many fuzzy decision tree induction algorithms have been proposed in the literature. A fuzzy decision tree allows the transverse of multiple branches of a node with different degrees within the range of [0; 1]. The most commonly used fuzzy decision tree algorithms is the Fuzzy ID3. [12] Aimed to provide a classification approach by using fuzzy ID3 algorithm for linguistic data. In this study, Weighted Averaging Based on Levels (WABL) method, fuzzy c-means, and fuzzy ID3 algorithm are combined. Other approaches include Min-Ambiguity algorithm, which aims to find the expanded attribute with the minimum uncertainty and the selection based on the Gini index. To further improve the accuracy of fuzzy decision tree, the authors of [13] proposed the strategy called Improved Second Order- Neuro- Fuzzy Decision Tree (ISO-N-FDT). ISO-N-FDT tunes parameters of FDT from leaf node to root node starting from left side of tree to its right and attains better improvement in accuracy with less number of iterations exhibiting fast convergence and powerful search ability. [14] Proposed a novel hybrid approach with combine of fuzzy set, rough set and ID3 algorithm called FuzzyRoughSetID3 classifier which is used to deal with uncertainties, vagueness and ambiguity associated with fuzzy datasets. Others proposed a modified fuzzy similarity measure developed for restricting the search space. [15] Found that linguistic representation of the training data with just the necessary and sufficient precision using fuzzy entropy can improve the reliability of the classification process. A multilabel fuzzy decision tree classifier named FuzzDTML is proposed by [16]. An empirical analysis shows that, although the algorithm does not yet incorporate neither pruning nor fuzzy interval adjustment phases, it is competitive with other tree based approaches for multilabel classification, with better performance in data sets having numerical features that can be fuzzified.

To the best of our knowledge, there are no studies involving decision tree for mixed fuzzy, numeric and nominal valued attributes. The method proposed in this work is able to speedily seek out the best threshold of every feature in simple way, sing fuzzy logic and achieving numeric data discretization to apply on back-end classification algorithm.

2.2 Problem Statement

2.2.1 Decision Tree's Essential Workflow

The process of building a Decision Tree is shown in the following steps:

Step1. Split the initial data into two parts, part is used as training data while another is used as testing data sets.
Step2. According to the Attribute Selection Measure, the attribute having the best score for the measure reflects the branching attribute.
Step3. From attributes not yet selected, the attribute with the best score is chosen as the decision tree's internal nodes, root nodes and non-leaf nodes for the given tuples.
Step4. Generate corresponding branches of the selected attribute (node splitting).
Step5. For every new branch generated, rearrange the training data and generate the next internal node.
Step6. Carry out the above steps recursively until the criteria for stopping the node is satisfied when all samples in the node have the same target or all samples in the node are locally constant.

2.2.2 Continuous Categorical and Fuzzy -Valued Attributes for Decision Tree Classification Learning

Let Security be one of the acquired data whose values are "Strong" and "Medium", Payment Alternative are "Prepaid Card" and "Mobile Payment" whereas Hour Availability are "normal" and "high". If the Hour Availability data we take is continuous values that lie between 10 and 20 and Security is fuzzy data set with corresponding membership degree. The decision tree will look like what is show in Fig. 2:

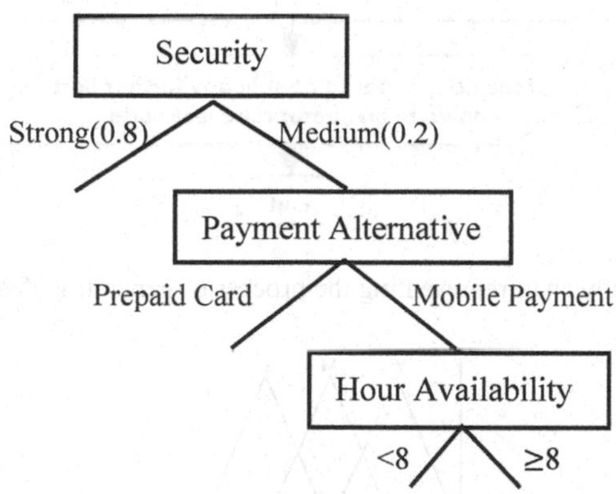

Fig. 2. Assumption of the acquired data

Handling of numerical, categorical and fuzzy valued attributes in decision tree generation process is the target of this paper. Here shows that different type of attribute and different splitting threshold value choices will lead to apparently different classification results.

How a suitable threshold value should be set to split continuous and fuzzy data is an important issue discussed in this study. For the purpose of clarifying this issue, our consideration is shown in Figs. 3 and 4.

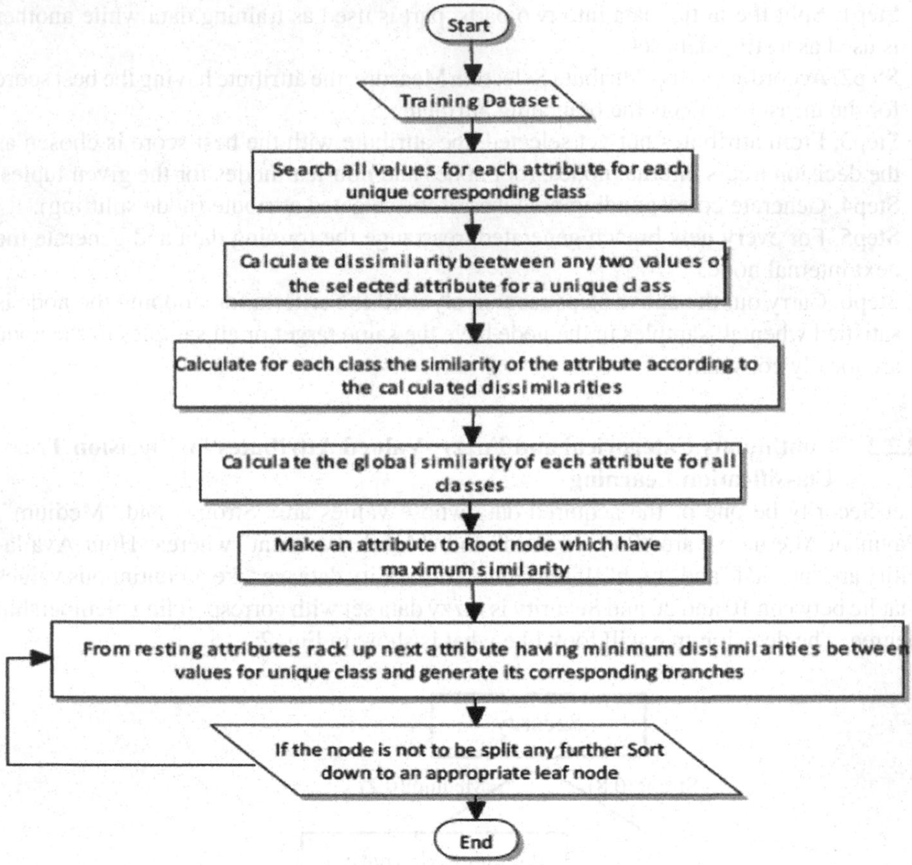

Fig. 3. Flowchart representing the process of generating decision tree

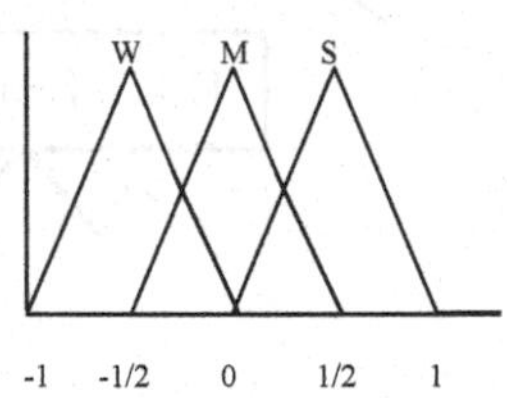

Fig. 4. Fuzzification of the fuzzy variable "Security"

3 New Splitting Criteria Method

The learning and classification steps of the proposed decision tree induction algorithm are developed by emphasizing the attributes with less values and higher similarity, and adulterating the attributes with more values and lower importance.

In this proposed method first of all we analyze hole training data and find the attribute for root node on the basis of maximum similarity with respect to class. Similarly find next node for second level from remaining attributes, and so on. Figure 3 shows flow chart of this work.

3.1 Flow Chart

Step 1: Select training dataset for learning process (numeric, categorical and fuzzy attributes belonging to different classes).

Step 2: Find mapping between all possible values for every attribute and that corresponding class.

Step 3: Calculate dissimilarity between any two values of the selected attribute for a unique class (dissimilarity differs according to the type of the attribute).

Step 4: Calculate the average similarity of the attribute for a unique class according to the sum of calculated dissimilarities.

Step 5: The global similarity is computed for all classes by the sum of similarities calculated in step 4.

Step 6: Make root node to the attribute which have maximum similarity.

Step 7: Similarly select other attribute for next level in decision tree from remaining attributes on the basis of minimum dissimilarity between values having unique class.

3.2 Preliminaries

For the better comprehension of the proposed work, firstly some basic concepts of is introduced. Training data set contains continuous, categorical and fuzzy valued features. Let T be the training dataset containing n samples belonging to k classes $\{c1, c2, \ldots, ck\}$ $(1 \leq k \leq p)$. $|C_k|$ is the size of C_k. And A_q the splitting feature whose value set is $\{a_1, \ldots a_u, \ldots, a_v\}$. Let A_q be a fuzzy variable and X the range of its values. Fuzzy sets are characterized by a membership function defined as: $\mu_A{:}X \rightarrow [0, 1]$ Subsets present expression to evaluate fuzzy criteria using linguistic terms, as "weak (W)", "medium (M)", "strong (S)". The center of the gravity of the area bounded by the membership function curve is computed to be the most crisp value of the fuzzy quantity. The fuzzy dissimilarity measure $d(a_u, a_v)$ on the given universe X, is then defined as the distance between center of gravity of the fuzzy values a_u and a_v.

Dissimilarity function between two A_q values for the class C_k can be computed by:

$$\mathrm{dis}(a_u, a_v) = \begin{cases} \dfrac{|a_u - a_v|}{\mathrm{Max}(A_q) - \mathrm{Min}(A_q)} & \text{if} A_q \text{is numeric} \\ 0 \text{ or } 1 & \text{if } A_q \text{is categorical} \\ \dfrac{d(GC(a_u), GC(a_v))}{d(GC(W), GC(S))} & \text{if } A_q \text{is fuzzy} \end{cases}$$

$d(GC(a_u), GC(a_v))$ is the distance between gravity center of fuzzy values a_u and a_v.

For d(GC(W), GC(S)): W and S refer to linguistic expressions which are represented by functions mapping the fuzzy attribute scale (Fig. 4).

3.3 Pseudo Code

The block diagram mentioned above provides a better understanding of the process of decision tree induction in data stream scenario, particularly focusing on the mathematical foundations of choosing the root and splitting continuous, categorical and fuzzy criteria in decision tree nodes (Fig. 5).

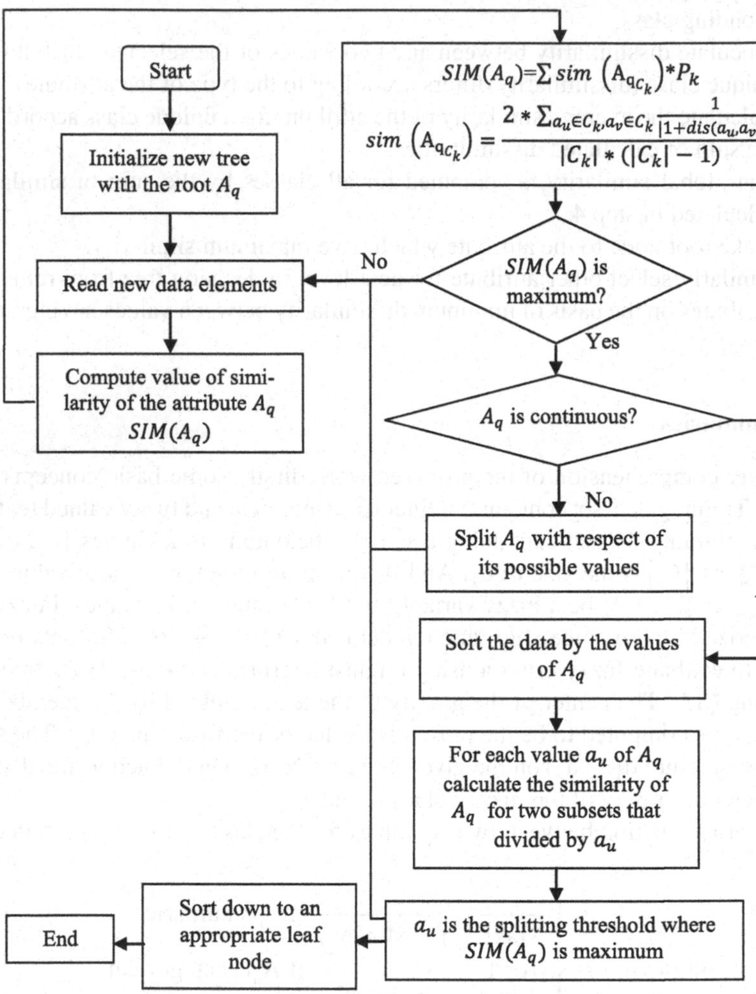

Fig. 5. Block diagram of the proposed splitting criteria method

Our approach suggests a fuzzification procedure to generate fuzzy decision tree for datasets with quantitative and qualitative attributes. This motivated us to design a similarity measure which is involved in the choice of the value of the split point. Our purpose is to find which threshold value candidate posses the largest Similarity and how much its corresponding continuous, fuzzy and categorical attribute value is.

The decision made at each node of the decision tree is whether the test attribute value is equal or not equal to the split value of the attribute at each node. According to the block diagram, the proposed algorithm is given as follows.

1. If the samples are all of the same class then
2. Turns the node into a leaf and return the leaf labeled with that class.
3. End If
4. For each attribute A_q in the dataset do
5. Calculate Similarity Function according to A_q values for each class C_k
6. End
7. Choose the attribute A_q with the maximum value of Similarity as the root node.
8. If splitting value is not met then
9. Constructing branches according to different split values of attribute A_q so that the samples are partitioned accordingly.
10. If the splitting attribute A_q is continuous then
11. Sort attribute's values along with class information
12. For each value a_u of A_q do
13. Calculate the similarity of two subsets that divided by a_u
14. End
15. Choose the value a_u with the maximum value of Similarity as the splitting threshold.
16. End
17. If the splitting attribute A_q is fuzzy then
18. Assign fuzzy and membership values of each class to this node.
19. End
20. If the splitting attribute A_q is nominal then
21. Assign corresponding categorical values of each class to this node.
22. End
23. End
24. While splitting attribute already the parent of the current node do
25. Select the next best attribute as the splitting attribute.
26. End
27. If none of the attributes are selected then
28. Make this node as leaf node
29. End
30. No more training samples to be classified, create a leaf belong to the class in majority among samples.
31. Output the decision tree with Mixed Fuzzy Categorical and Numeric Attributes.

4 An Illustration

The algorithm requires class prior probabilities which are made proportional to the training sample sizes. Table 1 present the training set, including 20 samples and 3 attributes, fuzzy one which is "Security", nominal attribute refers to "Payment Alternative" and "Hour Availability" is a continuous attribute. The aim is establishing the classification model that decided belonging to five classes.

Table 1. Descriptive example of used training dataset

Class	Security			Alternative Payment	Hour Availability
	W	M	S		
C5	1	0	0	Prepaid Card	10
C5	1	0	0	Cash Payment	10
C5	1	0	0	Cash Payment	12
C4	0	0.5	0.5	Cash Payment	14
C4	0.5	0.5	0	Cash Payment	14
C3	0	1	0	Prepaid Card	18
C3	0	0.5	0.5	Mobile Card	17
C3	0	0.7	0.3	Prepaid Card	18
C3	0	0.5	0.5	Prepaid Card	20
C2	0	0	1	Mobile Card	20
C1	0	0	1	Prepaid Card	22
C2	0	0	1	Prepaid Card	22
C2	0	0.6	0.4	Prepaid Card	22
C2	0	1	0	Prepaid Card	22
C1	0	0	1	Prepaid Card	24
C1	0	0.3	0.7	Prepaid Card	21
C2	0	1	0	Mobile Card	24
C1	0	0	1	Mobile Payment	24
C1	0	0	1	Prepaid Card	24
C1	0	0.5	0.5	Mobile Payment	21

Classification methods aim to identify the classes that belongs objects from some descriptive traits as mentioned in Table 1 to find utility in automated decision making. For this data set, we will split the continuous attribute and find the best threshold value. Before the threshold value search, a data preprocessing is carried out where fuzzy data is converted suitable analysis forms.

The algorithm takes as output a tree that resembles to an orientation diagram where each end node (leaf) is a decision (a class) and each non- final node (internal) represents a test.

First step, we calculate the similarity of each attribute. Next step, in the same way, the algorithm recursively calculates the similarity of each resting attributes on the subsets which are divided by the value of splitting attribute in the last step until all instances belong to the same class.

SIM (Payment Alternative) = 0.759
SIM (Hour Availability) = 0.722
SIM (Security) = 0.886

Root Node= Security

Weak (1,0,0)

Payment Alternative? (SIM (Payment Alternative) =0.099))
Delivery Time? (SIM (Delivery Time) =0.099))
$SIM_{\leq 10}$(Delivery Time)=0.1
$SIM_{>10}$(Delivery Time)=0.05
$SIM_{\leq 12}$(Delivery Time)=0.09

Splitting Threshold= 10

Medium (0, 0.5, 0.5)

Payment Alternative? (SIM (Payment Alternative) =0.1))
Delivery Time? (SIM (Delivery Time) = 0.107))
$SIM_{\leq 14}$(Delivery Time)=0.1 , $SIM_{>14}$(Delivery Time)=0.082
$SIM_{\leq 17}$(Delivery Time)=0.082 , $SIM_{>17}$(Delivery Time)=0.05
$SIM_{\leq 20}$(Delivery Time)=0.05 , $SIM_{>20}$(Delivery Time)=0.5
$SIM_{\leq 21}$(Delivery Time)=0.082

At this stage we firstly sort data according to the continuous attribute values and extract possible threshold value candidates. Secondly, Similarity measure is employed as the index for attribute classification ability calculation. Thirdly, the root, split attribute and the threshold value are found. Dataset are partitioned into groups in terms of the variable to be predicted.

To predict the class that a new input belongs to, a path of each leaf can be converted into a production rule IF-THEN:

Rule 1: **IF** Security is Weak (1, 0, 0) **AND** Hour Availability is <=10 **AND** Payment alternative is Prepaid Card **THEN** Class is C5

Rule 2: **IF** Security is Medium (0, 0.5, 0.5) **AND** Delivery Time is >20 **AND** Payment Alternative is Mobile Payment **THEN** Class is C1.

5 Conclusion

The paper is concerned with splitting method for decision tree based on similarity with mixed fuzzy categorical and numeric attributes. It proposes a fuzzy decision tree induction method for fuzzy data of which numeric attributes can be represented by continuous value, and nominal attributes are represented by categorical value. A decision tree algorithm, equipped with great noise eliminating ability, is based on finding the best split point. Performing the split considering fuzzy, continuous and nominal criteria is the main task in this paper. An example is used to prove the validity of our contribution. A comparison to outperform some classic algorithms in the classification accuracy, in tolerating imprecise, conflict, and missing information must to be further discussed.

Furthermore, using the proposed tree induction technique, marketing rules can be generated to match customer to satisfaction categories. The extracted decision rules provide personalized profiling when a customer visits an Internet store. An experiment will be performed to evaluate the effectiveness of the proposed approach with random selection and preference scoring.

References

1. Lian, K., Liu, R.-F.: A new searching method of splitting threshold values for continuous attribute decision tree problems (2015)
2. Sofeikov, K.I., Tyukin, I.Y., Gorban, A.N., Mirkes, E.M., Prokhorov, D.V., Romanenko, I.V.: Learning optimization for decision tree classification of non-categorical data with information gain impurity criterion (2014)
3. Wang, Y., Song, C., Xia, S.T.: Improving decision trees by Tsallis entropy information metric method (2016)
4. Wang, R., Kwong, S., Wang, X., Jiang, Q.: Segment based decision tree induction with continuous valued attributes. IEEE Trans. Cybern. **45**, 1262–1275 (2014)
5. Luo, Z., Yu, X., Yuan, C.: A new approach of constructing decision tree based on shortest path methods. In: ICALIP (2016)
6. Jaworski, M., Duda, P., Rutkowski, L.: New splitting criteria for decision trees in stationary data streams. IEEE Trans. Neural Netw. Learn. Syst. **29**, 2516–2529 (2017)
7. Song, Y., Yao, S., Yu, D., Shen, Y., Hu, Y.: A new K-ary crisp decision tree induction with continuous valued attributes. Chin. J. Electron. **26**, 999–1007 (2017)
8. Wang, Y., Song, C., Xia, S.: Improving decision trees by Tsallis entropy information metric method (2016)
9. Li, F., Zhang, X., Zhang, X., Du, C., Xu, Y., Tian, Y.: Cost-sensitive and hybrid-attribute measure multi-decision tree over imbalanced data sets. Inf. Sci. **422**, 242–256 (2018)
10. Cervantes, B., Monroy, R., Medina-Pérez, M.A., Gonzalez-Mendoza, M., Ramirez-Marquez, J.: Some features speak loud, but together they all speak louder: a study on the correlation between classification error and feature usage in decision-tree classification ensembles. Eng. Appl. Artif. Intell. **67**, 270–282 (2017)
11. Bekker, J., Davis, J.: Estimating the class prior in positive and unlabeled data through decision tree induction (2018)
12. Kantarci-Savaş, S., Nasibov, E.: Fuzzy ID3 algorithm on linguistic dataset by using WABL deffuzification method (2017)
13. Narayanan, S.J., Bhatt, R.B., Paramasivam, I.: An improved second order training algorithm for improving the accuracy of fuzzy decision trees. Int. J. Fuzzy Syst. Appl. (IJFSA) **5**, 96–120 (2016)
14. Raghuwanshi, S., Ahirwal, R.: An efficient classification based fuzzy rough set theory using ID3 algorithm. Int. J. Comput. Appl. **154**, 31–34 (2016)
15. Morente-Molinera, J., Mezei, J., Carlsson, C., Herrera-Viedma, E.: Improving supervised learning classification methods using multigranular linguistic modeling and fuzzy entropy. IEEE Trans. Fuzzy Syst. **25**, 1078–1089 (2017)
16. Prati, R.C., Charte, F., Herrera, F.: A first approach towards a fuzzy decision tree for multilabel classification (2017)

Mobility of Web of Things: A Distributed Semantic Discovery Architecture

Ismail Nadim[1(✉)], Yassine El Ghayam[2], and Abdelalim Sadiq[1]

[1] MISC Laboratory, Ibn Toufail University, Kenitra, Morocco
ismail.nadim.gi@gmail.com,
abdelalim.sadiq.ma@ieee.org
[2] SMARTILab EMSI-HONORIS, Rabat, Morocco
yassine.elgh@gmail.com

Abstract. The mobility of Internet of Things (IoT) objects, gateways and services is a challenging issue. Effectively, this phenomenon can hamper the interoperability and scalability of the network at many levels. Nevertheless, this phenomenon is a natural feature of IoT that cannot be neglected. In this paper, we present different mechanisms that can be used together to reduce the negative impact of this phenomenon in dynamic IoT environments. The contribution of this paper is twofold: firstly a semantic-based clustering method which takes into account the dynamicity of the services. Secondly, a spatial-based indexing method which considers the mobility of IoT objects and gateways. The performed experiments show the feasibility of our approach.

Keywords: Internet of Things · Mobility · Clustering · Semantic discovery

1 Introduction

The Internet of Things (IoT) is considerably accelerating the convergence between the real world and the digital world. Effectively, with the advancement of the information and communication technologies, it is now possible to transform the things around us from ordinary objects into actors that affect significantly our daily lives, offering services that help to preserve our time, energy, money or even our lives. However, the accessibility by users and applications to such quality services in a reliable manner is facing numerous challenges, especially interoperability and scalability.

The Web of Things (WoT) addresses these challenges leveraging the Web standards. Specifically, the WoT enables interaction of IoT things through Web APIs publishing things capabilities as services. Moreover, the use of semantic Web technologies such as RDF models and OWL ontologies enables inter-operable and scalable means to access WoT information [1]. However, the processing of a huge size of semantic data particularly in distributed and dynamic environments is very costly. Therefore, the semantic Web technologies must be considered in conjunction with efficient data structures and mechanisms such as indexing, ranking and clustering in order to optimize the cost of semantic data processing, the semantic discovery, the quality of results and to save energy.

Y. Tabii et al. (Eds.): BDCA 2018, CCIS 872, pp. 249–260, 2018.
https://doi.org/10.1007/978-3-319-96292-4_20

Due to the dynamic nature of the IoT environments and the geographic distribution of the devices, the status and the quality of the IoT services might change frequently. Effectively, service mobility, service registration and removing, device failure, wireless communication quality, battery depletion, as well as the effective mobility of IoT objects and gateways. All these factors, as well as the size of the network in term of nodes and data, generate a large number of costly computations and update operations that might need to be performed frequently.

According to [2], The WoT applications can be built on four layers stack, (1) the accessibility layer which guarantees the consistent access to all kinds of IoT objects, namely using Web APIs (2) The findability layer which enables the discovery of relevant services. (3) The security layer which guarantees the privacy and the security of the services. (4) And the composition layer which composes applications based on the discovered services. The mobility issue is present throughout the previously mentioned stack. Effectively, the access to a reliable data is greatly affected by the distribution of IoT objects and gateways. In addition to this, a device failure, a battery depletion or simply the mobility of a device from one place to another may affect to quality of the gathered data. Moreover, the services discovery implements some mechanisms such as the semantic annotation, the clustering and the indexing which are complex in term of deployment and computation processing. This complexity is increased in dynamic context, because many computation updates might need to be performed frequently to guarantee the system coherence. Last but not least, the composition layer need not only relevant services, but the most relevant ones to compose quality applications. Consequently, mobility can reduce the competitiveness of the device to provide a useful service at the composition level.

To overcome these difficulties, we present in this paper different mechanisms that can be used together to reduce the negative impact of the mobility in dynamic IoT environments. Precisely, this paper main contribution is to propose a semantic discovery architecture of WoT services suitable for dynamic environments. Through this architecture we explain how the mobility issue can be better handled. Our approach proposes:

- A WoT service clustering approach, which is suitable for dynamic services.
- An indexing Data Structure over Distributed Hash Tables, which reduces the number of updates of the gateways index even in presence of dynamic devices or gateways.

The remaining of this paper will be organized as follows: Sect. 2 presents the semantic model we will use to model a WoT service. The proposed semantic discovery approach is described in Sect. 3. Section 4 presents the experimental results and Sect. 5 concludes this paper.

2 Semantic Model for Web of Things

According to [1], WoT ontologies and models need to address the representation of not only the thing specific heterogeneity of the WoT with the necessary level of abstraction, but also capture the distributed environment context in which they operate.

Consequently, the data and services, the quality of these services (QoS), the mobility of objects etc. needs to be modelled and captured. In what follows, we cite only some WoT models and we direct the reader to this survey [1] for more details.

Numerous conceptual models have been proposed to model devices using generic vocabularies, but no standard is yet defined: [3] et al. grouped high-level concepts and their relations that describes three examples of real devices. CG1: Actuator, Sensor, System, CG2: Global and Local Coordinates, CG3: Communication Endpoint, CG4: Observations, Features of Interest, Units, and Dimensions, CG5: Vendor, Version, Deployment Time. [4] et al. formalized the typical semantic triples in IoT scenarios as: Sensor-observes-Observation, Observation-generates-Event, Actuator-triggers-Action, Action-changes-Observation (State), Object- locates-Location and Owner-owns-Object. [2] et al. proposed the web of things model which is a «conceptual model of a web Thing that can describe the resources of a web Thing using a set of well-known concepts». The authors specified four resources to describe a web thing: Model, Properties, Actions and Things. For our approach in this paper, we can summarize these different components into five sets: location, data, content, type and semantics (see Fig. 1 and Table 1).

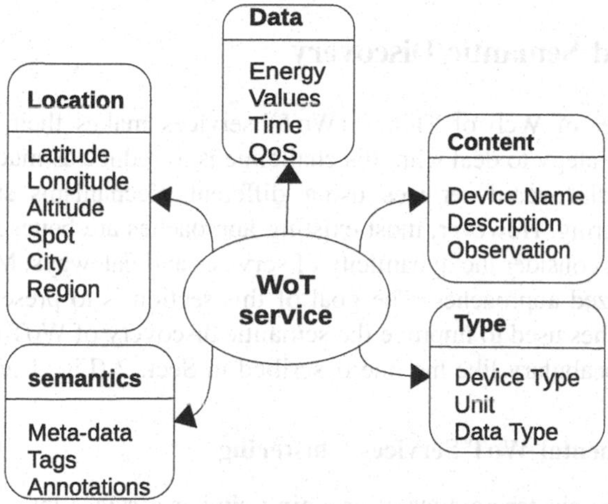

Fig. 1. Web of things services vocabulary.

Table 1. A description of each concept of WoT services vocabulary

Concept	Description
Location	The device's geographic location, city, region…
Latitude	The position of the sensor or thing that collects data in decimal degrees. For example, the latitude of the city of London is 51.5072
Longitude	The position of the sensor or thing that collects data in decimal degrees. For example, the longitude of the city of London is −0.1275

(*continued*)

Table 1. (*continued*)

Concept	Description
Elevation	The position of the sensor or thing that collects data in meters. For example, the elevation of the city of London is 35.052
Device name	A unique device name for a device
Description	A brief description of the device
Observation	Describe the device used to serve that scene
Device type	Describes what type of sensor the device is capable of detecting
Unit	The unit of measurement, e.g. Celsius
Data type	String, float, date…
Meta-data	Information about device data (Manufacturer, owner…)
Tags	Keywords that identify the device
Annotation	The semantics of the data
Energy	The energy consumption of the device (battery life time)
Values	The values of the observed data
Time	Time when the data has been captured
QoS	The quality of the service

3 Distributed Semantic Discovery

The huge number of Web of Things (WoT) services makes their discovery a real challenge. One strategy to deal with this challenge is to reduce as much as possible the number of the discovered services using different mechanisms such as semantic Web-based clustering. However, most existing approaches are better suitable for static context and don't consider the dynamicity of services and gateways. Moreover, most of them are centralized approaches. The goal of this section is to present the clustering, indexing approaches used to improve the semantic discovery of WoT services enriched by a semantic vocabulary like the one described in Sect. 2 (Fig. 1 and Table 1).

3.1 An Incremental WoT Services Clustering

The WoT services clustering aims at grouping similar services into clusters, and then execute queries in the selected cluster. Since the number of services in one cluster is relatively smaller, the overall discovery process is reasonably efficient. Different clustering approaches exist in the literature:

- **Static clustering:** (K-means, BIRCH, Hierarchical clustering) use similarity metrics to cluster services. Two problems are worth to be mentioned here: first, these clustering methods are applicable only for static context. Second, they present high complexity when coping with big datasets or semantic data.
- **Incremental clustering:** The principle of this clustering is simple: a service joins a cluster if some predefined criteria are verified. Otherwise, a new cluster is created to represent the new service. Thus, this clustering is more suitable for dynamic datasets [5, 6].

Our approach uses an incremental clustering based on three features: content, type and semantics as described in Sect. 2. These three features are extracted from the semantic description of the WoT service which is hosted in a semantic gateway. After that, a similarity computation is performed between the service to be clustered and other services according to the incremental clustering algorithm (see Fig. 2).

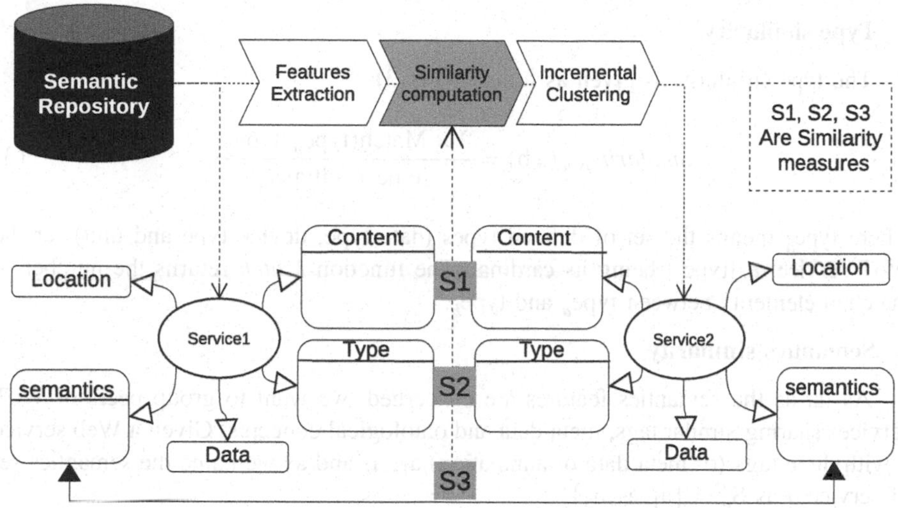

Fig. 2. Web of things services clustering architecture.

We present first the similarity metrics we will use in this clustering, after that we present the different functions of the clustering algorithm.

3.1.1 Similarity Metrics

In what follows we detail the different similarity metrics [7] we will use in the clustering.

- **Content similarity**

Given two WoT services a and b and their respective content vectors A and B of respective dimensions |A| and |B|. We use the Normalized Google Distance (NGD) to compute the content similarity between two WoT services as follows (Eq. 1):

$$Similarity_{content}(\mathrm{a,b}) = \frac{\sum_{c_i \in A} \sum_{c_j \in B} 1 - ngd(c_i, \mathrm{c}_j)}{|A| \times |B|} \quad (1)$$

where *ngd* is the normalized google distance (Eq. 2). The *ngd* function [8] compute the similarity between two words based on the word coexistence in the Web pages.

$$ngd(c_i, c_j) = \frac{max\left[\log f(c_i), \log f(c_j)\right] - \log f(c_i, c_j)}{\log N - min\left[\log f(c_i), \log f(c_j)\right]} \quad (2)$$

where $f(c_i)$,$f(c_j)$,$f(c_i, c_j)$ denote respectively the number of pages containing c_i, c_j, both c_i and c_j, as reported by Google. N is the total number of Web pages searched by Google.

- **Type similarity**

The type similarity is given as follows (Eq. 3):

$$Similarity_{type}(\text{a,b}) = \frac{2 \times \text{Match}(\text{type}_a, \text{type}_b)}{|\text{type}_a| + |\text{type}_b|} \quad (3)$$

where type_a means the set of defined types (data type, device type and unit) for the WoT service *a*. $|\text{type}_a|$ being its cardinal. The function *Match* returns the number of matched elements between type_a and type_b.

- **Semantics similarity**

As far as the semantics features are concerned, we want to group peers of WoT services sharing similar tags, meta-data and ontological concepts. Given a Web service *a* with three tags (or meta-data or annotation) a_1, a_2 and a_3 we name the semantics set of service *a* as $S_a = \{a_1, a_2, a_3\}$.

According to the Jacquard coefficient method, we can calculate the semantics similarity between two WoT services *a* and *b* as follows:

$$Similarity_{semantics}(\text{a,b}) = \frac{|S_a \cap S_b|}{|S_a \cup S_b|} \quad (4)$$

- **Global similarity**

The global similarity between *a* and *b* is defined as follows:

$$\begin{aligned} Similarity(a, b) = {} & w_1 Similarity_{\text{content}}(a, b) \\ & + w_2 Similarity_{semantics}(a, b) \\ & + w_3 Similarity_{type}(a, b) \end{aligned} \quad (5)$$

where $w_1, w_2, w_3 \in [0, 1]$ are the respective weights for the content, semantics and type similarities and $w_1 + w_2 + w_3 = 1$.

In what follows we present the incremental clustering algorithm we will use in conjunction with the calculated similarity to cluster WoT services.

3.1.2 Incremental Clustering

3.1.2.1 Cluster Representative

We note ∇_k the cluster number k where $k > 0$, containing N services: $\nabla_k = \{S_i \in S, i \in [1, N]\}$. We define the *representativity* $r_{k,i}$ of a WoT service $S_i \in \nabla_k$ and the *representative* $\Re_k$ of the cluster ∇_k as follows:

$$\begin{cases} r_{k,i} = \sum_{j=0, j\neq i}^{N} Similarity(S_i, S_j) \;, \; i \in [0, N] \\ \quad (S_i, S_j) \in \nabla_k \times \nabla_k \end{cases} \tag{6}$$

$$\Re_k = \underset{i \in [0,N]}{argmax} \; r_{k,i} \tag{7}$$

Especially, when a new cluster k is created for a service S_{new}, we have: $r_{k,new} = 0$ and $\Re_k = S_{\text{new}}$.

3.1.2.2 Cluster Representative Updating

Let S_{new} be a new service to be added to the cluster ∇_k. To update the representative $\Re_k$, we have to update each $r_{k,i}$ as follows: $r_{k,i} = r_{k,i} + \text{Similarity}(S_i, S_{\text{new}})$, $i \in [0, N]$. After that we recalculate the new $\Re_k$.

3.1.2.3 Services Internal Mobility

After the distribution of the cluster ∇_k by adding or removing a service S_{new}, the cluster ∇_k may change its representative $\Re_k$. In this case, all the services of the semantic gateway may change their clusters and migrate to the distributed cluster ∇_k. To optimize the internal mobility in term of computation time, we give the threshold of the internal mobility T_{imob} that we use as follows:

If $\forall S \in \nabla_{l \neq k}, d_S = \text{Similarity}(S, \Re_l) \geq T_{\text{imob}}$, the service S keeps its cluster. Else If $d_S > \text{Similarity}(S, \Re_k)$, the service S keeps its cluster. Else the service S moves to the cluster ∇_k.

3.1.2.4 Services External Mobility

To add a new service S_{new}, we give the threshold of external mobility T_{emob}.

$$\forall k, d_k = \text{Similarity}(S_{\text{new}}, \Re_k)$$

If $d \geq T_{\text{emob}}$, the service S is added to the cluster ∇_k. Else a new cluster ∇_{new} is created and S_{new} is added to this cluster.

3.1.2.5 Incremental Clustering Algorithm

Input :
- index : The index of the service
- op : indicates the operation to execute (op=1 to add the service , 0 to delete it)
- The thresholds T_{imob} and T_{emob}
- The set of clusters ∇

Output : The updated set of clusters ∇

```
If op = 1
If |∇|=0 create_cluster( S_index )                        # if there is no cluster
    Else
        k = nearest_cluster_index( ∇ , S_index )   # returns the index of the nearest
                                                   # representative to a given service.
        d=Similarity(S_index, ℜ_k)
        If (d> T_emob) create_cluster( S_index )   # create a new cluster
        Else
          add_to_cluster( S_index , ∇_k )
          update_representative( ∇_k );            # change the representative
          internal_mobility( ∇ , T_imob )  # moves a service from a cluster to another
        End If
End If
Else
          remove( S_index ) # removes a service from a cluster
          update_representative( ∇_k ); internal_mobility( ∇ , T_imob )
End If
```

3.2 An Indexing Data Structure Over DHTs

Indexing is a technique that organizes search key values and addresses of objects into catalogs to enable efficient lookup. The search functionality is provided by scanning the catalog first and then locating the desired objects via the addresses in the catalog [9]. In the WoT context, the use of spatial indexing is very useful. Effectively, the WoT services are by nature distributed over different geographical areas. Consequently, location-based indexing allows searching in particular data repositories following the location index value. However, the mobility of IoT objects and services makes this type of indexing complex and costly. Works like [10] focus on indexing the IoT objects like sensors. However, the mobility of the network (e.g. sensors failure) requires the frequent update of the index. This problem was taken into account by [11] that have indexed the IoT gateways instead of the IoT objects leveraging a geospatial index. This method reduces considerably the number of index updates since the index concerns only the gateways. However, as mentioned by the authors [11], this method only focuses on gateways installed at fixed locations. To overcome this lack, we propose a method based on distributed hash tables (DHTs), in which spatially indexed static gateways can volunteer to form an overlay peer-to-peer (P2P) network and provide distributed discovery for mobile gateways. DHTs have many advantages such as scalability, ease of deployment, self-organizing, requiring no centralized authority or manual configuration. Moreover, They are robust against node failures and easily accommodate new nodes [12]. However, DHTs suffer from one big problem: they don't support multi-attributes and range queries which is essential for systems and applications handling complex queries such as geo-spatial ones. Fortunately, numerous works have been proposed in order to handle complex queries. Namely, the Prefix Hash Tree (PHT) [12] which is a distributed data structure built on top of DHT implementation. However, this PHT system supports only a single attribute range queries. Our approach uses the PHT solution given in [13] which supports multi-attributes queries thanks to a linearization technique that maps a multidimensional domain into a one-dimensional one and offers an API to handle the PHT system. Moreover, we use a spatial hashing to optimize the management of the mobile gateways leveraging the static ones. Spatial hashing is a technique in which objects in a 2D or 3D domain space are projected into a 1D hash table allowing for very fast queries on objects in the domain space [14]. The advantage of this type of hashing is that it can compress 3D spatial data in such a way that there spatial coherency (Fig. 3).

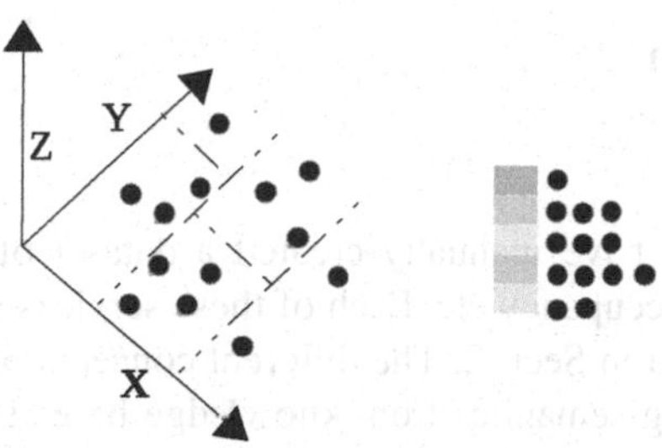

Fig. 3. 3D indices (in the left) near each other have paired values near each other in the hash table (in the right)

In our dynamic context, we have a P2P network composed of several static and mobile nodes. Our architecture first discovers the nodes (namely the static ones) based on their geographical position (lat, long, alt) through range queries. After that, the discovered nodes should be able to manage neighboring mobile nodes organized using the spatial hashing technique (see Fig. 4).

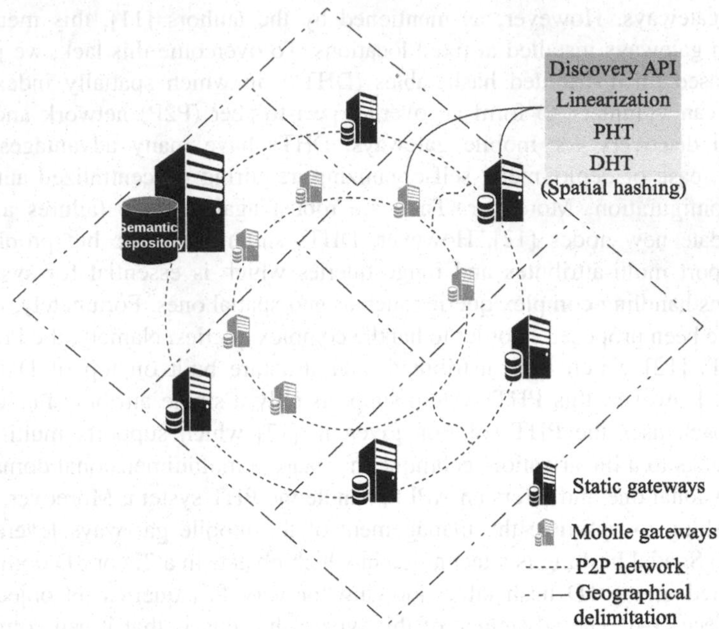

Fig. 4. Distributed discovery architecture to manage mobile gateways.

4 Experimentation

4.1 Clustering

For our experiment, we have manually created a dataset of 100 WoT services like humidity, temperature, occupancy etc. Each of these services was described using a set of meta-data as presented in Sect. 2. The different concepts of each services were also manually annotated using semantics from knowledge bases such as Dbpedia. W have inserted the 100 WoT services incrementally using the thresholds $T_{imob} = 0.5$ and $T_{emob} = 0.33$. To check the relevance of each feature (content, type, semantics), we have clustered the WoT services of our dataset using each feature separately. The obtained results have shown that the semantic coherence of the content has the most important impact on the clustering while the semantics factor has the lower impact. Consequently, we have chosen the weights of the global similarity as follows: $W_1 = 0.5$, $W_2 = 0.10$ and $W_3 = 0.40$. The result of the clustering using the incremental clustering and the global similarity is $K = 6$ clusters. To check the relevance of the obtained clusters, we have applied the static K-means (using Weka 3.9.1) on our dataset using the same obtained number of clusters $K = 6$. The comparison between the instances of the obtained clusters has shown the convergence only between three of them. We have explained that by the difference between our features and the Weka K-means features (Table 2).

Table 2. Comparison between static and incremental clustering

Cluster number	Incremental	Static	Instances convergence (Y/N)
0	20 (20%)	16 (16%)	Y
1	16 (15%)	19 (19%)	Y
2	31 (30%)	20 (20%)	Y
3	10 (10%)	6 (6%)	N
4	13 (13%)	17 (17%)	N
5	10 (20%)	22 (22%)	N

4.2 DHT Architecture

Each gateway in the network is defined with a key based on its three attributes (latitude, longitude, altitude). Moreover, the information record to store in these nodes is in form of pairs (key, value) where the value is a list of tuple (URL, timestamp) to indicate the semantic repositories URLs and the corresponding insertion times in the system. We have conducted two implementations, we first simulated the insertion, removing and lookup operations of the mobile gateways using a PHT implementation for PeerSim simulator [15]. For that, we have considered a network of 20 nodes and 20000 keys generated randomly. For the linearization process we have used a Z-order curve code to map multidimensional (lat, long, alt) data to one dimension while preserving locality of the data points. Furthermore, we have performed another implementation of a DHT using a spatial hashing [16] and Java Sockets. Clients has put and get methods, the put method hashes the key using the spatial hashing and send the hashed key to the corresponding server to store it. Figure (Fig. 5) shows the distribution of the inserted keys over the network. As we can note the distribution using spatial hashing is quite uniform and reflects the geographical distribution of gateways. In the opposite, we note that numerous PHT nodes have no keys inserted.

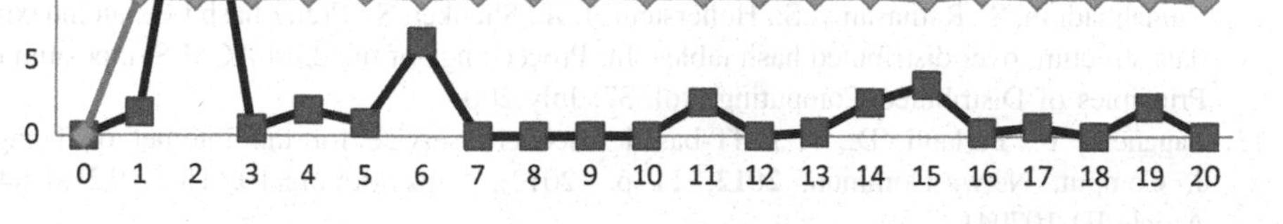

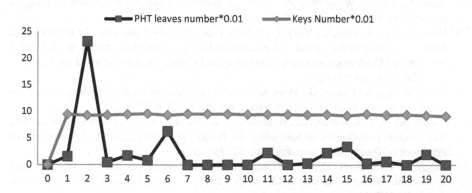

Fig. 5. Distribution of PHT leaves over 20 nodes without the spatial hashing (in black), distribution of keys over DHT (20 nodes) using spatial hashing (in orange). (Color figure online)

5 Conclusion

In this paper, we have proposed a semantic discovery architecture for WoT services, dealing with the dynamicity of both WoT services and IoT gateways. The description of the proposed approach shows that the number of discovered WoT services will decrease using semantics and services filtering mechanisms such as clustering and indexing. In addition to this, our architecture reduces the impact of services and IoT gateways mobility in term of computation process.

References

1. De, S., Zhou, Y., Moessner, K.: Ontologies and context modeling for the Web of Things, pp. 3–36 (2017)
2. Guinard, D.D., Trifa, V.M.: Building the Web of Things (2016)
3. Kolchin, M., et al.: Ontologies for web of things: a pragmatic review. In: Klinov, P., Mouromtsev, D. (eds.) KESW 2015. CCIS, vol. 518, pp. 102–116. Springer, Cham (2015). https://doi.org/10.1007/978-3-319-24543-0_8
4. Wu, Z., Xu, Y., Zhang, C., Yang, Y., Ji, Y.: Towards semantic web of things: from manual to semi-automatic semantic annotation on web of things. In: Wang, Y., Yu, G., Zhang, Y., Han, Z., Wang, G. (eds.) BigCom 2016. LNCS, vol. 9784, pp. 295–308. Springer, Cham (2016). https://doi.org/10.1007/978-3-319-42553-5_25
5. Charikar, M., Chekuri, C., Feder, T., Motwani, R.: Incremental clustering and dynamic information retrieval. SIAM J. Comput. **33**, 1417–1440 (2004)
6. Young, S., Arel, I., Karnowski, T.P., Rose, D.: A fast and stable incremental clustering algorithm. In: ITNG, pp. 204–209 (2010)
7. Wu, J., Chen, L., Zheng, Z., Lyu, M.R., Wu, Z.: Clustering web services to facilitate service discovery. Knowl. Inf. Syst. **38**(1), 207–229 (2014)
8. Cilibrasi, R.L., Vitnyi, P.M.B.: The Google similarity distance. IEEE Trans. Knowl. Data Eng. **19**(3), 370–383 (2007)
9. Zhou, Y., De, S., Wang, W., Moessner, K.: Search techniques for the web of things: a taxonomy and survey. Sensors **16**(5), 600 (2016)
10. Ding, Z., Gao, X., Guo, L., Yang, Q.: A hybrid search engine framework for the internet of things based on spatial-temporal, value-based, and keyword-based conditions. In: 2012 IEEE International Conference on Green Computing and Communications (GreenCom), pp. 17–25. IEEE, November 2012
11. Wang, W., De, S., Cassar, G., Moessner, K.: An experimental study on geospatial indexing for sensor service discovery. Expert Syst. Appl. **42**(7), 3528–3538 (2015)
12. Ramabhadran, S., Ratnasamy, S., Hellerstein, J.M., Shenker, S.: Prefix hash tree: an indexing data structure over distributed hash tables. In: Proceedings of the 23rd ACM Symposium on Principles of Distributed Computing, vol. 37, July 2004
13. Paganelli, F., Parlanti, D.: A DHT-based discovery service for the Internet of Things. J. Comput. Netw. Commun. **2012**, 11 p. (2012). https://doi.org/10.1155/2012/107041. Article ID 107041
14. Hastings, E.J., Mesit, J., Guha, R.K.: Optimization of large-scale, real-time simulations by spatial hashing. In: Proceedings of the 2005 Summer Computer Simulation Conference, vol. 37, no. 4, pp. 9–17 (2005)
15. https://github.com/nongbottom/Peersim-Pht
16. Lefebvre, S., Hoppe, H.: Perfect spatial hashing. In: ACM Transactions on Graphics (TOG), vol. 25, no. 3, pp. 579–588. ACM, July 2006

Comparison of Feature Selection Methods for Sentiment Analysis

Soufiane El Mrabti(✉), Mohammed Al Achhab, and Mohamed Lazaar

ENSA, Abdelmalek Essaadi University, Tetuan, Morocco
elmrabtisouf@gmail.com

Abstract. Sentiment analysis is process of deriving the opinion or attitude expressed in input text. For the classification problem, feature selection aims to select features that are capable of discriminating samples that belong to different classes. This paper evaluates the performance of three feature selection methods (MI, CHI and ANOVA) combined with three machine learning based classification techniques (NB, SVM and KNN) for sentiment analysis on online movie reviews dataset. The paper shows that feature selection is important task for sentiment based classification.

Keywords: Sentiment analysis · Feature selection · Text classification Natural language processing

1 Introduction

Turning data available on the internet into information and turning information into knowledge is the most challenge of the information age. The extracted knowledge can be utilized for different exploratory or predictive analysis purposes.

The purpose of data mining is to extract knowledge from large amounts of data by automatic or semi-automatic methods. Text mining refers to using data mining techniques for discovering useful patterns from texts. The overarching goal is, essentially, to turn text into data for analysis, via application of natural language processing (NLP) and analytical methods. Typical text mining tasks include text categorization, text clustering, document summarization and sentiment analysis.

In this context, Sentiment analysis (SA) is a sub-field of Natural Language Processing and involves automatically classifying input text according to the sentiment expressed in it [1] as shown in Fig. 1. It refers to the use of advanced text mining (TM), machine learning (ML), information retrieval (IR) and natural language processing (NLP) approaches to systematically identify, extract, quantify, and study affective states and subjective information. SA is widely applied to review-related websites [2], recommendation systems [3, 4], and politics for understanding what voters are thinking [5, 6].

One major challenge in the text classification especially Sentiment based classification is the high formal dimensionality of the data [7, 8]. For this reason feature selection (FS) is a crucial task for SA as illustrated in Fig. 1. The aim of feature selection technique is to reduce high dimensionality of the features by removing many

Y. Tabii et al. (Eds.): BDCA 2018, CCIS 872, pp. 261–272, 2018.
https://doi.org/10.1007/978-3-319-96292-4_21

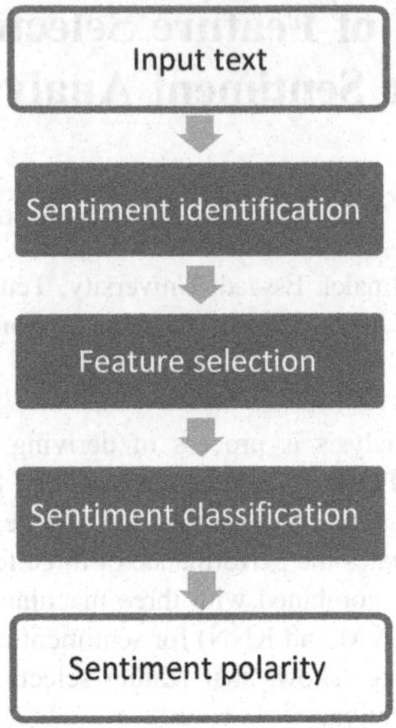

Fig. 1. Sentiment analysis process.

features that are considered irrelevant or redundant. This has resulted in further improvements in classification accuracy decrease the running time of learning algorithms [9, 10].

In this study, our primary objective is to find the appropriate combination of feature selection methods and machine learning based classifiers. This paper is an empirical comparison of feature selection methods combined with machine learning based classification techniques for sentiment analysis. We used three traditional feature selection methods i.e., Mutual Information (MI), CHI statistics (CHI) and Analysis of Variance (ANOVA). For the aim of classification, also three machine learning classifiers are experimented with in this study. Those three classifiers were Naïve Bayes (NB) [11], Support Vector Machine (SVM) [12] and K Nearest Neighbors (KNN) [13].

The rest of this paper is organized as follows: Sect. 2 introduces the related works. Feature selection and machine learning techniques are described in Sect. 3. Section 4 shows the experimental results. Finally Sect. 5 concludes this study and gives future directions.

2 Related Work

Sentiment analysis is a large area. This topic became the subject of many researches and discussions. Interested readers to surveys with thorough coverage of SA are invited to consult the papers such as the works of Bo and Lillian [2], Liu and Zhang [14], Mikalai and Themis [15] and Walaa [16].

Sentiment classification techniques can be divided into lexicon-based methods and machine-learning methods [17] as shown in Fig. 2. The first group collects an opinion word list to perform sentiment analysis, by counting and weighting sentiment-related words that have been evaluated and tagged [30]. In order to assemble this word list, two main approaches have been used: the dictionary-based approach and the corpus-based approach. In this paper, we focus only on machine-learning methods combined with feature selection methods. Machine learning approach (ML) relies on the famous ML algorithms to solve the SA as a regular text classification problem that makes use of syntactic and/or linguistic features, including sentiment lexicons [17]. Many studies on sentiment classification have used machine learning algorithms, with SVM and NB being the most commonly used [8]. For Naïve Bayes (NB) we find [18–20, 32] and for Support Vector Machine (SVM) we identify [19, 21, 22]. There are other ML algorithms used in SA such as Decision Trees (DT) [23, 24], K-Nearest Neighbors (KNN) [25] and Maximum Entropy (ME) [32]. In Table 1 it is described the amount of the studies including sentiment analysis, machine learning based classification techniques and feature selection methods.

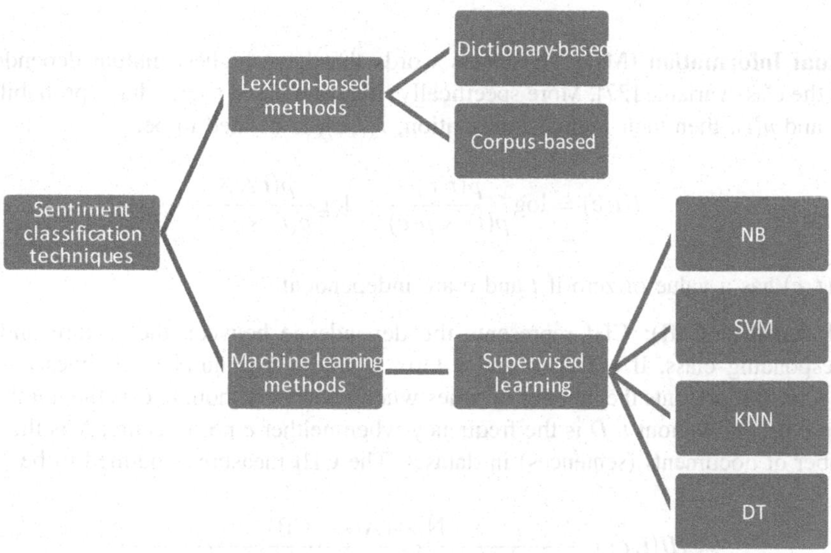

Fig. 2. Sentiment classification techniques.

Feature selection is an important part of machine learning. Is refers to the process of finding the most meaningful inputs. Feature Selection (FS) methods can be divided into lexicon-based methods that need human annotation and statistical methods which are automatic methods that are more frequently used [16]. Among the lexicon-based methods may be: single words [25] or N-grams [26]. For statistical methods, we find Mutual Information (PMI), information gain and CHI statistics [25].

Table 1. Summary of some articles using machine learning techniques and feature selection methods for sentiment analysis.

Algorithm	Dataset	Accuracy (%)	Year	Reference
SVM	Product reviews	85.8	2003	[31]
SVM	Movie reviews (IMDb)	86.4	2004	[19]
ME	movie review (IMDb)	87.40	2007	[32]
NBM	movie review (IMDb)	83.95	2007	[32]
SVM	Movie Reviews (IMDb)	92.2	2007	[33]
SVM	movie review (IMDB)	96.9	2010	[34]
NB	Restaurant review documents	83.6	2012	[11]
SVM	Twitter	87	2013	[35]
SVM	Facebook	83.27	2014	[36]

3 Feature Selection Methods

Mutual Information (MI): MI selects words that have highest mutual dependence with the class variable [27]. More specifically, if a class c and a term, have probabilities $p(c)$ and $p(t)$, then their mutual information, $I(t,c)$, is defined to be:

$$I(t,c) = \log \frac{p(t,c)}{p(t) \times p(c)} = \log \frac{p(t \wedge c)}{p(t) \times p(c)}$$

$I(t,c)$ has a value of zero if t and c are independent.

CHI statistic (CHI): CHI represents the dependence between the feature and the corresponding class. If a class c and a term t, where A is number of times c and t co-occur, B represents the number of times when t occurs without c, C is the number of times c occurs without t, D is the frequency when neither c nor t occurs; N is the total number of documents (sentences) in dataset. The CHI measure is defined to be [28]:

$$CHI(t,c) = \frac{\mathrm{N} \times (\mathrm{AD} - \mathrm{CB})^2}{(\mathrm{A}+\mathrm{C}) \times (\mathrm{B}+\mathrm{D}) \times (\mathrm{A}+\mathrm{B}) \times (\mathrm{C}+\mathrm{D})}$$

CHI has a natural value of zero if t and c are independent. The computation of CHI scores has a quadratic complexity.

Analysis of Variance (ANOVA): ANOVA rank the features by measuring the ratio between their variances between groups (documents or sentences) and within groups (dataset) [29]. The ratio reveals how strong the λ-th feature is related to the group variables. The ratio F value ($\mathrm{F}(\lambda)$) of λ-th g-gap dipeptide in two benchmark datasets is defined as the following equation:

$$F(\lambda) = \frac{S_B^2(\lambda)}{S_W^2(\lambda)}$$

Where $S_B^2(\lambda)$ and $S_W^2(\lambda)$ are the sample variance between groups and sample variance within groups.

4 Classifier

Naïve Bayesian (NB): is a simple probabilistic classifier based on applying Baye's theorem. For each document, the NB algorithm computes the probability that the sentences (document) belongs to different classes and assigns it to the class with the highest probability. The probability is defined as the following equation:

$$p(c|s) = \frac{p(c)p(d|k)}{p(d)}$$

Class (with the highest probability) of d is computes:

$$Class = \arg\max_{c}\{p(s|c)\}$$

A class's prior may be calculated by assuming equiprobable classes, or by calculating an estimate for the class probability from the training set. To estimate the parameters for a feature's distribution, one must assume a distribution or generate nonparametric models for the features from the training set [37]. The different naive Bayes classifiers differ mainly by the assumptions they make regarding the distribution of $p(s|c)$. In this paper, we used Multinomial Naive Bayes is one of the two classic naive Bayes variants used in text classification (where the data are typically represented as word vector counts). With a multinomial Naive Bayes the distribution is parameterized by vectors called multinomial $P_c = \left(P_{y1}, \ldots, P_{cn}\right)$ for class c where n is the number of features and P_{yi} is the probability $p(s|c)$ of feature P_i appearing in a sample belonging to class c. P_{yi} is estimated by the following equation:

$$P_{yi} = \frac{N_{ci} + \alpha}{N_c + \alpha n}$$

Where $N_{ci} = \sum_{t \in D} t_i$ is the number of times feature i appears in a sample of class c in the training set D. And $N_c = \sum_{t \in D} N_{ci}$ is the total count of all features for class c. The smoothing $\alpha \geq 0$ accounts for features not present in the learning samples and prevents zero probabilities in further computations.

Support Vector Machine (SVM): is supervised classification method. SVM algorithm consists of two types of versions: non-linear and linear versions. In linear version, Classes are separated using the hyperplanes. It finds the best decision hyperplane that separates two classes. The quality of a decision hyperplane is determined by the distance (referred as margin) between two hyperplanes that are parallel to the decision hyperplane and touch the closest data points of each class. The best decision hyperplane is the one with the maximum margin. In Fig. 3 there are 2 classes x, o and there are 3 hyperplanes A, B and C. Hyperplane A provides the best separation between the classes, because the normal distance of any of the data points is the largest, so it represents the maximum margin of separation [16]. In non-linear version, classes are not separated i.e. no straight lines can be found that separate the classes. Vladimir N. Vapnik suggested a way to create nonlinear classifiers by applying the kernel trick to maximum-margin hyperplanes. The resulting algorithm is formally similar to linear classifier, except that every dot product is replaced by a nonlinear kernel function. An SVM often maps data to a high dimensional space and then employs kernel techniques [38]. In this paper, we chose radial basis function (RBF) kernel, which maps data to an infinite dimensional space. It give better performance compared to polynomial kernels.

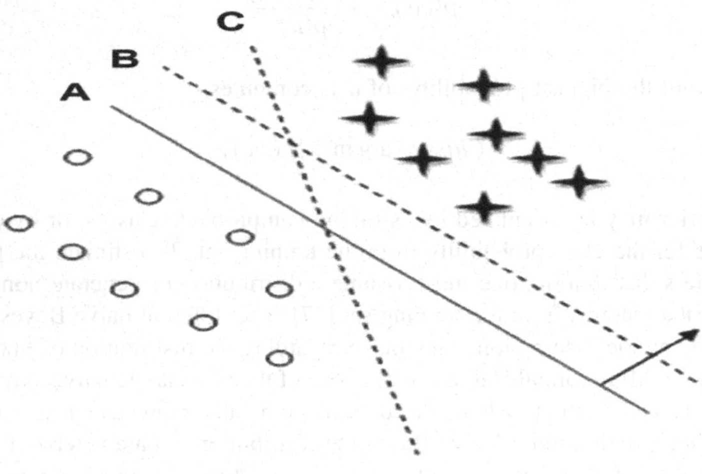

Fig. 3. Using support vector machine on a classification problem [16].

The RBF kernel on two samples x and x', represented as feature vectors in some input space, is defined as [39]:

$$K_{RBF}(x, x') = \exp\left(-\frac{\|x - x'\|^2}{2\alpha^2}\right)$$

Where α is a free parameter.

K nearest neighbors (KNN): is a type of instance-based learning or non-generalizing learning: it does not attempt to construct a general internal model, but simply stores instances of the training data. Classification is computed from a simple majority vote of the nearest neighbors of each point: a query point is assigned the data class which has the most representatives within the nearest neighbors of the point. The input consists of the k closest training examples in the feature space. The output is a class membership. An object is classified by a majority vote of its neighbors, with the object being assigned to the class most common among its k nearest neighbors (k is a positive integer, typically small). If k = 1, then the object is simply assigned to the class of that single nearest neighbor. KNN Algorithm is based on feature similarity: How closely out-of-sample features resemble our training set determines how we classify a given data point (Fig. 4):

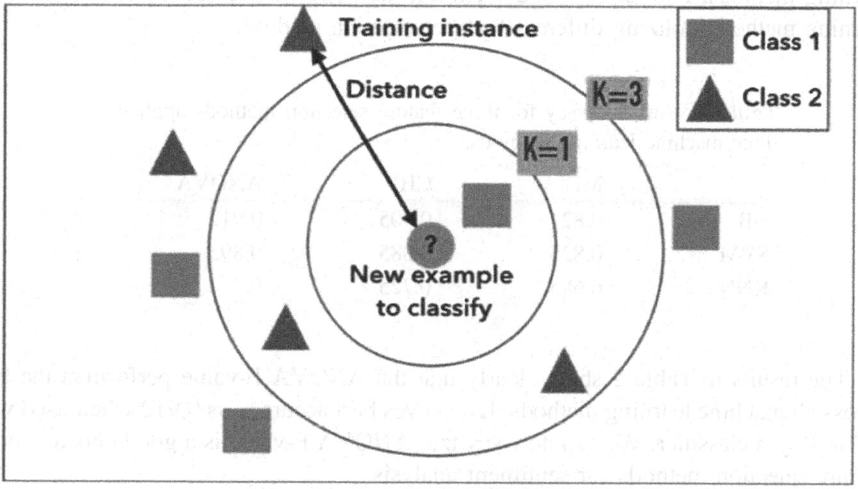

Fig. 4. Example of KNN classification. The test sample (green circle) should be classified either to the first class of blue squares or to the second class of red triangles. If k = 3 (solid line circle) it is assigned to the second class because there are 2 triangles and only 1 square inside the inner circle. If k = 5 (dashed line circle) it is assigned to the first class (3 squares vs. 2 triangles inside the outer circle) [40]. (Color figure online)

5 Experiment Results

5.1 Datasets and Evaluations

This study use a on movie review dataset comprising reviews of movies from the Internet Movie Database (IMDb) adopted from Pang and Lee [19]. It contains 2000 reviews (1000 positive and 1000 negative), and labels were created with an improved rating-extraction system. This paper aims to build a predictor that can distinguish between positive and negative reviews.

To evaluate the performance of sentiment classification, this work has adopted classification accuracy as an index. Accuracy in this study is used as a statistical measure of how well a sentiment based binary classification test correctly classifies a test document. The accuracy is the proportion of true results (both true positives and true negatives) to the total population. The classification accuracy was computed as follows:

$$classification\ accuracy = \frac{Number\ of\ Correctly\ Classified\ Reviews}{Total\ Number\ of\ Reviews}$$

5.2 Results Discussion

The results of the comparison are presented in the following tables. Table 2 presents the best performance of three feature selection methods applied on three machine learning methods. Figures 5, 6 and 7 exhibit the performance curves of two machine learning methods utilizing different feature selection methods.

Table 2. Best accuracy for three feature selection methods applied on three machine learning methods.

	MI	CHI	ANOVA
NB	0.827	0.905	0.912
SVM	0.825	0.885	0.895
KNN	0.685	0.725	0.7

The results in Table 2 show clearly that the ANOVA F-value performed the best across all machine learning methods. It achieves best accuracy as 0.912 when used with Naïve Bayes classifier. We can now say that ANOVA F-value is a good choice among feature selection methods for sentiment analysis.

From Fig. 6, we observe that the ANOVA F-value give the best accuracy with the three machine learning methods when used with nearly 10000 features. Generally, from Figs. 5, 6 and 7, we can note that when the number of features is between 5000 and 15000, NB and SVM realize desirable performance. On the other hand, we observe that the performance curves of KNN vary according to feature selection methods. For example. In the case the CHI or MI, it performed the best in range of 400 to 1000

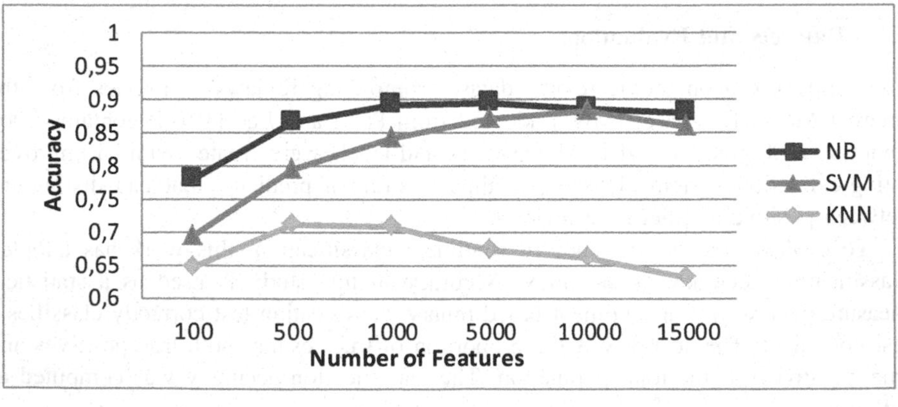

Fig. 5. Performance of machine learning techniques with Chi squared.

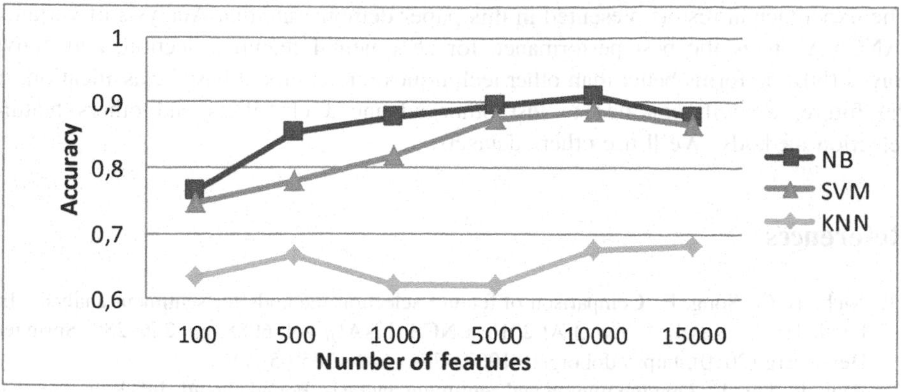

Fig. 6. Performance of machine learning techniques with ANOVA.

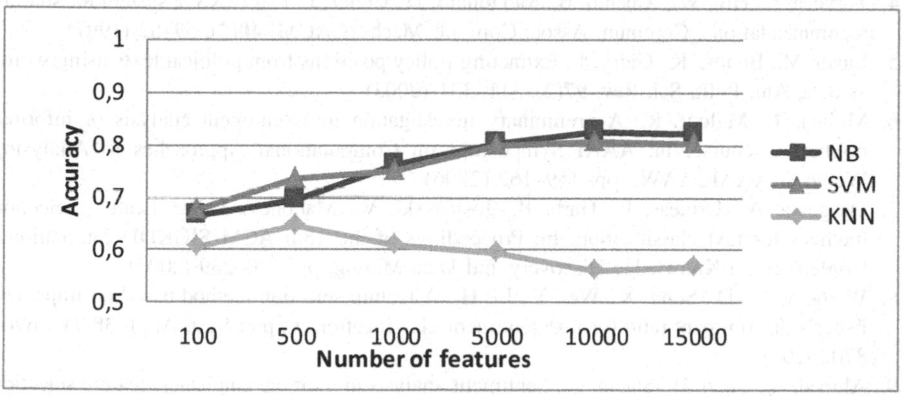

Fig. 7. Performance of machine learning techniques with mutual information.

features, whereas when KNN is combined with ANOVA, it provides good results in range of 10000 to 15000.

After comparing Figs. 5, 6 and 7, we observed that the performance curves of NB and SVM varies proportionally with the number of features. The accuracy gradually increases with the number of features before reaching its maximum value. Then beyond a 15000 features begin to decrease. In all, NB is the best in terms of accuracy whether it is the number of features, followed by the SVM. KNN is classified in last place in the rankings, far ahead of its competitors (NB and SVM).

6 Conclusion

In this study, we have used feature selection methods for sentiment analysis. We prepared a comparative study that examines the performance of feature selection methods combined with machine learning methods on online movie reviews dataset.

The experimental results presented in this paper demonstrate that Analysis of variance (ANOVA) gives the best performance for sentimental feature selection, and Naïve Bayes (NB) performs better than other techniques for sentiment based classification. In the future, we will continue to test other advanced classifiers and others feature selection methods. We'll use others datasets.

References

1. Nicholls, C., Song, F.: Comparison of feature selection methods for sentiment analysis. In: Farzindar, A., Kešelj, V. (eds.) AI 2010. LNCS (LNAI), vol. 6085, pp. 286–289. Springer, Heidelberg (2010). https://doi.org/10.1007/978-3-642-13059-5_30
2. Pang, B., Lee, L.: Opinion mining and sentiment analysis. Found. Trends Inf. Retr. **2**, 1–135 (2008)
3. Tatemura, J.: Virtual reviewers for collaborative exploration of movie reviews. In: Proceedings of Intelligent User Interfaces (IUI), pp. 272–275 (2000)
4. Terveen, L., Hill, W., Amento, B., McDonald, D., Creter, J.: PHOAKS: a system for sharing recommendations. Commun. Assoc. Comput. Mach. (CACM) **40**(3), 59–62 (1997)
5. Laver, M., Benoit, K., Garry, J.: Extracting policy positions from political texts using words as data. Am. Polit. Sci. Rev. **97**(2), 311–331 (2003)
6. Mullen, T., Malouf, R.: A preliminary investigation into sentiment analysis of informal political discourse. In: AAAI Symposium on Computational Approaches to Analysing Weblogs (AAAICAAW), pp. 159–162 (2006)
7. Dasgupta, A., Drineas, P., Harb, B., Josifovski, V., Mahoney, M.W.: Feature selection methods for text classification. In: Proceedings of the 13th ACM SIGKDD International Conference on Knowledge Discovery and Data Mining, pp. 230–239 (2007)
8. Wang, S., Li, D., Song, X., Wei, Y., Li, H.: A feature selection method based on improved fisher's discriminant ratio for text sentiment classification. Expert Syst. Appl. **38**(7), 8696–8702 (2011)
9. Ahmed, A., Chen, H., Salem, A.: Sentiment analysis in multiple languages: feature selection for opinion classification in web forums. ACM Trans. Inf. Syst. **26**(3), 12:21–12:25 (2008)
10. Sharma, A., Dey, S.: A comparative study of feature selection and machine learning techniques for sentiment analysis. In: Proceedings of the 2012 ACM Research in Applied Computation Symposium. ACM (2012)
11. Kang, H., Yoo, S.J., Han, D.: Senti-lexicon and improved Naïve Bayes algorithms for sentiment analysis of restaurant reviews. Expert Syst. Appl. **39**(5), 6000–6010 (2012)
12. Joachims, T.: Text categorization with support vector machines: learning with many relevant features. In: Proceedings of the ECML 1998, pp. 137–142 (1998)
13. Yang, Y., Lin, X.: A re-examination of text categorization methods. In: Proceedings of the SIGIR 1999, pp. 42–49 (1999)
14. Liu, B., Zhang, L.: A survey of opinion mining and sentiment analysis. In: Aggarwal, C., Zhai, C. (eds.) Mining Text Data, pp. 415–463. Springer, Boston (2012). https://doi.org/10.1007/978-1-4614-3223-4_13
15. Mikalai, T., Themis, P.: Survey on mining subjective data on the web. Data Min. Knowl. Discov. **24**, 478–514 (2012)
16. Medhat, W., Hassan, A., Korashy, H.: Sentiment analysis algorithms and applications: a survey. Ain Shams Eng. J. **5**, 1093–1113 (2014)

17. Maynard, D., Funk, A.: Automatic detection of political opinions in tweets. In: García-Castro, R., Fensel, D., Antoniou, G. (eds.) ESWC 2011. LNCS, vol. 7117, pp. 88–99. Springer, Heidelberg (2012). https://doi.org/10.1007/978-3-642-25953-1_8
18. Pang, B., Lee, L., Vaithyanathan, S.: Thumbs up? Sentiment classification using machine learning techniques. In: Proceedings of the ACL 2002 Conference on Empirical Methods in Natural Language Processing. ACL (2002)
19. Pang, B., Lee, L.: A sentimental education: sentiment analysis using subjectivity summarization based on minimum cuts. In: Proceedings of ACL (2004)
20. Xia, R., Zong, C., Li, S.: Ensemble of feature sets and classification algorithms for sentiment classification. Inf. Sci. **181**(6), 1138–1152 (2011)
21. Dave, K., Lawrence, S., Pennock, D.M.: Mining the peanut gallery: opinion extraction and semantic classification of product reviews. In: Proceedings of the 12th International WWW Conference, Budapest, Hungary, 20–24 May 2003, pp. 519–528 (2003)
22. Wilson, T., Wiebe, J., Hoffman, P.: Recognizing contextual polarity in phraselevel sentiment analysis. In: Proceedings of the Human Language Technology Conference and Conference on Empirical Methods in Natural Language Processing, British Columbia, Canada, pp. 347–354 (2005)
23. Annett, M., Kondrak, G.: A comparison of sentiment analysis techniques: polarizing movie blogs. Adv. Artif. Intell. **5032**, 25–35 (2008)
24. Jotheeswaram, J., Kumaraswamy, Y.S.: Opinion mining using decision tree based feature selection through Manhattan hierarchical technology. J. Theor. Appl. Inf. Technol. **58**(1), 72–79 (2013)
25. Tan, S., Zhang, J.: An empirical study of sentiment analysis for Chinese documents. Expert Syst. Appl. **34**(4), 2622–2629 (2008)
26. Gamon, M.: Sentiment classification on customer feedback data: noisy data, large feature vectors, and the role of linguistic analysis. In: Proceedings of the 20th International Conference on Computational Linguistics, Geneva, Switzerland. ACL (2004)
27. Cover, T.M., Thomas, J.A.: Elements of Information Theory. Wiley, New York (1991)
28. Yang, Y., Pedersen, J.O.: A comparative study on feature selection in text categorization. In: Proceedings of the ICML (1997)
29. Lin, H., Ding, H.: Predicting ion channels and their types by the dipeptide mode of pseudo amino acid composition. J. Theor. Biol. **269**, 64–69 (2011)
30. Zhang, H., Gan, W., Jiang, B.: Machine learning and lexicon based methods for sentiment classification: a survey. In: Yuan, X., Meng, X. (eds.) Proceedings of the 11th Web Information System and Application Conference, pp. 262–265. IEEE Press, Piscataway (2014)
31. Kushal, D., Lawrence, S., Pennock, D.: Mining the peanut gallery: opinion extraction and semantic classification of product reviews. In: Proceedings of WWW (2003)
32. Boiy, E., Hens, P., Deschacht, K., Moens, M.: Automatic sentiment analysis in on-line text. In: Chan, L., Martens, B. (eds.) ELPUB, pp. 349–360 (2007)
33. Zaidan, O., Eisner, J., Piatko, C.: Using annotator rationales to improve machine learning for text categorization. In: NAACL – HLT (2007)
34. Paltoglou, G., Thelwall, M.: A study of information retrieval weighting schemes for sentiment analysis. In: Proceedings of Annual Meeting of the Association for Computational Linguistics (ACL-2010) (2010)
35. Li, Y.-M., Li, T.-Y.: Deriving market intelligence from microblogs. Decis. Support Syst. **55** (1), 206–217 (2013)
36. Ortigosa, A., Martin, J.M., Carro, R.M.: Sentiment analysis in Facebook and its application to e-learning. Comput. Hum. Behav. **31**, 527–541 (2014)

37. John, G.H., Langley, P.: Estimating continuous distributions in Bayesian classifiers. In: Proceedings of the Eleventh Conference on Uncertainty in Artificial Intelligence, pp. 338–345. Morgan Kaufmann (1995)
38. Chang, Y.-W., Hsieh, C.-J., Chang, K.-W., Ringgaard, M., Lin, C.-J.: Training and testing low-degree polynomial data mappings via linear SVM. J. Mach. Learn. Res. **11**, 1471–1490 (2010)
39. Vert, J.-P., Tsuda, K., Schölkopf, B.: A primer on kernel methods. In: Kernel Methods in Computational Biology (2004)
40. Bronshtein, A.: A quick introduction to k-nearest neighbors algorithm (2017). https://medium.com/@adi.bronshtein/a-quick-introduction-to-k-nearest-neighbors-algorithm-62214cea29c7. Accessed 15 Jan 2018

A Hierarchical Nonlinear Discriminant Classifier Trained Through an Evolutionary Algorithm

Ziauddin Ursani[1,2(✉)] and David W. Corne[1,2]

[1] Heriot Watt University, Edinburgh, UK
ziaursani@yahoo.com
[2] Route Monkey Limited, Livingston, UK

Abstract. This work builds on our earlier two papers where we developed method to train nonlinear discriminant classifier for 4-feature datasets. In this paper, the method has been formalized to include any number of features. A hierarchical nonlinear discriminant classifier builds models using a constrained pattern of feature combinations. The model is far more expressive than naïve Bayes, for example, which does not consider feature combinations at all; and the model is far more parsimonious and scalable than unconstrained genetic programming (for example), which does not rule out any feature combinations. The method can be used for knowledge acquisition and decision-making expert system as it can retrieve 100% accurate model from the dataset. The method can also be used for classification of unseen data. The method has been tested on popular test datasets present in the UCI repository. Two approaches are presented to apply a learned model to the test set. The first method consists of application of a single exact hierarchical model on the test set; another method is the application of a weighted sum of models present in each hierarchy. Results of this approach on the datasets studied here are found to be very competitive with the results in recent literature.

Keywords: Hierarchical model · Weighted sum model · Nonlinear model Supervised learning

1 Introduction

Helping computers to learn classification task is the very important area of machine learning, which has now dominated the artificial intelligence literature since last several decades. Supervised Learning has remained subject of research throughout this period. To evaluate the performance of the supervised learning methodology, the dataset is divided into training set and the test set. The model is trained on the training set and then is applied on the test set. Though it is not guaranty that the more accurate model on the training set produces more accurate results on the test set but retrieving accurate models from the datasets has always been subject of interest for knowledge acquisition and decision-making problems [1, 2]. The most popular system in this area is C4.5 inductive decision tree learners [3]. In this paper, we propose a method which is capable of highly accurate low-complexity models of the training set (i.e. models have

Y. Tabii et al. (Eds.): BDCA 2018, CCIS 872, pp. 273–288, 2018.
https://doi.org/10.1007/978-3-319-96292-4_22

very few parameters, and achieved 100% accuracy in training on the cases studied here). High accuracy on a training set provides, of course, generally no information about generalization quality in machine learning; however, when such accuracy is regularly obtained with a low complexity model, it becomes of potential interest for fields such as knowledge acquisition, especially if the model also performs well on test sets. The method is extension of our preliminary work [4, 5], now rendered more scalable for datasets with many features. The model can be described as a hierarchical nonlinear discriminant classifier that exploits a constrained pattern of feature combinations in a fixed tree data structure. The model is far more expressive than, for example, naïve Bayes [6], which does not consider feature combinations at all; and the model is far more parsimonious and scalable than unconstrained genetic programming [7], which does not rule out any feature combinations. The nonlinear discriminant classifiers have been in the literature now for a considerable time, such as Kernel based nonlinear discriminant classifiers [8, 9]. However, in this paper hierarchical nonlinear discriminant classifier model is proposed, which is constructed automatically through randomized training procedure. The model is stochastic, trained via an evolutionary algorithm, therefore produces potentially different models in each run. However, it seems to reliably find 100% accurate models of the training set in the cases we have studied so far, and present herein. This paper contains some examples of these models produced on three datasets Iris Flower, Balance Scale and Car Evaluation. These datasets are popular test cases for classification and knowledge acquisition problems and are present in the UCI machine learning repository [10]. Later, the method is used for classification of unseen data on the same datasets. The model is trained on the training set which is a randomly chosen subset of the original set. The trained model is then applied to classify the test set, which is a subset of the original set complimentary to the training set. Therefore, data in the test set is not seen by the model during training. The paper proposes two methods for application of model on the test set. One method is to exactly apply same hierarchical model on the test set and another method is to produce a model that is weighted sum of models present in each hierarchy of the trained model. The results are competitive with the state of art literature.

The rest of the paper is structured as follows. In Sect. 2, a tree generation model for the feature set of any size is proposed. Section 3 consists of description of evolutionary algorithm that trains the tree data structure model. The detailed description of the three test datasets is given in the Sect. 4. Experimental design of supervised learning for classification of these datasets and their results are discussed in Sect. 5. Section 6 concludes the findings and speculates on the future work. Finally, an appendix is given which gives some examples of accurate models trained through an evolutionary algorithm on the complete test datasets.

2 Tree Generation Model

A tree generation model generates a tree that can represent a mathematical model consisting of full feature set of the dataset regardless of its size. The total number of nodes in the tree generation model is governed by Eq. 1.

$$n = 3 * f - 1 \quad (1)$$

where

n = number of nodes in the tree
f = number of features in the dataset

The tree essentially consists of three types of nodes.

2.1 Weight Nodes n_w

These are the tail nodes of the tree which contain the weight of the features; therefore, number of weight nodes is equal to number of features. The id numbers of these weight nodes start from $2 \times f$ and end at $3 \times f - 1$. The value of weight ranges between 0–1. All the weight nodes are present at the last level of the tree or they are leaf nodes.

2.2 Feature Nodes n_f

These are the nodes preceding to weight nodes. The feature nodes contain the actual feature values and hence are also equal to number of features. The id numbers of these nodes start from f and end at $2f - 1$. All the feature nodes are present at the second last level of the tree or one level before the leaf nodes.

2.3 Operator Nodes n_o

The nodes preceding to the feature nodes are operator nodes. These nodes contain the information about mathematical operator, which is supposed to be applied on the two expressions represented by two branches emanating from this node. The number of the operator nodes are one less than the feature nodes i.e., $n_o = n_f - 1$. The id numbers of operator nodes start from 1 and end at $f - 1$. The operator nodes are present at different hierarchy levels of the tree starting from the first level to the third last level. At the third last level, the operator nodes follow the following rule.

$$n_o^3 = INT\left(\frac{f}{2}\right) \quad (2)$$

where

n_o^3 = Number of operator nodes at the third last level

On the levels preceding to 3rd last level, the operator nodes follow following rule.

$$n_o^m = \begin{cases} INT\left(\frac{n_o^{m-1}}{2}\right) + 1, & if\ n_o^{m-1},\ n_x^{m-2}\ are\ odd \\ INT\left(\frac{n_o^{m-1}}{2}\right), & otherwise \end{cases} \quad (3)$$

where

n_o^m = number of operator nodes at m^{th} last level
n_x = can be any nodes i.e. feature nodes or operator nodes depending on the level of tree.

The Eq. 3 says that the number of operator nodes at any level of tree depends on the number of nodes at two succeeding levels. If the number of nodes at two succeeding levels are odd then the number of operator nodes will be one more than the number of nodes in the other case. The operator nodes contain integer value from 1–4, each representing each of four mathematical operators $+, -, \times, \div$ respectively.

Let us explain above model with the car evaluation dataset which has six features. The tree in Fig. 1 is representative of this model. The tree in Fig. 1 contains 17 nodes which follows the Eq. 1. The nodes 12–17 are weight nodes. The nodes 6–11 are feature nodes and the nodes 1–5 are operator nodes. At the third last level, there are three operator nodes 3–5, which follow the Eq. 2. At fourth last level (2nd level), there is only node 2 and at the fifth last level (1st level) again there is only node 1. The nodes at first and second level follow the Eq. 3. The node at 1st level follows conditional part of Eq. 3 and node at 2nd level follows otherwise part of Eq. 3.

Now if the weight nodes 12–17 contain weight values w_1–w_6 respectively, the feature nodes 6–11 contain values f_1–f_6 respectively, the operator nodes 4–5 contain the value +, the operator nodes 1–3 contain the values $\div, \times, -$ respectively then the phenotype equivalent $\in$ of this tree structure is given in Eq. 4.

$$\in = \frac{w_1 f_1 - w_2 f_2}{(w_3 f_3 + w_4 f_4) \times (w_5 f_5 + w_6 f_6)} \tag{4}$$

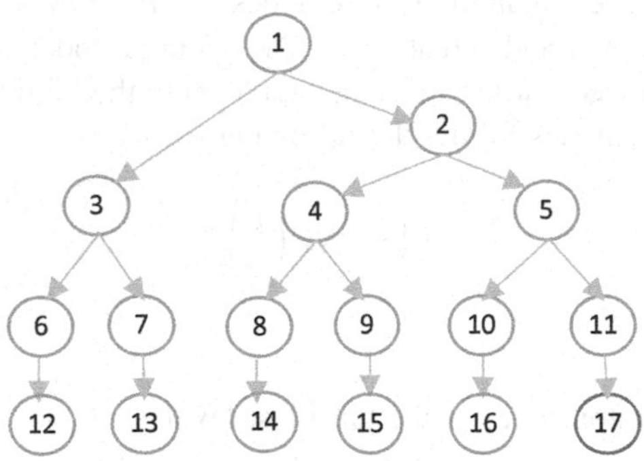

Fig. 1. A tree model for six feature set

It can be seen from the example Eq. 4, that values at weight nodes are multiplied with corresponding feature nodes and then resultant expressions are subjected to operators represented in the operator nodes.

3 Evolutionary Algorithm (EA)

The evolutionary algorithm trains the tree data structure explained in Sect. 2. The evolutionary algorithm can be applied on the whole dataset for knowledge acquisition or it can also be applied on the randomly chosen part of the dataset for training purpose. The algorithm follows the hierarchical procedure used in our earlier work [5], summarized here as follows.

a. Create two lists i.e. sample list and model hierarchy list
b. Store the number of samples under examination in the sample list.
c. Initialize model hierarchy list with level $n = 0$.
d. The EA starts with the random generation of population of solutions. Each solution consists of tree data structure presented in section 2.
e. The EA evaluates each solution of the population according to fitness and unfitness function, discussed in detail later in this section.
f. The individuals for reproduction of next generation are selected using binary tournament selection.
g. The next generation is produced through reproductive procedures consisting of crossover and mutation operators as described in [5].
h. If termination condition is false then go to step ***e***.
i. Set $n = n + 1$ and store the trained model in the model hierarchy list
j. Delete the classified samples from the sample list.
k. If sample list is still non-empty then go to step ***d***.
l. Terminate the program.

Procedure 1: Hierarchical application of evolutionary algorithm

It can be seen from the above procedure, that the algorithm continues to train models iteratively until all samples are classified. Finally, all the models can be put in a hierarchical way to represent decision model of the whole dataset or the training set under examination. The interesting thing about these models is that every single model correctly classifies some of the samples but it doesn't misclassify any of the samples. This is accomplished through combination of fitness and unfitness function (step *e*). The primary objective is to maximize fitness function and secondary objective is to minimize unfitness function. The fitness function is equal to number of classified samples. Unfitness function is the value of partition wall that is incorporated into the model to prevent model from misclassifying the samples. The model is probabilistic. It measures probability of sample to be member of each class. These probabilities are computed with the help of the probabilistic model based on the distance of phenotype value ∈ (example Eq. 4) of sample *i* from the phenotype mean of class *j*. Figure 2 along with Eq. 5 illustrates this probabilistic principle of membership.

$$p_i^j = \frac{\delta}{\mu} \tag{5}$$

where

p_i^j = probability that sample i is member of class j
δ = Distance of phenotype value for sample i from estimated maximum/minimum of class j
μ = Distance of estimated mean of phenotype value of all samples of class j in the training set from estimated minimum/maximum of the values of members of class j.

It is clear from the Fig. 2 and Eq. 5, that the sample will have greater probability of class membership when it is closer to the mean position of the class. Its probability of class membership decreases when it goes farther and becomes negative when it goes farther than the estimated minimum/maximum of the class phenotype value. We know that in standard probability theory probability ranges between (0–1), however, according to Eq. 5, its value can go much below zero and we keep it as it is because it is useful in our class membership function later discussed in Eq. 9. The estimated mean of phenotype value of class j is calculated from the training set as follows.

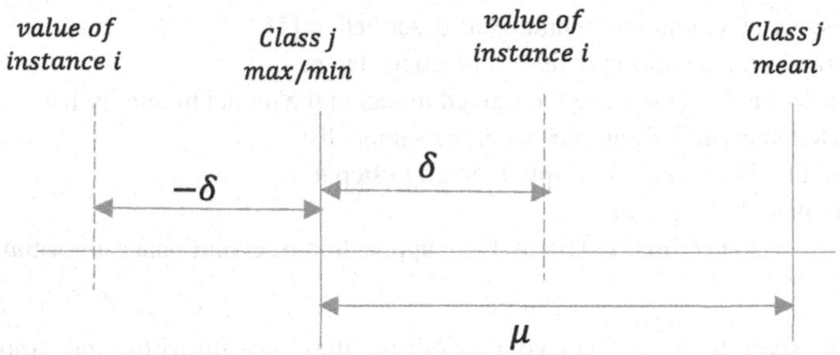

Fig. 2. A principle of probabilistic membership

$$\epsilon_{mean}^{j} = \frac{\sum_{i=1}^{i=t_j} \in_i}{t_j + \Delta} \tag{6}$$

where

$\in_i$ = Phenotype value for sample i according to evaluation of model described in Sect. 2 (for example, Eq. 4)
t_j = Number of samples in the training set of class j
Δ = Predictive parameter for larger sample = 1.0

The estimated maximum and minimum of phenotype value of class j are modelled as follows.

$$\epsilon_{\substack{max \\ min}}^{j} = \epsilon_{mean}^{j} \pm 3.0 * \epsilon_{sd}^{j} \tag{7}$$

where

ϵ^{j}_{mean} = estimated mean of set of phenotype values of member samples of class j in the training set

$\epsilon^{j}_{\substack{max\\min}}$ = estimated maximum/minimum of set of phenotype values of member samples of class j in the training set

ϵ^{j}_{sd} = estimated standard deviation of set of phenotype values of member samples of class j in the training set

The estimated standard deviation of phenotype value of class j is modelled as follows.

$$\epsilon^{j}_{sd} = \frac{\sum_{i=1}^{i=t_j}\left(\epsilon^{j}_{i} - \epsilon^{j}_{mean}\right)^2}{t_j - \Delta} \tag{8}$$

The task of classifying the sample i is achieved through class membership function as given below.

$$\emptyset_i = k \text{ iff } P^k_i > \forall^{j \neq k}_{j=1,n_c}\left(P^j_i + \nabla\right) \tag{9}$$

where

$\emptyset_i$ = class of sample i
∇ = Safety partition to avoid misclassification during training (unfitness function)
n_c = Total number of classes in the dataset

It is clear from the Eq. 9, that the sample is classified into the class with which it has highest probability of class membership among all the classes. However, it remains unclassified if highest probability of class membership is not greater enough than the second highest probability of class membership to overcome the obstacle of unfitness function ∇. Following are the steps of evaluation procedure of chromosome.

- **a.** The evaluation starts by setting unfitness function/safety partition $\nabla = 0$.
- **b.** Set sample number $i = 0$
- **c.** Increment $i = i + 1$
- **d.** Apply model in relation 9 to classify the sample i
- **e.** If the model misclassifies a sample i to a wrong class k, then $\nabla = P^k_i - \max\left(\forall^{j \neq k}_{j=1,n_c} P^j_i\right)$ go to step b.
- **f.** Terminate the procedure

Procedure 2: Evaluation procedure of chromosome

It is clear from the step e that the value of unfitness function is raised to minimum threshold level to avoid misclassification. Due to this raised value of safety partition none of the probability values of any class membership satisfy the condition placed in model (relation 9). Therefore, the sample i remains unclassified. Since the model has now been modified, therefore procedure of evaluation starts again from first sample with the new value of unfitness function. The procedure continues until all samples of training dataset are examined under same value of unfitness function and none of the samples are misclassified. Now the chromosome fitness value is composite of its fitness and unfitness function. The fitness function is number of classified samples and value of ∇ is unfitness function.

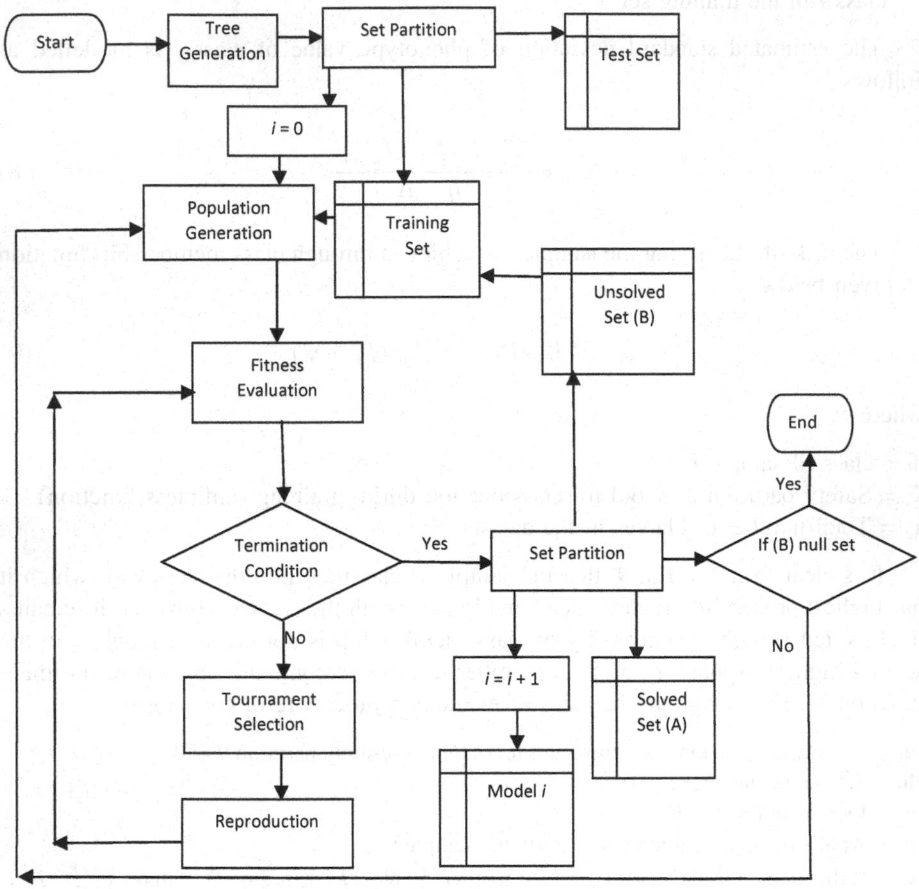

Fig. 3. Flowchart of hierarchical model evolution

Now the primary objective is to maximize fitness function i.e., maximize number of classified samples and the secondary objective is to minimize unfitness function i.e. value of ∇. Therefore, while comparing fitness of chromosomes, a chromosome with higher number of classified samples is considered better regardless of value of its unfitness function. The value of unfitness function is only considered when the two chromosomes have equal score in number of classified samples. The flowchart of whole procedure is depicted in Fig. 3.

The flowchart starts from the process of tree generation, which is described in Sect. 2. Understandably the tree is generated after reading the dataset. The dataset is then partitioned into training set and test set through the procedure of set partition, which is entirely random procedure but it ascertains the proportional representation of each class in the training set. The variable i is initialized with zero. This variable represents a model or hierarchy number, which will be incremented later with the generation of model. The evolutionary algorithm starts with generation of random population followed by typical cycle of evolutionary iteration consisting of fitness evaluation, selection and reproduction until termination condition is achieved. After the termination the training set is further partitioned into the solved set and unsolved set. The solved set consists of classified samples of the training set by the trained model while the unsolved set consists of samples which the model failed to classify. Now if this unsolved set is not a null set, then it is considered as a training set for the next phase of application of evolutionary algorithm, which is again starts from generation of random population of solutions. This iterative procedure continues until unsolved set becomes null set.

4 Description of Datasets

This paper considers three datasets which are taken from UCI repository [10] to analyze the performance of the method proposed. Following is the description of those datasets.

4.1 Iris Flower

This is a botanical dataset. The dataset contains 150 samples of 3 species of iris flower called Setosa, Virginica and Versicolour. The dataset has 50 samples of each class, with details of four features i.e., sepal width, sepal length, petal width and petal length. The dataset was created by Anderson in 1935 [11] and later was popularized by Sir Fisher in 1936 [12]. The dataset is most popular in pattern recognition and classification domain.

4.2 Balance Scale

This is a psychological dataset. This dataset was created by Siegler in 1976 [13] to model psychological experimental results. The dataset contains 625 examples of persons with attributes left weight, right weight, left distance and right distance. This data is helpful in determining whether person is balanced, right tipped or left tipped. The dataset contains 288 examples for each right and left tipped people while only 49 examples for the balanced people. This is a very popular test case in the classification domain.

4.3 Car Evaluation

This is a decision-making dataset. The dataset has six attributes namely buying price, maintenance cost, number of doors, maximum number of accommodable persons, size of lug-boot and level of safety measures. The dataset has total of 1728 samples. The dataset has four classes unacceptable, acceptable, good and very good. The unacceptable class has 1210 samples. The acceptable class has 384 samples. The good class has 69 samples and very good class has 65 samples.

Table 1 summarizes feature list of these datasets. Column 1 contains name of the dataset, column 2 provides number of features in the dataset and columns 3–8 provide name of the feature corresponding to label used in the column head. These labels are later used to represent classifier models of the dataset in Table 5 in the Appendix. Table 2 summarizes the class list of the dataset. Again column 1 contains name of the dataset, column 2 informs about number of classes in the dataset and columns 3–6 give name of the class corresponding to label used in the column head. These labels are later used in Table 6 in Appendix to give statistical data about generated models.

Table 1. Feature description for each dataset

Dataset	Number of features	f_1	f_2	f_3	f_4	f_5	f_6
(1)	(2)	(3)	(4)	(5)	(6)	(7)	(8)
Balance scale	4	Left weight	Left distance	Right weight	Right distance	-	-
Iris flower	4	Sepal length	Sepal width	Petal length	Petal width	-	-
Car evaluation	6	Buying cost	Maintenance cost	Number of doors	Number of seats	Size of lug-boot	Level of safety

Table 2. Class description for each dataset

Dataset	Number of classes	c_1	c_2	c_3	c_4
(1)	(2)	(3)	(4)	(5)	(6)
Balance scale	3	Balanced	Left tipped	Right tipped	
Iris flower	3	Setosa	Virginica	Versicolour	
Car evaluation	4	Unacceptable	Acceptable	Good	Very good

5 Experimental Design and Analysis

The experiments are performed on the datasets described in Sect. 4. The objective of experiments is two-fold. First objective is to retrieve 100% accurate models from complete datasets. The results of these experiments are included in the Appendix. The second objective is to develop models on the randomly generated training sets and then verify those models on the test set. On the test set trained models are applied in two different ways. First method is to apply models in hierarchical way as stored in model hierarchy list described in procedure 1. Following is the stepwise method for hierarchical application of models.

a. Create a sample list
b. Store the samples to be tested in the sample list.
c. Set pointer in the model hierarchy list with level $n = 1$.
d. Apply the pointed model on the sample list for classification (step explained further in appendix in procedure 4)
e. Delete the classified samples from the sample list.
f. If sample list is non-empty then increment the pointer in the model hierarchy list $n = n + 1$ and go to step d.
g. Terminate the program.

Procedure 3: Evaluation Procedure of the test set

The second method is weighted sum method, i.e., weighted sum of all models present in the model hierarchy list is produced and applied on the test dataset. The weights to the models are assigned based on the fitness i.e. number of classified samples by the model. The experiments are performed on randomly generated training sets of three different sizes equivalent to around 50%, 80% and 90% of the original size of the dataset. The training sets are generated in a way that samples of each class are chosen proportionally for proper representation of each class in the training set. 30 simulations are run on each dataset. However, each simulation has different randomly generated training set. The results of experiments are summarized in Table 3.

Table 3. Classification results on the datasets.

Dataset	Classification method	Size of training set	Best results	Average results	% age of accurate results
(1)	(2)	(3)	(4)	(5)	(6)
Iris flower	Weighted sum	50%	98.67%	94.31%	0.00%
		80%	100.00%	95.44%	23.33%
		90%	100.00%	96.44%	60.00%
	Hierarchical	50%	98.67%	93.51%	0.00%
		80%	100.00%	94.22%	6.67%
		90%	100.00%	94.44%	36.67%
Balance scale	Weighted sum	50%	100.00%	97.44%	3.33%
		80%	100.00%	98.53%	43.33%
		90%	100.00%	96.13%	40.00%
	Hierarchical	50%	100.00%	99.05%	23.33%
		80%	100.00%	99.76%	80.00%
		90%	100.00%	99.41%	73.33%
Car evaluation	Weighted sum	50%	85.19%	78.96%	0.00%
		80%	88.12%	79.78%	0.00%
		90%	86.05%	80.78%	0.00%
	Hierarchical	50%	95.14%	93.29%	0.00%
		80%	97.68%	94.88%	0.00%
		90%	98.84%	95.81%	0.00%

In Table 3, column-1 contains name of the dataset, column 2 provides name of the classification method, column 3 gives size of the training set in terms of percentage to original size, columns 4–5 informs about best and average result of 30 simulations respectively. The results are in terms of percentage of correctly classified samples. Finally, column 6 provides percentage of accurate results i.e., the percentage of number of simulations out of 30 simulations where 100% accurate results are obtained.

It can be seen from the Table 3, that better results are obtained with weighted sum method on the iris flower dataset while on the balance scale and car evaluation datasets better results are obtained with hierarchical method of classification. It can also be noticed that best results are obtained on training set of 80% size on balance scale and car evaluation dataset, while for iris flower dataset best results are obtained at the training set of 90% size. The hierarchical method has been most successful on the balance scale dataset with up to 99.76% average results on test set with the training set of 80% size, whereas accurate results on test set have been obtained on 80% of simulations.

Table 4, has also been prepared to compare results with other methods. In Table 4, column 1 gives reference of the method, column 2 provides name of the dataset, column 3 informs about number of simulations/cross validation, size of training set in terms of percentage to original dataset is given in column 4. Columns 5–6 give average and best results respectively of all the simulations in terms of percentage of correctly classified samples.

Table 4. Classification results in the literature

Ref.	Dataset	Sim/X-validation	Size of Tr. set	Average results	Best results
(1)	(2)	(3)	(4)	(5)	(6)
[12]	Iris	-	80%	-	100%
	Balance		50%	-	88.14%
[13]	Iris	10	90%	94.67%	-
	Balance		90%	78.88%	-
[14]	Iris	10-fold X-validation	90%	94.0%	94.0%
	Balance		90%	89.1%	89.1%
[15]	Iris	15x10-fold X-validation	90%	95.65%	-
	Balance		90%	85.28%	-
	Car		90%	98.48%	-
[16]	Iris	10-fold X-validation	90%	87.22%	-
	Balance		90%	71.27%	-
	Car		90%	70.12%	-
[17]	Iris	10-fold X-validation	90%	95.4%	-
	Balance		90%	97.15%	-
[18]	Iris	-	100%	-	98%
	Balance		100%	-	84%
[19]	Car	10x10-fold X-validation	90%	93.3%	-

It can be seen by comparing results in Tables 3 and 4 that proposed method has produced average of 96.44% correct results on the test set of iris flower dataset with the 90% of the training set, which is better than all the methods presented in Table 2. On the balance scale dataset, the proposed method has produced staggering average of 99.76% accurate results on test set with 80% training set, which is again best results among all the contemporary methods. On the car evaluation dataset, the proposed method has produced average of 95.81% correct results against 98.48% average of random forest method [15]. However, random forest method [15] has used 15x10-fold X-validation, whereas proposed method hasn't made any use of x-validation.

6 Conclusion and Future Work

In this paper, a hierarchical nonlinear discriminant classifier is presented. The method proposed automatically produces a tree data-structure according to number of features that can represent nonlinear discriminant classifier based on only four basic mathematical operators $+, -, \times, \div$. The method can retrieve 100% accurate model from the iris flower, balance scale and car evaluation datasets. The example retrieved models are given in appendix. Thus, the model can be useful in knowledge acquisition and decision-making expert systems. Those retrieved models are the array of models placed hierarchically in the model hierarchy list. They can be applied hierarchically to the dataset for the classification purpose. Further, the method is used for classification of the previously unseen data by the model. To achieve this the model was trained on the randomly chosen training set. To classify the test set two models were used i.e. hierarchical application of models present in the model hierarchy list and weighted sum model of all the models present in the model hierarchy list. Weighted sum model produced better results on the iris flower dataset while hierarchical application of models produced better results on the balance scale and car evaluation dataset. Also, the method produced competitive average results when compared with the state of art. Encouraged by these results, now the authors are determined to expand this method to make it applicable to more datasets. Furthermore, detailed analysis is needed to establish why on some datasets weighted sum application of model on the test set performs better than the actual hierarchical application.

Acknowledgments. The authors are grateful for financial support from Innovate UK and Route Monkey Ltd via KTP Partnership number 9839.

Appendix

This appendix contains 100% accurate models that have been retrieved from the iris flower and balanced scale datasets by the proposed computational model when trained on the whole list of samples contained in the datasets. Car evaluation models are not given because of space limitations. Since the method is randomized therefore each run produces different model however, each model when tested back on the datasets produced 100% accurate classification. The models are presented in favour of researchers to help them extract knowledge of the datasets so that they could use this knowledge to build expert systems or develop their own knowledge acquisition and decision-making tools. Table 5 contains these hierarchical models. One model from each dataset is given. For iris flower dataset the model has two hierarchies, while for the balance scale dataset the model has only one hierarchy. Only one model is presented from each dataset because of limited space but there can be many accurate hierarchical models for one dataset, a new model with each run. The beauty of the method is not only in generating many accurate models but also in generating them automatically with only four basic mathematical operators without any mathematical analysis and without any help of analytical tools.

In Table 5, column 1 gives name of the dataset, number of hierarchies in the model is given in column 2, column 3 provides level of model hierarchy, actual trained model in each hierarchy is in column 4, the fitness of model in each hierarchy in terms of number of classified samples is stated in column 5 and finally column 6 shares value of model unfitness or partition wall. Table 1 can be referred to see what feature of dataset corresponding symbols in the model represent.

Table 5. Accurate models of classification datasets

DS	NH	HL	Model description	MF	MUF
(1)	(2)	(3)	(4)	(5)	(6)
Balance scale	1	1	$\frac{0.7813f_4}{0.2571f_2} - \frac{0.9791f_1}{0.3225f_3}$	625	0.00
Iris flower	2	1	$0.9102f_1 - 0.0964f_4 + 0.7035f_2 + 0.0815f_3$	138	0.3439
		2	$\frac{0.5598f_3}{0.0802f_4} + 0.4826f_2 + 0.3099f_1$	12	0.00

Since the models presented in Table 5 are trained on the complete datasets therefore they are based on actual statistical parameters rather than estimated parameters. Therefore, for the development of these models the predictive parameter value in Eq. 6 is taken as $\Delta = 0$. Equation 7 is also replaced to compute actual minimums and maximums for each class member list. There is no need of standard deviation as it was used in Eq. 7 to estimate minimum and maximum value of the model. Procedure-3 should be followed to classify the datasets. The step *d* of procedure-3 i.e., application of relevant model can be broken down as follows in procedure 4.

a. Compute model value for each sample by putting its feature values into the model under consideration.
b. Compute actual mean, minimum and maximum for each class.
c. Compute probability for membership of each sample to each class according to equation 5.
d. Start classification of samples by using relation 9.

Procedure 4: Procedure of application of model

Model Solutions

To give complete sense of the method to readers solutions of above models are presented in Table 6 against one sample from each dataset. In Table 6, column 1 refers to the name of the dataset, level of hierarchy is given in column 2. Column 3 gives class label. For the corresponding class labels Table 2 can be referred. Columns 4–6 provide values of statistical parameters of the corresponding model for each class i.e., minimum, maximum and mean respectively. The feature dimensions of chosen samples are given in column 7. The computed probability of class membership is provided in column 8 and finally column 9 contains the resultant class assigned.

Table 6. Statistical parameters of models for each class of the dataset

Dataset	Hierarchy level	Class	Minimum	Maximum	Mean	Test sample dimensions	Probability of class membership	Class assigned
(1)	(2)	(3)	(4)	(5)	(6)	(7)	(8)	(9)
Balance scale	1	c_1	0.0007	0.0181	0.0044	1, 1, 1, 1	0.7927	c_1
		c_2	−14.5709	0.0000	−3.8166		−0.0009	
		c_3	0.1527	14.5898	3.8266		−0.0406	
Iris flower	1	c_1	6.9513	15.1915	10.4918	17, 45, 25, 49	−6.5829	Unclassified
		c_2	44.4055	64.1775	53.3945		0.0046	
		c_3	28.2416	47.2345	39.0089		0.3339	
	2	c_1	0.0000	0.0000	0.0000		$-\infty$	c_2
		c_2	30.5460	32.3623	31.8337		0.0000	
		c_3	32.5227	34.1201	33.0470		−5.7053	

In column 8, with the help of Eq. 5, statistical parameters of models in columns 4–6 are used to estimate class membership probabilities of samples whose dimensions are given in column 7. It can be seen from Table 6 that both the samples, one from each dataset are classified correctly. Please note that sample classification is based on relation 9. Class membership probabilities in column 8 should be used in conjunction with relation 9 to classify the sample. Balance scale model has only one hierarchy therefore it is classified in that hierarchy. The sample of iris flower could not be classified by the model in the first hierarchy. This is because unfitness value in the column-6 of Table 5 prevented it from classifying, as difference in probabilities of class membership was not great enough to surpass unfitness value. It should be noted that if unfitness value would not be there then method would have misclassified the sample as c_3 instead of c_2, as probability of class membership with c_3 has largest value in first hierarchy model. Since the sample remained unclassified in first hierarchy therefore it was tested again in the model in second hierarchy. This model classified it correctly. This is the beauty of hierarchical model that it stops any misclassifications through unfitness value and the sample is given a chance to be classified in the next hierarchy. All the models in the last hierarchy have unfitness value 0.0000. This is done to make sure no sample remains unclassified.

References

1. Bohanec, M., Rajkovic, V.: Knowledge acquisition and explanation for multi-attribute decision making. In: 8th International Workshop on Expert Systems and their Applications, Avignon, France, pp. 59–78 (1988)
2. Bohanec, M., Rajkovic, V.: DEX: an expert system shell for decision support. Sistemica **1** (1), 145–157 (1990)
3. Quinlan, J.R.: C4.5: Programs for Machine Learning. Morgan Kaufmann Publishers, Burlington (1993)
4. Ursani, Z., Corne, D.W.: Use of reliability engineering concepts in machine learning for classification. In: 4th International Conference on Soft Computing & Machine Intelligence (IEEE) (ISCMI 2017), Mauritius, November 2017
5. Ursani, Z., Corne, D.W.: A novel nonlinear discriminant classifier trained by an evolutionary algorithm. Accepted in the 10th International Conference on Machine Learning and Computing (ICMLC 2018), University of Macau, China, 26–28 February 2018, ACM Conference Proceedings (2018). ISBN 978-1-4503-6353-2
6. Farid, D.M., Zhang, L., Rahman, C.M., Hossain, M.A., Strachan, R.: Hybrid decision tree and naïve Bayes classifiers for multi-class classification tasks. Expert Syst. Appl. **41**, 1937–1946 (2014)
7. Espejo, P.G., Ventura, S., Herrera, F.: A survey on the application of genetic programming to classification. IEEE Trans. Syst. Man Cybern. Part C (Appl. Rev.) **40**(2), 121–144 (2010)
8. Camps-Valls, G., Bruzzone, L.: Kernel-based methods for hyperspectral image classification. IEEE Trans. Geosci. Remote Sens. **43**(6), 1351–1362 (2005)
9. Chao, Y.H., Wang, H.M., Chang, R.C.: A novel characterization of the alternative hypothesis using kernel discriminant analysis for LLR-based speaker verification. Comput. Linguist. Chin. Lang. Process. **12**(3), 255–272 (2007)
10. University of California Irvine Machine Learning Repository. https://archive.ics.uci.edu/ml/datasets.html
11. Anderson, E.: The irises of the Gaspe Peninsula. Bull. Am. Iris Soc. **59**, 2–5 (1935)
12. Fisher, R.A.: The utilization of multiple measurements in taxonomic problems. Ann. Eugen. **7**, 179–188 (1936)
13. Siegler, R.S.: Three aspects of cognitive development. Cogn. Psychol. **8**, 481–520 (1976)
14. Thamano, A., Moolwong, J.: A new computational intelligence technique based on human group formation. Expert Syst. Appl. **37**, 1628–1634 (2010)
15. Mohamed, W.N.H.W., Salleh, M.N.M., Omar, A.H.: A comparative study of reduced error pruning method in decision tree algorithms. In: IEEE International Conference on Control System, Computing and Engineering, Penang, Malaysia, 23–25 November (2012)
16. Kliegr, T., Kuchař, J., Sottara, D., Vojíř, S.: Learning business rules with association rule classifiers. In: Bikakis, A., Fodor, P., Roman, D. (eds.) RuleML 2014. LNCS, vol. 8620, pp. 236–250. Springer, Cham (2014). https://doi.org/10.1007/978-3-319-09870-8_18
17. Zhang, L., Ren, Y., Suganthan, P.N.: Instance based random forest with rotated feature space. In: IEEE Symposium on Computational Intelligence and Ensemble Learning (CIEL), pp. 31–35 (2013)
18. Ibrahim, S.P.S., Chandran, K.R., Kanthasamy, C.J.K.: Chisc-AC: compact highest subset confidence-based associative classification. Data Sci. J. **13**, 127–137 (2014)
19. Wang, B., Zhang, H.: Probability based metrics for locally weighted naive bayes. In: Kobti, Z., Wu, D. (eds.) AI 2007. LNCS (LNAI), vol. 4509, pp. 180–191. Springer, Heidelberg (2007). https://doi.org/10.1007/978-3-540-72665-4_16

A Feature Level Fusion Scheme for Robust Speaker Identification

Sara Sekkate(✉), Mohammed Khalil, and Abdellah Adib

Team Networks, Telecoms & Multimedia, LIM@II-FSTM, B.P. 146, 20650 Mohammedia, Morocco
sarasekkate@gmail.com, medkhalil87@gmail.com, adib@fstm.ac.ma

Abstract. For speaker identification purposes, features are first extracted and then compared with those of the training set to find the closest match. So, finding effective and robust features for classifying speakers is beneficial to improve the overall identification performance, especially in the presence of noise. In this paper, a new method of feature extraction based on feature fusion is proposed, where Gammatone Frequency Cepstral Coefficients (GFCC) and wavelet components are extracted and fused for training and testing the Support Vector Machines (SVM) classifier. The performance of the proposed scheme is validated and compared with conventional GFCC using clean and noise corrupted signals from Voxforge database. From the experimental results, it is evident that our algorithm has a higher identification accuracy compared to baseline GFCC.

Keywords: Speaker identification · DWT · SWT · GFCC · SVM

1 Introduction

With the ongoing research into biometric authentication systems, speaker recognition is gaining interest for a myriad of reasons but mostly due to the fact that biological identification and authentication is considered more and more important. From mobile banking to access control to voice mailing, the practical uses of speaker recognition technology are numerous [1].

Speaker recognition systems make use of physiological or behavioral characteristics for verification and identification of individuals [2]. The identification process is based on the classification of an unknown speaker to be identified relative to a reference database of different speaker models and reach one of two decisions: either to find the most probable identity of the unknown speaker (closed-set mode) or to consider that the unknown speech matches none of the previously known samples (open-set mode). The verification process (sometimes also called recognition) aims at making a true-false decision that the identity of the unknown speaker conforms to the claimed identity. Although, the identification and verification tasks are different from each other, they share much in technique. Depending on the linguistic constraints on what the testing speaker

Y. Tabii et al. (Eds.): BDCA 2018, CCIS 872, pp. 289–300, 2018.
https://doi.org/10.1007/978-3-319-96292-4_23

is allowed to say, both can be categorized as text-dependent or text-independent [3]. In text-dependent mode, the spoken text to be uttered is previously known to the system, while in text-independent mode, the system has no knowledge about the spoken utterance.

Any Speaker Identification System (SIS) involves two main stages namely feature extraction and classification. In spite of widespread efforts, finding effective and robust features is still a challenging task in Speaker recognition [4]. Mel Frequency Cepstral Coefficients (MFCC) [5] are probably the most popular features used in speaker identification [6,7]. However, it has been observed that the performance of MFCC based systems degrades drastically in the presence of noise or channel effects [8,9]. In this context, researchers have proposed alternative features to tackle noise issue. Amongst several others, we found Mean Hilbert Envelope Coefficient (MHEC) [10] and Gammatone Frequency Cepstral Coefficients (GFCCs) [11].

Several researches in speaker recognition systems reported that combining different biometric traits can improve the performance of the single biometric trait based system as it provides more useful information [12]. This combination is known as fusion. As shown in Fig. 1, fusion techniques can be divided into three groups: Pre-classification fusion, post-classification fusion, as well as a hybrid of both.

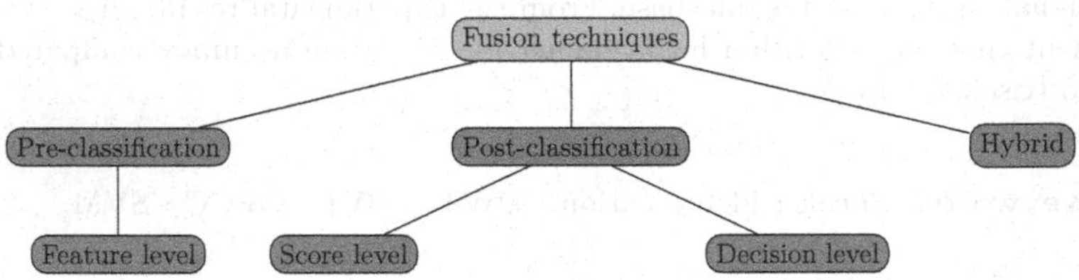

Fig. 1. Fusion techniques based classification

Fusion prior to classification includes fusion at the feature extraction level, it refers to the combination of several feature vectors, obtained by applying different feature extraction techniques to the same data. Approaches for combining information after the classification process can be divided into score level and decision level fusion. Score level fusion take place when matching scores provided by different classifiers are combined using for example mathematical operations (weighted sum or weighted product). In decision-level fusion, each of the extracted data is separately classified, then fusion consists of merging the output from the classification using logical operators (AND, OR) or majority voting.

Finally, a hybrid fusion can be done by employing the advantages of both pre-classification and post-classification strategies. The work presented in this paper is focused on fusion at the feature extraction level for robust closed-set text-independent speaker identification. The feature extraction process if performed using two features namely GFCC and Wavelet Transform, and classification using Support Vector Machines (SVM) because of their accuracy and good performance [13]. The viewpoint in this fusion is obtaining relatively better performance than single GFCC in noisy environments.

The organization of this paper is as follows. We introduce a brief review of some researches related to feature level fusion in Sect. 2. The proposed feature fusion based scheme is detailed in Sect. 3. Then, we apply this feature extraction method for closed-set text-independent speaker identification. The performances of the proposed fusion scheme is evaluated and compared to conventional GFCC features in Sect. 4. Finally, we conclude our paper and propose a scope for future work in Sect. 5.

2 Literature Review

The general form of a feature level fusion system is illustrated in Fig. 2. Feature level fusion involves concatenation of different feature sets originating from multiple information sources to form a new feature set. Capturing several features from the same data possibly incorporates some features those that were not captured by the first method. Thus, supplementary information on the same identity helps in achieving a higher performance.

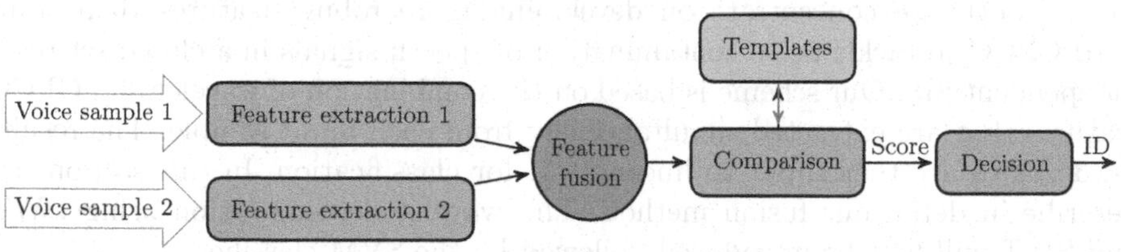

Fig. 2. Feature level fusion

The research in feature level fusion attracted a great deal of attention. Table 1 provides a non-exhaustive list of works related to this topic. Markov and Nakagawa [14] proposed a Gaussian Mixture Model (GMM) based text-independent speaker identification and verification systems integrating pitch and Linear Predictive Coding (LPC) residual with standard LPC derived cepstral coefficients. Their experimental results show that including the pitch parameter further improves the identification rate by 3–4%.

Most of the existing works have considered the use of MFCCs. Nakagawa et al. [15,16] proposed the combination of MFCC with the phase information in clean and noisy environments by adding stationary and non-stationary noise to utterances from Nippon Telegraph and Telephone (NTT) and Japanese Newspaper Article Sentences (JNAS) databases [17]. Sarangi and Saha [18] introduced Speech Signal based Frequency Cepstral Coefficients (SFCC) for robust speaker identification, its combination with MFCC showed a greater performance than using single MFCC or SFCC features in the presence of white, pink, babble, volvo and factory noises. Sadjadi and Hansen [19] considered the fusion of MHEC features with MFCC.

Since MHEC features have been shown to be an effective alternative to MFCCs in extremely degraded channel conditions, their combination with MFCC improved the speaker identification performance remarkably. Verma [20] suggested a multi-feature fusion method which uses Discrete Wavelet Transform (DWT) to extract the features and represent them using common statistics and entropy. The obtained feature vector is then fused with MFCC and input to a K-Nearest Neighbor (KNN) classifier. In [12], the authors investigated the combination of MFCC with several features namely Residual Phase Cepstrum Coefficients (RPCC), Glottal Flow Cepstrum Coefficients (GLFCC) and Teager Phase Cepstrum Coefficients (TPCC). Their experimental results showed an improvement of the identification rate about 7% compared to the baseline MFCC. The work presented by Kawakami et al. [21] explored several feature combinations based on MFCC and Linear Predictive Cepstral Coefficients (LPCC). These combinations include LPCC with LPC, MFCC with phase information, MFCC with LPCC and a fusion of all of these features.

3 Proposed Fusion Scheme

In our work, we concentrate on developing more robust features than standard GFCC to tackle noise contamination of speech signals in a closed-set text-independent SIS. Our scheme is based on the combination of wavelet and GFCC features that are extracted simultaneously from each input sample. The resulting features are then input to linear SVM for classification. In this section, we describe in detail our fusion method. The wavelet decomposition using DWT and SWT will first be introduced, followed by the SVM classifier.

3.1 Wavelet Decomposition

DWT is computed in practice by passing a signal $x[n]$ successively through a high-pass and a low-pass filter with impulse responses $h[n]$ and $l[n]$, respectively. Filtering a signal corresponds to convolving the signal with the impulse response of the filter. For each level of decomposition, the low-pass filter produces the approximation coefficients A, and the high-pass filter produces the detail coefficients D. The filter outputs are then downsampled by 2. This constitutes one level of decomposition and can mathematically be expressed as follows

$$\begin{aligned} D_1[n] &= \sum_{k=-\infty}^{\infty} x[k].h[2n-k] \\ A_1[n] &= \sum_{k=-\infty}^{\infty} x[k].l[2n-k] \end{aligned} \tag{1}$$

Table 1. Brief review on feature level fusion techniques

Work	Feature	Classifier	Database
[14]	LPC + LPC Residual + Pitch	GMM	NTT
[16]	MFCC + Phase information	GMM	NTT JNAS
[18]	MFCC + SFCC	GMM	POLYCOST
[19]	MFCC + MHEC	GMM	RATS
[20]	MFCC + DWT	KNN	Voxforge
[12]	MFCC + RPCC MFCC + GLFCC MFCC + TPCC MFCC + RPCC + GLFCC + TPCC	GMM	YOHO
[21]	LPC + LPCCLPCC + LPC residualMFCC + Phase information MFCC + LPCC	GMM	JNAS

where n and k denote discrete time coefficients. The approximation is then itself split into a second level approximation and detail coefficients. The process is repeated as many times as it is desirable resulting in N decomposition levels.

SWT was introduced by Holschneider et al. [22] to overcome the lack of translation invariance of DWT. SWT is computed by convolving the signal with the appropriate filters as in the DWT but without downsampling to achieve the translation invariance. Then the resulting approximation and detail coefficients at each level are the same as the length of the input signal.

The aptitude of wavelets to extract features from the signal relies on the choice of the mother wavelet function. Different types of wavelets have specific properties and thus it is always an issue how to select the best wavelet function for feature extraction. Standard wavelet families include Haar, Daubechies, Symlets, Morlet and Coiflet. Selecting the adequate wavelet basis for speaker identification is challenging. Since there is no well-defined rule stating that a wavelet function is more suitable than another one for a particular application, some guidelines could help make the selection easier. For example, Coiflet6 provides better data compression while the fourth member of Daubechies family (db4) is more preferable for feature extraction [23].

In this work, wavelet features are decomposed up to six levels using db4. Resulting in six details, D1 to D6, and one approximation coefficient, A6. These coefficients were further refined to a four-element vector by extracting statistical features. For each sub-band coefficients, the following features are extracted:

- The mean of the absolute value
- The average power
- Skewness
- Kurtosis

Mean and average features represent the signal frequency. Skewness is a measure of the asymmetry distribution of the signal around its mean value and Kurtosis describes the flatness of the spectral distribution around its mean.

3.2 GFCC

It is a recent technique introduced by [11] as an auditory based feature. The auditory model is represented by a bank of Gammatone filters that decompose the input speech into a time-frequency representation. GFCCs are computed as follows: First, the input speech signal is passed through a N-channel Gammatone filterbanks to get sub-band signals. This filter is derived from psychophysical and physiological observations of the auditory periphery and makes use of a set of band-pass filters to model the basiliar membrane. The impulse response of each Gammatone filter is defined by

$$g[f,t] = \begin{cases} at^{n-1}e^{2\pi bt}\cos(2\pi f_{c_i}t + \phi) & t \geq 0 \\ 0 & else \end{cases} \tag{2}$$

where f_c denotes the center frequency of the filter, t represents time, a and n are the gain and the order of the filter, respectively. b is the rectangular bandwidth and ϕ is the phase of the nth filter. The center frequencies f_{c_i} are equally spaced on the Equivalent Rectangular Bandwidth (ERB) scale between the filter bank boundaries. In the next step, a cubic root operation is performed on the decimated outputs to generate Gammatone Features (GF), followed by a Discrete Cosine Transform (DCT) to get GFCC features. In this work, 32-channel GFCC features were generated and were reduced by computing the mean before their concatenation with wavelet features to form the final feature vector.

3.3 SVM

SVM is a classification technique which relies on statistical learning theory that was first proposed by Boser et al. [24]. It is a binary classifier that attempts to find the equation of a hyperplane that divides the training set leaving the largest possible fraction of points of the same class on the same side, while keeping the greatest possible margin between either of the two classes and the hyperplane.

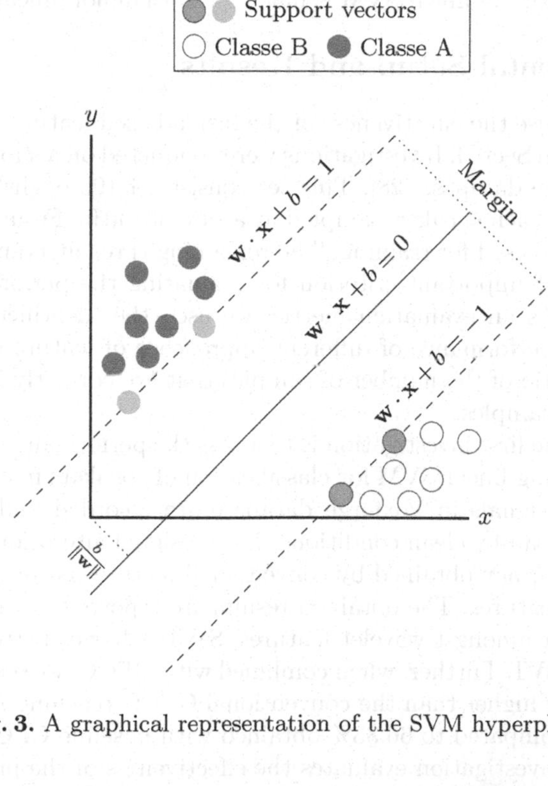

Fig. 3. A graphical representation of the SVM hyperplane

Any hyperplane can be described as the set of points satisfying $\mathbf{w.x} - b = 0$ where the vector $\mathbf{w}$ is perpendicular to the hyperplane and b is the bias value of the hyperplane. $\frac{b}{\|\mathbf{w}\|}$ determines the offset of the hyperplane from the origin along the normal vector $\mathbf{w}$. As shown in Fig. 3, maximum-margin hyperplanes are described by the following equations $\mathbf{w}.\mathbf{x} + b = 1$ (Class A) and $\mathbf{w}.\mathbf{x} + b = -1$ (Class B). Since SVM is a binary classifier, the best approach to deal with multiclass problems is to use a combination of several binary classifiers.

Two common strategies are distinguished: One-Versus-All (OVA) [25] and One-Versus-One (OVO) [26].

OVO approach, known also as pairwise decomposition, constructs $k(k-1)/2$ classifiers for k-class classification, each separates a pair of classes. During test, applying each classifier to the testing speech sample would give one vote to the winning class. The testing sample is then labeled to the class with the maximum number of votes.

OVA approach constructs k binary classifiers for k-class classification, each trained using data from a single class as positive examples and the remaining $k-1$ classes as negative ones. During test, the classifier with the higher output is chosen, and the corresponding class label is assigned to the testing speech. The number of classifiers constructed by this strategy is lower than that of the OVA approach. This justifies its employment in this work. Moreover, the use of linear kernel has been preferred because of its efficiency and fast classification speed. Also, the complexity of linear SVM is much lower than non-linear classifiers [27].

4 Experimental Setup and Results

In order to appraise the effectiveness of the fusion based feature extraction technique described in Sect. 3. Investigations were conducted on a subset of the online available Voxforge database [28]. This set consists of 100 english speakers with 10 utterances for each speaker, sampled at a rate of 8 kHz. From which, seven of the utterances are used for training. The remaining three utterances are used for testing. The most important criterion for evaluating the performance of a SIS is its accuracy. As an evaluation metric, we used the Identification Rate (IR) to compare the performance of different approaches of feature extraction. It is defined as the ratio of the number of samples that are correctly identified to the total number of samples.

The goal of the first investigation is to assess the performance of the proposed fusion scheme using linear SVM for classification of speakers in clean conditions. Although audio signals in Voxforge database are recorded under uncontrolled conditions, we mean by clean conditions that no signal alteration was done. The identification accuracy obtained by conventional features is compared with that of fusion based features. The obtained results are reported in Fig. 4.

It is seen that amongst wavelet features, SWT achieves better identification accuracy than DWT. Further, when combined with GFCC, we see that its performance is notably higher than the conventional GFCC reaching an identification rate of 92.66% compared to 66.33% obtained with baseline GFCC.

The second investigation evaluates the effectiveness of the proposed method in the presence of noise. In this context, clean speech signals were corrupted artificially by several background noises at different Signal-to-Noise-Ratio (SNR)

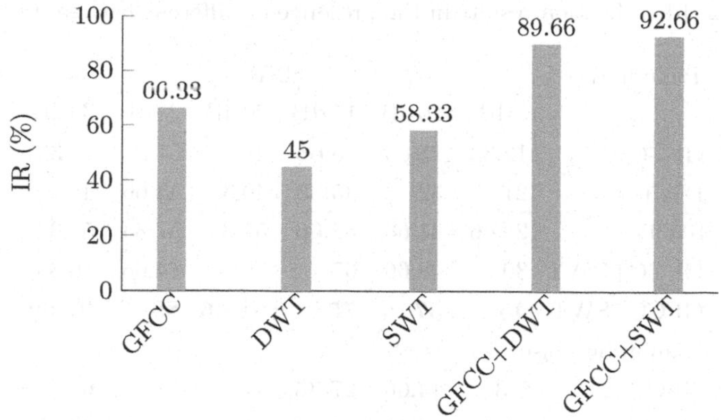

Fig. 4. Identification rates of different features in clean conditions

levels (5, 10, 15, 20, 25, 30 dB). These noises are: Airport, train, street, car, exhibition and restaurant noise. Street and babble (Mixture of a lot of speakers voices) noises are non-stationary and the remaining ones are stationary. A comparison study is held between five extraction methods: GFCC, DWT, SWT, GFCC+DWT and GFCC+SWT. Table 2 summarizes the obtained results.

This group of experiments indicate that globally, the introduction of wavelet analysis improves the system performance. The proposed GFCC+SWT features outperform other features in all conditions and at all SNR ranges. In terms of robustness to noise, the combined GFCC+SWT is shown to be more robust than baseline GFCC. Especially at lower SNRs (5, 10 and 15 dB), where an improvement of about 35% is reached. For example, in the presence of babble noise, we obtained 43% with GFCC+SWT at 5 dB against 6% with the single GFCC, which corresponds to an improvement of 37%. At higher SNRs (20, 25 and 30 dB), we reached an improvement of 42.33% in the presence of exhibition noise at 20 dB using GFCC+SWT.

5 Conclusion

In this paper, we aimed to find a robust set of features for closed-set text independent SIS. For this purpose, performance analysis of a wavelet fusion based feature extraction technique has been discussed using 100 speakers of the online Voxforge database. A linear SVM classifier has been used for assessing the performance of the proposed feature extraction technique for six decomposition levels by DWT and SWT. The obtained results were compared with those of conventional features. It has been revealed that the proposed fusion scheme based on wavelet analysis exhibits a high identification rate compared to conventional GFCC. Therefore, the obtained feature sets can be considered as more robust features. Further studies will aim at evaluating the impact of using non linear SVM kernels.

Table 2. Identification results in the presence of different background noises

Train noise	SNR					
	5 dB	10 dB	15 dB	20 dB	25 dB	30 dB
GFCC	12.33	25.66	35.66	47	57	61.33
DWT	21	32	35.33	40.33	43.66	45
SWT	25.66	41.66	52.66	57.33	57.33	58.3
GFCC+DWT	30	48.66	67	79	84.66	86.33
GFCC+SWT	**45**	**57**	**75**	**81.66**	**89**	**91.66**
Exhibition noise						
GFCC	7.33	14.66	27.33	41	57	63.66
DWT	15.33	25.33	35.66	41.33	43.33	44.66
SWT	21.33	37	46.66	54.33	57	57.66
GFCC+DWT	22.33	41.33	62	78	82.33	88
GFCC+SWT	**30.33**	**48.66**	**70.33**	**83.33**	**89**	**90.66**
Street noise						
GFCC	12.66	22.33	36.33	50.33	59	62
DWT	25	34.33	39.66	44.33	44.66	45
SWT	27.33	44	52.66	57.66	58.33	58.33
GFCC+DWT	25.33	47.33	64.33	76.66	84	87.33
GFCC+SWT	**28.33**	**54.33**	**71.66**	**83**	**88.33**	**90.66**
Car noise						
GFCC	13.33	20.66	36.66	50.66	57.66	61
DWT	20.33	33.33	38.33	41.33	43	43.66
SWT	22.66	42.66	52.33	56.33	57	58
GFCC+DWT	34	57.33	73.66	83.33	85	87.66
GFCC+SWT	**40.33**	**65.33**	**81.66**	**85.33**	**91.33**	**92.33**
Restaurant noise						
GFCC	9.66	21.66	36.66	50	60.33	62.33
DWT	27	36	40	45.33	44.66	45.33
SWT	27.66	40.66	52	56.33	57.66	58.33
GFCC+DWT	43.33	64	77.66	81.66	87	89.66
GFCC+SWT	**46.66**	**71**	**82.33**	**87**	**90.66**	**92**
babble noise						
GFCC	6	15.66	31	50	60	61.33
DWT	24.66	33.33	38.33	43.33	43.66	44.66
SWT	26.33	42	52	56.66	57.66	58
GFCC+DWT	32.66	55.33	73.66	83	85.33	89.33
GFCC+SWT	**43**	**65.33**	**81.33**	**86.66**	**88**	**90**
Airport noise						
GFCC	23	43.66	58.66	65.66	66.66	66.66
DWT	25	32	37	39	43.33	44.66
SWT	28.66	46	52.66	57	58.33	58.66
GFCC+DWT	56	72	79.33	85.66	87.66	89
GFCC+SWT	**58.66**	**76.66**	**85.66**	**87**	**88.66**	**89.33**

References

1. Reynolds, D.A.: An overview of automatic speaker recognition technology. In: 2002 IEEE International Conference on Acoustics, Speech, and Signal Processing, vol. 4, pp. IV-4072–IV-4075, May 2002
2. Faundez-Zanuy, M., Monte-Moreno, E.: State-of-the-art in speaker recognition. IEEE Aerosp. Electron. Syst. Mag. **20**(5), 7–12 (2005)
3. Gish, H., Schmidt, M.: Text-independent speaker identification. IEEE Sig. Process. Mag. **11**(4), 18–32 (1994)
4. Rao, K.S., Sarkar, S.: Robust Speaker Recognition in Noisy Environments. Springer, Cham (2014). https://doi.org/10.1007/978-3-319-07130-5
5. Davis, S., Mermelstein, P.: Comparison of parametric representations for monosyllabic word recognition in continuously spoken sentences. IEEE Trans. Acoust. Speech Sig. Process. **28**(4), 357–366 (1980)
6. Prasad, A., Periyasamy, V., Ghosh, P.K.: Estimation of the invariant and variant characteristics in speech articulation and its application to speaker identification. In: 2015 IEEE International Conference on Acoustics, Speech and Signal Processing (ICASSP), pp. 4265–4269, April 2015
7. Biagetti, G., Crippa, P., Falaschetti, L., Orcioni, S., Turchetti, C.: Robust speaker identification in a meeting with short audio segments. In: Czarnowski, I., Caballero, A.M., Howlett, R.J., Jain, L.C. (eds.) Intelligent Decision Technologies 2016. SIST, vol. 57, pp. 465–477. Springer, Cham (2016). https://doi.org/10.1007/978-3-319-39627-9_41
8. Zhao, X., Wang, D.: Analyzing noise robustness of MFCC and GFCC features in speaker identification. In: 2013 IEEE International Conference on Acoustics, Speech and Signal Processing, pp. 7204–7208, May 2013
9. Sekkate, S., Khalil, M., Adib, A.: Speaker identification: a way to reduce call-sign confusion events. In: 2017 International Conference on Advanced Technologies for Signal & Image Processing, May 2017
10. Sadjadi, S., Hansen, J.: Mean hilbert envelope coefficients (MHEC) for robust speaker and language identification. Speech Commun. **72**(6), 138–148 (2015)
11. Shao, Y., Srinivasan, S., Wang, D.: Incorporating auditory feature uncertainties in robust speaker identification. In: Proceedings of the IEEE International Conference on Acoustics, Speech, and Signal Processing, ICASSP 2007, Honolulu, Hawaii, USA, 15–20 April, pp. 277–280 (2007)
12. Wang, J., Johnson, M.T.: Physiologically-motivated feature extraction for speaker identification. In: 2014 IEEE International Conference on Acoustics, Speech and Signal Processing (ICASSP), pp. 1690–1694, May 2014
13. Wan, V., Campbell, W.M.: Support vector machines for speaker verification and identification. In: Proceedings of the 2000 IEEE Signal Processing Society Workshop on Neural Networks for Signal Processing X (Cat. No. 00TH8501), vol. 2, pp. 775–784 (2000)
14. Markov, K., Nakagawa, S.: Integrating pitch and LPC-residual information with LPC-cepstrum for text-independent speaker recognition. J. Acoust. Soc. Jpn. **20**(01), 281–291 (1999)
15. Nakagawa, S., Wang, L., Ohtsuka, S.: Speaker identification and verification by combining MFCC and phase information. IEEE Trans. Audio Speech Lang. Process. **20**(4), 1085–1095 (2012)

16. Wang, L., Minami, K., Yamamoto, K., Nakagawa, S.: Speaker identification by combining MFCC and phase information in noisy environments. In: 2010 IEEE International Conference on Acoustics, Speech and Signal Processing, pp. 4502–4505, March 2010
17. Itou, K., Yamamoto, M., Takeda, K., Takezawa, T., Matsuoka, T., Kobayashi, T., Shikano, K., Itahashi, S.: JNAS: Japanese speech corpus for large vocabulary continuous speech recognition research. J. Acoust. Soc. Jpn. (E) **20**(3), 199–206 (1999)
18. Sarangi, S.K., Saha, G.: A novel approach in feature level for robust text-independent speaker identification system. In: 2012 4th International Conference on Intelligent Human Computer Interaction (IHCI), pp. 1–5, Dec 2012
19. Sadjadi, S.O., Hansen, J.H.L.: Robust front-end processing for speaker identification over extremely degraded communication channels. In: 2013 IEEE International Conference on Acoustics, Speech and Signal Processing, pp. 7214–7218, May 2013
20. Verma, G.K.: Multi-feature fusion for closed set text independent speaker identification. In: Dua, S., Sahni, S., Goyal, D.P. (eds.) ICISTM 2011. CCIS, vol. 141, pp. 170–179. Springer, Heidelberg (2011). https://doi.org/10.1007/978-3-642-19423-8_18
21. Kawakami, Y., Wang, L., Kai, A., Nakagawa, S.: Speaker identification by combining various vocal tract and vocal source features. In: Sojka, P., Horák, A., Kopeček, I., Pala, K. (eds.) TSD 2014. LNCS (LNAI), vol. 8655, pp. 382–389. Springer, Cham (2014). https://doi.org/10.1007/978-3-319-10816-2_46
22. Holschneider, M., Kronland-Martinet, R., Morlet, J., Tchamitchian, P.: A real-time algorithm for signal analysis with the help of the wavelet transform. In: Combes, J.M., Grossmann, A., Tchamitchian, P. (eds.) Wavelets, pp. 289–297. Springer, Heidelberg (1990). https://doi.org/10.1007/978-3-642-75988-8_28
23. Walker, J.S.: A Primer on Wavelets and Their Scientific Applications. CRC Press, Boca Raton (2008)
24. Boser, B.E., Guyon, I.M., Vapnik, V.N.: A training algorithm for optimal margin classifiers. In: Proceedings of the Fifth Annual Workshop on Computational Learning Theory, COLT 1992, New York. ACM, pp. 144–152 (1992)
25. Vapnik, V.N.: Statistical Learning Theory. Adaptive and Learning Systems for Signal Processing, Communications, and Control. Wiley, New York (1998)
26. Kressel, U.H.G.: Advances in Kernel Methods, pp. 255–268. MIT Press, Cambridge (1999)
27. Yuan, G.X., Ho, C.H., Lin, C.J.: Recent advances of large-scale linear classification. Proc. IEEE **100**(9), 2584–2603 (2012)
28. Voxforge database. Technical report

One Class Genetic-Based Feature Selection for Classification in Large Datasets

Murad Alkubabji(✉), Mohammed Aldasht(✉), and Safa Adi(✉)

Hebron, Palestine
muradwk@gmail.com, {mohammed,safa_adi}@ppu.edu

Abstract. Feature selection is a key success factor for classification problems with high dimensional and large datasets. In this paper, we introduce an approach for enhancing classification performance of high dimensional datasets using a combination of genetic algorithms for feature selection and One-class SVM for classification. The proposed approach is suitable for high dimensional and large datasets. It can be used when we have only one class observations and when high classification accuracy is required. Two benchmark datasets were taken from the NIPS 2003 variable selection competition and the UCI Machine Learning Repository to span a variety of domains and difficulties. Results show that applying feature selection prior to classification gives a higher prediction accuracy than using classification without any feature selection. It can also outperform classifier like random forest especially when we have datasets with a very large number of instances and a small number of observations like the ARCENE dataset.

Keywords: Feature selection · Classification · One-class SVM
Large datasets · Genetic algorithm

1 Introduction

In supervised machine learning, data classification is "the problem of identifying to which set of categories a new observation belongs to, based on a training set of data containing observations whose category membership is known" [1].

Figure 1 illustrates the two phases of a general classification process [15], these phases are the training phase and the prediction phase.

Let the dataset D consists of a labeled training dataset D_{train} and unlabeled validation dataset D_{valid}. The D_{train} has n labeled instances pairs, $S = (x_i, y_i)$. Where $i = 1, ..., n$; $x_i \in R$ and $y_i \in \{-1, +1\}$ is a class label, the classification process is to find a hyperplane that separates D_{valid} positive testing sample from the negative ones.

Searching in the feature space has a high computational cost; for instance if we have M features in the search space, then the total search space is 2^M which

Y. Tabii et al. (Eds.): BDCA 2018, CCIS 872, pp. 301–311, 2018.
https://doi.org/10.1007/978-3-319-96292-4_24

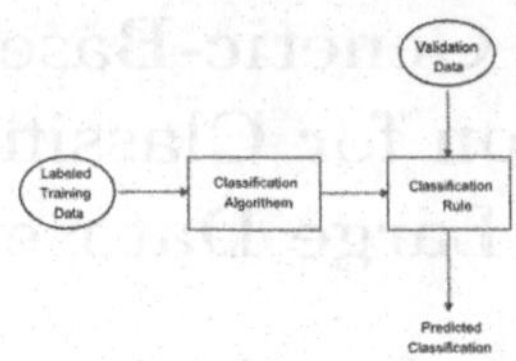

Fig. 1. General process of data classification

is a NP-hard problem for large value of M. Therefore, heuristic search is often used to deal with this problem [7]. Depending on the nature of the problem (whether there is only single or multiple solution), different approaches can be used to find the best features. According to Le et al. [6], two approaches often used in feature selection when there are only a single solution which are; forward selection and backward selection.

In forward selection; we start with no feature in the model at the beginning. After that we test the addition of each feature using a chosen model comparison criteria and adding the feature (if existed) that improves the model. The process keeps repeating until no improvement to the model [7].

The second approach which is the backward selection starts with all candidate features, then it tests the deletion of each feature using a chosen model comparison criteria and deleting the feature (if existed) that improves the model. The process keeps repeating until no further improvement is possible [5].

The used algorithms can be categorized into either a supervised and unsupervised according to whether the training set is labeled or not [8]. In this paper we exploit the advantages of one-class SVM model, which estimates the support of a distribution by identifying regions in input space where most of the target cases lie. One-class SVM is nonlinearly projecting the data into a feature space, and then separating the data from the origin by as large a margin as possible [21].

2 Related Work

The researchers used the genetic algorithm in feature selection to enhance classification process and reduce the computation time, like Lee et al. [10] who used the genetic algorithm to reduce the number of system inputs from 4,800 into much smaller set without performance degradation. Results show that the system accuracy using the subset of features selected by the proposed GA method is similar to the accuracy using the whole feature in the original data. However, using this methods reduced the computation time by 0.88 compared to all original data. Krupa et al. [11] proposed a method that uses evolutionary algorithms as a feature selectors. Their goal was to identify which combination of features are the most accurately subset that can predict consumer's willingness to purchase a hybrid vehicle. Küçükural et al. [12] used GA for selecting the most relevant factors (features) from genetic profiles which has a crucial importance in identifying complex disease and assessing drug efficiency. Results showed that

GA yield the highest classification accuracy comparing to other feature selection methods in their literature where the highest classification accuracy was 0.9194 and their accuracy reached 0.9677.

Chow et al. [4] used a hybrid feature selection model based on a combination of genetic algorithm and multi class support vector machine for large health-care databases. They introduced an efficient approach for reducing run time cost of a SVM-GA hybrid feature selection system for large databases without sacrificing classification performance. Despite the fact that they were able to reduce the cost of computational time by using parallel programming, their approach can't be used for novelty or abnormality detection where we have only one class observations available.

Reviewing previous literature showed that almost all the feature selection approaches based on GA-SVM are formed by combining the genetic algorithms with the multi class SVM classifiers, like in [22], but not the One-class SVM classifiers. The studies that focused on using one-class classification for feature selection didn't combined it with genetic algorithms. Rather, they used it alone or combined it with other methods like Recursive Feature Elimination (RFE), Principal Component Analysis (PCA), Q-a algorithm or some filter methods like in [3].

This paper is concerned with improving the classification performance by combining the genetic algorithm with One-class SVM classifier to be used for feature selection in situations where other classifiers can't be used because of the nature of the problem where we have only one class observation available.

3 Description of the Proposed Algorithm

Genetic Algorithm (GA) is a global search and optimization technique was developed by John Holland in 1975 based on natural evolution and Darwin concept of survival of the Fittest [2]. Figure 2 illustrates basic genetic algorithm where representing the candidate solutions can be expressed as genes and the process of obtaining a better solutions can be expressed as the evolution.

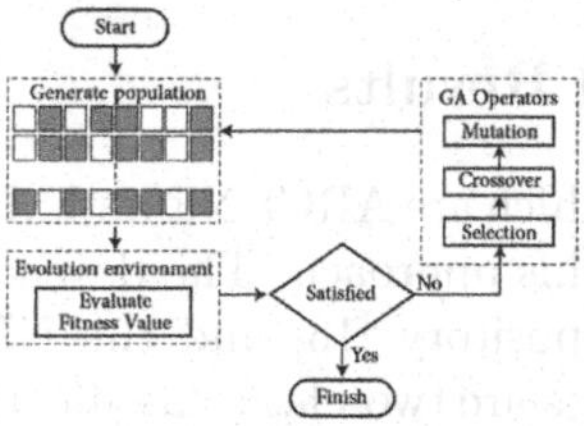

Fig. 2. Basic genetic algorithm's operations

We combined the genetic algorithm with one-class SVM classifier to reduce the computational complexity and to overcome the obstacle where we can't use classifiers like Random Forest (RF) and SVM if we have one-class classification problem.

We used the wrapper feature selection model suggested by Karegowda et al. [14]. As seen in Fig. 3, the first step in this model is to generate candidate subsets by using a search strategy. In our proposed approach we used the Genetic Algorithms.

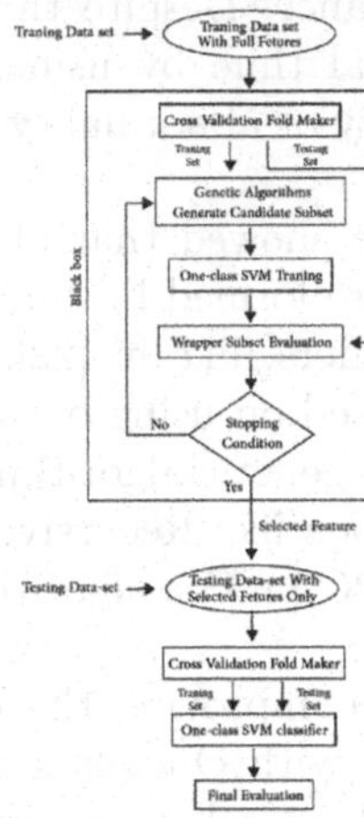

Fig. 3. Wrapper feature selection using one-class SVM and GA

The next step is to evaluate the generated candidate subsets using wrapper subset evaluator; the quality of the candidate subset is evaluated by the performance of the chosen classifier obtained on the training data which is in our case the One-class SVM classifier.

This process continues until reaching the stopping condition. We used the evaluation function (we use the classification accuracy (ACC) as a fitness function for Performance evaluation) as stopping criteria where the process stops if the addition or deletion of any feature doesn't produce a better subset.

4 Experiments and Results

Two benchmark datasets, which are ARCENE and MADELON have been chosen for the purpose of testing this approach. The datasets were taken from the the UCI Machine Learning Repository [13] and the NIPS 2003 variable selection competition [50]. All datasets are two-class classification problems and they were chosen to span a variety of domains and difficulties.

4.1 Experimental Settings

Due to the fact that we are working on very large and extremely high denominational benchmark dataset, our experiments couldn't be conducted on any regular personal computer. The solution was to use a powerful server that could run the experiments. This server has 32 ADM OPTERON 6132 processors at a speed of 2200 MHZ each, and 24605928 KB available memory, running 64bit Ubuntu 14.04 LTS server.

4.2 Optimal Parameter Selection Using Auto-WEKA

Finding the optimal or near-optimal parameter for a classification or regression machine learning problem has never been an easy task for researchers; due to the fact that there is a staggeringly large number of possible alternatives to take into consideration.

In our research we were only interested in classifier parameter optimization for the benchmark dataset. We discarded the option of trying alternative classifiers due to the extremely high complexity level of the experiment and hardware requirement. The parameter optimization problem in Auto-weka can be written as:

$$\lambda * \in \lambda \in Aargmin \frac{1}{k} \sum_{i=1}^{k} \tau(A_{\lambda}, D_{train}^{(i)}, D_{valid}^{(i)}) \quad (1)$$

where λ is the parameters for the learning algorithm A and $\tau(A_{\lambda}, D_{train}^{(i)}, D_{valid}^{(i)})$ is the loss (here: miss-classification rate) achieved by A when trained on $D_{train}^{(i)}$ and evaluated on $D_{valid}^{(i)}$ using k-fold cross-validation, the system is designed for robust optimization under noisy function evaluations since the function to be optimized is a mean over a set of loss terms (each corresponding to one pair of $D_{train}^{(i)} and D_{valid}^{(i)}$ constructed from the training set).

The key idea behind Auto-weka is to make progressively better estimates of this mean by evaluating these terms one at a time. But this approach trades off accuracy against computational cost [16]. In order to test their allegation on a classification problem, we conducted an experiment on the *krvskp* benchmark dataset from the UCI Machine Learning Repository [13]. This benchmark dataset has not been tested on this tool before, Table 1 shows the experiment results before and after parameter optimization by Auto-WEKA using SVM classifier with 10-folds cross validation.

Table 1. krvskp benchmark dataset parameter optimization using Auto-WEKA

	Accuracy	Absolute error
SVM classification results without parameter optimization	96.2422%	0.0376
SVM classification results after Auto-WEKA parameter optimization	99.7912%	0.0021

The optimization process on the *krvskp* benchmark dataset showed an improvement in SVM classification accuracy from 96.2422% to 99.7912% and improved the mean absolute error from 0.0376 to 0.0021.

In our experiment we used Auto-Waka to optimize our benchmarks datasets classifier parameters, Table 2 summarizes the parameter optimization results.

Table 2. Auto-Waka parameter optimization result

	ARCENE	MADELON
Time	93,687 s	97,650 s
Number of iterations	22,019	23,180
Parametr c	1.390	0.752
Parametr γ	0.379	0.624

Where c is known as the penalty parameter for classification errors and γ affects the width of the Gaussian functions of the RBF kernel.

4.3 Genetic Algorithm Parameter Setting

In situations where the characteristics of the problem are unknown, the used approach for finding the suitable GA parameters are typically trial and error. However, this requires more time and computational efforts [9,17].

For our experiments, we used the empirical studies method which is based on trial and error to calibrate the parameters; because the characteristics of the problem in our benchmark datasets are unknown. We set the population size to 250 with binary tournament selection. For the crossover and the mutation probability we used the default setting which are 0.6 and 0.01 respectively.

4.4 Random Forest Classifier

Tables 3 and 4 summarizes MADELON and ARCENE benchmark datasets classification results respectively.

The MADELON benchmarks dataset classification results in Table 3 shows that the best accuracy was 84.2308% and the classifier was able to correctly classify 2190 instances out of 2600.

A better result for ARCENE dataset can be seen in Table 4 where the classifier accuracy was 86% and the correctly classified instances was 172 out of 200.

Figures 4 and 5 show the random forest ROC (Receiver Operating Characteristic) Area curves of the best classification results for MADELON and ARCENE benchmark datasets respectively.

Table 3. RF classification results for MADELON dataset

MADELON benchmark (500 feature, 2600 instances)		
Number of trees in RF	Number of features in each tree	Classification accuracy
500	50	66.6538%
500	100	79.3077%
1000	200	83.7692%
1000	500	84.2308%

Table 4. RF classification results for ARCENE dataset

ARCENE benchmark (10000 feature, 200 instances)		
Number of trees in RF	Number of features in each tree	Classification accuracy
500	200	86%
500	500	85%
1000	700	86%
1000	1000	85.5%
1000	10000	85%

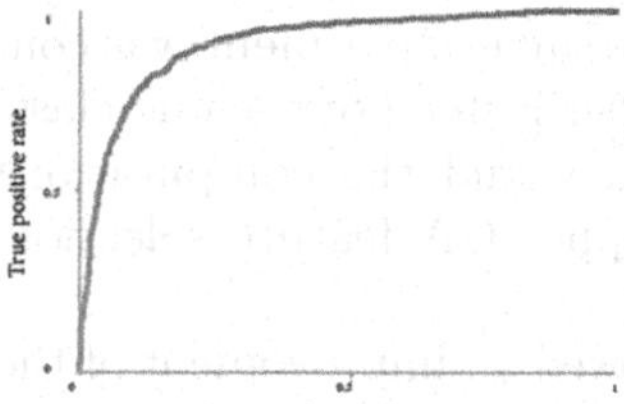

Fig. 4. Random forest ROC curve for MADELON dataset

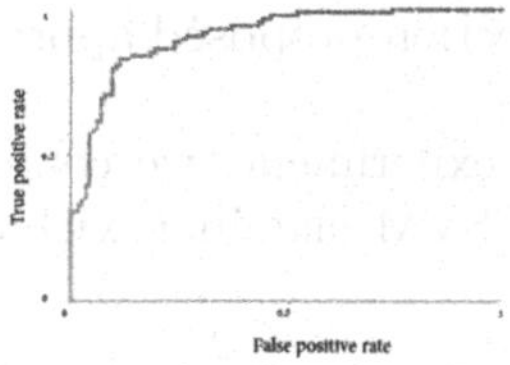

Fig. 5. Random forest ROC curve for ARCENE dataset

Table 5. Classification results for GA-One class SVM classifier

Dataset	ACC	Precision	Recall	F-Measure	ROC Area
ARCENE	70%	0.709	0.700	0.701	0.716
MADELON	65.7308%	0.648	0.657	0.668	0.686

Table 6. Classification results for GA-SVM classifier

Dataset	ACC	Precision	Recall	F-Measure	ROC Area
ARCENE	89.5%	0.860	0.909	0.884	0.897
MADELON	72.28%	0.748	0.734	0.741	0.810

Table 7. Computational time in hours

Classification method	ARCENE	MADELON
GA-One class SVM classifier	39:3:20 h	74:44:57 h
GA-SVM classifier	88:42:35 h	151:17:08 h

4.5 SVM Genetic-Based Feature Selection

In our experiment we used three phases to test the significant importance of our proposed approach.

- In the first phase: we used the Genetic Algorithm as wrapper feature selection method combined with one-class SVM classifier. Table 5 shows the classification results for our Wrapper GA feature selection approach using the one-class SVM classifier.
- In the second phase: The same experiment was conducted again, but this time we used the SVM classifier instead of the one-class SVM classifier to compare the classification accuracy and the computational cost, Table 6 shows the result of using our wrapper GA feature selection approach using the SVM classifier.
  As expected, results showed an improvement of the classification accuracy for the ARCEN and the MADELON dataset when we used the full dataset in the training of the SVM Classifier, where the MADELON dataset improved from 65.7308% to 74.28% and the ARCEN dataset from 70% to 89.5%. But regarding classifier training time, using the SVM instead of one-class SVM in our wrapper feature selection proposed approach exceeded the double a as seen in Table 7.
- In the third phase of our experiment, we compared our approach with the classification result of the SVM classifier without any feature selection and

Table 8. Classification accuracy results for the SVM classifier without any feature selection, followed by our proposed approach and the Random Forest classifier

Classification method	ARCENE	MADELON
SVM classifier (no feature selection)	56%	50%
GA with one-class SVM classifier	70%	65.7308%
GA with SVM classifier	89.5%	74.28%
RF classifier without GA	86%	84.2308%

the best classification results from the Random Forest classifier, Table 8 shows the classification accuracy for the two benchmark datasets.

We also compared our proposed approach ROC Area curves for the ARCENE and MADELON benchmark datasets with the Random Forest ROC Area curves as Figs. 6 and 7 show. In our experiments the ROC Area represents the distance to the hyperplane that separates the inliers from the outliers.

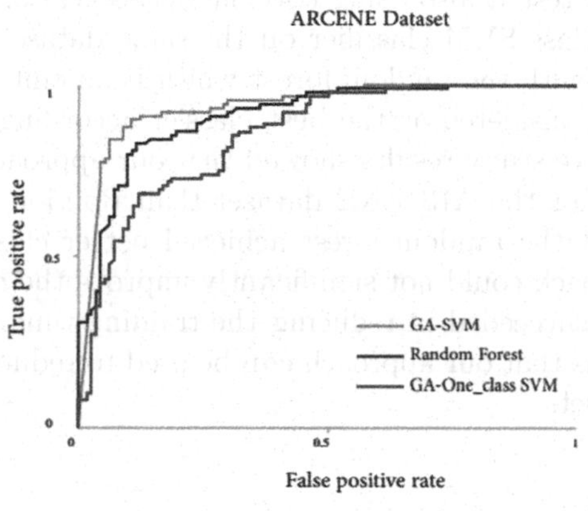

Fig. 6. Comparing ROC curves for ARCENE dataset

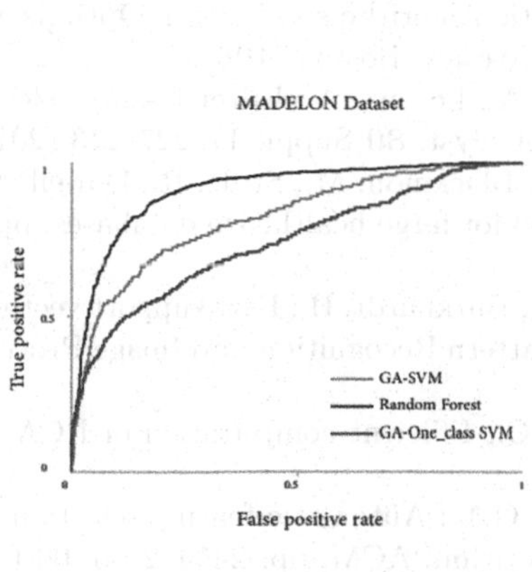

Fig. 7. Comparing ROC curves for MADELON dataset

Empirical results show that our proposed approach was able to surpass the Random Forest classifier on the ARCENE dataset, but for the MADELON dataset (which is a computer generated dataset made especially for the feature selection NIPS 2003 competition) the Random Forest classification accuracy was 84.2308% where our proposed approach accuracy was 74.28%.

5 Conclusion

The proposed approach enhances the accuracy of classification using feature selection for high dimensional and large datasets for one-class classification problem and reduce both the model training time and computational complexity. Two benchmark datasets were used in testing, ARCENE and MADELON. The experiments show that the approach can give better results than the classification without the using feature selection for all the benchmark datasets used.

The approach is tested also using two class classification using SVM classifier instead of one-class SVM classifier on the same dataset and compared the classification result with the random forest which is an embedded feature selection model that is considered as the best classier according to Cernadas et al. [18]. The comparative study results showed that our approach gives better classification accuracy for the ARCENE dataset than Random Forest results. For MADELON dataset the random forest achieved better classification accuracy. Although our approach could not significantly improve the classification results for MADELON, it succeeded in reducing the training time of the SVM significantly. Which means that our approach can be used to reduce the SVM training time for large datasets.

References

1. Michalski, R., Carbonell, J., Mitchell, T.: Machine Learning: An Artificial Intelligence Approach. Tioga Publishing Company (1983)
2. Goldberg, D.E.: Genetic Algorithms in Search, Optimization, and Machine Learning, 1st edn. Addison Wesley, Boston (1989)
3. Lorena, L., Carvalho, A., Lorena, A.: Filter feature selection for one-class classification. J. Intell. Robot. Syst. **80**(Suppl. 1), 227–243 (2015)
4. Chow, R., Zhong, W., Blackmon, M., Stolz, R., Dowell, M.: An efficient SVM-GA feature selection model for large healthcare databases, pp. 978–990, July 16. ACM (2008)
5. Fehr, J., Arreola, K.Z., Burkhardt, H.: Fast support vector machine classification of very large datasets. Pattern Recognition and Image Processing, Freiburg, Germany (2011)
6. Navas, M., Ordonez, C.: Efficient computation of PCA with SVD in SQL. ACM (2009)
7. Le, H.T., Yannakakis, G.N.: Automatic feature selection for named entity recognition using genetic algorithm. ACM, pp. 2454–2466, 06 December 2013
8. Dash, M., Liu, H.: Feature selection for classification. Intell. Data Anal. **1**, 131–156 (1997)
9. Cho, H.W., Kim, S.B., Park, Y., Ziegler, T.: Genetic algorithm-based feature selection in high-resolution NMR spectra. Expert Syst. Appl. **35**(3), 967–975 (2008)
10. Lee, J., Hong, S., Lee, J.H.: An efficient prediction for heavy rain from big weather data using genetic algorithm. ACM, pp. 1–5 (2014)
11. Krupa, J., Chatterjee, S., Eldridge, E.: Evolutionary feature selection for classification: a plug-in hybrid vehicle adoption application, pp. 978–1000. ACM, July 2012

12. Yeniterzi, R., Küçükural, A., Yeniterzi, S., Sezerman, U.: Evolutionary selection of minimum number of features for classification of gene expression data using genetic algorithms. ACM, vol. 1 (2007). ISBN 978-1-59593-697-4
13. Bache, K., Lichman, M.: UCI machine learning repository. University of California, School of Information and Computer Science, Irvine, CA (2013). http://archive.ics.uci.edu/ml
14. Karegowda, A.G., Jayaram, M.A., Manjunath, A.: Feature subset selection problem using wrapper approach in supervised learning. Int. J. Comput. Appl. **7**, 0975–8887 (2010)
15. Yugal, K., Sahoo, G.: Analysis of Bayes, neural network and tree classifier of classification technique in data mining using WEKA. In: CCSEA, pp. 359–369 (2012)
16. Thornton, C., Hutter, F., Hoos, H.H., Leyton-Brown, K.: Combined selection and hyperparameter optimization of classification algorithms. ACM, pp. 847–855 (2013)
17. Gibbs, M.S., Maier, H.R., Dandy, G.C., Nixon, J.B.: Minimum number of generations required for convergence of genetic algorithms. IEEE, vol. 9, no. 6, pp. 7803–9487 (2006)
18. Cernadas, E., Barro, S., Delgado, M.F.: Do we need hundreds of classifiers to solve real world classification problems? J. Mach. Learn. Res. **15**, 3133–3181 (2014)
19. Wolpert, D.H.: The lack of a priori distinctions between learning algorithms. Neural Netw. **9**, 1341–1390 (1996)
20. Ding, C., Peng, H.: Minimum redundancy feature selection from microarray gene expression data. J. Bioinform. Comput. Biol. **3**, 185–205 (2005)
21. Dreiseitl, S., Osl, M., Scheibbóck, C., Binder, M.: Outlier detection with one-class SVMs: an application to melanoma prognosis. In: AMIA Annual Symposium Proceedings, vol. 2010, pp. 172–176 (2010)
22. Gharaee, H., Hosseinvand, H.: A new feature selection IDS based on genetic algorithm and SVM. In: 2016 8th International Symposium on Telecommunications (IST), Tehran, Iran (2016)

Multiobjective Local Search Based Hybrid Algorithm for Vehicle Routing Problem with Soft Time Windows

Bouziyane Bouchra[✉], Dkhissi Btissam, and Cherkaoui Mohammad

National School of Applied Sciences, Abdelmalek Essaadi University, Tetuan, Morocco
bouziyaneensa@gmail.com

Abstract. The competition between companies requires finding the optimized vehicle routing, for this reason researches are more and more interested in transportation problems, this article attempts to address a practical variant of the vehicle routing problem (VRP), known as the VRP with soft time windows (VRPSTW), where deliveries are still possible outside the time windows, that often arise in practice.

Industrial problems have several antagonist objectives to optimize simultaneously, so we propose an improved multiobjective local search (MOLS) based on a hybrid approach, that simultaneously minimizes the transportation costs by producing better planning using a fleet of vehicles, and improve the quality of service by reducing the delay time for each customer and reduce time loss by increasing the stopping time for each vehicle. The algorithm is applied to a standard benchmark problem set, and expected to achieve competitive results compared with previously published studies.

Keywords: Multiobjective optimization
Vehicle routing problem with soft time windows (VRPSTW) · Hybrid approach

1 Introduction

The Vehicle Routing Problem with Time Windows (VRPTW) is an extension of the classic Vehicle Routing Problem (VRP) which consists of determining a set of optimum routes covering all the demands of a given set of customers without violation of the time and capacity constraints. The VRPTW is one of the most important variants of the VRP, which has arisen due to the growing importance of time constraints in the modern societies. Time windows constraints are indeed common in many applications, including bank deliveries, postal deliveries, grocery distribution, dial-a-ride service, bus routing, and repairmen scheduling.

City logistics focuses on practical logistics applications, which are often set in soft time windows environment where late deliveries are possible at some penalty cost, in practice this can be due to several hazards like a traffic jam causing a delay in delivery. In the vehicle routing problems with soft time windows, a vehicle can arrive late within the maximum allowed time, so we can produce solutions that reduce the transportation

Y. Tabii et al. (Eds.): BDCA 2018, CCIS 872, pp. 312–325, 2018.
https://doi.org/10.1007/978-3-319-96292-4_25

cost using fewer number of vehicle through small violations of the time windows. These conditions lead to the definition of the Vehicle Routing and scheduling Problem with soft Time Windows (VRPSTW).

The VRP and its variants are classified as NP-hard problems. Hence, the use of exact optimization methods does not appear experimentally efficient to solve large instances of the problems. So, we will use heuristics and meta-heuristics for finding good solutions, also, we will combine some of these methods, which could be termed hybrid methods.

In real world Applications, the multi-objective optimization that aims to optimize multiple objectives simultaneously is very important, it consider all objectives with the same importance and allows obtaining a set of Pareto optimal solutions that represent the tradeoffs among the objectives. On the other hand, the evolutionary algorithms are the well adapted to solving multi-objective optimization problems, so this paper presents a hybrid approach for dealing with multi-objective VRPSTW which combines a genetic algorithm with the Variable Neighborhood Search (VNS). We aim to minimize three objectives namely the delays, the stopping time and the total transportation cost. A multiobjective optimization provides a set of solutions that represent the tradeoffs among the objectives, and these solutions are compared using the pareto dominance.

This paper is organized as follows: Sect. 2 presents a literature review, and Sect. 3 introduces the multiobjective optimization and presents the problem formulation. Section 4 proposes the multiobjectif algorithm based on a hybrid method for VRPSTW. Finally, in Sect. 5 we make a conclusion of this research.

2 State of the Art

The vehicle routing problems with time windows are the most studied, because they are more practical in many industrial applications. The optimization of these problems allows especially a saving of time which ensure the satisfaction of customers, and represents a major objective for most modern societies. For a long time, several authors have been interested in the resolution of instances with clients related to time intervals, using exact methods, and other heuristics [1–4].

Many studies in the literature are concentrating on vehicle routing problem with hard time windows [5, 6], but other try to treat more practical problems such as vehicle routing problem with soft time windows [7–10]. This last article of Figliozzi proposes an iterative route construction and improvement algorithm to deal with vehicle routing problem with soft and hard time windows. The solution method is divided into two phases: route construction and route improvement. The primary objective function for the VRPSTW is the minimization of the number of routes (NV). A secondary objective is the minimization of the number of time window violations (%HTW). A third objective is the minimization of total time or distance plus penalties for early or late deliveries. Another recent article that is interested in this type of time window is that of Salani et al. [11], which proposes two exact algorithms to solve the vehicle routing problem with soft time windows. The first is based on standard branch-and-cut-and-price. The second algorithm uses concepts of bi-objective optimization and is based on the bisection method. The soft time windows can be also divided into many types by the penalties calculation method. The penalties can be calculated for the outside both early and late of the limited time interval. It can also be calculated only for a late arrival, which is referred to as the semi soft time windows. The solution to this problem is obtained through a CPLEX solver, a genetic algorithm, and a simulated annealing algorithm [12].

The most real problems have more than one objective function to be optimized; this is the case for Qiuyun et al. [13], their research object is the dynamic vehicle routing problem with time windows for distribution goods, which takes into consideration the random demand and the dynamic network. The problem has many objectives: maximize the number of customer serviced, minimize customer waiting time and the total vehicle driving distance, it's treated as a multiobjective optimization problem. The resolution is based on dynamic hill-climbing local search operator and genetic hybrid algorithm, while a standard test data from Solomon are used for simulation experiment.

The most of multi objective optimization problems used genetic algorithm as method of resolution. One of the oldest known approach is that of Deb et al. [14], in which the concept of pareto dominance is present in the design of their method, because in the multi-objective optimization, a good solution refers to his ability to dominate others. Then Ombuki et al. [15] use a genetic algorithm with pareto ranking technique to solve the multi objective VRPTW, the algorithm minimize the number of vehicles and total distance travelled and produce a set of unbiased solutions for both objectives against large number of standard benchmark instances. Other authors who have integrated the genetic algorithm in their approach of resolution: Ghoseiri and Ghannadpour [16], they derive a multi objective VRPTW, in which the total distance travelled and the number of vehicles used are minimized. They combine the genetic algorithm with goal programming approach for solving the problem. The algorithm was tested on huge number of Solomon's benchmark instances, and the results validate the effectiveness of the algorithm. The last example is that of Sivaram Kumar et al. [17], they treat a multi objective VRPTW with three objectives namely total distance travelled, total number of vehicles used and route balance. To solve this problem, the authors used a genetic algorithm, with new specifications that characterize the proposed approach, and makes it highly competitive, for example fitness aggregation approach to evaluate fitness function value for multiple objectives, and specialized genetic operators concerning selection, crossover and mutation. Not far from the principle of genetic algorithm, a novel multi-objective evolutionary algorithm was proposed by Najera and Bullinariaa [18], the approach is based on Darwin's theory of evolution to solve the multi objective VRPTW. The specific feature of this proposed method is the use of similarity Measure for maintaining population diversity by including the similarity measure in the recombination phase. For more powerful methods, the genetic algorithm are often combined with local search methods, for example Minocha and Tripathi [19] developed a model for multi objective VRPTW, in which minimization of total distance travelled and number of vehicles used are the components of the objective function. The genetic algorithm with local search heuristics (replacing next neighbour and reinserting random customer) was introduced to solve the problem. The results show that incorporation of local search heuristics improved the efficiency of the proposed approach.

Another strategy is to use only local search methods to solve the multi objective problems. Tricoire [20] proposes a new algorithmic framework for Multi-directional local search; the idea consists of selecting a solution, searching around it in each direction then updating the archive. For this reason, the author uses different local searches, each of them working on a single objective. To treat the multi-objective generalized consistent vehicle routing problem, Kovacs et al. [21] propose two exact solution approaches based on the ε-constraint method, and a metaheuristic algorithm referred to as MDLNS. This approach combines two methods: the variable neighborhood search algorithm and the multi directional local search framework. This last method consists in iteratively improving the solutions by using a local search algorithm for each objective. In this work, the non-dominated set of solutions is initialized by using the construction heuristics, while in our algorithm, we initialize the solutions by applying a hybrid method, and this is the most important novelties of this paper.

3 Multiobjective Optimization

This section briefly reviews the basic concepts of a multiobjective optimization, and presents the mathematical model of the problem.

A problem of multiobjective optimization is defined by:

$$\min F(x) = \{f_1(x), f_2(x), \ldots, f_m(x)\}$$

y pareto-dominates x if and only if:

$$f_i(y) \leq f_i(x) \forall i = 1, \ldots, m$$
$$f_j(y) < f_j(x) \exists j = 1, \ldots, m$$

y is an pareto optimal solution if there is no solution z that dominates y.

In this paper, the main goal is to serve all customer requests by minimizing:

- The transportation cost and the number of routes.
- The total sum of delay time for late deliveries, and the number of time window violations.
- The total sum of stopping time for vehicles to avoid early deliveries.

Before presenting the model of VRPSTW, we will clarify some assumptions, and identify the parameters that characterize this problem:

- Each customer is served exactly once by one vehicle.
- With only one depot, each vehicle starts from the depot and must return there after visiting the last customer.
- The vehicles have the same capacity, and this capacity constraint must be respected.
- The value of K (number of vehicles) is not specified initially, it is an output of the solution algorithm.
- This problem is considered with flexible time windows: it is allowed to arrive after the time window has closed.

- If the vehicle arrives too early at his destination, it has to wait until the window opens.

The vehicle routing problem with soft time windows (VRPSTW) studied in this research can be described as follows: Let $G = (V, A)$ be a graph, where $V = (v_0, \ldots, v_N)$ is a vertex set.

$A = \{(v_{i,}, v_j) : i \neq j \wedge i, j \in V\}$ is an arc set. Vertex v_0 denotes a depot at which the routes of K identical vehicles of capacity Q start and end. The set of vertices $\{v_1, \ldots v_N\}$ specify the location of a set of N customers. Each vertex in V has an associated demand $q_i > 0$, a service time $s_i \geq 0$, and a service time window $[e_i, l_i]$. Each arc (v_i, v_j) has an associated constant distance $d_{ij} \geq 0$ and travel time $t_{ij}(t_{ij} = d_{ij}/v)$, v is the speed of the vehicle. T is the length of the working day. The arrival time of a vehicle at customer i is denoted A_i, its departure time D_i and the goods quantity in the vehicle k visiting the customer i is denoted y_{ik}. The objective function for the VRPSTW is the minimization of the transportation cost (C is the transportation cost per unit distance), the minimization of the sum of stopping time and the minimization of the sum of delay time.

The decision variables are defined as follows:

$$x_{ijk} = \begin{cases} 1 \text{ If there is travel from i to j by the vehicle k} \\ 0 \text{ Otherwise} \end{cases}$$

$$z_{ik} = \begin{cases} 1 \text{ If the vehicle K visit the customer i} \\ 0 \text{ Otherwise} \end{cases}$$

$$\text{Minimize}\, f(x) = (f1(x), f2(x), f3(x)) \tag{1}$$

$$f1 = \sum_{k=1}^{K} \sum_{i=0}^{N} \sum_{j=0}^{N} \frac{d_{ij}}{v} x_{ijk}$$

$$f2 = \sum_{k=1}^{K} \sum_{i=0}^{N} \sum_{j=0}^{N} \max(0, e_j - A_j) x_{ijk}$$

$$f3 = \sum_{k=1}^{K} \sum_{i=0}^{N} \sum_{j=0}^{N} \max(0, A_j - l_j) x_{ijk}$$

Subject to

$$\sum_{k \in K} \sum_{i \in N_{T_l}} x_{ijk} = 1 \quad j = 2 \ldots N \tag{2}$$

$$\sum_{j=1}^{N} \sum_{k=1}^{K} x_{ijk} = 1 \quad i = 2 \ldots N \tag{3}$$

$$\sum_{i=0}^{N} x_{i0k} \leq 1 \quad \forall k \in K \tag{4}$$

$$\sum_{j=0}^{N} x_{0jk} \leq 1 \quad \forall k \in K \tag{5}$$

$$\sum_{i=0}^{N} x_{iuk} = \sum_{j=0}^{N} x_{ujk} \quad \forall k \in K, \forall u \in N \tag{6}$$

$$y_{jk} \leq Q_k \quad \forall j \in N, \forall k \in K \tag{7}$$

$$y_{ik} = y_{jk} z_{jk} + q_i x_{ijk} \quad \forall i,j \in N, \forall k \in K \tag{8}$$

$$D_0 = 0 \quad \forall k \in K \tag{9}$$

$$D_j = [\max(A_j, e_j)] + s_j \quad \forall j \in N \tag{10}$$

$$\sum_{i=1}^{N} \sum_{j=1}^{N} x_{ijk} t_{ij} + \sum_{i=1}^{N} z_{ik} s_i \leq T \quad \forall k \in K \tag{11}$$

The objective function (1) in this model is to minimize the transportation cost, the total sum of stopping time and the total sum of delay time. Constraints (2) and (3) restrict the assignment of each customer to exactly one vehicle route. Constraints (4) and (5) concern the availability of vehicles. Constraint (6) implies that the number of vehicles which have left the depot is equal to the number of vehicles coming back to the depot. Constraints (7), (8), (9) and (10) ensure the schedule feasibility with respect to time considerations and capacity constraints. The maximum route duration is limited by (11).

4 The Proposed Approach to Solve the VRPSTW

In this paper, the problem we want to tackle is to provide a good non-dominated front, because we are interested in multiobjective optimization.

On the one hand, the effectiveness of the multi-objective hybrid methods applied in several articles, on the other hand the strength of the multiobjective local search algorithms gave us the idea to combine the two approaches in order to propose a more powerful method, it's a multiobjective locale search, which uses methods of neighborhood search as LNS and VNS, with the starting point is a set of nondominated solutions, obtained by the application of a multiobjective hybrid method.

The proposed approach consists of three main steps: in the first, we apply the genetic algorithm that improves the initial population. Secondly, the VNS explore efficiently promising areas, and finally, a local search procedure (objectivewise local search) is designed for each objective (Fig. 1).

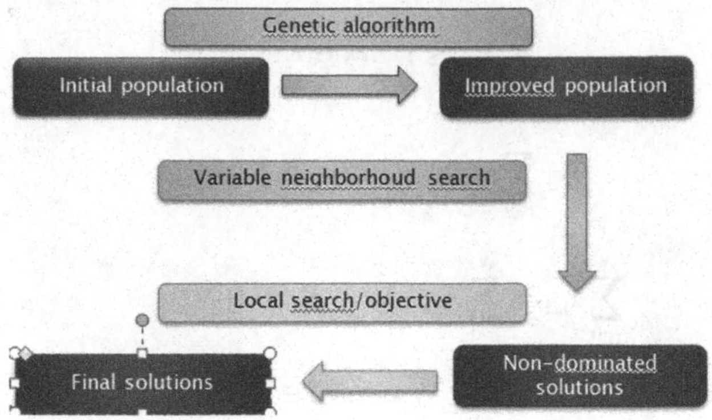

Fig. 1. Steps of the proposed approach

This approach allows combining the advantages of a hybrid multi-objective evolutionary algorithm and a multi objective local search.

4.1 Multiobjective Genetic Algorithm for the Resolution of the Problem

The first two steps allow exploiting a hybrid method to generate non-dominated set of solutions, in order to provide good approximation of the Pareto front. In what follows, we detail the specific features of the first part of this hybrid approach: the genetic algorithm.

Initialization Phase

Each solution in the initial population is the permutation of n positive integers, such that each integer is corresponding to a customer. We use a single line to represent each solution; it is a representation of several tours served by a set of vehicles.

We use a greedy constructive heuristic to generate a 50% of the initial population, the greedy method starts with one client and move systematically to the nearest client that has not yet been visited. The rest of the population is generated randomly with the aim of converting the entire search space. Among all the solutions of the initial population, we seek the nondominated solutions, we keep them in the A1 set.

To illustrate the transition from a solution in the form of a line to a solution in the form of tours, we present an example with seven customers, each with a request q_i. Knowing that the capacity of the vehicle is 20, so the chromosome may be broken into three parts. Customers are listed in their order of visitation (0 is the depot): (Fig. 2).

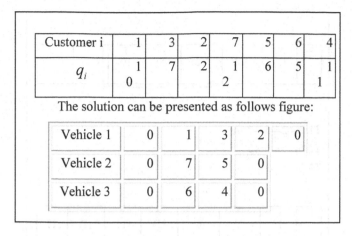

Customer i	1	3	2	7	5	6	4
q_i	10	7	2	12	6	5	11

The solution can be presented as follows figure:

Vehicle 1	0	1	3	2	0
Vehicle 2	0	7	5	0	
Vehicle 3	0	6	4	0	

Fig. 2. An example of encoding of a solution

Fitness Assignment

To evaluate them, every individual in the population must be assigned to fitness. In this paper, we are interested in multiobjective problems, so we use the non-dominance sorting criterion of Deb et al. [14].

This approach consists of distributing the population according to several fronts, based on the concept of pareto dominance. The first front contains the best solutions, called the non-dominated solutions in the case of minimization of f1 and f2.

Genetic Algorithm Operators

The performance of genetic algorithms is affected by genetic operators, we present thereafter the crossover and mutation operators applied to the initial population. But before that, we use Binary Tournament Selection for selecting parent individuals from the population. The first of two parent is chosen from the nomdominated solutions A1, and the second is randomly selected from the population.

Every two parent candidates are compared using pareto dominance in order to keep the parent who participates in the recombination process. To perform this process, a random swath of consecutive customers from parent P1 are copied into the offspring S1, and remaining values are placed in the child S1 in the order which they appear in parent P2. To get a second child S2 from the two parents, we flip Parent P1 and Parent P2. The crossover operator is described in Fig. 3 as follows:

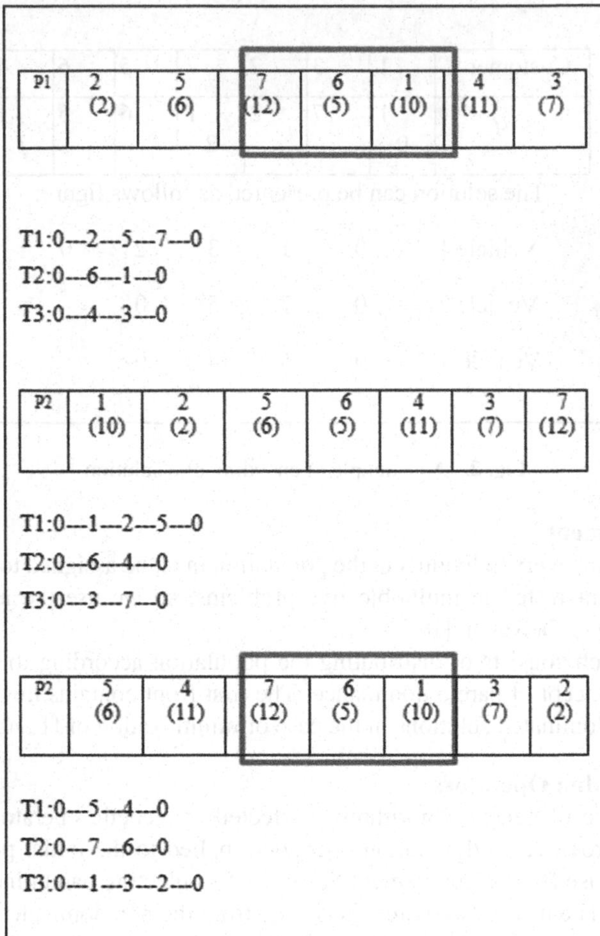

Fig. 3. Recombination process

A further stochastic change or mutation is applied to the offspring to avoid premature convergence of the algorithm to a local optimum.

For the permutation encoding already used, we apply Order changing which select two customers (customer 5 and customer 1 for example) and exchange them, the two chosen customers may belong to the same route, as they may belong to two different routes.

After we apply the crossing and mutation, we must determine the individuals who will be present in the following population.

At each iteration, we compare the new individual (offspring) with the nondominated solutions A1, if he dominates at least one solution, the offspring is inserted in the set of the nondominated solutions A1. The process is repeated until a fixed number of iterations.

At the end, all the solutions of the set A are compared with each other to keep only the nondominated solutions A2.

4.2 Implementation of Multiobjective VNS Algorithm

The second part of the proposed approach is based on a metaheuristic called variable neighborhood search (VNS), which the principle is the change of neighborhoods during the search. Our algorithm based on VNS to solve the proposed problem is inspired from the work of Geiger [22], who presents a Multi-objective Variable Neighborhood Search Algorithms for a Single Machine Scheduling Problem with Distinct due Windows(MOVNS). In our algorithm, we use the nomdominated solutions from the set A2 as initial solutions, and we use two neighborhood structures, one generate neighbor solutions by insert, other by exchange.

At the beginning, we randomly choose a solution X from A2, then, at each iteration, a neighbor X1 is generated using the neighborhood structure N1, and we apply 2 opt on X1 to get X2.

If X2 is a dominant solution, we will insert it into A2, and we evaluate another neighbor generated by the same neighborhood structure.

Otherwise we move to another neighbor generated by the other neighborhood structure, up to a maximum number of iterations.

This process is repeated n times with change of X which is randomly selected from set A2.

The procedure VNS applied to our problem is detailed in the following paragraphs. The description consists of the building of an initial solution, the shaking phase, the local search method, and the acceptance decision.

The Building of an Initial Solution. The initial solution is an element of the set of nondominated solutions A2.

The Shaking Phase. We use two neighborhood structures, one by generating neighbors using the insertion method, this by inserting a customer chosen randomly from the permutation in a new position also chosen randomly. In the other neighborhood structure, two randomly selected customers are simply swapped.

Local Search Method. This paper selects 2-opt as a local search operator in order to obtain a new nondominated solutions in a short period.

The Acceptance Decision. If the new solution dominate elements of the set A2, The latter is updated by adding the new solution, and we continue the search with the same neighborhood structure. Otherwise, we move to another neighborhood structure.

The pseudocode description of the steps of VNS, obtained by taking two neighborhoods structures is done in Algorithm 1:

Algorithm 1

```
A2 <--Set of nondominated solutions
N← Maximal number of iterations
Repeat
  i=i+1
  select randomly a solution X from A2
  while StoppingCriterion=False
      select a neighborhood structure N1
      generate a solution X1 using N1
      X2<--2-opt applied on X1
      Evaluate X2
      If  X2 is a nondominated solution then
          Update A2
          N←N1
      Else N←N2
  End while
Until (i=N)
Return A2
```

The set A is then sorted to keep only the nondominated solutions obtained after application of the multiobjective variable neighborhood search (MOVNS), the new set is named A3.

4.3 Recherche Locale Multiobjective

In this paper, the idea of MOLS was inspired from the paper of Wang et al. [23]. In the MOLS, the method search only in one direction at a time, i.e. to use single-objective local search, because if we want to find a neighbor x1 of x which is efficient, x1 must to be better than x for at least one objective.

So our approach is based on the multi objective local search framework, which consist, for a given solution, in applying different local search strategies, each for minimize one of the objectives in the order of finding new efficient solutions.

Set A of non-dominated solutions is initialized by using a multiobjective hybride method, then we select one of the solution and we apply a local search strategy for each objective. The update of the archive is done by adding new efficient solutions, and the algorithm stops when the maximum number of iterations is reached. All these steps are marked in Algorithm 1.

The algorithm that describes this third step of the proposed algorithm is presented in Algorithm 2:

Algorithm 2

```
Initialize Archive A3
  While (iteration number < maximum iteration number) do
        X=randomly select a solution from archive A3
        for obj=1 to 4 do
              perform objectivewise local search
              update archive A3
        End for
  End while
```

This part tries to optimize different objectives of a given solution in parallel. Archive A3 is initialized by the set of nondominated solutions obtained by application of MOVNS.

In this third part of the application of the proposed method, we add another objective to try to minimize the number of vehicles used.

Objectivewise Local Search for Minimizing the Number of Vehicles (MOLSV)
To minimize the number of vehicles, first, the route which has the fewest customers is selected. Then, we enumerate all customers in the selected route to try to insert them into other possible routes. So, one vehicle can be reduced if customers in the selected route are inserted into other routes successfully.

Objectivewise Local Search for Minimizing the Total Distance
We remove a random customer from a route, which is randomly selected and we try to reinserts it into the position which makes the resultant solution after insertion have the lowest total distance.

Objectivewise Local Search for Minimizing the Total Delay Time
We select the route which has the longest delay time, and we apply the Large Neighborhood Search (LNS), in order to obtain new solution with lowest total delay time.

Objectivewise Local Search for Minimizing the Total Waiting Time
We remove a random number of customers from a route selected randomly, and then we compare all the possibilities of insertion. Finally, these removed customers are reinserted into the best position to obtain solution that has the lowest total waiting time.

The algorithm considers the 4 objectives one after the other in the loop for. By improving one of these objectives, we try to find better solutions without deteriorating other objectives. Otherwise, we keep these solutions because they represent the entire pareto front.

5 Conclusion

This paper has introduced a multiobjective variant of VRPSTW. The choice of treating the problem according to a multi-objective approach is due to their advantage to be able to manage a vector of constraints, which makes it possible to envisage an optimization according to the different constraints. The proposed approach to solve the problem is based on a multiobjective local search, such as the solutions in the initial archive are obtained by the hybrid algorithm. The objective is to simultaneously minimize the delays, stops and the total cost of transportation.

References

1. Desrochers, M., Lenstra, J.K., Savelsbergh, M.W.S., Soumis, F.: Vehicle routing with time windows: optimization and approxinmation. In: Golden, B., Assad, A. (eds.) Vehicle Routing: Methods and Studies. Elsevier Science Publishers, Amsterdam (1988)
2. Golden, B.L., Assad, A.A.: Perspectives on Vehicle Routing: Exciting New Developments. Oper. Res. **34**, 803–809 (1986)
3. Golden, B.L., Assad, A.A.: Vehicle Routing: Methods and Studies. Elsevier Science Publishers, Amsterdam (1988)
4. Soloman, M.M., Desrosiers, J.: Time window constrained routing and scheduling problems. Transp. Sci. **22**, 1–13 (1988)
5. Bettinelli, A., Ceselli, A., Righini, G.: A branch-and-cut-and-price algorithm for the multi-depot heterogeneous vehicle routing problem with time windows. Transp. Res. Part C: Emerg. Technol. **19**, 723–740 (2011)
6. Yu, B., Yang, Z.Z., Yao, B.Z.: A hybrid algorithm for vehicle routing problem with time windows. Expert Syst. Appl. **38**, 435–441 (2011)
7. Hashimoto, H., Ibaraki, T., Imahori, S., Yagiura, M.: The vehicle routing problem with flexible time windows and traveling times. Discrete Appl. Math. **154**, 2271–2290 (2006)
8. Chiang, W.C., Russell, R.A.: A metaheuristic for the vehicle-routing problem with soft time windows. J. Oper. Res. Soc. **55**, 1298–1310 (2004)
9. Fu, Z., Eglese, R., Li, L.Y.: A unified tabu search algorithm for vehicle routing problems with soft time windows. J. Oper. Res. Soc. **59**, 663–673 (2008)
10. Figliozzi, A.: An iterative route construction and improvement algorithm for the vehicle routing problem with soft time windows. Transp. Res. Part C: Emerg. Technol. **18**(5), 668–679 (2010)
11. Salani, M., Battarra, M., Gambardella, L.M.: Exact algorithms for the vehicle routing problem with soft time windows. In: Lübbecke, M., Koster, A., Letmathe, P., Madlener, R., Peis, B., Walther, G. (eds.) Operations Research Proceedings 2014. ORP, pp. 481–486. Springer, Cham (2016). https://doi.org/10.1007/978-3-319-28697-6_67
12. Setak, M., Azizi, V., Karimi, H., Jalili, S.: Pickup and delivery supply chain network with semi soft time windows: metaheuristic approach. Int. J. Manag. Sci. Eng. Manag. 1–7 (2016)
13. Qiuyun, W., Wenbao, J., Gang, Z.: A novel model and algorithm for solving dynamic vehicle routing problem on goods distribution. J. Appl. Sci. **13**(22), 5410–5415 (2013)
14. Deb, K., Pratap, A., Agarwal, S., Meyarivan, T.: A fast and elitist multiobjective genetic algorithm: NSGA-II. IEEE Trans. Evol. Comput. **6**(2), 182–197 (2002)
15. Ombuki, B., Ross, B.J., Hanshar, F.: Multi-objective genetic algorithms for vehicle routing problem with time windows. Appl. Intell. **24**, 17–30 (2006)

16. Ghoseiri, K., Ghannadpour, S.F.: Multi-objective vehicle routing problem with time windows using goal programming and genetic algorithm. Appl. Soft Comput. **10**, 1096–1107 (2010)
17. Sivaram Kumar, V., Thansekharb, M.R., Saravananc, R., Miruna Joe Amalid, S.: Solving multi-objective vehicle routing problem with time windows by FAGA. Procedia Eng. **97**, 2176–2185 (2014)
18. Najera, A.G., Bullinariaa, J.A.: An improved multi-objective evolutionary algorithm for the vehicle routing problem with time windows. Comput. Oper. Res. **38**(1), 287–300 (2011)
19. Minocha, B., Tripathi, S.: Solution of time constrained vehicle routing problems using multi-objective hybrid genetic algorithm. Int. J. Comput. Sci. Inf. Technol. **2**, 2671–2676 (2011)
20. Tricoire, F.: Multi-directional local search. Comput. Oper. Res. **39**, 3089–3101 (2012)
21. Kovacs, A., Parragh, S.N., Hartl, R.F.: The multi-objective generalized consistent vehicle routing problem. Eur. J. Oper. Res. **247**, 441–458 (2015)
22. Geiger, M.J.: Randomized variable neighborhood search for multi objective optimization. In: 4th EU/ME: Design and Evaluation of Advanced Hybrid Meta-Heuristics, pp. 34–42 (2004)
23. Wang, J., Zhou, Y., Wang, Y., Zhang, J., Chen, C.L.P., Zheng, Z.: Multiobjective vehicle routing problems with simultaneous delivery and pickup and time windows: formulation, instances, and algorithms. IEEE Trans. Cybern. **46**(3), 582–594 (2016)

Dimension Reduction Techniques for Signal Separation Algorithms

Houda Abouzid(✉) and Otman Chakkor(✉)

National School of Applied Sciences, Abdelmalek Essaadi University, Tetouan, Morocco
abzdhouda@gmail.com, o.chakkor@gmail.com

Abstract. While collecting data information, this received data, in most cases, are recorded with multiple number of variables, thus, this large dimension dataset will be so hard to visualize and then to be analysed for the purpose to be interpreted properly. The graphical representation may also not be helpful in case the dataset is too many. In this paper we will present a broad overview of two famous data reduction techniques known as the Principal Component Analysis and the Factorial Analysis. These two methods facilitate the interpretation of the data for the user, in a more meaningful form. Also this work highlights the big key differences existing between them and then, make easier the choice of using one of them according to different cases. In the context of ICA, this dimension reduction of the dataset represents a main first step for the famous problem known as Blind Source Separation (BSS).

Keywords: BSS · Factorial Analysis (FA)
Principal Component Analysis (PCA) · OFDM
Signal separation algorithms

1 Introduction

Statistical methods are today used in almost all areas of human activity and are part of the basic knowledge of the researcher, the engineer, the manager, the economist, etc. They are existing in two types known as: Factorial methods and Classification methods. In this work, we are interested in studying Factorial methods. This latter are among the descriptive or unsupervised methods of Datamining which consist in the projection on a space of lower dimension in order to give a clear viewing of all the links between variables while guaranteeing the minimization of loss of the informations. Those Factorial methods are classified into two groups:

1. Principal Component Analysis or PCA
2. Factor Analysis or FA

By contrast on linear data, there are also other many dimensionality reduction techniques used for nonlinear dimensionally reduction structure like the Self

Y. Tabii et al. (Eds.): BDCA 2018, CCIS 872, pp. 326–340, 2018.
https://doi.org/10.1007/978-3-319-96292-4_26

Organizing Maps (SOM) used to visualize corrective actions of failure modes and effects analysis (FMEA) [1], Kernel PCA which could be used for de-noising image or either novelty detection and many others applications [2,3]. In the context of Independent Component Analysis (ICA), supposing the assumption of source independence, is the main factor to apply this method instead of PCA which assumes that the sources are uncorrelated. ICA is the well known method often used as a solution of blind source separation (BSS) problem [4,5]. In this study, the goal of using PCA or FA is to reduce the dimension space to separate signals from its mixtures (observations) and then, these techniques will be applied for linear dataset as a whitening step before the separation process. To clarify the idea of using PCA or FA: knowing the difference between the data types is a major step, which means that, if the one have a table of numerical or ordinary variables, the one should apply the principal component analysis, but if the table contains the qualitative or nominal variables, the factor analysis should be used instead. In the following, a detailed study of those two previous methods is provided.

1.1 Applications of Signal Separation Algorithms in Telecommunications Systems Based on OFDM

Orthogonal frequency-division multiplexing (OFDM) is a method of encoding digital data on multiple carrier frequencies. OFDM has developed into a popular scheme for wideband digital communication, used in applications such as digital television and audio broadcasting, DSL internet access, wireless networks, power line networks, and 4G mobile communications.

In statistical wireless signal processing, extraction of unobserved signals from observed mixtures can be achieved using Blind Source Separation (BSS) algorithms. OFDM can be considered as a good established predominant air interface communication technique. It is used for encoding digital data on multiple carrier frequencies.

Due to the high data rate transmission and the ability to against frequency selective fading, OFDM is usually applied in the current broadband wireless telecommunication system.

In the mobile communication environment we have to deal with multipath transmission channels due to the reflections of wavefronts. In order to apply existing source separation algorithms for mobile communication signals, some modifications of the classical narrow band data model have to be done. In this paper a modification of the data model using PCA or FA techniques is presented. After the classification of the data, the OFDM-technique could be used for such many telecommunication systems such as:

- Digital audio broadcasting (DAB) (1995).
- Digital video broadcasting (DVB) (1997).
- High-definition television (HDTV) terrestrial broadcasting.
- Wireless LAN and PAN like: IEEE 802.11a and IEEE 802.11g.
- Optical communications.

- Now, OFDM technique has been adopted as the new European DAB standard, and HDTV standard.
- OFDM/UWB (802.15.3a) (2004).
- IEEE 802.16 broadband wireless access system (2004).
- IEEE 802.20 mobile broadband wireless access (MBWA).
- 4G mobile communication (2005).

Nowadays, OFDM is representing the key technology for beyond 3G, 4G and 5G communications, promising robust, high capacity, and high speed wireless broadband multimedia networks. A source separation algorithms named PCA and FA will be considered in this paper for data transmission through random multipath channels like mobile communication channels. Simulation results will show the separation and classification efficiency.

2 Methods

2.1 Principal Component Analysis

Definition. The PCA (*Hotelling* [6]) is a part of the multidimensional descriptive techniques which consists in passing from a table of complex and large data containing all the information of a certain phenomenon studied, to visual representations (graphs) and optimal as much as possible of the data. This passage aims to reduce this number of data while projecting these cloud points on a principal or factorial axis, a plane or a hyperplane without using any particular hypothesis or model, which allowed the user to interpret these results [7]. This reduction of the number of variables will allow to form a linear combination that each one of it is related to a principal component [8,9]. It operates through a mathematical process that transforms a number of variables that are likely to be correlated to a number of uncorrelated variables called Principal Component, because of their character to absorb as much information as possible or variance in the starting variables. So Principal Component Analysis is really a good name because it does what it says; the PCA finds the Principal Component Analysis of the data.

Problematic 1. The measurement table is presented as follows: the columns contain variables of type numerical values, and the rows represent the observations (individuals) on which these variables are observed, in the form of a matrix of type (p, q).

$$X = \begin{pmatrix} x_{11} & x_{12} & \cdots & x_{1j} & x_{1q} \\ x_{21} & x_{22} & \cdots & x_{2j} & x_{2q} \\ \vdots & & & & \\ x_{i1} & x_{i2} & \cdots & x_{ij} & x_{iq} \\ \vdots & & & & \\ x_{p1} & x_{p2} & \cdots & x_{pj} & x_{pq} \end{pmatrix} = \begin{pmatrix} X_1 \\ X_2 \\ \vdots \\ X_q \\ X_p \end{pmatrix} \tag{1}$$

As one can observe, this matrix is a linear combination of the rows and columns of the initial table as follows:

$$\begin{aligned} Y_1 &= e_{11}X_1 + e_{12}X_2 + \cdots + e_{1p}X_p \\ Y_2 &= e_{21}X_1 + e_{22}X_2 + \cdots + e_{2p}X_p \\ &\vdots \\ Y_p &= e_{p1}X_1 + e_{p2}X_2 + \cdots + e_{pp}X_p \end{aligned} \tag{2}$$

These new components are linear combinations of variables and must be uncorrelated.

About the coefficients e_{ij} they are collected into the vector:

$$e_i = \begin{pmatrix} e_{i1} \\ e_{i2} \\ \vdots \\ e_{ip} \end{pmatrix} \tag{3}$$

- Goals of applying PCA:
  - The most important thing is to reduce the dimensions of the data set.
  - Have an idea about the structure of the data set and also point out the similarities or oppositions of behaviour between individuals.
  - Graph the point cloud in the plane or space, respecting:
    * The distances between individuals.
    * The structure of correlations between variables.
- *Variance-Covariance matrix*

A variance-covariance matrix is a square and symmetric matrix that contains the variance and covariance associated with several variables. The diagonal elements of the matrix contain the variances of the variables, while the off-diagonal elements contain the covariance between all possible pairs of variables.

This matrix is used to evaluate the variance between different variables, that covariance measures the linear link that may exist between a couple of statistical variables or a couple of quantitative random variables, so that one can calculate the covariance of each couple of variables and then indicate them in a symmetric matrix:

$$cov(x,y) = \frac{1}{n}\left(\sum_{i=1}^{n}(x_i - \bar{x})(y_i - \bar{y})\right) \tag{4}$$

2.2 Factor Analysis

Definition. In general, the Factorial Analysis is also a data reduction tool, the term factor analysis was first introduced by (*Thurstone* [10]) and used for modulate the data set and to detect the relationships between qualitative and nominal variables to classify them [11] and determine the covariance of variables reconstructed with less latent variables called *factors* independent one another, to well describe an observed phenomenon involved in many fields such as intelligence, science, psychology, health, ecology, sociology and others. It is similar to Principal Component Analysis in the term of reducing the data. In Factor Analysis there is two types of variables: the latent variables (factors) and the observed variables. Note that The PCA is a particular type of FA.

More especially, there are many types of Factorial Analysis, the famous one is called *Factorial Analysis of correspondence.*

The Factorial Analysis of Correspondence (*Benzekri* [12]) is used for the processing of information contained in a so-called contingency (dependency) table of qualitative, quantitative and positive variables of different kinds, and it is used mainly for nominal variables. This table can thus be represented by a cloud of points with probabilities [13]. This correspondence analysis is descriptive when there are two way tables or multi tables having correspondence between rows and columns. The final result produced is similar to the Factorial Analysis method exploring the categories of variables contained in the specific table.

- So what is "correspondence"?

When the variables are quantitative, a correlation study have to be done (PCA). However, when there are qualitative or nominal variables, the one must make a study of the correspondences (FCA).

Problematic 2. The notation of the Factorial Analysis model is like the regression model and each data-subject is a linear function of the unobserved factors $f_1, f_2, \ldots, f_m$ which determine the variation of the data set. In general, the matrix notation of the FA model is like:

$$X = \mu + Lf + \epsilon \tag{5}$$

We have the data X with the expression in Eq. (1), μ is the X_i variables mean vector denoted:

$$\mu = \begin{pmatrix} \mu_1 \\ \mu_2 \\ \vdots \\ X_p \end{pmatrix} \tag{6}$$

f represents the factors collected in the vector of common factors:

$$f = \begin{pmatrix} f1 \\ f2 \\ \vdots \\ fm \end{pmatrix} \tag{7}$$

With $m \prec\prec p$ And the matrix of factor loadings is represented like:

$$L = \begin{pmatrix} l_{11} & l_{12} & \cdots & l_{1m} \\ l_{21} & l_{22} & \cdots & l_{2m} \\ \vdots & & & \\ l_{p1} & x_{p2} & \cdots & x_{pm} \end{pmatrix} \quad (8)$$

And finally the measurement error:

$$\epsilon = \begin{pmatrix} \epsilon_1 \\ \vdots \\ \epsilon_p \end{pmatrix} \quad (9)$$

To know more about the model assumptions for the mean, variance and correlation, see [14] (Table 1).

Now let's consider the example of a collect information table applied for the Factorial Analysis of Correspondence. The following table contains variables of two sets I and J (the entries):

Table 1. Contingency table

Set J (the parameters)	1	...	j	...	m
Set I (the individuals)					
1	x_{11}	...	x_{1j}	...	x_{1m}
i	x_{i1}	...	x_{ij}	...	x_{im}
n	x_{n1}	...	x_{nj}	...	x_{nm}

∗ *Example*:
The technique of the FCA is mainly used for large data tables all expressed in the same unit. For the qualitative case, the preceding table is presented in the form of a table of the ones and the zeros (depending on whether or not the individual i has the parameter j).

And we have: $p_{ij} = \frac{x_{ij}}{\sum_{i=1}^{n}\sum_{j=1}^{m} x_{ij}}$ which replace x_{ij} in the previous table.

- Goals of Factorial Analysis:
  - First, we use Factorial Analysis in the purpose of measuring the unobserved (latent) and error-free variables.
  - Reduce the number of variables.
  - Determine and prioritize all the dependencies between the rows and the columns of the table on one hand, and on the other hand, it serves to appear some abstract synthetic non correlated variables (reduction of dimensionality). For this purpose, the projection of transformed cloud must be on a space of smaller dimension.

We have the observations which are classified in the contingency table in the boxes following two sets presented in rows and columns. In contrast to PCA, the representative cloud of individuals can not be visualized using a Cartesian coordinate system since the population in this case is defined by nominal criteria. On the other hand, the analysis of the correspondences will make it possible to visualize links between the variables on one or two factorial planes using the metric.

3 PCA and FA Differences

- The Factorial Analysis offers the uniqueness (unlike the PCA) of providing a space of representation common to variables and individuals. In addition, the FA can process nominal data, which is not possible for the PCA.
- In Principal Components Analysis we assume that all variability in an item should be used in the analysis, while in Factor Analysis we only use the variability in an item that it has in common with the other items.
- The Factorial Analysis studies the link between two qualitative and quantitative variables, However, The PCA analyses only the quantitative variables.
- A double PCA on lines and columns leads to obtain the Factorial Correspondence Analysis.
- In the PCA, the used distance for the computation is the Euclidian method but for the FCA it is the *Khi-deux* test [15].
- As the number of variables used to study such a phenomenon is huge, application result of PCA and FA become more and more similar. This observation has been proved by many researchers in this field, thus (*Snook* and *Gorsuch* [16]) have found out that variable table with at least 40 variables result in minor differences.

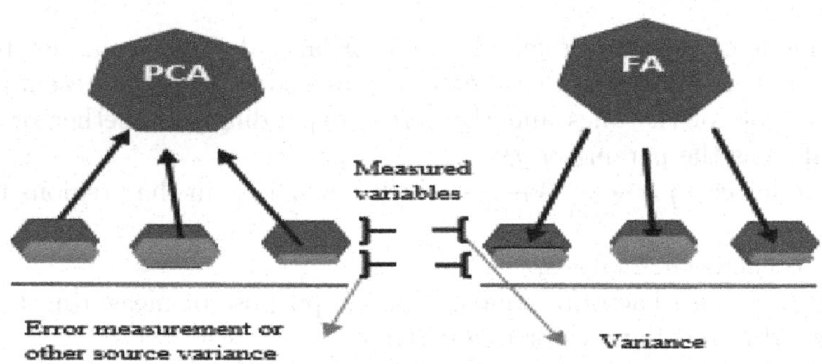

Fig. 1. Simple comparison of PCA and FA

The following figure shows the principal distinguish between PCA and FA in a very easier and shortest way: Noticing that, the arrows point the measured variables to the principal component and it is the inverse for the FA. The variability in the measured variables in the Principal Component Analysis lead to the variance for the Principal Component, by contrast, in the Factorial Analysis the *latent factors* are the mean raison of variance and correlation between the measured variables (*Marcoulides* and *Hershberger* [17]) (Fig. 1).

4 Results and Interpretations

4.1 Analyzing General Data

In this section, we will show some result of statistical analyses and the projection data obtained by the two techniques studied in this paper; the Principal Component Analysis and the Factorial Analysis presented in the type of Factorial Correspondence Analysis (FCA). First we begin with example 1 where the dataset have been collected in a table presenting a series of completely fictitious data concerning the stays of several patients in a hospital center. We are looking to analyze these data by using PCA.

Note that this data is chosen for the pedagogic purpose of study and not for comprehensive or limited analyses.

In the first example we present the results of PCA technique. Our original first table contains 10 (ordinary and nominal) variables presented below:

Table 2. Descriptive statistics

Variables	Mean	Standard deviation	n	n missing
ID	10.60	6.08	20	0
Age	46.58	16.96	20	1
Disability test	2.05	1.28	20	0
Hospitalized	2.75	2.90	20	0
Hour of entry	11:28	6:42	20	0
Cholesterol level	1.56	0.50	20	1

The Table 2 shows the descriptive statistics of each variable, here, we have replaced all the missing variables by their means.

In this example, the study of the data has been done for 20 samples, and thus, the purpose of analysing the structure of this data is to perform a meaningful interpretation of the results after applying the PCA technique. The matrix presented in Table 3 regroups the set of the variation that exists between the variables i.e., for example, there is a strong correlation that is equal to 0.22 between the variable age and the variable hospitalized, which could be interpreted in the way of that the aged people are more hospitalized than the young people. This correlation determines all the variables that will decompose the main components, all the variables that are correlated will be grouped into factors.

Table 3. Correlation matrix

Correlation	ID	Age	Disability test	Hospitalized	Entry	Level of cholesterol
ID	1	0.05	0.24	−0.08	0.2	−0.43
Age	0.05	1.0	−0.23	0.22	−0.4	−0.17
Disability test	0.24	−0.23	1	0.05	0.19	0.21
Hospitalized	−0.08	0.22	0.05	1	0.09	−0.07
Hour of entry	0.2	−0.40	0.19	0.09	1	0.27
Cholesterol level	−0.43	−0.17	0.21	−0.07	0.27	1

The total variance explained in Table 4 gives us an idea of the degree of information presented by each component or factor, so that 10 variables have been replaced by 6 components, but the first component represents only itself, 29% of the total information of the set of all variables, then the second represents 23% of the total information and that the third one itself represents 18%, so then if we regroup the three components that will give us 71% of the set of variables so, as a result, we are no longer able to work on the set of all variables.

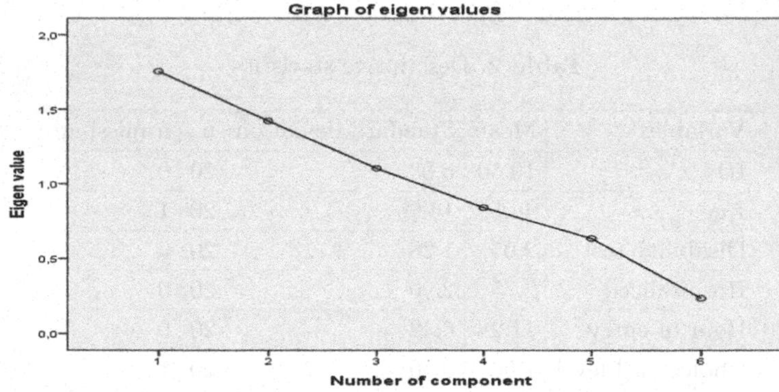

Fig. 2. The eigen value graph

The Table 4 presents the correlation values between variables and the Principal Component grouped in the Component matrix after rotation.

The graph of the Fig. 2 shows us the eigenvalues of each calculated component. As one can observe the tree first component choosen by PCA have the high values from the six total component computed. These tree components have the high variance PC1, PC2 and PC3 calculated from the Table 4 with the eigen values 29.26, 23.72 and 18.41 respectively.

Table 4. Total variance

Initial eigenvalues sum of squares of factors selected for rotation						
PC	Total	% of variance	% commulated	Total	% of variance	% commulated
1	1.8	29.26	29.26	1.7	27.80	27.806
2	1.4	23.72	52.98	1.5	24.30	52.105
3	1.1	18.41	71.39	1.2	19.3	71.39
4	0.8	14.05	85.44			
5	0.6	10.7	96.05			
6	0.2	3.95	100			

The rotation type used in this case is Varimax with Kaiser normalization.

After 5 iterations the rotation matrix converged, and we obtained this component matrix shown in the Table 5 presenting the tree axes that influence on each variable, so that the Hour of entry, the disability test and the cholesterol level are having the high correlation with the first axe, the ID has a correlation of 0.875 with the second axe and finally the variables age and hospitalized have the high correlation with the third axe (0.520 and 0.936) respectively.

Table 5. The component matrix after rotation

Variables	PC1	PC2	PC3
Hour of entry	0.793	−0.065	0.008
Disability test	0.689	0.100	0.077
Age	−0.581	0.187	0.520
ID	0.316	0.875	−0.042
Cholesterol level	0.338	−0.800	−0.056
Hospitalized	0.117	−0.050	0.936

Now one can plot the projection points of two first components according to ID variables. Here in the Fig. 3, each small circle represents the projection of the data following the two dimentions represented by the first two components having the highest eigen values (variance) of the data.

Now we present the result of the second example analyzed with FCA. This example offers data on the composition of products sold in fast food outlets in the United States. Here, we have 117 types of hamburger products with 16 variables. So, the set of all types of hamburgers sold constitutes the population we seek to study by FCA.

At the beginning, we can show the relation between the calories and proteins in the following graph.

That type of analyses is called *bivariate analysis*.

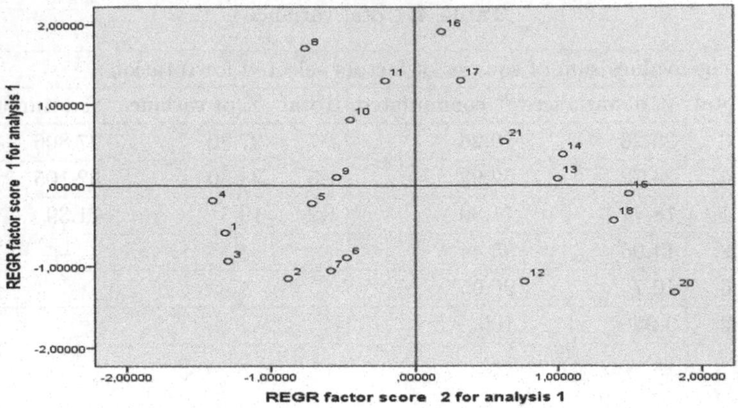

Fig. 3. Projection of two first component according to ID variable

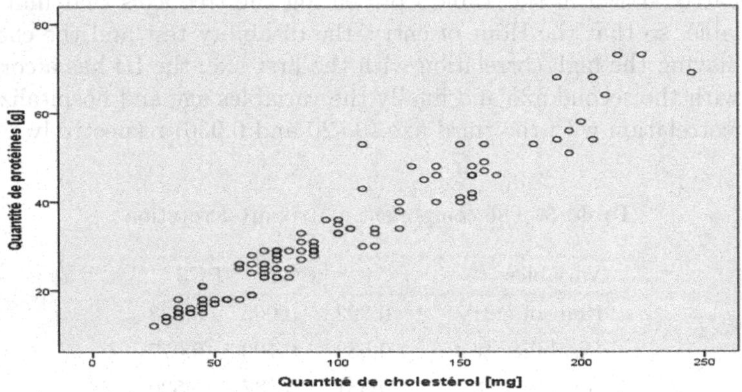

Fig. 4. Graph of relation between two variables (cholesterol and proteins)

This graph presented in Fig. 4 shows a positive linear relationship between the two variables: The more cholesterol in a hamburger, the more protein there is. The correlation coefficient of Pearson is 0.966, which shows a strong but not perfect relationship. Now we will weigh the observations of 117 types of marks of hamburgers by the numerical identifier ID and then project the data on two dimensions.

The Fig. 5 shows the statistical link between the three variables: marks of hamburgers, the fast food offering this hamburger and the total calories recorded into 4 categories presented in Table 6.

As we can observe from Table 6, the Marge active is the fast food chain that proposed more hamburgers with high total of calories (>820), Burger King comes after with 1036 fast food chain, Jack in the box with 739, McDonalds with no hamburger which exceed 820 calories and finally Wendy's is the last fast food chain ranking with 281 hamburgers. We notice also, that Marge active is the

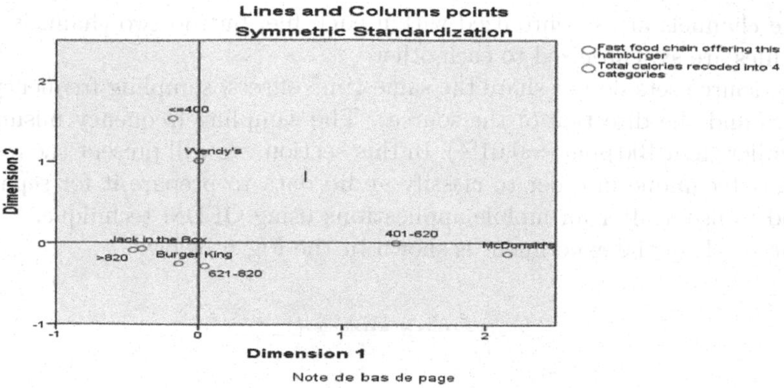

Fig. 5. Graph of projection points in two dimensions

Table 6. Correspondance table

Total number of calories recoded into 4 categories					
Chain of fast food offering this hamburger	≤400	401–620	621–820	>820	Active margin
Wendy's	97	105	73	281	556
McDonald's	10	235	80	0	325
Jack in the Box	86	90	291	739	1206
Burger King	68	269	319	1036	1692
Marge active	261	699	763	2056	3779

only fast food chain which proposed high number of hamburgers with less total of calories (<40). This table shows the importance correspondence between the fast food chain and the number of total calories.

4.2 Analyzing Audio Data

In the telecommunication systems as OFDM technique, audio data is widely used to analyse the recordings of different types of signals and since those audio signals belongs to some audio classes, such as speech, noise and music, it can be useful for several applications, like audiovisual indexing, retrieval system and automatic classification of multimedia contents. In our case, we suppose that we have only speech signals represented in three mixtures of two male speakers. The condition of the experiment is mentioned below:

The recording of those four male speakers is represented in a stereo WAV audio file where all the microphone elements are spaced in a linear arrangement. The spacing of each stereo microphone pair is about 2.15 cm. The reverberation time is about 150 ms [18].

The channels are synchronized within each file, but no two channels in different files are synchronized to each other.

The source sets do not share the same time offsets, sampling frequency mismatches and the direction of the sources. The sampling frequency mismatches are smaller than 100 ppm (=0.01%). In this section, we will present the result of the PCA technique in order to classify audio data to prepare it for separation method to use it after for mobile applications using OFDM technique.

The result of the experiment is shown in the Fig. 6 below:

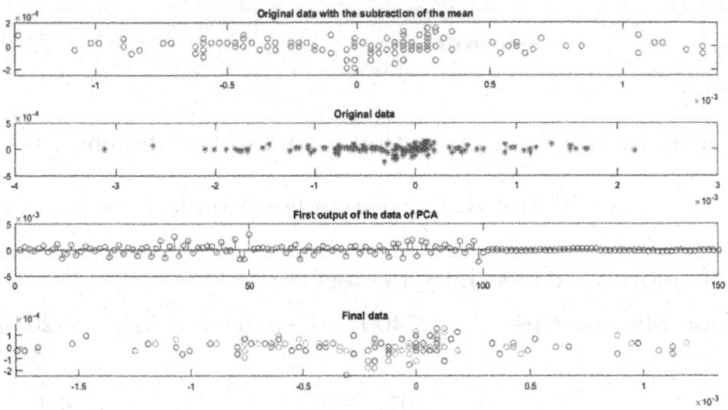

Fig. 6. Principal component analysis of audio data

This figure demontrates that the PCA reduces the number of dataset on 6 components according to 6 different colors representing all the original data. In this experiment, we choosed 50 samples of each column of the mixtures among 64000 samples for every mixture alone, which is of course a huge number that will complicates the operation of the computation and need much more memory in the computer, so in order to simplify this operation we reduced this number

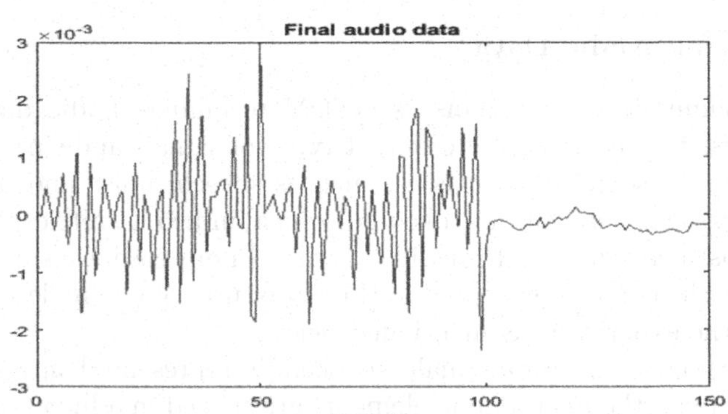

Fig. 7. Final data

of samples just to compute quickly and see the perspicuous results. The final data is seen in the Fig. 7.

The covarience matrix is:

$$CovMat = \begin{pmatrix} 6.572699270125735e-07 & 1.396525492870834e-09 \\ 1.396525492870834e-09 & 4.054649297556355e-09 \end{pmatrix} \quad (10)$$

5 Conclusion

To sum up, we have demonstrate that the techniques of PCA and FA are both tools of reduction and Processing data, in which PCA aims to group together a large number of variables in a limited number of components in order to facilitate the analysis of the data and to detect the set of relations of independence between the various variables in the major objective of obtaining the most relevant summary of the initial data. Otherwise, FA method, is also a dimension reduction technique used especially for measuring the impact of un-observed variables called *factors* on a large number of observed variables. Those data are defined by qualitative variables and notably of the nominal variables.

Finally, we conclude that the choice of the method of analysis depends fundamentally on the type of the data, and consequently, the principal component analysis (PCA) is used to process the quantitative variables meanwhile, the analysis factorial correspondence is used for qualitative and nominal variables. This differences will be so helpful to decide which method is most appropriate for a given variables. Choosing improperly might lead to have a bad interpretation results or incorrect understanding of the data.

References

1. Chang, W.L., Pang, L.M., Tay, K.M.: Application of self-organizing map to failure modes and effects analysis methodology. Neurocomputing **249**, 314–320 (2017)
2. Wang, Q.: Kernel principal component analysis and its applications in face recognition and active shape models. CoRR, abs/1207.3538 (2012)
3. Roweis, S.T., Saul, L.K.: Nonlinear dimensionality reduction by locally linear embedding. Science **290**(5500), 2323–2326 (2000)
4. Abouzid, H., Chakkor, O.: Blind audio source separation: state-of-art. Int. J. Comput. Appl. **130**(4), 1–6 (2015)
5. Abouzid, H., Chakkor, O.: A novel method based on gaussianity and sparsity for signal separation algorithms. Int. J. Electr. Comput. Eng. (IJECE) **7**(3), 1906–1914 (2017). https://doi.org/10.11591/ijece.v7i3. ISSN 2088-8708
6. Hotelling, H.: Analysis of a complex of statistical variables into principal components. J. Educ. Psychol. **24**(6), 417 (1933)
7. Abdi, H., Williams, L.J.: Principal component analysis. WIREs Comput. Stat. **2**, 433–459 (2010)
8. Besse, P.C.: PCA stability and choice of dimensionality. Stat. Probab. Lett. **13**, 405–410 (1992)
9. Jolliffe, I.: Principal Component Analysis, 2nd edn. Springer, New York (2002). https://doi.org/10.1007/b98835

10. Thurstone, L.L.: Multiple factor analysis. Psychol. Rev. **38**(5), 406 (1931)
11. Yong, A.G., Pearse, S.: A beginner's guide to factor analysis: focusing on exploratory factor analysis. Tutor. Quant. Methods Psychol. **9**(2), 79–94 (2013)
12. Benzekri, J.P.: Analyse des données. Dunod, Paris (1973)
13. Hoffman, D.L., Franke, G.R.: Correspondence analysis: graphical representation of categorical data in marketing research. J. Mark. Res. **23**(3), 213–227 (1986)
14. Manly, B.F.J.: Multivariate Statistical Methods: A Primer, 3rd edn. Chapman and Hall, London (2005)
15. Confais, J., Grelet, Y., Le Guen, M.: Test d'intependance et mesure d'association dans un tableau de contingence. Revue Modulad (2005)
16. Snook, S.C., Gorsuch, R.L.: Component analysis versus common factor analysis: a Monte Carlo study. Psychol. Bull. **106**, 148–154 (1989)
17. Marcoulides, G.A., Hershberger, S.L.: Multivariate Statistical Methods: A Fast Course. Psychology Press, New York (1997)
18. Liutkus, A., et al.: The 2016 signal separation evaluation campaign. In: Tichavský, P., Babaie-Zadeh, M., Michel, O.J.J., Thirion-Moreau, N. (eds.) LVA/ICA 2017. LNCS, vol. 10169, pp. 323–332. Springer, Cham (2017). https://doi.org/10.1007/978-3-319-53547-0_31

Neural Networks

A Probabilistic Vector Representation and Neural Network for Text Classification

Mariem Bounabi[1(✉)], Karim El Moutaouakil[2], and Khalid Satori[1]

[1] Computer Sciences, Imaging and Numerical Analysis Laboratory (LIIAN), Fez, Morocco
mariem.bounabi@usmba.ac.ma, khalidsatori@gmail.com
[2] Hoceima National School of Applied Sciences (ENSAH), University Mohammed First, Al-Hoceima, Morocco
karimmoutaouakil@yahoo.fr

Abstract. The increasing of the textual databases and its representation in large spaces prevents the automation of the treatment of these great masses and the extraction of knowledge. In order to address the challenges of high dimensionality which using the methods and technics of the text mining. Where the term frequency-inverse document frequency (TF-IDF), weighting method, is the most required approach to represent the document. Unfortunately, TF-IDF produces descriptors of large sizes (generally greater than 1000), which requires models with great complexity. However, the texts classification systems based on these models suffer from the overfitting phenomenon and are very slow. Therefore, to overcome these problems, we use the select attributes methods; by giving the deterministic aspect of this latter, we risk to lose huge information. Thus, to recover from this loss, we propose a probabilistic vector representation of each document, based on the relevant terms selected previously. Then, we associate a set of features to each document composed by local and global probabilistic coefficients basing on the selected terms. More specifically and precisely, the components formulas are composed by the frequency of each descriptor, the length of each document and the size of the corpus. To show the performance of this treatment we propose comparative studies between TF-IDF representation and the new probabilistic representation, to classify the BBCSPORT corpus. Moreover, in the classification phase, we use several versions of Bayesian Network and Multilayer Perceptron. The obtained results are satisfied, where the neural network classifier, multilayer perceptron, gives 100% as a recognition rate, using the new representation and 94.69%, using the simple TF-IDF weighting.

Keywords: Feature selection · Text classification · Probabilistic representation
Select attributes · Bayes Net · Multilayer perceptron

1 Introduction

Recently, the growth of online-unstructured knowledge resources and the diversification of forms used for their storage and transmission is still an issue in the search for textual documents. However, the text mining has coming to solve the problem, where the textual information can be automatically acquired and processed by the machine [1]. Typically,

Y. Tabii et al. (Eds.): BDCA 2018, CCIS 872, pp. 343–355, 2018.
https://doi.org/10.1007/978-3-319-96292-4_27

text-mining tasks include document classification, document clustering, sentiment analysis and document summarization. Therefore, in order to classify a corpus of textual documents, is following the main steps of the text mining [2, 3] sited in Fig. 1.

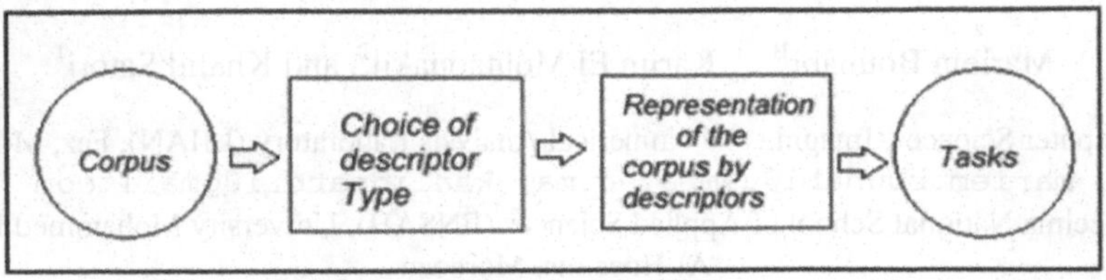

Fig. 1. Important steps in the text mining.

The word is not the only way to describe a document. There are many forms of descriptors as radicals and n-gram forms. The choice of the descriptor depends on the nature of the language treated, and it has a crucial role in the relevance of the obtained results. To address the challenges of high dimensionality, we use the methods of selecting attributes that are critical to classify documents and to improve the accuracy of clustering algorithms by identifying the relevant and informative attributes. In this sense, the extraction methods are combined with the selected attributes methods to reduce the size of the feature set [4]. Thereafter, it is necessary to represent each descriptor of the corpus by weights, who are in general the mathematical representation [5]. The set of the obtained terms, called features, are represented as input to several classification tools, in order to classify each document of the corpus in the correct class.

This work fits in texts classification field. Most of the proposed texts classification systems are based on vector representation methods [5–7]. In this regard, the TF-IDF weighting method remains the most required approach to represent document [5, 6]. Unfortunately, TF-IDF produces descriptors of large sizes (generally greater than 1000), which requires models with great complexity. The texts classification systems based on these models suffer from the overfitting phenomenon and are very slow. In this work, to overcome this problem, we use the select attributes methods [4, 8]. Given the deterministic aspect of this latter, we risk a huge loss of information. To recover the lost information, we propose a probabilistic vector representation of each document, based on the relevant terms selected previously. The adopted formulas are used to calculate some scores in the matching process [9]. In our case, we associate a set of features to each document composed by a local and global probabilistic coefficients basing on the selected terms. More precisely, the components formulas are composed by the frequency of each descriptor, the length of each document and the size of the corpus.

View the diversity of its architectures and its performances, Bayes Network (BNet) and neuronal network (MLP) are used in the classification phase. Various Bayesian network classifier-learning algorithms [10] are proposed in the literature as the search algorithm option and the estimator option. The first one can be used to select a structure-learning algorithm and specify its options. Three well-known local research methods, to know Hill climbing, K2, Tabu Search, are detailed later. The second one is the estimator option, who are used to select the method for estimating the conditional probability distributions [10]. The artificial neural network MLP is used in several applications based on the static classification [11]. These networks are easy to use and they can approximate any input-output card. Generally, the MLP is composed of three kinds of layers: the input layer, the hidden layer and the output layer. Concerning the learning phase, the researchers use the gradient back-propagation methods [12]. To select the architecture of the MLP, several methods were proposed in the literature; see for example [11–14].

The set of processes used in this approach will be detailed in the rest of the paper as follows: we start first by the description of classical classification systems; thereafter we delineate all necessary preprocessing steps for our new approach where we describe the main methods of selecting and representation for final descriptors. A description of the two-used classification method, BNet and MLP, is given in the fourth part illustrated by some experimental results given in the last part.

2 Classical Text Classification System

Typically, there are three traditional and necessary steps in the system of text classification; one summarizes them in Analysis as a first step, weighting and Classification Tools. In this section, we describe the classical preprocessing operations used to prepare the corpus and select features, as it is shown in Fig. 2, in order to classify, in a traditional way, the content of the documentary database.

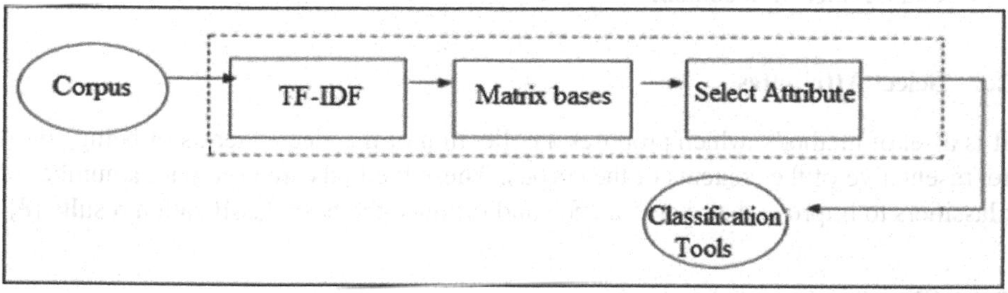

Fig. 2. The preprocessing operations used to prepare the corpus and select features.

2.1 Analysis

The analysis procedure process in three steps. In the first one, the documents are substituted by a linear sequence of characters. Then, the stop words are eliminated using a stop list. Finally, stemming algorithms are required to find the radicals of the obtained list. This procedure is useful in many areas of computational linguistics and information retrieval.

2.2 Weighting

The content of the document is, generally, represented by the mathematical representation basing, for example, in the Boolean theory; the binary is one of this representation where the content of a document is represented by 0 and 1. This latter is easy to implement but not given much informative [15]. Another type of the weighing term is the probabilistic model which is a mathematical model based on the theory of probability. However, the basic idea is to select documents that have both a high probability of being relevant and a low probability of being irrelevant to the user request. This model unifies the representations of documents and concepts and allows an approximate matching of documents and request but it uses a complex conditional probability calculation [16]. It should be noted that the probabilistic search model is more efficient than the Boolean search model. Moreover, the most famous and most used type is the vector representation where the terms of each document are represented by a vector, its components are the weights calculated by the TF-IDF formula [17] defined by:

$$\mathrm{tf} * \mathrm{idf} = (0.5 + \frac{0.5 * \mathrm{tfij}}{max\,\mathrm{tfij}}) * log(\frac{N - \mathrm{ni}}{N}) \quad (1)$$

Where:

tfij: is the number of occurrences of the term in the document;
ni: the number of documents containing term ti;
N: total number of document.

2.3 Select Attributes

It is a set of methods, which proposes a collection of the elected terms of beings most representative of the contents of the corpus. These methods are used with a number of classifiers to improve their performance and produce the best classification results [8].

2.4 Classification

Once the features are prepared, there are represented as input to the classifier which gives the most appropriate class as a response.

3 Our Approach

Most of the proposed texts classification systems are based on vector representation methods [5–7]. In this regard, the TF-IDF weighting method remains the most required approach to represent document [5, 6]. Unfortunately, TF-IDF produces descriptors of large sizes (generally greater than 1000), which requires models with great complexity. The texts classification systems based on these models suffer from the overfitting phenomenon and slowness. Thus, in this part, we propose a new approach to select features of a given document taking into a count the context. Our approach selects a set of probabilistic features, which the components are probabilistic scores. In fact, we will follow three steps: In the first step, we use the TF-IDF to transform the corpus to term of matrix bases. In the second step, we use the select attributes method to select a set of the relevant terms noted B. Finally, for each Document, we calculate the probabilistic weights for each element among B. Figure 3 shows the said steps:

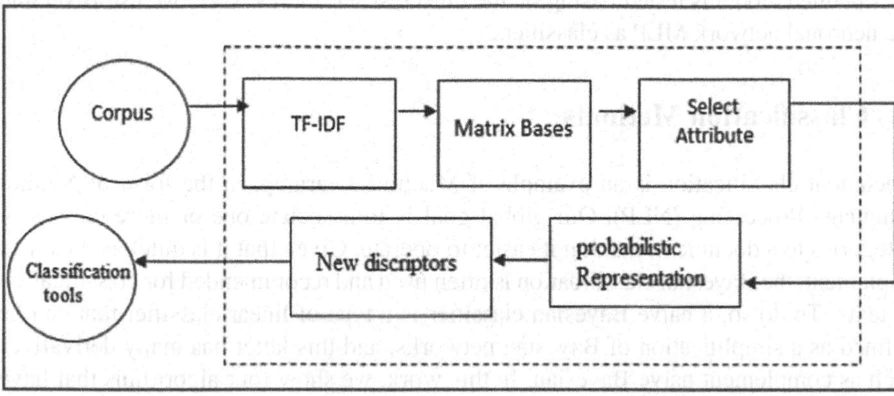

Fig. 3. The preprocessing of our new classification system.

Let T be the set of terms obtained using TF-IDF, which represent the corpus basing on T. To reduce T we use Correlation Based Feature Selection (SBF) [8], which is a popular technique for selecting the most relevant attributes based on Pearson's correlation. It calculates the correlation between each attribute and the output variable and selects only those attributes that have a moderate-to-high positive or negative correlation (close to −1 or 1) and drop those attributes with a low correlation (a value close to zero).

Let $B = \{d_1, d_2 \ldots d_n\}$ be the set of the obtained terms. For each element D_j from our corpus and di from B, a vector $Wj = \{w_{1,j}, \ldots, w_{n,j}\}$ is calculated by the formula:

$$Wij = \log\left(\frac{N}{\text{dfij} + \varepsilon}\right) * \frac{\dfrac{(k+1)dfij}{k(1-b) + b * k * dlj}}{avgl} + tfij \tag{2}$$

Where:

Local parameters:

dfij: Frequency of the descriptor i in the document j; to avoid calculation redundancy, we keep the dfij calculated by TF-IDF.
The frequency dfij is initialized by $0 < \varepsilon << 1$ to take into account the case dfij = 0.
dlj: Number of the descriptor in de document j.

Global parameters:

N: number of the documents in de collection;
avgl: Average number of the descriptors in the document j;
Constants K = typically is set around 1.2 to 2

b = 1 is relative frequency (fully scale by document length) generally it's set around 0.75.

After the extraction feature process, we obtained a new descriptor of the corpus, which is divided into three sets, which are, learning set, validation set and test set. The first and the second sets are used to select the appropriate model. The performance of the obtained model is tested basing on the third test set. In this work, we use BNet and the neuronal network MLP as classifiers.

4 Classification Methods

Document classification is an example of Machine Learning, in the form of Natural Language Processing (NLP). Our global goal is to associate one or more classes or categories to a document, making it easier to operate. Given that it is quick and easy to implement, the Bayesian classification is often used and recommended for classification of texts. To do so, a naive Bayesian classifier is a type of linear classifier that can be defined as a simplification of Bayesian networks, and this latter has many derivatives such as complement naïve Bayesian. In this work, we show four algorithms that have given better classification.

4.1 Bayes Networks

Bayesian networks (BNet) are acyclic probabilistic graphs, where the nodes are random variables; the structure of the network defines their conditional dependencies. In order to use this classification tools, we process in four phases [21]:

1. Modeling the problem n terms of a set of random variables $X = \{x_1, x_2,\ldots, x_n\}$. In our case, we have n random variables, which represent the set of features, and an additional random variable for the class.
2. Choosing adequate network architecture. As we do not know the dependencies between features random variables, we test several kinds of architectures. First, we adopt the naïve assumption. Then, we select the Bayes network architecture using K2, Hill climbing, simulated Annealing, Tabu Search and genetic Search.
3. Constructing the conditional probabilities matrix of node i, knowing the state of its parents: $\theta i = P\ (Xi/Pa\ (Xi))$. In this work, we use Maximum a Posteriori (MAP) estimation to estimate P(y) and P (xi/y) directly from data.
4. Interfering with response to a given request, such task is based on the following joint distribution: $P(x_1, x_2,\ldots, x_n) = \prod P\ (Xi/Pa\ (Xi))$.

Given a class variable y and a dependent feature vector x1 through xn, Bayes theorem states the following relationship [21]:

$$P\left(y/x_1, x_2, \ldots, x_n\right) = \left(P(y)\, P\left(x_1, x_2, \ldots, x_n/y\right)\right)/\left(P\left(x_1, x_2, \ldots, x_n\right)\right) \tag{3}$$

Naïve Bayes (NB) is a set of supervised learning algorithms based on applying Bayes theorem with the "naive" assumption of independence between every pair of features [22]. Basing on this naïve assumption, the Eq. (3) is simplified to:

$$P(y/x_1, x_2, \ldots, x_n) = \left(P(y) \prod P(x_i/y)\right)/P(x_1, x_2, \ldots, x_n) \quad (4)$$

Since $P(x_1, x_2, \ldots, x_n)$ is constant given the input, we can use the following classification rule:

$$Y = \text{Arg. maxy } P(y) \prod P(xi/y) \quad (5)$$

Local research methods to select the Bayes Net architecture This Bayes Network learning algorithm uses Tabu search for finding a well scoring Bayes network structure. To find a well scoring Bayes network structure, thus, to find a well scoring Bayes network structure, several researchers have used local research methods. In this paper, we compare between three well-known local research methods, to know Hill climbing, K2, and Tabu Search [10].

The *Hill Climbing algorithm* (HC) consists adding, deleting and reversing arcs. Where, in each iteration, HC conserves the best architecture.

Unlike the HC method, the Bayes Network learning *algorithm K2* use a fixed ordering of variables to add arcs. However, the network starts as a Naive Bayes network and proceed from there. It also allows the user to designate the maximum number of parents each node can have.

The *Tabu Search method* (TS) defines the notion of the neighborhood and initializes the research by a set of solutions. Hence, to avoid the production of the same set of solution, TS use a set of forbidden movement.

For each feature i, let SPi the set of the selected parents for i using one of the mentioned local method. Following this notation, the Eq. (3) is simplified to:

$$P(y/x_1, x_2, \ldots, x_n) = \left(P(y) \prod P(xi/SPi)\right)/P(x_1, x_2, \ldots, x_n) \quad (6)$$

Since $P(x_1, x_2, \ldots, x_n)$ is constant given the input, we can use the following classification rule:

$$Y = \text{Arg. maxy } P(y) \prod P(xi/SPi) \quad (7)$$

4.2 Multilayer Perceptron

The multilayer perceptron is an artificial neural network oriented, with supervised learning, used to model n Nonlinear functions, each Classification of documents in relation to one of the topics. Let f: IR n → IR p nonlinear function modeled using MLP. We have to determine three kinds of layers:

1. Input layer: is composed of n neurons and it is a virtual layer associated with the system input. This means, the number of the selected terms is 68, and then the number of the input layer neurons is 68.
2. Hidden layer: a multilayer perceptron can have any number of hidden layers and any number of neurons per hidden layer, but it should be noted that using one hidden layer is sufficient to solve a non-linear complex problem and the choice of the number of hidden layers is still a challenging issue. Different approaches for hidden neurons selection are proposed in the literature [11, 13]. As the size of the BBCSPORT corpus is 731, we use the simple validation method to select the number of hidden layer neurons.
3. Output layer: this layer is called decision layer and contains p neurons. As the BBCSPORT corpus has 5 class, the number of decision neurons is 5. It should be noted that the neurons of the MLP are connected together by weighted connections. Figure 4 gives the architecture of the adopted multilayer perceptron.

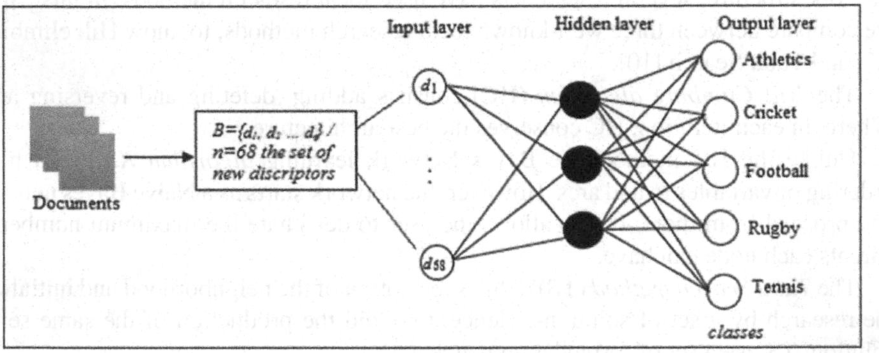

Fig. 4. The architecture of the adopted multilayer perceptron.

The weights of these connections govern the operation of the network and program an application from input space to the output space through a non-linear transformation. The creation of a multilayer perceptron solve a given problem requires the inference of the best possible application as defined by a set of training data consisting of pairs of input vectors and desired outputs. The algorithm called back propagation can realize this inference, among others [14].

5 Result and Discussion

For the sake of the proving effectiveness of the proposed descriptors, selected and represented by the methods cited above, we propose a textual classification based on a set of classifiers. Several experiments have been conducting all algorithms with different Configurations under a Dell compatible, Intel (R) Core i5-CPU 2.50 GHz, and 4 GB of RAM. The whole of the algorithms has been implemented with Java language, which favors our study.

5.1 Dataset

For the test, we used a database of 737 documents organized as follows (Table 1):

Table 1. BBCSPORT class and number of articles.

Class	Number of articles
Athletics	101
Cricket	124
Football	265
Rugby	147
Tennis	100

5.2 Experimentations Setup

It should be noted that 80% of the data is reserved for the training of the classifiers and 20% for the test.

To select the satisfactory Bayes Net architecture, we tested with different Local research methods (Hill Climber, Tabu Search and K2); the obtained results are noted in Table 7.

For multilayer perceptron, we tried to increase the number of neurons in the hidden layer in order to select the best classification results. This number must be selected to be high enough to model the problem but not very high to avoid the overfitting. For that, we stood at three layers, were the results, of both systems, are maximized and stabilized. (Consult Table 8 and Fig. 5 in the appendix).

5.3 Results

A set of evaluation measures was used to evaluate the improvement of results by changing the weighting method. Table 2 shows a global comparison of differently used classifiers, combined with the proposed set of features, using the precision, recall and accuracy as evaluation measure.

Table 2. Classification results from NB, BNET and MLP.

	Probabilistic representation			TF-IDF		
	Precision	Recall	Accuracy	Precision	Recall	Accuracy
BNet	98.30%	98.3%	98.29%	94.30%	92.9%	92.89%
NB	98.4%	98.3%	98.29%	94.10%	92.3%	92.30%
MLP	100%	100%	100%	94.80%	94.7%	94.67%

Confusions Matrix

Another way to evaluate the improvement of the results of the classification is the Confusion Matrix. Tables: 3, 4, 5 and 6 give the confusion matrix of the classifiers: NB and MLP using probabilistic representation and TF-IDF as methods of representation of the descriptors obtained by Best-first search as a selecting attributes method.

Table 3. Confusions matrix of the NB classifier using probabilistic representation.

Class	Athletics	Cricket	Football	Rugby	Tennis
Athletics	17	0	0	0	0
Cricket	0	20	0	0	0
Football	0	0	38	0	0
Rugby	0	0	1	21	0
Tennis	0	0	0	0	20

Table 4. Confusions matrix of the NB classifier using the simple TF-IDF representation

Class	Athletics	Cricket	Football	Rugby	Tennis
Athletics	17	0	0	0	0
Cricket	0	20	0	0	0
Football	0	0	38	0	0
Rugby	0	1	1	20	0
Tennis	0	0	0	0	20

Table 5. Confusions matrix of the MLP classifier using probabilistic representation

Class	Athletics	Cricket	Football	Rugby	Tennis
Athletics	17	0	0	0	0
Cricket	1	13	1	5	0
Football	0	0	38	0	0
Rugby	0	0	0	22	0
Tennis	0	0	0	0	20

It is notable that the matrix, for each classifier, becomes hollow by changing the simple TF-IDF weighting method by the new probabilistic method.

Table 6. Confusions matrix of the MLP classifier using the simple TF-IDF representation.

Class	Athletics	Cricket	Football	Rugby	Tennis
Athletics	16	0	0	0	1
Cricket	1	25	2	0	0
Football	0	1	36	1	0
Rugby	0	0	0	22	0
Tennis	0	0	1	0	19

6 Conclusion

In this work, we have proposed a new approach to select an optimal set of features for text classification. The proposed approach consists of selecting the relevant terms in a given corpus using TF-IDF representation and selecting attributes method. Then a vector of probabilistic weight is calculated basing on the selected terms. In the classification phase, we have used Bayesian network and multilayer perceptron. The envisaged systems were testing on BBCSPORT databases. As it was mentioned in the experimental part, the best systems, which processes a large amount of data, are the ones based on the probabilistic presentation and the neural network MLP with an optimal number of hidden layers (=3). Incoming work, to avoid the true negative response, we will use a rejection class besides and we will test our system on others database.

Appendix

See Tables 7 and 8 and Fig. 5.

Table 7. Results for different algorithms for learning the network structure using the new probabilistic method

Structure of Bayesian network	Accuracy on test set (%)	Recall (%)	F-Measure (%)
Tabu search	98.29	98.30	98.30
K2 Algorithm	98.00	98.01	98.01
Hill Climber Algorithm	98.29	98.30	98.30

Table 8. Results for different Number of hidden nodes

	Probabilistic representation	TF-IDF
Number of hidden nodes	Accuracy on test set (%)	Accuracy on test set (%)
2	88.03	85.56
3	100	95.85
5	100	94.67
10	100	94.67
50	100	94.67

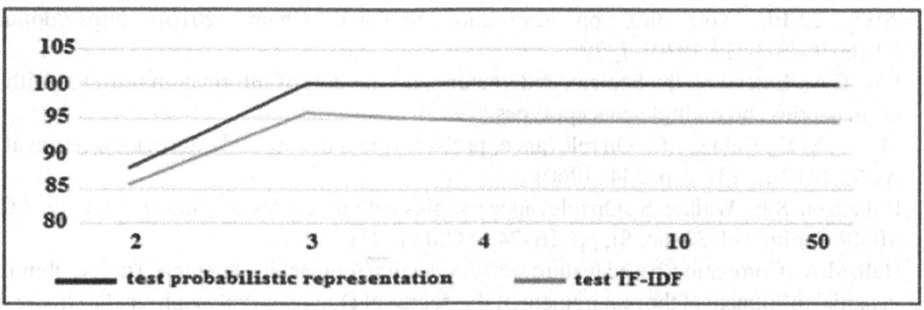

Fig. 5. Change of the accuracy according to number of nodes in the hidden layer of the MLP using the booth systems.

References

1. Ahmad, M.: Machine learning approach to text mining: a review. Int. J. **4**(6), 1125–1131 (2014)
2. Tan, A.H.: Text mining: the state of the art and the challenges. In: Proceedings of the PAKDD 1999 Workshop on Knowledge Disocovery from Advanced Databases, vol. 8, pp. 65–70. Sn (1999)
3. Kumar, L., Bhatia, P.K.: Text mining: concepts, process and applications. Int. J. Global Res. Comput. Sci. (UGC Approv. J.) **4**(3), 36–39 (2013)
4. Hall, M.A., Smith, L.A.: Practical feature subset selection for machine learning. J. Comput. Sci. **98**, 4–6 (1998)
5. Trinh, A.P.: Classification de texte et estimation probabiliste par Machine à Vecteurs de Support. Actes du troisième DÉfi Fouille de Textes, pp. 77 (2007)
6. Vu, T., Denoyer, L., Gallinari, P.: Un modèle statistique pour la classification de documents structurés (2003)
7. Eensoo, E., Nouvel, D., Martin, A., Valette, M.: Combiner analyses textométriques, apprentissage supervisé et représentation vectorielle pour l'analyse de la subjectivité. In: 11e Défi Fouille de Texte (DEFT 2015), Caen, France (2016)
8. Li, Y., Luo, C., Chung, S.M.: Text clustering with feature selection by using statistical data. IEEE Trans. Knowl. Data Eng. **20**(5), 641–652 (2008)
9. Salton, G., Buckley, C.: Term-weighting approaches in automatic text retrieval. Inf. Process. Manage. **24**(5), 513–523 (1988)
10. Bouckaert, R.R.: Bayesian network classifiers in weka for version 3-5-7. Artificial Intelligence Tools **11**(3), 369–387 (2008)
11. Panchal, G., Ganatra, A., Kosta, Y.P., Panchal, D.: Behaviour analysis of multilayer perceptronswith multiple hidden neurons and hidden layers. Int. J. Comput. Theory Eng. **3**(2), 332 (2011)
12. Buscema, M., Tastle, W.J., Terzi, S.: Meta Net: a new meta-classifier family. In: Tastle, W. (ed.) Data Mining Applications Using Artificial Adaptive Systems, pp. 141–182. Springer, New York (2013). https://doi.org/10.1007/978-1-4614-4223-3_5
13. Ettaouil, M., Ghanou, Y.: Neural architectures optimization and Genetic algorithms. Wseas Trans. Comput. **8**(3), 526–537 (2009)
14. Dahmouni, A., El Moutaouakil, K., Satori, K.: Robust face recognition using local gradient probabilistic pattern (LGPP). In: El Oualkadi, A., Choubani, F., El Moussati, A. (eds.) MedCT 2015. LNEE, vol. 380, pp. 277–286. Springer, Cham (2016). https://doi.org/10.1007/978-3-319-30301-7_29
15. Fox, E.A.: Extending the boolean and vector space models of information retrieval with P-norm queries and multiple concept types (1983)
16. Maron, M.E., Kuhns, J.L.: On relevance, probabilistic indexing and information retrieval. J. ACM (JACM) **7**(3), 216–244 (1960)
17. Robertson, S.E., Walker, S.: On relevance weights with little relevance information. In: ACM SIGIR Forum, vol. 31, no. SI, pp. 16–24. ACM (1997)
18. Hall, M.A.: Correlation-based feature subset selection for machine learning. Thesis submitted in partial fulfillment of the requirement of the degree of Doctor of Philosophy at the University of Waikato (1998)
19. Kjaerulff, U.B., Madsen, A.L.: Bayesian Networks and Influence Diagrams: A Guide to Construction and Analysis. Springer, New York (2008). https://doi.org/10.1007/978-0-387-74101-7. vol. 200, p. 114

20. Rennie, J.D., Shih, L., Teevan, J., Karger, D.R.: Tackling the poor assumptions of naive bayes text classifiers. In: Proceedings of the 20th International Conference on Machine Learning (ICML-2003), pp. 616–623 (2003)
21. Aharrane, N., Dahmouni, A., El Moutaouakil, K., Satori, K.: A robust statistical set of features for Amazigh handwritten characters. Pattern Recognit. Image Anal. **27**(1), 41–52 (2017)
22. Raschka, S.: Naive bayes and text classification I-introduction and theory. arXiv preprint arXiv:1410.5329 (2014)

Improving Implementation of Keystroke Dynamics Using K-NN and Manhattan Distance

Farida Jaha(✉) and Ali Kartit

Laboratory LTI, Department TRI, Chouaïb Doukkali University,
ENSAJ Avenue Jabran Khalil Jabran, BP 299 El Jadida, Morocco
Jaha.farida@gmail.com, alikartit@gmail.com

Abstract. Keystroke dynamics is a heavy field for researches; a lot of solutions have been proposed in this domain using different implementations usually based on Euclidean distance for measuring similarity between features vectors. However, the Euclidean distance method has a higher error equal rate comparing with other classification methods which makes the method less effective. Therefore, in the following paper, we propose our version of keystroke dynamics implementation based on K-NN, F-NN and Manhattan distance as classifiers to improve the authentication efficiency. The flight times and dwell time between keys are used in this study.

Keywords: Keystroke dynamics · Behavioral biometric · Threshold · BYOD K-NN · K-FN · Manhattan distance

1 Introduction

Employees use more and more their mobiles devices in work specifically after having introduced a new trend called BYOD (Bring your own devices) that allows workers to provide their own devices and use the same materials for both personal and professional purposes. Therefore it is very important to use an authentication platform like authentication based on knowledge (password, etc.), physical biometric authentication (iris, etc.) or behavioral biometric authentication (keystroke dynamics, etc.).

This paper concerns biometric authentication based on keystroke dynamics. The method consists to analyze the typing patterns of a claimed user and then decide to accept or reject the user authentication attempt.

The main advantages of keystroke dynamics are: (1) it improves productivity by using a known device, (2) As the user is typing his login and password; biometric data is extracted and compared to a reference profile stored in the system database without the need for an extra time to verify the user, (3) it allows a reduction in investment, it does not require external hardware. Keystroke dynamics implementation is based essentially on software, which is the subject of this paper.

We propose an implementation with an interactive graphic interface, it allows (1) to capture the user features and (2) to give to the system administrator to modify some parameters to improve the software efficiency (see Sect. 4).

Y. Tabii et al. (Eds.): BDCA 2018, CCIS 872, pp. 356–366, 2018.
https://doi.org/10.1007/978-3-319-96292-4_28

2 Related Work

Keystroke dynamics was and remains a strong field for research, the first documented research [6] dated back on 1977. Just after, many others researches [9, 12, 13, 21, 23] were appeared. For instance, Patil and Renke [17] published a paper where they better cleared up keystroke dynamics, they mentioned some drawback of this biometric method and they distinguished two different keystroke dynamics authentications: static and continuous. On the same page, Avasthi and Sanwal [19] gave the existing approaches, security and challenges in keystroke dynamics in order to motivate the researches to further come with more novel ideas. Some other researchers like [16] devoted their studies to compare different keystroke dynamics databases and to test if the same algorithm running on two theoretically identical databases gives the same results.

Other approaches were looking to improve the EER (Error Equal Rate) [4] or the security level of the devices using keystroke biometric by combining keystroke dynamic with other sensors. Nagargoje et al. [20] combined keystroke and mouse movement to authenticate the user and increase the device confidentiality. While Trojahn et al. [24] combined keystroke biometric and the finger area.

Systems with touchscreens, which are replacing more and more traditional computer systems, arouse researchers [8] who redirect their studies in this direction. They try to adapt keystroke dynamics authentication to this kind of screen. [15] is one of those researches; it gives us an overview and survey of a touch dynamics authentication system available for devices with touchscreen.

Morales et al. [3] focused on reporting the results of 31 different algorithms evaluated according to accuracy and robustness.

Ali et al. [12] presented a detailed survey of the most recent researches on keystroke dynamic authentication. They analyzed different methods, algorithms used, the accuracy rate, and the shortcomings of those researches. In the same direction, [18, 28] presented a survey of user authentication using keystroke dynamics.

Further, new researches are concentrated on analyzing keystroke recognition method for smartphones [2, 7, 22], Android platform [11], web-based applications [14, 27], or even for mobile cloud computing [10, 25, 26].

Our Contribution:

(1) Most available software in keystroke dynamics fields use Euclidean distance in their algorithm. However, according to many searches such as [11, 16], k-Nearest Neighbor (K-NN) and Manhattan distance are the most top-performing methods comparing with the Euclidean distance. Which makes the software using the last method less precise and the results obtained less exact.

Thus, to improve the keystroke algorithm, we use k-Nearest Neighbor (K-NN) as a classification method. KNN, a straight forward classifier, has been used in statistical estimation and pattern recognition. It identifies the k closest neighbors of feature value. In our case, we use 1-NN to search one nearest neighbor of a user's typing pattern.

In addition, we adopt K-NN and K-FN (K-Further Neighbor) algorithm based on Manhattan distance instead Euclidean distance to calculate the distance between the claimed user typing pattern and the original user feature values.

(2) Most research remains theoretical. In this paper, we propose complete software that can be used in mobile devices that need a biometric system for authentication besides password especially devices without two-factor authentication method. The software is based on the pseudo code already discussed in our previous paper [5].

3 Methodology

3.1 Keystroke Dynamics

Keystroke recognition is a biometric technique which can automatically identify a person by typing his login and password. It describes exactly when each key was pressed and when it was released as a device user is typing.

There are many keyboard features that we can use to authenticate a person using typing pattern: keystroke pressure, keystroke speed, typing sound, dwell time and flight time.

Studies like [12, 20] demonstrate that the use of dwell time and digraph times (flight times) gives the best FAR (False Acceptance Rate) and FRR (False Rejection Rate) combination. Therefore, for identifying the genuine user from impostors, we have adopted dwell time noted f_i^d and different digraph times noted f_i^{L1}, f_i^{L2} and f_i^{L3} in which:

- f_i^d: Is the time difference between pressing and releasing the same keyboard.
- f_i^{L1}: Is the difference between releasing the ith key and pressing the (i + 1)th key.
- f_i^{L2}: Is the difference between the pressure of the ith button and pressure the (i + 1)th button.
- f_i^{L3}: Is the difference between the release of the ith key and the release of (i + 1)th key.

The Fig. 1 is a good demonstration of these four functions:

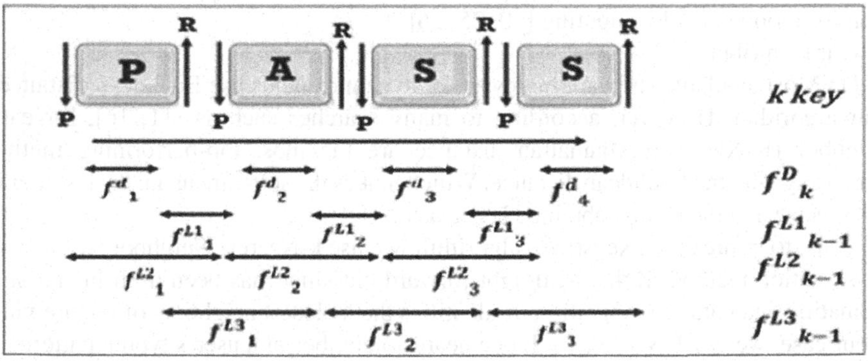

Fig. 1. Keystroke dynamics extraction of password « pass »

3.2 Proposed Work Architecture

Figure 2 shown the general approach used in this study. During his first access to the computer system, the user has to create his own account (Registration phase) and then he is asked to type his login and his password n times (enrollment phase). As the user is typing, the system records his biometric features (features collection) and stores his reference profile in the system database.

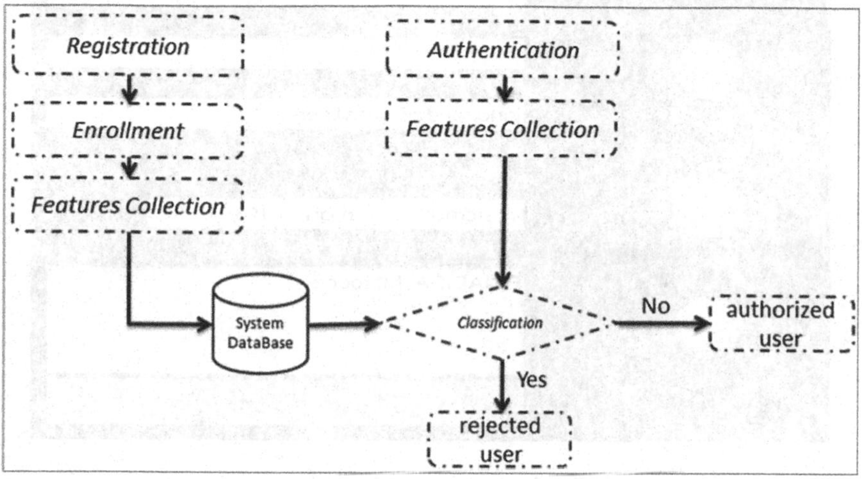

Fig. 2. Keystroke dynamics software's architecture

At every attempt connection to the computer system, the software captures and recalculates the keystroke biometric of a claimed user (authentication phase). This phase involves the use of a classification method; we have used KNN with Manhattan distance, to compare new data against the recorded signature (classification phase). Then, the user will be accepted or rejected based on a predetermined threshold value.

4 Proposed Work

4.1 Registration

The registration process is the first step to accomplish, as shown in Fig. 3, before reaching other phases. The user has to fill some information including his full name, his login and password that will be used to authenticate to the system, his gender, his date of birth, and his full address. The account created will be used in authentication and enrollment phases.

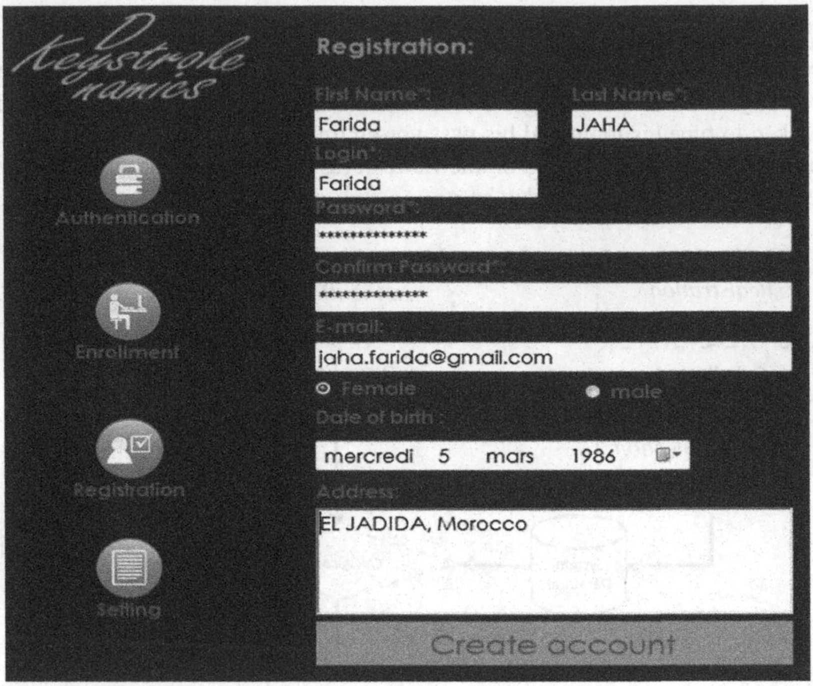

Fig. 3. Authentication windows

Those Data will be stored in the system database for future use.

4.2 Enrollment Phase and Features Collection

The next step is enrollment phase; the user clicks on enrollment button and the features collection began. Most research capture features data for user password only, in our software we propose to record biometric data during all identification and authentication processes in order to increase the extracted features which means more accuracy. The Fig. 2 is a screenshot demonstration of user biometric data; the password tested is "ensajschool".

While the user is typing on keyboard for submitting a sample, factors like dwell time (time interval between consecutive key press and key release), digraph time 1, digraph time 2 and digraph time 3 and While the user is typing the login + password 20 times the reference profile is stored in the respective database tables. The stored profile will be noted "fg" for genuine user.

In our example, we have chosen 20 as the number of enrollment attempts. The system administrator can increase or decrease the value in setting section.

Figure 4 shows different graphs for dwell time and digraph times, we record those function for the 17 login + password keys.

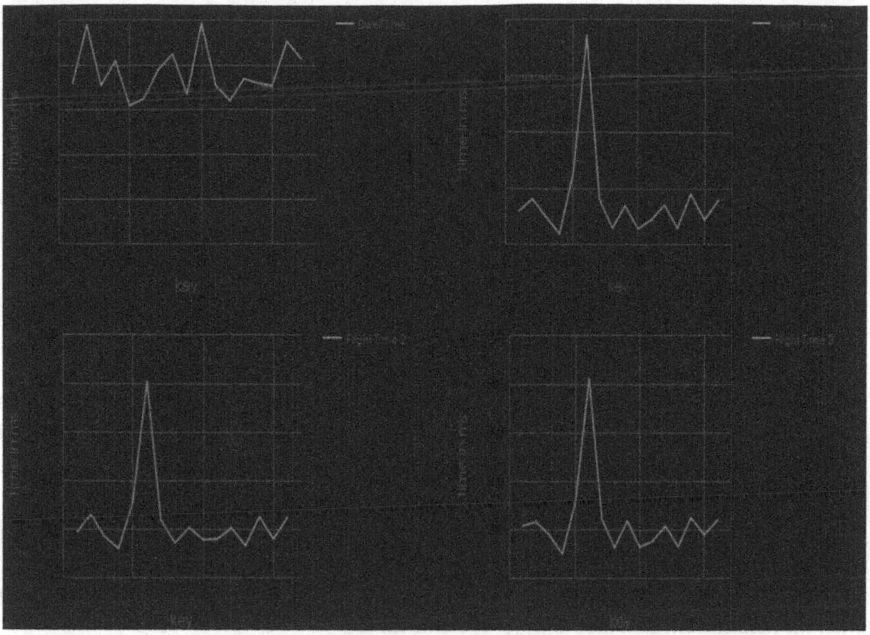

Fig. 4. Dwell time and flight times of user

4.3 Authentication

Each access to the system requires an authentication from the user, he must provide his login and password as the user is typing we record and calculate his new biometric data $f_i^d, f_i^{L1}, f_i^{L2}$ and f_i^{L3}.

Those functions present the user's temporary profile that will be noted "fc" for claimed user.

4.4 Classification

Classification phase is the most important step, it answers the following question: the claimed user is he the original user or an impostor? To answer this question, we have equipped the software by two classification methods: K-NN and K-FN based on Manhattan distance.

To decide if the user will be allowed or rejected we have to:

(1) Calculate de Manhattan distance, based on the Eq. (1) between $f_i^d, f_i^{L1}, f_i^{L2}$ and f_i^{L3} of the temporary profile and each $f_{ij}^{d}, f_{ij}^{L1}, f_{ij}^{L2}$ and f_{ji}^{L3} captured during enrollment phase according to the Eq. (2).

$$\sum_{i=1}^{k} |x_i - y_i| \quad (1)$$

$$D_i = \begin{cases} \sum_{j=1}^{k} \left| fg_{ij}^{d} - fc_i^{d} \right| \\ \sum_{j=1}^{k-1} \left| fg_{ij}^{\partial} - fc_i^{\partial} \right| \end{cases} \quad (2)$$

With:

$$\partial \in \{11, 12, 13\}$$

$k = 1, \ldots, K$: Number of pressed keys.
$i = 1, \ldots, n$: Number of enrollment attempts.

(2) We have to choose the 1-NN (One-Nearest Neighbor), the K factor in our case is equal to 1, by selecting the one minimum Manhattan distance D_{min}(3) from all D_i, with $i = 1, \ldots, n$, of all feature acquisitions stored in enrollment phase.

$$D_{min} = MIN(D_i(f^{\partial}), \text{with } \partial \in \{d, 11, 12, 13\} \quad (3)$$

(3) We have also to calculate 1-FN (One-Furthest Neighbor) by determining the one maximum Manhattan distance D_{max}(4) from all D_i.

$$D_{max} = MAX(D_i(f^{\partial}), \text{with } \partial \in \{d, 11, 12, 13\} \quad (4)$$

(4) Then we compare D_{max} and D_{min} with thresholds, so if the $D_{max} \leq MAX_{Threshold}$ and $D_{min} \leq MIN_{Threshold}$ the user will be accepted, as shown in Fig. 5, else the user will be rejected, as shown in Fig. 6.

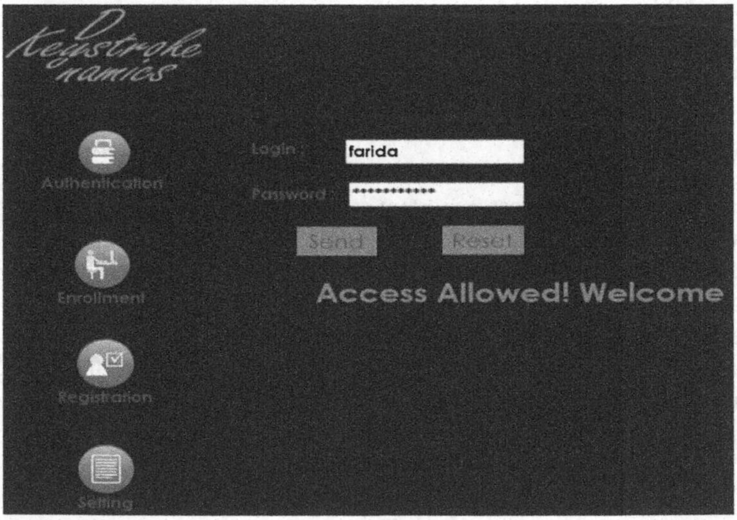

Fig. 5. Allowed access for the genuine user

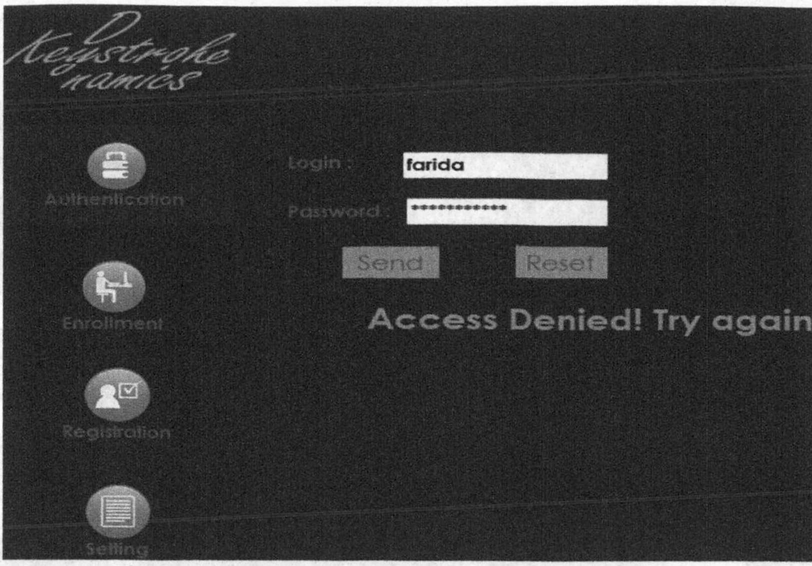

Fig. 6. Denied access for an imposter

The reason to add F-NN to the classification phase is to better identify the genuine user and determine the lower and upper limits not to exceed.

4.5 Setting

We allowed the administrator to change some parameters to improve the result accuracy. These changes are made either to increase the security of access or to allow a tired or sick user whose typing pattern are changing to access his system.

The Fig. 7 shows the four variables that can be modified:

(1) The password length has an important effect to decrease the software's FAR and FRR. The longer the password is, the better we can capture the user features. Thus, longer phrase allowed obtaining much better accuracy.
(2) According to [1] threshold has to be variable. One of the conclusions this team reached is that using individual thresholds could improve the performance of the system. For our implementation, we calculated a threshold for each user using the same algorithm used in authentication phase.
(3) The next parameter is the number of entries used to generate the reference patterns, so a user's template is created. What we said for the password applies for number of enrollment attempts which has to be more than 10 times to capture different state of mind of user (comfortable, tired, etc.).
(4) The last parameter is number of authentication, the user has not an infinite authentication attempts. Administrator can increase or decrease the authentication attempts to give more security for the system against impostor and another attempt

for the genuine user to type his login and password correctly with the same rhythm as stored in the system database.

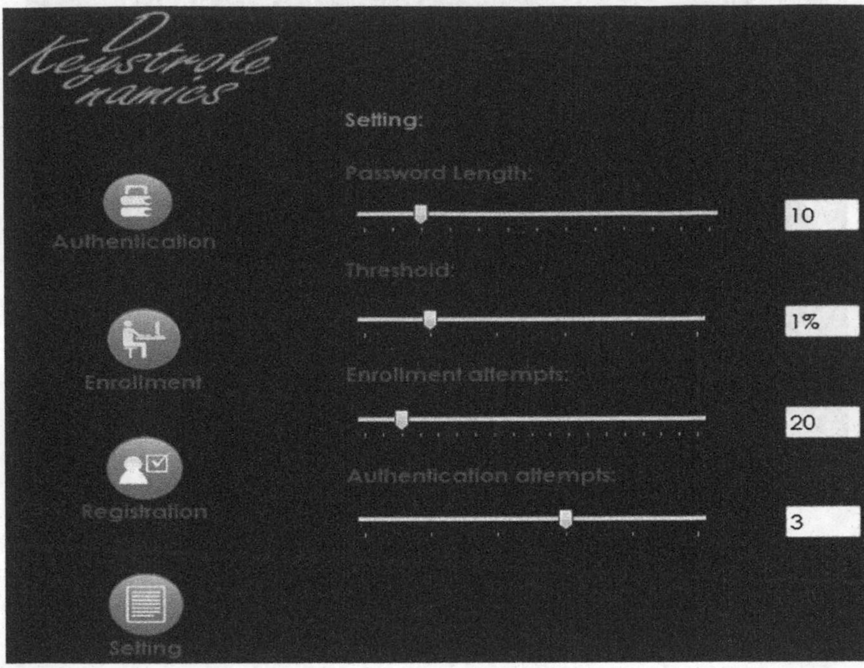

Fig. 7. Setting window

The most powerful part in our software is its flexibility, the administrator can modify different setting values (password length, threshold, enrollment attempts and authentication attempts) to:

(1) Increase software security and eliminate all malicious attempts, by increasing the password length, threshold and enrollment attempts and decreasing the authentication attempts
(2) Decrease the appropriate parameters to allow an employee which has an illness that has had an impact on his keystroke biometric to access the system.

5 Conclusion and Future Work

This paper presented an Improving implementation of keystroke dynamics using KNN, FNN and Manhattan distance. We have discussed keystroke's biometric architecture and phases (registration, enrollment, authentication and classification) and showed the logic followed to transform the pseudo code, which we presented in a previous article [5], to an operational software.

Our next steps are:

(1) We will improve the software by optimizing the code for faster response time, and by adding some other useful features for the user and system administrator.
(2) Since the quality of each biometric system is characterized by: FAR, FRR and EER, we will add another window dedicated to calculate those three rates to examine performance and quality of the software.
(3) In order to conclude which method between K-NN using Manhattan distance and Euclidean distance gives the lower FAR, FRR and EER results, we will use the current code and replace K-NN with Euclidean distance then compare FAR, FRR and EER of the two methods.

References

1. Mhenni, A., Rosenberger, C., Cherrier, E., Amara, N.E.B.: Keystroke template update with adapted thresholds. In: International Proceedings on Advanced Technologies for Signal and Image Processing (ATSIP), Tunisia (2016)
2. Alzubaidi, A., Kalita, J.: Authentication of smartphone users using behavioral biometrics. J. IEEE Commun. Surv. Tutor. **18**, 1998–2026 (2015)
3. Morales, A., Fierrez, J., Tolosana, R., Ortega-Garcia, J., Galbally, J., Gomez-Barrero, M., Anjos, A., Marcel, S.: Keystroke biometrics ongoing competition. IEEE Access **4**, 7736–7746 (2016)
4. Morales, A., Falanga, M., Fierrez, J., Sansone, C., OrtegaGarcia, J.: Keystroke dynamics recognition based on personal data: a comparative experimental evaluation implementing reproducible research. In: 7th International Proceedings on Biometrics: Theory, Applications and Systems, Arlington, USA, pp. 1–6 (2015)
5. Jaha, F., Kartit, A.: Pseudo code of two-factor authentication for BYOD. In: International Proceedings on Electrical and Information Technologies (ICEIT), IEEE Conferences, pp. 1–7, Marocco (2017)
6. Forsen, G., Nelson, M., Staron Jr., R.: Personal attributes authentication techniques. Technical Report RADC-TR-77-333, Rome Air Development Center, October 1977
7. Ho, G.: Tapdynamics: strengthening user authentication on mobile phones with keystroke dynamics. Technical report, Stanford University (2014)
8. Kambourakis, G., Damopoulos, D., Papamartzivanos, D., Pavlidakis, E.: Introducing touchstroke: keystroke-based authentication system for smartphones. Secur. Commun. Netw. **9**, 542–554 (2014)
9. Gascon, H., Uellenbeck, S., Wolf, C., Rieck, K.: Continuous authentication on mobile devices by analysis of typing motion behavior. In: Proceeding GI Conference "Sicherheit", Germany, pp. 1–12 (2014)
10. Babaeizadeh, M., Bakhtiari, M., Aizaini Maarof, M.: Keystroke dynamic authentication in mobile cloud computing. Int. J. Comput. Appl. (0975 – 8887), **90**(1) (2014)
11. Antal, M., Zsolt Szabo, L., Làszlo, I.: Keystroke dynamics on Android platform. Procedia Technol. **19**(2015), 820–826 (2015)
12. Ali, M.L., Monaco, J.V., Tappert, C.C., Qiu, M.: Keystroke biometric systems for user authentication. J. Sig. Process. Syst. **86**(2–3), 175–190 (2017)
13. Kaur, K., Virk, R.S.: Security system based on user authentication using keystroke dynamics. Int. J. Adv. Res. Comput. Commun. Eng. **2**(5), 2111–2117 (2013)

14. Michael, O.B., Missah, Y.M.: Utilizing keystroke dynamics as an additional security measure to password security in computer web-based applications - a case study of UEW. Int. J. Comput. Appl. (0975 – 8887), **149**(5) (2016)
15. Teh, P.S., Zhang, N., Teoh, A.B.J., Chen, K.: A survey on touch dynamics authentication in mobile devices. Comput. Secur. **59**, 210–235 (2016)
16. Panasiuk, P., Dąbrowski, M., Saeed, K., Bocheńska-Włostowska, K.: On the comparison of the keystroke dynamics databases. In: Saeed, K., Snášel, V. (eds.) CISIM 2014. LNCS, vol. 8838, pp. 122–129. Springer, Heidelberg (2014). https://doi.org/10.1007/978-3-662-45237-0_13
17. Patil, R.A., Renke, A.L.: Keystroke dynamics for user authentication and identification by using typing rhythm. Int. J. Comput. Appl. (0975 – 8887), **144**(9) (2016)
18. Vinayak, R., Arora, K.: A survey of user authentication using keystroke dynamics. Int. J. Sci. Res. Eng. Technol. (IJSRET), **4**(4) (2015)
19. Avasthi, S., Sanwal, T.: Biometric authentication techniques: a study on keystroke dynamics. Int. J. Sci. Eng. Appl. Sci. (IJSEAS), **2**(1) (2016)
20. Nagargoje, Y.R., Lomte, S.S., Auti, R.A., Rokade, A.H.: Security using fusion of keystroke and mouse dynamics. Int. J. Sci. Res. Educ. **2**(7), 1185–1194 (2014)
21. Zhong, Y., Deng, Y.: Recent advances in user authentication using keystroke dynamics. In: Science Gate Publishing, vol. 2, pp. 59–70 (2015)
22. Trojahn, M., Ortmeier, F.: Toward mobile authentication with keystroke dynamics on mobile phones and tablets. In: Advanced Information Networking and Applications Workshops (WAINA), pp. 697–702. IEEE (2013)
23. Ali, M.L., Monaco, J., Tappert, C., Qiu, M.: Authentication and identification methods used in keystroke biometric systems. In: IEEE International Symposium on Big Data Security on Cloud (Big Data Security 2015), pp. 1424–1429. IEEE (2015)
24. Trojahn, M., Arndt, F., Ortmeier, F.: Authentication with keystroke dynamics on touchscreen keypads—effect of different N-Graph combinations. In: 3rd International Proceedings on Mobile Services, Resources, and Users, pp. 114–119 (2013)
25. Bondada, M.B., Bhanu, S.: Analyzing user behavior using keystroke dynamics to protect cloud from Malicious insiders. In: International Proceedings on Cloud Computing in Emerging Markets (CCEM), pp. 1–8. IEEE (2014)
26. Xi, K., Tang, Y., Hu, J.: Correlation keystroke verification scheme for user access control in cloud computing environment. Comput. J. **54**(10), 1632–1644 (2011). https://doi.org/10.1093/comjnl/bxr064
27. Giot, R., El-Abed, M., Rosenberger, C.: Web-based benchmark for keystroke dynamics biometric systems: a statistical analysis. In: 8th International Proceedings on Intelligent Information Hiding and Multimedia Signal Processing (IIH-MSP), pp. 11–15. IEEE (2012)
28. Alsultan, A., Warwick, K.: Keystroke dynamics authentication: a survey of free-text methods. Int. J. Comput. Sci. **10**(4), 1–10 (2013)

SARIMA Model of Bioelectic Potential Dataset

Imam Tahyudin[1,2](✉), Berlilana[2], and Hidetaka Nambo[1]

[1] Artificial Intelligence Laboratory, Division of Electrical Engineering and Computer Science, Graduate School of Natural Science and Technology, Kanazawa University, Kakumamachi, Kanazawa, Ishikawa Perfecture, Japan
imam@blitz.ec.t.kanazawa-u.ac.jp
[2] Department of Information System, STMIK AMIKOM Purwokerto, Jl. LetjendPol Soemarto, Purwokerto, Central Java, Indonesia

Abstract. Bioelectric potential of plant produces a low electrical signal because of the plant activities like photosynthesis and respiration. Furthermore, the electrical signal will change because of the environmental factors such as temperature, humidity and human behavior. Some authors successfully used the bioelectric potential of plant for detecting the various human activities, like walking, jumping, open the door, and etc. They used decision tree (DT) J48, multi layer perceptron (MLP) and convolution neural network (CNN) as the analysis method. However, the previous accuracy was no satisfied and estimating the human position globally not specifically an exact location. This research has aim to construct a time series model for bioelectric potential dataset which is SARIMA model and to build infrastructure design of human position estimation in an exact location. For constructing the SARIMA model we use one observation location and obtained the best model is SARIMA (1,0,0) with accuracy of 80%. In addition, this research successfully designed the infrastructure of human position estimation using three locations.

Keywords: SARIMA · Bioelectric potential dataset · Forecasting
Location estimation design

1 Introduction

The study of bioelectric potential of plant already conducted in some approaches. For instance, The study about bioelectric potential by using artificial neural network algorithm. The author successfully detected a distance of person within the plant of bioelectric potential [1]. Then, the study utilized bioelectric potential for determining the position in a room. This study uses several algorithms including decision tree (DT) for the classification and multilayer perceptron (MLP) to determine a position and then make a regression model for the matching process. The results obtained that a person's position can be estimated with an accuracy rate of 60% [2,4]. Another research with the purpose for estimating

Y. Tabii et al. (Eds.): BDCA 2018, CCIS 872, pp. 367–378, 2018.
https://doi.org/10.1007/978-3-319-96292-4_29

human position also conducted using convolution neural network (CNN), deep learning approach [5]. However, the accuracy was not satisfied and the research only estimate people existance near the plants globally. They did not estimate people position in each location specifically. We performed another approach for analyzing bioelectric potential data set using time series method. Because the characteristics of data set are sequential data. Therefore, it is interesting to use time series method, SARIMA model.

Time series is one of the studies in the field of statistics. It is usually expressed in a data interval streak. Time series data are found in a variety of fields such as in the economics field which are the unemployment data, and the cash flow data of hospital; in the financial field which are the daily average of stock exchange, the data distribution of dividends, and etc.; in the environment field which are on daily data of rainfall, air quality readings, the phenomenon El Nino, and etc., then, in the fields of geology which like the river level prediction [6,7].

We have been studied time series for bioelectric potential of data set using some models which were autoregressive (AR), moving average (MA), AR with grid search optimization, and ARMA model. However, the results of average mean square error (MSE) and mean absolute error (MAE) values were still high and the average of forecasting accuracy were around 75% [8–10]. Therefore, the purpose of this research is to improve the accuracy by constructing the SARIMA model for bioelectric potential data set. In addition, that model also is used for building the infrastructure design of bioelectric potential of plant for estimating the human position in specific location.

The remain sections are arranged as follows: Sect. 2 describes about previous research; Sect. 3 explains proposed method; Sect. 4 presents results and discussion; and finally, the conclusion is in Sect. 5.

2 Related Work

Bioelectric potential of plant has been discussed by previous authors by some approaches. For example, for determining the distance using ANN, and for estimating the human position using DT, MLP, and CNN [1–5]. This research presented a new approach using time series method, SARIMA model.

The use of time series for bioelectric potential data set has been conducted using some models which are autoregressive (AR), moving average (MA), AR with grid search optimization, and ARMA model. Their average of forecasting accuracy were around 75% [8–10]. Furthermore, time series has been applicated in some fields. For instance, in 2015 an author discussed about AR modelling. In this study showed various types of AR models such as univariate and multivariate AR models, a radial base function autoregressive model and so on [11]. Another research tried to improve accuracy by combining with another method. This research combined time series algorithms with Particle Swarm Optimization method [12]. Next, the research about PSO base neural network compared with traditional classic models for seasonal time series forecasting. The result performed that the proposed method was better than traditional classic time series model [13]. In addition, the paper "Time series prediction using PSO-optimized neural network and hybrid feature selection algorithm for IEEE load data". This research used two feature selection methods which are Genetic Algorithm and Ant Colony Optimization. And then, to analyze the data using ANN which was optimized by PSO method. The result performed that the proposed method has extremely improved of accuracy by using MAPE (mean absolute percentage error) parameter [14].

The other implementation of time series is the study about the discovery knowledge in time series databases. This study has aim to predict important attributes and extract rules in association analysis [7]. Another author used the moving average technique to predict personal power consumption [15]. And then, The study used MA to predict Playout delay control in VoIP [16]. Next, the study about ARMA(p, q) type which has high order fuzzy time series forecast method based on fuzzy logic relations. This research has purpose to show that the result of the forecast will increase significantly if not utilizing MA variables [17]. More over, the research discussed MA method based on fuzzy resource scheduling (MV-FRS) for virtualized cloud environment to optimize the scheduling of resources through virtual machine [18]. Furthermore, some authors studied about "A hybrid ARIMA and support vector machines model in stock price forecasting". They tried to capture non linear pattern using ARIMA combine with support vector machine. Their research showed the good result [19]. In addition, the combination of ARIMA and GA for forecasting the non linear problem. Their proposed method is better than the previous methods such as ARIMA-ANN, ARIMA-SVM etc. [20].

According to those previous research, time series has robust ability to estimate and to predict some cases in many fields even when it combines with other methods. Therefore, this research is intereseted for solving bioelectric potential of data set that to obtain the best model and to estimate the human position.

3 Proposed Method

3.1 Measurement of Bioelectric Potential

To perform measurements is using a data logger. Specifications data logger used is GRAPHTEC GL400-4 (Fig. 1). It measures the low voltage at an average altitude of sampling (approximately 512 Hz). For the measurement of electrical potential of plants by attaching electrodes on two different leaves then measured the voltage generated between both the leaves. The measurement results are stored on a PC in real time via the local network (Fig. 2).

3.2 Dataset

Data were obtained by using one plant and one observation location in a room of size 3.45 m × 5.75 m (Fig. 3). The process of recording data is conducted by walking around the position point for 30 s. Data obtained is spectrum data. In addition, the observed data is voltage data, so we use this raw data for the analysis.

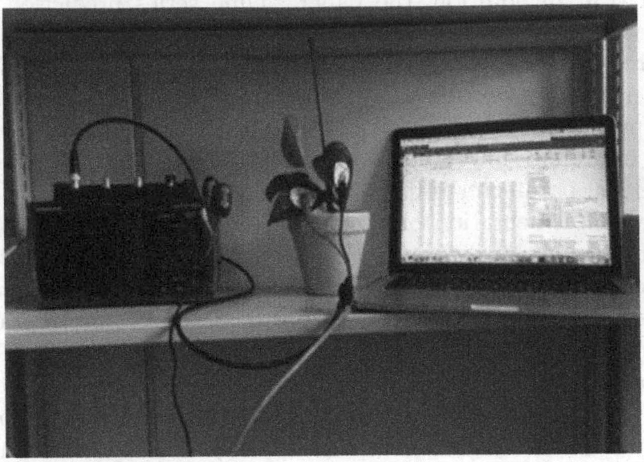

Fig. 1. Measurement process using data logger

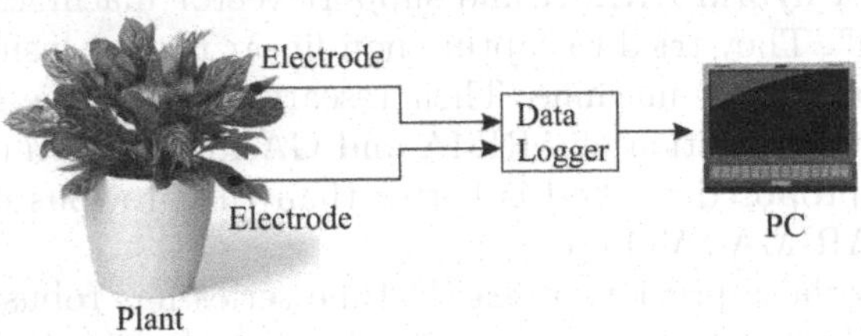

Fig. 2. Bioelectric potential plant

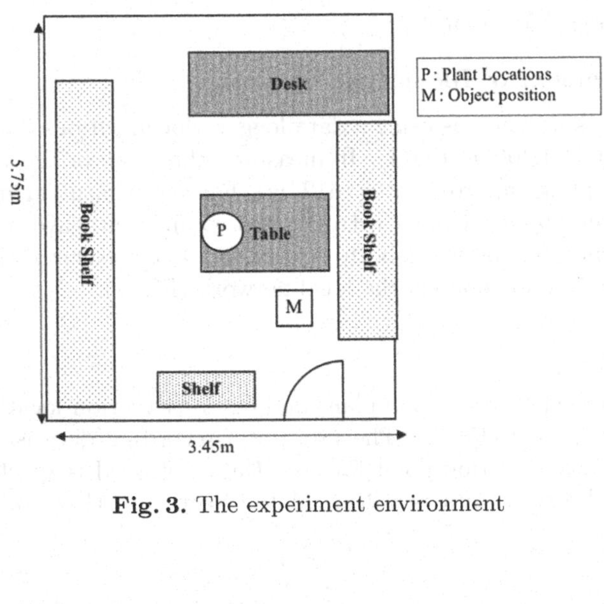

Fig. 3. The experiment environment

3.3 ARIMA Model

ARIMA is a time series model which consist of Autoregressive (AR), Integration (I), and Moving average (MA). Generally there are two kinds of ARIMA model which are ARIMA non seasonal and ARIMA seasonal. This proposed method uses the second ARIMA type. The ARIMA model is written as ARIMA(p,d,q) which p is the number of AR term, d is the number of I, and q is the number of MA term. The general model of ARIMA(p, d, q) is see in Eq. 1 [21].

$$(1 - \phi_1 B .... - \phi_p B^p)(1 - B)^d Y_t = c + (1 + \theta_1 B ..... + \theta_q B^q) e_t \qquad (1)$$

There are three main components, which are the first is AR(p) term,

$$(1 - \phi_1 B .... - \phi_p B^p) \qquad (2)$$

the second is integration for differentiation (d),

$$(1 - B)^d Y_t \qquad (3)$$

and the third is MA(q) term,

$$(1 + \theta_1 B ..... + \theta_q B^q) e_t \qquad (4)$$

In addition, c is a constant value.

3.3.1 Seasonal ARIMA Model

Seasonal ARIMA or SARIMA is a pattern which repeated in an interval time constantly. For stationary data set, seasonal is can be detected from ACF plot. If ACF visualization shows a seasonal pattern then it should to analyze by different solution [22,23].

The general equation of seasonal ARIMA is shown in Eq. 5.

$$ARIMA(p, d, q)(P, D, Q)^S \qquad (5)$$

where (p, d, q) is non seasonal of ARIMA model, (P, D, Q) is seasonal of ARIMA model, and S is the number of period in seasonal model.

For example, if ARIMA (1,0,0) then the model is as Eqs. 6 and 7 below:

$$(1 - \phi_1 B) Y_t = c \qquad (6)$$

where BYt=Y$t - 1$. Therefore,

$$Y_t = c + \phi_1 Y_{t-1} \qquad (7)$$

For detecting the data set is seasonality is by some graphical techniques, such as a run sequence plot, a seasonal subseries plot, multiple box plot, and autocorrelation plot. This research will use autocorrelation plot to detect seasonality. One of the solutions to solve this problem is by using differentiation operator of seasonality [23].

3.3.2 Constructing SARIMA Model

For constructing SARIMA model in this research is explained as below:

1. Visualization process. This step is to make sure the bioelectric potential dataset is stationary series. Stationary dataset can be seen in visual if the mean, variance and covariance graph are constant.
2. For determining the order of ARIMA model is by checking value of auto correlation function (ACF) and partial auto correlation function (PACF) graphs. We decide the appropriate order of AR(p), I(d) and MA(q) based on the visual of ACF and PACF graphs.
3. Choosing the best model by comparing the value of Bayesian information criterion (BIC) and Akaike information criterion (AIC). The best model is obtained if the BIC and AIC values is less than others.
4. Validation process by checking the accuracy of bioelectric potential dataset. This dataset is divided into 30 groups. After that, Finding the best model from each groups. Finally, calculating the accuracy value from all groups.
5. Forecasting process. This step is performed by using testing dataset. This dataset is inserted to the choosen ARIMA model and calculating the value of MAE and MSE. From the graph of testing dataset and model can be seen the precision of the model. The smaller MAE and MSE values then the ARIMA model is more excellent precision.
6. Constructing the infrastructure for estimating the human position using bioelectric potential of plants.

4 Results and Discussion

4.1 Experimental Setup

The data used is bioelectric potential dataset from one plant. Data analysis was performed using a MacBook Pro with specification: 2.7 GHz Intel Core i5, 8 GB 1867 MHz, and DDR3.

4.2 SARIMA Model

For constructing the SARIMA model, the first step is by confirming the dataset visualisation. The bioelectric potential dataset is seen in Fig. 4.

Figure 4 shows that the dataset performs stationary because mean and variance of bielectric potential data set runs constantly. After that, we check the visualization of ACF dan PACF value. Both of figures are presented in Figs. 5 and 6.

According to acf plot we detected that the data set is seasonal because every eight leg has the same pattern. Therefore, we should get rid this seasonality using differentiation. By using R software, we obtain the SARIMA model (1,0,0) from 15.000 instances. It means the order of seasonal AR is 1, integrated and MA orders are zero.

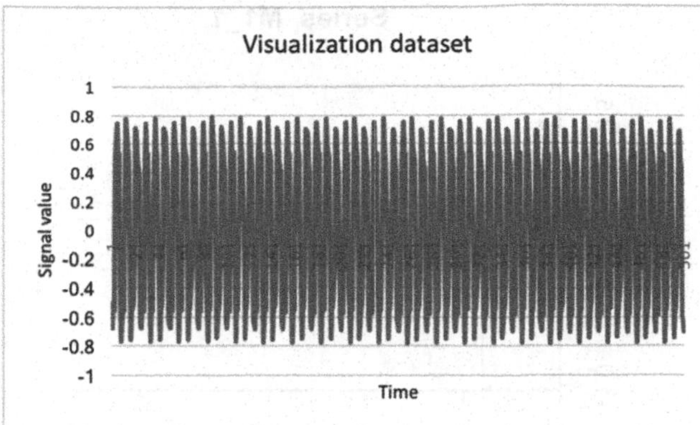

Fig. 4. Bioelectric potential dataset

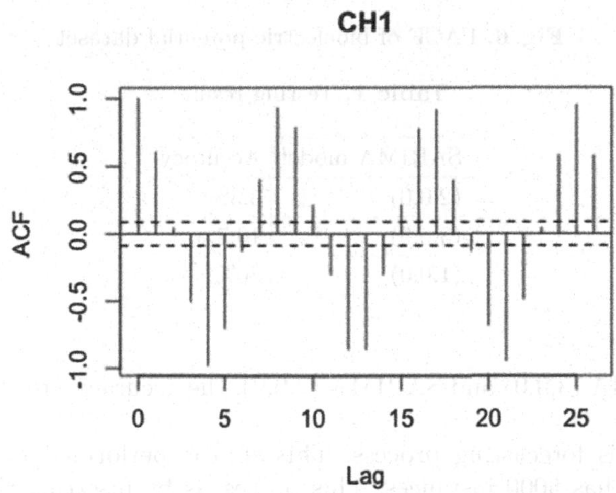

Fig. 5. ACF of bioelectric potential dataset

SARIMA model (1,0,0) is the best model which is obtained by comparing among the other models because the AIC and log likelihood is the less one. In other word, It can be explained clearly that SARIMA (1,0,0) consists p = 1, d = 0 and q = 0. According to the result the coefficient and intercept values are 0.9374 and −0.6997 respectively. Furthermore, the AIC value is −56285.83 and log likelihood value is 28146.92. For make sure that this model is better than others by calculating the accuracy. This is conducted using bioelectric potential dataset which is divided into 30 groups. Each group is 500 instances and we obtained the best SARIMA model from all groups. After that, we calculate the accuracy by calculating the proportion. The result is presented in the Table 1.

This table compare three SARIMA model that SARIMA (1,0,0) is the best model because it has the highest accuracy of 80%. The remain SARIMA

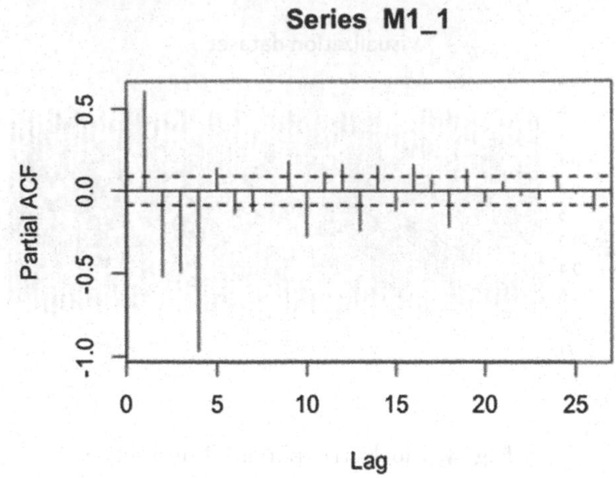

Fig. 6. PACF of bioelectric potential dataset

Table 1. Testing result

SARIMA model	Accuracy
(2,0,0)	3.3%
(3,0,0)	16.7%
(1,0,0)	80%

model, SARIMA (3,0,0) and SARIMA (2,0,0), the accuracy are 16,7% and 3.3% respectively.

The Next is forecasting process. This step is performed by using testing dataset which has 5000 instances. This process is by inserting the data to the SARIMA (1,0,0) model. Afterward, we calculate the forecasting performance using MAE and MSE. Finally, we obtained the MAE and MSE were 0.2089 and 0.0487 respectively. The forecasting result can be seen in Fig. 7.

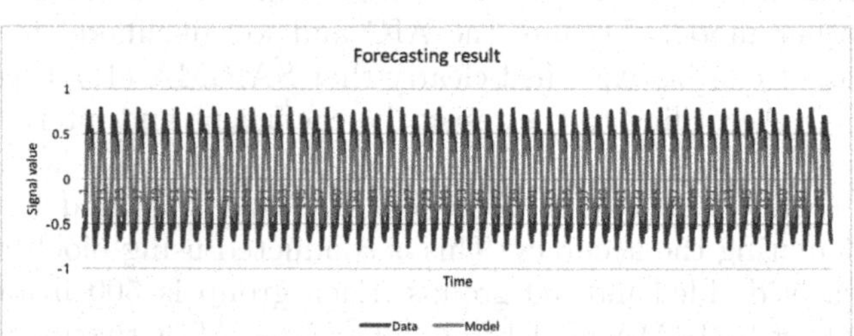

Fig. 7. Forecasting result

Figure 7 described the forecasting result which compared testing data with SARIMA model (forecasting value). The testing data is seen in blue line and forecasting value is the red line. This comparison presents an excellent result of SARIMA (1,0,0) because it has less value of MAE and MSE. Therefore, The SARIMA (1,0,0) model for bioelectric potential dataset performs a promise forecasting result. In addition, the accuracy of SARIMA (1,0,0) is better than previous research [7–9].

4.3 Infrastructure Design of Human Position Estimation

The next study is that the SARIMA model will be used as a new approach for constructing the design infrastructure of human position estimation using bioelectric potential of plant. The infrastructure is shown in Fig. 8.

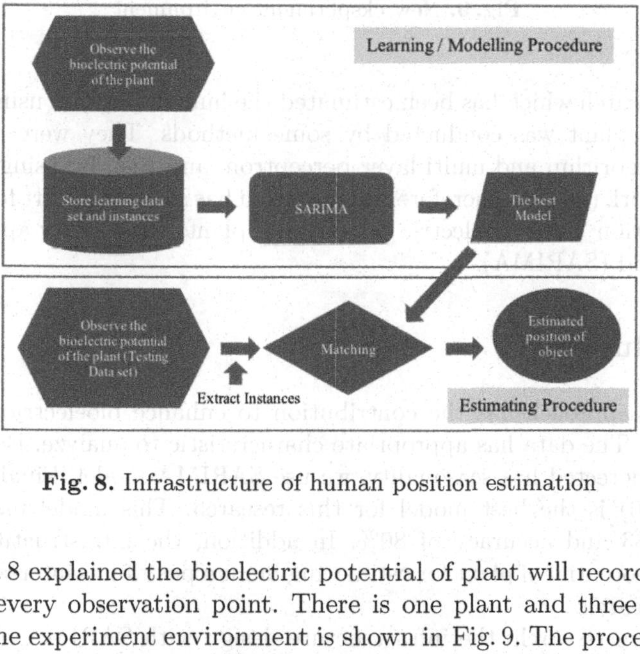

Fig. 8. Infrastructure of human position estimation

This Fig. 8 explained the bioelectric potential of plant will record the human position in every observation point. There is one plant and three observation locations. The experiment environment is shown in Fig. 9. The process recording is the same like explanation in Sect. 3.2. Therefore, there are three data set from three observation locations. The next, building the model for each position using SARIMA and the best model will be used for matching process. We use another data randomly from three data set for testing data and inserted to the SARIMA model for matching process. We determine the exact location of testing data set which has clostest position with training data set.

The differentiation between Figs. 9 and 3 is the number of observation point. In Fig. 9 the are three number of locations. The range one plant can detect a person position is very short, about 1.5 m is the maximum. In this paper, one plants is used. It is enough using three locations for the experiment. If we want to detect more locations, we need to use more plants. In summary, the

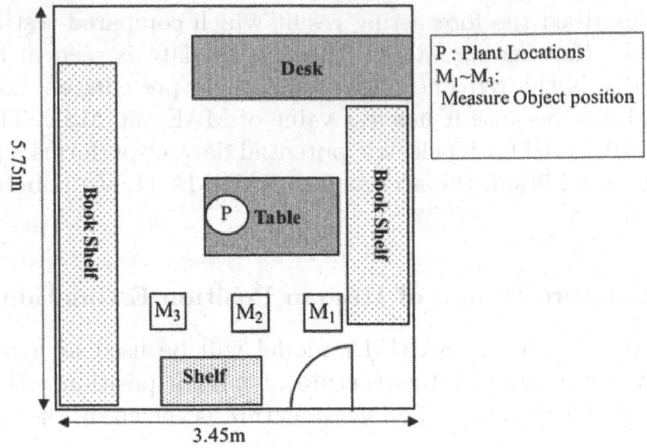

Fig. 9. New eksperiment environment

previous research which has been estimated the human position using bioelectric potential of plant was conducted by some methods. They were decision tree using J48 algorithm and multi layer perceptron, and then by using convolution neural network (CNN). Therefore, this research has state of the art for estimating human position using bioelectric potential of plants with a new approach, time series method (SARIMA).

5 Conclusion

Time series approach has the contribution to enhance bioelectric potential of plant study. The data has appropriate characteristic to analyze. Because of the data set is detected has seasonality, we use SARIMA model. Finally, SARIMA model (1,0,0) is the best model for this research. This model has AIC value of −56285.83 and accuracy of 80%. In addition, the infrastructure design of bioelectric potential of plant for estimating human position is interested to follow for next research.

For future research, the infrastructure design with SARIMA model will be used for determining human position. And then, it is also interested to compare with deep learning method (long short term memory (LSTM) algorithm). Furthermore, for improving the accuracy both of SARIMA and LSTM method will be combined in order to solve either linear or non linear data set.

Acknowledgements. This research supported by various parties. We would like to thank for scholarship program from Kanazawa University, Japan and Ministry of Research and Technology and Directorate of Higher Education (RISTEKDIKTI) and also STMIK AMIKOM Purwokerto, Indonesia. In addition, we thank for anonymous reviewers who gave input and correction for improving this research.

References

1. Jin, X.: Recognition of the distance between plant and human by plant bioelectric potential. In: APIEMS, pp. 602–606 (2014)
2. Nambo, H., Kimura, H.: Development of the estimation method of resident's location using bioelectric potential of living plants and knowledge of indoor space. In: Xu, J., Hajiyev, A., Nickel, S., Gen, M. (eds.) Proceedings of the Tenth International Conference on Management Science and Engineering Management. AISC, vol. 502, pp. 431–444. Springer, Singapore (2017). https://doi.org/10.1007/978-981-10-1837-4_37
3. Nambo, H.: A study on the estimation method of the resident's location using the plant bioelectric potential. In: APIEMS, pp. 1896–1900 (2015)
4. Nambo, H., Kimura, H.: Estimation of resident's location in indoor environment using bioelectric potential of living plants. Sens. Mater. **28**(4), 369–378 (2016)
5. Nambo, H.: Development of a human sensor using living plant and bioelectric potential. In: APIEMS, pp. 19–22 (2017)
6. Borkowf, C.B.: Time-series forecasting. Technometrics **44**(2), 194–195 (2002). Chateld, C.: Time-Series Forecasting. Chapman and Hall/CRC, Boca Raton (2001). ISBN 1-58488-063-5, xi 267 p. $69.95
7. Schluter, T.: Knowledge discovery from time series, April 2012
8. Tahyudin, I., Nambo, H.: An optimized time series model of bioelectric potential dataset. In: APIEMS, pp. 1–5 (2017a)
9. Tahyudin, I., Nambo, H.: Estimating position of bio electric potential dataset as a natural sensor using time series approach. In: IJCAI Workshop (2016)
10. Tahyudin, I., Nambo, H.: Comparison study of time series model on bioelectric potential data set. In: SOPEJ, pp 1–5 (2017b)
11. Ohtsu, K., Peng, H., Kitagawa, G.: Time Series Modeling for Analysis and Control (2015)
12. Abdurrahman, A.: An algotithm for time series prediction using particle swarm optimization (PSO). Int. J. Sci. Knowl. **4**(6), 26–33 (2014)
13. Adhikari, R., Agrawal, R.K., Kant, L.: PSO based Neural Networks vs. traditional statistical models for seasonal time series forecasting. In: 2013 3rd IEEE International Advance Computing Conference, pp. 719–725 (2013)
14. Sheikhan, M., Mohammadi, N.: Time series prediction using PSO-optimized neural network and hybrid feature selection algorithm for IEEE load data. Neural Comput. Appl. **23**(3–4), 1185–1194 (2013)
15. Kim, J., Kang, S., Kim, H.-M.: Prediction of personal power consumption using the moving average technique. In: Kim, T., Stoica, A., Chang, R.-S. (eds.) SUComS 2010. CCIS, vol. 78, pp. 230–234. Springer, Heidelberg (2010). https://doi.org/10.1007/978-3-642-16444-6_29
16. Ramos, V.M.R., Barakat, C., Altman, E.: A moving average predictor for playout delay control in VoIP. In: Jeffay, K., Stoica, I., Wehrle, K. (eds.) IWQoS 2003. LNCS, vol. 2707, pp. 155–173. Springer, Heidelberg (2003). https://doi.org/10.1007/3-540-44884-5_9
17. Kocak, C.: ARMA (p, q) type high order fuzzy time series forecast method based on fuzzy logic relations. Appl. Soft Comput. **58**, 92–103 (2017)
18. Priya, V., Babu, C.N.K.: Moving average fuzzy resource scheduling for virtualized cloud data services. Comput. Stand. Interf. **50**, 251–257 (2017)
19. Pai, P.F., Lin, C.S.: A hybrid ARIMA and support vector machines model in stock price forecasting. Omega **33**(6), 497–505 (2005)

20. Lee, Y.S., Tong, L.I.: Forecasting time series using a methodology based on autoregressive integrated moving average and genetic programming. Knowl.-Based Syst. **24**(1), 66–72 (2011)
21. Hamilton, J.: Time Series Analysis. Princeton University Press, Princeton (1994)
22. NIST/SEMATECH: Seasonality (2012). http://www.itl.nist.gov/div898/handbook/pmc/section4/pmc443.htm. Accessed 23 Feb 2018
23. Srivastava, T.: A Complete Tutorial on Time Series Modeling in R (2015). https://www.analyticsvidhya.com/blog/2015/12/complete-tutorial-time-series-modeling/. Accessed 23 Feb 2018

New Starting Point of the Continuous Hopfield Network

Khalid Haddouch(✉) and Karim El Moutaouakil

Artificial Intelligence, Complex Systems and Modeling Team,
National School of Applied Sciences of Al Hoceïma,
University Mohammed First, Oujda, Morocco
haddouchk@yahoo.fr, yassirkarimimane@gmail.com

Abstract. In recent years, the continuous Hopfield network has become the most required tool to solve quadratic problems (QP). But, it suffers from some drawbacks, such as, the initial states. This later affect the convergence to the optimal solution and if a bad starting point is arbitrarily specified, the infeasible solution is generated. In this paper, we examine this issue and try to provide a new technique to choose a good starting point in order to give a good optimal solution for any quadratic problems (QP). Numerical simulations are provided to demonstrate the performance of this new technique applied to task assignment problems.

Keywords: Quadratic 0-1 programming · Continuous Hopfield network
Energy function · Starting point · Task assignment problems

1 Introduction

In the beginning of the 1980s, Hopfield published two scientific papers, which attracted a lot of interest. These papers are considered as the starting point of the new neural networks area, which continues today. It has been extensively studied, developed and has found many applications in many areas. This type of neural networks is characterized by the output functions. Based on these later, HNNs can be classified into two popular forms: discrete and continuous models. In general, the continuous HNN has dominated the solving techniques for optimization problems that are popular in various areas. It is a major artificial neural network for solving optimization problems [3].

In order to use CHN for optimization, Hopfield and Tank presented the energy function approach as dynamic system. This function is the key for using the continuous Hopfield networks (CHN) in order to dress a large class of the constraints optimization problems. In this regard, the optimization problem must be mapped onto a CHN in such a way that an energy function is associated with this resolved problem. In this context, three common methods, penalty functions, Lagrange multipliers, and primal and dual methods to construct an energy function are studied in the literature [6]. Recently, A new energy function is proposed so that any 0-1 linear constrains programming with quadratic objective function can be solved [5]. This problem, denoted as the generalized quadratic knapsack problem (GQKP) [5].

Y. Tabii et al. (Eds.): BDCA 2018, CCIS 872, pp. 379–389, 2018.
https://doi.org/10.1007/978-3-319-96292-4_30

Nevertheless, the CHN suffers from some drawbacks and difficulties in optimization phases [7]. Based on our expertise in this field, theses major drawbacks are caused by several points such as the starting point of CHN. This later influences the convergence of the system towards a stability point which guarantees a good solution to the treated problem. In this context, they have two cases: a bad starting points leads to an unfeasible solution and a good one gives a good solution which correspond to optimal value. So, the question that arises, how to choose a good starting point that guarantee good convergence?. So, our objective is to study, theoretically and practically, the influence of starting point on the convergence to the optimal solution and to conduct an analytical and comparative study for this one.

This paper is organized as follows: In Sect. 2, an introduction of CHN for optimization is presented. In the last section, we propose a new techniques for specify a good starting point. Finally, the implementation details of the analytical and comparative study for a different way to specify the starting point are presented in the last section.

2 Continuous Hopfield Networks for Constrained Optimization Problems

Hopfield and Tank proposed a neural network named as Hopfield network to solve a wide variety of combinatorial problems. This neural model is inspired by physical systems like Ising's magnetic model. This formalism comes from statistical physics describing a magnetic system with two-state units called spins [3, 6]. This network allows accept an exact and complete theoretical analysis. It has also contributed to develop research on neural networks. Recall that, the most important contribution in this case is the introduction of the energy function notion based on magnetic systems. This energy function is usually used to solve several optimization problems [3]. Their results encouraged a number of researchers to apply this network for solving different problems [5, 6].

The Hopfield network is a fully interconnected system of n neurons [3, 6]. The output of each neuron is looped back to the inputs of the others. The connection between two neurons i and j is determined by the weight W_{ij}, which can be a positive or a negative depending on the state of the array (excitatory or inhibitory). The input state of each neuron u_i is equivalent to the weighted sum of the output states of all other neurons. The output of the neuron is given by x_i, with $0 \leq x_i \leq 1$. An external input I_i to each neuron is also introduced. The relationship between u_i and x_i is determined by an activation function $g_i(u_i)$. Generally, this activation function is given by []:

$$x_i = g(u_i) = \frac{1}{2}(1 + \tanh(\frac{u_i}{u_0})) \quad u_0 > 0$$

It is a hyperbolic tangent, where u_0 is a parameter used to control the gain (or slope) of the activation function.

Hopfield used electrical circuits to simulate the actions of biological neurons. So, the basic electronic model can be implemented by interconnecting a set of resistors, non-linear amplifiers with symmetrical output, and the bias of an external current. Then, the dynamic of the CHN is described by the differential equation [5]:

$$\frac{du}{dt} = -\frac{u}{\tau} + Wx + i^b$$

With τ is the constant time value for the amplifiers. For the continuous Hopfield network, a Lyapunov function can be constructed for the system, which guarantees convergence to stable states. Consider the energy function:

$$E(x) = -\frac{1}{2}x^T Wx - (i^b)^T x + \frac{1}{\tau}\sum_{i=1}^{n}\int_0^{x_i} g^{-1}(z)dz$$

The proof of stability of such continuous Hopfield networks relies upon the fact that $E(x)$ is a Lyapunov function, provided that the inverse function of $g'(u)$ (the first derivative of the activation function), exists. The existence of this equilibrium points for the CHN is guaranteed if a Lyapunov function exists, where the function $g^{-1}(z)$ is a monotone increasing function. The idea is that the networks Lyapunov function, when $\tau \rightarrow \infty$, is associated with the cost function to be minimized in the combinatorial problem. In this way, the CHN output can be used to represent a solution of the combinatorial problem. Then, for solving any combinatorial problem via the continuous Hopfield networks, we will write this problem in the following form:

$$E(x) = -\frac{1}{2}x^T Wx - (i^b)^T x$$

Using the proposed CHN, the energy function is equivalent to the objective function of the optimization problem which must be minimized, while the constraints of the problem are included in the function under the control of the penalty terms. Next, many researchers have developed the CHN to solve optimization problems, especially problems with mathematical programming. In general, the type of mathematical programming problem handled by continuous Hopfield networks is defined by [5]:

$$(GQKP)\quad \begin{cases} Min & \frac{1}{2}\sum_{i=1}^{n}\sum_{j=1}^{n} q_{ij}x_i x_j + \sum_{i=1}^{n} q_i x_i \\ s.c & \\ & \sum_{i=1}^{n} a_{k,i}x_i \leq b_k \quad k = 1,\ldots,m_1 \\ & \sum_{i=1}^{n} a_{k,i}x_i = b_k \quad k = m_1+1,\ldots,m \\ & x_i \in \{0,1\} \qquad i = 1,\ldots n \end{cases}$$

At first, the resolution of this quadratic program (GQKP) via continuous Hopfield networks (CHN) requires the transformation of the set of linear inequality constraints to a set of linear equality constraints, using the slack variables $x_{n+1},\ldots,x_{n+m_1}$, belonging to the interval [0,1]. These variables are included in the previous model with the coefficients $a_{1,n+1}, \ldots, a_{m_1,n+m_1}$ defined by:

$$a_{k,n+k} = b_k - \sum_{j:a_{k,j}<0}^{n} a_{k,j} \qquad \forall\, k \in \{1, \ldots, m_1\}$$

Then, this problem can be written in the following form:

$$(GQKP) \quad \begin{cases} Min & \frac{1}{2}\sum_{i=1}^{n}\sum_{j=1}^{n} q_{ij}x_ix_j + \sum_{i=1}^{n} q_ix_i \\ s.c & \\ & e_k(x) = \sum_{i=1}^{n} a_{k,i}x_i + a_{k,n+k}x_{n+k} = b_k \quad k = 1, \ldots, m_1 \\ & e_k(x) = \sum_{i=1}^{n} a_{k,i}x_i = b_k \quad k = m_1+1, \ldots, m \\ & x_i \in \{0,1\} \quad i = 1, \ldots n \\ & x_{k+n} \in [0,1] \quad k = 1, \ldots m_1 \end{cases}$$

Without loss of generality, we consider the following quadratic program with linear constraints according to [5]:

$$(GQKP) \quad \begin{cases} Min & f(x) = \frac{1}{2}x^TQx + q^Tx \\ s.c & \\ & Ax = b \\ & x_i \in \{0,1\} \quad i = 1, \ldots n \\ & x_{k+n} \in [0,1] \quad k = 1, \ldots m_1 \end{cases}$$

Typically, the generalized energy function allows representing mathematical programming problems with quadratic objective function and linear constraints. This energy function includes the objective function $f(x)$ and it penalizes the linear constraints $Ax = b$ with a quadratic terms and a linear terms. Then, the generalized energy function must also be defined by [5]:

$$E(x) = E^O(x) + E^C(x) \qquad \forall\, x \in [0,1]^n$$

Where:

- $E^O(x)$ is directly associated with the objective function of the QP problem,
- $E^C(x)$ is a quadratic function that penalizes the violated constraints of the QP problem.

There are many different way to map the QP problem into energy function of CHN [6]. In this paper, we use the following generalized energy function proposed in [5]:

$$E(x) = \frac{\alpha}{2}x^T Qx + \frac{1}{2}(Ax)^T \Phi(Ax) + x^T diag(\gamma)(1-x) + \beta^T Ax$$

Where $\alpha \in R^+$, $\beta \in R^N$, $\gamma \in R^n$, Φ is an $N \times N$ symmetric matrix and $diag(\gamma)$ denotes the diagonal matrix constructed from the vector γ.

In order to ensure the feasibility of the equilibrium point associated with the stability of the continuous Hopfield, a parameter adjustment procedure called hyperplane procedure is proposed [5]. The objective of this procedure is to determine the control parameters in order to ensure the feasibility of the solution. Finally, we use the Newton algorithm or the algorithm proposed in [5] to compute an equilibrium point of the constructed *CHN* model, so generate the solution of the QP problem.

3 New Starting Point of CHN

According to our studies, the application of continuous Hopfield networks to solve quadratic programming problems has gaps that need to be improved to effectively solve large problems. These shortcomings can be summarized in four questions then the important is: How do you choose the initial state (starting point)?. Then, our objective is to get, theoretically and experimentally, a good answer to this question.

In the natural case, the starting point is chosen inside the hamming hypercube. Or, this choice influences the convergence towards optimal solutions. In this case, some of research suggest that the initial state should be chosen in a region where the final solution can be reserved without dissipating it. On the other hand, others propose that the starting point can be generated as a feasible solution. Stressed that the initial state must be close to the optimal solution [6]. However, according to our experimental studies, an estimation of a starting point approximately to the solution can help CHN to get an optimal solution. In this context, we can study the nature of resolved problems in order to get a good indication and chosen a good starting points. In this context, we have realised a series of experimentals study to clarify the importance of starting point and define a new technique based on the problem properties. In order to demonstrate the importance of starting point selection, we tried an example.

Example 1. Let us give the following problem [5]

$$\min\{v_1^2 + 4v_1v_2 + 3v_2^2 - 2v_2v_3 + v_1 - v_3\}$$

$$s.t\begin{Bmatrix} v_1 - v_2 \le 0 \\ v_2 + v_3 = 1 \end{Bmatrix}$$

There is one slack variable v_4, which is introduced with the factor:

$$r_{1,4} = b - (r_{1,2}) = 0 - (-1) = 1$$

In this way, this instance is characterized by the parameter values

$$Q=\begin{pmatrix}1 & 2 & 0 & 0\\ 2 & 3 & -1 & 0\\ 0 & -1 & 0 & 0\\ 0 & 0 & 0 & 0\end{pmatrix}\quad q=\begin{pmatrix}1\\ 0\\ -1\\ 0\end{pmatrix}\quad R=\begin{pmatrix}1 & -1 & 0 & 1\\ 0 & 1 & 1 & 0\end{pmatrix}\quad b=(0\ \ 1)$$

In order to optimize this problem with CHN, we have three ways to chose a starting point:

- The first one, the starting point can be chosen inside the hamming hypercube. Then, we can generate randomly starting point in the interval [0, 1].
- The second one, the starting point can be generated as a feasible solotion. Then, an example of starting point is (0,1,0,1).
- Finally, the thread way to chose the starting is proposed in [5]. This manner consist to favorite each decision variable to take 1 than others basing on problem characteristics.

$$v_i = 0.8 + 0.19\frac{(N+1-k)}{N} + 10^{-10}U$$

Where u is a random uniform variable in the interval [−0.5, 0.5] and N is the number of problem variables.

However, an estimation of a starting point approximately to the solution can help CHN to get an optimal solution. In this context, we can study the nature of resolved problems in order to get a good indication and chosen a good starting points. In this regard, all informations of problem, mathematically, are represented in matrices Q, R and vectors q, b. The important idea in this paper, is to based on this parameter values for chose the good starting point that garant the feasible and optimal value.

Then, based on these matrices and vectors we can define a technique allowing the estimation of a good starting point. In this framework, if we have summed rows of the matrix P and the vector q, we can notice that there is an order between the coefficients of the variables. Then this order can be used as an indicator to favor certain variables taking *1* opposite to others. Take example 1, the sum of the i-th row of the matrix P and the i-th element of the vector q gives the following results:

- 1st line gives 3
- 2nd line gives 4
- 3eme ligne donne -2
- 4 eme ligne donne 0

You can notice that the third variable takes the smallest value. So, we can favorite the third variable to take *1* which will allow us to have an optimal value of the problem. This reflects the real case because the optimal solution for this example is the following: (0,0,1,0). To do this, we have based on the formula proposed in paper [10] while favoring the variables which have the summation of the smallest coefficients. This way of choosing the starting point gives a better chance of finding the optimal solution.

$$v_i = 0.1 + \frac{\left(1 - \sum_{i=1}^{n} P_{ij} + q_i\right)}{\sum_{i,j=1}^{n} P_{ij} + \sum_{i=1}^{n} q_i} 10^{-1} U$$

Where U is a random uniform variable in the interval $[-0.5, 0.5]$. In this context, we have realised a series of experimentals study to clarify the importance of starting point. Finally, we can define a new technique based on the problem properties.

4 Experimental Result: Task Assignment Problem

The task assignment problem play a vital role in a computation system with a number of distributed processors, where a set of tasks must be assigned to a set of processors minimizing the sum of execution costs and communication costs between tasks [1].

The task assignment problem with non uniform communication costs consists in finding an assignment of N tasks to M processors such that the total execution and communication costs is minimized. This problem is stated as a two sets and two parameters where: $T = \{T_1, \ldots, T_N\}$ a set of N tasks, $P = \{P_1, \ldots, P_M\}$ a set of M processors, The execution cost e_{ik} of task i if is assigned to processor k and the communication cost c_{ikjl} between two different tasks i and j if they are respectively assigned to processors k and l. This problem with non-uniform communication costs can be modeled as 0-1 quadratic programming which consists in minimizing a quadratic function subject to linear constraints (QP) [1, 2].

$$(QP) \begin{cases} Min & f(x) = \frac{1}{2} x^t Q x + e^t x \\ Subject\ to & \\ & Ax = b \\ & x \in \{0,1\}^n \end{cases}$$

In order to solve the task assignment problem using the continuous Hopfield networks, we define the generalized energy function for the TAP problems basing on the model. This generalized energy function includes the objective function $f(x)$ and it penalizes the linear constraints $Ax = b$ with a quadratic term and a linear term. The generalized energy function for the QP problem is defined by [2]:

$$E(x) = \frac{\alpha}{2} \sum_{i=1}^{N} \sum_{k=1}^{M} \sum_{j=1}^{N} \sum_{l=1}^{M} c_{ijkl} x_{ik} x_{jl} + \alpha \sum_{i=1}^{N} \sum_{k=1}^{M} e_{ik} x_{ik} + \frac{1}{2} \varphi \sum_{i=1}^{N} \sum_{k=1}^{M} \sum_{l=1}^{M} x_{ik} x_{il}$$
$$+ \beta \sum_{i=1}^{N} \sum_{k=1}^{M} x_{ik} + \gamma \sum_{i=1}^{N} \sum_{k=1}^{M} x_{ik}(1 - x_{ik})$$

In this way, the quadratic programming has been presented as an energy function of continuous Hopfield network.

To solve an instance of the QP problem, the parameter setting procedure is used. This procedure, based on the partial derivatives of the generalized energy function, assigns the particular values for all parameters of the network, so that any equilibrium points are associated with a valid affectation of all variables when all constraints are satisfied [2]:

$$\frac{\partial E(x)}{\partial x_{ik}} = E_{ik}(x) = \alpha \sum_{j=1}^{N} \sum_{l=1}^{M} c_{ikjl} x_{jl} + \alpha e_{ik} + \varphi \sum_{l=1}^{M} x_{il} + \beta + \gamma(1 - 2x_{ik})$$

This procedure uses the hyperplane method, so that the Hamming hypercube H is divided by a hyperplane containing all feasible solutions. Consequently, we can determine the parameters setting by resolving the following system [2, 5]:

$$\begin{cases} \alpha > 0 \\ \phi \geq 0 \\ -\phi + 2\gamma \geq 0 \\ \alpha d_{\min} + 2\varphi + \beta - \gamma = \varepsilon \\ \alpha d_{\max} + \beta + \gamma = -\varepsilon \end{cases}$$

Where $d_{\min} = M(N-1)C_{\min} + e_{\min}$ and $d_{\max} = M(N-1)C_{max} + e_{max}$ with $C_{min} = Min\{\, c_{ikjl} \,/\, (i,j) \in \{1,\ldots,N\}^2 \text{ and } (k,l) \in \{1,\ldots,M\}^2 \,\}$
$e_{min} = Min\{\, e_{ik} \,/\, i \in \{1,\ldots,N\} \text{ and } k \in \{1,\ldots,M\} \,\}$
$C_{max} = Max\{\, c_{ikjl} \,/\, (i,j) \in \{1,\ldots,N\}^2 \text{ and } (k,l) \in \{1,\ldots,M\}^2 \,\}$
$e_{max} = Max\{\, e_{ik} \,/\, i \in \{1,\ldots,N\} \text{ and } k \in \{1,\ldots,M\} \,\}$

Finally, we obtain an equilibrium point for the CHN using the algorithm described in [4], so compute the solution of task assignment problem.

A demonstrative table corresponds to the resolution of 20 TAP type problems in a 10,000 experiment run with $\alpha = 1/2$ and $\varepsilon = 10^{-3}$ is represented in Table 1. In order to understand and compare different techniques used for choosing a starting point, we have drawn up a suitable experience plan. This plan can be divided into two levels contains very specific measures. These measures are considered as performance indicators. For the first level, we proposed the following measures (see Table 1):

- The first measure is the number of times that the CHN didn't violate the constraints of the problem.
- the second measure is whether CHN found the optimal solution or not? This last measure is completed by two other measures: mode and average.
- Finally, to compare the speed of each used techniques, we compute the number of iterations and the execution time.

For the second level, we have opted for following measures (see Table 2):

- The first corresponds to the average of measures mentioned in the first level.
- The second is the number of times that CHN generate the optimal solution.

Table 1. First level of experiment plan

Instances name	Benchmarks optimal value	PSP					
		NSR	OV	Mean	Mode	Sum iteration	Sum time
tassnu_10_3_1	−719	8134	−719	−504,74	−659	764083	3561
tassnu_10_3_2	−790	8425	−790	−490,00	−611	780301	3356
tassnu_10_3_3	−624	7867	−614	−332,70	−362	714981	3170
tassnu_10_3_4	−734	8186	−619	−454,56	−603	751908	3329
tassnu_10_3_5	−871	7743	−801	−571,09	−775	751835	3342
tassnu_10_3_6	−677	8908	−677	−336,84	−376	862569	3735
tassnu_10_3_7	−613	8651	−613	−398,18	−481	821542	3578
tassnu_10_3_8	−495	9963	−479	−171,72	−287	974442	4173
tassnu_10_3_9	−750	8446	−730	−495,62	−669	727686	3187
tassnu_10_3_10	−486	8616	−452	−174,16	−161	805300	3502
tassnu_15_5_1	−1985	9181	−1783	−943,64	−1323	866612	17596
tassnu_15_5_2	−1568	9579	−1389	−728,83	−911	971735	19374
tassnu_15_5_3	−1892	9427	−1565	−1000,79	−1194	909723	18366
tassnu_15_5_4	−1806	9513	−1539	−767,23	−819	928863	18531
tassnu_15_5_5	−1881	9416	−1796	−1177,47	−1382	922772	18346
tassnu_15_5_6	−1950	9515	−1822	−1055,78	−1225	943855	18999
tassnu_15_5_7	−1893	9432	−1817	−1040,90	−1186	958541	18660
tassnu_15_5_8	−1733	9463	−1698	−766,04	−883	921775	17984
tassnu_15_5_9	−1798	9387	−1512	−761,70	−927	949422	18675
tassnu_15_5_10	−1763	9508	−1481	−850,44	−891	936690	18502

Table 2. Second level of experiment plan

Starting point type		PSP	0-1	PSP [10]	Feasible
Mean	NSR	8838	8779	8316	9956
	Best optimal value	−1043,60	−922,25	−954,85	−1177,30
	Mean optimal value	−339,00	6,00	−783,00	−659,00
	Mode	−405,30	15,45	−782,10	−683,35
	Sum time	722726	463929	716434	980319
	Sum iteration	8010	5029	7708	10912
NTBOV		6	4	0	2

Legend of table

- NTBOV: Number of Time that CHN give an Optimal Value specified in benchmarks
- NSR: Number of Successful Resolution
- PSP: Proposed starting point.

Concerning the NSR, the results presented in the first graph show that the feaseble type is the best, which is normal because the starting point is only a feasible solution. So, the average of all solutions will be the best. Subsequently, the PSP type is ranked second which shows the performance of this type. This performance is validated in the second graph because PSP gives good results compared to others. This type help the CHN to generate 6 times the optimal solution known in the literature. Or, type 0-1 is ranked second with 4 times (Figs. 1, 2 and 3).

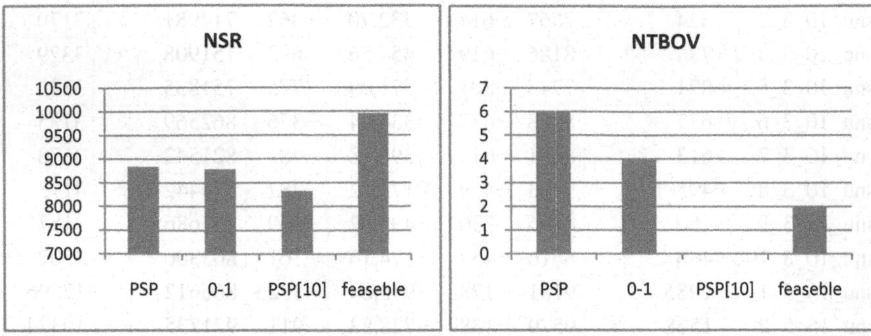

Fig. 1. Number of Successful Resolution (NSR) and Number of Time that CHN give an Optimal Value specified in benchmarks (NTBOV) for different starting point

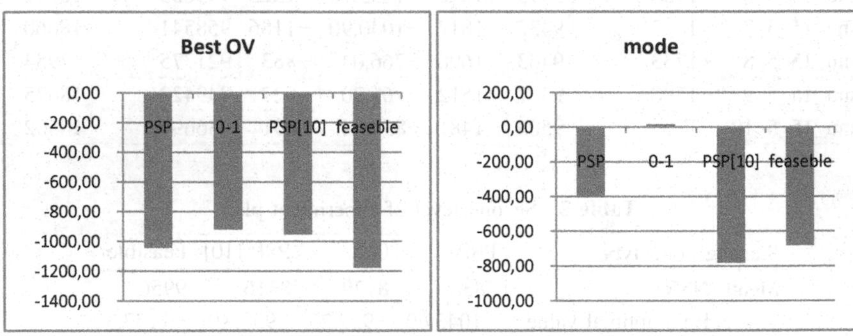

Fig. 2. Best optimal value and mode for different starting point

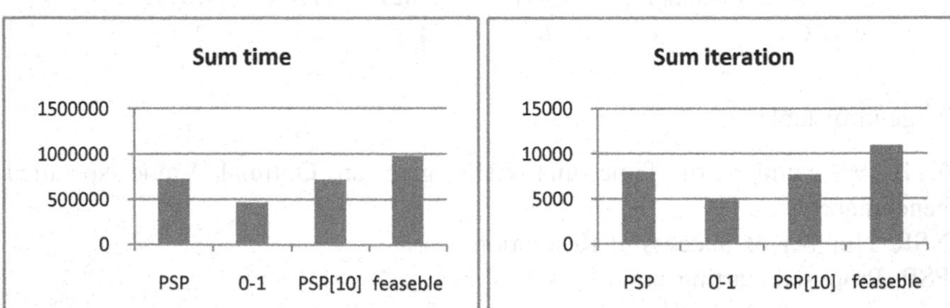

Fig. 3. Sum time and iteration for different starting point

For the Best OV presented in the third graph shows that the feaseble type is the best due to its NSR. On the other hand, the type PSP is ranked second in comparison with the others which shows the performance of this type.

For the two indicators of performance sum time and sum iteration shows that a technique 0-1 is the best, while the technique PSP is ranked second which shows that the proposed starting point help the CHN to converge in less time opposite to other techniques.

Finally, the technique of the proposed starting point is very interesting, it helped CHN to generate better solutions in comparison with the other techniques. This performance is measured in terms of NSR and computed time. The Table 3 shows this performance in terms of ranking.

Table 3. Rank of different starting point for different performance indicators

Indicators	Starting point			
	PSP	0-1	PSP [10]	Feasible
NSR	2	3	4	1
NTVOB	1	2	4	3
Best OV	2	4	3	1
Sum time	2	1	3	4

5 Conclusion

In this paper, we have proposed a new approach for choosing a good starting point for CHN. This new technique is validated experimentally. The experimental results show that the proposed starting point can find a good solution in a short time. Future directions of this research is using this technique to solve other problems such as graph coloring problem, constraint programming in order to improve the obtained results.

References

1. Elloumi, S.: The task assignment problem, a library of instances (2004). http://cedric.cnam.fr/oc/TAP/TAP.html
2. Ettaouil, M., Loqman, C., Hami, Y., Haddouch, K.: Task assignment problem solved by continuous Hopfield network. IJCSI Int. J. Comput. Sci. Issues **9**(2), 206–212 (2012)
3. Hopfield, J.J., Tank, D.W.: Neural computation of decisions in optimization problems. Biol. Cybern. **52**, 1–25 (1985)
4. Talavàn, P.M., Yànez, J.: A continuous Hopfield network equilibrium points algorithm. Comput. Oper. Res. **32**, 2179–2196 (2005)
5. Talavàn, P.M., Yànez, J.: The generalized quadratic knapsack problem. A neuronal network approach. Neural Netw. **19**, 416–428 (2006)
6. Wen, U.P., Lan, K.M., Shih, H.S.: A review of Hopfield neural networks for solving mathematical programming problems. Eur. J. Oper. Res. **198**, 675–687 (2009)
7. Takahashi, Y.: Mathematical improvement of the Hopfield model for TSP feasible solutions by synapse dynamic systems. IEEE Trans. Syst. Man. Cybern. Part B **28**, 906–919 (1998)

Information System And Social Media

A Concise Survey on Content Recommendations

Mehdi Srifi[1](✉), Badr Ait Hammou[1], Ayoub Ait Lahcen[1,2], and Salma Mouline[1]

[1] LRIT, Associated Unit to CNRST (URAC29), Faculty of Sciences, Mohammed V University, Rabat, Morocco
mehdisrifii@gmail.com
[2] LGS, National School of Applied Sciences, Ibn Tofail University, Kenitra, Morocco

Abstract. A recommender system is often perceived as an enigmatic entity that seems to guess our thoughts, and predict our interests. It is defined as a system capable of providing information to users according to their needs. It is enable them to explore data more effectively. There are several recommendation approaches and this domain remains to date an active research area that aims improving the quality of recommended contents. The main goal of this paper is to provide not only a global view of major recommender systems but also comparisons according to different specifications. We categorize and discuss their main features, advantages, limits and usages.

Keywords: Recommender systems · Content recommendation
Collaborative filtering · Survey

1 Introduction

Recommender systems are powerful tools widely deployed to cope with the information overload problem. These systems are used to suggest relevant items to targeted users based on their past preferences [1].

Currently, the effectiveness of recommender systems has been demonstrated by their use in several domains, such as E-commerce [2], E-learning [3], News [5], Search engines [6], Web pages [7], and so on.

In the literature, several methods have been proposed for building recommender systems, which are based on either the content-based or collaborative filtering approach [8]. However, in order to improve the performance of recommender systems, these two approaches can be combined to define the so-called hybrid recommendation approach. The implementation of the hybrid approach requires a lot of effort in parameterization [9]. In recent years, several recommendation approaches based user reviews have been developed [10], which aim to solve the sparsity and cold start problems by incorporating textual information generated by users (i.e. reviews).

Y. Tabii et al. (Eds.): BDCA 2018, CCIS 872, pp. 393–405, 2018.
https://doi.org/10.1007/978-3-319-96292-4_31

The rest of paper is organized as follows: Sect. 2 presents the backgrounds. Section 3 describes the different recommendation approaches based on the traditional sources of information: ratings, item data, demographic-data and knowledge-data. Section 4 describes the content recommendation approaches. Section 5 presents the evaluation metrics. Finally, Sect. 6 concludes the paper.

2 Backgrounds

In order to recommend interesting items to targeted users, recommender systems collect and process the useful information about the users and items [11].

2.1 Item Profiles

In the personalized recommendation, the item profile is intimately linked to the recommendation technique used, that is to say according to whether or not the content of the item is taken into account in the recommendation process [1,11,12]:

- In the case of a technique that does not take into account the content of the item, the latter can be represented by a simple identifier to distinguish it in a unique way.

- In the opposite case, the latter can be described according to three representations: structured, unstructured or semi-structured, for these last two representations, a step of pre-processing of text, which is the indexing, becomes necessary, in order to transform this text into a structured representation.

2.2 User Profiles

The main purpose of the personalized recommendation is to provide the user with items that meet his needs [11]. To do this, the recommendation system exploits the user's interactions with the e-service, in order to build him a specific profile, modeling his preferences [13–15].

Explicit Feedback. In this method, the user is involved in the process of collecting data about him. The recommender system prompts the user to fill out forms, or to note items, in order to directly specify his preferences to the system. The information provided by the user can take several forms, namely [11]:

Numeric : defined on a scale generally from 1 to 5.

Binary : the user must specify if the item is "good" or "bad".

Ordinal : the user chooses from among a list of terms the one describing the best his feeling with respect to the item in question.

Descriptive : Also called reviews, they represent the textual comments left by users on items. Their exploitation can make it possible to know the preferences of a user in a more refined way. There are many types of review elements [10], such as the contextual information, the multi-faceted nature of opinions, comparative opinions, discussed topics, and reviewers' emotions. Furthermore, several methods for their extraction are described in [10].

Implicit Feedback. In this method, the user is not involved in the process of collecting data about him [13]. This type of method uses the appropriate analysis of the user's history, thus informing about the frequency of consultation of the item, based on the number of visits or only the number of clicks on the corresponding page at item [15]. Other criteria can also be taken into account, including the time spent on the page in question, the list of favorite sites of the user, its downloads, its backups of pages, etc.

Hybrid Feedback. In this method, a combination of the two feedbacks (implicit and explicit) is made [16], in order to be able to fill the gaps of each of them, in terms of lack of information about the user. To do this, it is possible to use the implicit data as check on explicit data provided by the user, in order to understand well his behavior towards the system.

3 Standard Recommendation Approaches

There is a wide variety of recommendation approaches presented in the literature [8]. In this section, we present the most used approaches, with their advantages and limitations [17].

Content-Based Recommendation Approach. The content-based approach directs the user into his decision-making process by suggesting him, items that are close to the content of items he has appreciated in the past [19]. Indeed, it consists of matching the attributes of a given item with the attributes of the user profile (the ideal item). To do this, this approach is based on the representation of items by a profile in the form of a vector of terms obtained from either the item's textual description, keywords, or meta-data. A weighting strategy, such as the Term Frequency/Inverse Document Frequency (TF-IDF) measure, can be used to determine each term's representativeness [18]:

$$W_{i,d} = TF_{i,j} \times IDF_i = \frac{f_{i,d}}{\sum(f_{i,d})} \times \log(\frac{N}{n_i}) \tag{1}$$

where N is the number of documents, n_i is how many times term i is appears in the documents, and $f_{i,d}$ is the number of times term i is appears in the document d.

The content-based approach then tries to recommend the most similar items to the user profile (ideal item) by using for example, the Cosine similarity measure described as follows:

$$sim(item_1, item_2) = \frac{\overrightarrow{item_1}.\overrightarrow{item_2}}{|\overrightarrow{item_1}| * |\overrightarrow{item_2}|} \tag{2}$$

There are other methods derived from the machine learning domain, such as the Bayesian classifier, neural networks, decision trees [18]. These methods can also be used to measure the similarity between profiles of items and users [18,20].

The content-based approach has advantages, each user in such an approach is independent of others, only his behavior affects his profile [19]. Moreover, this approach is able to recommend newly items introduced in the system, even before they are evaluated by users (item cold-start problem) [21]. However, this approach has limitations, namely, the complexity of the representation of the items [11], which must be described in a manner that is both automatic and well structured. Another problem is the limitation of the user to recommendation of similar items to those appreciated in the past [13], which prevents him from discovering new items that may interest him (serendipity). In addition, for a new user, who has not yet sufficiently interacted with the e-service, the system can not develop him its own profile (user cold-start problem) [22].

Collaborative Filtering Approach. The collaborative filtering approach attempts to orient the user in his process of choice by recommending him items that other users with similar tastes have appreciated in the past [23]. The main goal of collaborative filtering systems is thus to guess the user-item connections of the rating matrix [15]. Two main axes stand out in the literature [8]. The first axis is relative to the memory-based approaches that act only on user-item rating matrix, and usually use similarity metrics to obtain the distance between users, or items [24]. The second axis concerns the model-based approaches, which use the machine learning methods, to generate the recommendations. The most used models are Bayesian classifiers, neural networks, matrix factorization, genetic algorithms, among others [8,16,25]. The model-based approaches yield better results, but their implementation cost is higher than that of memory-based approaches [21].

• ITEM-BASED COLLABORATIVE FILTERING APPROACH: The item-based approach aims to search for items that are neighbors, those who have been appreciated by the same users [21]. To do this, the k-nearest neighbor algorithm (K-NN) can be used to determine the k items closest to the target item, for which the Cosine similarity [16], can be applied to identify the similarity, between two items i and j.

$$sim(i,j) = \frac{\sum_{u \in U_{i,j}} r_{u,i} \times r_{u,j}}{\sqrt{\sum_{u \in U_{i,j}} r_{u,i}^2} \cdot \sqrt{\sum_{u \in U_{i,j}} r_{u,j}^2}} \tag{3}$$

Where $r_{u,i}$ and $r_{u,j}$ are the user's notes u for item i and j respectively. After that, the prediction of the note that the user u will assign to item i is calculated as follows:

$$P_{u,i} = \frac{\sum_{i \in I_u} sim(i,j) r_{u,j}}{\sum_{i \in I_u} |sim(i,j)|} \tag{4}$$

Items with the highest predicted ratings are then recommended to the user.

• User-based collaborative filtering approach: The principle of this technique is that users who have shared the same interest in the past are likely to share in a similar way their future affinities [22]. The k-NN algorithm can be used to select the k-nearest neighbors of the target user, based on the Pearson similarity measure [26], to determine the similarity between two users u and v.

$$sim(u,v) = \frac{\sum_{i \in I_{u,v}} (r_{u,i} - \bar{r_u}).(r_{v,i} - \bar{r_v})}{\sqrt{\sum_{i \in I_{u,v}} (r_{u,i} - \bar{r_u})^2}.\sqrt{\sum_{i \in I_{u,v}} (r_{v,i} - \bar{r_v})^2}} \quad (5)$$

Where $r_{u,i}$ and $r_{v,i}$ are the users's notes u and v for the item i. $\bar{r_u}$ and $\bar{r_{vu}}$ are the averages rating of the user u and v respectively. After that, the user's note prediction u for an item i, is done as follows:

$$P_{u,i} = \bar{r}_u + \frac{\sum_{v \in Neighbor(u)} (r_{v,i} - \bar{r_v}).sim(u,v)}{\sum_{v \in Neighbor(u)} |sim(u,v)|} \quad (6)$$

Items with the highest predicted ratings are then recommended to the user.

In contrast to content-based approaches, in this two collaborative filtering approaches mentioned above, the item can be represented only by a simple identifier [11]. This avoids the system to go through the analysis phase of the contents of the items, which can sometimes lead to bad recommendations [13]. Thus, by using these approaches and thanks to their independence of the content, various types of items can be recommended to the user on the same e-service (diversity) [17]. In addition, this kind of approaches makes possible the effect of surprise to the user, by offering him items totally different from items previously appreciated [21]. However, these approaches have limitations [25], namely, the need to have a database containing a large number of user interactions with the e-service, in order to be able to generate recommendations. Thus, these approaches are limited to short-lived items such as news, products containing promotions because this type of items appears and disappears before having a sufficient number of ratings by users of the system [21].

• Matrix Factorization: Matrix factorization models aim to put in a latent factorial space of dimension f, the profiles of users and products directly deduced from the rating matrix [27]. Thus, a note $P_{u,i}$ is predicted by performing the dot product between the latent profiles q_i of the item i and the latent profiles p_u of the user u: $P_{u,i} = q_i^T p_u$.

Several matrix factorization techniques exist [18], namely, the SVD (Singular Value Decomposition), PCA (principal Component Analysis) and (NMF) (Non-negative Matrix Factorization) models that are used to identify latent factors from explicit users feedback. Another enhancement to basic SVD model is SVD++ [18]. This asymmetric variation enables adding implicit feedback which in turn allows to improve the precision of the predictions of the SVD.

In recent years, matrix factorization models are becoming more efficient [27], thanks to consideration of various factors such as social links [28], text or time [29], allowing a better tracking of user behavior. Matrix factorization techniques give better precisions in the prediction than the recommendation approaches based on the neighborhood mentioned above [18,28,30]. In addition, they offer an efficient model in terms of memory, thus, easy to learn by the systems [31].

Demographic Recommendation Approach. The principle on which this approach is based, is that users who have common demographic-attributes (gender, age, city, job, etc) will necessarily also have common trends in the future [8,24]. Several works [32–34] have shown that the exploitation of demographic data instead of the user evaluation history, solves the problem of cold start of the user. However, this approach does not always provide users with recommendations that meet their needs in a precis way, because it does not take into account their preferences [21].

Knowledge-Based Recommendation Approach. This technique is based on a set of knowledge that defines the user's preference domain [15]. In the literature, this type of approach is sometimes considered to belong to the same family of content-based approach [35]. The only difference is that in the knowledge-based approach, the user explicitly specifies criteria for the recommendation system, that define conditions on items of interest [18], unlike the content-based recommendation approach that relies only on the user's history. Therefore, the knowledge-based approach takes as input: the user's specifications, item attributes, and the domain of knowledge (domain-specific rules, similarity metrics, utility functions, constraints). The use of this approach becomes useful, in the case of items rarely sold and therefore rarely noted as for example, very expensive products [18]. Recommendation systems based on this approach can be classified into two classes: *Constraint-based recommender systems*, which takes as input, the user-defined constraints on the attributes(eg: min or max limits...) of the item [36]. *Case-based recommender systems*, in which, the recommendation is made by calculating the similarity between the attributes of the items and the cases specified by the user [37].

Hybrid Recommendation Approach. Hybrid approaches are techniques that combine two or more different recommendation techniques [9,15], in order to overcome the limitations posed by each of them. For instance, several works [38–40] have shown that the use of an hybrid recommendation approach can solves the users/items cold-start problem encountered when using an individual recommendation approach. However, the implementation of hybrid approaches requires a lot of effort in parameterization allowing the combination between different approaches [9], so the process of explaining these recommendations to users becomes difficult [41].

4 Content Recommendation Approaches

4.1 Preference-Based Product Ranking

The preference-based product ranking approach, becomes useful when the items are described by a set of attributes, for example, for a movie (Producer, actors, genre) [25]. In this approach, the user's preference can be represented by ($\{V_1, \ldots, V_n\}$, $\{w_1, \ldots, w_n\}$), where V_i is the value function (criterion) that a user specifies for the attribute a_i [25], and w_i is the relative importance (i.e., the weight) of a_i. Then, the utility of each product a_i is calculated, using the multi-attribute utility (MAUT) as follows:

$$U(< a_1, a_2, \ldots, a_n >) = \sum_{i=0}^{n} w_i \times V_i(a_i) \quad (7)$$

Products with large utility values, are classified and then recommended to the user.

Based on the utility of each item characteristic for the user in question, this approach allows to filter items, in a finer and more tailored way, than other classical recommendation approaches [18]. However, the major challenge of this technique is in defining the most appropriate utility function for the user at hand [25].

4.2 Exploiting Terms on Reviews for Recommender Systems

In [42] the authors presented an approach called index-based approach, in which, each user is characterized by the textual content of his reviews. The term-based user profile $\{t_1, \ldots, t_n\}$ is constructed by extracting keywords from user reviews, followed by assignment of a weight $U_{i,j}$ to each extracted term, by using TF-IDF technique. This weight indicates how important each term is to the user. Similarly, each item is represented by a set of terms extracted from the reviews published on this item P_i. During the recommendation process, the user's profile serves as a query to retrieve items that are most similar to the user profile. The index-based approach has been evaluated [42] using a dataset collected from Flixster. The evaluation shows that this approach outperforms the user/item based collaborative filtering approaches, in terms of diversity, coverage, and novelty, but its accuracy is lower than that of user/item based collaborative filtering approaches.

4.3 Exploiting Emotions on Reviews for Recommender Systems

In [43], a new recommendation approach has been proposed, with the aim of improving the results of standard collaborative filtering approaches, by exploiting the emotions left by these users in reviews relating to given items. The principle of this approach is the following: given the user-item rating matrix R and emotion E towards others' reviews, the goal is to deduce the missing values in R.

To do this, the proposed approach (Mirror framework) aims to minimize the following equation [43]:

$$\begin{aligned} &\min_{U,V} ||\widetilde{W} \odot (R - U^T V)||_F^2 + \alpha(||U||_F^2 + ||V||_F^2) \\ &+ \gamma \min \sum_{i=1}^{n} \sum_{j=1}^{m} max(0, (u_i^T v_j - \bar{R}_{*j}^{ip})^2 - (u_i^T v_j - \bar{R}_{*j}^{in})^2) \end{aligned} \quad (8)$$

where U denotes the preference latent factors of each user u_i, and V denotes the characteristic latent factors of each item v_j. $\widetilde{W}$ is function that controls the importance of $R_{i,j}$. The term $\alpha(||U||_F^2+||V||_F^2)$ is introduced to avoid over fitting. γ is introduced to control its local contribution of emotion regularization to model emotion on other users' reviews. $\bar{R}_{*j}^{ip}$ and $\bar{R}_{*j}^{ip}$, are denoted as the average rating of positive and negative emotion reviews from u_i to v_j, respectively.

The results of experience and comparison [43] of this approach with standard approaches [44,45], show that when training sets (Ciao, Epinions) are more sparse, this approach allows to provide more precise recommendations than those returned by the standard approches. Thus its performance decreases more slowly, when cold-start users are involved in both training sets.

4.4 Exploiting Contexts on Reviews for Recommender Systems

Starting from the following idea: "the utility of choosing an item may vary according to the context", the authors of [46] have defined the utility of an item for the user, by two factors, namely, the *predictedRating*, calculated using standard item-based collaborative filtering algorithm, and the *contextScore*, measuring the convenience of an item i to the target user u's current context. The context is mined from a textual description of user's current situation and the features that are important to him. The utility score of item i for user u is calculated as:

$$utility(u, i) = \alpha \times predictedRating(u, i) + (1 - \alpha) \times contextScore(u, i) \quad (9)$$

where α is a constant, representing the weight of the predicted rating. Products with large utility values, are classified and then recommended to the user.

The results of the tests performed by the authors in [46] on a data set (hotels on TripAdvisor), show that this approach gives better predictions than the standard non-context based rating prediction using the item-based collaborative filtering algorithm. In [47] another approach was developed, which associate the latent factors with the contextual information inferred from reviews, to enhance the standard latent factor model.

4.5 Exploiting Topics on Reviews for Recommender Systems

In [48], the authors proposed an approach in which each user is assigned a profile of preferences grouping the topics (aspects of the item, for example: the location of the hotel, the cleanliness, the view of the room, etc.) mentioned by the user in his reviews, and having a large number of opinions (exceeding a certain threshold ts). More precisely, the profile of the user is represented by Z_i = {z| *count*(z, R_i)>ts}, where *count*(z, R_i) indicates the number of opinions associated with the aspect z in the set of reviews R_i written by the user i, and ts is a threshold defined as zero in their experience. Thus, the relevance of a review $r_{j,A}$ belonging to the set of reviews R_A associated with a product candidate A(j $\in 1, \ldots, | R_A$ |), is defined by $Z_{i,r_{j,A}}$, which consists of aspects appearing both in the user's profile Z_i and in the review $r_{j,A}$. Finally, the interest of an item for the user is calculated by weighting the average of the already existing ratings of this item by $Z_{i,r_{j,A}}$.

The results of the experiments [48] of this technique on a set of data collected from TripAdvisor, showed that this technique surpasses the non-personalized technique of product classification, with regard to the Mean Absolute Error (MAE) as well as Kendall's tau, which measures the fraction of items with the same order in the classification provided by the system and the one wanted by the user [49].

5 Evaluation Metrics for Recommendation Approaches

There are several criteria for evaluating recommendation approaches, the most important of which are [8,15,16]:

Statistical Accuracy Metrics. Its principle is based on the fact of verifying if the predicted scores for the user with respect to given items are correct [8], to do this two measurements have been reported namely the Mean Absolute Error (MAE) and the Root Mean Square Error (RMSE). Let $p_{u,j}$ a user note prediction u for item i and $n_{u,j}$ the actual note assigned by the user u for the item i:

MAE: measure the difference between predicted and true notes, small values of MAE means that the recommendation system accurately predicts the ratings. It is calculated as follows:

$$MAE = \frac{1}{N} \sum_{u,j} |p_{u,j} - n_{u,j}| \tag{10}$$

RMSE: puts more importance on larger absolute error. The recommendation is more accuracy when the RMSE is smaller. It is calculated via:

$$RMSE = \sqrt{\frac{1}{N} \sum_{u,j} (p_{u,j} - n_{u,j})^2} \tag{11}$$

Decision Support Accuracy Metrics. These measures allow users to find the items that interest them most, among all those available [18]. Several measures exist [16], namely, Weighted errors, Reversal rate, Precision Recall Curve (PRC), Receiver Operating Characteristics (ROC) and Precision, Recall and F-measure. The most used are Precision, Recall and F-measure.

Precision: the precision determines among the set of recommended items those who are the most relevant, its calculated via:

$$Precision = \frac{Correctly\ recommended\ items}{Total\ recommended\ items} \tag{12}$$

Recall: the Recall determines the proportion of recommended items among all relevant items, its calculated as follows:

$$Recall = \frac{Correctly\ recommended\ items}{Total\ useful\ recommended\ items} \tag{13}$$

F-measure: another way exists making the computation much simpler and easier [16], it is the F-measure which groups the two previous metrics into one, it is defined as follows:

$$F - measure = \frac{2PrecisionRecall}{Precision + Recall} \tag{14}$$

Coverage. It consists in determining the proportion of users for whom the recommender system can actually recommend items, as well as the proportion of items that can be recommended by this system [18].

Novelty, Diversity and Serendipity. Anothers measures [8,25] can be taken into consideration as, the novelty criterion which represents a very important aspect in the recommendation process especially if this element has not been seen before. Another important criterion is diversity, the absence of this criterion can generate a feeling of boredom in the user who is sentenced to receive similar items. In addition, the criterion of serendipity, it brings a surprise effect it can recommend users unexpected and surprising items.

6 Conclusion

The recommendation systems present tools for personalization and filtering of the information sought by the user. Several approaches on which these systems are based, exist in the literature, the best known of which are content-based recommendation approaches and collaborative filtering approaches presenting the problem of sparsity and cold start. The hybrid approach remains however an alternative trying to merge the advantages of these methods to fill their weak points. Recently, new approaches have been developed to fill the gaps in standard approaches. These new approaches in turn have some limitations, which presupposes the possibility of intervention by the researchers' community in order to reinforce and develop other approaches likely to adequately meet users' expectations. Thus, the present work can serve as a platform for exploring and developing new methods that can bridge the gaps in the presented approaches.

References

1. Cliquet, G.: Innovation method in the Web 2.0 era. Dissertation, Arts et Métiers ParisTech (2010)
2. Linden, G., Smith, B., York, J.: Amazon.com recommendations: item-to-item collaborative filtering. IEEE Internet Comput. **7**(1), 76–80 (2003)

3. Bobadilla, J.E.S.U.S., Serradilla, F., Hernando, A.: Collaborative filtering adapted to recommender systems of e-learning. Knowl.-Based Syst. **22**(4), 261–265 (2009)
4. Miller, B.N., et al.: MovieLens unplugged: experiences with an occasionally connected recommender system. In: Proceedings of the 8th International Conference on Intelligent User Interfaces. ACM (2003)
5. Billsus, D., et al.: Adaptive interfaces for ubiquitous web access. Commun. ACM **45**(5), 34–38 (2002)
6. Pass, G., Chowdhury, A., Torgeson, C.: A picture of search. In: InfoScale, vol. 152 (2006)
7. McNally, K., et al.: A case study of collaboration and reputation in social web search. ACM Trans. Intell. Syst. Technol. (TIST) **3**(1), 4 (2011)
8. Bobadilla, J., et al.: Recommender systems survey. Knowl.-Based Syst. **46**, 109–132 (2013)
9. Burke, R.: Hybrid recommender systems: survey and experiments. User Model. User-Adap. Interac. **12**(4), 331–370 (2002)
10. Chen, L., Chen, G., Wang, F.: Recommender systems based on user reviews: the state of the art. User Model. User-Adap. Interac. **25**(2), 99–154 (2015)
11. Ben Ticha, S.: Hybrid personalized recommendation. Dissertation, Université de Lorraine (2015)
12. Goldberg, D., et al.: Using collaborative filtering to weave an information tapestry. Commun. ACM **35**(12), 61–70 (1992)
13. Wei, C.-P., Shaw, M.J., Easley, R.F.: Recommendation systems in electronic commerce. In: E-Service: New Directions in Theory and Practice, p. 168 (2002)
14. Burke, R.: Hybrid web recommender systems. In: Brusilovsky, P., Kobsa, A., Nejdl, W. (eds.) The Adaptive Web. LNCS, vol. 4321, pp. 377–408. Springer, Heidelberg (2007). https://doi.org/10.1007/978-3-540-72079-9_12
15. Lemdani, R.: Hybrid adaptation system in recommendation systems. Dissertation, Paris Saclay (2016)
16. Isinkaye, F.O., Folajimi, Y.O., Ojokoh, B.A.: Recommendation systems: principles, methods and evaluation. Egypt. Inf. J. **16**(3), 261–273 (2015)
17. Sharma, M., Mann, S.: A survey of recommender systems: approaches and limitations. Int. J. Innov. Eng. Technol. **2**(2), 8–14 (2013)
18. Ricci, F., Rokach, L., Shapira, B.: Introduction to recommender systems handbook. In: Ricci, F., Rokach, L., Shapira, B., Kantor, P.B. (eds.) Recommender Systems Handbook, pp. 1–35. Springer, Boston, MA (2011). https://doi.org/10.1007/978-0-387-85820-3_1
19. Louëdec, J.: Bandit strategies for recommender systems. Dissertation, University Paul Sabatier-Toulouse III (2016)
20. Schafer, J.B., Konstan, J.A., Riedl, J.: E-commerce recommendation applications. Data Min. Knowl. Discov. **5**(1–2), 115–153 (2001)
21. Quba, R.C.A.: On enhancing recommender systems by utilizing general social networks combined with users goals and contextual awareness. Dissertation, Université Claude Bernard-Lyon I (2015)
22. Adomavicius, G., Tuzhilin, A.: Toward the next generation of recommender systems: a survey of the state-of-the-art and possible extensions. IEEE Trans. Knowl. Data Eng. **17**(6), 734–749 (2005)
23. Lousame, F.P., Sánchez, E.: A taxonomy of collaborative-based recommender systems. In: Castellano, G., Jain, L.C., Fanelli, A.M. (eds.) Web Personalization in Intelligent Environments, pp. 81–117. Springer, Heidelberg (2009). https://doi.org/10.1007/978-3-642-02794-9_5

24. Croft, W.B., Metzler, D., Strohman, T.: Search Engines: Information Retrieval in Practice. Addison-Wesley, Reading (2010)
25. Aggarwal, C.C.: Recommender Systems. Springer, Heidelberg (2016). https://doi.org/10.1007/978-3-319-29659-3
26. Zhang, F., et al.: Fast algorithms to evaluate collaborative filtering recommender systems. Knowl.-Based Syst. **96**, 96–103 (2016)
27. Dias, C.E., Guigue, V., Gallinari, P.: Recommendation and analysis of feelings in a latent textual space. In: CORIA-CIFED (2016)
28. Hammou, B.A., Lahcen, A.A.: FRAIPA: a fast recommendation approach with improved prediction accuracy. Expert Syst. Appl. **87**, 90–97 (2017)
29. Dias, C.-E., Guigue, V., Gallinari, P.: Recommendation and analysis of feelings in a latent textual space, Sorbonne University, UPMC Paris univ 06, UMR 7606, LIP6, F-75005 (2016)
30. Hammou, B.A., Lahcen, A.A., Aboutajdine, D.: A new recommendation algorithm for reducing dimensionality and improving accuracy. In: 2016 IEEE/ACS 13th International Conference of Computer Systems and Applications (AICCSA). IEEE (2016)
31. Koren, Y., Bell, R., Volinsky, C.: Matrix factorization techniques for recommender systems. Computer **42**(8), 43–47 (2009)
32. Safoury, L., Salah, A.: Exploiting user demographic attributes for solving cold-start problem in recommender system. Lect. Notes Softw. Eng. **1**(3), 303 (2013)
33. Wang, Y., Chan, S.C.-F., Ngai, G.: Applicability of demographic recommender system to tourist attractions: a case study on trip advisor. In: Proceedings of the The 2012 IEEE/WIC/ACM International Joint Conferences on Web Intelligence and Intelligent Agent Technology, vol. 03. IEEE Computer Society (2012)
34. Sun, M., Li, C., Zha, H.: Inferring private demographics of new users in recommender systems. In: Proceedings of the 20th ACM International Conference on Modelling, Analysis and Simulation of Wireless and Mobile Systems. ACM (2017)
35. Smyth, B.: Case-based recommendation. In: Brusilovsky, P., Kobsa, A., Nejdl, W. (eds.) The Adaptive Web. LNCS, vol. 4321, pp. 342–376. Springer, Heidelberg (2007). https://doi.org/10.1007/978-3-540-72079-9_11
36. Felfernig, A., Burke, R.: Constraint-based recommender systems: technologies and research issues. In: Proceedings of the 10th International Conference on Electronic Commerce. ACM (2008)
37. Bridge, D., et al.: Case-based recommender systems. Knowl. Eng. Rev. **20**(3), 315–320 (2005)
38. De Pessemier, T., Vanhecke, K., Martens, L.: A scalable, high-performance algorithm for hybrid job recommendations. In: Proceedings of the Recommender Systems Challenge. ACM (2016)
39. Strub, F., Gaudel, R., Mary, J.: Hybrid recommender system based on autoencoders. In: Proceedings of the 1st Workshop on Deep Learning for Recommender Systems. ACM (2016)
40. Braunhofer, M., Codina, V., Ricci, F.: Switching hybrid for cold-starting context-aware recommender systems. In: Proceedings of the 8th ACM Conference on Recommender systems. ACM (2014)
41. Kouki, P., et al.: User preferences for hybrid explanations. In: Proceedings of the Eleventh ACM Conference on Recommender Systems. ACM (2017)
42. Esparza, S.G., O'Mahony, M.P., Smyth, B.: Effective product recommendation using the real-time web. In: Bramer, M., Petridis, M., Hopgood, A. (eds.) Research and Development in Intelligent Systems XXVII, pp. 5–18. Springer, London (2011). https://doi.org/10.1007/978-0-85729-130-1_1

43. Meng, X., et al.: Exploiting emotion on reviews for recommender systems. AAAI (2018)
44. Zhang, S., et al.: Learning from incomplete ratings using non-negative matrix factorization. In: Proceedings of the 2006 SIAM International Conference on Data Mining. Society for Industrial and Applied Mathematics (2006)
45. Raghavan, S., Gunasekar, S., Ghosh, J.: Review quality aware collaborative filtering. In: Proceedings of the Sixth ACM Conference on Recommender Systems. ACM (2012)
46. Hariri, N., et al.: Context-aware recommendation based on review mining. In: Proceedings of the 9th Workshop on Intelligent Techniques for Web Personalization and Recommender Systems (ITWP 2011) (2011)
47. Li, Y., et al.: Contextual recommendation based on text mining. In: Proceedings of the 23rd International Conference on Computational Linguistics: Posters. Association for Computational Linguistics (2010)
48. Musat, C-C., Liang, Y., Faltings, B.: Recommendation using textual opinions. In: IJCAI International Joint Conference on Artificial Intelligence, No. EPFL-CONF-197487 (2013)
49. Kendall, M.G.: A new measure of rank correlation. Biometrika **30**(1/2), 81–93 (1938)

Toward a Model of Agility and Business IT Alignment

Kawtar Imgharene[1(✉)], Karim Doumi[1,2], and Salah Baina[1]

[1] ENSIAS, Mohamed V Rabat University, Rabat, Morocco
imgharene.kawtar@gmail.com, karim.doumi@um5.net.com, Sbaina@um5s.net.ma

[2] FSJESR, Mohamed V Rabat University, Rabat, Morocco

Abstract. Strategic alignment must remain active in the long term and dynamic with unforeseen changes. This is how agility at this level requires a projection into the future which must be instrumented by formal techniques as rational anticipation. It is important to find the right balance between the agile part, which is necessary for the rapid and appropriate transformation of the information system and strategic alignment, which ensures the coherence, durability, and relevance of an information system. By contrast, it should be obvious that the key to evolution in an approach between strategic alignment and agility is the dynamism of the process. Following an improvement in the state of the art, our article proposes a process that will be a good balance for a harmonized system that is agile enough to be able to maintain a strategic alignment with frequent evolutions.

Keywords: Alignment business IT · Agility · Change · Dynamism process

1 Introduction

Today, companies are faced with rapid and radical changes thus making the agility of the company a crucial step to obtain a competitive advantage and a performance of the company. They must adapt and respond to different types of transformation on the agility. In most cases, the agility has an effect on the elements of the organization of companies and information technology (IT).

Organizations are faced with the execution of current strategy for survive the challenges of today while being agile enough to adapt to the turbulence of tomorrow.

During the review of the literature in the field of research of alignment, there is not the stewardship of the impact of agility on the different work of strategic alignment. Indeed, the main research in this area offer:

- Modeling of strategic alignment between the different entities of the Enterprise Architecture [1–5]
- The harmonization of the assessment of approaches to strategic alignment: enabling organizations to measure the alignment between the different areas of enterprise architecture. So, Impact of the agility must be managed in a way to maintain the organizational system aligned [6, 7]

Y. Tabii et al. (Eds.): BDCA 2018, CCIS 872, pp. 406–416, 2018.
https://doi.org/10.1007/978-3-319-96292-4_32

Recent research continues to rely on empirical evidence that reveals the positive effects of the strategic alignment on the performance of the company. [2, 4, 7–9] have approached the strategic alignment from a point of modeling and evaluation with a proper result, but little research has been maintained on the evolution of this strategic alignment with the events and the unexpected changes. The problem occurs in this direction: the impact agility on the strategic alignment to be dynamic in the long term.

Strategic Alignment Model (Fig. 1) [10] includes the definition general of strategic alignment, it articulates around 4 fundamental domains and the nature of the link between its domains: (1) Business Strategy (2) It Strategy (3) Organization, Infrastructure and Process (4) Information System, Infrastructure and Process.

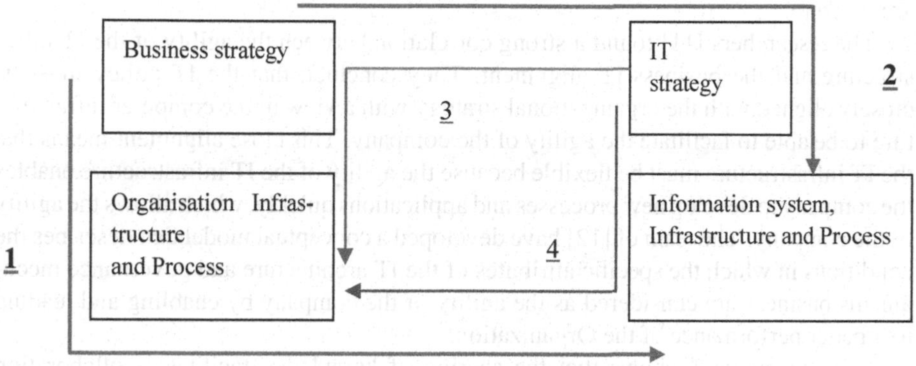

Fig. 1. Strategic Alignment Model [10]

If we propagate agility on the SAM model, we focus more specifically on arrows 1 and 2 which have the common step processes that will help us acquire a new strategy if a change is prescribed and thus have dynamic processes to conceal agile and aligned architecture.

The levels of abstraction are touching by this discontinuity of change; an offset develops and decreases the slowdown in the implementation of the evolution. To do this, a synchronization of the Domains With this change in process must always be in the listening and anticipatory.

The current work is motivated by the maintenance of a strategic alignment between strategy and enterprise information system despite the changes internal or external that will make the agility a primary issue.

In order to respond to the problem, the article is structured as follows: we have a literature review about the agility, a comparative table of definitions of agility for contributing to an aspect of change, and then we will discuss strategic alignment in relation to this change which will give us a track for an approach that accepts quickly the events by demonstrating according to a process approach which allows the resolution of several areas, but at the same time a cycle of a capture of unforeseen events.

2 Related Work

2.1 Alignment Business IT

The strategic alignment must be evolved for its retention in the long term. In effect, the changes often influence the organization in its entirety as well as the business processes in the information system. However, it is important for the organizations if they want to remain competitive to respond quickly and with the flexibility to change.

To be able to adapt to new opportunities, it requires agility on the business level of an organization, this flexibility leads to the use of the evolutionary business process by the information system and this agility allows you to have the flexibility of the enterprise architecture.

The researchers [11] found a strong correlation between the agility of the IT infrastructure and the business-IT alignment. They conclude that the IT policy must be closely aligned with the organizational strategy with a view to the computer infrastructure to be able to facilitate the agility of the company. This close alignment means that the IT infrastructure must be flexible because the agility of the IT infrastructure enables the company to develop new processes and applications quickly, which allows the agility of the company. The team of [12] have developed a conceptual model that describes the conditions in which the specific attributes of the IT architecture and governance mechanisms business are considered as the agility of the company by enabling and leading to a better performance of the Organization.

Previous research shows that the sharing of knowledge facilitates collaboration between business and IT which makes it easier for businesses in order to detect changes before deciding to a common line for the best way to react [13, 14].

The resulting alignment between IT and the company strategy can activate the agility since essential changes in the strategy of the company that can be easily communicated to IT managers. In this way, the path of dependencies and routines provided by alignment can allow increasing the adaptability and innovation [15, 16].

Various arguments based on resources also indicate a positive relationship between the alignment and agility. Key resources must be deployed in order to implement the changes. The sharing of knowledge, as noted earlier, allows companies to better understand their needs in terms of resources and potentially the limits of their resources, but it could also motivate the frames to move the resources to the areas of the business that are the most likely to experience change. Resources for having integrated into business processes and in the vicinity of the locus of the change mean that, in addition to facilitating the alignment, firms are more likely to be agile to respond to change [17].

Business alignment it is a continuous process of adaptation and change, but it is not known if it is to an improvement or to an alteration of the agility saw that the number of researcher each its opinion.

The following section it's about the concept of agility, explores the reason for which the strategic alignment needs to be agile, as well it handles different definitions business agility to begin to the challenge of change.

2.2 Agility

The world turns, not necessarily very round but certainly more and more quickly, the man in the middle of all its, if it creates the conditions of this acceleration must also cope.

Everything changes and quickly, so here is the great principle of the business of tomorrow: the agility. In our days, the instability makes this necessary quality even indispensable.

The need for the enterprise is enabled toward a new model, which controls the difficulty of the strategy and the evolution of the process of the company where the concept of the agility appears. The agility is not only a quality but a necessity for companies that wish to keep listening to its environment [18]. The agility is the ability to detect and respond quickly to points suggesting perpetual for the environment [19–23].

The agility is often mention with the flexibility, the management of change and adaptability, [33] define the agility like the ability of detection of a change in the environment and responds as appropriate. [24] Have classified the agility in two ways. First, according to the main attributes of agility: (1) The flexibility and adaptability, (2) responsiveness, (3) the speed, (4) The integration and low complexity, (5) the mobilization of basic skills, (6) high-quality products and custom products, and (7) the culture of change.

The table that follows shows some definition of agility that will thus be able to determine the change that will affect the strategic alignment.

During the review of the definitions of the agility (Table 1), the vast majority of researchers who have addressed the subject of agility defined as the ability of a business to adapt quickly to external changes [11, 18], and the agility is always defined as a response to the turmoil and instability of the markets and business environments. As argued [28] the main engine of agility is the change, therefore, one of the main characteristics of the agility is the change. These changes can be predictable (e.g. a new regulation affecting the industry) or unpredictable (e.g. the volatility of the market caused by a descriptive innovation).

Table 1. Definition of agility

Author	Definition
Dove [21]	An effective integration of knowledge and ability to answer and precision to adapt quickly, efficiently to changes in both proactive and reactive to the needs and opportunities
Sambamurthy et al. [25]	Two main factors (i) Respond to changes (anticipated or not) to time, (ii) the exploitation of changes and taking advantage of the possibilities of changes
Ashrafi et al. [19]	The ability of an organization to detect environmental changes and to respond efficiently and effectively to this change
Fartash et al. [26]	Agility is defined as the possibility of revising or reinvents the company and its strategy in adapting to the unexpected changes in the business environment, moving quickly and also, in an easy mode
Di Minin et al. [27]	Agile companies are able to maintain the cap and preserve the momentum that they follow the ambitious objectives while remaining flexible enough to quickly and effectively respond to opportunities to break through innovation

This change can affect the entire industry or a single level of the company (e.g. change of a process the process level) More specifically all levels of abstractions of the company.

The common idea among its definitions that there was a change in each agility, and therefore we must know detecting and know that it domain this change will impact, in the next section we will address the management of change for a business IT alignment.

2.3 Change in Business IT Alignment

Prof Dr Knut Hinkelmann [29] has cited that the objective of the IT strategic it is to align with the objectives of the enterprise and the requirements of the business and make it flexible enough to cope with the constant changes in the business and its environment.

To improve their chances of life, companies need to be agile, agility is the ability of companies to adapt quickly to changes in their environment and to seize the opportunity, and they have the necessary flexibility to cope with the specific needs of customers, reduce the time and response to external applications and to react on the events [29].

Forces at the source of organizational change can be classified by their nature into two groups: external and internal. Next subsections review the existing literature into the two mentioned groups and describe the most relevant forces.

Dr. Knut has clarified the changes internal and external environment that may impact the strategic alignment (Table 2).

- External change: Aguilar [30] argues that evaluating the external environment is essential to understand the external forces that can impact an organization.
- Internal change: it is possible to identify that the main internal change forces are related to the power of internal actors, emerging internal issues as well as evolution of the internal needs.

The external changes it's to seize the opportunities to react on the threats.
The internal changes to exploit the strengths for delineating the weaknesses.

Table 2. Internal and external change which can impact the strategic alignment [29]

External change	Internal change
Market opportunities	Business process optimization
New model of the company	Reorganizations
New regulation	Increase the flexibility of Information Systems
Request for new product and service	Change in the IT infrastructure

An external event (e.g. the development of a new technology or a new customer requiring) may trigger the need to change. This reactive behavior of the organization (i.e., recognize this need) is one aspect of the agility. The need for change can result in either the IT policy change or business. Transformation of activities and/or computer strategy based on external events is another attribute of the flexibility of the Organization. Agility provides a contribution for the alignment: a change of strategy (according to which the Enterprise Architecture must, therefore, be updated) can lead to an organization poorly aligned to the internal.

According to [31] there are four prospects how re-alignment takes place in such a case, the agility of the Organization is in the process of changing its business strategy or computing based on external developments. If the IT strategy is the leader, the strategy of the company can be adapted to new developments in the IT market.

The infrastructure is therefore affected by the new objectives of the company, linked to the skills. It is the competitive potential perspective. Another perspective is that of the alignment of the level of service, in which the strategy is directly translated to the IT infrastructure, exploiting the processes of the Organization to be able to cope with the demand of end customers to appropriately. If the company strategy is the leader, the IT infrastructure can be based on the IT strategy supporting the strategy directly.

The alignment must take place as soon as possible, ensuring the quality [21], which in their turn are aspects of the agility (that implies the word in an appropriate way in the definition of [32].

In conclusion, Enterprise Architecture should ensure the internal alignment quickly, based on the strategy of the changes triggered by external events, while guaranteeing a high quality and in a timely manner. In the next section, we will try to propagate the agility on the enterprise architecture to draw the level that will make the link between strategic alignment and agility.

2.4 Enterprise Architecture

Agility can be integrated with each layer of the Enterprise architecture Fig. 2. The main challenge for the achievement the agility is to obtain the alignment through the different layers and the components of the enterprise architecture.

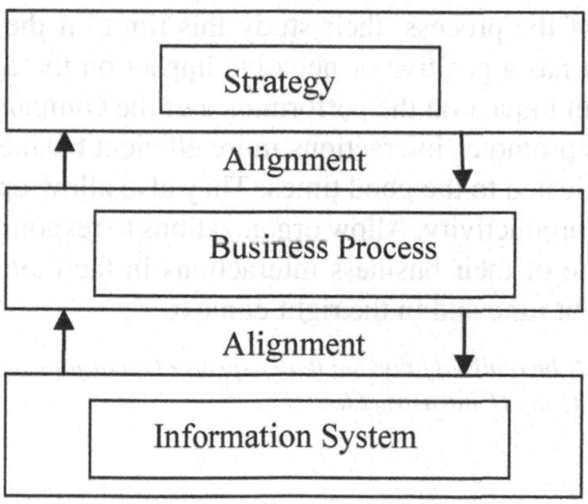

Fig. 2. Harmonization entity in Enterprise Architecture

Enterprise Architecture is not a concrete set and must be reviewed constantly in most businesses; it provides the guidelines (technical) rather than the rules for making decisions. The enterprise architecture must face the commercial Uncertainty and technological change.

Agility can be incorporated in each layer of the architecture of the business of the organization and in the enterprise architecture as a whole. The main challenge for the achievement of the agility is the obtaining of the alignment through the different layers and of the components of the enterprise architecture to drive.

The objective of the Enterprise Architecture is to strengthen the alignment pins transverse to facilitate the overall efficiency and contribute to the overall control of the risks, for this, it focuses on the cross-cutting circuits of information that feed and pass through the business processes including the fluidity of execution determines the performance of the company.

Table 3. Impact of agility on the levels of abstraction

Abstraction level	Agility impact
Strategy	Change the strategy of the company
Business process	Make business processes extremely agile, editable quickly and applicable for the entire organization remaining aligned
Information System	Flexible Information System to accompany the mutations that will continue oblige them to transform, extend (movement, process,…) and deploy (new actors, partner …)

The Table 3 above will include the impact of agility on the different layers of the architecture of the enterprise.

The level the most reactive and I dared the appoint the "*core*" of the enterprise architecture to make as well the combination easy and dynamic: **Business Process.**

The researchers [14] have mentioned in their studies in order to obtain an understanding more clear on the way in which the alignment business it can facilitate the agility on the level of the process, their study this limit on the made to know if the alignment business it has a positive or negative impact on the agility of the company where the latter has an impact on the performance of the company.

The agile process promotes interactions more efficient business, based on the good information communicated to the good times. They also allow optimizing the time and resources to increase productivity. Allow organizations to respond quickly to events and to maximize the value of their business interactions in facilitating access to valuable information at the right time and in the right context.

These benefits can only be realized fully that if all aspects of an organization are interconnected since the Strategy up to the IT infrastructure.

3 Proposed Approach - Global View

During our previous research [33] it was concluded that there was very little work empirically validated, which have been maintained on the relationship between the strategic alignment and agility relative to the criteria that was found during the search. In focusing on the dynamic evolution of strategic alignment any in affecting the agility of a system aligned, we deduced that when are faced by the dynamic developments of the organizations and the changes that affect the business process, the alignment is confronted with the same difficulties seen its levels of abstraction are related to one another.

Taking into account the review of the literature, we propose in this section the proposal approach.

The model focuses on the core of the enterprise architecture because we must concentrate on the principal of the business processes in order to optimize the operations and ensure a better functioning.

On this, a none-evolving alignment, a firm's process will not use the technological resources implemented in a favorable manner.

A life cycle mentioned in Fig. 3 of implementation of a business process dynamic which will affect all levels of abstraction because when there is an unscheduled change it is all the system that moves, it is largely difficult to modify a relationship that is in relationship with another relationship, this collision is a pure harmonization between the business process and the information system, this is where the impact of agility persists.

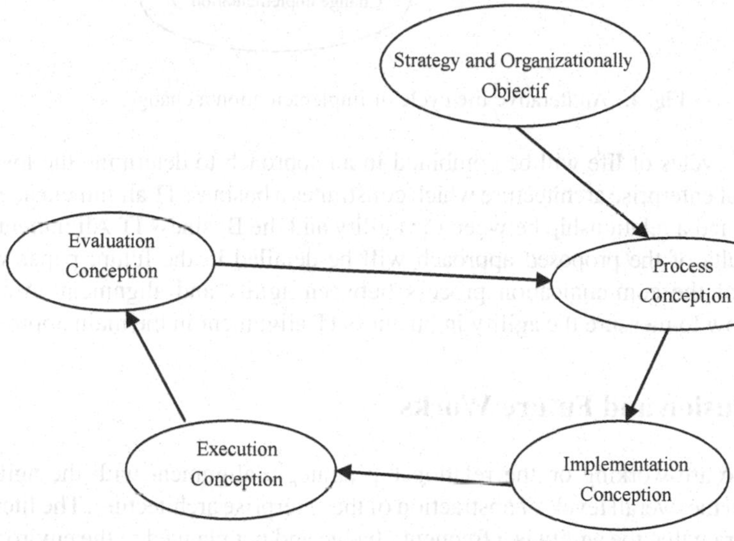

Fig. 3. A life cycle of implementation business process in a favorable manner

At the time of making the business process progressing within a system aligned, an iterative lifecycle will be managed the permanent changes, random and for the speed of the unforeseeable changes in the environment mentioned in Fig. 4.

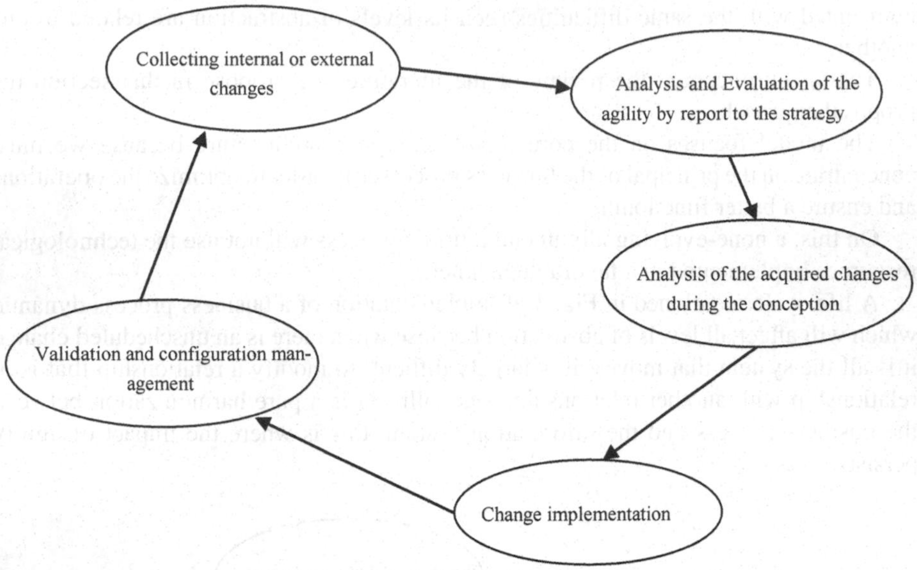

Fig. 4. An Iterative life cycle of implementation a changes

The two cycles of life will be combined in an approach to determine the levels of abstraction of enterprise architecture which constitutes a business IT alignment adequate with mentioned a relationship between the agility and the Business IT Alignment.

The results of the proposed approach will be detailed in the future paper with a simulation of the communication process between agility and alignment. And also propose a how to measure the agility in business IT alignment in the main approach.

4 Conclusion and Future Works

Actually, we are working on the relationship strategic alignment with the agility to propagate on the overall levels of abstraction of the enterprise architecture. The literature we demonstrate that the agility is a frequent change and not planned to the environment and that it little be external or internal, and to make the strategic alignment agile and dynamic, it is focused on the business processes that allow the harmonization and the communication between the different level of abstraction. In this paper, we aim to give a global view on the process of the collection of changes to their implementation and thus a cycle that manages the events of a business process. We will target a method that will be able to apply to our approach, analyze the impact of agility on the gap between Strategy and process and between process and information system, and to define by the result of the metrics that will calculate the agility on the strategic alignment.

References

1. Luftman, J.: Assessing IT/business alignment. Inf. Syst. Manag. **20**(4), 9–15 (2003)
2. Doumi, K., Baïna, S., Baïna, K.: Modeling approach using goal modeling and enterprise architecture for business IT alignment. In: Bellatreche, L., Mota, P.F. (eds.) Model and Data Engineering, pp. 249–261. Springer, Heidelberg (2011). https://doi.org/10.1007/978-3-642-24443-8_26
3. Thevenet, L.-H.: Proposition d'une modélisation conceptuelle d'alignement stratégique: la méthode INSTAL. Université Panthéon-Sorbonne-Paris I (2009)
4. Etien, A.: Ingénierie de l'alignement: concepts, modèles et processus: la méthode ACEM pour l'alignement d'un système d'information aux processus d'entreprise, Paris 1 (2006)
5. Engelsman, W., Quartel, D., Jonkers, H., van Sinderen, M.: Extending enterprise architecture modelling with business goals and requirements. Enterp. Inf. Syst. **5**(1), 9–36 (2011)
6. Gmati, I., Nurcan, S.: A framework for analyzing business/information system alignment requirements. In: International Conference on Enterprise Information Systems, p. 1 (2007)
7. Doumi, K., Baïna, S., Baïna, K.: Strategic business and it alignment: representation and evaluation. J. Theor. Appl. Inf. Technol. **47**(1), 41–52 (2013)
8. Couto, E.S., Lopes, M.F.C., Sousa, R.D.: Can IS/IT Governance contribute for business agility? Procedia Comput. Sci. **64**, 1099–1106 (2015)
9. Silvius, A.G.: Business & IT alignment in theory and practice. In: 2007 40th Annual Hawaii International Conference on System Sciences. HICSS 2007, p. 211b (2007)
10. Henderson, J.C., Venkatraman, H.: Strategic alignment: leveraging information technology for transforming organizations. IBM Syst. J. **32**(1), 472–484 (1993)
11. Chung, S.H., Rainer Jr., R.K., Lewis, B.R.: The impact of information technology infrastructure flexibility on strategic alignment and application implementations. Commun. Assoc. Inf. Syst. **11**(1), 44 (2003)
12. Oosterhout, M.: Business agility and information technology in service organizations. Erasmus Research Institute of Management (ERIM) (2010)
13. Barki, H., Pinsonneault, A.: A model of organizational integration, implementation effort, and performance. Organ. Sci. **16**(2), 165–179 (2005)
14. Tallon, P.P., Pinsonneault, A.: Competing perspectives on the link between strategic information technology alignment and organizational agility: insights from a mediation model. MIS Q. **35**(2), 463–486 (2011)
15. Lavie, D., Rosenkopf, L.: Balancing exploration and exploitation in alliance formation. Acad. Manage. J. **49**(4), 797–818 (2006)
16. Zahra, S.A., George, G.: The net-enabled business innovation cycle and the evolution of dynamic capabilities. Inf. Syst. Res. **13**(2), 147–150 (2002)
17. Tallon, P.P.: Inside the adaptive enterprise: an information technology capabilities perspective on business process agility. Inf. Technol. Manag. **9**(1), 21–36 (2008)
18. Krotov, V., Junglas, I., Steel, D.: The mobile agility framework: an exploratory study of mobile technology enhancing organizational agility. J. Theor. Appl. Electron. Commer. Res. **10**(3), 1–7 (2015)
19. Ashrafi, N., et al.: A framework for implementing business agility through knowledge management systems. In: 2005 Seventh IEEE International Conference on E-Commerce Technology Workshops, pp. 116–121 (2005)
20. Conboy, K., Fitzgerald, B.: Toward a conceptual framework of agile methods: a study of agility in different disciplines. In: Proceedings of the 2004 ACM Workshop on Interdisciplinary Software Engineering Research, pp. 37–44 (2004)

21. Dove, R.: Response Ability: the Language, Structure, and Culture of the Agile Enterprise. Wiley, Hoboken (2002)
22. Hobbs, G., Scheepers, R.: Agility in information systems: enabling capabilities for the IT function. Pac. Asia J. Assoc. Inf. Syst. **2**(4) (2010)
23. Raschke, R.L., David, J.S.: Business process agility. In: AMCIS 2005 Proceedings, p. 180 (2005)
24. Sherehiy, B., Karwowski, W., Layer, J.K.: A review of enterprise agility: Concepts, frameworks, and attributes. Int. J. Ind. Ergon. **37**(5), 445–460 (2007)
25. Sambamurthy, V., Bharadwaj, A., Grover, V.: Shaping agility through digital options: reconceptualizing the role of information technology in contemporary firms. MIS Q. 237–263 (2003)
26. Fartash, K.: Google Scholar Citations. https://scholar.google.com/citations?user=yaS3Mw0AAAAJ&hl=en. Accessed 14 Mar 2017
27. Di Minin, A., Frattini, F., Bianchi, M., Bortoluzzi, G., Piccaluga, A.: Udinese Calcio soccer club as a talents factory: strategic agility, diverging objectives, and resource constraints. Eur. Manag. J. **32**(2), 319–336 (2014)
28. Yusuf, Y.Y., Sarhadi, M., Gunasekaran, A.: Agile manufacturing: the drivers, concepts and attributes. Int. J. Prod. Econ. **62**(1), 33–43 (1999)
29. prof. Hinkelmann, K.: Alignment and agility - Recherche Google, March 14 2017. https://www.google.com/?gws_rd=ssl#safe=off&q=prof.+knut+hinkelmann+alignment+and+agility. Accessed 14 Mar 2017
30. Aguilar, F.J.: Scanning the Business Environment. Macmillan, New York (1967)
31. Henderson-Sellers, B., Serour, M.K.: Creating a dual-agility method: the value of method engineering. J. Database Manag. **16**(4), 1 (2005)
32. Overby, E., Bharadwaj, A., Sambamurthy, V.: Enterprise agility and the enabling role of information technology. Eur. J. Inf. Syst. **15**(2), 120–131 (2006)
33. Imgharene, K., Baina, S., Doumi, K.: Impact of agility on the business IT alignment. In: The International Symposium on Business Modeling and Software Design, BMSD (2017)

Integration of Heterogeneous Classical Data Sources in an Ontological Database

Oussama El Hajjamy[1(✉)], Larbi Alaoui[2], and Mohamed Bahaj[1]

[1] University Hassan I, FSTS, Settat, Morocco
elhajjamyoussama@gmail.com, mohamedbahaj@gmail.com
[2] International University of Rabat, 1110 Sala Al Jadida, Morocco
larbi.alaoui@hotmail.de

Abstract. The development of semantic web technologies and the expansion of the amount of data managed within companies databases has significantly expanded the gap between information systems and amplified the changes in many technologies. However, this growth of information will give rise to real obstacles if we cannot maintain the pace with these changes and meet the needs of users. To succeed, researchers must administrate properly these sources of knowledge and support the interoperability of heterogeneous information systems. In this perspective, it is necessary to find a solution for integrating data from traditional information systems into richer systems based on ontologies. In this paper, we provide and develop a semi-automatic integration approach in which ontology has a central role. Our approach is to convert the different classical data sources (UML, XML, RDB) to local ontologies (OWL2), then merge these ontologies into a global ontological model based on syntactic, structural and semantic similarity measurement techniques to identify similar concepts and avoid their redundancy in the merge result. Our study is proven by a developed prototype that demonstrates the efficiency and power of our strategy and validates the theoretical concept.

Keywords: Integrating data · Ontologies · UML · XML · RDB · OWL2

1 Introduction

Currently, the applications based on ontologies are more numerous and continuously changing thanks to the development of semantic web technologies. These applications play an important role in business development because they make the content of data accessible and usable by programs and software agents. However, gigantic volumes of data (billions of pages) are identified on the Internet and the developed applications do not use the same vocabulary or the same development model (the Entity/association model for conceptual modeling, the XML model for the exchange of data, as well as the relational model for data management are the most used to present, store and process data). This situation results in two difficulties. On the one hand, the distance between the model of existing data sources and the ontological model, which is linked to a set of types of reasoning applicable to modeled knowledge. On the other hand, many

Y. Tabii et al. (Eds.): BDCA 2018, CCIS 872, pp. 417–432, 2018.
https://doi.org/10.1007/978-3-319-96292-4_33

companies still want to keep their data in existing systems bearing in mind the time and money already spent on them and the multiple software tools associated with. Unfortunately, the developed applications that are using traditional methods of design, exchange or storage of data do not allow the use of explicit ontologies in order to explicitly share knowledge and make their content understandable by machines. As a result, the integration problem becomes an active research field. However existing works on making classical data available as ontologies are not dealing with the integration of such data issued from various sources. Each of these works mainly deals separately, and not within a global integration framework, with a specific task in one of the various steps of the process of integration: mapping (RDB to OWL [5, 8, 11, 16], XSD 2 OWL [4, 9, 10, 13, 17, 24], UML 2 OWL [14, 22, 23, 28]), alignment between ontologies (syntactic similarity [18, 31, 32], semantic similarity [2, 12, 25, 27] and structural similarity [3, 26, 30, 33]) and fusion of ontologies [5, 6, 21].

Our aim is to tackle the aforementioned integration problem to come up with an approach leading to a system that is based on a uniform view of various data sources providing a single access interface for data stored in multiple data sources. Such data are however designed differently and do not use the same vocabulary which leads to the following problems:

Mapping Problem: A mapping consists in indicating, by a transformation of models, how one can present a modelization of a source model in the most equivalent way possible in a destination model. In this case, domain researchers encounter an important problem, because some types of reasoning and/or possible constraints in the source model may no longer be possible in the destination model.

Heterogeneity Problem: The heterogeneities problems of the information sources are classified as follow:

Heterogeneity of Models: The UML model for conceptual modeling, the XML model for data exchange, and the relational model for data management and storage are ubiquitous and adopted, hitherto, by a large majority of applications constituting the kernels of business information systems, in addition to their permanent presence in the background of the majority of websites. The problem here is the transformation of their different data sources into a common model (OWL in our case) that is used to represent data from their associated heterogeneous sources.

Heterogeneity of Data: The models to be integrated were, a priori, built independently of each other, and each needs a specific collector that uses his own vocabulary to express its needs. As a result, conflicts may arise during the integration process because of heterogeneities that may exist between model elements. These conflicts can be of different types:

- Syntactic conflicts: This conflict stems from the fact that each collector uses his own terminologies. These terminologies may be identical or syntactically close.

- Semantic conflicts: corresponds to the differences related to the interpretation and meaning associated with the elements of the models. This type of conflict occurs when different models use different names to represent the same concept.
- Structural Conflicts: This type of conflict is evaluated by the distance that separates the objects in the OWL common model. It makes it possible to identify the subsumption relationships between the concepts of local ontologies to enrich the global ontology.

Fusion Problem: The ontology merge problem consists in creating a new global ontology representing the union of local ontologies so as to group all the similarities and dissimilarities contained in the local ontologies and avoid their redundancy in the merge result.

To answer these problems, we propose a semi-automatic integration approach, via a global schema located in an ontological database, integrating all aspects: semantic, syntactic, structural. Semi-automatic since our method requires human intervention to validate the results obtained by the similarity identification system on the base of its own needs. Our approach has three subsystems:

- A mapping system: to convert the elements of classical data sources into local ontologies.
- A similarity identification system: to identify similar elements that will be merged with the last subsystem.
- A fusion system: to merge local ontologies into a global ontology based on distinctive graph grammars.

The rest of this paper is organized as follow. Section 2 present an overview of existing work that we consider to be major related to the integration and fusion of ontological data. Section 3 describes our integration process; it is divided into three sub-parts describing the three subsystems of our integration method. The experimental part of our prototype is presented in Sect. 4. Finally Sect. 5 concludes our work by summarizing the main contributions and presenting a discussion of our perspectives.

2 Existing Integration Approaches

As we already mentioned, there is not any work that really deals with the problem of integrating of various classical data sources into ontologies. During the last years, because of the importance of ontologies many research works have been dealing with just a particular task, not within a global integration framework. We first addressed existing works related to the mapping task of one type of such data sources into ontologies. In a second step we give a discussion on relevant works on similarities between ontologies. Finally we also give an overview of solutions existing for ontology Fusion.

2.1 Mapping Systems

In order to evaluate the existing approaches, we highlight in this section, the different methods that were interested in the construction of ontologies from classical data sources:

- **UML-to-Ontology:** Due to the widespread use of UML and OWL languages, it is no wonder that there are many works in the literature whose goal is to study the different relationships between UML and OWL and propose a transformation from UML to OWL. Cranefield [28] provide a UML-based visual environment for modeling web ontology. He creates an OWL ontology in a UML tool and then save it as an XMI-coded file. Then an XSLT stylesheet translates the XMI-coded file into the corresponding RDF Schema (RDFS). In [14] Zedlitz considered the mapping between UML elements and OWL2 constructs such as disjoint and complete generalization, generalization between associations, composition and enumeration. However, we believe that our method UML2OWL2 [23] give a solution to all aforementioned limitations of existing approaches in order to provide the semantic world as complete as possible conversion technique that allow to easily and fully deduce all conceptual details of the considered UML specifications relative to the analysis, conception and design of the associated modeled systems.
- **XML-to-Ontology:** We can found several approaches that deal with XML to OWL mapping: Jyun-Yao propose in [13] a template that can handle extremely large XML data and provides user friendly templates composed of RDF triple patterns including simplified XPath expressions. Ferdinand et al. [17] propose a mechanism to lift XML structured data to semantic web. This approach is twofold: mapping concepts from XML to RDF and from XML Schema to OWL. Bedini et al. [10], propose a tool called "Janus", this last provides automatic derivation of ontologies from XS files by applying a set of derivation rules. Then, the same group proposed a method based on patterns [9] that deals with 40 patterns and convert each pattern to equivalent OWL ontology. All aforementioned ontology based transformation present limitations in treating various important XSD elements related to the art of elements, relations or constraints. Our approach [24] aims at defining a correspondence between the xml schema and OWL2 ontology. It maintains the structure as well as the meaning of XML schema. Moreover, our mapping method provides more semantics for XML instances via adding more definitions for elements and their relationships in OWL ontology by using OWL2 functional-style syntax.
- **RDB-to-Ontology:** there are many researches that have been proposed to achieve RDB to OWL conversion [8, 11, 15] but most of them contain simple and limited cases, rules, and doesn't cover most complex relations and constraints. This has allowed us to build an associated general and complete mapping algorithm [16] that covers different aspects of the relational model which are relevant for the mapping process. The algorithm deals among others with various multiplicities for relationships, relation transitivity, circular relationships, self-referenced relationships, binary relations with additional attributes including many-to-many relations and constraints such as check constraints (Check values, Check in)

2.2 Identification of Similarities

In the literature, the similarity measure of two or more ontologies is the ability to detect a set of correspondences between the concepts of these ontologies. We present the existing work according to the Heterogeneity of Data classification as follow:

Syntactic similarity: is based on the calculation of the distance between two characters. Different syntactic similarity distance calculation algorithms exist in the literature such as those of Levenstein [31], Hamming [32], Jaro [18] and others. They are all based on the same hypothesis described by [1] who states that two terms are similar if they share enough important elements. We chose the distance of Jaro because it is adapted to the treatment of short chains.

Semantic similarity: is a human ability that machines can only reproduce very poorly. Various methods have been proposed for semantic similarity detection techniques: Resnik [25] has used the notion of informational content that measures semantic similarity by the amount of information they share. The informational content is obtained by calculating the frequency of the object in Wordnet. To address the problem presented at the Resnik measurement level, Jiang in [12] combined a thesaurus knowledge source with Wordnet to improve the semantic similarity calculation results. Another method is proposed by Leacock and Chodorow [2] which is based on calculating the length of the shortest path between two synsets of Wordnet. Armouch in [27] used Wordnet to construct a synonymy vector for each concept of the first ontology, and then compares it with all the concepts of the second to find the concept that is most similar to the concept in question. We chose to use this method because it combines the results of two lexical and semantic similarity measurement techniques.

Structural similarity: the objective of this technique is to obtain results for concepts related to each other by a subsumption relation. Among the works in this field we can mention: the measure of Rada et al. [26] which is based on the hierarchical "is-a" links to calculate the minimum number of arcs separating two concepts. Lin [3] performed a comparison between the methods of structural similarity measures. He deduced that the technique proposed by Wu and Palmer [33] has the advantage of being simple to compute and more efficient. However, it has a limit because with this measure it is possible to obtain a higher similarity between a concept and its surroundings with respect to this same concept and a child concept. To solve this problem Slimani [30] has developed a similarity measure extension based on the Wu and Palmer measurement that penalizes the similarity of two distant concepts that are not located in the same hierarchy. That is why we adopted this measure in our integration method

2.3 Fusion Systems

Different ontology merge tools exist in literature. Most of these are semi-automatic and require the intervention of a knowledgeable engineer to validate the results obtained. The most known are:

FCA-Merge: is a symmetric approach proposed by Stumme and Maedche [6] that allows merging ontologies based on the formal analysis of concepts. Its process is as follows: first, perform a linguistic analysis of the two ontologies and extract their instances. Once instances are retrieved, use FCA techniques to merge the two contexts and calculate the trellis. Then, generate the global ontology from the constructed trellis. Finally, to resolve conflicts and eliminate duplications, the user is invited through a "question-and-answer" mechanism to choose the proposals that suit him the most.

PROMPT [21]: is a protégé plugin for ontology merge. It looks for linguistic similarity points between the concepts of the two source ontologies and proposes a list of all the possible merging actions (to-do list). Then the user can choose the proposals that suit him the most.

MMOMS: Framework proposed by Li et al. [5] to merge OWL ontologies. It is based on learning machines, Wordnet and structural techniques to look for similarity. It uses a merge algorithm that addresses the concepts, relationships, and attributes of both ontologies.

3 Our Integration Process

Our approach aims to provide a unique and transparent interface of classical data sources (UML, RDB, XML) via a global schema (OWL) located in ontological database. To deal with the heterogeneities of models and data, we have chosen ontologies as a common model. The latter ensures a semantic equivalence between the different models. Our strategy consists of three distinct phases, as shown in Fig. 1.

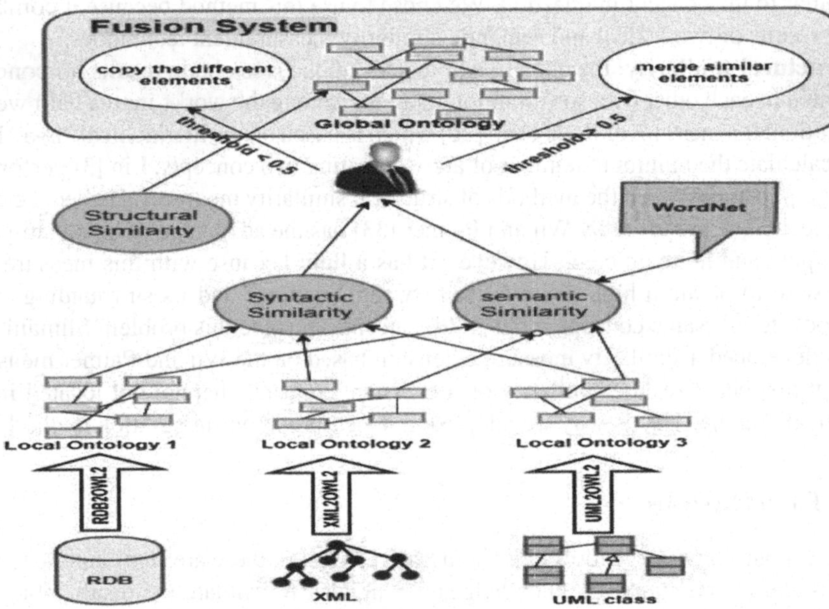

Fig. 1. Proposed general approach

In the first step, the system loads files from existing data sources, and applies our mapping algorithms [16, 23, 24] to create their OWL2 equivalents. It should be noted that the use of OWL2 to generate the resulting ontology allows us to benefit from a more powerful inference system, as well as OWL2 extends OWL1 with new features based on actual use in applications. It is indeed possible with OWL2 to define more constructs to express additional restrictions and obtain new characteristics on the properties of the modeled object. In the second step, our tool imports the generated ontologies and uses Syntactic, Semantic and Structural Similarity techniques to determine the correspondences between the concepts of the ontologies to merge. The final step is to merge the local ontologies based on the matches found in the previous step. We present ontologies with the formalism of typed graph grammars to merge ontologies using the SPO (Simple PushOut) algebraic approach.

Our approach is asymmetrical; it requires the choice of the source ontology. The concepts of the source ontology will be preserved while the non-redundant concepts of the other ontologies will be added to the global ontology.

3.1 Mapping from Classic Data Sources to Local Ontologies

This step consists of designing local ontological models from classical models, while keeping the operating principle of source models and while minimizing the loss of information:

From the point of view of entity/association models for conceptual modeling, we use our UML2OWL2 [23] method. This method aims to generate OWL ontologies from an existing UML class diagram. It is based on the XMI format, which provides a storage and knowledge exchange standard for UML model.

From the point of view of semi-structured models, we use our XSD2OWL2 [24] approach. This solution takes an existing XML schema (XSD) as input, loads the XSD document, and parses it using the DOM parser. Then, it extracts its elements with as many constraints as possible and applies our mapping algorithm to create the resulting OWL2 document. For a complete transformation the mapping of XML elements is added to our approach.

From the point of view of relational models, we use our approach RDB2OWL2 [16], which makes it possible to automatically build OWL2 ontologies via a transformation process of relational databases. The goal of this solution is to provide a general transformation algorithm that covers all constraints, preserves the semantics of the source RDB, and maintains data consistency and integrity. This process operates on two levels: The schema level in which the terminology part or TBOX of the ontology is generated from a schema of the source RDB. The level of data instances in which data stored as records is converted to the factual level or ABOX of the ontology.

3.2 The Similarity Search Techniques

Our objective is to design a semi-automatic local ontology fusion algorithm (generated in the previous step) based on a set of similarity search techniques. The similarity identification module covers all the elements of the comparison types in order to detect all the matches, and combines all the comparison types (syntactic, semantic and structural) in order to increase the probability of having real correspondences and real differences.

Syntactic Similarity: To measure the degree of syntactic equivalence, we compare the elements of the models syntactically. To do so, we chose the distance of Jaro. This distance between two chains C_1 and C_2 is defined as follows:

$$d_j(C_1, C_2) = \frac{1}{3}\left(\frac{m}{|C_1|} + \frac{m}{|C_2|} + \frac{m-t}{m}\right)$$

m: the number of corresponding characters. Two chains C_1 and C2 are considered as corresponding if their distance does not exceed: $\left[\frac{max(|C_1|, |C_2|)}{2}\right] - 1$

$|C_1|$: the length of the chain C_1.

t: the number of transpositions. It is calculated by comparing the i-th corresponding character of C_1 with the i-th corresponding character of C_2. The number of times these characters are different, divided by two, gives the number of transpositions.

The two concepts C_1 and C_2 are considered syntactically similar if d_j is greater than a threshold that will be determined empirically. Example: Calculate the syntax distance between "conveyance" and "conv", and "conveyance" and "transport". Assuming that (threshold = 0.5) we get:

$$d_j(\text{conveyance}, \text{conv}) = \frac{1}{3}\left(\frac{5}{10} + \frac{5}{4} + \frac{5-0,5}{5}\right) = 0,88 > 0,5$$

Then "conveyance" and "conv" are syntactically similar. And since

$$d_j(\text{conveyance}, \text{transport}) = \frac{1}{3}\left(\frac{2}{10} + \frac{2}{10} + \frac{2-0,5}{2}\right) = 0.39 < 0.5,$$

Then "conveyance" and "transport" are syntactically different.

Semantic Similarity: When several symbolic names cover the same concept but their names are different (synonymy), the distance dj < threshold does not reflect the reality. To solve this problem, semantic similarity measurement is essential (example: conveyance and transport). To do so, we use a lexical database (English Wordnet dictionary or EuroWordNet multilingual dictionary) so that we can deduct the meaning of a word. By articulating on WordNet two concepts are equal if their synset overlap. For example: synset = {transport, conveyance}.

The measurement of semantic similarity between two concepts C_1 and C_2 is defined by calculating the number of common synonymy relations (synset) as follows:

$$\text{SimSem}(C_1, C_2) = \frac{2 \times card(synset(C_1) \cap synset(C_2))}{card(synset(C_1)) + card(synset(C_1))}$$

C_1 and C_2 are considered semantically similar if SimSem is greater than a threshold that will be determined empirically. SimSem(transport, conveyance) = 2 × 2/4 = 1, then "transport" et "conveyance" are semantically similar.

Structural Similarity: Structural similarity identification methods use the hierarchical structure of the ontology and are based on arc counting techniques. We also use it to enrich the global ontology. The similarity between the entities is determined according to their positions in their hierarchies. It is calculated once for each pair of nodes. The nodes of the two ontologies are classified by category (or type). The method [30] which inspires advantages of the work [33] is based on the following principle: Let C_1 and C_2 two elements of the global ontology and C their subsuming concept, the principle of calculating similarity is defined by the following formula:

$$\mathrm{SimStr}(C_1, C_2) = \frac{2 \times depth(C)}{depth(C_1) + depth(C_2)} \times \mathrm{fp}(C_1, C_2)$$

If C_1 and C_2 are not in the same path, then: $\mathrm{fp}(C_1, C_2) = \frac{1}{|depth(C_1) - depth(C_2)| + 1}$

Else if C1 is ancestor of C2 or the opposite, then: fp $(C_1, C_2) = 1$

The advantage of this measurement is that one can obtain a higher similarity between a concept and a child concept compared to this same concept and its surroundings.

3.3 Fusion of Local Ontologies

The ontology fusion is the creation of a global ontology from several existing ontologies. However this step can cause the following conflicts:

- Redundancy of elements that have syntactically close names, for example "conveyance" and "conv".
- Ontologies can share concepts that are semantically close (synonymies), for example "conveyance" and "transport".
- Ontologies can share subsumption relationships (inheritance).

In order to resolve these conflicts, we have developed a set of guidelines based on the similarity measurement techniques introduced in the previous chapter. These directives indicate the actions to be applied to decide how the elements will appear in the result model, for example the creation, the deletion and the renaming of the elements.

Our fusion approach is based on typed graph grammars and Simple PushOut algebraic approach (SPO). We first present the definitions of the concepts used in our merge approach.

Definition 1. An oriented graph is defined as a system G (N, E) where N, E correspond respectively to the sets of nodes and edges of the graph, and an application s: $E \rightarrow N \times N$ which associates for each edge a source and target node.

Definition 2. An oriented and assigned graph is defined as a system G (N, E, A) where A is a set of attributes.

Definition 3. A morphism m(f, g) of an unattributed graph from G(N, E) to H(NH, EH) is an application from G to H defined by two applications f: N → NH and g: E → EH, such that if e = (a, b) and g(e) = e′ = (a′, b′), then a′ = f(a) and b′ = f(b).

Definition 4. A graph grammar is a system defined by GG(G, Re), where G is the initial graph and Re is the set of rewriting rules. These rules make it possible to transform the initial graph G. Re is defined by Re(LHS, RHS), LHS and RHS respectively specify the left and right sides of a rule. The left side shows the structure that must be found in a host graph G to be able to apply the rule and the right part describes the rewriting rule that replaces L in G.

A rewrite rule may have an additional requirement called Negative Application Conditions NAC. It defines the conditions that should not be checked for the rewriting rule to be applied.

Définition 5. A typed graph grammar is defined by GGT(GT, G, R) where GT(NT, ET) is a type graph specifying the type of nodes and edges of the initial graph.

Définition 6. Simple PushOut (SPO) is an algebraic method of graph transformation proposed by Löwe [19]. The stages of the transformation are as follows:

- Identify the graph LHS in G according to a morphism m: LHS → G.
- Remove from the graph G, the graph m(LHS) – m(LHS ∩ RHS) and delete all the suspended edges.
- Add the graph m(RHS) – m(LHS ∩ RHS) to the initial graph G

In order to represent ontologies and ontological changes, we used respectively TGGOnto model [20] based on typed graph grammars: TGGOnto(GTO, GO, RO) with:

- GTO: type graph representing the OWL2 ontology meta-model.
- GO: initial graph representing the source ontology.
- RO(NAC, LHS, RHS, CHD): rewrite rules describing ontological changes. CHD presents the derived changes. Example: AddObjectProperty(OP_2, C_2, C_3) in Fig. 2.

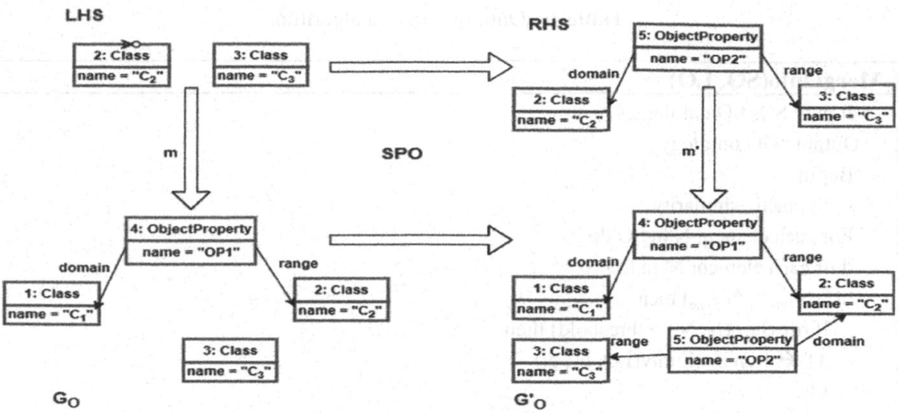

Fig. 2. Rewriting rules of "AddObjectProperty" change with the SPO approach

Our approach is asymmetrical, then for two ontologies O_1 and O_2 $\text{Merge}(O_1, O_2) \neq \text{Merge}(O_2, O_1)$. The fusion method adopts the "one pair at time" strategy (Fig. 3) and requires the definition of the source ontology whose elements will be preserved and only the non-redundant elements of the other ontology will be added to the global ontology.

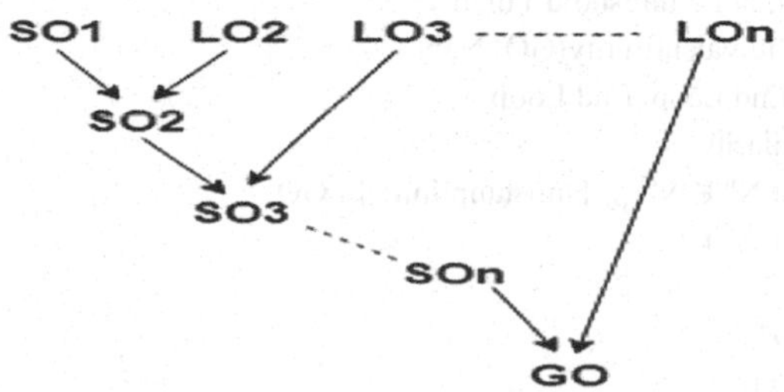

Fig. 3. One pair at time fusion strategy

We propose an algorithm called MergeOnto (Table 1) that takes as input two ontologies SO and LO, and returns a third GO ontology. Our algorithm starts with the identification of similar concepts, it takes into consideration the types of elements to compare their similarities (for example: the two elements must be classes). Elements of the same type are analyzed in two steps: two elements can be equal if their Jaro distance is greater than the threshold, and they are equivalent if their semantic similarity defined from Wordnet is greater than the threshold. Then, our algorithm merges the elements deemed syntactically similar and accepted by the Knowledge Engineer, copies the elements deemed different and adds "EquivalentEntity" to elements deemed semantically similar and accepted by the Knowledge Engineer. Finally, by applying the structural similarity measurement rule, we add "EquivalentEntity" to elements deemed similar and accepted by the Knowledge Engineer. Thus, we obtain a global and more comprehensive ontology that covers a wider field of application.

Table 1. Ontology fusion algorithm

```
MergOnto(SO, LO)
  Input : SO, LO ontologies
  Output : GO ontology
  Begin
  /* Syntactic similarity
  For each element N in SO do
   For each element N' in LO
    If (N_Type = N'_Type) then
      If (distJaro(N, N') > threshold) then
        O' ← RenameEntity(LO, N', N)
      Else
        O' ← Entity(LO, N')
      End If  EndIf  End Loop  End Loop
  /* Fusion function merge the similar entities and copy the different entities in SO
  GO ← Fusion(O', SO)
  /* Semantic similarity
  For each element N in SO do
   For each element N' in LO
    If (NType = N'Type) then
      If ( distSem(N, N') > threshold ) then
       GO ← AddEquivalentEntity(GO, N, N')
   End If  EndIf  End Loop  End Loop
  /*Structural Similarity:
  For each element N" ∈ N"_Type{subsumption} in GO
  O" ← Entity(GO, N")
  End Loop
  For each N" in O"
   For each Ni" in O"
    If (SimStr(N", Ni" ) > threshold) then
     GO ← AddEquivalentEntity(GO, N", Ni")
    End If  End Loop End Loop End
```

4 Experimental Results

To evaluate our model a tool has been developed. This tool takes as input different classical data sources. Then, it applies our mapping algorithms [16, 23, 24] to create the local ontologies. Finally it merges these ontologies into a global ontological model based on the similarity measurement techniques.

To illustrate the functioning of our tool, we present an example of CIT, ATM and Cash Center data sources, extracts from Cash Solution domain (Fig. 4).

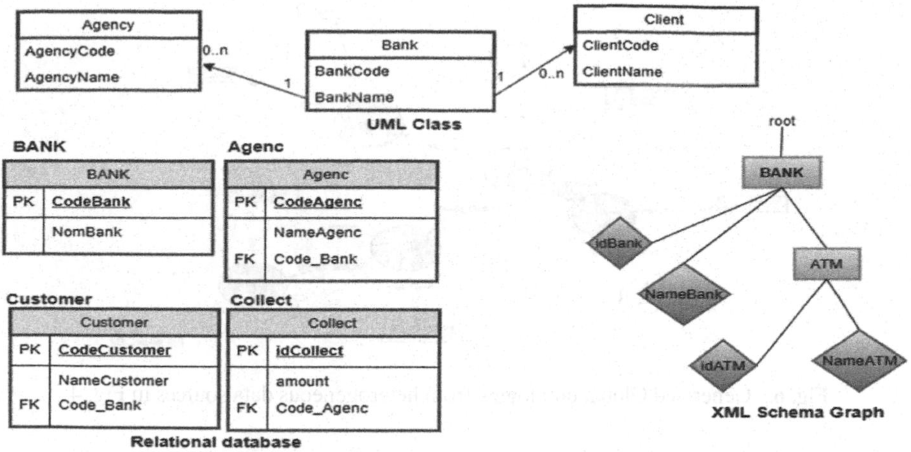

Fig. 4. Heterogeneous data sources for Cash Solution domain

The prototype (Fig. 5) implements the three steps of the integration solution. The first contains a "Choose File" button that allows the user to choose which data sources to embed. The second interface generates in OWL2 the Local ontologies. The Third interface merges local ontologies using our ontology fusion algorithm to generate the global ontology. The local ontology is loaded in the Protégé OWL editor. The figure below (Fig. 6) obtained using the plugin VOWL protégé shows the results obtained by our tool.

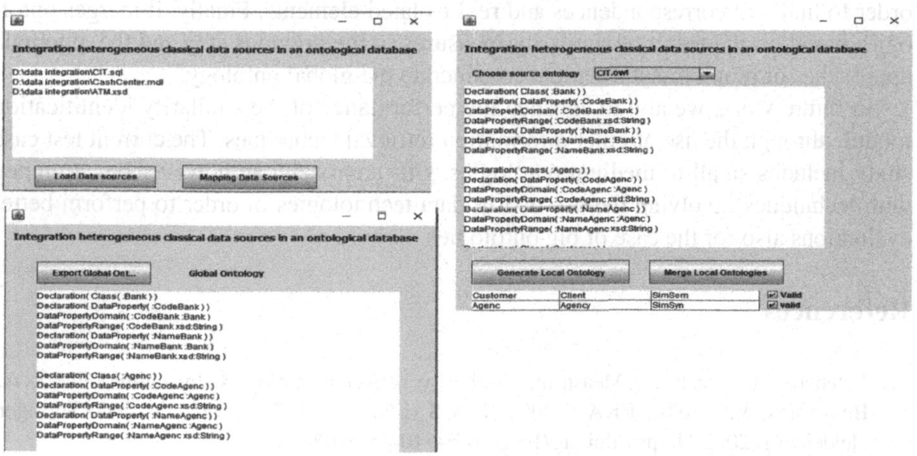

Fig. 5. Screenshots of our tool

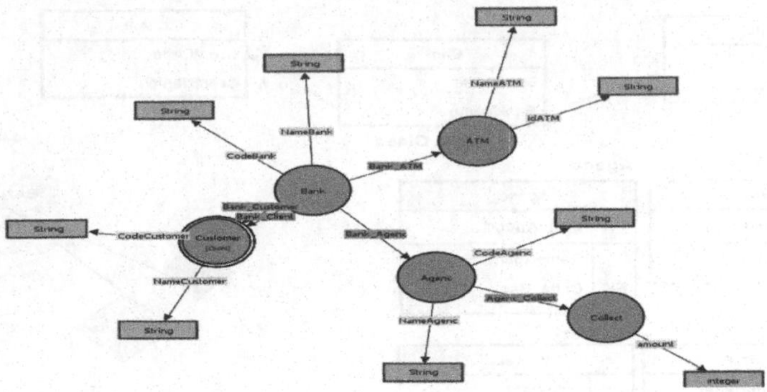

Fig. 6. Generated Global ontologies from heterogeneous data sources in Fig. 4

5 Conclusion

The general context of this work is the integration of classical data sources into an ontological database. In order to answer this problem, we have proposed a semi-automatic approach in which human intervention is promising to validate the results. This approach starts with a transformation of the different classical sources (UML, XML and RDB) to local ontologies (OWL2). Then, it combines syntactic similarity measures based on the computation of the distance between the characters describing the concepts, semantics based on the semantic enrichment of local ontologies from Wordnet and structural between pairs of objects in a hierarchical network (subsumption relation) in order to find real correspondences and real isolated elements. Finally, it merges ontologies based on the result of similarity measures in the previous step and the algebraic approaches of graph transformations to generate the global ontology.

In future work, we aim to enhance the performance of the similarity identification module through the use of other information retrieval techniques. The current test case study includes small to medium ontologies. Our approach can however be combined with techniques involving the use of Big data technologies in order to perform better evaluations also for the case of big ontologies.

References

1. Maedche, A., Staab, S.: Measuring similarity between ontologies. In: Gómez-Pérez, A., Benjamins, V.R. (eds.) EKAW 2002. LNCS (LNAI), vol. 2473, pp. 251–263. Springer, Heidelberg (2002). https://doi.org/10.1007/3-540-45810-7_24
2. Leacock, C., Chodorow, M.: Combining local context and WordNet similarity for word sense identification. In: Fellbaum, C. (ed.) WordNet: An Electronic Lexical Database. MIT Press, Cambridge (1998)
3. Lin, D.: An information-theoretic definition of similarity. In: Proceedings of the Fifteenth International Conference on Machine Learning (ICML 1998). Morgan Kaufmann, Madison (1998)

4. Breitling, F.: A standard transformation from XML to RDF via XSLT. Astron. Nachr. **330**(7), 755–760 (2009)
5. Li, G., Luo, Z., Shao, J.: Multi-mapping based ontology merging system design. In: 2nd International Conference on Advanced Computer Control (ICACC), June 2010
6. Stumne, G., Maedche, A.: FCA-MERGE: bottom-up merging of ontologies. In: The 17th International Joint Conference on Artificial Intelligence, vol. 1, pp. 225–230, August 2001
7. Wiederhold, G.: Mediators in the architecture of future information systems. IEEE Comput. **25**(3), 38–49 (1992)
8. Ling, H., Zhou, S.: Mapping relational databases into OWL ontology. Int. J. Eng. Technol. **5**(6), 4735–4740 (2013)
9. Bedini, I., Matheus, C., Patel-Schneider, P.F.: Transforming XML schema to OWL using patterns. In: 2011 Fifth IEEE International Conference on Semantic Computing (ICSC), October 2011
10. Bedini, I., Benjamin, N., Gardarin, G.: Janus: Automatic Ontology Builder from XSD files. arXiv preprint arXiv:1001.4892 (2010)
11. Sequeda, J.F., Arenas, M., Miranker, D.P.: On directly mapping relational databases to RDF and OWL. In: International World Wide Web Conference Committee (IW3C2), WWW 2012, 16–20 April 2012, Lyon, France (2012)
12. Jiang, J., Conrath, D.: Semantic similarity based on corpus statistics and lexical taxonomy. In: Proceedings of International Conference on Research in Computational Linguistics, Taiwan (1997)
13. Huang, J.Y., Lange, C., Auer, S.: Streaming transformation of XML to RDF using XPath based mappings. In: Proceedings of the 11th International Conference on Semantic Systems, SEMANTICS 2015, 15–17 September, Vienna, Austria (2015)
14. Zedlitz, J., Jörke, J., Luttenberger, N.: From UML to OWL 2. In: Lukose, D., Ahmad, A.R., Suliman, A. (eds.) KTW 2011. CCIS, vol. 295, pp. 154–163. Springer, Heidelberg (2012). https://doi.org/10.1007/978-3-642-32826-8_16
15. Alaoui, L., EL Hajjamy, O., Bahaj, M.: Automatic mapping of relational databases to OWL ontology. Int. J. Eng. Res. Technol. (IJERT), **3**(4) (2014)
16. Alaoui, L., El Hajjamy, O., Bahaj, M.: RDB2OWL2: schema and data conversion from RDB into OWL2, Int. J. Eng. Res. Technol. (IJERT), **3**(11) (2014)
17. Ferdinand, M., Zirpins, C., Trastour, D.: Lifting XML schema to OWL. In: Koch, N., Fraternali, P., Wirsing, M. (eds.) ICWE 2004. LNCS, vol. 3140, pp. 354–358. Springer, Heidelberg (2004). https://doi.org/10.1007/978-3-540-27834-4_44
18. Klein, M., Fensel, D.: Ontology versioning on the semantic web. In: The First Semantic Web Working Symposium, Stanford, CA (2001)
19. Löwe, M.: Algebraic approach to single-pushout graph transformation. Theor. Comput. Sci. **109**(1–2), 181–224 (1993)
20. Mahfoudh, M., Forestier, G., Hassenforder, M.: A benchmark for ontologies merging assessment. In: Lehner, F., Fteimi, N. (eds.) KSEM 2016. LNCS (LNAI), vol. 9983, pp. 555–566. Springer, Cham (2016). https://doi.org/10.1007/978-3-319-47650-6_44
21. Noy, N.F., Muzen, N.A.: PROMPT: algorithm and tool for automated ontology merging and alignement. Stanford University (2000)
22. Gherabi, N., Bahaj, M.: A new method for mapping UML class into OWL ontology. Spec. Issue Int. J. Comput. Appl. (0975 – 8887) Softw. Eng. Databases Expert Syst. – SEDEXS, (2012)
23. EL Hajjamy, O., Alaoui, L., Bahaj, M.: Mapping UML to OWL2 Ontology. J. Theor. Appl. Inf. Technol. (JATIT), **90**(1) (2016)

24. EL Hajjamy, O., Alaoui, L., Bahaj, M.: XSD2OWL2: automatic mapping from XML schema into OWL2 ontology. J. Theor. Appl. Inf. Technol. (JATIT), **95**(8) (2017)
25. Resnik, P.: Using information content to evaluate semantic similarity in taxonomy. In: Proceedings of 14th International Joint Conference on Artificial Intelligence, Montreal (1995)
26. Rada, R., Mili, H., Bichnell, E., Blettner, M.: Development and application of a metric on semantic nets. IEEE Trans. Syst. Man Cybern. **19**, 17–30 (1989)
27. Amrouch, S., Mostefai, S.: Un algorithme semi-automatique pour la fusion d'ontologies basé sur la combinaison de stratégies. In: International Conference on Education and e-Learning Innovations (2012)
28. Cranefield, S.: UML and the semantic web. In: The First Semantic Web Working Symposium, pp. 113–130. Stanford University, California (2001)
29. Raunich, S., Rahm, E.: ATOM: automatic target-driven ontology merging. In: 2011 IEEE 27th International Conference on Data Engineering (ICDE), May 2011
30. Slimani, T., Yaghlane, B.B., Mellouli, K.: Une extension de mesure de similarité entre les concepts d'une ontologie. In: 4th International Conference: Sciences of Electronic, Technologies of Information and Telecommunications, March 2007
31. Levenshtein, V.I.: Binary codes capable of correcting deletions, insertions and reversals. Sov. Phys. Dokl. **6**, 707–710 (1966)
32. Winkler, W.E.: Overview of record linkage and current research directions. In: Research Report Series, RRS (2006)
33. Wu, Z., Palmer, M.: Verb semantics and lexical selection. In: Proceedings of the 32nd Annual Meeting of the Associations for Computational Linguistics, pp. 133–138 (1994)

Toward a Solution to Interoperability and Portability of Content Between Different Content Management System (CMS): Introduction to DB2EAV API

Abdelkader Rhouati(✉), Jamal Berrich, Mohammed Ghaouth Belkasmi, and Toumi Bouchentouf

Team SIQL, Laboratory LSEII, ENSAO, Mohammed First University, 60000 Oujda, Morocco
abdelkader.rhouati@gmail.com, jberrich@gmail.com, ghaouth@gmail.com, tbouchentouf@gmail.com

Abstract. Content Management Systems, recognized by the acronym CMS, have evolved lots with development of the internet in the 2000s. Several new versions and systems are created annually. Interoperability between these systems has become a necessity for enterprise using a variety of CMS. It concerns data in general. The solution most used is Web Services. The disadvantage is that we have to develop two components a client and a server. Furthermore, those elements are not compatible with another system, and in case version of system or all system change we must re-develop all components. In this paper, we present an innovative solution to the problem of data interoperability between CMS. It is an alternative to Web Services with more performance, and a lower cost of maintenance, and compatibility with variety of systems. Our solution is called DB2EAV. DB2EAV is an API of mapping database to Entity-Attribute-Value model. The idea is inspired by the fact that most of the CMS uses the Entity-Attribute-Value model as a conception of their databases. The API DB2EAV provides also the ability to recover data directly from the database of CMS. DB2EAV API is compatible with any type or version of CMS that it implements the Entity-Attribute-Value model.

Keywords: Interoperability · CMS · EAV · Web-Services · DB2EAV Web application · Database mapping

1 Introduction

The content management systems (CMS) are now the most used tools for creating content websites on the internet. Since the explosion of the Internet in the early 2000s a multitude of CMS have been created, each with a different technical design on the one hand, and functional direction on the other. A CMS cannot solve all the problems of content management, which continues to evolve with the evolution of the Internet and its use in our everyday life. All CMS then tends to the specialty. On last year's almost all CMS are focused on one main feature while providing additional features that are

Y. Tabii et al. (Eds.): BDCA 2018, CCIS 872, pp. 433–443, 2018.
https://doi.org/10.1007/978-3-319-96292-4_34

not usually complete. As an example of this situation, we can list the Magento CMS specialized in e-commerce, WordPress which is recognized by its features related to Blogging and Drupal or Ezpublish specialists in the management of editorial content.

An enterprise can use several CMS solutions for implement its information system. The communication between these solutions is therefore necessary to avoid duplication of data, and to build access to each site from another (Example: a user that accesses to a corporate website can view the products offered for sale on the e-commerce website). The communication may also be necessary in the case of site migration from one CMS to another or from one version to another version [1].

We conclude that communication between CMS is no longer a choice, it has become a necessity: It is interoperability [2].

The interoperability can be defined as a problem related to the interaction and communication between two incompatible systems [2]. Which is compatible with the IEEE's definition "the ability of two or more systems or components to exchange information and to use the information that has been exchanged" [10]. By focusing on the ontology of interoperability from a technical point of view, we can deduce two types of solutions: a priori solution by homogenization of the system's components and a posteriori solution by construction of bridge between two systems [2]. The bridges are protocols used by systems to communicate with other remote systems. In the case of Web Sites in general and in particular those designed and built by CMS, we talk about bridge as Web Services [3]. Several solutions are available, the most used are: SOAP, REST and XML [3].

In this paper, we propose a solution to the problem of data interoperability between CMS. Our solution is an alternative to Web-Services and based on the fact of using the Entity-Attribute-Value model (EAV) [4] as the conception of database by almost all CMS. Compared to web service our solution is faster and a low cost for evolutivity and maintainability.

This article is organized in different sections. Section 2 presents the Entity-Attribute-Value model (EAV) and its use in content management systems (CMS). Section 3 introduces our DB2EAV API solution with an illustration of a case study of communication between three CMS Drupal, Magento and EzPublish. Finally, a comparative discussion between DB2EAV and Web Services, and views on the prospects of our solution will be presented respectively in Sects. 4 and 5.

2 The Conception of Databases CMS Based on the Entity-Attribute-Value Model

2.1 The Presentation of the Entity-Attribute-Value Model (EAV)

The classical model of relational database of an information system, which is based on the principle that a data structure X is modeled by a single table X, is a non-flexible model. In other words, if we change the data structure X by adding, deleting or modifying fields for example, we must change the definition of the table X. Furthermore, we can imagine the impact and cost of this change on the source code of our system [5].

The EAV model was created in part to address this problem [4]. It transforms a non-flexible classical model to an open one, allowing flexibility and scalability on database. In fact, using the EAV model make changing any data structure possible without any modification in database tables, unlike the classical model that could handle this with an "alter table".

To understand this principle, Fig. 1 illustrates an example of conception of an article, following the classical model and the EAV model.

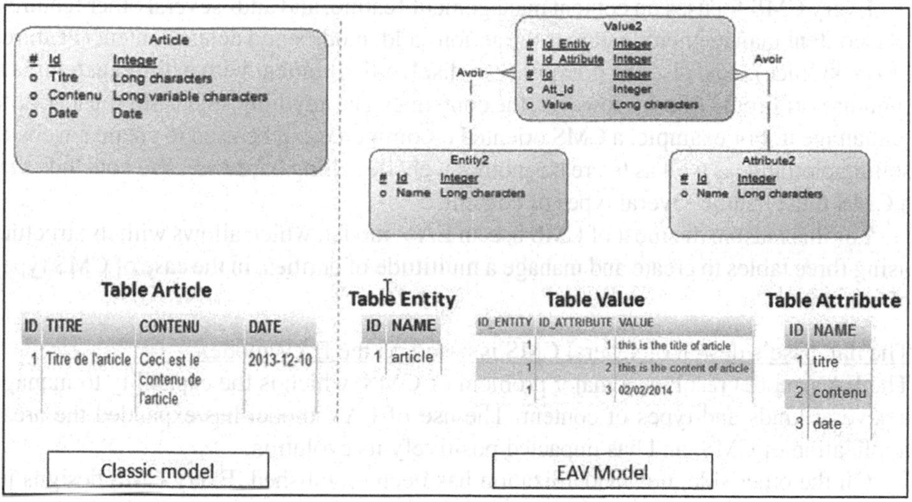

Fig. 1. Comparison between the classical conception database model and the Entity-Attribute-Value (EAV).

As its name indicate, EAV model is based on three components:

- The "entity" refers to any item, it's can be an event of sale, a merchant or a product. Entities in EAV are managed via an Objects table that handles data about each item, such as name, description, and so on. This table have a unique identifier for each entity which is used across foreign key in other tables of the model.
- The "attribute" is stored in a dedicated attributes table. This table handle a set of attribute of every entity. It's also used to automate generation of user interfaces for browsing and editing data of entities.
- The "values" is a one or several tables, which is used to store data values.

The main advantage of using EAV is its flexibility. However, EAV is less efficiency when retrieving data in bulk comparing with classic models. Another limitation of EAV is that we need additional logic to complete tasks which can be done automatically by conventional schemas.

2.2 The Use of EAV Model as Design of CMS Databases

Acronym for Content Management System, CMS [6] are a tool created with the bursting of the Internet bubble in the early 2000s. CMS can be considered as new tools, which is why most of them have not yet reached technical and functional maturity. Therefore, they evolve every day with the evolution of our use of internet. So, some versions of CMS come with a radical change of the technical and conceptual architecture (Example: version 5 of EzPublish integrates Symfony2 Framework).

Every CMS focuses on content management feature, and adds several other features. The content management feature is the actions add, modify and delete content (Features of BackOffice), And also the possibility to display this content with a different template (Features of Front Office). However, the content can be anything, and CMS must be able to manage it. For example, a CMS oriented e-commerce can be used to create a website selling clothing, as well as to create another website selling hardware. We conclude that a CMS must handle several types of content.

For this reason, the most of CMS use an EAV model, which allows with its structure using three tables to create and manage a multitude of entities, in the case of CMS types of content.

The database's design of several CMS is based on the EAV model:
The EAV model resolves a major problem of CMS, which is the capability to manage a several kinds and types of content. The use of EAV model has expanded the areas application of CMS, and has impacted positively its evolution.

On the other side, no standardization has been established. Every CMS designs its database with the EAV model differently, and try to give solutions to the limitations of the model by adapting it to their needs according to the priorities drowned: performance, advanced search, data normalization, etc.

3 Introduction to the DB2EAV API

3.1 The API DB2EAV: Mapping Database to the EAV Model

The DB2EAV API is created with the aim of providing a solution to the data interoperability between CMS that implements an EAV model as design of their databases. The DB2EAV is an API of mapping databases to EAV model. we have been inspired by [11], however the API is for a specific design of Database who is EAV, in order to described with details how every database have implement the design.

The mapping is based on an XML [12] file that describes the implementation of the three components of the EAV model: Entity, Value and Attribute. In addition to database mapping, the API allows access to a CMS data directly from database with SQL queries. The Fig. 2 explains how the DB2EAV API works.

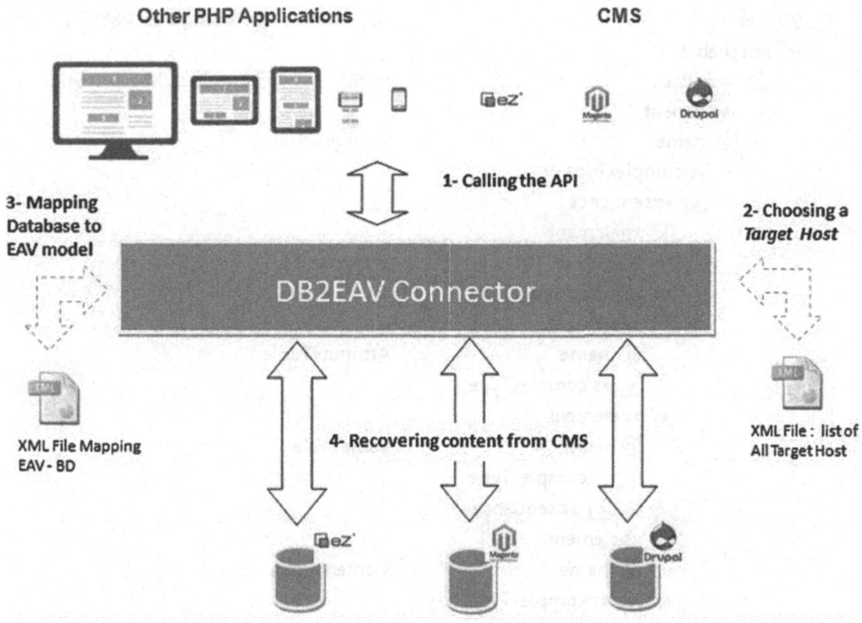

Fig. 2. Operating process of the API DB2EAV

The DB2EAV API operates in four steps:

1 - Calling the API: the API is based on language PHP, and compatible with 5.3.0 version or higher.
2 - Choosing a Target Host: A Target Host is a Web Site based on CMS. It is used to define access settings of the CMS's database. A list of all available Target Hosts is defined in an XML file.
3 - Mapping database to EAV model: in this step, the API uses an XML mapping file, corresponding to the Target Host defined in step 2, to build all SQL queries needed to get content from CMS's database. This mapping file describes how a CMS implements the three components of the EAV model.
4 - Recovering content from CMS: using API we can retrieve data from remote CMS's database. The data is retrieved width SQL queries in associative arrays.

The XML [12] file for mapping databases to EAV model is specific to one CMS and must respect the following XML schema (Fig. 3):

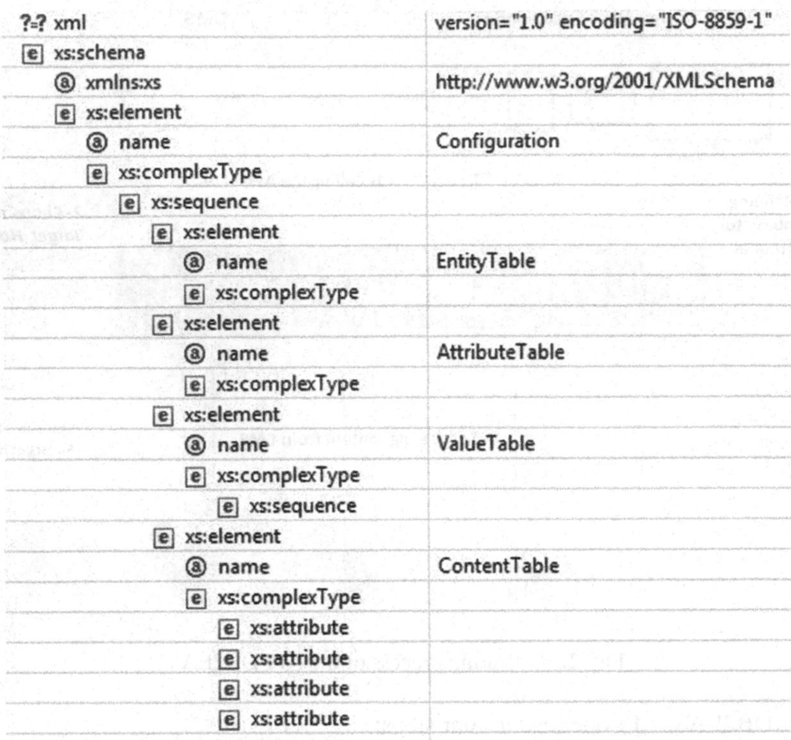

Fig. 3. XSD schema of XML mapping file of Database to EAV model

3.2 Case Study of the DB2EAV API: Solution to Data Interoperability Between CMS

This section describes a concrete example of using the DB2EAV API as solution of data interoperability between CMS.

In this scenario, we suppose an enterprise system composed of three different web sites: an e-commerce web site based on Magento CMS [7], a corporate site by Drupal [8] and a portal built using the Ezpublish CMS [9]. The interoperability between the three CMS is necessary to improve the visibility of company data by users. The DB2EAV API is used then from the CMS EzPublish, to get products from the Magento CMS and news items from the Drupal CMS. The following figure illustrates this case study (Fig. 4).

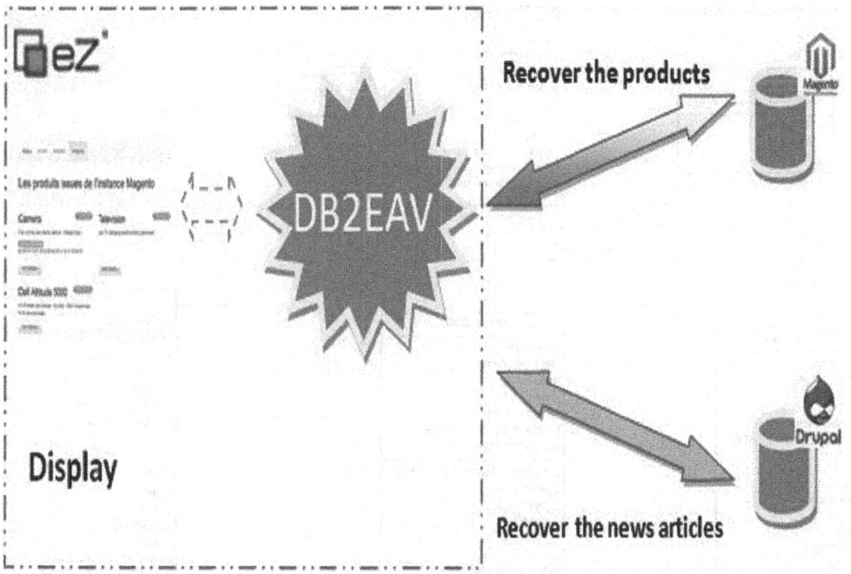

Fig. 4. Using the API as solution to data interoperability between 3 CMS - EzPublish, Magento and Drupal

4 Technical Design of DB2EAV API

DB2EAV API is based on the PHP language. This choice is related to the fact that PHP is the most used on the web and also because the main CMS taken as a case study are based on the same language PHP, as Drupal, Magento and Ezpublish.

In the Fig. 5, we expose the class diagram of the DB2EAV API. "Entity", "Attribute" and "Value" classes correspond to ENTITY, ATTRIBUTE, VALUE of the EAV model, and class "Content" matches the content which means a record corresponding to an entity. These four classes are dedicated to a specific treatment, and inherit respectively from the classes "EntityBase", "AttributeBase", "ValueBase" and "Contentbase" which contains the code source that make possible to manipulate the EAV Data-Bases.

- EntityBase: it is a class containing functions allowing manipulation of the table entities, as creating, editing and removing.
- AttributeBase: it is a class containing functions to manipulate attribute of entities.
- ContentBase: it is a class containing functions to manipulate content as instance of entity.

The configuration system is the most important part of the API, because it's explaining how the target database of CMS has implemented the EAV model. All setting files are grouped in a "config" folder, as shown in The Following figure (Fig. 6).

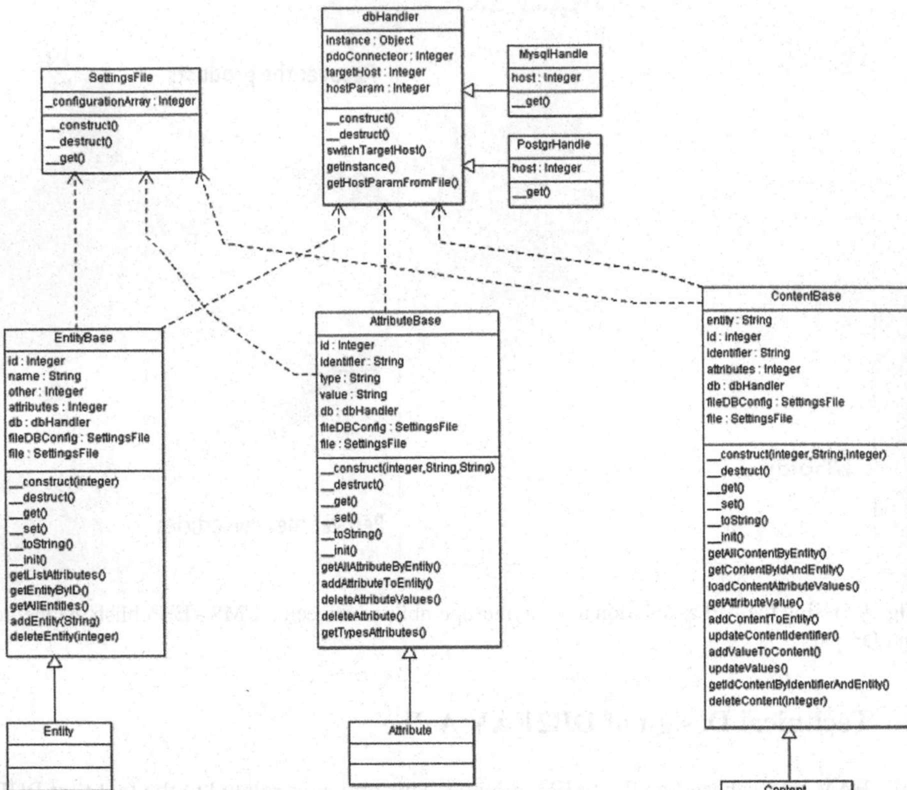

Fig. 5. The class diagram of DB2EAV API

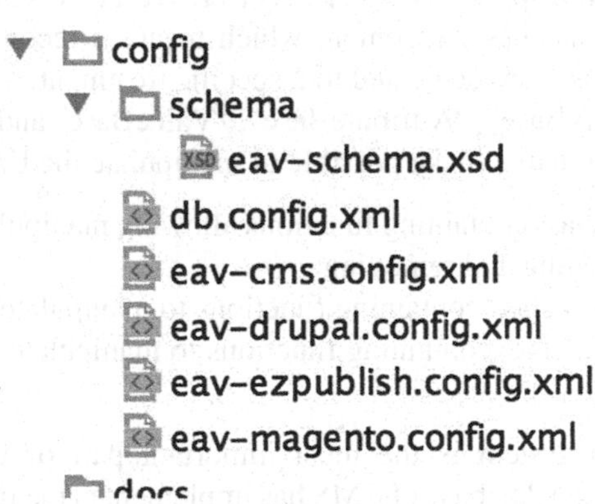

Fig. 6. List of setting files

The setting file are:

- db.config.xml: the database access configuration file of the target CMS.
- eav-schema.xsd: it presents the XML schema of setting files that explains how the EAV model has been implemented on the database of the target CMS.
- eav-cms.config.xml: it is an example of a configuration file based on the schema XSD.
- eav-drupal.config.xml: it is the setting file that illustrates the model EAV as implemented on Drupal CMS.
- eav-ezpublish.config.xml: it is the setting file that illustrates the model EAV as implemented on EzPublish CMS.
- eav-magento.config.xml: it is the setting file that illustrates the model EAV as implemented on Magento CMS.

The DB2EAV API is available for contributing under the apache license (ASL), and its code source is on: https://github.com/arhouati/DB2EAV.

5 A Comparative Discussion Between DB2EAV and Web Services

5.1 Disadvantages of Web Services: REST, SOAP and XML

From a technical point of view, the interoperability between two systems can generally be solved with a system of "Bridge." [2] In the case of CMS, which are tools for creating web site or application, the bridge systems are Web Services. In fact, a Web Service can be defined as a program for communication and data exchange between heterogeneous systems on the Internet [3].

The implementation of Web Services gives rise to several protocols and technologies. The most used with the CMS's are REST, SOAP and XML.

The diagram in Fig. 7 explains the principle of Web Services.

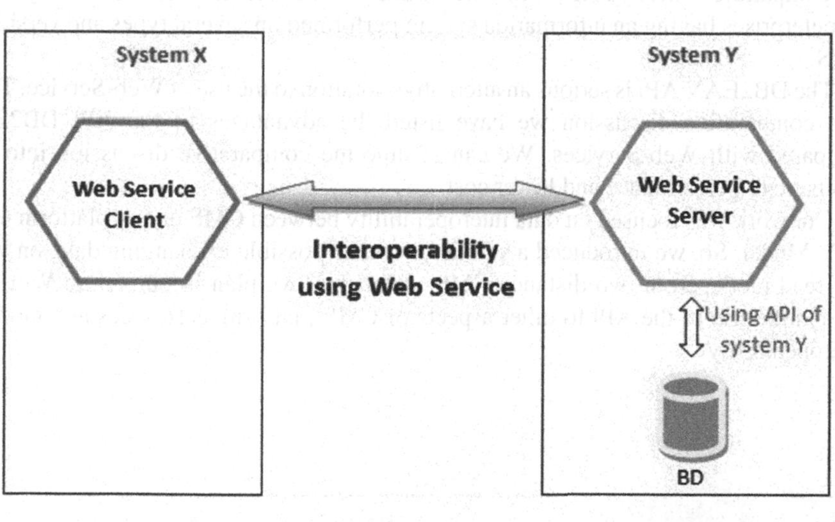

Fig. 7. Descriptive diagram of the operation process of Web Services

Then we can easily detect weak links in the operation of Web Services. First, we need two components to use a Web Service; a server component who is a program that receives requests, processes them, and returns answers, and client component who consumes the data received from the server. In addition, the server uses the API system to recover the data.

In conclusion, if the entire system and/or version are changed, even if the Web Service is achieved by a portable language like PHP, it is essential to re-develop the entire code specially to retrieve the data. the same thing for the client side.

Further a Web Service made for a given system cannot work on another system. in this case an adaptation is required.

5.2 Advantages of DB2EAV API

In one hand, the major advantage of DB2EAV API is more performance, since that this API recover data directly from database using SQL queries, unlike to Web Service that have two layers, a server component and the API persistence of system which depends on the target platform. On the other hand, the API DB2EAV is completely independent of the CMS systems. Changing version or whole of system does not affect the operation of the API, provided that the design of the database is still based on the EAV model. However. in the case of Web-Services we need to adapt it to the new adopted system.

6 Conclusion and Future Works

In this paper, we have presented the DB2EAV API, its functional and technical operation and its application on a case study. In fact, DB2EAV API is a solution to data interoperability between CMS having a design database based on EAV model. It is a portable and compatible with any PHP CMS. The DB2EAV API is a solution which is very useful for enterprises having an information system performed on several types and version of CMS.

The DB2EAV API is serious an alternative solution to the use of Web-Service. Thus, in a comparative discussion we have listed the advantages of the API DB2EAV compared with Web-Services. We can resume the comparative discussion into two points more performance and lower cost.

Our work was focused on data interoperability between CMS or any platform using EAV Model. So, we introduced a solution to make possible exchanging data, on write and read mode, from two distance CMS. After that, we plan in our future Works to expand the use of the API to other aspects of CMS platform as services and modules interoperability.

References

1. Chen, D., Doumeingts, G., Vernadat, F.: Architectures for enterprise integration and interoperability: past, present and future. Comput. Ind. **59**, 647–659 (2008)
2. Naudet, Y., Latour, T., Guedria, W., Chen, D.: Towards a systemic formalization of interoperability. Comput. Ind. **61**, 176–185 (2010)
3. Web Services Architecture: W3C Working Group Note, 11 February 2004. http://www.w3.org/TR/ws-arch/
4. Nadkarni, P.M., Brandt, C.A., Marenco, L.: WebEAV: automatic metadata-driven generation of web interfaces to entity–attribute–value databases. J. Am. Med. Inform. Assoc. **7**, 343–356 (2000)
5. Codd, E.F.: A relational model of data for large shared data banks. Commun. ACM **13**(6), 377–387 (1970)
6. Laleci, G.B., Aluc, G., Dogac, A., Sinaci, A., Kilic, O., Tuncer, F.: A semantic backend for content management systems. Knowl.-Based Syst. **23**, 832–843 (2010)
7. Magento (2017). http://magento.com/
8. Drupal (2017). http://drupal.org/
9. Ezpublish (2017). http://ez.no/
10. The Institute of Electrical and Electronics Engineers: Standard Glossary of Software Engineering Terminology, Std 610.12, New York (1990)
11. Murthy, R., Krishnaprasad, M., Chandrasekar, S., Sedlar, E., Krishnamurthy, V., Agarwal, N.: Mechanism for mapping XML schemas to object-relational database systems. Google Patents, US Patent 7,096,224 (2006). http://google.com/patents/US7096224
12. XML 1.0: Extensible Markup Language (XML) 1.0, W3C Recommendation, World Wide Web Consortium (2008). http://www.w3.org/TR/xml/

Image Processing and Applications

Reconstruction of the 3D Scenes from the Matching Between Image Pair Taken by an Uncalibrated Camera

Karima Karim[1(✉)], Nabil El Akkad[1,2(✉)], and Khalid Satori[1(✉)]

[1] LIIAN, Department of Computer Science, Faculty of Science, Dhar El Mahraz, Sidi Mohamed Ben Abdellah University, B.P 1796 Atlas, Fez, Morocco
karima.karim35@gmail.com, nabil.elakkad@usmba.ac.ma, khalid.satori@gmail.com

[2] Department of Mathematics and Computer Science, National School of Applied Sciences (ENSA) of Al-Hoceima, University of Mohamed First, B.P 03 Ajdir, Oujda, Morocco

Abstract. In this paper, we will study a new approach of reconstruction of three-dimensional scenes from an auto calibration method of camera characterized by variable parameters. Indeed, obtaining the 3D scene is based on the Euclidean reconstruction of the interest points detected and matched between pair of images. The relationship between the matches and camera parameters is used to formulate a nonlinear equation system. This system is transformed into a nonlinear cost function, which will be minimized to determine the intrinsic and extrinsic camera parameters and subsequently estimate the projection matrices. Finally, the coordinates of the 3D points of the scene are obtained by solving a linear equation system. The results of the experiments show the strengths of this contribution in terms of precision and convergence.

Keywords: Auto calibration · Reconstruction · Variable parameter Fundamental matrix

1 Introduction

In this work, we will investigate about the three-dimensional reconstruction being a technique that allows obtaining a 3D representation of an object from a sequence of images of this object taken by different views. In fact, several 3D reconstruction techniques use calibration or Auto-calibration methods.

During this work, we will presented a new approach to reconstructing three-dimensional scenes from a method of autocalibration of cameras characterized by variable parameters. In general, the determination of the 3D scene is based on the euclidean reconstruction of the interest points detected and matched by the ORB descriptor [20]. The intrinsic parameters of the cameras are estimated by the resolution of a nonlinear equation system (using the nonlinear equations of the Levenberg-Marquart algorithm [18]), and they are used with the fundamental matrices (estimated from 8 pairings between the image couples by the RANSAC algorithm [11]) to determine the extrinsic camera parameters, and finally to estimate the projection matrix

Y. Tabii et al. (Eds.): BDCA 2018, CCIS 872, pp. 447–463, 2018.
https://doi.org/10.1007/978-3-319-96292-4_35

(expressed according to the intrinsic and extrinsic parameters of the cameras used). The relationships between camera parameters, projection matrix elements, pairing coordinates, and 3D point coordinates gives a linear equation system and the resolution of this system permits to obtain a cloud of 3D points.

In this introduction, we have therefore provided the general ideas that will be investigated in this paper. The rest of this work is organized as follows:

A diagram of different steps of our method is presented in the second part, the scene and the camera model are presented in the third part, the fourth part treats the auto calibration of the cameras, the fifth part explains the reconstruction of the 3D scene, the experiments will be discussed in the sixth paragraph and the conclusion is presented in the last part.

2 Diagram of Different Steps of Our Method

The Fig. 1. below represents a diagram of different steps of the reconstruction of 3D scene:

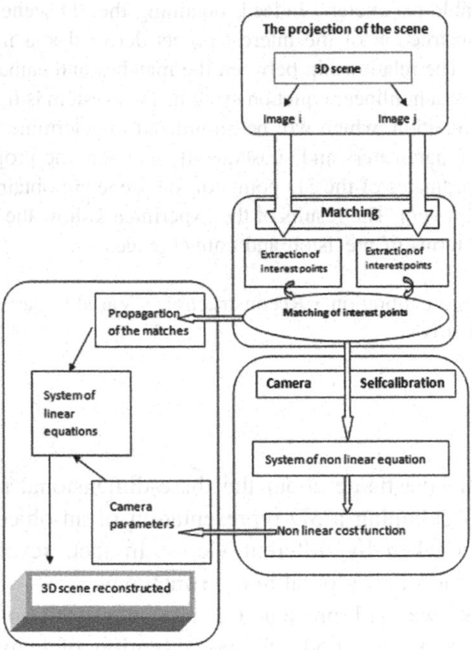

Fig. 1. Diagram of the reconstruction of the 3D scene

3 Scene and Camera Model

3.1 Presentation of the Scene

We consider two points S_1 and S_2 of the 3D scene, there is a single point S_3, such as $S_1S_2S_3$: is an equilateral triangle. $R_e(OX_eY_eZ_e)$ is the euclidean reference associated to the triangle wich O is its center and b its side.

3.2 Model of the Camera

We are using the pinhole model of the camera Fig. 2. so that we project the points of the 3D scene in the planes of images, this model is characterized by a matrix $K_i(R_it_i)$ of size (3 × 4), with:

R_i : the rotation matrix
t_i : the translation vector
K_i : The matrix of intrinsic parameters defined by:

$$K_i = \begin{pmatrix} f_i & s_i & u_{oi} \\ 0 & \varepsilon_i f_i & v_{oi} \\ 0 & 0 & 1 \end{pmatrix} \quad (1)$$

with f_i : focal length
ε_i : the scaling factor
s_i : the skew factor
(u_{0i}, v_{0i}) : the coordinates of the principal point.

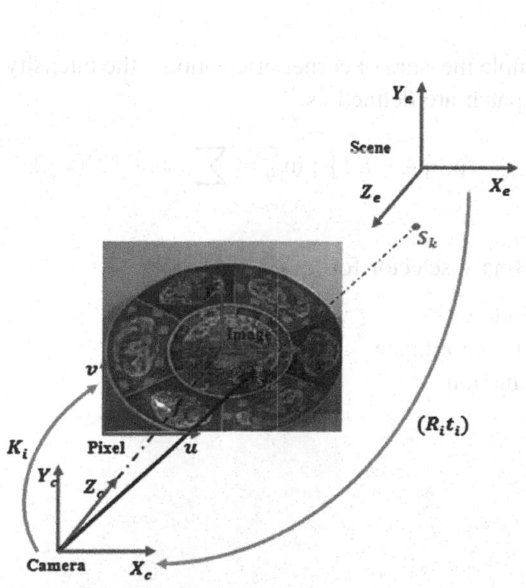

Fig. 2. Representation of the scene

4 Camera Autocalibration

The auto Calibration [1–10] is a technique that allows us to estimate the parameters of the cameras without any prior knowledge on the scene.

4.1 ORB Descriptor: Oriented FAST and Rotated BRIEF

The detection [12–14] and the matching [15–17] of the interest points are important steps in the autocalibration and the reconstruction of 3D scenes, in this paper we based on the ORB descriptor: Oriented FAST and rotated BRIEF [21] (ORB: Binary Robust Independent Elementary Features) which is a fast robust local feature detector, first presented by Rublee et al. in 2011 [20], that can be used in computer vision tasks like object recognition or 3D reconstruction. It is a fusion of the FAST key point detector and BRIEF descriptor with some modifications [9]. Initially to determine the key points, it uses FAST. Then a Harris corner measure is applied to find top N points. FAST does not compute the orientation and is rotation variant. It computes the intensity weighted centroid of the patch with located corner at center. The direction of the vector from this corner point to centroid gives the orientation. Moments are computed to improve the rotation invariance. The descriptor BRIEF poorly performs if there is an in-plane rotation. In ORB, a rotation matrix is computed using the orientation of patch and then the BRIEF descriptors are steered according to the orientation.

The ORB descriptor is a bit similar to BRIEF. It doesn't have an elaborate sampling pattern as BRISK [26] or FREAK [27]. However, there are two main differences between ORB and BRIEF:

1. ORB uses an orientation compensation mechanism, making it rotation invariant.
2. ORB learns the optimal sampling pairs, whereas BRIEF uses randomly chosen sampling pairs.

ORB uses a simple measure of corner orientation – the intensity centroid [28]. First, the moments of a patch are defined as:

$$\forall p, q \in \{0, 1\} : m_{pq} = \sum\nolimits_{x,y} x^p y^q \, I(x,y) \tag{2}$$

With:
$p, q \in \{0, 1\}$ Binary selector for x and y direction

x,y Circular window
$x^p y^q$ weighted by coordinate
$I(x, y)$ image function

Image moments help us to calculate some features like center of mass of the object, area of the object etc.

With these moments we can find the centroid, the "center of mass" of the patch as:

$$C = \left(\frac{m_{10}}{m_{00}}, \frac{m_{01}}{m_{00}}\right) \tag{3}$$

and by constructing a vector from the patch center O to the centroid C, we can define the relative orientation of the patch as:

$$\underset{OC}{\rightarrow}\theta = \operatorname{atan2}(m_{01}, m_{10}) \tag{4}$$

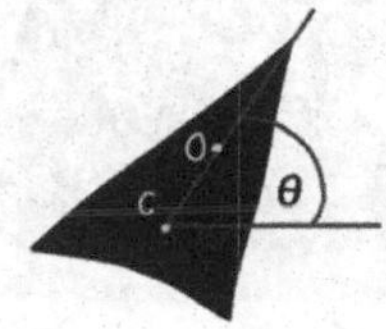

ORB discretize the angle to increments of $\frac{2\pi}{30}$ (12°), and construct a lookup table of precomputed BRIEF patterns. As long as the keypoint orientation θ is consistent across views, the correct set of points will be used to compute its descriptor.

To conclude, ORB is binary descriptor that is similar to BRIEF, with the added advantages of rotation invariance and learned sampling pairs. You're probably asking yourself, how does ORB perform in comparison to BRIEF. Well, in non-geometric transformation (those that are image capture dependent and do not rely on the view-point, such as blur, JPEG compression, exposure and illumination) BRIEF actually outperforms ORB. In affine transformation, BRIEF perform poorly under large rotation or scale change as it's not designed to handle such changes. In perspective transformations, which are the result of view-point change, BRIEF surprisingly slightly outperforms ORB.

4.2 The Projection Matrix

We consider S_1 and S_2 two points of the 3D scene and π the plan which contains these two points.

$R_e(O\ X_eY_eZ_e)$ is the Euclidian reference which is associated to the triangle of the center O and side b

The coordinates of points S_1, S_2 and S_3 Fig. 3 are given as below:

$$S_1 = \left(\frac{b}{2}, \frac{\sqrt{3}}{2}b, 1\right)^T$$

$$S_2 = (b, 0, 1)^T$$

$$S_3 = (0, 1, 1)^T$$

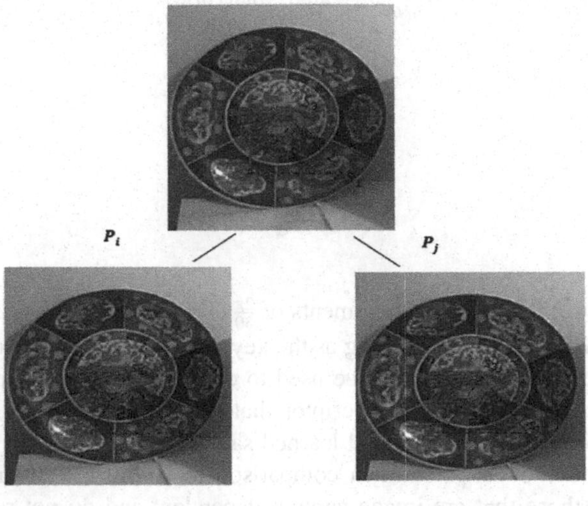

Fig. 3. Representation of points S_1, S_2 and S_3 in the two images i and j.

We consider the two homography H_i and H_j that can be used to project the plan in the images i and j, so the projection of the two points can be represented by the following expressions:

$$s_{im} \sim H_i S_m \tag{5}$$

$$s_{jm} \sim H_j S_m \tag{6}$$

With $m = 1, 2$. s_{im} and s_{jm} represent respectively the points in the images i and j which are the projections of the two summits S_1 and S_2 of the 3D scene, and H_n represents the homography matrix defined by:

$$H_n = K_n R_n \begin{pmatrix} 1 & 0 & \\ 0 & 1 & R_n^T t_n \\ 0 & 0 & \end{pmatrix};\ n = i, j \tag{7}$$

With:
R_n : the rotation matrix
t_n : the translation vector
K_n : The matrix of intrinsic parameters.

The expressions (5) and (6) can be written as :

$$s_{im} \sim H_i B S'_m \tag{8}$$

$$s_{jm} \sim H_j B S'_m \tag{9}$$

With : $B = \begin{pmatrix} b & \frac{b}{2} & 0 \\ 0 & \frac{\sqrt{3}}{2} b & 0 \\ 0 & 0 & 1 \end{pmatrix}$

$$S'_m = \begin{pmatrix} a \\ b \\ 1 \end{pmatrix}$$

For:

$$\begin{cases} m = 1 <=> a = 0 \textit{ and } b = 1 \\ m = 2 <=> a = 1 \textit{ and } b = 0 \end{cases}$$

We put:

$$P_n \sim H_n B\ ;\ n = i, j \tag{10}$$

With P_i and P_j are the projections matrix of the two points S_1' and S_2' in the images i and j Figs. 3 and 6.

From the Eq. (10) we have:

$$P_j \sim H_{ij} P_i \tag{11}$$

With:

$$H_{ij} \sim H_j H_i^{-1} \tag{12}$$

H_{ij} is the homography between the images i and j.

The Eqs. (8), (9) and (10) give:

$$s_{im} \sim P_i S'_m \tag{13}$$

$$s_{jm} \sim P_j S'_m \tag{14}$$

And from the Eqs. (11) and (14) we have :

$$s_{jm} \sim H_{ij} P_i S'_m \tag{15}$$

The Eq. (15) gives:

$$e'_j s_{jm} \sim e'_j H_{ij} P_i S'_m \tag{16}$$

This later gives:

$$e'_j s_{jm} \sim F_{ij} P_i S'_m \tag{17}$$

With F_{ij} is the fundamental matrix between the images i and j.

$$e'_j = \begin{pmatrix} 0 & -e_{j3} & e_{j2} \\ e_{j3} & 0 & -e_{j1} \\ -e_{j2} & e_{j1} & 0 \end{pmatrix}$$

$(e_{j1} e_{j2} e_{j3})^T$ are the coordinates of the epipole of the right image, this epipole can be estimated by the fundamental matrix.

The expression (18) gives:

$$s_{i1} \sim P_i S'_1 \tag{18}$$

$$s_{i2} \sim P_i S'_2 \tag{19}$$

So from the two last relationships, we gets four equations with eight unknowns that are the elements of P_i

The expression (17) gives:

$$e'_j s_{j1} \sim F_{ij} P_i S'_1 \tag{20}$$

$$e'_j s_{j2} \sim F_{ij} P_i S'_2 \tag{21}$$

From the two last relationships, we get four other equations with eight unknowns which are the parameters of P_i. So we can estimate the parameters of P_i, because we have a total of eight unknown equations that are the elements of P_i.

The Eq. (11) gives:

$$e_j^{'}P_j \sim e_j^{'}H_{ij}P_i \tag{22}$$

That gives:

$$e_j^{'}P_j \sim F_{ij}P_i \tag{23}$$

The previous expression gives eight unknown equations that are the elements of P_j. So we can estimate the parameters of P_j from these eight equations with eight unknown.

4.3 Autocalibration Equations

In this part, we will determine the relationship between the images of the absolute conic (ω_i and ω_j), and a relationship between the two points (S_1, S_2) of the 3D scene and their projections (s_{i1}, s_{i2}) and (s_{j1}, s_{j2}) in the planes of the left and right images respectively, the different relationships are established from some techniques of projective geometry. A nonlinear cost function will be defined from the determination of these relationships. The formulated cost function will be minimized by the Levenberg-Marquardt algorithm [18] to estimate ω_i and ω_j and finally the intrinsic parameters of the cameras used [24].

The Eq. (11) gives:

$$\lambda_{im}s_{im} = P_iS_m^{'} \tag{24}$$

With: $P_i = \begin{pmatrix} P_{11} & P_{12} & P_{13} \\ P_{21} & P_{22} & P_{23} \\ P_{31} & P_{32} & P_{33} \end{pmatrix}$

$$s_{im} = \begin{pmatrix} x_{im} \\ y_{im} \\ 1 \end{pmatrix}$$

$$P_i^T\omega_iP_i \sim \begin{pmatrix} B'^TB' & B'^TR_i^Tt_i \\ t_i^TR_iB' & t_i^Tt_i \end{pmatrix} \tag{25}$$

With:

$$B' = \begin{pmatrix} b & \frac{b}{2} \\ 0 & \frac{\sqrt{3}}{2}b \\ 0 & 0 \end{pmatrix} \tag{26}$$

K_i is an upper-triangular matrix normalized as $\det K_i = 1$

$\omega_i = \left(K_i K_i^T\right)^{-1}$ is the image of the absolute conic.

The same for P_j:

$$P_j^T \omega_j P_j \sim \begin{pmatrix} B'^T B' & B'^T R_j^T t_j \\ t_j^T R_j B' & t_j^T t_j \end{pmatrix} \quad (27)$$

We can deduce that the first rows and columns of the matrix $P_i^T \omega_i P_i$ and $P_j^T \omega_j P_j$ are the same.

We put X_i and X_j the two matrix corresponding respectively to the first two rows and columns of the two previous matrices.

$X_m = \begin{pmatrix} x_{1m} & x_{3m} \\ x_{3m} & x_{2m} \end{pmatrix}$, with $m = i, j$.

So we conclude the 3 following equations:

$$\begin{cases} x_{1i} = x_{2i} \\ x_{1j} = x_{2j} \\ x_{1i} x_{3j} = x_{1j} x_{3i} \end{cases} \quad (28)$$

Each image pair gives a system of 3 equations with 8 unknown (4 unknown for ω_i and 4 unknown for ω_j), so to solve the equation system (28), we need at least 4 images.

The equation system (28) is nonlinear, so to solve this system of equations we minimize the following nonlinear cost function:

$$\min_{\omega_k} \sum_{j=i+1}^{n} \sum_{i=1}^{n-1} \left(\alpha_{ij}^2 + \beta_{ij}^2 + \gamma_{ij}^2\right) \quad (29)$$

With: $\propto_{ij} = q_{1i} - q_{2i}$; $\beta_{ij} = q_{1j} - q_{2j}$; $\gamma_{ij} = q_{1i} q_{3j} - q_{1j} q_{3i}$, and : n is the number of images.

The Eq. (29) will be minimized by the Levenberg–Marquardt algorithm [18], this algorithm requires an initialization step. So the camera parameters are initialized as follows:

Pixels are squares, so: $\varepsilon_i = \varepsilon_j = 1$, $s_i = s_j = 0$,

The principal point is in the centre of the image so: $x_{0i} = y_{0i} = x_{0j} = y_{0j} = 256$ (because the images used are of sizes 512×512), and the focal distances f_i and f_j are obtained by the resolution of the equation system (29).

4.4 General Algorithm

1. Detecting and matching of interest points respectively by ORB algorithm.
2. Determination of the Fundamental matrix by Ransac algorithm using eight matches.
3. Calculation of the projection matrices used by the projection of two points.
4. Formulation of the non-linear cost function
5. Minimization of non-linear cost function by the Levenberg-Marquardt algorithm.
   - 5.1. Initialization: we suppose that the principal point is in the center of the image, the pixels are squared, and we calculate the focal length.
   - 5.2. Optimization of the non-linear cost function.

5 Reconstruction of the 3D Scene

This part is dedicated to the 3D reconstruction to determine a cloud of 3D points from the matching between the pairs of images [19, 22, 23, 25]. In theory, getting the position of 3D points from their projections in the images is trivial. The matching 2D point pair must be the projections of the 3D points in the images.

This reconstruction is possible when the geometric relationship between the cameras is known and when the projection of the same point is measured in the images.

The reconstruction of a few points of the 3D scene requires the estimation of the projection matrix of this scene in different images.

We have: P_0 and P_1 two projection matrices of the 3D scene, respectively in the plane of the images, such as:

$$s_{0m} \sim P_0 S_m \tag{30}$$

$$s_{im} \sim P_i S_m$$

We have $P \sim K(R\ t)$
So,

$$P_0 \sim K_0(I_3 O) \tag{31}$$

$$P_1 \sim K_1(R_1 t_1)$$

The essential matrix [29] is the specialization of the fundamental matrix to the case of normalized image coordinates. Historically, the essential matrix was introduced (by

Longuet-Higgins) before the fundamental matrix, and the fundamental matrix may be thought of as the generalization of the essential matrix in which the (inessential) assumption of calibrated cameras is removed. The essential matrix has fewer degrees of freedom, and additional properties, compared to the fundamental matrix.

The defining equation for the essential matrix is:

$$\widehat{X}_1^T E \widehat{X}_0 = 0$$

With $\widehat{X} = K^{-1}X$.

In terms of the normalized image coordinates for corresponding points $X_0 \leftrightarrow X_1$

Substituting for $\widehat{X}_0$ and $\widehat{X}_1$ gives $X_1^T K_1^T E K^{-1} X_0 = 0$. Comparing this with the relation $X_1^T F_{12} X_0 = 0$ for the fundamental matrix, it follows that the relationship between the fundamental and essential matrices is

$$\mathrm{E}_{12} = \mathrm{K}_1^{\mathrm{T}} \mathrm{F}_{12} \mathrm{K}_0 \tag{32}$$

With: F_{12} represent the fundamental matrix between the first and second images, It is estimated from 8 matches between this couple of images.

E_{12} is decompose into singular value in the following equation:

$$\mathrm{E}_{12} = \lambda \mathrm{L}_1 \mathrm{U}(1 \quad 1 \quad 0) \mathrm{L}_2^{\mathrm{T}} \tag{33}$$

With

λ is a non-zero scalar,

And $\mathrm{U}(1 \quad 1 \quad 0)$ is written in the following form:

$$\mathrm{U}(1 \quad 1 \quad 0) = \mathrm{N}_1 \mathrm{N}_2^{\mathrm{T}} = -\mathrm{N}_1 \mathrm{N}_2^{\mathrm{T}} \tag{34}$$

$$\mathrm{N}_1 = \begin{pmatrix} 0 & 1 & 0 \\ -1 & 0 & 0 \\ 0 & 0 & 0 \end{pmatrix}, \mathrm{N}_2 = \begin{pmatrix} 0 & -1 & 0 \\ 1 & 0 & 0 \\ 0 & 0 & 1 \end{pmatrix} \tag{35}$$

From (33) and (34), we have:

$$\mathrm{E}_{12} = \lambda \mathrm{L}_1 \mathrm{N}_1 \mathrm{N}_2^{\mathrm{T}} \mathrm{L}_2^{\mathrm{T}} = -\lambda \mathrm{L}_1 \mathrm{N}_1 \mathrm{N}_2^{\mathrm{T}} \mathrm{L}_2^{\mathrm{T}} \tag{36}$$

L_1 is orthonormal, so the matrix E_{12} can be written as the following form:

$$\mathrm{E}_{12} \sim \mathrm{L}_1 \mathrm{N}_1 \mathrm{L}_1^{\mathrm{T}} (\mp \mathrm{L}_1 \mathrm{N}_2 \mathrm{L}_2^{\mathrm{T}}) \sim -\mathrm{L}_1 \mathrm{N}_1 \mathrm{L}_1^{\mathrm{T}} (\mp \mathrm{L}_1 \mathrm{N}_2^{\mathrm{T}} \mathrm{L}_2) \tag{37}$$

On the other hand, E_{12} is expressed as follows:

$$\mathrm{E}_{12} \sim [\mathrm{t}_1]_{\wedge} \mathrm{R}_1 \tag{38}$$

$$[t_1]_\wedge = \begin{bmatrix} 0 & -t_{13} & t_{12} \\ t_{13} & 0 & -t_{11} \\ -t_{12} & t_{11} & 0 \end{bmatrix} \quad (39)$$

And $(t_{11}t_{12}t_{13})^T$ are the coordinates of the translation vector t_1.

From the two latest expressions, we can conclude the vector t_1 that admits an unique solution:

$$[t_1]_\wedge \sim L_1 N_1 L_1^T \quad (40)$$

And the rotation matrix R_1 admits 4 solutions

$$R_1 \sim \mp L_1 N_2 L_2^T \text{ or } R_1 \sim \mp L_1 N_2^T L_2^T \quad (41)$$

But the determinant of the rotation matrix must be equal to 1, which allows fixing a sign for the two matrices:

$$\mp L_1 N_2 L_2^T \text{ and } \mp L_1 N_2^T L_2^T$$

So the number of solutions for R_1 becomes 2.

We use the two solutions to reconstruct the 3D scene, and finally we choose the solution that gives the best Euclidean reconstruction.

From the Eq. (30), we obtain the following linear system of equations:

$$M(X\ Y\ Z)^T = N \quad (42)$$

M : Matrix of size 4 x 3
N : Vector of size 4

These two matrices are expressed in function of the elements of the projection matrices and the coordinates of the matches.

$(X\ Y\ Z)^T$: The vector of the coordinates of the searched 3D point.

The coordinates of the 3D points (the solution of the Eq. (42)) are obtained by the following expression:

$$\det M^T M \neq 0 \text{ so } M^T M \text{ is no singular}$$

$$(X\ Y\ Z)^T = \left(M^T M\right)^{-1} M^T N \quad (43)$$

6 Experimentations

In this part, we have taken two images of an unknown three-dimensional scene by a CCD camera characterized by variable intrinsic parameters Fig. 4. In the first step, we applied the ORB descriptor to determine the interest points Fig. 5. And the matching between the two selected images Fig. 6. Subsequently and after implementation the algorithms of Ransac and Levenberg-Marquardt while relying on the Python programming language, we got the result of the 3D reconstruction below Fig. 7:

Fig. 4. Two images of unknown 3D scene

Fig. 5. The interest points in the two images (blue color) (Color figure online)

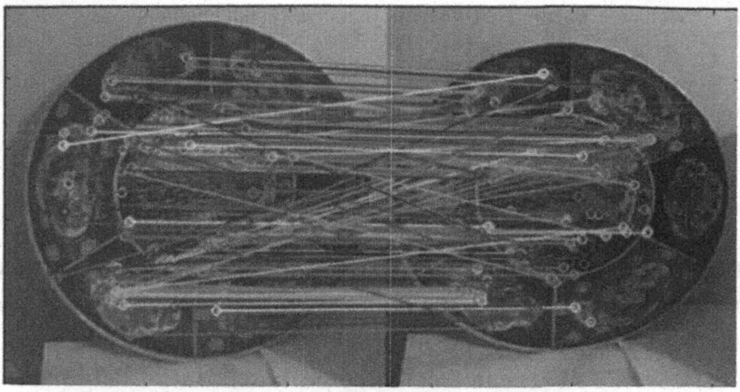

Fig. 6. The matches between the two images

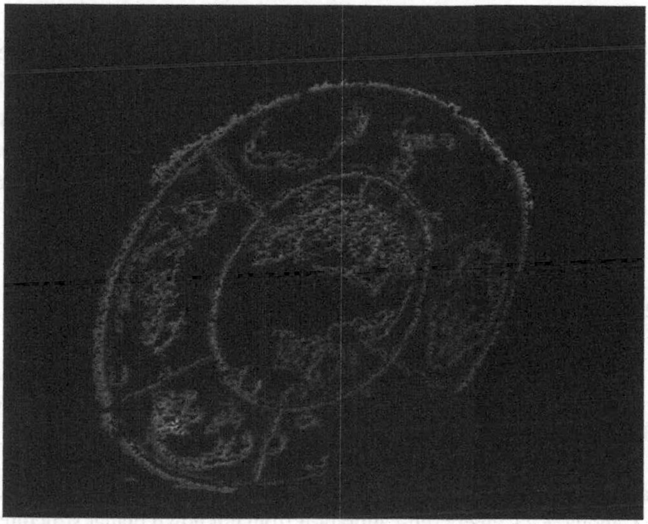

Fig. 7. The reconstructed 3D scene

The detection of interest points, Fig. 5. And the mapping Fig. 6 are carried out by the descriptor ORB [20]. The determination of the relationship between the matches and the camera parameters permit to formulate a system of non-linear equations. This system is introduced in a non-linear cost function. The minimization of this function by Levenberg-Marquardt algorithm [18] allows finding an optimal solution of the camera parameters. These parameters are used with the matches to obtain an initial point cloud Fig. 7.

We have a lot of values to estimate, every parameters have a minimum value.

The intrinsic camera parameters (focal lengths, coordinates of the principal points, scale factors, skew factors) and the rotation matrices.

This population is chosen in a way that each parameter belongs to a specific interval Table 1.

Table 1. Intervals of camera parameters

Parameters	Intervals
f_τ	[800 2000]
ϵ_τ	[0 1]
s_τ	[0 1]

The usefulness of our contribution is to obtain a 3D scene reconstructed just from 2 images taken from an uncalibrated camera and with variable intrinsic parameters. The next steps will be the 3D modeling in order to finalize our work and find a robust results and a very well a 3D scene reconstructed based on a triangulation construction and a texture mapping.

7 Conclusion

In this work we have treated a new approach of the reconstruction of three-dimensional scenes from a method of autocalibration of cameras characterized by variable intrinsic parameters. The interest points are detected and matched by the ORB descriptor, and it's used later with the projection matrix (expressed according to camera settings) of the scene in the planar images to determine coordinate of the point cloud, so that we can reconstruct the scene.

References

1. Lourakis, M.I.A., Deriche, R.: Camera self-calibration using the kruppa equations and the SVD of the fundamental matrix: the case of varying intrinsic parameters. Technical report 3911, INRIA (2000)
2. Sturm, P.: Critical motion sequences for the self-calibration of cameras and stereo systems with variable focal length. Image Vis. Comput. **20**(5–6), 415–426 (2002)
3. Malis, E., Capolla, R.: Camera self-calibration from unknown planar structures enforcing the multi-view constraints between collineations. IEEE Trans. Pattern Anal. Mach. Intell. **4**(9) (2002)
4. Gurdjos, P., Sturm, P.: Methods and geometry for plane-based self-calibration. In: CVPR, pp. 491–496 (2003)
5. Liu, P., Shi, J., Zhou, J., Jiang, L.: Camera self-calibration using the geometric structure in real scenes. In: Proceedings of the Computer Graphics International (2003)
6. Hemayed, E.E.: A survey of camera self-calibration. In: Proceedings of the IEEE Conference on AVSS (2003)
7. Zhang, W.: A simple method for 3D reconstruction from two views. In: GVIP 05 Conference, CICC, Cairo, Egypt, December 2005
8. Boudine, B., Kramm, S., El Akkad, N., Bensrhair, A., Saaidi, A., Satori, K.: A flexible technique based on fundamental matrix for camera self-calibration with variable intrinsic parameters from two views. J. Vis. Commun. Image R. **39**, 40–50 (2016)
9. El Akkad, N., Merras, M., Saaidi, A., Satori, K.: Camera self-calibration with varying intrinsic parameters by an unknown three-dimensional scene. Vis. Comput. **30**(5), 519–530 (2014)

10. El Akkad, N., Merras, M., Saaidi, A., Satori, K.: Camera self-calibration with varying parameters from two views. WSEAS Trans. Inf. Sci. Appl. **10**(11), 356–367 (2013)
11. Torr, P.H.S., Murray, D.W.: The development and comparison of robust methods for estimating the fundamental matrix. IJCV **24**, 271–300 (1997)
12. Trajkovic, M., Hedley, M.: Fast corner detection. Image Vis. Comput. **16**, 75–87 (1998)
13. Harris, C., Stephens, M.: A combined corner et edge detector. In: 4th Alvey vision Conference, pp. 147–151 (1988)
14. Smith, S.M., Brady, J.M.: A new approach to low level image processing. Int. J. Comput. Vis. **23**(1), 45–78 (1997)
15. Saaidi, A., Tairi, H., Satori, K.: Fast stereo matching using rectification and correlation techniques. In: ISCCSP, Second International Symposium on Communications, Control And Signal Processing, Marrakech, Morrocco, March 2006
16. Chambon, S., Crouzil, A.: Similarity measures for image matching despite occlusions in stereo vision. Pattern Recognit. **44**(9), 2063–2075 (2011)
17. Mattoccia, S., Tombari, F., Di Stefano, L.: Fast full-search equivalent template matching by enhanced bounded correlation. IEEE Trans. Image Process. **17**(4), 528–538 (2008)
18. Moré, J.J.: The Levenberg-Marquardt algorithm: implementation and theory. In: Watson, G. A. (ed.) Numerical Analysis. LNM, vol. 630, pp. 105–116. Springer, Heidelberg (1978). https://doi.org/10.1007/BFb0067700
19. El Akkad, N., El Hazzat, S., Saaidi, A., Satori, K.: Reconstruction of 3D scenes by camera self-calibration and using genetic algorithms. 3D Res. **7**, 6 (2016)
20. Rublee, E., Rabaud, V., Konolige, K., Bradski, G.: ORB: an efficient alternative to SIFT or SURF. In: 2011 IEEE International Conference on Computer Vision (ICCV), pp. 2564–2571. IEEE (2011)
21. Calonder, M., Lepetit, V., Strecha, C., Fua, P.: BRIEF: binary robust independent elementary features. In: Daniilidis, K., Maragos, P., Paragios, N. (eds.) ECCV 2010. LNCS, vol. 6314, pp. 778–792. Springer, Heidelberg (2010). https://doi.org/10.1007/978-3-642-15561-1_56
22. Merras, M., Saaidi, A., El Akkad, N., Satori, K.: Multi-view 3D reconstruction and modeling of the unknown 3D scenes using genetic algorithms. Soft Comput. (2017). https://doi.org/10.1007/s00500-017-2966-z
23. El Hazzat, S., Merras, M., El Akkad, N., Saaidi, A., Satori, K.: 3D reconstruction system based on incremental structure from motion using a camera with varying parameters. Vis. Comput. (2017). https://doi.org/10.1007/s00371-017-1451-0
24. El Akkad, N., Merras, M., Baataoui, A., Saaidi, A., Satori, K.: Camera self-calibration having the varying parameters and based on homography of the plane at infinity. Multimed. Tools Appl. (2017). https://doi.org/10.1007/s11042-017-5012-3
25. El Akkad, N., El Hazzat, S., Saaidi, A., Satori, K.: Reconstruction of 3D scenes by camera self-calibration and using genetic algorithms. 3D Res. **7**(6), 1–17 (2016)
26. Leutenegger, S., Chli, M., Siegwart, R.Y.: BRISK: binary robust invariant scalable keypoints. In: 2011 IEEE International Conference on Computer Vision (ICCV). IEEE (2011)
27. Alahi, A., Ortiz, R., Vandergheynst, P.: Freak: fast retina keypoint. In: 2012 IEEE Conference on Computer Vision and Pattern Recognition (CVPR). IEEE (2012)
28. Rosin, P.L.: Measuring corner properties. Comput. Vis. Image Underst. **73**(2), 291–307 (1999)
29. Hartley, R., Zisserman, A.: Multiple View Geometry in Computer Vision. Cambridge University Press, Cambridge (2004)

An Enhanced MSER Based Method for Detecting Text in License Plates

Mohamed Admi, Sanaa El Fkihi(✉), and Rdouan Faizi

IRDA Group, ADMIR Laboratory, Rabat IT Center, ENSIAS, Mohammed V University of Rabat, Rabat, Morocco
elfkihi.s@gmail.com

Abstract. In this paper, we propose a novel method for detecting license plates (LP) in images. The proposed algorithm is an extension of Maximally Stable Extremal Regions (MSER) for extracting candidate text region of LP. The approach is more robust to edge and more powerful thanks to its stability, and robustness against the changes of scale and illumination. We propose a novel method based on a bilateral filter as well as an adaptive dynamic threshold so as to improve the MSER results. Besides, we consider the outer tangent of circles intersection for filtering the region with the same orientation, and finally a character classifier based on geometrical and statistical constraints of character to eliminate false detection. Thus, our proposal consists of three steps namely, image preprocessing, candidate license plate character detection, and finally filtering and grouping to eliminate false detection.

Experimental results showed that our approach results in significant improvement compared to another compared method. Indeed, the recall rate of our method is equal to 96% and the standard measure of quality F rate is equal to 97%.

Keywords: VLP detection · MSER region · Image text detection
License plate recognition · Component · Plate region extraction

1 Introduction

Text detection in real-world images is an open problem that is considered as the first and a critical step in a number of computer vision applications such as reading labels in map applications, auto driving (detecting street panels), and License Plate (LP) detection.

Basically, the existing text detection approaches can be grouped into two major categories: The first category is based on detection from general to particular as in detecting license plate shapes [1], and horizontal changes of the intensity [2,3] while the second set relies on detection from particular to general like detecting character content of LP [4–6].

In this paper we propose a novel approach for detecting License Plate content by using Maximally Stable Extremal Regions (MSER). The basic idea of our

Y. Tabii et al. (Eds.): BDCA 2018, CCIS 872, pp. 464–474, 2018.
https://doi.org/10.1007/978-3-319-96292-4_36

proposal is to take into account regions that remain nearly the same through a wide range of thresholds. This approach is more robust to edge and more powerful thanks to its stability, and robustness against changes of scale and illumination.

Our proposal uses both the MSER and the adaptive threshold with bilateral filter. The remainder of this paper is organized as follows: In Sect. 2, we provide a related work based on MSER. In Sect. 3, we detail the properties of the proposed approach. In Sect. 4, we evaluate the performance of our proposal compared to another method. The conclusion and some perspectives are drawn in Sect. 5.

2 Related Work

In this section, we provide a brief overview of some related research works that are based on the MSER. [7–11] have proposed a method for scene text detection and recognition that uses MSER as blob detection. The MSER performs well but has problems on blurry images and when characters have low contrast. To overcome these problems, many approaches have been put forward. Indeed, many MSER extensions have been proposed in order to enhance regions in the component tree: [12] proposes a new enhanced MSER feature detector. It consists in replacing the Max and Min-trees with the tree of shapes. [13] makes use of the MSER tree as a character proposal generator with a deep CNN text classifier. Besides, [14] proposes to combine the canny edge detector with MSER to cope with blurred and low-quality text. [15] proposes an enhanced MSER based detection on the intersection of canny edge and MSER region to locate regions that are more likely to belong to text; canny edge lets to cope with the weakness of MSER to blur and removes all pixels outside boundaries formed by canny edges. [16] detects MSER regions from the input image then fed result as input to the canny edge detector. [17] presents a novel algorithm to identify text in natural and complex images; first the MSER image is obtained on which canny edge detection is performed for edge enhancement then combine results with stroke width transformation for an accurate detection of text. [18] uses the MSER structure of rooted tree to discard repeating noises, and with the directed graph, they built upon the connected component nodes with edges comprising of unary and pairwise cost function. [19] introduces Maxima of Gradient Magnitudes (MGMs). The latter are defined as the points that are mostly around the boundaries of the MSER regions. They completed the boundaries of the regions which are important for detecting repeatable extremal regions.

3 The Proposed Method

Before moving on, it is worth noting that the main objective behind the proposal of this approach is to detect License Plates. Our proposed approach is mainly based on the next three properties of characters: (1) The pixels presenting LP's characters contour usually have a height contrast compared to their neighbor pixels. (2) Contours of characters are always closed. And (3) there is a relationship between characters.

Our method consists of three main steps. These are outlined below.

3.1 First Step: Image Preprocessing

Most license plate images that are acquired from real environments are colored. These images are transformed into gray ones to cut down the amount of calculation, and get their negatives to detect dark MSER regions.

Fig. 1 gives the results of the first step.

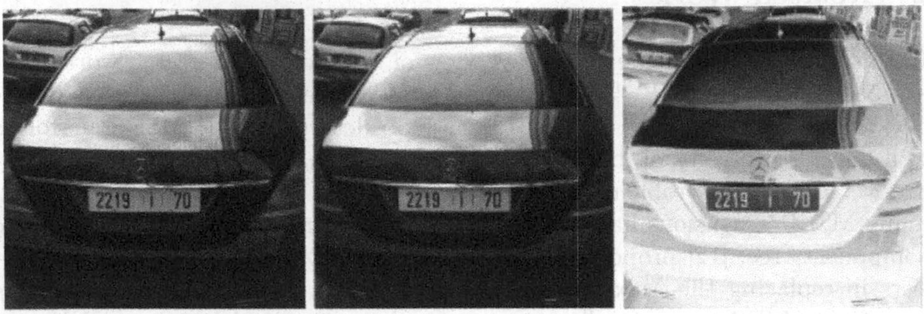

(a) (b) (c)

Fig. 1. (a) Input color image. (b) Gray level image. (c) Negative image (the output of our method first step).

3.2 Second Step: Candidate License Plate Character Detection

We use MSER to detect a set of distinguished regions which are defined by an extremal property of their intensity functions in the region and on their outer boundary.

In order to overcome the MSER problems and to enhance detected MSER regions, we propose to combine it with an adaptive threshold by mean after noise reducing. Unlike a fixed threshold, the adaptive threshold gives a good threshold where the image has different lighting conditions in different areas. The threshold value at each pixel location depends on the neighboring pixel intensities. To calculate the threshold $T(x, y)$ i.e. the threshold value at pixel location (x, y) in the image, we perform the following stages:

- A *bxb* region around the pixel location is selected. The value of b is defined by the user.
- The weighted average of the bxb region is calculated. To this end, we can either use the average (mean) of all the pixel locations in the *bxb* box or use a Gaussian weighted average of the pixel values in the box. In the latter case, the pixel values that are near the center of the box will have higher weight. We will represent this value by $WA(x, y)$.

- The next stage is to find the Threshold Value $T(x, y)$ by subtracting a constant parameter; let's note this parameter param1 for the weighted average value $WA(x, y)$ calculated for each pixel in the previous stage. The threshold value $T(x, y)$ at pixel location (x, y) is then calculated using the formula given below:

$$T(x, y) = WA(x, y) - param1 \tag{1}$$

We used the Adaptive Threshold with mean weighted average because we generally have different lighting conditions in license plate images, and we need to segment a lighter foreground object from its background. In many lighting situations shadows or dimming of light cause thresholding problems as traditional thresholding considers the entire image brightness. Adaptive Thresholding will perform binary thresholding by analyzing each pixel with respect to its local neighborhood (see Fig. 2). This localization allows each pixel to be considered in a more adaptive environment.

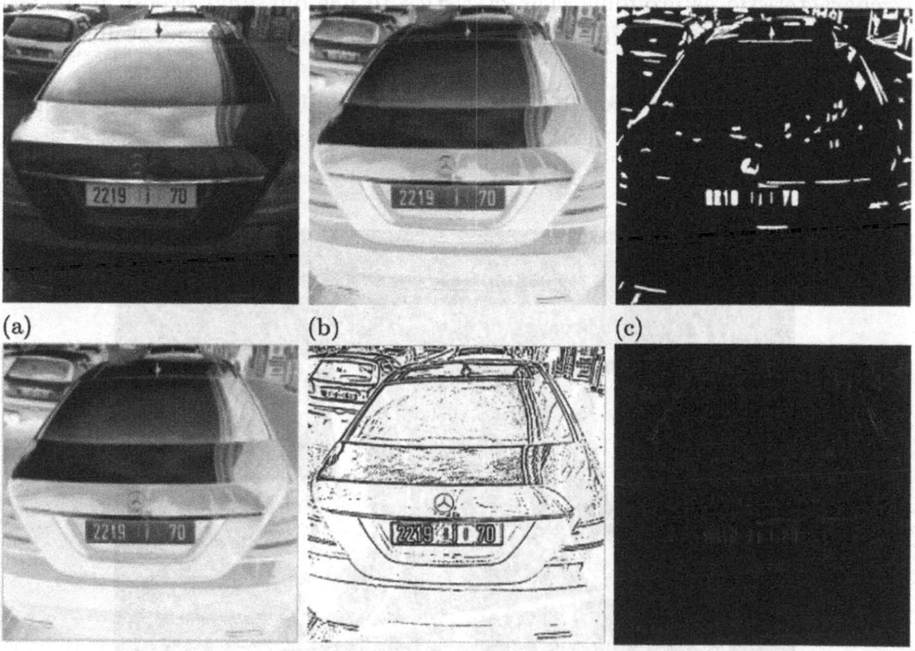

(a) (b) (c) (d) (e) (f)

Fig. 2. (a) The input of our method. (b) Output of the first step of our proposal. (c) MSERs extraction result. (d) Bilateral Filter result. (e) Adaptive Threshold result. (f) Contour result (the output of our method second step).

In order to reduce the image noise, we chose to use the bilateral filter which is a non-linear filter. The reason behind our choice is to avoid to smooth away the edges. Besides, this filter considers the neighboring pixels with weights assigned to each of them. These weights have two components; the first of which is the same weighting used by the Gaussian filter while the second component takes into account the difference of intensities between the neighboring pixels and the evaluated one.

Figure 2 gives an example of the input of our nethod and details of the input and the output of our method second step.

3.3 Third Step: Filtering and Grouping

The second step results in detecting candidate License Plates. These are our final candidate contours and regions of interest. Unfortunately, we can have some false detection. So as to deal with this, we propose to:

- eliminate non-character regions by taking into account some geometrical properties of characters (height, width, Orientation).
- use the outer tangent of circles around each blob and the closed geometry characteristic as grouping characteristics to get our final license plate (see Fig. 3). Indeed, we assume that LP characters consist of horizontally aligned line.
  In order to find subsets of regions which are aligned horizontally a grouping step is applied.

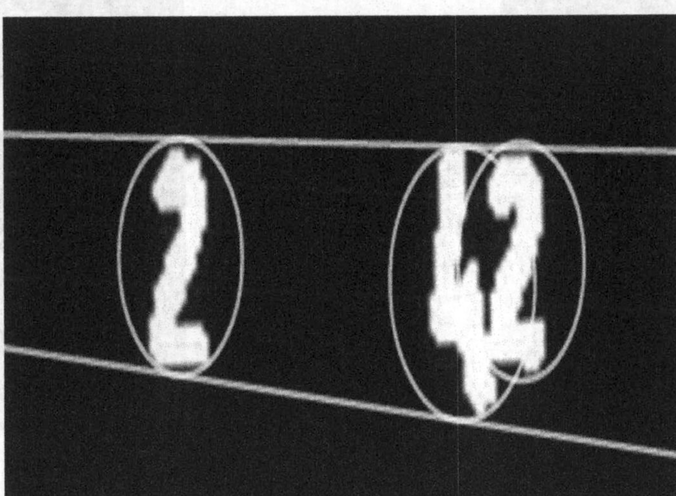

Fig. 3. An example of outer tangent of circles around blobs.

Figure 4 shows an example of the input of our method (see Fig. 4(a)) and its output (see Fig. 4(d)). In addition, details of the third step of our proposal are given in Figs. 4(b), (c) and (d).

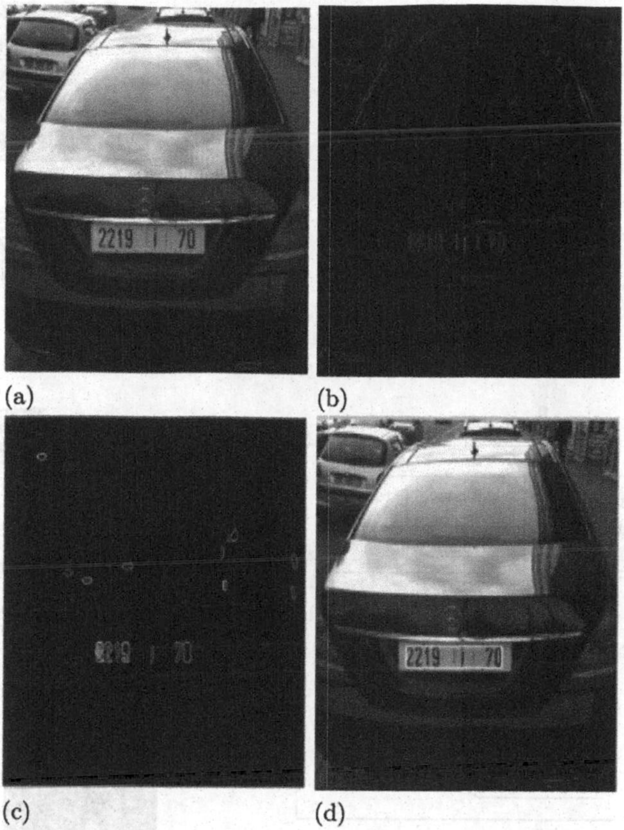

Fig. 4. (a) The input of our method. (b) Output of the second step of our proposal. (c) Filtering result. (d) Grouping by outer tangent result (the output of our method).

An overview of our proposed method is given by the flowchart displayed in Fig. 5. This flowchart gives details of the different steps of our proposal that are:

- Image Preprocessing.
- Candidate License Plate Character Detection.
- And Filtering and Grouping.

The proposed flowchart also gives an example of the result of each stage of the approach by considering an example of a query input image.

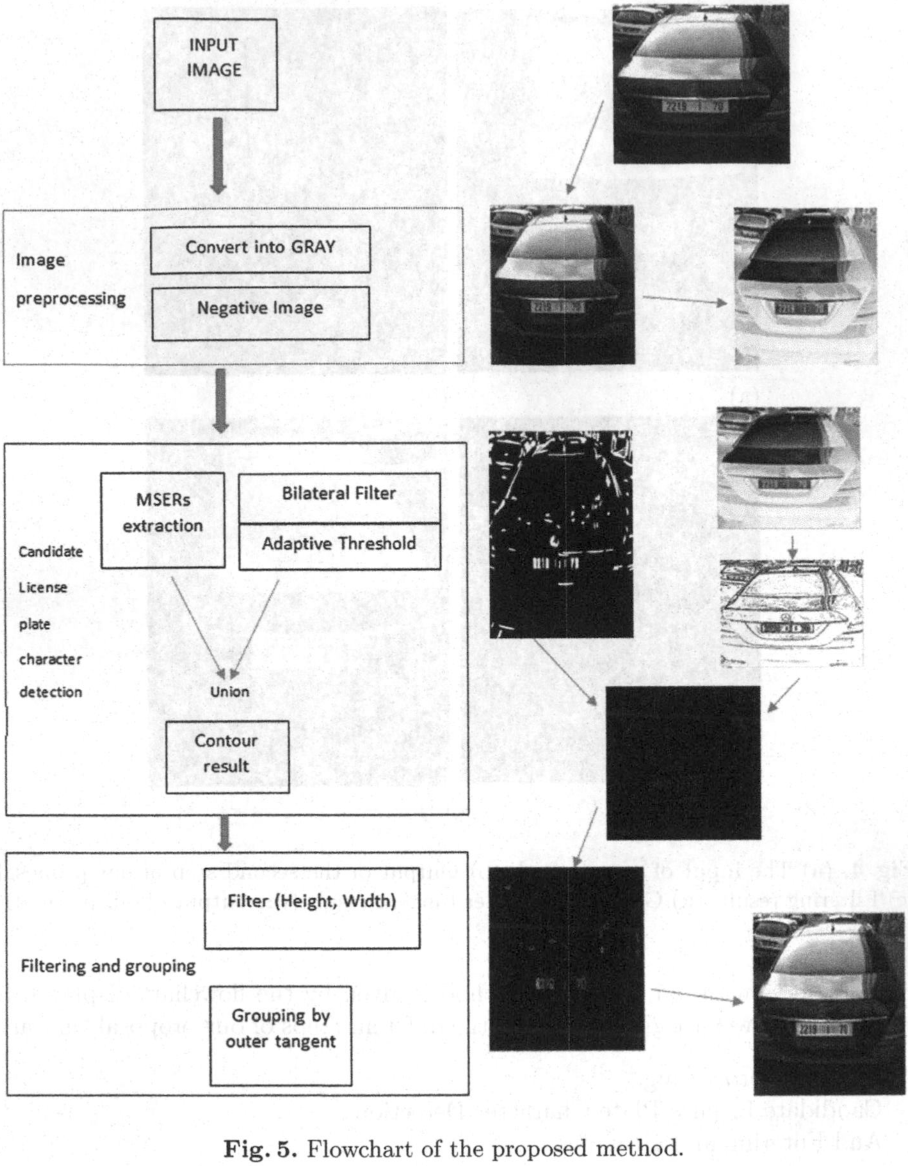

Fig. 5. Flowchart of the proposed method.

4 Experiments

In this section we evaluate our method on a dataset that includes a large variety of images with different conditions and from various positions of the camera as well as distinct vehicle License Plates (VLP) used by [20].

We compare the result of our method to that of [21], which is an open source approach (European license plate).

We notice that the block size (bxb) of a pixel neighborhood that is used to calculate a threshold value for the pixel is fixed to 7. Besides we fixed $param1$ of Eq. (1), which is subtracted from the mean, to 2.

To measure the VLP localization performance, we adopted the evaluation method based on recall/precision. In this aim we define:

- Recall is defined as the ratio between the number of true VLP detected plates and the number of real VLP in image. Thus, the recall is given by:

$$Recall = \frac{trueVLP}{realVLP} \tag{2}$$

- Precision is defined as the ratio between the number of true VLP detected and the sum of true VLP detected and false detected VLP. This is formulated by the next equation:

$$Precision = \frac{trueVLP}{trueVLP + falseVLP} \tag{3}$$

After collecting the testing result of the two methods, we plot the Recall/Precision graph (see Fig. 6). This figure highlights that the new approach offers more precision for all recall values.

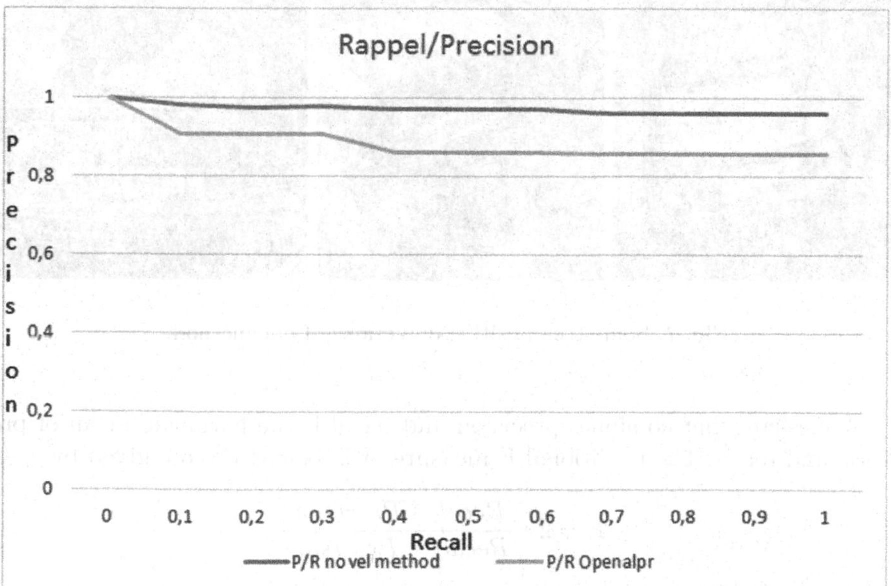

Fig. 6. Recall/Precision curves of the two compared approaches.

Some results of our method are given in Fig. 7. The examples belowpresent images that contain VLP with different complex back ground.

Fig. 7. Some true positive detections of our method.

A measure that combines precision and recall is the harmonic mean of precision and recall. The traditional F-measure or balanced F-score given by:

$$F = 2 * \frac{Recall * Precision}{Recall + Precision} \tag{4}$$

The table below summarizes the results of the two considered compared approaches (Table 1).

As MSER can detect some blob with the same characteristic of LP component, we have obtained some false detection with our approach. Figure 8 gives some of the false detection LP.

Table 1. Performances of the two compared methods.

	Precision	F-score
Our approach	0.96	0,97
Operalpr	0.856	0,92

Fig. 8. Some false detections of our method.

5 Concluding Remarks

In this paper we proposed an efficient method to detect and locate text in LP. We adopted the MSER method as a region detector and overcome its sensitivity to blurred text, low contrast, and complex background by adding a parallel step of adaptive Threshold to enhance MSER result and bilateral filter to reduce noise without smoothing edge. The combination of MSER and adaptive threshold together with the bilateral filter allows improving the existing LP detectors. Our experimental results demonstrated that the proposed method gives better results that other methods. Thus, we obtained a precision rate equal to 96% and an F-score equals to 0, 97 with our approach.

Further works remain to study other ways to tackle the MSER shortcomings.

References

1. Ullah, I., Lee, H.J.: License plate detection based on rectangular features and multilevel thresholding. In: International Conference on Image Processing, Computer Vision, and Pattern Recognition, IPCV 2016 (2016)
2. Fazekas, B., Konyha-Kálmán, E.-L.: Real time number plate localization algorithms. J. Electr. Eng. **57**(2), 69–77 (2006)
3. Joshi, R., Kourav, D.: Efficient license plate recognition using dynamic thresholding and genetic algorithms. Int. Res. J. Eng. Appl. Sci. (IRJEAS), **5**(2), April-June 2017
4. Zhang, C., Sun, G., Chen, D., Zhao, T.: A rapid locating method of vehicle license plate based on characteristics of characters. In: 2nd IEEE Conference on Industrial Electronics and Applications (ICIEA 2007) Harbin, China, pp. 23–25, May 2007

5. Anoual, H., Fkihi, S., Jilbab, A., Aboutajdine, D.: Vehicle license plate detection in images. In: International Conference on Multimedia Computing and Systems (ICMCS 2011), pp. 1–5, 7–9 April 2011
6. Samra, G.A., Khalefah, F.: Localization of license plate number using dynamic image processing techniques and genetic algorithms. IEEE Trans. Evol. Comput. **18**(2), 1–14 (2014)
7. Donoser, M., Arth, C., Bischof, H.: Detecting, tracking and recognizing license plates. In: Yagi, Y., Kang, S.B., Kweon, I.S., Zha, H. (eds.) ACCV 2007. LNCS, vol. 4844, pp. 447–456. Springer, Heidelberg (2007). https://doi.org/10.1007/978-3-540-76390-1_44
8. Neumann, L., Matas, J.: A method for text localization and recognition in real-world images. In: Kimmel, R., Klette, R., Sugimoto, A. (eds.) ACCV 2010. LNCS, vol. 6494, pp. 770–783. Springer, Heidelberg (2011). https://doi.org/10.1007/978-3-642-19318-7_60
9. Novikova, T., Barinova, O., Kohli, P., Lempitsky, V.: Large-lexicon attribute-consistent text recognition in natural images. In: Fitzgibbon, A., Lazebnik, S., Perona, P., Sato, Y., Schmid, C. (eds.) ECCV 2012. LNCS, vol. 7577, pp. 752–765. Springer, Heidelberg (2012). https://doi.org/10.1007/978-3-642-33783-3_54
10. Alsharif, O., Pineau, J.: End-to-End Text Recognition with Hybrid HMM Maxout Models, CoRR, Volume abs/1310.1811
11. Yin, X.-C., Yin, X., Huang, K., Hao, H.-W.: Robust text detection in natural scene images. IEEE Trans. Pattern Anal. Mach. Intell. **36**(5), 970–983 (2014)
12. Bosilj, P., Kijak, E., Lefévre, S.: Beyond MSER: maximally stable regions using tree of shapes. In: British Machine Vision Conference, Swansea, United Kingdom, Sep 2015 (2015)
13. Huang, W., Qiao, Y., Tang, X.: Robust scene text detection with convolution neural network induced MSER trees. In: Fleet, D., Pajdla, T., Schiele, B., Tuytelaars, T. (eds.) ECCV 2014. LNCS, vol. 8692, pp. 497–511. Springer, Cham (2014). https://doi.org/10.1007/978-3-319-10593-2_33
14. Chen, H., Tsai, S.S.: Robust text detection in natural images with edge-enhanced maximally stable extremal regions. In: 18th IEEE International Conference on Image Processing (2011)
15. Islam, M.R., Mondal, C., Azam, M.K., Islam, A.S.M.J.: Text detection and recognition using enhanced MSER detection and a novel OCR technique. In: 5th International Conference on Informatics, Electronics and Vision (ICIEV) (2016)
16. Kethineni, V., Velaga, S.M.: Text detection on scene images using MSER. Int. J. Res. Comput. Commun. Technol. **4**(7), 452–456 (2015)
17. Tabassum, A., Dhondse, S.A.: Text detection using MSER and stroke width transform. In: Fifth International Conference on Communication Systems and Network Technologies, 4–6 April 2015
18. Wang, L., Fan, W., Sun, J., Uchida, S.: Globally optimal text line extraction based on KShortest paths algorithm. In: 12th IAPR Workshop on Document Analysis Systems. Santorini, Greece, 11–14 April 2016
19. Faraji, M., Shanbehzadeh, J., Nasrollahi, K., Moeslund, T.B.: Extremal regions detection guided by maxima of gradient magnitude. IEEE Trans. Image Process. **13**(9), 5401–5415 (2015)
20. Srebric, V.: Enhancing the contrast in greyscale images (2003)
21. openalpr: https://github.com/openalpr/openalpr

Similarity Performance of Keyframes Extraction on Bounded Content of Motion Histogram

Abderrahmane Adoui El Ouadrhiri(✉), Said Jai Andaloussi, El Mehdi Saoudi, Ouail Ouchetto, and Abderrahim Sekkaki

LR2I, FSAC, Hassan II University of Casablanca,
B.P 5366, Maarif, Casablanca, Morocco
{a.adouielouadrhiri-etu,said.jaiandaloussi,ouail.ouchetto, abderrahim.sekkaki}@etude.univcasa.ma, elmehdi.saoudi@gmail.com

Abstract. The paper studies the influence on the similarity by extracting and using m from n frames on videos, the purpose is to evaluate the amount of the proportion similarity between them, and propose a new Content-Based Video Retrieval (CBVR) system. The proposed system uses a Bounded Coordinate of Motion Histogram (BCMH) [1] to characterize videos which are represented by spatio-temporal features (eg. motion vectors) and the Fast and Adaptive Bidimensional Empirical Mode Decomposition (FABEMD). However, a global representation of a video is compared pairwise with all those of the videos in the Hollywood2 dataset using the k-nearest neighbors (KNN). Moreover, this approach is adaptive: a training procedure is presented, and an accuracy of 58.1% is accomplished in comparison with the state-of-the-art approaches on the dataset of 1707 movie clips.

Keywords: Content-Based Video Retrieval (CBVR)
Bounded Coordinate of Motion Histogram (BCMH)
Structural similarity (SSIM) · Information search and retrieval · kNN

1 Introduction

Currently, many digital multimedia data are created in diverse areas and in several application frameworks. Imagine when we could use all these data to construct a smart environment, maybe a computer-aided, or a robot assistant that is able to understand and recognize many motion or actions at a level that they might really support us in finding things without the need to any intervention. Thus, this kind of assistance could help us in surveillance systems, web searching, entertainment, geographic information systems, medicine, etc.

If our imagination leads us to this interesting point, so we will need to exceed the traditional method, which has been to make a relationship between the video context and the title (e.g. Youtube). Really, a great number of web users rely on

Y. Tabii et al. (Eds.): BDCA 2018, CCIS 872, pp. 475–486, 2018.
https://doi.org/10.1007/978-3-319-96292-4_37

textual keyword to perform their searches. Youtube searches look principally at the title of each video and its description, and sometimes the user will not know the "*tag or name*" of what he/she is looking for, but is knowing some contents, for instance, the visual appearance of an artist, or what an object looks like, etc.

Perhaps, it was easy to find some resources in the last century, because multimedia databases have been really smaller, but recently, the situation has changed, and there are several disadvantages to use this kind of search. For the reason that this textual data is often inexact, inadequate or incomplete, the massive amounts of new multimedia data in a large variety of formats (e.g. videos and images) are made available worldwide on a daily basis, and the complexity, quantity and high dimensionality of this information are all exponentially increasing. Thus, we should find the alternative model, the solution to perform this search is to refer to Content-based Video Retrieval (CBVR).

What a challenge awaits us? There are several causes that CBVR proves more challenging. First, we don't have just one image or one object to analyze. Second, there are successive images and many video shots that have different background, which need the pairwise comparisons. Additionally, the algorithms should be highly efficient to be practical on the wide video datasets.

In CBVR, many works have been presented, such as Herath et al. [2], present many research areas including human dynamics, semantic segmentation, object recognition, domain adaptation, and give surveys on Motion and Action Analysis. Rossetto et al. [3] present a system that exploits a high-level spatial-temporal features and a variety of low-level image (video) features; include motion, color, edge and that all be jointly used in any combination. Droueche et al. [4] used the wavelet and region trajectories, respectively, to provide a video characterization by fast dynamic time warping distance. Jones and Shao [5] tried to make the combination between several techniques like vocabulary guided, spatiotemporal pyramid matches, Bag-of-Words for action representation, and also SVMs/ABRS-SVMs for relevance feedback using the datasets of the realistic action like "*UCF Sports, UCF YouTube and HOHA2*". Jai-Andaloussi et al. [6] already suggested Content-Based Image Retrieval (CBIR) using a distributed computing system to benefit the computation time.

Gao et al. [7] discussed about the feature transformation and the learning techniques in high-dimensional which need to know and apply if we would reduce the dimensionality, and keep the growth of the performance and the robustness of domain applications. Frikha et al. [8] present an original unsupervised appearance key-frame selection approach using the similarity between HOG features vectors for multi-shot person re-identification problem. Huang et al. [9,10], provide practical measurement algorithms for capturing the dominating content of a video. Because of the full scale of the CBVR problem, this paper focuses on one subdomain in which the key idea is to minimize the redundancy of frames of videos by choosing efficient frames. Then, these selected keyframes will be modeled into a global video signature represented by the motion and the characterization of the image decomposed into multiple hierarchical components, and we will study its influence about the computational time, processing and the similarity by the matching score of the average of all pairwise distances. Therefore, we present two issues in this work, the first one is about finding the centroid image that can be the keyframe of group of pictures (GOP), so we calculate the similarity between *n-windows* frames; in our application, we choose n-windows= $\{1, 3, 5, 7, 9\}$, for n-windows= 1 that means that we utilize all frames of the video, and for n-windows= 3 that means that we choose the first frame and all frames that can be modulo 3, and so on for others. The second part is for extracting the efficient features using different techniques to construct the global video signature representation and calculate the similarity between videos utilizing k-nearest neighbors (kNN) approach.

The remainder of the paper is organized as follows. The different steps of the proposed approach are described in Sect. 2. The experimental results and discussions are reported in Sect. 3. Finally, Sect. 4 is the conclusion.

2 System Overview and Proposed Method

Generally, Group of Pictures (GOP) is a type of terminology related to MPEG video encoding. Thus, every coded video stream has groups of GOPs. GOPs include various types such as I, P and B (Intra-compressed, forward Predicted and Bi-directional predicted, respectively). I-frame contains a lot of information from the image and it is not referenced to any frame of the stream, for that reason, the motion vector is extracted from the coding of the two other type of frames. The B or P frames contain motion-compensated difference information relative to decoded frames, therefore, each B-frame can reference on any frame from the previous and following images, rather the P-frame makes the same process of B but it is just with the previous images [4].

In the following subsections, we present the technique of selection the keyframes, the motion histogram, and the representation of the relevant data by the Bounded Coordinate System (BCS), we have also Non-negative least squares (NNLS) as a kind of pairwise comparison between the video signatures to give a coordinate to the video and kNN for the similarity purpose.

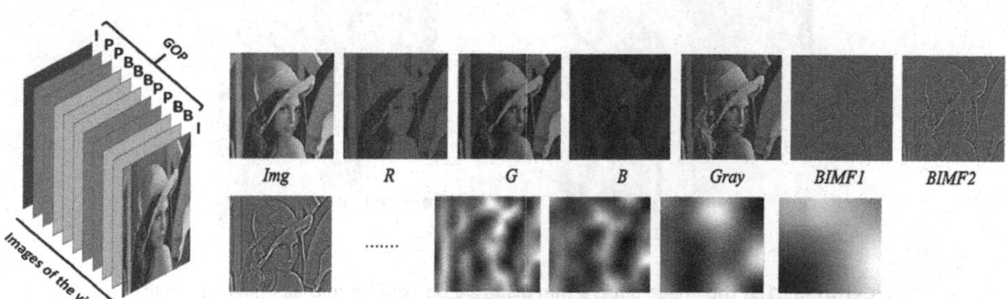

Fig. 1. Low-level appearance features

2.1 Key Frame Selection

In this subsection, we try to present the technique that we made to choose the relevant keyframes from video stream applying $n-windows$ concept. First, every image will be represented by its intensity of low-level appearance (Fig. 1).

$$Rep_{i,j,k} = (Intensity_{Red}, Intensity_{Green}, Intensity_{Blue}, Intensity_{Gray}) \quad (1)$$

The Eq. (1) means the representation of image i in GOP j of video k, the centroid image i is that has a minimum distance between all frames in GOP j.

$$Centroid_{i,w,k} = Min\left(\sum_{i=1}^{n}\sum_{r=1}^{n} DTW(Rep_{i,j,k}, Rep_{r,j,k})\right)_{i \neq j} \quad (2)$$

Where the DTW is the *Dynamic Time Warping* distance for the measuring multidimensional time series, and n is the number of frames in GOP. The application takes n-windows= $\{1, 3, 5, 7, 9\}$, so we have five windows, and w identifies which n-windows utilized in our application. After that, we match between $Centroid_{i,w,k}$ to find which window is closest to the representation of n-windows= 1; In this matching (Table 1), the PSNR and SSIM are two approaches to use. Well, the PSNR limitations are from the borders of the MSE (mean squared error). Thus, the SSIM (structural similarity index) is proposed by Wang et al. [11,12] as a kind of involved solution to the problem of "*image quality assessment*" [13].

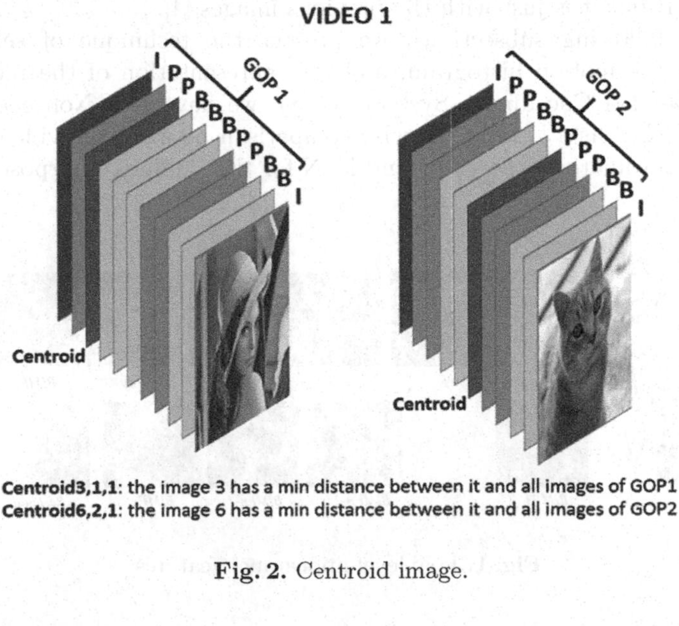
VIDEO 1
GOP 1
GOP 2
Centroid
Centroid
Centroid3,1,1: the image 3 has a min distance between it and all images of GOP1
Centroid6,2,1: the image 6 has a min distance between it and all images of GOP2

Fig. 2. Centroid image.

"*SSIM correlates extraordinarily well with perceptual image quality and handily outperforms prior state-of-the-art HVS-based metrics*" [14]. For that reason, we apply SSIM.

2.2 Motion Histogram

The motion histogram is based on the motion vectors that we could extract from P and/or B frames. Every motion histogram represents one frame, due to a lot of directions of motion (360°) which can find in the frames, 12 possibilities and a separate bin $M = 0$ for zero-length motion vectors are considered like 13 bins of directions [15]. The direction of motion vector μ(x,y) is calculated by the Eq. (3).

The Eq. (3) is considered true, if μ(x,y) $\neq$ (0,0) with length $|\mu|$. With Eq. (4), the motion histogram is calculated. The first part of our signature will take three values:

- Direction: the value of the prevalent motion vectors μ,
- Class: the ID of the Direction,
- Intensity: the median of a dominant motion vectors (5).

$$\Omega(\mu) = \begin{Bmatrix} \arccos \frac{x}{|\mu|} & ,y \geq 0 \\ 2\pi - \arccos \frac{x}{|\mu|} & ,y < 0 \end{Bmatrix} \tag{3}$$

$$Histogram(\mu) = \begin{cases} 0 & ,\mu = (0,0) \\ 1 + ([\Omega(\mu)\frac{M}{2\Pi} + \frac{1}{2}]modM) & ,otherwise \end{cases} \tag{4}$$

$$Intensity_{\mu} = \frac{1}{D}\sum_{i=1}^{D} |\mu| \, ; (D : Direction) \tag{5}$$

2.3 FABEMD

With the decomposition of the images from high to low frequencies components by the Fast and Adaptive Bidimensional Empirical Mode Decomposition (FABEMD) [16], no information is lost. The original image is exactly the reconstruction of the BIMF images (Bidimensional Intrinsic Mode Functions) [17,18]. Moreover, any image follows the generalized Gaussian model, it will represent by suitable parameters, which can facilitate the comparison.

Table 1. Proportion of similarity between the n-windows

Similarity between	{n= 1 & 3}	{n= 1 & 5}	{n= 1 & 7}	{n= 1 & 9}
Average	86.6%	83.1%	80.8%	79.4%
SD	13.8%	14.7%	14.7%	15.2%

BIMFs. BIMFs and a residue are decomposition of an original image using the FABEMD method. The highest local frequencies of oscillation are found in the first BIMF, and the last BIMF holds the lowest, but the *residue* includes the rest of data [17,18].

Generalized Gaussian Distribution (GGD). Different statistical models of the motion and the residual information have been proposed, for instance, the Gaussian and the zero-mean Laplacian distributions, but Gaussian distributions are more close to random Gaussian noise [4], then, the best probability density function which can be conveniently reached by Generalized Gaussian Distribution (GGD) [19], defined by (4).

$$P(x, \alpha, \beta) = \frac{\beta}{2\alpha\Gamma(\frac{1}{\beta})} e^{-(\frac{|x|}{\alpha})\beta} \tag{6}$$

The gamma function is $\Gamma(x) = \int_0^\alpha e^{-t} t^{x-t} dt; x > 0$, where:

- α: a scale factor, it corresponds to the standard deviation of the Gaussian distribution [20].
- β: a shape parameter.

Well, with a maximum likelihood estimator of the GGD $(\widehat{\alpha}, \widehat{\beta})$, we find these parameters. Supposing that, each x_i (coefficient for one BIMF) is independent and L is the total of frame's blocks, and the digamma function is $\Psi(t) = \frac{\Gamma'(t)}{\Gamma(t)}$. Varanasi and Aazhang [21] demonstrated that the unique solution of $(\widehat{\alpha}, \widehat{\beta})$ is taken by the following equations:

$$\begin{cases} \hat{\alpha} = (\frac{\hat{\beta}}{L} \sum_{i=1}^{L} |x_i|)^{\frac{1}{\hat{\beta}}} \\ 1 + \frac{\Psi(\frac{1}{\hat{\beta}})}{\hat{\beta}} - \frac{\sum_{i=1}^{L} x_i^{\hat{\beta}} log|x_i|}{\sum_{i=1}^{L} |x_i|^{\hat{\beta}}} + \frac{log(\hat{\beta} \frac{\sum_{i=1}^{L} |x_i|^{\hat{\beta}}}{L})}{\hat{\beta}} = 0 \end{cases} \tag{7}$$

2.4 Signature Extraction and Signature Matching

Due to the results of [18], the runtime grows exponentially when the procedure of the decomposition goes to the end, however, the extraction of first BIMFs need relatively low computation time. Thus, to integrate the FABEMD method in the real-time system, we should take consideration of this limitation. Typically, three levels are ideal and the representation of our signature will be (8). Indeed, according to the n-windows of the Key Frame Selection Sect. 2.1, every row of $Sign_{V_k}$ represents the features of the *Centroid* image of GOP j (Eq. (2), Fig. 2).

$$Sign_{V_k} = \begin{bmatrix} D_1 & C_1 & I_1 & \alpha_1^1 & \beta_1^1 & \alpha_1^2 & \beta_1^2 & \alpha_1^3 & \beta_1^3 \\ D_2 & C_2 & I_2 & \alpha_2^1 & \beta_2^1 & \alpha_2^2 & \beta_2^2 & \alpha_2^3 & \beta_2^3 \\ D_3 & C_3 & I_3 & \alpha_3^1 & \beta_3^1 & \alpha_3^2 & \beta_3^2 & \alpha_3^3 & \beta_3^3 \\ . & . & . & . & . & . & . & . & . \\ . & . & . & . & . & . & . & . & . \\ D_n & C_n & I_n & \alpha_n^1 & \beta_n^1 & \alpha_n^2 & \beta_n^2 & \alpha_n^3 & \beta_n^3 \end{bmatrix} \tag{8}$$

Where k is the number of the video, and n is the number of the last frame in the video, D is the Direction, C is the Class, I is the Intensity, α_n^i and β_n^i are the scale factor, and the shape parameter of an image for BIMF i, respectively. On the other hand, the representation of 2 dimensions makes the interpretation of $Sign_{V_k}$ much easier than 9 dimensions, and it is more suitable for the large number of videos.

Bounded Coordinate System (BCS). Bounded Coordinate System (BCS) is linear system of feature space (not depending on the video length), that makes the real-time search from big video collections feasible. [9,10] present the BCS model that captures the distribution of the tendency of content of a video bounded by the range of data projections on the length of the axis. Thus, the using of PCA is to get the corresponding axes of BCS of dominating content. Well, the complexity of data is notable reduced.

$$D(BCS(X), BCS(Y)) = \|O_X - O_Y\| + \left(\sum_{i=1}^{d^Y} \left\|\ddot{\Phi}_{X_i} - \ddot{\Phi}_{Y_i}\right\| + \sum_{d^Y+1}^{d^X} \left\|\ddot{\Phi}_{X_i}\right\|\right)/2 \quad (9)$$

Let $X = (x_1, x_2, x_3, ..., x_n)$ a video clip, the mean for all x_i denoted as ranges, orientations and origin O of the bounded axes of coordinate system (Φ_i). Let X and Y videos, $BCS(X) = (O_X; \ddot{\Phi}_{X_1}; \ddot{\Phi}_{X_2}; ...; \ddot{\Phi}_{X_d})$ and $BCS(Y) = (O_Y; \ddot{\Phi}_{Y_1}; \ddot{\Phi}_{Y_2}; ...; \ddot{\Phi}_{Y_d})$, to calculate the similarity between BCS(X) and BCS(Y), two distances will be calculated. Where $d^X = d^Y$, $\|O_X - O_Y\|$ is the translation distance betwixt two origins, and it indicates the global difference betwixt two sets of frames representing the video clips, and the average difference of all the content-changing indicated by the distance betwixt each pair of bounded axes by rotation $\left\|\ddot{\Phi}_{X_i} - \ddot{\Phi}_{Y_i}\right\|/2$, else if $d^X > d^Y$, a scaling distance $\left\|\ddot{\Phi}_{X_i}\right\|/2$ will be added to a translation and rotation distance, therefore, the rotation and scaling indicate the content tendencies. The length of bounded principal component $\left\|\ddot{\Phi}_i\right\|$ is $2c\sigma_i$ [9].

Non-Negative Least Squares (NNLS). In data modeling, the fundamental problem is to estimate and describing the data. The objective here is to remodel the vector x, which presents the observed values as better as possible. This requirement probably executed by the linear system:

$$Mx = y \quad (10)$$

The unknown model parameters need to be indicated by $x = (x_1, x_2, ..., x_n)^T$. Thus, the different experiments relating x are encoded by the measurement matrix $M \in \mathbb{R}^{m \times n}$, and y is given by the set of observed values [22].

2.5 K-Nearest Neighbors (kNN)

kNN is an algorithm for regression and classification, the predictions are made using directly the training dataset. Through the training set, each instance x searches for the k most closer neighbors using the Euclidean Distance. This might be the mean output variable for regression, and the mode for classification. In the testing part, the result is given by the value of the summarizing for k neighbors using the Mean Average Precision (MAP) (11). The computational complexity of kNN increases with the size of the training dataset.

Other popular distance measures include: Manhattan Distance, Minkowski Distance, and Hamming Distance are used as like as Euclidian distance.

$$MAP = \frac{\sum_{j=1}^{n}(P(j) \times rel(j))}{Number\,of\,relevant\,video} \tag{11}$$

With n is the number of retrieved videos, j is the rank in the sequence of retrieved videos. *P(j)* is the precision at cut-off j in the list, *rel(j)* is an indicator function equaling 1 if it is a relevant video, and 0 in the otherwise[1]. The scenario to compute MAP is:

- Every video played, in turn, the role of the query video in a test subset. The algorithm found the most relevant videos in the training subset (the videos minimizing the distance to the query video, in the training subset),
- The average precision was calculated for every query in the test subset. The average precision was obtained by averaging all precision values.

3 Video Dataset, Experimentation and Results

In this part, we present the proposed framework and the dataset which is used in our experiment, the chronology of using the methods (Fig. 3) and the discussion about the results.

The framework is applied on the movie clip dataset, called HOLLYWOOD2[2] [23] which consists of 1,707 video sequences of human action with 12 types of class divided in 2 sections. The training set and the test subset consist of 823 and 884 video sequences, respectively. The computations were executed on an Intel processor with 2 cores, 4 threads, running at 2.6 GHz, with 4 GB of RAM. The first step is to extract the global signature from the video set. Thus, we could create a set of signatures with each n-windows used (Signature (8)).

The difficulty of the interpretation of data in 9 dimensions leads us to BCS, which can give an acceptable representation of the data in low dimension (2 dimensions) with the conservation of more than 90% of relevant data. Well, the scatter represents and gives the specificity of each video by the center and the length of bounded principal component. Sometimes, these two signs don't present

[1] https://www.wikipedia.org/wiki/Information_retrieval.
[2] http://www.di.ens.fr/~laptev/actions/hollywood2/.

Table 2. Performance evaluation of the proposed approach

	Proposed approach n= n-window, p= parameters (equ. (8))												RegTraj EFDTW [4]	SIFT HOG/F [23]	BCMH [1]
	n=5 p=3	n=5 p=5	n=5 p=7	n=5 p=9	n=7 p=3	n=7 p=5	n=7 p=7	n=7 p=9	n=9 p=3	n=9 p=5	n=9 p=7	n=9 p=9			
SitUp	86.4%	81.2%	78.3%	**87.2%**	64.6%	75.3%	70.45%	64.0%	85.4%	77.3%	75.4%	67.8%	**12.5%**	**07.8%**	**34.2%**
DriveCar	70.8%	61.6%	53.3%	**56.2%**	70.3%	60.4%	60.7%	52.2%	69.1%	71.9%	55.5%	64.2%	**35.0%**	**75.0%**	**91.9%**
GetOutCar	52.0%	44.5%	54.4%	**46.9%**	51.5%	62.0%	47.0%	43.7%	49.8%	49.2%	49.8%	65.2%	**18.9%**	**11.6%**	**90.5%**
Eat	34.5%	27.9%	31.6%	**36.7%**	63.9%	32.5%	29.4%	29.3%	45.6%	36.2%	46.9%	37.6%	**22.5%**	**28.6%**	**78.5%**
StandUp	70.0%	51.7%	63.4%	**64.6%**	53.6%	54.6%	60.8%	66.0%	68.9%	63.8%	61.8%	59.9%	**31.0%**	**32.5%**	**77.7%**
AnswerPhone	33.2%	44.2%	45.1%	**45.5%**	43.6%	35.2%	36.1%	51.6%	63.6%	28.0%	44.4%	36.9%	**17.8%**	**10.7%**	**45.7%**
Kiss	50.5%	55.5%	55.0%	**37.4%**	44.4%	34.0%	37.6%	31.6%	54.7%	55.0%	40.6%	44.0%	**27.8%**	**55.6%**	**65.4%**
Run	68.4%	60.3%	60.5%	**66.1%**	64.6%	78.0%	73.5%	64.3%	71.2%	63.2%	62.1%	56.9%	**21.0%**	**56.5%**	**85.0%**
SitDown	48.2%	32.7%	54.9%	**50.3%**	44.7%	59.4%	43.4%	49.5%	62.1%	52.5%	60.4%	48.1%	**25.2%**	**27.8%**	**65.7%**
FightPerson	57.9%	50.5%	76.5%	**76.9%**	71.2%	58.7%	76.4%	74.9%	62.5%	46.9%	56.9%	56.6%	**25.0%**	**57.1%**	**31.6%**
HandShake	69.2%	62.0%	66.2%	**71.1%**	59.3%	56.0%	64.0%	63.1%	67.2%	68.2%	70.5%	80.1%	**52.3%**	**14.1%**	**30.0%**
HugPerson	48.7%	41.1%	39.6%	**58.6%**	46.4%	46.2%	50.4%	43.2%	61.2%	51.6%	51.8%	45.3%	**23.0%**	**13.8%**	**31.6%**
Total Average	***57.5%***	***51.1%***	***56.6%***	***58.1%***	***56.5%***	***54.4%***	***54.1%***	***52.8%***	***63.4%***	***55.3%***	***56.4%***	***55.2%***	*26.0%*	*32.6%*	*64.1%*

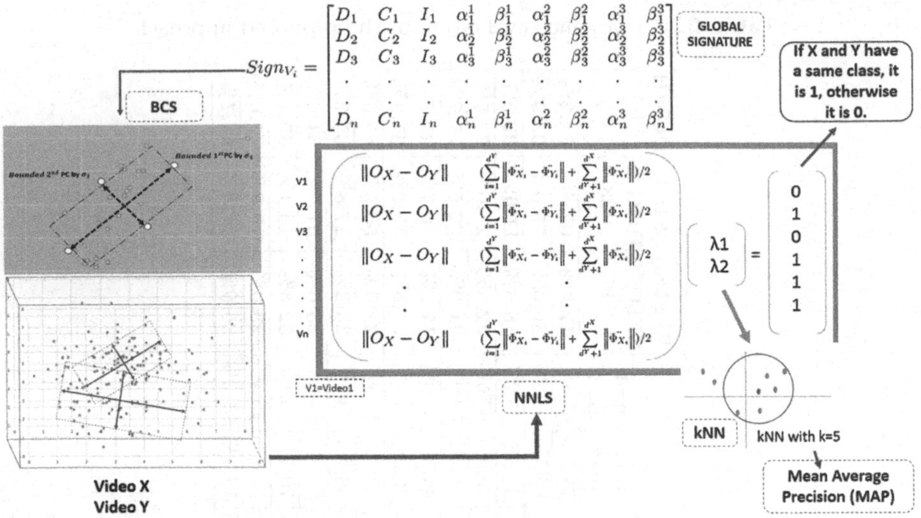

Fig. 3. Signatures and measurement process

the correct information, maybe with the missing of the data (the video is short, the using of a predefined number of frames, not all), or the video's model (many actions or classic), or by the lighting, certain values are influenced. Therefore, the comparative model with all videos in the training part is important. Thus, the system can compare them and accumulate the values of the neighbors in the testing part.

According to Table 1, we can see that the average between the using n-windows= $\{3, 5, 7, 9\}$ and all frames does not exceed 20% of the difference of the similarity, in this way, we can benefit the computation time by choosing a predefined number of frames. The standard deviation represents the percent that shows *how closer/far the data around the mean is ?*. Except n-windows= $\{3\}$, because the frames are closer to n-windows= $\{1\}$, we think that n-windows= $\{5\}$ and n-windows= $\{7\}$ are more useful, but we should experiment their performance. According to Table 2, we present the results of our experiment on 12 types of class, we have used different modes n-windows= $\{5, 7, 9\}$ and for each one, we test with 3, 5, 7, and all parameters, for instance $(Direction, Class, Intensity)$, $(Direction, Class, Intensity, \alpha, \beta)$, etc. In Table 2, we can notice also that the results of n-windows= $\{5\}$ preserve their performance with 3 parameters, and when we add others, we could see the growth of the performance. In the other n-windows, we have some fluctuations that can not be explained without a deep study. However, we have a good percent similarity if we choose n-windows= 9 frames with just 3 parameters. Unfortunately, 3 parameters can't represent efficiently the images and so on for the video. On the other side, we can say that 6 from 12 classes have the good percent by using all parameters with n-windows= 5, but the other classes are also closer, the difference almost 2%

between them (between 3 and 9 parameters with n-windows= 5). This confirms that the proposed method is good in comparison with the state-of-the-art. Thus, we can consider the choosing n-windows= {5} with all parameters as the ideal choice to have the best similarity with a reasonable computation time that does not exceed 3 min on average than 9 min in the first version of BCMH [1].

Overall, our results are compared to those obtained in [4,23]. Generally, ours considered as better by more than 30% with $k = 5$ of neighbors and {*n-windows=5, parameters=9*}, but in comparison to [1], the advantage of computational time is indicated. This leads us to go on to the real time searches environment. Furthermore, the CBVR using a distributed computing system, and an improved version of this framework are both our area of research for future work.

4 Conclusion

In this paper, the focus is to choose the efficient keyframes, and construct a global signature, firstly, by motion vectors with 3 parameters, the following parameters are extracted by using FABEMD in 3 levels. This combination presents an *upgrade version* of Bounded Coordinate of Motion Histogram (BCMH) that characterizes a video by its scattered data in low dimension. To get an adequate form of video and all that belong to the same category, the NNLS presents its performance and with the efficient of KNN we find the closest neighbors. The Mean Average Precision (MAP) is applied to classify the relevant videos. Despite using 3 BIMFs, the results show that our approach is faster than BCMH, and the performance of MAP is 30% higher in comparison with the combination of SIFT-HOG-HOF and the Region Trajectories EFDTW. Honestly, a theoretical analysis proves that the computation time will be reduced with the distributed system. Thus, the real-time process should be more feasible.

References

1. Ouadrhiri, A.A.E., Saoudi, E.M., Andaloussi, S.J., Ouchetto, O., Sekkaki, A.: Content based video retrieval based on bounded coordinate of motion histogram. In: 2017 4th International Conference on Control, Decision and Information Technologies (CoDIT), pp. 0573–0578, April 2017
2. Herath, S., Harandi, M.T., Porikli, F.: Going deeper into action recognition: a survey. CoRR abs/1605.04988 (2016)
3. Rossetto, L., et al.: IMOTION — a content-based video retrieval engine. In: He, X., Luo, S., Tao, D., Xu, C., Yang, J., Hasan, M.A. (eds.) MMM 2015. LNCS, vol. 8936, pp. 255–260. Springer, Cham (2015). https://doi.org/10.1007/978-3-319-14442-9_24
4. Droueche, Z., Quellec, G., Lamard, M., Cazuguel, G., Cochener, B., Roux, C.: Computer-aided retinal surgery using data from the video compressed stream. Int. J. Image Video Process.: Theory Appl. **2014**, 1–10 (2014). http://www.orb-academic.org/index.php/journal-of-image-and-video-proc/issue/view/24
5. Jones, S., Shao, L.: Content-based retrieval of human actions from realistic video databases. Inf. Sci. **236**, 56–65 (2013)

6. Jai-Andaloussi, S., Elabdouli, A., Chaffai, A., Madrane, N., Sekkaki, A.: Medical content based image retrieval by using the Hadoop framework. In: 2013 20th International Conference on Telecommunications (ICT), pp. 1–5. IEEE (2013)
7. Gao, L., Song, J., Liu, X., Shao, J., Liu, J., Shao, J.: Learning in high-dimensional multimedia data: the state of the art. Multimed. Syst. **23**(3), 303–313 (2017)
8. Frikha, M., Chebbi, O., Fendri, E., Hammami, M.: Key frame selection for multi-shot person re-identification. In: Ben Amor, B., Chaieb, F., Ghorbel, F. (eds.) RFMI 2016. CCIS, vol. 684, pp. 97–110. Springer, Cham (2017). https://doi.org/10.1007/978-3-319-60654-5_9
9. Huang, Z., Shen, H.T., Shao, J., Zhou, X., Cui, B.: Bounded coordinate system indexing for real-time video clip search. ACM Trans. Inf. Syst. (TOIS) **27**(3), 17 (2009)
10. Shen, H.T., Zhou, X., Huang, Z., Shao, J., Zhou, X.: UQLIPS: a real-time near-duplicate video clip detection system. In: Proceedings of the 33rd International Conference on Very Large Data Bases, pp. 1374–1377. VLDB Endowment (2007)
11. Wang, Z., Bovik, A.C., Sheikh, H.R., Simoncelli, E.P.: Image quality assessment: from error visibility to structural similarity. IEEE Trans. Image Process. **13**(4), 600–612 (2004)
12. Wang, Z., Bovik, A.C., Simoncelli, E.: Structural approaches to image quality assessment, pp. 961–974, December 2005
13. Dosselmann, R., Yang, X.D.: A comprehensive assessment of the structural similarity index. Signal Image Video Process. **5**(1), 81–91 (2011)
14. Kalpana Seshadrinathan and Alan C Bovik. New vistas in image and video quality assessment
15. Schoeffmann, K., Lux, M., Taschwer, M., Boeszoermenyi, L.: Visualization of video motion in context of video browsing. In: 2009 IEEE International Conference on Multimedia and Expo, ICME 2009, pp. 658–661. IEEE (2009)
16. Bhuiyan, S.M.A., Adhami, R.R., Khan, J.F.: Fast and adaptive bidimensional empirical mode decomposition using order-statistics filter based envelope estimation. EURASIP J. Adv. Signal Process. **2008**(1), 728356 (2008)
17. Nunes, J.C., Guyot, S., Deléchelle, E.: Texture analysis based on local analysis of the bidimensional empirical mode decomposition. Mach. Vis. Appl. **16**(3), 177–188 (2005)
18. Mahraz, M.A., Riffi, J., Tairi, H.: Motion estimation using the fast and adaptive bidimensional empirical mode decomposition. J. Real-Time Image Process. **9**(3), 491–501 (2014)
19. Lamard, M., Cazuguel, G., Quellec, G., Bekri, L., Roux, C., Cochener, B.: Content based image retrieval based on wavelet transform coefficients distribution. In: 2007 29th Annual International Conference of the IEEE Engineering in Medicine and Biology Society, EMBS 2007, pp. 4532–4535. IEEE (2007)
20. Jai-Andaloussi, S., et al.: Content based medical image retrieval: use of generalized gaussian density to model BEMD's IMF. In: Dossel, O., Schlegel, W.C. (eds.) World Congress on Medical Physics and Biomedical Engineering, vol. 25/4, pp. 1249–1252. Springer, Heidelberg (2010). https://doi.org/10.1007/978-3-642-03882-2_331
21. Varanasi, M.K., Aazhang, B.: Parametric generalized Gaussian density estimation. J. Acoust. Soc. Am. **86**, 1404–1415 (1989)
22. Boutsidis, C., Drineas, P.: Random projections for the nonnegative least-squares problem. Linear Algebra Appl. **431**(5–7), 760–771 (2009)
23. Marszalek, M., Laptev, I., Schmid, C.: Actions in context. In: 2009 IEEE Conference on Computer Vision and Pattern Recognition, CVPR 2009, pp. 2929–2936. IEEE (2009)

Natural Language Processing

Modeling and Development of the Linguistic Knowledge Base DELSOM

Fadoua Mansouri[1(✉)], Sadiq Abdelalim[1], and Youness Tabii[2]

[1] SIM Team of MISC Laboratory, Faculty of Science, University IBN TOFAIL, Kenitra, Morocco
mansourifadoua@gmail.com

[2] New Technology Trends (NTT) ENSA, University Abdelmaled Essadi, Tetouan, Morocco

Abstract. Information and communication technology has changed rapidly over the past 20 years with a key development being the emergence of social media. The growing popularity of social media networks has revolutionized the way we view ourselves, the way we see others and the way we perceive the world and interact with one another. More than that, we have witnessed that opinionated postings in social media have helped reshape businesses, and sway public sentiments and emotions, hence the importance of sentiment analysis on social media.

We are interested in studying the opinions of Moroccan Internet users, so this article presents a new electronic dictionary called "DELSOM" that is intended for the sociolect language used by Moroccan Internet users on the web and social networks. It presents in detail the process of developing this dictionary, namely the general features of this knowledge base, the morphological and syntactic specifications that characterize this first draft of the characterization of this new language, the different grammatical and phonetic rules, and the modeling schemes adopted to define the entries of this dictionary.

Keywords: Electronic dictionaries · Sentiment analysis
Arabic opinion mining · Moroccan sociolect language

1 Introduction

The Web has become a huge ground for posting and sharing emotions about any subject; and understanding this phenomenon represents a major challenge at many levels. Therefore the influence of social networks has taken a considerable place since they represent an undeniable power in today's global society.

The web including social networks occupies a very important place in Morocco. According to the National Telecommunication Regulatory Agency (ANRT) statistics [1], Morocco had 18.5 million Internet users in 2016, which is almost 58.3% of its population and this number continues to increase, nearly two in three Internet users using networks social networks access it daily.

The main uses of Moroccan Internet users are participation in social networks (90%), so Morocco is the fifth largest user of the Facebook network in Africa.

Y. Tabii et al. (Eds.): BDCA 2018, CCIS 872, pp. 489–499, 2018.
https://doi.org/10.1007/978-3-319-96292-4_38

So as part of our work on the analysis and detection of feelings of Internet users from their publications on the web and social networks, we were interested in studying the opinions of the Moroccan Internet community on an event, a political decision or a commercial product, etc. Therefore, for a better analysis and follow-up of the opinion of the Moroccan Internet users it was essential first of all to understand this sociolect language used by the Moroccan Net surfers on the social networks.

This sociolect language is characterized by the combination of numbers and letters to transcribe words from the French, Arabic and English languages or even to transcribe emoticons expressing a given feeling, it has even become very common to write the Arabic language in Latin letters.

Since the use of this type of language that calls for both numbers and languages is a new trend of communication, we do not really find on the market a dictionary that meets this need, hence the idea to develop this first version of dictionary for this Moroccan sociolect language.

This work of elaboration of a dictionary specific to the sociolect language used by the Moroccan Net surfers on the web is a complementary work to another work in progress that aims the application of text classification algorithms to the Moroccan sociolect language for opinion analysis.

In the literature there are many research studies that have dealt with Sentiment Analysis applied to the variations of Arabic language.

In this respect, Itani et al. [2] have developed resources for sentiment analysis specifically for Arabic text in social media. A distinctive feature of the corpora and lexicons developed are that they are determined from informal Arabic that does not conform to grammatical or spelling standards.

Harrat et al. [3] present a first linguistic study of the Arabic Algerian dialect, a non-resourced language for which no known resource is available to date. They introduce its most important features and describe the resources that they created from scratch for this dialect.

El-Masria et al. [4] proposed a new tool that applies sentiment analysis to Arabic text tweets using a combination of parameters (the time of the tweets, preprocessing methods like stemming and retweets, n-grams features, lexicon-based methods, and machine-learning methods). Users can select a topic and set their desired parameters. The model detects the polarity (negative, positive, both, and neutral) of the topic from the recent related tweets and display the results.

The rest of this paper is organized as follows: Sect. 2 is about the Moroccan sociolect language and a presentation of the linguistic situation in morocco, and Sect. 3 is a definition of the linguistic knowledge base "DELSOM" and its content. Furthermore the Sect. 4 is devoted to present the steps of modeling of grammatical rules of the sociolect language. Section 5 is about the modeling of phonetic rules of this language. And the final Sect. 6 is a conclusion of all the work done is this paper.

2 Moroccan Sociolect Language and the Linguistic Situation in Morocco

As part of Morocco presents a very complex linguistic situation [5]: classical Arabic and modern Arabic for the most educated, Arabic dialect or Moroccan Arabic, called in Morocco "darija", for almost all the population,, the Berber, called "Amazigh" for about 40% of Moroccans, French for those who attend schools, Spanish for a small part of the population of the North, and English which tends to prevail as a vehicle for modernity.

The interaction [6] of all these languages that coexist in Morocco has given birth to a new language that combines all these languages and associates them even with Latin numbers, it is what we call here the Moroccan sociolect language which aims essentially at facilitating and accompanying the increased speed of communication required by new exchange technologies.

As a conceptual clarification, we have opted for the word "sociolect" because it corresponds better to the linguistic situation that we propose to describe in view of the fact that the specific linguistic uses in chat and blogs are widely shared by the community of young Internet users.

In sociolinguistics [7], a sociolect or social dialect is a variety of language associated with a social group such as a socioeconomic class, an ethnic group, an age group, etc.

Sociolects [8] involve both passive acquisition of particular communicative practices through association with a local community, as well as active learning and choice among speech or writing forms to demonstrate identification with particular groups.

The sociolect in question is characterized by the use of at least three different idioms, namely Moroccan Arabic, modern Arabic and French both in oral and in writing.

Moroccan Arabic is constituted of a lexical background from classical Arabic, Tamazight and French in consideration of to the history of the country [9]. And with the advent of web 3.0 including social networks and blogs, in addition to SMS, new modes of communication have emerged, and Moroccan Internet users have begun to use this new language, which is characterized by the combination of numbers and letters to transcribe words from the French, Arabic and English languages in order to free themselves from the obligations and complications that come with the grammatical and syntactic rules imposed by the formal languages.

Indeed, this work is the result of another work [10] where we proposed a new modeling methodology for Moroccan sociolect recognition used on the social media. It is based on detecting the language of each word in the text: classical Arabic, Tamazight, French or English, determination of the dominant language and processing the words belonging to the Moroccan sociolect language. Thus the creation of a dictionary dedicated to the Moroccan sociolect language used on the web came as the next step in this work aiming to analyze the opinions of Moroccan Internet users.

3 Definition of the Linguistic Knowledge Base "DELSOM" and Its Content

The electronic dictionary of the Moroccan sociolect language DELSOM is a reference book containing a maximum of words belonging to the sociolect language used by Moroccan Internet users to communicate on the web and social networks.

We have chosen to call this dictionary by the name of "DELSOM", the term "DELSOM" stands for "Dictionnaire Electronique du Langage SOciolecte Marocain" in French which means "electronic dictionary of Moroccan sociolect language" in English.

This first version of the dictionary contains lexical (nouns, adjectives, verbs, etc.) and grammatical units (word-tools, such as pronouns, conjunctions, prepositions…), and providing for each entry a definition, an explanation and a correspondence in the French language.

Our ultimate goal is to analyze the opinion trends of Moroccan Internet users, whether they have a positive or negative reaction on a subject or an event, so having a dictionary of Moroccan sociolect language will allow us in addition to understand a sociolect text, to have an idea on the polarity of the text, whether it carries a positive or negative opinion or neutral. Thus this dictionary DELSOM will offer us a way to annotate our corpus of study in order to apply and compare thereafter the different algorithms of classification of texts we chose.

It should be noted that we do not just rely on this dictionary to analyze the data we extracted from social networks because Moroccan Internet users can use the sociolect language, French and English or another language simultaneously, thus and as explained in another article (see reference no 10) we proceed by a detection of the language, so each time we detect a language we use an existing dictionary of this language, but when it is social language that is not recognized and has no dictionary or rules to frame it, we use the dictionary DELSOM.

According to Alexa Ranking [11] which provides a regular update of the most visited websites in Morocco, we opted for the site of Facebook and Hespress to extract comments of Moroccan Internet users, for this we used data extraction software like Facepager [12] that was created to fetch public available data from Facebook, Twitter and other JSON-based API. All data is stored in a SQLite database and may be exported to csv. The extracted data have undergone several cleaning and decomposition processes to obtain a first version of valid units to be entries of the sociolect dictionary DELSOM.

Since the sociolect language is the result of the interaction between the Arabic language and mainly French and other languages of course because of its history, it was necessary to standardize the entries of the dictionary to have something exploitable and reliable. Thus we tried to combine the grammatical, syntactic, phonetic… rules of these languages to deduce rules that are specific to this sociolect language.

Arabic language has a very complex and rich morphology in which a word may carry important information. As a space delimited token, a word in Arabic reveals several morphological aspects: derivation, inflection, and agglutination [13].

Table 1. Correspondence table between Arabic letters and sociolect graph (letters and numbers)

Numbers and Latin letters	Arabic letters	IPA[a]
a, e, é, è	ا	aː
b, p	ب	b
t	ت	t
th, s	ث	θ
j, g	ج	ʤ , ʒ g
h, 7	ح	ħ
kh, 5, 7'	خ	x
d	د	d
z, th, dh	ذ	ð
r	ر	r
z	ز	z
s, c	س	s
ch, sh	ش	ʃ
s	ص	sˤ
d	ض	dˤ , ðˤ
t	ط	tˤ
th	ظ	zˤ , ðˤ
3	ع	ʔˤ
gh	غ	ɣ
f	ف	f
k, 9	ق	q
k	ك	k
L	ل	l
m	م	m

(*Continued*)

Table 1. (*Continued*)

n	ن	n
h, ha, he, eh	ه	h
t, at	ة	t
w, ou, u	و	w , u:
i, y, ei, ai	ي	j , i:
2a	أ	ʔ
2o	ؤ	ʔ
2i	إ	ʔ
2	ئ	ʔ

[a]**IPA :** stands for the International Phonetic Alphabet

The notation for Arabic [14] is the same as for French with one exception, namely the dual (couple) which does not exist in French, so we can say that the same rules can be applied to the sociolect language. Thus the first step in the process of elaboration of the electronic dictionary of the Moroccan sociolect language DELSOM was to find the canonical form of each entry.

For verbs in sociolect language, the adopted canonical form corresponds to the third person masculine singular of the completed form, because Arabic is a non-temporal aspectual language, a language that expresses more the verbal aspect than verbal time. So the most important in Arabic is the expression of the completed or uncompleted state of the action expressed by the verb.

For the nominal entries of the sociolect language, the adopted form is the masculine singular form, with one exception, which is the so-called "broken" plural because the latter is built by internal derivation which leads to a new entry completely different from the original word.

For deverbals, also called "immediate verbo-nominal derivatives", such as the infinitive form, the active participle, the passive participle, we keep the form of the masculine singular.

Another aspect that needed to be handled is the phonetic rules of the sociolect language.

Moroccan Internet users tend to express the long vowels by repetition of the vowel several times, so for reasons of economy and standardization we tolerate a single repetition of the vowel concerned by vocal elongation.

To express gemination in sociolect language, we have chosen opts for the repetition of the consonant concerned only once.

In the sociolect language a letter can have several writings as shown in the following table:

Thus each word of the sociolect language can have several writings, so after having applied all these rules above on each entry of the dictionary, we have proceeded, based on the table of correspondences presented over, with a combinatorial analysis to determine all the writings possibilities of each word that will be added as dictionary entries on one side and as synonyms of the original word on the other side.

To find all possible writing combinations for each entry in the dictionary, the principle of multiplication has been applied which makes it possible to count the number of results of experiments which can be broken down into a succession of sub-experiments.

So if we suppose that an experiment is the succession of m sub-experiments, and if the ith experiment has n_i possible results for i = 1, …, n, then the total number of possible outcomes of the overall experience is:

$$n = \prod_{i=1}^{m} ni = n_1 n_2 n_3 \ldots n_m \quad (1)$$

All these rules presented above represent a first step towards building an electronic dictionary that is scalable, reliable and usable by different languages and platforms.

4 Modeling of Grammatical Rules of the Sociolect Language

The following model aims at modeling the grammatical rules presented in the previous section, so these rules can be considered as a first characterization of the Moroccan sociolect language (Fig. 1 and Table 2).

Each time we collect an entry for the DELSOM dictionary, we proceed by detecting the grammatical category of the sociolect word.

We have two major categories, the nominal one that has two sub categories: noun and adjective, and the verbal onc that has also two sub categories: verb and deverbale.

So as explained before, for the noun, the adjective and the deverbale sub categories, we look for the masculine singular corresponding form, with one exception which is the broken plural sub category that we keep it as it is. As for the verb category we look always for the form that corresponds to the third masculine person singular.

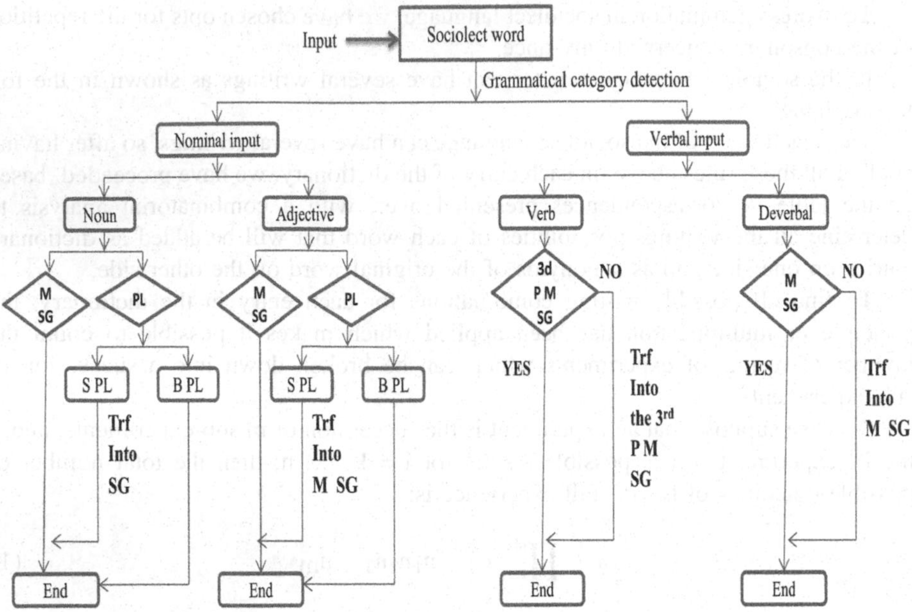

Fig. 1. A modeling scheme of grammatical rules of the sociolect language

Table 2. Explanation of the abbreviations used in the modeling scheme

Abbreviation	Meaning
M SG	masculine singular
PL	Plural
S PL	Simple plural
B PL	Broken plural
Trf Into M SG	transformation into singular masculine
3d P M SG	third masculine person singular

5 Modeling of Phonetic Rules of the Sociolect Language

The following diagram is a modeling of the phonetic rules adopted for the elaboration of the DELSOM dictionary entries (Fig. 2).

After applying the grammar rules to each entry of the dictionary, we proceed to the application of the phonetic rules presented above.

Each phoneme of the sociolect word can undergo modifications because of the specific nature of sociolect language.

When the pronunciation of the sociolect word does not contain any vocal elongation, then the vowel is used in its usual simple form, but when there is a vocal elongation during the pronunciation of the sociolect word, and for reasons of economy and standardization, a single repetition of the vowel concerned with elongation is

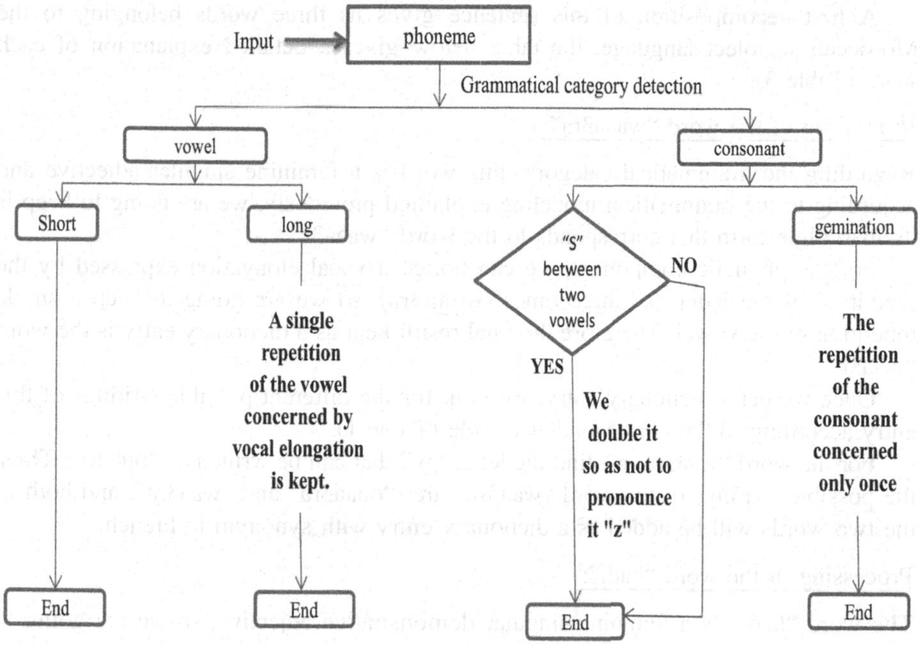

Fig. 2. A modeling scheme of phonetic rules of the sociolect language

tolerated. And since the sociolect language is very influenced by the French language, then when we have the letter "s" between two vowels we double it so as not to pronounce it "z".

In the sociolect language, we also witness the use of consonants repeated several times and this when there is a gemination during the pronunciation of the sociolect word, so for the same reasons of standardization we opt for a single repetition of the letter concerned by the gemination.

Example:

We extracted the following sociolect sentence from Facebook: **"waaa3ra hadi 3andak"** that can be translated by "it is a nice one!"[1].

Table 3. Explanation of the example of the sociolect sentence

Word	Signification
Waaa3ra	Arabic adjective having undergone a semantic sliding to be part of the new language of the young Moroccans to say "top or superb" in English
hadi	A demonstrative whose reference depends on the situation of enunciation, and it means "this one"
3andak	A word that combines the characteristics of the preposition and the possessive pronoun

[1] It's our translation as native speakers (see generative grammar of Noam Chomsky).

A first decomposition of this sentence gives us three words belonging to the Moroccan sociolect language; the table below gives a detailed explanation of each word (Table 3).

Processing of the word "waaa3ra":

Regarding the grammatical category, this word is a feminine singular adjective and according to the grammatical modeling explained previously, we are going to keep is its masculine form that corresponds to the word "waaa3r".

For the phonetic component, we can notice a vocal elongation expressed by the repetition of the letter "a" three times (w**aaa**3ra), so we are going to keep a single repetition of the vowel. Therefore the final result kept as a dictionary entry is the word "waa3r".

Once we get a dictionary entry, we look for the different possible writings of this entry according to the correspondence table (Table 1).

For the word "waa3ra, we find the letter "w" that can be written as "ou" too, Thus, the possible writings of the word "waa3ra" are: "ouaa3ra" and "waa3ra", and both of the two words will be added as a dictionary entry with synonym in French.

Processing of the word "hadi":

The word "hadi" is a feminine singular demonstrative adjective, so we are going to keep its masculine form that corresponds to the word "hada".

Furthermore, the word does not present any phonetic concerns, and the letter composing this word have no other writings according to the correspondence table (Table 1), so we obtain the final entry for our dictionary which is the word "hada".

Processing of the word "3andak":

The word "3andak" combines the characteristics of the preposition and the possessive pronoun, so we keep it as it is.

This word does not have phonetic aspects that need to be handled, but due to the Moroccan spelling features that are shown in the correspondence table (Table 1), the word "3andak" can be also written as "3andek". So by the end of this processing we get two finale entries: "3andak" and "3andek".

6 Conclusion

The purpose of our research is to be able to better analyze the trends of the opinions of the Moroccan Internet users, so it was essential first to better understand this language used by this community of Internet users.

This Moroccan sociolect language is a kind of combination of numbers with classical Arabic, Moroccan or "darija", French and other languages that have influenced the history of Morocco. Thus we had the idea to build a first electronic dictionary of this sociolect language.

In this article we tried to present the content of this dictionary, the process of its development and the different models that contributed to its realization, we also have devoted a section to talk about the historical context that have led to the birth of this sociolect language.

Certainly to build a dictionary of a new language that is neither recognized nor structured is not something obvious, so this first version of the dictionary can be very enriched, for example we can define synonyms in other languages, also the dictionary entries can be classified according to grammatical category, gender, number, etc.

References

1. The annual Report The National Agency for the Regulation of Telecommunications ANRT-2015. https://www.anrt.ma/lagence/actualites/rapport-annuel-2015. Accessed 10 June 2017
2. Itani, M., Roast, C., Al-Khayatt, S.: Developing resources for sentiment analysis of informal arabic text in social media. In: 3rd International Conference on Arabic Computational Linguistics, ACLing 2017, 5–6 November 2017, Dubai, United Arab Emirates, vol. 117, pp. 129–136. Elsevier (2017)
3. Harrat, S., Meftouh, K., Abbas, M., Hidouci, K., Smaili, K.: An algerian dialect: study and resources. Int. J. Adv. Comput. Sci. Appl. 7(3), 384–396 (2016)
4. El-Masria, M., Altrabsheh, N., Mansour, H., Ramsay, A.: A web-based tool for Arabic sentiment analysis. In: 3rd International Conference on Arabic Computational Linguistics, ACLing 2017, 5–6 November 2017, Dubai, United Arab Emirates, vol. 117, pp. 38–45. Elsevier (2017)
5. La situation linguistique au Maroc: Enjeux et état des lieux, Saïd BENNIS Centre des Etudes et Recherches en Sciences Sociales, Faculté des Lettres et des Sciences Humaines, Université Mohammed V, 16 Juin 2011
6. Zouhir, A.: Selected Proceedings of the 43rd Annual Conference on African Linguistics. Edited by O.O. Orie, K.W. Sanders, pp. 271–277. Cascadilla Proceedings Project, Somerville (2012)
7. Wolfram, W.: Social varieties of American English. In: Finegan, E., Rickford, J.R. (eds.) Language in the USA: Themes for the Twenty-first Century. Cambridge University Press, Cambridge (2004). ISBN 0-521-77747-X
8. Durrell, M.: Sociolect. In: Ammon, U., et al. (eds.) Sociolinguistics: An International Handbook of the Science of Language and Society, pp. 200–205. Walter de Gruyter, Berlin (2004)
9. Marley, D.: Language attitudes in Morocco following recent changes in language policy. Lang. Policy **3**, 25 (2004). https://doi.org/10.1023/B:LPOL.0000017724.16833.66
10. Mansouri, F., Abdelalim, S., Ikram, E.A.: A modeling framework for the Moroccan sociolect recognition used on the social media. In: BDCA, pp. 34:1–34:5 (2017)
11. Alexa Ranking: statistics on the most visited websites in Morocco. http://www.alexa.com/topsites/countries/MA. Accesssed 1 May 2017
12. Facepager: Data extraction software. https://github.com/strohne/Facepager. Accessed 5 Aug 2017
13. Boudad, N., et al.: Sentiment analysis in Arabic: a review of the literature. Ain Shams Eng. J. (2017). https://doi.org/10.1016/j.asej.2017.04.007
14. Ibrahim, M.N.: Statistical Arabic grammar analyzer. In: Gelbukh, A. (ed.) CICLing 2015. LNCS, vol. 9041, pp. 187–200. Springer, Cham (2015). https://doi.org/10.1007/978-3-319-18111-0_15

Incorporation of Linguistic Features in Machine Translation Evaluation of Arabic

Mohamed El Marouani(✉), Tarik Boudaa, and Nourddine Enneya

Laboratory of Informatics Systems and Optimization, Faculty of Sciences, Ibn-Tofail University, Kenitra, Morocco
mohamed.elmarouani@gmail.com, tarikboudaa@yahoo.fr, enneya@uit.ac.ma

Abstract. This paper describes a study on the contribution of some basic linguistic features to the task of machine translation evaluation of Arabic as a target language. AL-TERp is used as a metric dedicated and tuned especially for Arabic. Performed experiments on a medium sized corpora show that linguistic knowledge improves the correlation of metric results with human assessments. Also a detailed qualitative analysis of the results highlights a number of resolved issues related to the use of linguistic features.

Keywords: Arabic MT · MT evaluation · AL-TERp · Linguistic features

1 Introduction

Evaluation in machine translation (MT) is critical and challenging for developers of MT systems to monitor progress of their work as well as for MT users to select among available MT engines for their language pairs of interest. Added to the human evaluation which is costly and time consuming, several automatic methods and tools have been developed by the research community. These methods are based on the comparison of a hypothesis to translation references.

Evaluating the MT system output quality in regard to its similarity to human references is not a trivial task. We observe that different human translators can generate different outputs, all of them are considered valid. Hence, the language variability is an issue in this context. A considerable effort has been made to integrate deeper linguistic knowledge in automatic evaluation metrics in order to tackle this language variability. The used features cover the syntactic similarities by using part-of-speech information for example in [1] and the semantic similarities by using synonyms in [2], paraphrases in [3] or textual entailment in [4]. The morphology aspect is also handled in [5] where the studied language is English-to-Arabic.

Machine translation into Arabic language, especially English-to-Arabic, does not provide a high quality output in comparison to other closed languages pairs. This low quality is due, among others, to the complex morphology of Arabic [6]. Thus, the adoption of a metric using linguistic information, namely AL-TERp [7], allows us to analyze the effect of each linguistic information type and to estimate the interest of their combination.

Y. Tabii et al. (Eds.): BDCA 2018, CCIS 872, pp. 500–511, 2018.
https://doi.org/10.1007/978-3-319-96292-4_39

The issues related to the morphology of Arabic can be viewed under two angles: the first angle is the morphology richness where words sharing the same core meaning (represented by the lemma or lexeme) can be said to inflect for different morphological features, e.g., gender and number. These features can realize using concatenative (affixes and stems) and/or templatic (root and patterns) morphology. The second angle is morphological ambiguity where words with different lemmas can have the same inflected form. As such, a word form can have more than one morphological analysis represented as a lemma and a set of feature-value pairs.

In this paper, we examine the impact of linguistic features in the evaluation of MT outputs for Arabic and we argue that taking into account the semantic and morphological sides of the target sentences is beneficial in MT evaluation. The second section presents some related works like TER metric [8], TER-Plus [9] and the version dedicated for Arabic AL-TERp. AL-BLEU [10] an extension of the classical metric BLEU [11] is also described in this section. The third section describes a comparative study involving some baselines metrics and AL-TERp by focusing on its different features. The fourth section provides a preliminary qualitative analysis of the impact of some linguistic features. The last section concludes the paper with brought contributions and the eventual improvements in the future.

2 Related Work

Since the manual evaluation of machine translation results is, practically, not possible in regard to its high cost, researchers have been designed automatic evaluation metrics trying to align with the basic evaluation criteria, like adequacy or fluency. BLEU is actually the most used metric and de-facto standard, at least in research community. This metric is calculated as a function of n-gram matching precision associated to a brevity penalty that reduces the score if the output is too short.

The most-know and worldwide workshops and shared tasks in MT like WMT [12] or IWSLT [13] involve several metrics and language pairs but do not tackle Arabic and do not focus on languages that represent issues in richness of morphology.

We are concerned in this literature reviewing, especially, by present the state-of-art of the metrics treating the particularities of morphologically complex languages and representing a high correlation with human assessment. In the same way, we will present metrics providing good results for evaluating machine translation into Arabic.

In order to put our work in its context, we present in the remaining subsections TER metric and how TER-Plus improves on it. Then we describe improvements brought by our tool AL-TERp. Finally, we discuss also AL-BLEU which is an extended version of BLEU to evaluate Arabic MT.

2.1 TER and TER-Plus

For a hypothesis, Translation Edit Rate (TER) is defined as the minimum edit distance over all references, normalized by the average reference length as the following:

$$TER(h,r) = \frac{C_{edit}(h,r)}{|r|} \tag{1}$$

$C_{edit}(h, r)$ is the number of edit operations needed to transform hypothesis h into a reference r. These equally-weighted operations can be: word insertion, word deletion, word substitution and block movement of words called shifts. Shifts are performed in TER under some constraints that reduce computational complexity. In the case of multiple references, TER scores the hypothesis against each reference individually. It uses the minimum number of edits of the closest reference to the hypothesis as the numerator, and the average number of words across all references as the denominator. In contrast to BLEU, TER is an error measure. So, the lower it scores, the higher the metric is better.

TER-Plus (notated as TERp henceforth) is an improved extension of TER which brings an added-value among the following mechanisms:

- TERp uses, in addition to the edit operations of TER, three new relaxing edit operations: stem matches, synonym matches, and phrases substitutions.
- The cost of each edit is optimized according to human judgments data set.
- As TERp added other features, its shifting criteria have also been extended. Thus, shifts operations are allowed if the words being shifted are: (i) exactly the same, (ii) synonyms, stems or paraphrases of the corresponding reference words, or (iii) any such combination.
- Furthermore, a set of stop-words is used to constrain the shift operations such that common words and punctuation can be shifted if and only if non-stop word is also shifted.
- TERp is insensitive to casing information.
- TERp is capped at 1 while the formula for TER allows it to exceed 1 if the number of edits exceeds the number of words.

In TERp, stems are computed by Porter stemmer [14], and synonyms using Wordnet [15] resources. Phrase substitutions are determined by looking up in a pre-computed phrases table of phrases and its paraphrases. This phrase table is extracted using the pivot-based method [16] with several additional filtering mechanisms to increase the precision.

With the exception of phrase substitutions, all of edit operations used by TERp have fixed cost edits, i.e., the edit cost does not depend on the used words.

For a phrasal substitution between a reference phrase r and a hypothesis phrase h where P is the probability of paraphrasing r as h, and $edit(r, h)$ is number of edits needed to align r and h without any phrasal substitutions, the edit cost is specified by four parameters ω_1, ω_2, ω_3 and ω_4 as follows [17]:

$$\cos t(r,h) = \omega_1 + edit(r,h)(\omega_2 Log(P) + \omega_3 P + \omega_4) \tag{2}$$

While TER uses uniform edit costs −1 for all edits except matches that is equivalent to 0, TERp uses seven optimized edit cost in plus of the fixed exact matching cost to 0. The paraphrase substitution cost is equivalent to four parameters as viewed in the formula below. The optimization of these ten parameters is done via a hill-climbing search algorithm [18] in order to maximize the correlation of human judgments with TERp scores.

Added to the score provided, TERp generates a hypothesis and reference sentences alignment, indicating which words are correct, incorrect, misplaced or similar to the reference translation. Experiments lead by [9] demonstrate that TERp achieves significant gains in correlation with human judgments over other MT evaluation metrics (TER, METEOR [19], and BLEU).

TERp is used in some shared tasks for several European languages pairs with English as a target language, but does not support Arabic given that it uses components running only under a restricted list of languages. These components are Porter stemmer, English Wordnet and a pre-computed English paraphrases database. Also, its weights deeply depend on the evaluated language which is English.

2.2 AL-TERp

Evaluation plays a crucial role in all NLP tasks, especially in machine translation. Thus, it is necessary that machine translation evaluation tools reach for Arabic high accuracy. For this purpose, it is important to take into account the linguistic specificities of Arabic in order to achieve a high correlation with human judgment. In this context, an improved version of TERp that supports Arabic is created which is called AL-TERp [7]. The main improvements are summarized in the following:

Normalization
This operation is necessary to reduce the negative effect on the score, due to random variations in some informal texts that depend generally on the author style. Since TERp normalizer doesn't support Arabic, a handcrafted normalizer dedicated to Arabic texts is implemented and is integrated as a part of this improved tool.

Paraphrase Database
In order to integrate paraphrases as a component in the Arabic version, namely AL-TERp, Arabic paraphrases database (PPDB) provided by [20] is used. This database is constructed via the usual method by pivoting through parallel corpora: Two expressions in language *F*, f_1 and f_2, which are translated to a shared expression e in another language E can be assumed to have the same meaning, i.e. paraphrases.

In this case, only two main informations among others are extracted from the database: $p(e|f)$ which is the probability of the paraphrase given the original phrase (in negative log value) and the reciprocal probability $p(f|e)$. Phrasal paraphrases set which is multi-words paraphrases has been chosen, this set includes cases where a single word maps onto a multiword paraphrase and many-to-many paraphrases. For AL-TERp, required customizations have been made in order to consume files of this new paraphrases database.

Synonyms
It is required to take into account synonyms to assign a precise cost while computing the AL-TERp metric. For this purpose, an API under Arabic WordNet [21] that allows checking synonyms of Arabic words is built, among others.

Stemming
To reflect what already exists for English in TERp, the baseline Arabic stemmer Khoja's stemmer [22] is adopted in order to replace the Porter stemmer and to allow AL-TERp to identify if two words having the same stem.

Parameters' Optimization
AL-TERp is a tunable metric. Thus, the optimization of its parameters regarding to human judgments is required. This task is performed via adapting the module provided by the original metric TERp. Therefore, a hill-climbing algorithm is rained in order to obtain high correlation in terms of Kendall coefficients [23] between metric scores and a ranks' range given by a human annotator for outputs of a set of MT systems.

2.3 AL-BLEU

AL-BLEU is one of the important works in MT evaluation which is designed especially for taking into account the richness of morphology of Arabic. It adopted the standard metric BLEU as the basis and extends its exact n-gram matching to morphological, syntactic and lexical levels with optimized partial credits. After exact matching, AL-BLEU examines the following: (a) morphological and syntactic feature matching, (b) stem matching. The set of checked morphological features are: (i) POS tag, (ii) gender, (iii) number, (iv) person, (v) definiteness. Unlike of BLEU, this tool provides a partial credit capped to 1 following this formula:

$$m(t_h, t_r) = \begin{cases} 1, \; \text{\textit{if}} \; t_h = t_r \\ \omega_s + \sum_{i=1}^{5} \omega_{f_i} \; \text{\textit{otherwise}} \end{cases} \tag{3}$$

m(t_h, t_r) is the matching credit of a hypothesis token t_h and its reference token t_r. This credit is equal to 1 in the case of exact matching. Otherwise, we provide partial credit for matching at stem ω_s and morphological level ω_{fi}. In order to avoid over-crediting, the range of weights is limited with a set of constraints.

Bouamor et al. [10] compare average Kendall's τ correlation to human judgments for three metrics: BLEU, METEOR and AL-BLEU. The results show a significant improvement of AL-BLEU against BLEU and a competitive improvement against

METEOR. The stem and morphological matching of AL-BLEU, gives a score and ranking much closer to human judgments.

The performances realized by AL-BLEU give more confidence in the ability of automatic MT evaluation metrics improvement by the introduction of linguistic knowledge.

3 Linguistic Features Impact

3.1 Data

The data set used in our experiments is the same used in [7]. It is composed of 1383 sentences selected from two subsets: (i) the standard English-Arabic NIST 2005 corpus, commonly used for MT evaluations and composed of political news stories; and (ii) a small dataset of translated Wikipedia articles. This corpus contains the source and target text along with the automatic translations produced by five English-to-Arabic MT systems: three research-oriented phrase-based systems with various morphological and syntactic features (QCRI, CMU, Colombia) and two commercial systems (Google, Bing). The corpus contains annotations that assess the quality of the five systems, by ranking their translation candidates from best to worst for each source sentence in the corpus. The annotation is performed by two annotators for each sentence with a mutual agreement in terms of Kendall's τ of 49.20 [4].

In this paper, we have reported the results of the previous experiments performed in [2] and we have extended our tests by the same data set partition (composed of 383 sentences) in order to further analyze the impact of the studied linguistic features.

3.2 Correlation Coefficient

The correlation scores are calculated following the Kendall tau coefficient [15]. This correlation coefficient is calculated for each sentence as follows:

$$\tau = \frac{conc - disc}{n(n-1)/2} \tag{4}$$

where *conc* is the number of cases where the agreement between the two ranks is perfect, *disc* is the number where the disagreement between the two ranks is perfect and *n* is the number of systems used to translate our datasets. Ranges of ranks provided in the raw data are normalized firstly taking into account ties, that are in fact ignored for the calculation of Kendall's tau.

The tau coefficient of Kendall is calculated in the corpus level using the Fisher transformation [24]. This method allows us to find the average correlation of a corpus using correlations at the sentence level. Fisher's Z transformation is one of several weighting strategies recommended in the literature for computing weighted correlations, and regardless of dataset size, back-transformed average of Fisher's transformation for each sentence is always less biased.

3.3 Results and Discussion

Firstly, we provide bellow (Table 1) AL-TERp parameters resulting from the optimization process under the dataset presented in the previous sub-section. These parameters are specific to Arabic language as target language in MT.

Apart from the exact matching cost which is null, these parameters vary from 0.0906 as the minimal cost (stem cost) to 1.5339 as the maximum cost (deletion cost). ω_1, ω_2, ω_3 and ω_4 are the parameters used in computing the paraphrasing cost as indicated in the above mentioned formula.

Table 1. AL-TERp parameters

Parameter	Cost
Deletion cost	1.5339
Insertion cost	0.5083
Substitution cost	1.4936
Match cost	0.0
Shift cost	0.8705
Stem cost	0.0906
Synonym cost	0.36700
ω_1	−0.5935
ω_2	−0.3135
ω_3	0.2643
ω_4	0.0554

In the previous work, we argued that AL-TERp is the best in term of Kendall's correlation. AL-TERp outperformed, as mentioned in Table 2, the results provided by BLEU, AL-BLEU, METEOR and TER. It is worth noting that METEOR is used in its universal mode but without using paraphrasing that require compiling a paraphrase database using a parallel corpus with Arabic in one side. These correlations are calculated in the corpus level.

Table 2. Corpus-level correlation with human rankings (Kendall's τ)

Metric	Kendall's tau
BLEU	0.2011
AL-BLEU	0.2085
METEOR	0.1782
TER	0.2619
AL-TERp	0.3242

An advanced study is conducted by watching the impact of each feature: using only paraphrasing, stemming or synonyms. We observe that all features bring an improvement even if small to the correlation coefficient of the best one metric, namely TER (cf. Table 3). Stems feature achieves a correlation of 0.3121 (+0.0502), paraphrases feature achieves 0.2851 (+0.0232) Kendall tau and synonyms feature arrives only at 0.2747 (+0.0128). Stemming realizes the best correlation which confirms the importance of morphology in evaluating Arabic MT output sentences. Also, this important result (equal correlations) is observed also when stemming is combined with the two other semantic features: paraphrases and synonyms.

Table 3. Corpus-level correlation using different features (Kendall's τ)

Metric	Kendall's tau
AL-TERp (All features)	0.3242
AL-TERp (Para)	0.2851
AL-TERp (Syn)	0.2747
AL-TERp (Stem)	0.3121
AL-TERp (Stem + Syn)	0.3193
AL-TERp (Para + Syn)	0.2871
AL-TERp (Para + Stem)	0.3193

On the other hand, the realized correlations are not additive but the combination of features improves further correlation coefficients.

4 Qualitative Analysis

We are not aiming at restricting our research to handling the correlations with human judgments, nor focusing only on the quantitative approach, we try in this part to shed some light on the suitability and influence of integration of linguistic features. Our study is not exhaustive, since we analyze only a data set sample which allows us to focus on issues that represent MT evaluation of Arabic as a target language, and to employ the detailed output that generates AL-TERp for each sentence's evaluation.

We find bellow an example of the detailed output provided by AL-TERp metric. The line *Alignment* indicates the set of performed edits: the blank digit is for exact matching, *T* digit is for stems matching, *P* digit is for paraphrases matching, *S* is for substitution and *I* is for insertion. Using the file of this detailed evaluation, we can perform a qualitative analysis of the different aspects involved by the edit operations.

```
Sentence ID: [nist][0814]
Original Reference: كما التقى تانغ ، وزير الخارجية الصينى
السابق ، مع الرئيس الإسرائيلى موشيه كاتساف اليوم ، وتبادل
الجانبان وجهات النظر بشأن الوضع الإقليمى الراهن .
Original Hypothesis: كما التقى تانغ، وزير الخارجية صيني
سابق، مع الرئيس الإسرائيلي موشي كاتساف اليوم. وقد تبادل
الجانبان وجهات النظر حول الوضع الحالي في المنطقة.
Reference: كما التقي تانغ وزير الخارجية الصيني السابق مع
الرئيس الاسرائيلي موشيه كاتساف اليوم وتبادل الجانبان وجهات
النظر بشان الوضع الاقليمي الراهن
Hypothesis: كما التقي تانغ وزير الخارجية صيني سابق مع
الرئيس الاسرائيلي موشي كاتساف اليوم وقد تبادل الجانبان
وجهات النظر حول الوضع الحالي في المنطقة
Hypothesis After Shift: كما التقي تانغ وزير الخارجية صيني
سابق مع الرئيس الاسرائيلي موشي كاتساف اليوم وقد تبادل
الجانبان وجهات النظر حول الوضع الحالي في المنطقة
Alignment: (      TT   T  P SSI)
HypErrs: 0.000 0.000 0.000 0.000 0.000 0.572 0.572 0.000
0.000  0.000  0.572  0.000  0.000  0.000  0.000  0.000  0.000
0.000 0.000 0.000 1.371 1.371 0.153
OtherErr: 0.000
HypLocMap: 0 1 2 3 4 5 6 7 8 9 10 11 12 13 14 15 16 17 18
19 20 21 22

NumShifts: 0
Num Phrase Substitutions: 1
  NewCost: 0.0 OrigCost: 2.16496 <p>وتبادل الجانبان وجهات
النظر بشان</p> <p>وقد تبادل الجانبان وجهات النظر حول</p>

Score: 0.220 (4.611 / 21.000)
```

The performed analysis confirms the utility of taking into consideration linguistic knowledge. We present bellow only an example that illustrates how stemming can provide good results in terms of correlation with ranks provided by the human annotator (Tables 4 and 5).

For Bing MT system for example, we have in the case of AL-TERp (Stem) 4 couples of words having the same stems: صيني/الصيني , سابق/السابق , موشي/موشيه , تبادل/وتبادل.. In the case of AL-TERp (Syn) these edits are considered as substitutions. The edit cost of stems is 0.0906 and the edit cost of substitutions is 1.496. This big difference between costs generates different scores then different ranks. Consequently, the metric version of AL-TERp which does not take into account stems in computing of its scores correlates negatively with the human judgments ($\tau = -0.4$).

Table 4. Example of MT outputs with corresponding annotations

		Human annotation ranks
Source	**Tang, a former Chinese foreign minister, also met with Israeli President Moche Katsav today. The two sides exchanged views on the current situation in the region.**	
Reference	**كما التقى تانغ ، وزير الخارجية الصينى السابق ، مع الرئيس الإسرائيلى موشيه كاتساف اليوم ، وتبادل الجانبان وجهات النظر بشأن الوضع الإقليمى الراهن.**	
CMU	تانغ ، وزير الخارجية الصيني السابق ، اجتمع أيضا مع الرئيس الإسرائيلي كاتساف mocheاليوم . وتبادل الجانبان وجهات النظر حول الوضع الحالي في المنطقة.	4
QCRI	تانغ , وزير الخارجية الصيني السابق , التقي الرئيس الاسرائيلي كاتساف moche اليوم . وتبادل الجانبان وجهات النظر حول الوضع الراهن في المنطقة.	5
Google	التقى تانغ، وزير الخارجية الصيني السابق، وأيضا مع الرئيس الاسرائيلي موشي كاتساف اليوم. وتبادل الجانبان وجهات النظر حول الوضع الحالي في المنطقة.	2
Bing	كما التقى تانغ، وزير الخارجية صيني سابق، مع الرئيس الإسرائيلي موشي كاتساف اليوم. وقد تبادل الجانبان وجهات النظر حول الوضع الحالي في المنطقة.	1
Columbia	تانغ ، وزير الخارجية الصيني السابق ، مع الرئيس الإسرائيلي موتشيه كتساف اليوم . وتبادل الجانبان وجهات النظر حول الوضع الحالي في المنطقة.	3

Table 5. Scores of two versions of AL-TERp

		CMU	QCRI	Google	Bing	Columbia	Kendall tau
AL-TERp (Stem)	Scores	50.511	45.315	33.914	27.905	45.910	0.6
	Ranks	5	3	2	1	4	
AL-TERp (Syn)	Scores	50.511	45.315	40.595	54.628	52.591	−0.4
	Ranks	3	2	1	5	4	

5 Conclusions

We studied in this paper the elementary impact of basic linguistic features introduced on a baseline error-oriented MT evaluation metric. The obtained results confirm our hypothesis regarding a rich morphology language like Arabic, namely we can take profit from linguistic oriented comparisons that overcome the lexical similarities. Also the detailed output of AL-TERp is a basis of an error analysis study that involves the linguistic characteristics of the evaluated language.

In the ongoing work, we plan to improve AL-TERp by introducing deep-level linguistic knowledge and exploring other ways of combination of these features especially by using deep learning algorithms and developed data structures.

References

1. Dahlmeier, D., Liu, C., Ng, H.T.: TESLA at WMT2011: translation evaluation and tunable metric. In: WMT 2011 Proceedings of the Sixth Workshop on Statistical Machine Translation, Edinburgh, pp. 78–84 (2011)
2. Denkowski, M., Lavie, A.: Extending the METEOR machine translation evaluation metric to the phrase level. In: Human Language Technologies: The 2010 Annual Conference of the North American Chapter of the Association for Computational Linguistics, pp. 250–253. Association for Computational Linguistics, June 2010
3. Snover, M.G., Madnani, N., Dorr, B., Schwartz, R.: TER-Plus: paraphrase, semantic, and alignment enhancements to translation edit rate. Mach. Transl. **23**(2–3), 117–127 (2009). https://doi.org/10.1007/s10590-009-9062-9
4. Padó, S., Galley, M., Jurafsky, D., Manning, C.D.: Textual entailment features for machine translation evaluation. In: Proceedings of the Fourth Workshop on Statistical Machine Translation, pp. 37–41. Association for Computational Linguistics, March 2009
5. Guzmán, F., Bouamor, H., Baly, R., Habash, N.: Machine translation evaluation for Arabic using morphologically-enriched embeddings. In: Proceedings of COLING 2016, the 26th International Conference on Computational Linguistics: Technical Papers, pp. 1398–1408 (2016)
6. Habash, N.Y.: Introduction to Arabic natural language processing. In: Synthesis Lectures on Human Language Technologies, vol. 3, pp. 1–187 (2010)
7. El Marouani, M., Boudaa, T., Enneya, N.: AL-TERp: extended metric for machine translation evaluation of Arabic. In: Frasincar, F., Ittoo, A., Nguyen, L., Métais, E. (eds.) NLDB 2017. LNCS, vol. 10260, pp. 156–161. Springer, Cham (2017). https://doi.org/10.1007/978-3-319-59569-6_17
8. Snover, M., Dorr, B., Schwartz, R., Micciulla, L., Makhoul, J.: A study of translation edit rate with targeted human annotation. In: Proceedings of the AMTA (2006)
9. Snover, M., Madnani, N., Dorr, B.J., Schwartz, R.: Fluency, adequacy, or HTER?: exploring different human judgments with a tunable MT metric. In: Proceedings of the Fourth Workshop on Statistical Machine Translation, pp. 259–268. Association for Computational Linguistics (2009)
10. Bouamor, H., Alshikhabobakr, H., Mohit, B., Oflazer, K.: A human judgement corpus and a metric for Arabic MT evaluation. In: EMNLP, pp. 207–213 (2014)
11. Papineni, K., Roukos, S., Ward, T., Zhu, W.J.: BLEU: a method for automatic evaluation of machine translation. In: Proceedings of the 40th Annual Meeting on Association for Computational Linguistics, pp. 311–318. Association for Computational Linguistics (2002)
12. Bojar, O., Chatterjee, R., Federmann, C., Graham, Y., Haddow, B., Huang, S., Huck, M., Koehn, P., Liu, Q., Logacheva, V., Monz, C., Negri, M., Post, M., Rubino, R., Specia, L., Turchi, M.: Findings of the 2017 conference on machine translation (WMT17). In: Proceedings of the Second Conference on Machine Translation, pp. 169–214 (2017)
13. Proceeding of IWSLT 2017 International Workshop on Spoken Language Translation. http://workshop2017.iwslt.org/downloads/iwslt2017_proceeding_v2.pdf
14. Snowball: a language for stemming algorithms. http://snowball.tartarus.org/texts/introduction.html
15. Miller, G.A., Fellbaum, C.: WordNet then and now. Lang. Res. Eval. **41**, 209–214 (2007)
16. Bannard, C., Callison-Burch, C.: Paraphrasing with bilingual parallel corpora. In: Proceedings of the 43rd Annual Meeting on Association for Computational Linguistics, pp. 597–604. Association for Computational Linguistics (2005)

17. Dorr, B., Snover, M., Madnani, N., Schwartz, R.: TERp system description. In: MetricsMATR Workshop at AMTA (2008)
18. Russell, S.J., Norvig, P.: Artificial Intelligence: A Modern Approach, 3rd edn (2009)
19. Lavie, M.D.A.: Meteor universal: language specific translation evaluation for any target language. In: ACL 2014, p. 376 (2014)
20. Ganitkevitch, J., Callison-Burch, C.: The multilingual paraphrase database. In: LREC, pp. 4276–4283 (2014)
21. Elkateb, S., Black, W., Rodríguez, H., Alkhalifa, M., Vossen, P., Pease, A., Fellbaum, C.: Building a wordnet for Arabic. In: Proceedings of the Fifth International Conference on Language Resources and Evaluation (LREC 2006), pp. 22–28 (2006)
22. Shereen, K.: Stemming Arabic Text. http://zeus.cs.pacificu.edu/shereen/research.htm
23. Kendall, M.G.: A new measure of rank correlation. Biometrika **30**, 81–93 (1938)
24. Silver, N.C., Dunlap, W.P.: Averaging correlation coefficients: should Fisher's z transformation be used? J. Appl. Psychol. **72**, 146 (1987)

Effect of the Sub-graphemes' Size on the Performance of Off-Line Arabic Writer Identification

Nabil Bendaoud(✉), Yaâcoub Hannad, Abdelillah Samaa, and Mohamed El Youssfi El Kettani

Ibn Tofail University, Kenitra, Morocco
Na.bendaoud@gmail.com, y.hannad@gmail.com,
semma_abdelillah@yahoo.fr, elkettani@univ-ibntofail.ac.ma

Abstract. In this paper, we address the issue of writer identification related to Arabic handwritten text using the approach of small fragments. The main contribution of this work is the analysis conducted about the impact of the window's size of small fragments on the effectiveness of the Arabic writer identification. The proposed system is evaluated according to three scenarios applied on 40 writers from the Arabic IFN/ENIT database through the use of similarity measures. The experiments are conducted by varying the size of the segmentation window allowing us to conclude that the fragments' size affects considerably the results of Arabic writer identification.

Keywords: Writer identification · Small fragments · Arabic text
Text independent

1 Introduction

Identification of writers of handwritten documents is a promising area of research that are of use to many specialists who are involved in jobs that rely on writer identification such as forensic experts and historical archives examiners. Although many studies have been realized on the subject of writer identification, there is still much to be done in this domain especially when the Arabic text is involved given that the results of writer identification vary depending on the language of the text being examined.

Writer identification can be categorized into two types; text dependent and text independent writer identification. The first category requires that the writer produces the same text in both training and evaluation steps, whereas the second type has not constraint on the textual content of the trained and tested samples. On the other hand, offline writer identification seeks the identity of the writer using scanned images of the writing. In our study, text independent writer identification of offline Arabic handwritten text is tackled.

The state-of-the-art approaches for off-line Arabic writer identification rely basically on two kinds of features, structural and textural. The structural features, like in the works of [6, 16, 17], are aimed to extract the structural properties of writing such as average

Y. Tabii et al. (Eds.): BDCA 2018, CCIS 872, pp. 512–522, 2018.
https://doi.org/10.1007/978-3-319-96292-4_40

line height, inclination etc. Whereas, the treatment of handwriting from textural perspective takes each writing as a whole texture and extracts the features from different regions of interest (blocks) or the complete image. The works of [5, 7, 9, 15, 18] illustrate such kind of subject. Sometimes, the combination of structural and textural features is possible, like in the works of [11, 12].

In [8], the authors have introduced new features, including textural-based and grapheme-based features. Evaluating these features have provided promising results from four different perspectives to understand handwritten documents beyond OCR (optical character recognition), by writer identification, script recognition, historical manuscript dating and localization.

On the other hand, some researchers have achieved notable results with respect to offline Arabic writer identification. [1, 2] have relied on the using of features extracted from graphemes (Fragments of text) clustered as codebooks. Their works have achieved an identification rate of 90% and 89% respectively.

Since the using of codebooks of graphemes has proved to be successful in writer identification, Khalifa et al. have addressed in [10] an improved approach that allows the generation of a combined codebook built from the writings of the same author. The researchers, on one hand, made use of SR-KDA (Kernel Discriminant Analysis using Spectral Regression) to generate such combined codebooks. On the other hand, they took advantage of the Nearest Neighbor classifier in order to evaluate the effectiveness of their proposed system. The latter has provides identification rate of 92% on 650 writers.

The work of [4], which is inspired from two other achievements on Latin text [3, 19] using direct comparison of small fragments via similarity measures, has yielded satisfactory results concerning the Arabic text either by extracting unvarying shapes of an Arabic text sample or by using redundant patterns within it termed as writer's invariants. The identification rate attained in [4] is 93.93%.

Fiel and Sablatnig [6] presented a work based on the codebook method to generate clustering features extracted by using the Scale Invariant Feature Transform (SIFT) using various pages of handwriting. The advantage of using SIFT from the authors point view is to eliminate the negative effects of binarization. An identification rate of 90.8% using the IAM dataset of 650 writers was achieved.

In [3], Daniels and Baird proposed a technique to investigate the performance of five highly discriminating features. These features include slant and slant energy, skew, pixel distribution, curvature, and entropy. The performance obtained by combining these features showed identification rates competitive with other state-of-the-art methods for writer identification.

In this paper, starting from the works of [1, 4], we provide a profound analysis of the approach relying on direct comparison of small fragments taking into account the peculiarities of the Arabic handwritten text.

It is worthy of note that the basis of this analysis is the use of features extracted from fragments of the text which in their turn are clustered as codebooks. Also, our work relies on the method of direct comparison of the small fragments via the similarity measures. The proposed system is evaluated according to three scenarios applied on 40 writers from the Arabic IFN/ENIT database. The experiments were conducted by varying the size of the segmenting window, which have allowed us to get to the conclusion that the size of the fragments being compared has a substantial impact on the results for Arabic writer identification.

This paper is organized as follows: We present the details of the system being evaluated in Sect. 2. The third section provides the experimental results. Finally, the conclusion is found in the last section.

2 Proposed Methodology

As presented above, some notable achievements have seen the day concerning offline Arabic writer identification. [1, 2] have taken advantage of features extracted from graphemes (Fragments of text) clustered as codebooks. [4], however, opted for direct comparison of sub-graphemes (smaller fragments) by using similarity measures. The latter work has yielded promising results either by extracting invariants of an Arabic text sample or by using redundant patterns of writings.

In this paper, we take up the issue of direct comparison of small fragments and thereby we propose an approach that consists of an improvement of the one proposed in [4] especially concerning the way the small fragments are extracted since we opt for the segmentation approach used in [19] by moving the cutting window along the ink trace. That system is next evaluated according to three scenarios depending on how we do perform the clustering of the small fragments.

As many similar systems do, the system includes three main phases that are preprocessing, feature extraction and writer identification.

2.1 Pre-processing

The scanned handwritten document is dealt with through the use of a global threshold calculated based on Otsu algorithm [13]. As the document contains Arabic text, the segmentation is performed by separating the connected components which are examined in the phase of feature extraction (Fig. 1).

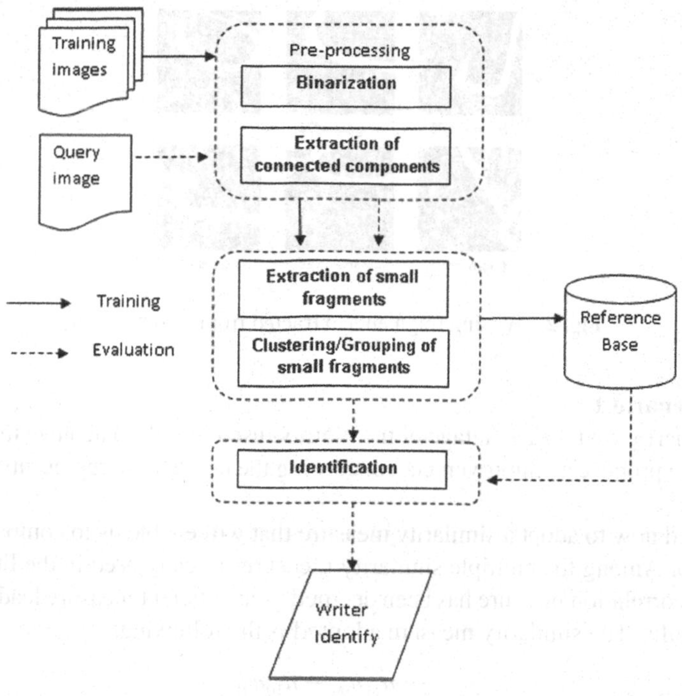

Fig. 1. Schematic diagram of the proposed method

2.2 Feature Extraction

Feature extraction plays a vital role in bettering the identification ability and computational performance. It consists of representing a given piece of writing by a set of features. For that, we have adopted small fragments of writing (sub-graphemes) to be the basic unit allowing us to extract the features and perform subsequent comparison of two basic units and eventually two writings.

These basic units are generated through dividing each component into small windows (blocks) of N * N size (N pixels). This task requires adding some white ink trace on the edges of the images to get windows of N * N size. The window size N is selected empirically and according to multiple experiments (Fig. 2).

After the normalization of the connected components, we proceed by the segmentation task based on the method proposed by [19]. Since the images are offline, we will seek to follow the ink trace. This method pinpoints the beginning of the ink trace of each connected component in order to place the window on it. Next, the window slides following the ink trace till the next position is found. The windows containing scant information are discarded as they are considered as noise.

Once the segmentation is done, it is time to group them into clusters containing small fragments of similar features. In order to attain such clustering, we have considered three scenarios.

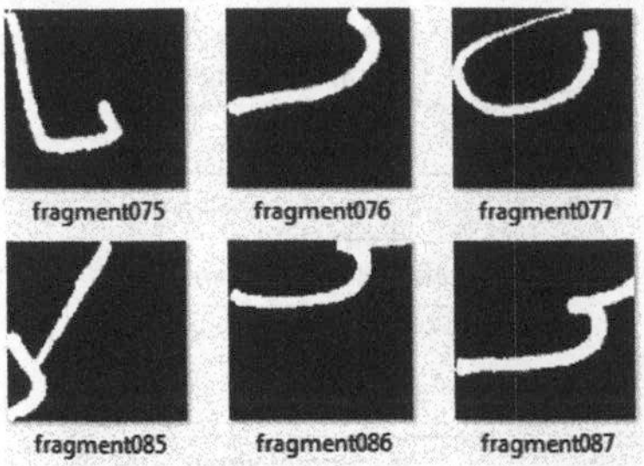

Fig. 2. Writing fragments extracted from a component

2.2.1 Scenario 1

In this scenario, we take advantage of the method used in [19] to achieve the clustering in which we propose an improvement concerning the manner the representing fragment is selected.

We need now to adopt a similarity measure that will enable us to compare two sub-images. For Among the multiple similarity measures already used in the literature, the following correlation measure has been deemed as an efficient measure leading to satisfactory results. The similarity measure adopted is the following:

$$\text{sim(x,y)} = \frac{n_{11}n_{00} - n_{10}n_{01}}{\sqrt{(n_{11} + n_{10})(n_{01} + n_{00})(n_{11} + n_{01})(n_{10} + n_{00})}} \tag{1}$$

With n_{ij} being the number of pixels for which the two sub-images X and Y have values i and j respectively, at the corresponding pixel positions. This measure will be close to 1 if the two compared sub-images are similar and ideally, it will equal 1 meaning that the two shapes are exactly the same.

In the end, and after discarding the clusters containing less than five elements, we choose a representing fragment for each cluster. The set of those representing fragments will be assigned to the concerned document. In other words, those representing fragments are characterizing the writer of the requested document.

2.2.2 Scenario 2

This time we make use of the sequential clustering algorithm as described in [4] which is similar to the one presented in scenario 1 with a small difference with respect to the way a fragment is included in a given cluster.

In this algorithm, the fragment is not linked to a cluster until it is close all the elements of that cluster. The correlation measure mentioned in scenario 1 is also used in our case. In the end, we keep all the resulting clusters without removing any of them. Consequently, a given document is represented by a set of small fragments which are the representing fragments of each cluster. Those representing fragments are the ones that are the closest to all the other elements in the same cluster.

2.2.3 Scenario 3

Contrary to the two other scenarios, this scenario considers all the generated fragments as one big cluster (except for the ones deemed as noise).

2.3 Writer Identification

With the aim of identifying a writer of a test document Q, we proceed by extracting the features of that document by the same way (scenario) used in the step of creating the reference base as well as the training step. The document Q is made under comparison against the documents saved in the reference base using the same similarity measure (1) and the authorship is known as the writer who is similar to one of the input document Q.

$$\text{Writer (Q)} = \underset{Di \in BaseRef}{\text{ArgMax}}\left(\text{SIM(Q, Di)}\right) \tag{2}$$

$$\text{with} \quad \text{SIM (Q, D)} = \frac{1}{\text{Card(Q)}} \sum_{i=1}^{\text{Card(Q)}} \underset{h_j \in D}{\text{Max}} \left(\text{sim}(x_i, y_j)\right) \tag{3}$$

Where x, y are two fragments and $\text{sim}(x_i, y_j)$ is the similarity measure defined in (1).

3 Experiments and Results

This section details the experiments and the corresponding results along with a comparison and discussion. We first present the database used in our study followed by the experimental results and discussion.

3.1 Database

In our study, we have tested our system on one of the most known Arabic handwritten database, namely the IFN/ENIT DataBase [14]. It contains forms with handwritten Arabic town/village names (more than 26,000 words) collected from 411 different writers (Fig. 3).

Fig. 3. Samples of words contained in the IFN/ENIT data base

3.2 Results

As forehand-mentioned, we have used the content of the IFN/ENIT Data Base in order to evaluate the effectiveness of the proposed system. However, It is worthy of note that we have only used a sub data base of 40 writers. Then, for each writer we randomly select a sample of 30 words in the training step and 20 in the test step. This way we make sure that on one hand, we are operating under text Independent mode and on the other hand, we almost emulate the reality in which there are only few handwritten documents available to be examined. We also envisaged showing the impact of the window's size in the segmentation step on the reported results.

3.2.1 Results Obtained for the Scenario 1

In this scenario, after discarding the clusters with less than 5 elements, we chose the 1st element of each cluster as the representing fragment of that cluster. Figure 4 represents the identification rates (TOP 1) obtained for this first scenario in which we used the segmentation window of size N * N. The best result is achieved for size 19 * 19 with an identification rate of 86%. Moreover, we can see that the rates decreases considerably when the size of the segmentation window gets wider. The underlying motive for that behaviour is that as we make bigger the window size, the likelihood of a cluster containing less than 5 elements to be discarded is bigger.

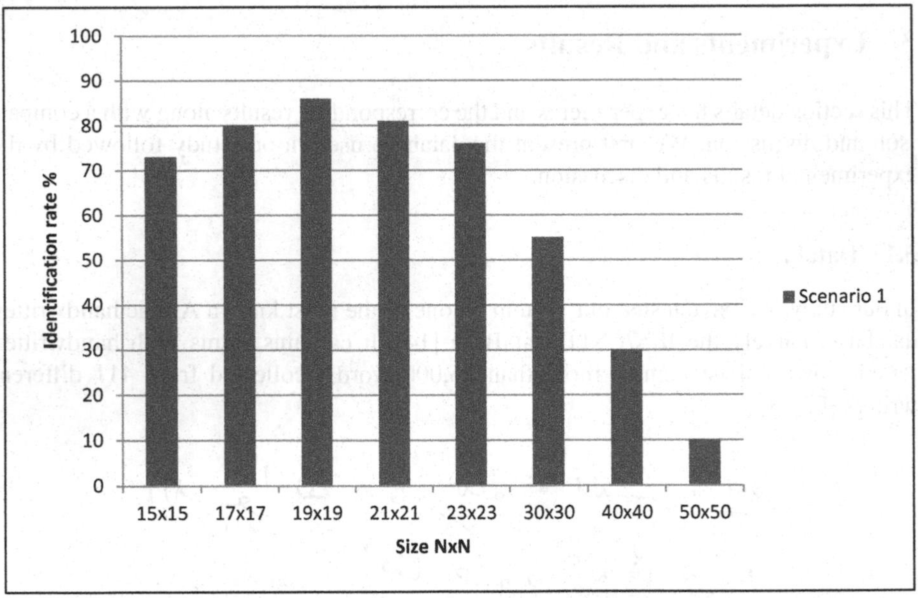

Fig. 4. Identification rates for the scenario 1

3.2.2 Results Obtained for the Scenario 2

This scenario is characterized by the fact that we name as the representing fragment of a cluster the one that is the closest to all the other elements in that cluster. Also, more importantly, we don't discard any of the clusters. Figure 5 shows the results.

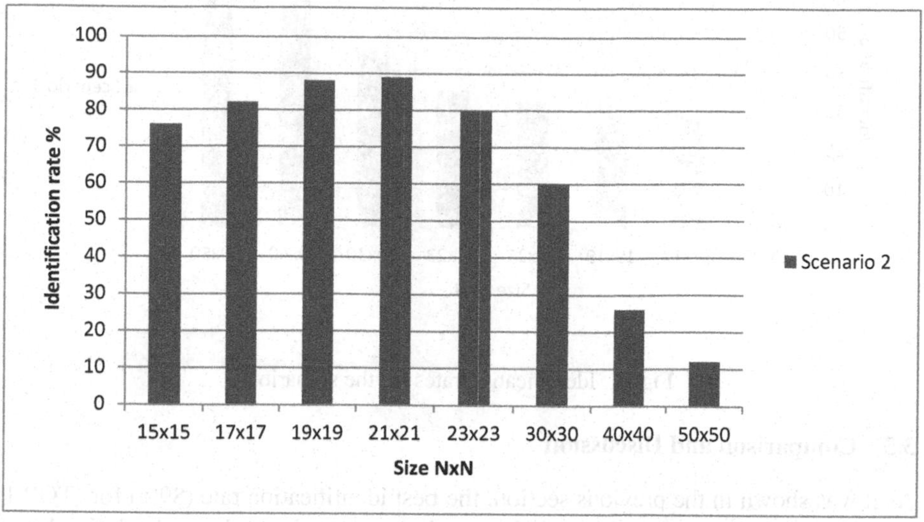

Fig. 5. Identification rates for the scenario 2

As shown, the best result is when the window size reaches 21 * 21 with an identification rate of 89% (TOP 1). A remarkable fall of the rate is noticed as the window size goes beyond 30 * 30 due to the broad variability between the small fragments with bigger window which affects the process of selecting a reliable representing fragment.

3.2.3 Results Obtained for the Scenario 3

This third scenario makes use of all the fragments that have been extracted from the scanned documents. No kind of clustering is performed. Also the notion of the representing fragment is not used. This scenario aims to analyse the impact of this case on the system performance which is based on direct comparison of small fragments. The results are shown in Fig. 6.

Our system has behaved differently this time compared to the first two scenarios. Indeed, the using of small size of the segmenting window impacts negatively the results. This is explained by big similarity among the small fragments related to different images. However, it is important to bring up that the identification rate increases when the window size gets wider. The best result reaches a rate of 78% for a size of 50 * 50.

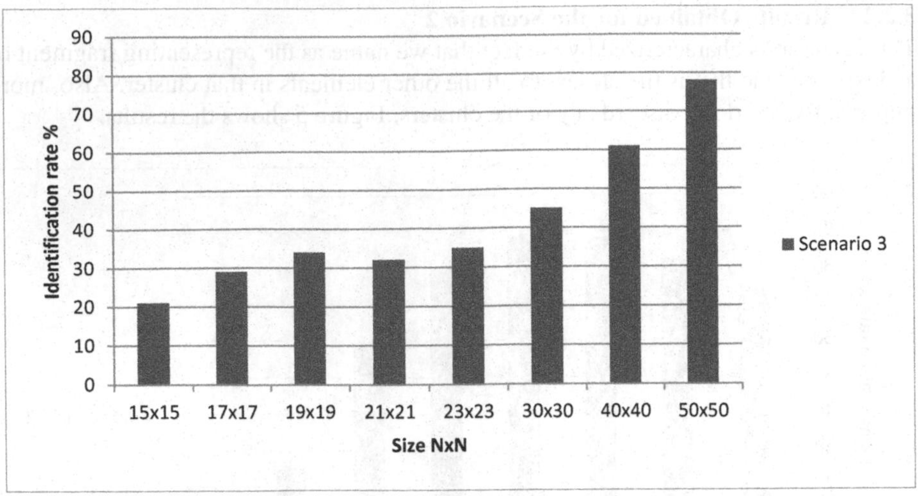

Fig. 6. Identification rates for the scenario 3

3.3 Comparison and Discussion

As it was shown in the previous section, the best identification rate (89%) for (TOP 1) applied on 40 writers was achieved when we have adopted an enhanced solution based on the one proposed in [4].

It is obvious from Fig. 7 presented above that the first two scenarios provide the same behaviour of the system under study. In these cases, the best results are obtained for the smaller windows. This attitude sounds reasonable given that fragments that have small size may contain enough recurrent information leading to sets of redundant forms characterizing the writer concerned.

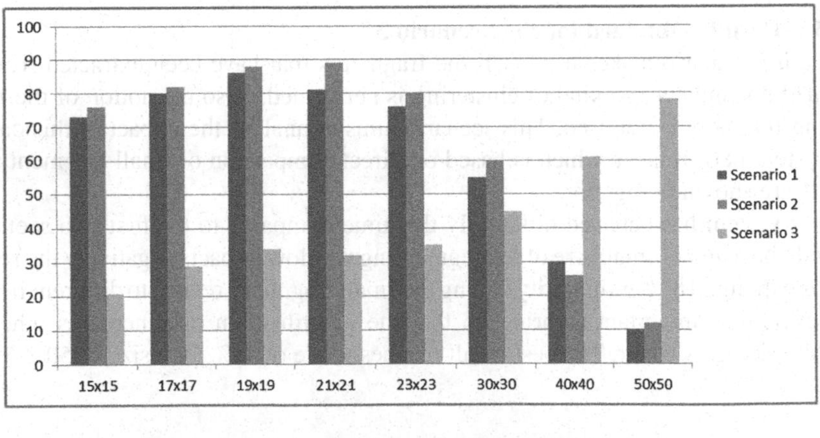

Fig. 7. Comparison results of the three studied scenarios

In contrast to the first two scenarios, the third scenario, which uses all the generated fragments, provides poor identification rates for small windows and better results for bigger windows. This is due to the fact that big fragments might contain more meaningful information that describes each author habits of Arabic writing.

Nevertheless, there is a major drawback to be taken in account when studying such kind of systems that are relying on comparison of fragments. The downside is the fact that the approach adopted is time consuming due to the multiple and complex comparisons needed to be performed vis-a-vis the fragments.

Consequently, this issue can be overcome if we opt for the third scenario. This is explained by the low number of comparison operations of fragments that are relatively of bigger size. This opens the door for further investigation of that last scenario applied on Arabic text knowing that the more the fragments are big, the better we expect as results for that scenario.

4 Conclusion

This paper gave a detailed description of the new system proposed which relies on direct comparison of small fragments. It has allowed assessing how effective this kind of systems is if applied on Arabic text. Also, we have presented a study of how such a system performs if we change the size of the segmentation window. This study was conducted according to three different scenarios that differs one another by the way the fragments are clustered.

In our future work, we intend to capitalize on this third scenario for further investigation with respect to the Arabic text. Therefore, the experiments conducted for that scenario will be tested against the entire IFN/ENIT DataBase. Moreover, rather than direct comparison used in this work, we envisage exploiting other classifiers such as Support Vector Machines (SVM) and K nearest-neighbour (K-NN).

References

1. Abdi, M.N., Khemakhem, M.: A model-based approach to offline text-independent Arabic writer identification and verification. Pattern Recogn. **48**(5), 1890–1903 (2015)
2. Bulacu, M., Schomaker, L., Brink, A.: Text-independent writer identification and verification on offline Arabic handwriting. In: Ninth International Conference on Document Analysis and Recognition (ICDAR 2007), vol. 2, pp. 769–773. IEEE, September 2007
3. Daniels, Z.A., Bairs, H.S.: Discriminating features for writer identification. In: Proceedings of 12th International Conference on Document Analysis and Recognition, pp. 1385–1389 (2013)
4. Djeddi, C., Labiba, S.M.: Une approche locale en mode indépendant du texte pour l'identification de scripteurs: Application à l'écriture arabe. In: Colloque International francophone sur l'ecrit et le document, pp. 151–156. Groupe de Rechercheen Communication Ecrite, October 2008
5. Djeddi, C., Labiba, S.M.: A texture based approach for Arabic writer identification and verification. In: IEEE International Conference on Machine and Web Intelligence, pp. 115–120 (2010)

6. Fiel, S., Sablatnig, R.: Writer retrieval and writer identification using local features. In: Proceedings of 10th IAPR International Workshop on Document Analysis Systems DAS 2012, pp. 145–149 (2012)
7. Hannad, Y., Siddiqi, I., El Kettani, M.E.Y.: Writer identification using texture descriptors of handwritten fragments. Expert Syst. Appl. **47**, 14–22 (2016)
8. He, S., Schomaker, L.: Beyond OCR: multi-faceted understanding of handwritten document characteristics. Pattern Recogn. **63**, 321–333 (2017)
9. He, S., Schomaker, L.: Writer identification using curvature-free features. Pattern Recogn. **63**, 451–464 (2017)
10. Khalifa, E., Al-Maadeed, S., Tahir, M.A., Bouridane, A., Jamshed, A.: Off-line writer identification using an ensemble of grapheme codebook features. Pattern Recogn. Lett. **59**, 18–25 (2015)
11. Bulacu, M., Schomaker, L., Brink, A.: Text-independent writer identification and verification on offline Arabic handwriting. In: Proceedings of 9th International Conference on Document Analysis and Recognition (ICDAR 2007), Curitiba, Brazil, 23–26 September 2007, vol. II, pp. 769–773. IEEE Computer Society (2007)
12. Nidhal Abdi, M., Khemakhem, M., Ben-Abdallah, H.: An effective combination of MPP contour-based features for off-line text-independent Arabic writer identification. In: Ślęzak, D., Pal, S.K., Kang, B.-H., Gu, J., Kuroda, H., Kim, T. (eds.) SIP 2009. CCIS, vol. 61, pp. 209–220. Springer, Heidelberg (2009). https://doi.org/10.1007/978-3-642-10546-3_26
13. Noboyuki, O.: A threshold selection method from gray level histogram. IEEE Trans. Syst. Man Cybern. **9**, 62–66 (1979)
14. Pechwitz, M., Maddouri, S.S., Märgner, V., Ellouze, N., Amiri, H.: IFN/ENIT-database of handwritten Arabic words. In: Proceedings of CIFED, vol. 2, pp. 127–136 (2002)
15. Said, H.E.S., Tan, T.N., Baker, K.D.: Personal identification based on handwriting. Pattern Recogn. **33**, 149–160 (2000)
16. Awaida, S.M., Mahmoud, S.A.: Writer identification of Arabic text using statistical and structural features. Cybern. Syst. **44**(1), 57–76 (2013)
17. Gazzah, S., Ben Amara, N.: Neural networks and support vector machines classifiers for writer identification using Arabic script. In: The second International Conference on Machine Intelligence (ACIDCA-ICMI 2005), Tozeur, Tunisia, pp. 1001–1005 (2005)
18. Shahabi, F., Rahmati, M.: Comparison of gabor-based features for writer identification of Farsi/Arabic handwriting. In: Tenth International Workshop on Frontiers in Handwriting Recognition (2006)
19. Siddiqi, I., Vincent, N.: Writer identification in handwritten documents. In: Ninth International Conference on Document Analysis and Recognition (ICDAR 2007), vol. 1, pp. 108–112. IEEE (2007)

Arabic Text Generation Using Recurrent Neural Networks

Adnan Souri(✉), Zakaria El Maazouzi, Mohammed Al Achhab, and Badr Eddine El Mohajir

New Trend Technology Team, National School of Applied Sciences, Abdelmalek Essaadi University, Tetouan, Morocco
adnan.souri@gmail.com, z.elmaazouzi.ma@ieee.org, {alachhab,b.elmohajir}@ieee.ma

Abstract. In this paper, we applied Recurrent Neural Networks (RNNs) Language Model on Arabic Language by training and testing it on "Arab World Books" and "Hindawi" free Arabic text datasets. While the standard architecture of RNNs does not match ideally with Arabic, we adapted a RNN model to deal with Arabic features. Our proposition in this paper is a gated Long-Short Term Memory (LSTM) model responding to some Arabic language criteria. As originality of the paper, we demonstrate the power of our LSTM model in generating Arabic text comparing to the standard LSTM model. Our results, comparing to English and Chinese text generation, have been promising and gave sufficient accuracy.

Keywords: Arabic NLP · Recurrent Neural Networks · Text generation

1 Introduction

Natural Language Processing (NLP) has shown a progressing interest in relation to Arabic language in the last few years [1]. Several fields such as machine translation, information retrieval and text summarisation have shown their need to Arabic language resources [1, 2]. In fact, Arabic language resources are available with big quantity of information contained on the web. Thus, there is a permanent need to interpret correctly this quantity of information, especially text written in Arabic. This interpretation would lead to an appropriate text comprehension, which motivates the need to Arabic NLP tools dealing with semantic analysis.

The aim of an Arabic NLP tool is to analyse Arabic text, to give the sense of its parts (paragraphs, sentences, words or any parts of the text) depending the context of the text. The process of analysing a text can take several aspects; word segmentation, morphological analysis, syntactic analysis and semantic analysis [3]. Given these points, Arabic texts cannot yet be efficiently exploited by machines, chiefly at semantic level [4]. Researches in the field of semantic analysis push towards the extraction of text meanings and by the way the retrieval of more understanding units from the text [5]. In other words, the hidden knowledge in the text can be shown after a semantic analysis of the text [6]. The consequence of that procedure is that machines can understand correctly the meanings of data as humans do or the nearest possible way [7].

Y. Tabii et al. (Eds.): BDCA 2018, CCIS 872, pp. 523–533, 2018.
https://doi.org/10.1007/978-3-319-96292-4_41

One of the recent and promising research domains at this level is applying Recurrent Neural Networks (RNNs) on text models to prove learning process. To measure text comprehension, at the semantic analysis level, we proceeded by the use of RNNs. RNN models have the abilities to learn text structures by training on a dataset at the input and then to produce (to generate) an acceptable (more or less) text in the output. The text generation operation proves the learning process success of the RNN model at semantic level.

Otherwise, the process of learning is mainly based on words meaning (or text units meaning when we note that in Arabic a text unit can be a letter, a word or a sentence as shown in the examples below: <"و": and>, <"كتب": books> and <"فستكتبونها": you will write it>).

Our idea is based on child language learning process, especially learning words meanings and expression meanings. This process matches ideally with the RNN operating principle. We recall here the words of Ibn Taymiya in his book "Al Iman" (The Faith, page 76): If the discrimination appears from the child, he heard his parents or his educators utter verbally, and refer to the meaning, he understand so that word is used in that meaning, i.e.: the speaker wanted that meaning [15] (Fig. 1).

فالمولود إذا ظهر منه التمييز، سمع أبويه أو من يربيه ينطق باللفظ ، ويشير إلى المعنى، فصار يفهم أن ذلك اللفظ يستعمل في ذلك المعنى، أي: أراد المتكلم به ذلك المعنى،

Fig. 1. Excerpt from Ibn Taymiya's book "Al Iman". Page 76.

By analogy to this, RNN models take a text dataset at their inputs and try to learn the meaning by training on. At the output, RNN models produce new sequences of text according to their learning process. The success of the learning process increases while increasing the quantity of input data and increasing the training operation, too.

In this paper, we used the Long-Short Term Memory (LSTM) model, as it is a more tools equipped neural network, to deal with Arabic text generation. The choice of LSTM model was motivated by its ability in steps memorization, which was a required task for our experiments while generating text at each step. In another side, given Arabic language features and specificities, the standard architecture of RNNs was not suitable for our test requirements on Arabic text. Our model had been so built basing on standard LSTM definition as described in [18]. Moreover, we modified the model to support some Arabic language features such as word schemes and the non-adjacency of letters. We fed up our model by these features in its input. The main challenge of our contribution was to prove that our modification on the LSTM model dealing with Arabic text gives a satisfactory accuracy results.

The organization of this document is as follows. In Sect. 2 (Related Work), we present some work dealing with Neural Networks, especially LSTM model, and their application on text processing in general. In Sect. 3 (Recurrent Neural Networks), we put the focus on RNNs and their efficiency dealing with text processing. In Sect. 4 (Experiments), we present our experiments in preparing data, creating the model and generating Arabic text. We give some promising results. In Sect. 5 (Conclusion), we conclude our research works as well as we discuss some further application as perspectives.

2 Related Work

The task of language modelling increases performance by applying it on RNNs [8, 9]. The implementation of RNN models is based on the idea of next element prediction, which could be in a character-level model or in a word-level model.

In [11], authors use a bidirectional LSTM model. The model is introduced as a character-to-word model that takes as input character-level representation of a word and generates vector representation of the word. Moreover, a word–character hybrid language model had been applied on Chinese using a neural network language model in [19]. A deep neural network produced high performance part-of-speech taggers in [20]. The network learns character-level representation of words and associates them with usual word representations. In [21], authors use RNN models to predict characters based on the character and word level inputs. In [22], authors present word–character hybrid neural machine translation systems that consult the character-level information for rare words.

3 Recurrent Neural Networks

Recurrent neural networks (RNNs) are sets of nodes, with inputs and outputs, linked together for the purpose of communicating and extracting results that respond to specific problems such as sequences generation [13, 14]. RNNs highlight is the large number of hidden layers, between inputs and outputs, that exchange information from and towards inputs and outputs nodes each time step in order to give more performing results (Fig. 2).

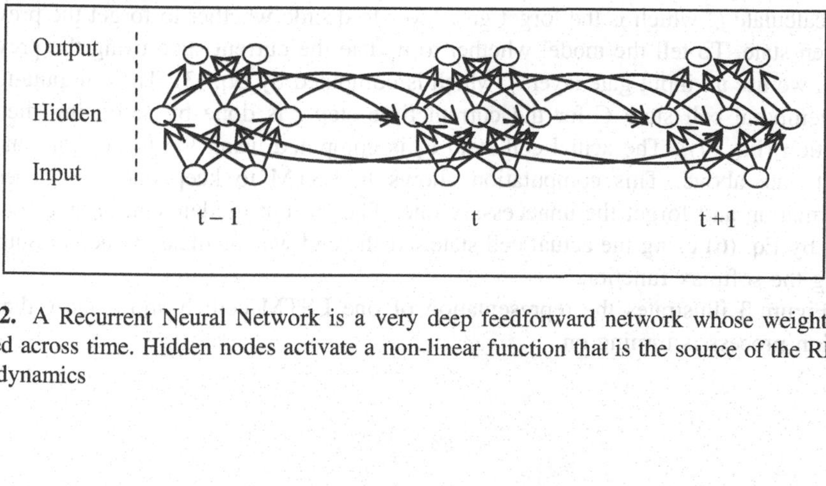

Fig. 2. A Recurrent Neural Network is a very deep feedforward network whose weights are shared across time. Hidden nodes activate a non-linear function that is the source of the RNN's rich dynamics

In general, RNNs are able to generate sequences of arbitrary complexity, but are unable to memorize information about past inputs for very long [14]. This memorization task helps to formulate better predictions and to recover from past mistakes. An effective solution will be then another kind of architecture designed to be better at storing and accessing information than standard RNNs.

Long-Short Term Memory (LSTM) is a RNN architecture, equipped with memory cells, that has recently given state-of-the-art results in a variety of sequence processing. It is both used as a predictive and a generative model; it can learn the sequences of a given text, in its input, and then generate new possible sequences by making predictions.

In principle, to predict the next element, RNN use the hidden layer function; an element wise application of a sigmoid function. LSTM do, too. Moreover, LSTM are better at finding and exploiting long-range dependencies in the data [14].

The LSTM model definition had been inspired from [18] judged as a basic reference. It is based on equations below:

$$o_t = \sigma(W_o[h_{t-1}, x_t] + b_O) \quad (1)$$

$$f_t = \sigma(W_f[h_{t-1}, x_t] + b_f) \quad (2)$$

$$i_t = \sigma(W_i[h_{t-1}, x_t] + b_i) \quad (3)$$

$$\check{C} = tanh(W_C[h_{t-1}, x_t] + b_C) \quad (4)$$

$$C_t = f_t * C_{t-1} + i_t * \check{C}_t \quad (5)$$

$$h_t = o_t * tanh(C_t) \quad (6)$$

$$y_t = softmax(W_{hy}h_t) \quad (7)$$

Where x_t, h_t and o_t are respectively input, hidden and control state at time step t. the parameter W_s is corresponding to the weights of the state s and b_s is the initial value given to a state s. Equation (1) computes the control state, and then after, in Eq. (2), we can calculate f_t, which is the forget gate layer to decide whether to forget the previous hidden state. To tell the model whether to update the current state using the previous state, we use an input gate layer i_t, which is computed by Eq. (3). The computation of the temporal cell state $\check{C}$ for the current time step t is done by activating the tanh function (Eq. (4)). The actual cell state C_t is computed using the forget gate and the input gate above. This computation allows to LSTM to keep only the necessary information and forget the unnecessary one. The current hidden state h_t is calculated then by Eq. (6) using the actual cell state. At the end we calculate the actual output y_t using the softmax function.

Figure 3 illustrates the representation of one LSTM cell. It shows how the prediction process is turning on.

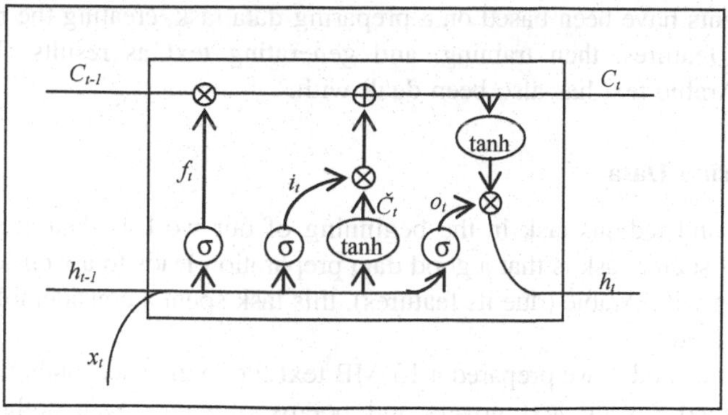

Fig. 3. A LSTM cell modelisation showing the prediction process architecture using equations presented above.

Briefly, previous equations assume the LSTM model is required to compute the hidden state at a time step (t). It is also able to decide whether to forget (f_t) the previous hidden state and to update the current state using the previous state. Moreover, LSTM is able to compute the temporal cell state ($\check{C}_t$) for the current time step using the **tanh** activation function as well as to compute the *actual* cell state (C_t) for current time step, using the forget gate and input gate. Intuitively, doing so makes LSTM be able to keep only the necessary information and forget the unnecessary one.

The computation of the current cell state is then used to compute the current hidden state. Consequently, comes the computation of the *actual* output (y_t).

4 Experiments

The main goal of these experiments is to demonstrate that LSTM model application on Arabic text gives satisfactory results in generating complex, realistic sequences containing long-range structure.

In our experiments, we have used LSTM as a predictive and a generative model; it can learn the sequences of a given text and then generate new possible sequences by making predictions. Thus, our model respects two rule-based methods, which are "scheme meanings" and "letters non-adjacency" explained in paragraph C (Creating model). These rules are implemented to the model as input gates. In the same way, LSTM is required then to learn language features respecting given specificities in input gates. Under those circumstances, the results accuracy of the generated text shows how the model has learned the problem (language features, text structure, words writing, and characters writing depending on their word position) as well as it generates text.

By training our model on "Arab World Books" and "Hindawi" datasets, we aim to achieve acceptable Arabic language learning. Comparing our model to the classic model from one side, and comparing Arabic text generation to English and Chinese text generation from another side, we demonstrate a high-quality learning language of our model.

Experiments have been based on a preparing data task, creating the model dealing with Arabic features, then training, and generating text as results. The encoding problem of Arabic text has also been dealt with.

4.1 Preparing Data

A necessary and tedious task in the beginning of our work is data preparation. The motivation of such a task is that a good data preparation leads to a well-learned model. While dealing with Arabic (due its features), this task spent a considerable time until it had been worked.

To train our model, we prepared a 13 MB text file to give acceptable results. In this file, we merged several text novels and poems of some Arab authors and poets (Mahmoud Darweesh, Taha Hussein, May Ziyada, Maarof Rosafi and Jabran Khalil Jabran). Texts have been freely downloaded from both “Arab World Books”[1] dataset at http://www.arabworldbooks.com/index.html [10] and “Hindawi”[2] foundation dataset at https://www.hindawi.org [12].

First, novels and poems were each in a PDF file format with a global size of 127 MB. We proceeded by converting these files to a text format using “Free PDF to Text Converter” tool available at: http://www.01net.com/telecharger/windows/Multimedia/scanner_ocr/fiches/115026.html. The target files (.txt) merged in one text file, with about 13 MB size, make up then our dataset of prepared text.

The next step is creating the LSTM model then feeding it up by the prepared text in its input and let it training by generating Arabic sequences basing on prediction method.

4.2 Arabic Features

The creation of the LSTM model is based on its definition as cited in paragraph III (Recurrent Neural Networks). Moreover, as additional inputs, we added two gates respecting some Arabic language criteria. It is a kind of rule-based method. Our idea is to feed the model by (1) schemes meaning and (2) letters non-adjacency principle. The application of this idea gave more performance to text generation process. We explain below the advantages we can draw from (1) and (2).

(1) Schemes meaning is one of the highlights of the Arabic language. We can get the meaning of such a word for example just by interpreting its scheme meaning and without having known the word before. The word <“كاتب”: author> has the

[1] Arab World Books is a cultural club and Arabic bookstore that aims to promote Arab thought, provide a public service for writers and intellectuals, and exploit the vast potential of the Internet to open a window in which the world looks at Arab thought, to identify its creators and thinkers, and to achieve intellectual communication between the people of this homeland and abroad.

[2] Hindawi Foundation is a non-profit organization that seeks to make a significant impact on the world of knowledge. The Foundation is also working to create the largest Arabic library containing the most important books of modern Arab heritage after reproduction, to keep them from extinction.

scheme "فاعل", which means that the word refers to someone who is responsible of the writing act. In like manner, the word <"جالس": sitting> has also the scheme "فاعل", which means that it refers to someone who is responsible of the sitting act and so on.

Table 1 below shows some of schemes meaning we used in our LSTM model implementation.

Table 1. The association scheme-meanings

Schemes	Translitteration	The associate meaning
فاعل	fAîl	The subject, the responsible of such an action
مفعول	mafôl	The effect of an action
مِفعَلة	mifâala	A noun of an instrument, a machine
فَعلة	faâla	Something done for once

(2) The principle of letters non-adjacency indicates what letter cannot be adjacent (before or after) to another letter. It is due to pronunciation criteria in Arabic. We mention here the couple (ع , خ). These two letters cannot be adjacent (ع before خ by respecting this order for next couples, too) in a word or a writing unit. Our idea was then proposed to reduce the tuning of prediction proceeding by elimination. So, once the model in front of the ع letter, it cannot predict the خ letter. Couples like (ع , غ), (ض, د) and (س , ص) respect the same rule.

4.3 Creating the Model

First, our model reads the text file and then split the content into characters. The characters then are stored in a vector *v_char*, which represents data. In a next step, we store unique values of data in another vector *v_data*. Information about features gates is stored in associative tables *scheme_meaning* and *nadj_letters*. The two tables fed up the model by schemes word meanings and by non-adjacency letter specifications. As learning algorithm deals with numeric training data, we choose to assign an index (numerical value) to each data character. Once done, variables *v_char, v_data, scheme_meaning* and *nadj_letters* form the input of the LSTM model. To complete the model, we created the model with three LSTM layers; each layer has 700 hidden states, with Dropout ratio 0.3 at the first LSTM layer.

Under those circumstances, we have implemented our model under Python programming language using Keras API with TensorFlow library as backend. We present briefly Keras and TensorFlow.

Written in Python, Keras is a high-level neural networks API. It can be running whether on top of TensorFlow, Theano or CNTK. Implementation with Keras leads to results from idea with the least possible delay, which enables fast experimentation comparing to other tools [16].

Using data flow graphs, TensorFlow is an open source software library dedicated to numerical computation [17]. Mathematical operations are represented by graph nodes while multidimensional data arrays (tensors) are represented by edges communicating between them [17]. This flexible architecture allows deploying computation to one or more CPUs or GPUs in a device with a single API. TensorFlow had been developed for the purposes of conducting machine learning and deep neural networks research. Thus, the system is general enough to be applicable in a wide variety of other domains as well [17].

In our case, we deployed computation to one CPU machine. We discuss next material criteria and performance concerning time execution.

4.4 Training Data

Three cases had been evaluated to validate our approach and to calculate the accuracy given by our proposed method:

- LSTM applied on Arabic text: We applied the standard LSTM architecture on Arabic text and tested it on our dataset.
- Gated LSTM applied on Arabic text: As originality of this paper, we added two gates to the LSTM model dealing with two Arabic features in order to give more performance to text generation process and to compare with the case (1) above.
- LSTM applied on English text and on Chinese text: Moreover, we applied the standard LSTM architecture on our dataset translated to English and Chinese in order to realise a kind of accuracy comparison.

Experiments have been performed on a PC using a single core i5 3.6 GHz CPU either for case 1, 2 and 3 above. We have encountered some encoding problems due to Arabic. We have used both utf-8 encoding to encode and decode "Hindawi" texts and Windows-1256 encoding for "Arab World Book" texts.

We trained our model using the data we prepared above. We launched training about a hundred times during 2 weeks. The model is slow to train (about 600 s per epoch on our CPU PC) because of data size and because of materiel performance. I addition to this slowness, we require more optimization, so we have used model check pointing to record model weights after each 10 epochs. Likewise, we observed the loss at the end of the epoch. The best set of weights (lowest loss) is used to instantiate our generative model.

After running the training algorithm, we gather 500 epochs each in a HDF5 file. We keep the one of the smallest loss value. We used it then to generate Arabic text. First, we define the model in the same way as in paragraph C (Creating model), except model weights are loading from the checkpoint file. The lowest loss encountered was 1.43 at the last epoch. We have used then the file to generate text after training.

4.5 Results

Here, we present some results from our three cases of experiments:

Figure 4 illustrates the loss function behaviour after each 10 epochs of applying the model on Arabic text dataset. We show values between epoch 140 and 240. The curve keep the same shape (tending to zero) while applying the model on English and Chinese.

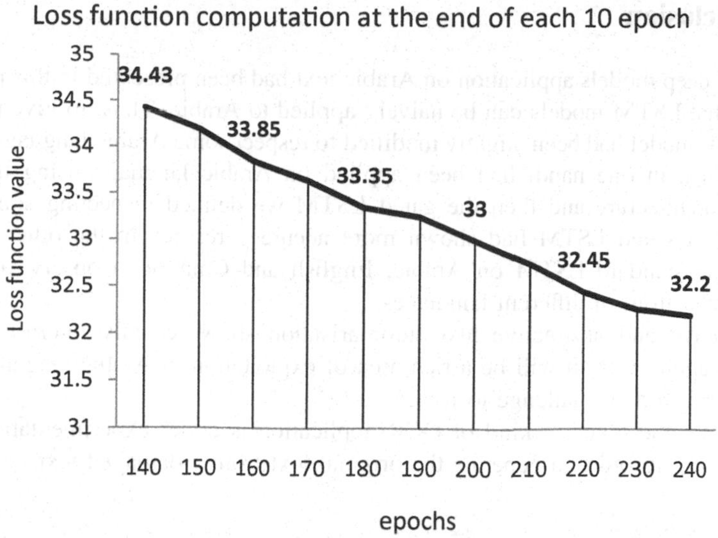

Fig. 4. The shape of loss function curve for some arbitrarily chosen epochs.

Surely, the standard model gives more accuracy for English than Arabic, because of the model, in his standard architecture, is more suited to Latin languages than other languages. Thus we attend a notable accuracy concerning loss function which we present in Table 2 below.

Table 2. Minimal loss function value while applying standard LSTM on different languages

Schemes	Languages	Loss function value
Languages	Arabic	1.43
	Chinese	2.13
	English	1.2

To attend more accuracy applying our model on Arabic text, we have built our gated model that gave a lower loss function value (0.73) after 500 epochs. We show in Table 3 below the comparison between both standard model application and gated model application on Arabic text.

Table 3. Minimal loss function value while applying both standard and gated LSTM models on Arabic

RNN model	Loss value	Epoch
Standard LSTM	1.43	500
Gated LSTM	0.73	500

5 Conclusion

A start of deep models application on Arabic text had been presented in this paper. We showed that LSTM models can be naively applied to Arabic. Thus, to give promising results, our model had been slightly modified to respect some Arabic language features. Experiments, in one hand, had been applied on Arabic language using the LSTM standard architecture and then the gated LSTM we defined respecting some Arabic criteria. Our gated LSTM had shown more accuracy results. In the other hand, we applied the standard LSTM on Arabic, English and Chinese to observe the model behaviour in front of different languages.

Extractive and abstractive text summarisation show recently interest in neural networks application. It will be a rich area of exploitation in Arabic language, which makes for us a new challenge to face.

By the same token, a kind of OCR application is under experimentation by our LSTM model in order to generate the original text from a damaged text.

References

1. Alansary, S., et al.: Building an International Corpus of Arabic (ICA): Progress of Compilation Stage. Bibliotheca Alexandrina (2008)
2. Souri, A., et al.: A study towards a building an Arabic corpus (ArbCo). In: The 2nd National Symposium on Arabic Language Engineering (JDILA 2015). National School Applied Sciences, University Sidi Mohammed Ben Abdellah Fez, Morocco (2015)
3. Souri, A., et al.: A proposed approach for Arabic language segmentation. In: 1st International Conference Arabic Computational Linguistics, Cairo, Egypt, 17–20 April 2015. IEEE Computer Society (2015). https://doi.org/10.1109/acling.2015.13
4. Elarnaoty, M., et al.: A machine learning approach for opinion holder extraction in Arabic language. Int. J. Artif. Intel. Appl. **3**, 45–63 (2012). https://doi.org/10.5121/ijaia.2012.3205
5. Chang, Y., Lee, K.: Bayesian feature selection for sparse topic model. In: IEEE International Workshop Machine Learning for Signal Processing, Beijing, China, pp. 1–6. IEEE (2011)
6. Faria, L., et al.: Automatic preservation watch using information extraction on the web: a case study on semantic extraction of natural language for digital preservation. In: 10th International Conference Preservation of Digital Objects, Lisbon, Portugal (2013)
7. Alghamdi, H.M., et al.: Arabic web pages clustering and annotation using semantic class features. J. King Saud Uni. Comput. Inf. Sci. **26**, 388–397 (2014). https://doi.org/10.1016/j.jksuci.2014.06.002
8. Józefowicz, R., et al.: Exploring the limits of language modeling. CoRR abs/1602.02410 (2016)
9. Zoph, B., et al.: Simple, fast noise-contrastive estimation for large RNN vocabularies. In: NAACL (2016). https://doi.org/10.18653/v1/n16-1145
10. Arab world Books dataset. http://www.arabworldbooks.com/index.html. Accessed 22 Feb 2018
11. Ling, W., et al.: Finding function in form: compositional character models for open vocabulary word representation. In: EMNLP (2015). https://doi.org/10.18653/v1/d15-1176
12. Hindawi Database. https://www.hindawi.org. Accessed 22 Feb 2018
13. Sutskever, I., et al.: Generating text with recurrent neural networks. In: International Conference on Machine Learning, ICML 2011 (2011)

14. Graves, A.: Generating sequences with recurrent neural networks. arXiv preprint arXiv: 1308.0850 (2013)
15. Taymiya, I.: Book of Al Iman, 5 edn (1996)
16. Keras. http://www.keras.io. Accesses 19 Jan 2018
17. TensorFlow. http://www.tensorflow.org. Accessed 19 Jan 2018
18. Hochreiter, S., Schmidhuber, J.: Long short-term memory. Neural Comput. **9**(8), 1735–1780 (1997). https://doi.org/10.1162/neco.1997.9.8.1735
19. Kang, M., et al.: Mandarin word-character hybridinput neural network language model. In: 12th Annual Conference International Speech Communication Association, INTERSPEECH 2011, Florence, Italy, pp. 625–628 (2011)
20. dos Santos, C.N., Zadrozny, B.: Learning character-level representations for part-of-speech tagging. In: Proceeding of the 31st International Conference on Machine Learning, ICML 2014, Beijing, China, pp. 1818–1826 (2014)
21. Bojanowski, P., et al.: Alternative structures for character-level RNNs. CoRR abs/1511.06303 (2015)
22. Luong, M.T., Manning, C.D.: Achieving open vocabulary neural machine translation with hybrid word-character models. CoRR abs/1604.00788 (2016). https://doi.org/10.18653/v1/p16-1100

Integrating Corpus-Based Analyses in Language Teaching and Learning: Challenges and Guidelines

Imad Zeroual(✉), Anoual El Kah, and Abdelhak Lakhouaja

Faculty of Sciences, Mohamed First University, Oujda, Morocco
mr.imadine@gmail.com, Elkah.anoual.mri@gmail.com,
abdel.lakh@gmail.com

Abstract. Over years, the major concern of researchers was using corpus linguistics as a source of evidence for linguistic description and argumentation, creating dictionaries, and language learning, among a wide range of research activities in several fields. However, this study focuses on the corpus-based studies that have a pedagogical purpose especially for an old Semitic language which recognized by a proud heritage, lexical richness, and speakers' growth, the Arabic language. This latter is relatively a poor-resourced language and the integration of artificial intelligent techniques such as corpus-based analyses in its teaching and learning process has not made much progress and fall far behind compared to other languages. Therefore, this paper is another contribution that shed lights on the challenges faced by specialists working in the field of teaching and learning Arabic language. Further, the authors aim to increase awareness of the greatest advantage of integrating corpus-based analyses in education. Besides, some guidelines are proposed and relevant available resources for use are introduced to help in preparing efficient materials for language teaching and (self)-learning primarily for learners of Arabic.

Keywords: Corpus-based analyses · Language teaching materials
Arabic language · Serious games

1 Introduction

Whether the corpus linguistics is considered a scholarly field or only a methodology, many researchers tend to agree that the focus of corpus linguistics is essentially divided into designing, compiling, analysing, and inferring information from language data. Even though the first time the name corpus has been used was in the decade of the sixties, compiling naturally occurring samples of both a spoken or a written language is deeply rooted in history. To the best of our knowledge, it can be traced back to Al-Khalil ibn Ahmad al-Farahidi, the lexicographer and philologist, who, in the 8th century, assembled a large corpus to build the first Arabic dictionary called "Kitab al-'Ayn". Since then, the major concern was using corpus linguistics as a source of evidence for linguistic description and argumentation, creating dictionaries, and language learning, among a wide range of research activities in several fields.

Since the Quranic scripture is used in daily prayers of 1.6 billion Muslims worldwide [1] in which 80% of them are not Arabic native speakers, learning Arabic

Y. Tabii et al. (Eds.): BDCA 2018, CCIS 872, pp. 534–545, 2018.
https://doi.org/10.1007/978-3-319-96292-4_42

has become paramount. Also, due to cultural and commercial perspectives, teaching Arabic as a foreign language is becoming a global educational enterprise [2]. At the same time, the literature on Arabic materials and resources used for educative purposes are still in a weak standing and fall far behind compared to other languages.

Among the most obvious problems faced by Arabic language learners is the vocabulary. Typically, when language novices explore a dictionary, they want to learn the most important and frequent words used during actual daily life activities. Whereas, most entries in dictionaries are listed in an alphabetical order which is a problematic for novices especially for second language learners. On the other hand, the interference between Arabic language varieties (i.e., Modern standard and colloquial Arabic dialects) leads to diglossic situations which in turn have a significant impact on the learning progress of Arabic [3]. Generally, the starting point for most learners of Arabic as a foreign language is the Modern Standard Arabic (MSA), the language used in writing and in most formal speech. Then, they usually need to learn a local dialect which is used in everyday oral communication. Furthermore, the mixture of both MSA and dialects is widely present in the media and the web. On the contrary, the native speakers start learning the MSA for the first time in their primary schools. Thus, the learning process is reliably and strongly influenced by dialectal Arabic [4].

In order to enhance the teaching effectiveness and develop new research-based teaching practices, language teachers, alongside lexicographers and linguists, always strive to investigate the language variation and observe the vocabulary growth. Although the value of the inferred insights is very beneficial, it is challenging in case of Arabic since it is an under-resourced language and undertaking such observations over time requires large and well-defined samples of both a spoken and a written language.

This paper is another contribution to the field of Arabic language teaching. The authors aim to provide some guidelines that will boost the creation of high quality corpus-informed teaching materials and resources. In doing so, relevant resources are highlighted and central corpus linguistics analyses are performed using LancsBox [5] on the Arabic Learner Corpus V2 (ALC) [6]. ALC is a collection of written and spoken data produced by Arabic learners. It is a balanced corpus that consists of two sub-corpora, the first one is NAS (i.e., L1) that refers to a Native Arabic Speakers corpus, whereas, the second one is NNAS (i.e., L2) that refers to a Non-Native Speakers corpus. Furthermore, a set of language-based games is proposed based on the inferred insights from the performed corpus-based analyses and other resources such as the frequency dictionary of Arabic [7].

In addition to the previous Introduction, this article is arranged as follows: In Sect. 2, the major difficulties faced by the learners of Arabic language are stated providing some insights of Arabic diglossia. Then, an overview of available data for teaching Arabic language, namely learner corpora and a frequency dictionary, is given in Sect. 3. In Sect. 4, some corpus-based statistical analyses are introduced with an application on the ALC. Furthermore, the authors propose some tools to create serious games for learning language and examples are provided in Sect. 5. Finally, some concluding remarks are included in Sect. 6.

2 Difficulties in Arabic Language Acquisition

2.1 For Arabic Dialect Speakers

The MSA language is an official language of 29 countries in an area extending from the Arabian/Persian Gulf in the East to the Atlantic Ocean in the West. This language is basically used for writing and formal language functions. On the other hand, Arabic is among the strongest examples of the world languages that are considered as a fertile ground for the emergence of diglossia [8]. There are basically four major dialects: The Eastern dialect, the Gulf dialect, the Egyptian dialect, and the North African dialect. However, each Arabic country has many dialects which relatively differ from one another. For instance, it is a big challenge for an Eastern dialect speaker to understand the North African dialect and vice versa. This leads to the emergence of diglossia in the Arabic-speaking communities, in which children must first learn the vernacular of everyday communication (Spoken Arabic or SA), then, they start learning the MSA in their primary schools [9]. Consequently, this diglossic situation influences the acquisition of basic language and literacy skills during the learning process of MSA due to several issues mainly related to the language phonological structure. Indeed, at early learning stages, children usually predict many MSA words based on their vocabulary affected by their Spoken language [10].

2.2 For Non-native Speakers

Many factors have made learning MSA as a second language paramount. For example, it is among the six official United Nations languages; it is used for prayer sermons of over 1.2 billion of non-Arabic Muslims; it is used for formal reading and writing; yet, for international and national news broadcast, and adopted by the educated Arabs. However, paradoxically, many of its learners fail to understand or use the spoken dialects for daily communications. What's more, the challenge increases more and more since no enough learning materials are available, no established rules, and those dialects are always susceptible to change over time and across geographical regions.

It is worth mentioning that some second language learners focus on the acquisition of spoken Arabic rather than MSA. For this kind of learning, the adopted teaching materials are usually transliterated, i.e., they are written in Latin alphabet especially that several Arabs use this alphabet to write Arabic in social networks and daily messages. However, this method of learning Spoken Arabic has its own complexities as the learner cannot read or write Arabic alphabets [11]. Besides, those learners could negatively have affected by the presence of various Arabic dialects as they find it a challenging task to learn those varieties of Arabic rather learning one language. These complexities occur as a result of diglossia since the words used in Spoken Arabic are derived from different origins such as MSA, English, French, Spanish, Turkish, and Tamazight.

3 Data for Arabic Language Teaching

3.1 Arabic Learner Corpora

The use of learner corpora is strongly involved in the mechanism of designing teaching and learning materials especially for second and foreign language education research [12]. Also, these corpora help L2 theoreticians and practitioners to perform contrastive interlanguage analysis which involves comparative studies using both native and non-native productions.

In the last few years, a major progress has been made in building Arabic corpora and developing robust processing tools [13]. However, Arabic learner corpora as well as different corpus-based studies that have a pedagogical purpose are still in a weak standing and fall far behind compared to other languages. Further, this kind of corpora is an essential resource for specialists seeking to develop materials for second language acquisition and teaching. They are especially useful when they are annotated with morpho-syntactic of error tags.

Concerning the literature of Arabic learner corpora, there have been only a few published works, but some of them are promising. To the best of our knowledge, the Arabic Learner Corpus V2 (ALC) [6], Arabic Learners Written Corpus (ALWC) [14], Malaysians Arabic Learners Corpus (MALC) [15], and the Pilot Arabic Learner Corpus (PALC) [16] are the most relevant resources of this type of corpora.

The PALC covers eight different texts written by American native speakers of English during their studying Arabic as a foreign language in the United States and abroad in Arab countries. This corpus comprises in total 8,559 words of Arabic written texts produced by two levels, intermediate (3,818 words) and advanced (4,741 words). Yet, it is annotated in terms of learners' error adopting FRIDA tagset [17].

The MALC was mainly compiled to give an accurate description of Arabic conjunctions used among Malaysians learners of Arabic. This corpus contains about 240,000 words, produced by 60 university students, mostly Malaysians, during their first and second year of their Arabic major degree at the Department of Arabic Language and Literature, International Islamic University Malaysia. Furthermore, similar corpus has been developed using materials of 19 Malaysian students at Al-Bayt University [18].

The ALWC compiled at the University of Arizona Center for Educational Resources in Culture, Language, and Literacy. This corpus consists of written samples produced by L2 and heritage students from the USA and collected over 15 years of teaching. Comprising approximately 35,000 words, the corpus targets several categories according to levels (beginning, intermediate, advanced), learners (L2 vs. heritage), and text genres (description, narration, instruction). The corpus developers intended to annotate the collected data with orthographic errors tagset alongside the morpho-syntactic information. Their aim was offering a data source that helps for hypothesis testing and developing teaching materials. It is worth mentioning that the ALWC was freely available for download in PDF format files, even though that makes its content difficult to process. However, at the time of writing this paper, it is no longer available.

The last and most recent corpus is the ALC V2, it is the only corpus that has been collected from an Arab country. Further, it is a balanced corpus in many aspects. First, it covers a collection of written and spoken data; second, it consists of data produced by both native (790 text materials) and non-native (795 text materials) learners of Arabic. The average length of a text is 178 words. All in all, the corpus contains 282,732 words produced by 942 students from 67 nationalities in which only one Arab nationality was covered, Saudi. However, covering other Arab nationalities probably will be more useful for corpus linguistics researches. In addition, the size of the ALC is basically enough to conduct many investigations in the second language acquisition field. According to Granger, researchers in the second language acquisition field usually rely on smaller samples and minute, therefore, a corpus of 200,000 words is generally considered big. Moreover, the ALC includes other key factors such as the level of education of learners (Pre-university and University), the place of production (in class or at home), and text genres (narratives and discussions). To our knowledge, none of PLAC, MALC, and ALWC are available for public use. Whereas, the ALC V2 is freely available[1] for download either one file or for each text individually in TXT or XML formats; yet, the audio recordings are available in MP3 format as well as their transcripts are in TXT and XML formats.

3.2 A Frequency Dictionary of Arabic

A lexicon or a dictionary is probably one of the best resources for language learners. However, learning the words that are frequently used in conversation and writing is a very good starting point. That is the philosophy behind producing frequency dictionaries derived from collected language data. i.e., they are derived from large and representative corpora that include both written text and transcribed speech. Furthermore, the data of those corpora must be compiled from common resources used in real life as opposed to textbook language which often distorts the frequencies of features in a language, see Ljung [19].

These frequency dictionaries have been shown to be beneficial for teachers and learners of languages. For example, Nation [20] reported that the 4,000–5,000 most frequent words account for up to 95% of a written text and the 1,020 most frequent words account for 85% of speech. Although Nation's results were only for English, they are accepted as a global standard. For instance, the recent provided dictionaries as a general guide for vocabulary learning are of German [21], Russian [22], Mandarin Chinese [23], and Korean [24], among others. Of course, there is the frequency dictionary of Arabic [7] that contains the 5,000 highly-frequent MSA and dialect words. This dictionary is developed based on a corpus of 30 million words that includes written and spoken materials from the entire Arab world. It provides the user with detailed information for each of the 5,000 entries to allow the user to access the data in different ways. These information include English equivalents, a sample sentence, its English translation, usage statistics, an indication of genre variation, and usage distribution over several major Arabic dialects. Also, there are thematically-organized lists

[1] http://www.arabiclearnercorpus.com/.

of the top words from a variety of key topics such as sports, weather, clothing, and family terms. The following Figure (see Fig. 1) exhibits an example of the entry for the word "طَرِيق".

This entry shows that the word in rank position 115 is "طريق", which is glossed as "road", "way", and "via", among other English glosses. The word "طريق" is categorized as a feminine (fem) and masculine (masc) noun, with an explanation that this word is often feminine in the Levantine (lev) corpus while it is mostly masculine in the MSA corpus. Further, its plural form (pl) is "طُرُق" and "طُرُقَات" and by mentioning the plural it means that it was also attested in the corpus. Besides, an Arabic sentence from the corpus illustrates the usage of the word —in this case the plural form "الطرق"— and is followed by an English translation. The last line in the entry presents the range count figure of 99, meaning that the usage of this word was distributed over 99% of the corpus; the raw frequency figure of 24,751, which is the total number of occurrences for the singular and plural forms combined. Finally, the word "طريق" is listed among the top words of the fifth topic "Transportation".

115 طَرِيق fem./masc.n. (MSA rarely fem.; Lev. mostly fem.) pl. طُرُق, طُرُقَات
road, course; way, method; عَن طَرِيق via, by way of; by means of, by using
التاريخ الآن على مفترق الطرق فلا القديم قد انتهى تماما ولا الحديث قد بدأ بعد — History now is at a crossroads, since the old has not completely ended, and the new has not yet started
99 | 24,751 |

Fig. 1. An example of the entry for the word "طَرِيق".

4 Corpus Linguistics Analyses

The corpus linguistics is a scholarly field that focuses essentially on designing, compiling, analysing, and inferring information from corpora for studying languages. Alongside the linguistic description and lexicography, corpora significantly affect a wide range of research activities that have a pedagogical purpose. Many scientific groups emphasize the potential relevance of corpus-based analyses for language teaching and learning in all its forms and uses [25]. For instance, the obtained results of such analyses could be used as a resource by both advanced learners majoring in the language as well as learners with lower levels of proficiency especially those who need learning a language for specific purposes and aim to reduce the time that would be necessary in learning process. However, to date it has been difficult for those teaching the Arabic language to apply corpus linguistics analyses in designing and preparing language teaching materials due to the lack of data and the appropriate processing tools.

4.1 Corpus-Based Analysis

Although learner corpora are relatively small, other types of corpora are generally containing millions or even billions of words. Thus, processing and analysing these large data requires appropriate and robust tools. Among relevant corpus-based statistical analyses, in this paper, we are focusing on concordance queries, word frequency lists, and collocation statistics. All these analyses and others are integrated into LancsBox. In the following, these analyses are explained with an application on the ALC.

Concordance queries aim to search the text and find all occurrences of a particular word or a clause together and displaying them vertically along with their immediate context in which they appear. It is worth noting that this is what text analysts painstakingly did for many years. For instance, It is reported that the first concordance, completed in 1230, was produced based on the Bible [26], it has been said that 500 monks engaged upon its preparation. Furthermore, concordances can be produced in several formats, but the most usual form is the Key-Word-In-Context (KWIC) concordance [27]. What is important is that concordance has a great impact on teaching or learning vocabulary and several empirical evidences demonstrate that receiving vocabulary through concordance performed is statistically significant compared to traditional vocabulary instruction [28, 29]. Today, thanks to LancsBox and ALC, we can find and recognize every example of a particular Arabic word from both native and non-native texts and also infer insights to prepare teaching materials. For instance, the obtained concordances for the word "مِثْل", which is ranked 86th in the Arabic frequency dictionary and it is glossed as "like", "similar", and "such as", shows that the number of occurrences of the word "مِثْل" in the NAS corpus is 81 while it is 141 in the NNAS corpus. Whereas for both corpora, in about 72% of cases, the word is used to give examples and for the remaining cases it is used to express a similarity.

Regarding the frequency lists, which are beneficial for vocabulary teaching as we discussed previously, the lists of the top 100 words in both NAS and NNAS showed some similarities as well as differences. Since the learners were mostly describing their journeys, they used same words such a "رحلة" <rhlp> "journey", "سفر" <sfr> "travel", "ذهبنا" <*hbnA> "we went", and "وصلنا" <wSlnA> "we arrived", among similar words. Consequently, we can conclude, to some extent, that both native and non-native Arabic speakers usually use the same key-words to describe a journey rather than other synonyms. On the other hand, we found that NAS and NNAS do not share some key-words. For example, the words "كلية" <klyp> "college", "الشريعة" <Al$ryEp> "Islamic law", "بلدي" <bldy> "my country", and "السعودية" <AlsEwdyp> "Saudi" are frequently appear in NNAS since the learners usually choose to describe their journeys while travelling from their country to Saudi in order to study in the College of Islamic law. Whereas, the top key-words of NAS are "السيارة" <AlsyArp> "car", "والدي" <wAldy> "my father", "أبي" <Aby> "my dad", and "عمي" <Emy> "my uncle". These findings provide sociolinguistics hypotheses such as the most Arabic native learners were taking their journeys with family members while driving a car. Yet, the word "my father" is often used rather than "my dad".

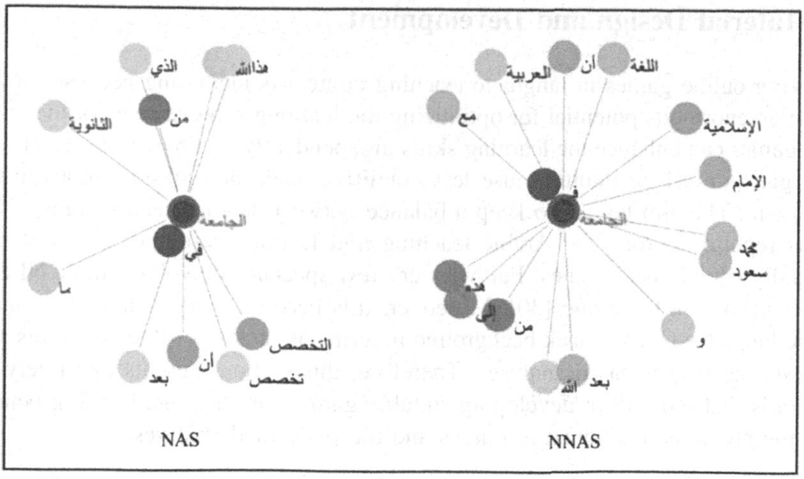

Fig. 2. Collocation statistics for the word "الجامعة".

Another experiment is performed using collocation statistics for both NAS and NNAS corpora are calculated. Figure 2 illustrates the collocations of the word "الجامعة" <AljAmEp> "University" in both NAS and NNAS corpora.

After reviewing the learners' texts, we come up with the following explanation for the obtained results. If we ignore the Particles, all that is left are the following words: For NNAS, the words that draw the attention are "الإمام" <AlAmAm> "Al-Imam", "محمد" <mhmd> "Muhammad", "سعود" <sEwd> "Saud", "الاسلامية" <AlAslAmyt> "Islamic", "اللغة" <Allgp> "Language", and "العربية" <AlErbyp> "Arabic". Based on the words' positions in the collocation graph, we can infer some insights to predicts the associations between the collocated words. Then, the hypothesises can be confirmed by checking the original texts. For this example, this collocation is reasonable since most non-native Arabic speakers were attending the "Al-Imam Muhammad Ibn Saud Islamic University" to learn the Arabic language. On contrary, the Arabic native speakers were talking about their high schools, attending or planning to register in different disciplines in several Universities. As a result, the most collocated words with the token "University" were "الثانوية" <AlvAnwyp> "high school", and "تخصص" <txSS> "discipline". Again, these findings are undoubtedly a valuable source of evidence for sociolinguistics as well as language education especially that the ALC provides situational characteristics of the learners such as gender, nationality, and study level.

Finally, many other analyses can be applied or even better, involving other language resources if they are available. However, selecting appropriate corpora and dictionaries and applying corpus-based statistical analyses are essential but not sufficient. The other and major challenge is how and when to transfer the obtained results into teaching materials and presented to learners in a meaningful and intuitive way.

5 Material Design and Development

Involving online games in language teaching context is increasing because they have shown an enormous potential for optimizing the learning achievements of the learners. Such games can enhance the learning skills independently on time or places. However, these games must be intuitive, use less cognitive load, and consider motivation and enjoyment. The aim here is to keep a balance between learning and gaming.

As reported before, the Arabic teaching and learning resources are very limited especially edutainment games. Further, very few specialists involve Arabic NLP tools in its teaching and learning [30]. Moreover, this becomes very challenging since the Arabic language teachers lack background in terms of games development tools as well as mastering corpus-based analyses. Therefore, this section presents two freely available tools that will aid in developing suitable games for language learning benefiting from the previous mentioned resources and the performed analyses.

5.1 Tools

Nowadays, lack of access to the Internet is no longer a barrier in front of learning resources seekers especially educated ones. Moreover, specialists are focusing more on cross-platform applications instead of device dependent applications. The main concept is building once and publishing everywhere. Among the available tools and platforms that provide suitable environment to develop appropriate language-based games, we suggest:

- Construct2[2]: It is using a 2D game engine based on HTML5. Construct2 provides an environment to develop games using a visual editor and a behaviour-based logic system. The exportation from this editor to most major platforms is allowed and the access from different devices is assured through its supported platforms like Android and Windows. Further, Construct2 is available in free and paid versions.
- LearningApps[3]: It is a Web 2.0 application that provides public interactive modules to generate Apps with no specific framework or a specific learning scenario, also, to be reused and adapted to the users' suitable objectives. Currently, the LearningApps system is available in 21 languages.

5.2 Proposed Games

The following set of games is developed to provide a model and examples to whom interested. The introduced set of games is created to be used as language teaching materials for vocabulary building and enhancement of words' collocation for Arabic learners. Furthermore, most games are developed with the concept drag-and-drop data binding and easy target selection facility which make using the games efficient and comfortable by either normal learners or those with fine motor skills.

[2] http://www.scirra.com.

[3] https://learningapps.org/.

Fig. 3. A learning game based on collocation statistics.

Benefiting from the previous collocation statistics, a game is developed using Constract2 (see Fig. 3). This game consists of binding words with their collocates. The number of the main words is restricted to four and the others are candidate collocates, yet, this number increases accordingly to advanced levels of the game.

Regarding the vocabulary, a set of games are created using the web application LearningApps. They are gathered in one block since they share the same concept and objective (see Fig. 4). The objective is linking words and their represented pictures. The concept is to use the frequency dictionary of Arabic to select top ranked words taking into consideration the topics classification namely Sports, Body, Animals, Colours, Nature, Materials, Professions, and Geometric forms. Finally, illustrative images are included to enhance the learning process especially for second language learners.

Fig. 4. A set of games for learning vocabulary.

For all proposed games, failure or success sound effects are involved in addition to the instructions. Besides, learners are restricted by timing that varies according to the game level, also, successful players are rewarded with high marks and golden stars.

6 Conclusion

This paper highlights the Arabic language teaching and learning from two aspects. The first one is the shortage of Arabic learner corpora and available tools that can be used to generate teaching materials automatically based on specified criteria such as the level of language complexity, readability, genre, and discourse style. In this regard, the authors aim to shed lights on the available resources and suggest applying corpus linguistics analyses that could fill this gap. Some experiments have been performed using appropriate resources namely ALC V2 and the frequency dictionary of Arabic. Then, the findings are presented and discussed.

The second aspect was focusing on how to successfully transform the inferred insights and observation of using corpus linguistics analyses in language teaching. Thus, free and effective tools which can be used to develop suitable teaching materials are introduced; yet, a set of serious games are proposed in this regard.

Finally, this is another contribution that shed lights on the challenges faced by researchers working in the field of the Arabic language teaching and learning. Further, the aim is to increase awareness of the greatest advantage of using corpus linguistics analyses and language-based games in this regard.

References

1. Yassein, M.B., Wahsheh, Y.A.: HQTP v. 2: holy Quran transfer protocol version 2. In: 2016 7th International Conference on Computer Science and Information Technology (CSIT), pp. 1–5. IEEE (2016)
2. Sakho, M.L.: Teaching Arabic as a Second Language in International School in Dubai a case study exploring new perspectives in learning materials design and development (2012). http://bspace.buid.ac.ae/handle/1234/177
3. Ferguson, C.A.: Diglossia. Word **15**, 325–340 (1959)
4. Maamouri, M.: Language Education and Human Development: Arabic Diglossia and Its Impact on the Quality of Education in the Arab Region (1998)
5. Brezina, V., McEnery, T., Wattam, S.: Collocations in context: a new perspective on collocation networks. Int. J. Corpus Linguist. **20**, 139–173 (2015)
6. Alfaifi, A.Y.G., Atwell, E., Hedaya, I.: Arabic learner corpus (ALC) v2: a new written and spoken corpus of Arabic learners. In: Proceedings of Learner Corpus Studies in Asia and the World 2014, vol. 2, pp. 77–89 (2014)
7. Buckwalter, T., Parkinson, D.: A Frequency Dictionary of Arabic: Core Vocabulary for Learners. Routledge, New York (2014)
8. Bassiouney, R.: Redefining identity through code choice in "Al-Ḥubb fī'l-manfā" by Bahā' Ṭāhir. J. Arab. Islam. Stud. **10**, 101–118 (2010)
9. Khamis-Dakwar, R., Makhoul, B.: The development of ADAT (Arabic Diglossic Knowledge and Awareness Test): a theoretical and clinical overview. In: Saiegh-Haddad, E., Joshi, R. Malatesha (eds.) Handbook of Arabic Literacy. LS, vol. 9, pp. 279–300. Springer, Dordrecht (2014). https://doi.org/10.1007/978-94-017-8545-7_13

10. Schiff, R., Saiegh-Haddad, E.: When diglossia meets dyslexia: the effect of diglossia on voweled and unvoweled word reading among native Arabic-speaking dyslexic children. Read. Writ. **30**, 1089–1113 (2017)
11. Palmer, J.: Arabic diglossia: student perceptions of spoken Arabic after living in the Arabic-speaking world. Ariz. Work. Pap. Second Lang. Acquis. Teach. **15**, 81–95 (2008)
12. Granger, S.: Learner corpora in foreign language education. In: Thorne, S., May, S. (eds.) Language, Education and Technology, pp. 1–14. Springer, Cham (2017). https://doi.org/10.1007/978-3-319-02328-1_33-2
13. Zeroual, I., Lakhouaja, A.: Arabic corpus linguistics: major progress, but still a long way to go. In: Shaalan, K., Hassanien, A.E., Tolba, F. (eds.) Intelligent Natural Language Processing: Trends and Applications. SCI, vol. 740, pp. 613–636. Springer, Cham (2018). https://doi.org/10.1007/978-3-319-67056-0_29
14. Farwaneh, S., Tamimi, M.: Arabic learners written corpus: a resource for research and learning. Center for Educational Resources in Culture, Language and Literacy (2012)
15. Hassan, H., Daud, N.M.: Corpus analysis of conjunctions: Arabic learners difficulties with collocations. In: Proceedings of the Workshop on Arabic Corpus Linguistics (WACL), Lancaster, UK (2011)
16. Abuhakema, G., Faraj, R., Feldman, A., Fitzpatrick, E.: Annotating an Arabic learner corpus for error. In: LREC (2008)
17. Granger, S.: Error-tagged learner corpora and CALL: a promising synergy. CALICO J. **20**, 465–480 (2003)
18. Abu al-Rub, M.: تحليل الأخطاء الكتابية على مستوى الإملاء لدى متعلمي اللغة العربية الناطقين بغيرها "Taḥlīl al-akhṭā' al-kitābīyah 'ala mustawá al-imlā' ladá muta'allimī al-lughah al-'arabīyah al-nāṭiqīna bi-ghayrihā" (Analysis of written spelling errors among non-native speaking learners of Arabic). Dirasat Hum. Soc. Sci. **34**(2), 1–14 (2007)
19. Ljung, M.: A study of TEFL vocabulary. Almqvist & Wiksell International (1990)
20. Nation, I.S.P.: Teaching & Learning Vocabulary. Heinle Cengage Learning, Boston (2013)
21. Jones, R., Tschirner, E.: A Frequency Dictionary of German: Core Vocabulary for Learners. Routledge, Abingdon (2015)
22. Sharoff, S., Umanskaya, E., Wilson, J.: A Frequency Dictionary of Russian: Core Vocabulary for Learners. Routledge, Abingdon (2014)
23. Xiao, R., Rayson, P., McEnery, T.: A Frequency Dictionary of Mandarin Chinese: Core Vocabulary for Learners. Routledge, Abingdon (2015)
24. Lee, S.-H., Jang, S.B., Seo, S.K.: A Frequency Dictionary of Korean: Core Vocabulary for Learners. Routledge, Abingdon (2016)
25. Boulton, A., Landure, C.: Using Corpora in Language Teaching, Learning and Use. Rech. Prat. Pédagogiques En Lang. Spéc. Cah. Apliut. **35**(2) (2016). https://doi.org/10.4000/apliut.5433
26. James, O.: The International Standard Bible Encyclopedia. Delmarva Publications Inc., Harrington (2015)
27. Kennedy, G.: An Introduction to Corpus Linguistics. Routledge, Abingdon (2014)
28. Soruç, A., Tekin, B.: Vocabulary learning through data-driven learning in an english as a second language setting. Educ. Sci. Theory Pract. **17**, 1811–1832 (2017)
29. Yılmaz, E., Soruç, A.: The use of concordance for teaching vocabulary: a data-driven learning approach. Procedia-Soc. Behav. Sci. **191**, 2626–2630 (2015)
30. El Kah, A., Zeroual, I., Lakhouaja, A.: Application of Arabic language processing in language learning. In: Proceedings of the 2nd International Conference on Big Data, Cloud and Applications, pp. 35:1–35:6. ACM, New York (2017)

Arabic Temporal Expression Tagging and Normalization

Tarik Boudaa(✉), Mohamed El Marouani, and Nourddine Enneya

Laboratory of Informatics Systems and Optimization, Faculty of Sciences, University of Ibn-Tofail, Kenitra, Morocco
tarikboudaa@yahoo.fr, mohamed.elmarouani@gmail.com, enneya@uit.ac.ma

Abstract. The tasks of tagging temporal expressions, normalizing numbers and extracting related countables are useful in many natural language processing applications. This paper describes the newly system named AraTimex, a natural language processing tool for recognizing and normalizing temporal expressions and literal numbers, for modern standard Arabic language. It is a rule-based extensible system that can be integrated easily in many other Arabic natural language applications. The system is designed to deal with complexity of the Arabic language and some of its special characteristics like the use of two calendar types Hijri and Gregorian for writing temporal expressions. To evaluate the system two new annotated datasets have been constructed, the first is based on news articles extracted from Wikinews, and the second contains articles dealing with historical events. This system is tested in these two different datasets and it achieved highly satisfactory results comparing to the state of the art tagger.

Keywords: Arabic temporal expressions tagging · Temporal information
Arabic number normalization · Arabic natural language processing

1 Introduction

The temporal information plays an important role in the semantics of the text, so it is necessary to have powerful tools that process temporal information while building natural language processing applications which aim to automatically understand human languages. In fact, many applications of natural language processing, such as information extraction and question answering systems [1], need to extract temporal information from documents. Extracting such temporal information requires the capacity to recognize and tag temporal expressions (TE), and to evaluate and convert them from text to a normalized form that is easy to process and to exchange between applications as well.

The temporal tagging is a sub-task of the full task of temporal annotation (or temporal information extraction), it consists of two subtasks, Extraction and Normalization.

This work concentrates on the temporal tagging task for Modern Standard Arabic language (MSA), and present our newly system named AraTimex. This system is built

Y. Tabii et al. (Eds.): BDCA 2018, CCIS 872, pp. 546–557, 2018.
https://doi.org/10.1007/978-3-319-96292-4_43

with paramount importance to extensibility and scalability, as well as using a rule based approach to identify temporal expressions and transform them into a normalized time tags based on TIMEX3, which is a part of TimeML annotation language [2]. The system is designed to deal with explicit, implicit or relative temporal expressions, and it supports the Arabic language specificities like the use of Hijri Calendar. The evaluation showed that our new system is more accurate than the current state-of-the-art tool. We included other useful features in this system, like Arabic literal number normalization, extraction of pairs constituted of numbers and their countables. Furthermore, we introduced two different domain datasets to evaluate temporal expression taggers.

2 Related Work

The annotation standards with detailed guidelines are essential when dealing with the task of temporal tagging. Researchers have commonly used two annotation standards for annotating temporal expressions in documents: TIDES TIMEX2 [3] and TimeML [2]. TimeML is a specification language for temporal annotation using TIMEX3 tags for temporal expressions. There is also, ISO-TimeML that is a revised and interoperable version of TimeML [4]. Actually, due to a lot of research on temporal relation extraction, TimeML is more widely used than TIDES TIMEX2 [5].

Manually annotated corpora play a crucial role in many NLP tasks, especially for the development and evaluation of temporal taggers. Thus, a significant number of annotated corpora have been created, but few of them cover Arabic language.

The ACE Multilingual 2005 training corpus [6] consists of English, Arabic, and Chinese documents annotated using TIMEX2, but only extent information and no normalization information is provided in the original datasets [5].

Due to the lack of normalization information, Strötgen et al. [7] re-annotated a part of this corpus using TIMEX3 standard and they added normalization. The new corpus is called (ACE 2005 Arabic) test-50* corpus, it contains 298 TIMEX3 expressions, and it is publicly accessible.

Another corpus that covers Arabic is ACE Multilingual 2007 Training Corpus [8], in addition to the extents, normalization information has also been annotated, however the annotation standard used is TIMEX2.

Another corpus was created in the context of a study on temporal tagging of texts about history, known as AncientTimes [9], it is based on TIMEX3 tags and it is publicly available and covers Arabic and some other languages. However, it contains a small number of documents (5 documents), and does not cover the diversity for the Arabic temporal expressions, for instance, it does not contain expressions using the Hijri calendar.

Although, the majority of existing temporal taggers concentrated on processing English documents, for example, GUTime/TARSQI [10, 11], SUTime [12] and DANTE [13]. There is also works that treat other languages, either as systems built from scratch or as resources added in existing systems or by translating resources of other languages. For instance, [14] describe a rule based system for recognition and normalization of temporal expressions for Hindi language. [15] adapts the HeidelTime system and manually evaluates its performance on a small subset of Swedish intensive care unit documents.

One of the challenges that the research community has tried to overcome is to build multilingual or language-independent systems. One of these systems that handle multilinguality is called HeidelTime, it is a multilingual, domain-sensitive temporal tagger that extracts temporal expressions from documents and normalizes them according to the TIMEX3 annotation standard. HeidelTime contains hand-crafted resources for 13 languages, including Arabic, Vietnamese, Spanish, Italian [7], French [16], Chinese [17] and Croatian [18]. In addition, HeidelTime contains automatically created resources for more than 200 languages [19]. The system is designed so that the addition of other languages can be done without changing the source code [20].

For the Modern Standard Arabic Language (MSA) there is still a great lack of annotated corpora and there is little work in temporal tagging. To the best of our knowledge, HeidelTime is the only tool publicly available that performs the full task of temporal tagging for Arabic documents [7]. There are other tools named ZamAn and Raqm systems that extract temporal phrases and numerical expressions using a machine learning approach [21]. However, the extraction is neither based on TIMEX2 nor on TIMEX3, and the normalization was not addressed. Besides, these tools are not publicly available. Moreover, [22] present a technique for temporal entity extraction from Arabic text based on morphological analysis and finite state transducers, however, like ZamAn and Raqm the extraction is neither based on TIMEX2 nor on TIMEX3, and the normalization was not addressed.

3 Complexity of Arabic Temporal Expressions

Building a rule-based temporal tagger for Arabic remains a challenging task. Indeed, Arabic is a rich language, since it leads to a significant number of temporal expressions. Diacritics represent short vowels, but in MSA they are often omitted. This lack of diacritics results in many ambiguities. For instance, the same word "مارس", without diacritics, can have at least these two different meanings: "practice" if it is diacritised "مَارَسَ" or March if it is diacritised "مَارِس".

Furthermore, a date in Arabic can be expressed using the Gregorian calendar, the Hijri calendar or both at the same time. The Hijri calendar or Islamic calendar is a lunar calendar consisting of 12 months (Safar, Rabi al-Awwal, Rabi al-Thani, Jumada al-Awwal, Jumada al-Thania, Rajab, Sha'ban, Ramadan, Shawwal, Dhul-Qa'dah, Dhul-Hijjah) in a year of 354 or 355 days. This calendar is widely used (concurrently with the Gregorian calendar) in Arabic. The following example shows a date expression mixing the two calendars:

الثلاثاء 29 نوفمبر2016 م الموافق ل 28 صفر 1438 هـ
Tuesday November 29, 2016 Corresponding to Safar 28, 1438

Unlike HeidelTime, AraTimex supports this particularity of the Arabic language during the extraction of information related to dates and it produces a single TIMEX3 tag for this kind of mixed expressions.

There are multiple ways for writing Gregorian month names in Arabic, such as, the phonetically English names and the Arabic names. To write a date in Arabic, we can use numerals, literal numbers or ordinal numbers, and generally the literal numbers can be mixed with numerals to write dates.

All previous possibilities are applied also for dates written in Hijri calendar, and we can also find other variations and more complicated examples that mix Hijri and Gregorian calendars. This leads to a large number of possibilities and involves a great effort while defining rules for extracting and evaluating expressions containing dates.

Another difficulty comes from the fact that the names of Hijri months are often used as name of persons, for instance, the word "رجب" in the next sentence is ambiguous and it can indicate either the name of a person or the name of Rajab Hijri month: "منذ دخول رَجَب والأطفال يلعبون/The children have been playing, since Rajab's arrival".

In general, there are other difficulties related to several challenges for Arabic natural language processing described with more details in [23, 24].

4 Arabic Temporal Expressions Tagging in AraTimex

To meet the standard TIMEX3 our system focuses on four types of expressions namely, DATE, TIME, SET and DURATION.

According to TIMEX3 a date expression describes a calendar time and a time expression refers to a time of the date. AraTimex recognizes both, relative times (e.g. first example in Table 1), as well as absolute dates times (e.g. second example in Table 1). In the first example in Table 1, we assumed that we know that the current date is "2018-01-06".

TIMEX3 doesn't support the Hijri calendar. Thus, we added an optional attribute altVal to TIMEX3 tag, which contains an alternative value that can include, amongst others, the normalized value of Hijri date (e.g. second example in Table 1).

Furthermore, since prayer times are often used to express time in Arabic language, we integrated rules allowing our system to recognize expressions based on prayer times.

Our system can recognize two categories of durations. The first category includes duration expressions specified as a combination of a unit and a quantity (e.g. ثلاثة أشهر/ three months), and the second category covers duration expressions defined as temporal range (*e.g. من الاثنين إلى الجمعة/ from Monday to Friday*).

The system can recognize also other forms of duration expressions, for example, duration defined as Non-Whole number (e.g. شهر و نصف/month and a half). According to TIMEX3, a temporal expression is a SET type if it describes a set of times. AraTimex supports temporal sets representing times that occur with some frequency (e.g. يزور الطبيب 3 مرات كل عام/he visits the doctor 3 times a year). AraTimex can recognize also temporal expressions related to holidays. In the current version a set of temporal expressions related to holidays are extracted automatically from Arabic Wikipedia. This operation is based on the observation that the first sentences of a Wikipedia article related to a holiday name contain the associated date. For instance, the article returned by Wikipedia for the holiday "عيد الاضحى" (Eid al-Adha), contains the associated date in the second sentence.

Table 1. Arabic time tagging examples

Arabic text	English translation	Normalization output
مساء اليوم المنصرم	Last evening	<TIMEX3 tid="t1" type="TIME" value="2018-01-05TEV" > مساء اليوم المنصرم </ TIMEX3>
الإثنين الواحد و الثلاثون يناير 2016 الموافق 5 شعبان 1415 ه	The 31st January 2016, corresponding to 5 Sha'ban 1415 AH	<TIMEX3 tid="t2" type="DATE" value="2016-01-31" altVal="2016-01-31 /1415-08-05" > الإثنين الواحد و الثلاثون يناير 2016 الموافق 5 شعبان 1415 ه </ TIMEX3>

5 Number Normalization in AraTimex

For many applications it's useful to extract numbers and their related countables. For example to compute semantic text similarities, one can compare the common pairs (number/countable) between two texts and use the result as feature in a classification based approach. In AraTimex we used this list of pairs to disambiguate some temporal expressions. For instance, in the sentence "قام بإعادة نشرها في 1990 كتابا رقميا" (he republished them in 1990 digital books), without extracting separately the pair (number = 1990, countable = رقميا كتابا) most systems can tag mistakenly the number 1990 as a date.

AraTimex extracts the countable of each number in the text based on a set of rules that make use of the part-of-speech (POS) tagging based on Stanford Tagger[1]. For illustration, we give bellow an example of rules used to extract the pairs (number, countable), and Table 2 illustrates an application of this rule:

Number + "من" + word (noun) having POS= NN OR DTNN → (number,word) is an acceped pair.

On the other hand, the POS tagger is used to help in disambiguation while normalizing literal numbers, for instance, the word "سبع" in Arabic can be used to mean the lion (e.g. first example in Table 3) or the number seven (e.g. second example in Table 3). Using the POS tagger we can conclude that the word in the first example doesn't mean the number 7, since the word "كبير" (big) is an adjective and cannot be considered as countable in most cases in Arabic (there are exceptions to this rule). Thus we avoid a bad normalization, in most cases, that can change completely the meaning of the sentence.

[1] nlp.stanford.edu/software/tagger.shtml.

Table 2. Example of using POS based rules to extract number/countable pairs

Arabic text	Tagged text	Applied rule
اشتريت 3 من الكتب الجيدة I bought 3 good books	اشتريت/NN 3/CD من/IN الكتب/DTNN الجيدة/DTJJ	Number + "من" + word having POS= DTNN → (3, كتب)

Table 3. Example of using POS for disambiguation

Arabic text	Tagged text	English translation
كان هناك سبع كبير	كان/VBD هناك/RB سبع/CD كبير/JJ	There was a big lion
اشتريت سبع مظلات	اشتريت/VBD سبع/CD مظلات/NN	I bought seven umbrellas

6 Technical Description and Design

AraTimex is a rule-based temporal tagger built on regular expression patterns and designed to deal with a maximum of difficulties presented previously. It is provided as a Java library, and to ensure its modularity and scalability, a multi-layered architecture has been adopted to separate the concerns. The next sub-sections describe the role of each layer.

6.1 Preprocessing Layer

The first step is to make some preprocessing and normalization operations, such as:

- Normalize Eastern Arabic Numerals: both Arabic numerals, also called Hindu–Arabic numerals (1, 2, 3 …) and Eastern Arabic numbers, also called Arabic–Indic numerals (١،٢،٣ …), are often used in Arabic texts, so for normalization purpose, the system converts Eastern Arabic numbers to Western Arabic numbers (١ → 1, ٢ → 2 …).
- Normalize the comma of decimal numbers: 19.00 → 19; 6, 14 → 6.14.
- Remove diacritics: since diacritics are often omitted in written MSA, we remove them to avoid any disruption.
- Normalize literal numbers: in general, Arabic documents, including date expressions, numbers are literally written. Thus, the system performs a conversion of numbers from literal to numerical value: خمسون فاصلة ثلاثة عشرة (fifty comma thirteen) → 50.13; ناقص ثلاثة في المئة (Minus three percent) → −3%.
- Segment the text and add POS tags: to make these tasks we used some existing NLP tools. The current version of AraTimex uses Stanford Tools (Segmenter, POS Tagger), but the system can work with any other tool easily, thanks to the widely

used design pattern known as dependency injection, which is a design principle that is claimed to increase software design quality attributes such as extensibility, testability and reusability. For instance, we integrated easily AraTimex with Farasa Segmenter [25].

6.2 Core Layer

This layer executes a set of rules responsible for the extraction of pairs (number, countable), temporal expressions, their evaluation and their mapping to data structures. This layer is connected to a set of resources that provide, among others, patterns to extract temporal expressions and typical dates like holidays, etc.

AraTimex performs some post-processing to filter out ambiguous expressions that are probably not temporal expressions, especially those that have already appeared in the list of pairs number/countable. Each incomplete temporal object is completed using a heuristic function that depends on the type of documents (news, historical events…), the other temporal objects of the text and the tense of verbs.

6.3 Formatter Layer

This layer is responsible for formatting the output results, its role is to make transparent the underlying annotation standard used to format the output. The current version contains only one implementation that renders the result in TIMEX3 format. Theoretically, we could add support to other annotation standard in AraTimex without making any changes in the core layer code.

6.4 AraTimex Rules Definition and Extensibility

To ensure extensibility of AraTimex, we separate the temporal expression tagging rules from the rest of the code. These rules are declarative, and they are defined using a syntax based on regular expressions in an external XML file. This allows adding new rules without changing or recompiling the source code. For flexibility purposes, AraTimex allows writing rules using Arabic letters or their equivalents by transliteration.

The rules are iteratively executed respecting a certain order defined by the priority of each rule. Ultimately, each rule has the following main properties:

- Pattern: the regular expression allowing extraction of a set of temporal expressions.
- Normal: the pattern that defines the normalized form of the extracted temporal expressions.
- MethodName: the method invoked automatically using Java reflection if an expression matches the extraction pattern. It processes this temporal expression and maps it to the corresponding data structures.
- Class: the Java class where the processing method is defined. This is an optional property assigned only in the case of extending AraTimex.
- Priority: defines the execution order for each rule. It is a crucial property, indeed the rules must be executed in a certain order. The priority is set manually for each rule based on the expression examples encountered in the development dataset.

For instance, the XML code below gives an example of one of rules used to extract a date expression written in Hijri Calendar, the associated method extractDate will be invoked dynamically using Java reflection to normalize the expression and map it to the corresponding data structures using the normalization pattern given by the attribute normal. In this example, the keywords beginning with "set" (e.g. set_monthYear Separation), will be replaced by the AraTimex regular expressions compiler with a set of elements that will be loaded from a resource file (such as week days, month names, etc.).

```
<rule id="hijriDateRule5"
type="date" pattern=
"\b(?:(?:Al)?(set_weekdays))?(?:set_weekdayMonthSeparation)?(set
_monthDays|\d{1,2})(?:set_dayMonthSeparation)(set_hijrimonths)?(
?:set_monthYearSeparation)?(\d{1,4}|set_years)(?:(?:set_hijriMar
ker))?(set_tense)?\b"
normal="H:gr(5)-gr(4)-gr(3)-gr(2)-gr(1)"
methodName="extractDate"
priority="5" />
```

To explain this expression, we split it and comment in Table 4. This separation between rules and resources improves scalability and maintainability. For instance, set_monthYearSeparation defines the texts that can appear between month and year in Arabic dates, these texts are defined; using regular expressions in a resource file.

Table 4. Explanation of an example of rule

<table>
<tr><td>(?:(?:Al)?(set_weekdays))?</td><td>This part of the regular expression matches weekdays</td></tr>
<tr><td>(?:set_weekdayMonthSeparation)?</td><td>This part of the regular expression matches the texts that can appear between weekdays and months</td></tr>
<tr><td>(set_monthDays|\d{1,2})</td><td>This part of the regular expression matches a day of the month</td></tr>
<tr><td>(?:set_dayMonthSeparation)</td><td>This part of the regular expression matches the texts that can appear between day of the month and months</td></tr>
<tr><td>(set_hijrimonths)?</td><td>This part of the regular expression matches Hijri months</td></tr>
<tr><td>(?:set_monthYearSeparation)?</td><td>This part of the regular expression matches the texts that can appear between month and year</td></tr>
<tr><td>(\d{1,4}|set_years)</td><td>This part of the regular expression matches years</td></tr>
<tr><td>(?: (?:set_hijriMarker))?</td><td>This part of the regular expression matches expressions used to indicate Hijri calendar type</td></tr>
</table>

7 Evaluation and Results

7.1 Evaluation Datasets Preparation

To ensure a good coverage of the various types of Arabic temporal expressions, we constructed two new real world datasets, the first one is based on news articles extracted randomly from Wikinews[2], and the second contains articles extracted randomly from Arabic Wikipedia which deal with historical events. Two volunteers were asked to annotate collected articles following TE annotation guidelines of TimeML [26] and guidelines for Hijri dates. The statistics related to annotated evaluation datasets are presented in Tables 5, 6 and 7:

Table 5. Number of temporal expressions and documents in evaluation datasets

Dataset	Number of documents	Number of expressions
News	127	512
Historical events	19	281

Table 6. Distribution of expressions types in datasets

Dataset	Set	Duration	Time	Date
News	6	125	51	330
Historical events	3	62	34	182

Table 7. Percentage use of Hijri in temporal expressions of datasets

Dataset	Percentage use of Hijri
News	0.48%
Historical Events	34.88%

7.2 Evaluation Metrics

To evaluate the system, we need to evaluate separately the extraction and the normalization tasks. We followed the same procedure as in TempEval-3 [27], but taking into account only; in achievement status of this work; the case of strict match comparisons, nevertheless, for HeidelTime that doesn't support Hijri dates, a temporal expression that mixes Gregorian and Hijri calendar is considered correctly extracted if at least the Gregorian part is correctly extracted. For AraTimex the rule is more stringent, indeed in the case of mixed Hijri/Gregorian temporal expressions, the extraction is considered correct only if AraTimex extracts correctly the two parts Hijri and Gregorian and produces a single associated TIMEX3 tag.

We used classical precision and recall to evaluate the extraction task, whereas for normalization we adopted the following rules:

[2] https://ar.wikinews.org.

- Only the values of the Type and Value attributes are taken into account while evaluating the normalization of temporal expressions.
- It is considered that normalization is correct, if the tag TIMEX3 produced has a correct value for both attributes Type and Value.

7.3 Results

We tested AraTimex and Heideltime in the two evaluation datasets described previously. The evaluation results are given in Tables 8 and 9.

Table 8. Temporal expressions tagging results in NEWS dataset

	Extraction			Normalization		
	P	R	F1	P	R	F1
AraTimex	**95.610**	**97.470**	**96.531**	**93.320**	**95.136**	**94.219**
Heideltime	78.517	80.350	79.423	70.722	72.373	71.538

Table 9. Temporal expressions tagging results in HISTORICAL EVENTS dataset

	Extraction			Normalization		
	P	R	F1	P	R	F1
AraTimex	**97.454**	**93.055**	**95.204**	**89.090**	**85.069**	**87.033**
Heideltime	41.210	52.573	46.203	36.023	45.955	40.387

7.4 Discussion

Experimental results show that AraTimex has the highest precision and recall for extraction and normalization in both datasets. We can conclude from Tables 8 and 9 that the results obtained for HeidelTime in the news datasets are very close to the results obtained in the datasets ACE used for HeidelTime official tests [7], whereas it's clear that HeidelTime shows its critical limit if the processed document may contains some Hijri temporal expressions as can be seen from results related to historical events dataset (Extraction P = 41.210% and R = 52.573%) and (Normalization P = 36.023% and R = 45.955%). Indeed, the Hijri temporal expressions cause a lot of confusions to HeidelTime, for example the date "في شهر ربيع الأول من السنة الرابعة من الهجرة" (In "Rabi Al-Awwal" of the fourth Hijri year), while Rabi Al-Awwal (ربيع الأوّل) is the third month in the Hijri calendar, will be tagged by Heideltime as follows:

```
في
<TIMEX3 tid="t1" type="DURATION" value="P1M">شهر</TIMEX3>
<TIMEX3 tid="t2" type="DATE" value="XXXX-SP">ربيع</TIMEX3>
الأول من
<TIMEX3 tid="t3" type="DURATION" value="P1Y">السنة الرابعة</TIMEX3>
من الهجرة
```

As can be seen from this example, HeidelTime annotates this expression as if it is a Gregorian date, which leads to overmuch extraction and normalization errors. This impacts greatly the accuracy of the system by extracting a lot of incorrect expressions. Furthermore, as temporal expressions appearing in the text are most likely dependent, these errors can influence also the value assigned to other Gregorian temporal expressions. All these problems are addressed by AraTimex, and as we can see, the results obtained in the both datasets are good and almost similar.

8 Conclusions

AraTimex tool is developed with the aim of having an efficient, extensible and fast temporal tagger dedicated for the Arabic language and which addresses some limitations of existing tools like for example handling of temporal expressions referring to the Hijri calendar. On the other hand, we addressed the normalization of literal numbers and we extract the information referred by numbers and we use it to disambiguate some temporal expressions. The obtained results demonstrate the high quality of our new tool. We plan to make this tool and data freely available, improve them and optimize them continuously. Otherwise, we plan to use AraTimex to improve Arabic NLP applications like machine translation and answer question answering systems.

References

1. Sanampudi, S.K., Guda, V.: A question answering system supporting temporal queries. In: Unnikrishnan, S., Surve, S., Bhoir, D. (eds.) ICAC3 2013. CCIS, vol. 361, pp. 207–214. Springer, Heidelberg (2013). https://doi.org/10.1007/978-3-642-36321-4_19
2. Pustejovsky, J., Castano, J.M., Ingria, R., Sauri, R., Gaizauskas, R.J., Setzer, A., Katz, G., Radev, D.R: TimeML: robust specification of event and temporal expressions in text. In: New Directions in Question Answering, vol. 3, pp. 28–34 (2003)
3. Ferro, L., Gerber, L., Mani, I., Sundheim, B., Wilson, G.: TIDES 2005 standard for the annotation of temporal expressions (2005)
4. Pustejovsky, J., Lee, K., Bunt, H., Romary, L.: ISO-TimeML: an international standard for semantic annotation. In: LREC, vol. 10, pp. 394–397 (2010)
5. Strötgen, J., Gertz, M.: Domain-sensitive temporal tagging. In: Synthesis Lectures on Human Language Technologies, vol. 9, pp. 1–82. Morgan & Claypool, San Rafael (2016)
6. Walker, C., et al.: ACE 2005 Multilingual Training Corpus LDC2006T06. DVD. Linguistic Data Consortium, Philadelphia (2006)
7. Strötgen, J., Armiti, A., Van Canh, T., Zell, J., Gertz, M.: Time for more languages: temporal tagging of Arabic, Italian, Spanish, and Vietnamese. ACM Trans. Asian Lang. Inf. Process. (TALIP) **13**(1), 1 (2014)
8. Song, Z., et al.: ACE 2007 Multilingual Training Corpus LDC2014T18. Web Download. Linguistic Data Consortium, Philadelphia (2014)
9. Strötgen, J., Bögel, T., Zell, J., Armiti, A., Van Canh, T., Gertz, M.: Extending HeidelTime for temporal expressions referring to historic dates. In: LREC, pp. 2390–2397 (2014)
10. Mani, I., Wilson, G.: Robust temporal processing of news. In: Proceedings of the 38th Annual Meeting on Association for Computational Linguistics, pp. 69–76. Association for Computational Linguistics (2000)

11. Verhagen, M., Pustejovsky, J.: Temporal processing with the TARSQI toolkit. In: 22nd International Conference on Computational Linguistics: Demonstration Papers, pp. 189–192. Association for Computational Linguistics (2008)
12. Chang, A.X., Manning, C.D.: SUTime: a library for recognizing and normalizing time expressions. In: LREC, vol. 2012, pp. 3735–3740 (2012)
13. Mazur, P., Dale, R.: The DANTE temporal expression tagger. In: Vetulani, Z., Uszkoreit, H. (eds.) LTC 2007. LNCS (LNAI), vol. 5603, pp. 245–257. Springer, Heidelberg (2009). https://doi.org/10.1007/978-3-642-04235-5_21
14. Kapur, H., Girdhar, A.: Detection and normalisation of temporal expressions in Hindi. Int. Res. J. Eng. Technol. (IRJET) **4**(7), 1231–1235 (2017)
15. Velupillai, S.: Temporal expressions in swedish medical text–a pilot study. In: Proceedings of BioNLP, pp. 88–92 (2014)
16. Moriceau, V., Tannier, X.: French resources for extraction and normalization of temporal expressions with HeidelTime. In: Proceedings of the Ninth International Conference on Language Resources and Evaluation (LREC 2014) (2014)
17. Li, H., Strötgen, J., Zell, J., Gertz, M.: Chinese temporal tagging with HeidelTime. In: EACL, vol. 2014, pp. 133–137 (2014)
18. Skukan, L., Glavaš, G., Šnajder, J.: HEIDELTIME.HR: extracting and normalizing temporal expressions in Croatian. In: Proceedings of the 9th Slovenian Language Technologies Conferences (IS-LT 2014), pp. 99–103 (2014)
19. Strötgen, J., Gertz, M.: A Baseline temporal tagger for all languages. In: EMNLP, pp. 541–547 (2015)
20. Strötgen, J., Gertz, M.: Multilingual and cross-domain temporal tagging. Lang. Resour. Eval. **47**(2), 269–298 (2013)
21. Saleh, I., Tounsi, L., van Genabith, J.: ZamAn and raqm: extracting temporal and numerical expressions in Arabic. In: Salem, M.V.M., Shaalan, K., Oroumchian, F., Shakery, A., Khelalfa, H. (eds.) AIRS 2011. LNCS, vol. 7097, pp. 562–573. Springer, Heidelberg (2011). https://doi.org/10.1007/978-3-642-25631-8_51
22. Zaraket, F., Makhlouta, J.: Arabic temporal entity extraction using morphological analysis. Int. J. Comput. Linguist. Appl. **3**, 121–136 (2012)
23. Farghaly, A., Shaalan, K.: Arabic natural language processing: challenges and solutions. ACM Trans. Asian Lang. Inf. Process. **8**, 1–22 (2009)
24. Habash, N.Y.: Introduction to Arabic natural language processing. Synthesis Lectures on Human Language Technologies, vol. 3, no. 1, pp. 5–112. Morgan & Claypool, San Rafael (2010)
25. Darwish, K., Mubarak, H.: Farasa: a new fast and accurate arabic word segmenter. In: LREC (2016)
26. Saurí, R., Littman, J., Knippen, B., Gaizauskas, R., Setzer, A., Pustejovsky, J.: TimeML annotation guidelines. Version, vol. 1, no. 1, p. 31 (2006)
27. UzZaman, N., Llorens, H., Derczynski, L., Verhagen, M., Allen, J., Pustejovsky, J.: SemEval-2013 Task 1: TEMPEVAL-3: Evaluating time expressions, events, and temporal relations. In: Second Joint Conference on Lexical and Computational Semantics (*SEM), Seventh International Workshop on Semantic Evaluation (SemEval 2013), vol. 2, pp. 1–9 (2013)

Author Index

Printed in the United States
By Bookmasters